SHAKESPEARE STUDIES

Advisory Board

SHAKESPEARE STUDIES

An Annual Gathering of Research, Criticism, and Reviews

IX

EDITOR   J. Leeds Barroll III

ASSOCIATE EDITORS

Barry Gaines

Ann Jennalie Cook

BURT FRANKLIN & CO., INC.

All editorial correspondence concerning *Shakespeare Studies* should be addressed to:
The Editorial Office, *Shakespeare Studies*, Department of English, University of Tennessee,
Knoxville, Tennessee 37916. Correspondence concerning orders and subscriptions should
be addressed to: Burt Franklin & Co., 235 East 44th Street, New York, New York
10017 U.S.A.

ISBN: 0–89102–070–5
ISSN: 0582–9399
Library of Congress Card Catalog Number: 66–4496
Library of Congress classification PR2885.S64
Manufactured in the United States of America

Contents

Contributors

Roy W. Battenhouse
Professor of English, Indiana University

Robert B. Bennett
Associate Professor of English, University of Delaware

David Bergeron
Professor of English, University of Kansas

Herbert Berry
Professor and Chairman of the Department of English, University of Saskatchewan

W. F. Bolton
Professor of English, Douglass College, Rutgers University

J. S. Dean
Associate Professor of English, University of Wisconsin, Parkside

R. W. Dent
Professor of English, University of California, Los Angeles

Austin C. Dobbins
Professor and Head of Department of English and Journalism, Samford University

John Freehafer
Professor of English, Temple University

Roland Mushat Frye
Professor of English, University of Pennsylvania

Robert C. Fulton, III
Assistant Professor of English, University of Tennessee, Chattanooga

S. N. Garner
Associate Professor of English, University of Minnesota, Twin Cities

W. L. Godshalk
Professor of English, University of Cincinnati

Duncan S. Harris
Assistant Professor of English, University of Wyoming

Joan Hartwig
  Associate Professor of English, University of Kentucky

S. K. Heninger, Jr.
  Professor of English, University of British Columbia

Mary P. Hiatt
  Associate Professor of English, Baruch College, CUNY

J. Dennis Huston
  Associate Professor of English, Rice University

Paul A. Jorgenson
  Professor of English, University of California, Los Angeles

Coppélia Kahn
  Associate Professor of English, Wesleyan University

Joel H. Kaplan
  Associate Professor of English, University of British Columbia

H. M. Klein
  Associate Professor of English, School of European Studies, University of East Anglia, Norwich, England

Erika Lindemann
  Assistant Professor of English, University of South Carolina

George M. Logan
  Assistant Professor of English, Queen's University, Kingston, Ontario

Robert P. Merrix
  Associate Professor of English, University of Akron

Kenneth Muir
  King Alfred Professor of English Literature, Liverpool University

Michael Mullin
  Assistant Professor of English, University of Illinois

D'Orsay Pearson
  Associate Professor of English, University of Akron

Morse Peckham
  Distinguished Professor of English and Comparative Literature, University of South Carolina

Moody E. Prior
  Professor Emeritus of English, Northwestern University

Jeanne Addison Roberts
  Professor of Literature, American University

Norman Sanders
  Professor of English, University of Tennessee, Knoxville

Wayne Shumaker
  Professor of English, University of California, Berkeley

Christopher Spencer
  Professor of English, University of North Carolina, Greensboro

Albert H. Tricomi
  Assistant Professor of English, State University of New York, Binghamton

Raymond V. Utterback
  Associate Professor of English, Georgia State University

Kent van den Berg
  Assistant Professor of Comparative Literature, Ohio State University

Marvin L. Vawter
  Executive Director, Illinois Humanities Council

George Walton Williams
  Professor of English, Duke University

SHAKESPEARE STUDIES

American Criticism of Shakespeare's Comedies

JEANNE ADDISON ROBERTS

Shakespeare criticism is one world. The biennial conferences at Stratford-upon-Avon have long insured cross-national stimulation to Shakespeare study. More recently the International Shakespeare Congresses provide visible verification of the reality of Shakespeare and his critics as citizens of the world. Internationally circulated publications like the *Shakespeare Jahrbuch's, Shakespeare Survey, Shakespeare Quarterly, Shakespeare Newsletter,* and the *Shakespeare Studies* of America and Japan make articles and reviews widely available and sometimes used; and, despite the awesome multiplication of titles, there is some evidence that we read each other's books.

Clearly to isolate and describe a distinctive "American" contribution to Shakespeare study is impossible. Even if directions of influence and movement of ideas could be charted, there would remain the difficulty of defining "American." In an essay celebrating the bicentennial of the founding of the United States, I have been regretfully constrained by logic to exclude Canadians and Latin Americans from my focus, but even this has not solved my problem. Modern critics have a habit of astonishing mobility which makes them very hard to categorize geographically. I have claimed or rejected, sometimes capriciously, and, no doubt, on occasion wrongly. I apologize in advance for offenses of inclusion or exclusion.

Rather to my surprise I have found that some of the oldest clichés about the American character can be usefully applied to our criticism of the comedies. In the most simplistic and reductive terms, it is, I think, fair to say that in their criticism Americans have tended to be individualistic, concerned with function, and specific rather than general. They have showed a continuing fascination with their Edenic vision, both realized and threatened. They have retained in disguised form some vestiges of their Puritan heritage. And, finally, in ways which would have distressed Ralph Waldo Emerson, they have remained remarkably provincial.

Turning more specifically to the question at hand, we discover that detailed commentary on the comedies as a whole was a late development worldwide. Although the 1623 Folio defined the genre by its grouping (except for *Pericles* and *Two Noble Kinsmen),* no full-scale discussions of these plays as a group appeared until the twentieth century. The pioneer Ameri-

can editions of Shakespeare's works in the nineteenth century by Gulian
Verplanck (New York: Harper, 1847), H. N. Hudson (Boston: Monroe,
1851–56), Richard Grant White (Boston: Little, 1857–66), and William G.
Rolfe (New York: Harper, 1882) contained useful introductions to individual plays or general commentary but no attempts at discussing the comedies as a group. H. H. Furness, Sr. and Jr., created a major landmark in
the Variorum editions (Philadelphia: Lippincott, 1871–1928),[1] bringing together criticism of the various plays but still attempting no larger synthesis.
In the great proliferation of twentieth-century American editions, there are
a few brief sections on comedy or groups of comedies but no sustained
analysis of the genre.

The first important book on *Shakespearean Comedy* (H. B. Charlton, London: Methuen, 1938) was British, and it is a curious fact that none of the
major subsequent works on the genre as a whole has been American.[2]
Ralph Berry, who is Canadian, may be speaking for us when he denies the
possibility of meaningful discussion of the genre, explaining, "I regard
Shakespearean comedy as a theoretician's Grail, the pursuit of which may
lead to a misjudgment of the individual comedy."[3] Although there are a
number of short essays by Americans on Shakespearean comedy and frequent discussions of Shakespeare in general books on comedy, we seem to
have resisted comprehensive efforts at synthesis and definition. (Many
good studies of individual plays have been rather arbitrarily omitted from
the present brief survey.)

The special genius of American criticism of the comedies to date lies,
for whatever reason, not in all-embracing theory, but more particularly in
its attention to subdivisions of the genre, its provocative juxtapositions of
plays, and its concentration on function and themes. A number of other
traditional approaches to comedy are notable for their absence or their rarity. The old interest in character criticism survives in a number of British
works but in only a few American ones.[4] E. E. Stoll early[5] denounced
oversophistication of analysis and insisted on the primacy of dramatic action, and A. H. Gilbert joined him in emphasis on performance over character analysis.[6] Robert Langbaum used the venerable plot versus character
controversy only to illustrate the vagaries of the history of taste.[7] Plot
seems to have been of small interest to American critics, although a
number of general works on the drama of the age, most notably Richard
Levin's *The Multiple Plot in English Renaissance Drama* (Chicago: Univ. of
Chicago Press, 1971), are useful on this subject even without a specific
focus on Shakespearean comedy.

T. W. Baldwin, O. J. Campbell, and Willard Farnham have done some important investigations into the origins and sources of the comedies,[8] but here again the work has been individualistic and atypical. Little has been done by Americans on the language of the comedies.

I think there can be no doubt that the single most influential work on modern American criticism of the comedies (and here I am sorely tempted to expand my definition of American to include Canadian) was Northrop Frye's English Institute Essay of 1948, "The Argument of Comedy" (New York: Columbia Univ. Press, 1949). Frye's work, later developed in *The Anatomy of Criticism* (Princeton: Princeton Univ. Press, 1957) and *A Natural Perspective* (New York: Columbia Univ. Press, 1965), focused the attention of critics on the function of comedy. He saw it as reinforcing in general the wishes of society and celebrating in particular the consummation of sex. He pointed to the special efficacy of Shakespearean comedies in achieving these ends through temporary retreat into a "green world." His principles[9] were astonishingly illuminating of Shakespearean comedy. Reductive though they doubtless were, they could be applied to all the comedies; they were immensely stimulating, and they did not challenge competition.

They did, however, inspire application and amplification. They appealed to and stimulated American concern with the function of comedy. The great flowering of American interest in the pastoral and perhaps our emphasis on sex and love in our criticism may be traced in part to Frye. Curiously, one real American, Susanne Langer, writing at almost the same time as Frye, probably independently[10] and much less specifically about Shakespeare, comes to some similar conclusions. Describing the essence of comedy as "human-life feeling," closely intertwined with the sex-impulse, she adds that it "arises naturally wherever people are gathered to celebrate life, in spring festivals, triumphs, birthdays, weddings, or initiations" (p. 331). Although Langer's work points in some of the same directions as Frye's (and as C. L. Barber's later), I have the impression that it has not been such a direct influence.

One might argue that the breaking down of the comedies into farces, romantic comedies, problem comedies, and romances is a universal twentieth-century trend. However, there have been relatively few American studies based explicitly on these divisions. Nor have Americans been drawn to chronological studies of early and late Shakespeare.[11] Rather, they have been notably occupied with divisions which describe function. Perhaps it is not too fanciful to suggest that in literature as in architecture this has been a peculiarly American concern. It is tempting to speculate further that such concern may be a lingering effect of our Puritan past. We seem eager to be sure that dramatic art will instruct as well as please, though we have broadened the concept of instruction to mean not just that drama teaches directly but that it serves a useful ritual purpose for readers, spectators, and society as a whole.

It is, at least in part, this attention to function which accounts for the popularity of Frye. It also helps to explain the great impact and influence of the single most important American book on Shakespearean comedy, C. L. Barber's *Shakespeare's Festive Comedy: A Study of Dramatic Form and its Relation to Social Custom* (Princeton: Princeton Univ. Press, 1959). Barber's idea of relating comedy to Saturnalian festivals was not entirely new. Stoll had suggested as early as 1927[12] a connection between Restoration comedy and the "Saturnalian spirit of rebellion against the code," and the parallels with the Feast of Fools under a Lord of Misrule. But Barber brilliantly illuminated Shakespeare by the application of this suggestion to six plays, relating them to the spirit of holiday times of year and showing how each of them takes its audience through a recurring human cycle—from tension to release through clarification. Barber also showed how stimulating the unusual juxtaposition of plays (the addition of *Henry IV, I* and *II* to a discussion of the romantic comedies) could be. Another book based on function, Robert G. Hunter's *Shakespeare and the Comedy of Forgiveness* (New York: Columbia Univ. Press, 1965), relates certain of the comedies to the medieval plays of forgiveness developed to meet a didactic and spiritual need of its Christian audience, reassuring them of mercy and grace even to sinners. Like Barber's, this work gains interest also from its unusual arrangement of plays *(Much Ado About Nothing, All's Well, Cymbeline, The Winter's Tale, Measure for Measure* and *The Tempest).*

Stoll's *Shakespeare's Young Lovers* (New York: Oxford Univ. Press, 1937), although it deals chiefly with the heroines of the comedies—and deals with them with a vividness which almost contradicts his insistence on the primacy of plot—begins with a discussion of *Romeo and Juliet.* Again the juxtaposition illuminates the total view. The subject of the book, love and sex, has been one of the chief interests of American critics. Karl F. Thompson and William G. Meader wrote[13] on the relation of the plays to the tradition of courtly love. David G. Stevenson dealt with *Love's Labour's Lost, As You Like It, Much Ado,* and *Troilus* in his *The Love-Game Comedy* (New York: Columbia Univ. Press, 1946). Peter G. Phialas contributed a fairly predictable study of *Shakespeare's Romantic Comedies* in 1966 (Chapel Hill: Univ of North Carolina Press). Most recently Hugh M. Richmond has readdressed the subject in *Shakespeare's Sexual Comedy: A Mirror for Lovers* (Indianapolis: Bobbs-Merrill, 1971). Richmond (considered here as an American because his book is especially directed at the students at Berkeley) includes *Othello* and *Antony and Cleopatra,* as well as a chapter on Edward Albee, in his discussion of comedy and attempts to show how Shakespeare provides models of successful sexuality. "Provocative" is perhaps the best term for this book. Never dull and beguilingly relevant, it is sufficiently peppered with eccentric prejudices against unmarried professional women and James Joyce to keep both sexes aroused to argument.

The most striking characteristic of the criticism of comedies in the twentieth century is the overwhelming amount of attention that has been devoted to the last plays. On this subject we have been visited with a proliferation of commentary which, though difficult to lament, is impossible to encompass. Whether included in studies of romance, tragicomedy, or pastoral, the final plays have occupied what seems an inordinate amount of critical time and energy. Curiously, British writers have tended to write on the plays as romances, whereas Americans have favored the categories of tragicomedy and pastoral, again with some illuminating combinations of late plays with earlier ones. I would venture the hypothesis that this variation of national points of view suggests a more traditional British concern with forms and influences as opposed to the recurring American tendency to define form in terms of function.

This may, however, be a tide which is turning. Four American books on the romances appeared between 1970 and 1973. The first, Carol Gesner's *Shakespeare and Greek Romance: A Study of Origins* (Lexington: Univ. of Kentucky Press, 1970) gives useful background materials and less useful analyses, centered on details of plot, of a large number of plays, including such disparate examples as *The Comedy of Errors, Romeo and Juliet,* and *Othello.*

The best of these books is Howard Felperin's *Shakespearean Romance* (Princeton: Princeton Univ. Press, 1972). Curiously flat for a work focused on the processes of the poetic mind is Hallett Smith's *Shakespeare's Romances: A Study of Some Ways of the Imagination* (San Marino: The Huntington Library, 1972). The two works are similar in their analyses of the poet's use and development of the romance form as it grows out of the materials of the earlier plays. Felperin's book is distinctively American, in spite of its emphasis on form, in its insistence on the "worldly ends" of the romance as used by Shakespeare, but it is notable for its attempt to use the Frye vision objectively and sometimes critically. Smith is unlike other Americans in his lack of concern with function and his concentration on art, but a chapter on the pastoral associates him with an American trend. Most notable, perhaps, are his two appendices against mythic and symbolic interpretation and against the idea of topicality in *Cymbeline* and *The Winter's Tale*.

The movement against excessive anthropology and theology is supported by Douglas Peterson in his *Time, Tide and Tempest: A Study of Shakespeare's Romances* (San Marino: The Huntington Library, 1973, p. xii) but in his discussion he ends by recharting what seems by now a fairly familiar landscape. Whether British or American, and whatever the approach, the results of the discussions of romance are often similar. Nearly all of them repeat conclusions about the natural and the artificial, the use of time, and the movement toward reconciliation and forgiveness.

The extensive American discussion of tragicomedy may seem to signal an interest in form in the conventional sense, but in fact this is really evident only in Madeleine Doran's *Endeavors of Art* (Madison: Univ. of Wisconsin Press, 1954). The early works on tragicomedy[14] are primarily histories with little special attention to Shakespeare. The two best treatments of Shakespeare's tragicomedy, Cyrus Hoy's and Joan Hartwig's,[15] both exhibit strong concern with the recurringly efficacious effects of experiencing vicariously the process by which man becomes aware of his fallibility and of his capacity to endure.

Another manifestation of attention to the last plays is interest in the pastoral. Such interest is certainly not uniquely American. The works of W. W. Greg, William Empson, and Raymond Williams[16] have amply evidenced the quality of British scholarship on the topic. But literary images of the pastoral have always had special reverberation for Americans, for reasons both historical and contemporary. Leo Marx says "The pastoral ideal has been used to define the meaning of America ever since the age of discovery, and it has not yet lost hold upon the native imagination."[17] The "meaning" has had to do with the vision of the American as the new Adam, inheritor of a new Eden, and with disillusionment with that ideal.[18] Currently the concern for ecology and the recurrent dream of the return to nature seem to have stimulated special interest in the Shakespearean pastoral.

Early in the century Edwin Greenlaw felt the need of persuading his readers that the pastoral element in Shakespeare was significant, demonstrating his point chiefly by reference to *As You Like It, Cymbeline,* and *The Winter's Tale.*[19] By 1936 Erwin Panofsky, later to qualify as an American, had written his widely influential essay, "Et in Arcadia Ego" (in *Philosophy and History, Essays Presented to Ernst Cassirer,* Oxford: Clarendon Press, 1936), not specifically on Shakespeare but full of insights illuminatingly applicable to the pastoral comedies. Hallett Smith discussed contemporary pastorals in *Elizabethan Poetry* (Cambridge: Harvard Univ. Press, 1952) and Shakespeare's pastorals in his earlier cited book. With the 1960s came the real acceleration of work on the relation of the pastoral to the comedies. Naomi Conn's "The Promise of Arcadia: Nature and the Natural Man in Shakespeare's Comedies," appeared in *Shakespeare Encomium: 1564–1964.* [20] Leo Marx included a splendid chapter on *The Tempest* in his work which was cited earlier. In 1969 Richard Cody's *The Landscape of the Mind* (Oxford: Clarendon Press) dealing especially with the earlier comedies, provided new insights and perspectives on the pastoral.

The banner year for the form was 1972, with two new books on the subject. Again the juxtaposition of the plays is of special interest. David Young in *The Heart's Forest: A Study of Shakespeare's Pastoral Plays* (New Haven: Yale Univ. Press) discusses *As You Like It, King Lear, The Winter's Tale;* and *The Tempest,* while Thomas McFarland in *Shakespeare's Pastoral Comedy* (Chapel Hill: Univ. of North Carolina Press) includes *Love's Labour's Lost, A Midsummer Night's Dream, As You Like It, The Winter's Tale,* and *The Tempest.* Both works are learned and stimulating; McFarland emphasizes the pastoral function of sustaining hope, and Young reminds us of the shadows in Arcadia. Most recently Rosalie Colie's posthumous *Shakespeare's Living Art* (Princeton: Princeton Univ. Press, 1974) devotes two chapters to Shakespeare's sophisticated use and modification of the pastoral tradition, including, as does Young, a section on *King Lear.* I foresee that none of these works will be the last word. The uses of the "green world" continue to fascinate, and we will probably yet see more results of this particular American obsession.

Our scholars suffer from no dearth of contributions to the study of Shakespearean comedy. If there are problems, they are due to a combination of proliferation and isolation. Our single greatest problem may be simply our number. I suspect that McFarland may be more typical than we would like to believe when he candidly announces that his book "arose quite without reference to the work of other critics and scholars" (p. 26). Until quite recently there has been no real community of American Shakespeareans, and it is greatly to the credit of the organizers of present national and international Shakespeare meetings that this condition is beginning to be remedied. Deliberately or helplessly we have often followed the pattern of American individualism, sometimes pushing back new frontiers and sometimes rediscovering the wheel. The result has been occasional brilliance but frequent repetitiveness and little sense of cooperative progress in the solution of problems. Casebooks abound, but we have to my knowledge no original and coherent books by collective authors to compare with the British Stratford-upon-Avon Studies (London: Arnold).

Perhaps because of our number, our geographic spread, and the backlog of our journals, we have remained provincially dependent upon

England in many ways. Until the last four years we went to Stratford for our only real Shakespeare meetings (two thousand people at an annual two-hour MLA meeting, while moving evidence of the intensity of our interest, is hardly community) and for our standards of dramatic production. Our many annual Shakespeare festivals have remained regional and have aimed more at popular than scholarly audiences. Our bibliographies are splendid, but we have frequently relied on the British for evaluation and analysis, reading *Shakespeare Survey, TLS,* and *Notes and Queries* for reasonably rapid reviews and commentaries. The effects have not been all bad. They have served to promote the idea of Shakespeareans as one world. Some Americans feel more at home internationally than nationally. But, because things have been done well elsewhere, we have been slow to learn to do them for ourselves.

As for the future, we are in need of such strong new energies as those released by Frye and Barber. Meanwhile we may be wise to continue our attentions to individual plays and interesting subgroups. It would be useful to have more done in the direction of efforts such as Rosalie Colie's and Mark Rose's[21] to relate Shakespearean form to Renaissance thought. Some attention to the differences between the poet's time and our own might prove more fruitful than an insistence on the similarities. Much more could be done with the language of the comedies, and it is quite possible that we are ready for new approaches to the characters, such as that suggested for tragedy by Leeds Barroll in *Artificial Persons: The Formation of Characters in the Tragedies of Shakespeare* (Columbia: Univ. of South Carolina Press, 1974). I know that creativity does not brook such restraints, but I personally would welcome a moratorium on "green worlds," seasonal analogies, festive influences, and even sex. I share the American addiction to our current form of moralizing Shakespeare by dwelling on the useful functions of his art; and, indeed, I admire the exercise inordinately when it is performed with perception and grace. However, I suspect that there are many other ways of studying both the function and the form of comedy which might well prove illuminating, if less immediately useful. It would be exhilarating if we could relax enough to legitimize without guilt the pure delight of scholarly inquiry—for its own sake and for the sake of some mysterious and uncharted future.

Notes:

1. Work on Variorum editions has continued to the present under the successive general editorship of Joseph Q. Adams, Hyder E. Rollins, James G. McManaway, and Robert K. Turner.

2. Four apparent exceptions do not disprove this rule. Thomas M. Parrott's *Shakespearean Comedy* (New York: Oxford Univ. Press, 1949) was actually a kind of handbook introduction to all the plays. Larry Champion's *The Evolution of Shakespeare's Comedy: A Study in Dramatic Perspective* (Cambridge: Harvard Univ. Press, 1970), emphasizing nine comedies, is only moderately successful and rather narrowly focused on the dubious contention that Shakespeare's evolution in comedy is marked by increasing complexity of characterization. (His notes are an impressive compendium of bibliography on the comedies.) William J. Martz's *Shakespeare's Universe of Comedy* (New York: David Lewis, 1971) is, in fact, a not-very-helpful effort to trace the intersection of a "comic point of view" and a "view of reality" in five plays. Elkin C. Wilson's *Shakespeare, Santayana, and the Comic* (University: Univ. of Alabama Press, 1973) is a very general book aimed apparently at a popular audience.

3. *Shakespeare's Comedies: Explorations in Form* (Princeton: Princeton Univ. Press, 1972), pp. 4–5.

4. Notably Leo Kirschbaum's *Character and Characterization in Shakespeare* (Detroit: Wayne State Univ. Press, 1962). Out of ten essays, only three are on the comedies. See also the Champion book referred to in note 2.

5. *Art and Artifice in Shakespeare* (Cambridge: Cambridge Univ. Press, 1933), p. 1.

6. *The Principles and Practice of Criticism* (Detroit: Wayne State Univ. Press, 1959), pp. 68–69, 75, 86–93.

7. "Character Versus Action in Shakespeare," *Shakespeare Quarterly,* 8 (1957), 57–69.

8. T. W. Baldwin, *William Shakspere's Five-Act Structure* (Urbana: Univ. of Illinois Press, 1947); O. J. Campbell, *Studies in Shakespeare, Milton and Donne,* University of Michigan Publications in Language and Literature I (New York: Macmillan, 1925); Willard Farnham, *The Shakespearean Grotesque: Its Genesis and Transformation* (Oxford: Clarendon Press, 1971).

9. Cogently summarized, clarified, and enlarged by Susan Snyder in "Othello and Romantic Comedy Conventions," *Renaissance Drama* 5 (1972), 124–25. Another excellent analysis of Shakespearean comedy, using Frye but going beyond him is Sherman Hawkins, "The Two Worlds of Shakespearean Comedy," *Shakespeare Studies* 3 (1967), 62–80.

10. She does not include him in the bibliography of her *Feeling and Form: A Theory of Art Developed from "Philosophy in a New Key"* (New York: Scribner's, 1953).

11. A few exceptions are W. W. Lawrence's *Shakespeare's Problem Comedies* (New York: Macmillan, 1931); William B. Toole's *Shakespeare's Problem Plays: Studies in Form and Meaning* (The Hague: Mouton, 1966); David Grene's *Reality and the Heroic Pattern: Last Plays of Ibsen, Shakespeare, and Sophocles* (Chicago: Chicago Univ. Press, 1967); Blaze Bonazza's *Shakespeare's Early Comedies: A Structural Analysis* (The Hague: Mouton, 1966), and Theodore Weiss's *The Breath of Clowns and Kings: Shakespeare's Early Comedies and Histories* (New York: Atheneum, 1971).

12. *Shakespeare Studies: Historical and Comparative in Method* (New York: Macmillan, 1927), p. 52.

13. Karl F. Thompson, "Shakespeare's Romantic Comedies," *PMLA,* 67 (1952, 1079–93; William G. Meader, *Courtship in Shakespeare: Its Relation to the Tradition of Courtly Love* (New York: Columbia Univ. Press, 1954).

14. Frank H. Ristine, *English Tragicomedy: Its Origin and History* (New York: Columbia Univ. Press, 1910); Marvin T. Herrick, *Tragicomedy: Its Origin and Development in*

Italy, France, and England (Urbana: Univ. of Illinois Press, 1955).

15. Cyrus Hoy, *The Hyacinth Room: An Investigation into the Nature of Comedy, Tragedy, and Tragicomedy* (New York: Knopf, 1964); Joan Hartwig, *Shakespeare's Tragicomic Vision* (Baton Rouge: Louisiana State Univ. Press, 1972.

16. W. W. Greg, *Pastoral Poetry and Pastoral Drama* (London: A. H. Bullen, 1906); William Empson, *Some Versions of Pastoral* (London: Chatto & Windus, 1950); Raymond Williams, *The Country and the City* (New York: Oxford Univ. Press, 1973). In the introduction (p. 7) to their recent anthology, *A Book of Pastoral Verse* (New York: Oxford Univ. Press, 1975), John Barrell and John Bull express what may be the current British attitude toward the pastoral: "As the possibility of social mobility and of economic progress increases, so the pastoral tradition, which had originally rested on a separation of social worlds, is first threatened and finally almost fades away." Americans, on the contrary, are more likely to see the pastoral as a living ideal.

17. *The Machine in the Garden: Technology and the Pastoral Ideal in America* (New York: Oxford Univ. Press, 1964), p. 3.

18. For an analysis of the progress of these ideas, see R. W. B. Lewis, *The American Adam: Innocence, Tragedy and Tradition in the Nineteenth Century* (Chicago: Univ. of Chicago Press, 1955).

19. "Shakespeare's Pastorals," *Studies in Philology,* 13 (1916), 122–54.

20. Anne Paolucci, ed., (New York: Enterprise Press, 1964), City College Papers, 1, pp. 113–22.

21. Rosalie Colie, *The Resources of Kind: Genre-Theory in the Renaissance,* ed. Barbara K. Lewalski (Berkeley: Univ. of California Press, 1973); Mark Rose, *Shakespearean Design* (Cambridge: Harvard Univ. Press, 1972).

American Criticism of Shakespeare's History Plays

NORMAN SANDERS

During the momentous events of the years following 1776, the two nations most immediately involved in them would appear to have been in agreement on at least one small point: namely, the continuing interest and entertainment afforded by the history plays of William Shakespeare. On the one side, British naval and military officers found time, during their occupation of Philadelphia in 1778, to stage a performance of the First Part of *Henry IV* at the Southwark Theater. And on the other, only five years after Cornwallis's surrender at Yorktown and some five before Washington's inauguration, the best-known theatrical company of the new United States—that of the younger Henry Hallam and John Henry—included *Richard III* among the first plays of its 1786 season in the Hall of Quesnay's Academy at Richmond.

In these early years of America's history and throughout the next century, Shakespeare's works generally were of course considered as much a part of the new nation's literary heritage as they were of England's. Shakespeare clubs were a feature of American life by the mid-nineteenth century, and his works figured as prominently in magazine analyses as they did in the theaters. Many of the nation's literary and political great made their own contributions to that period's deification of the playwright. Washington, Jefferson, and even Franklin all quoted and praised; Lowell set him firmly above his European peers in being uniquely "unitary with human nature"; Emerson typically saw the Revolutionary War as no barrier to the nation's claim to the writer who "drew the man of England and Europe; the father of the man in America," and Melville, with his characteristic ease in moving directly into the metaphysical, made up for his late coming to the plays at the age of twenty-nine by roundly asserting, "if another Messiah ever comes 'twill be in Shakesper's person."

One might have suspected that for many new Americans the historical plays, with their feudal materials and monarchical assumptions, would have provided at least a stumbling block to total admiration, particularly as it was during the nineteenth century that these plays were coming to be recognized for the first time as large expressions of the English national spirit which, as Schlegel argued, constituted a continuous patriotic work of art of a very special kind.

Yet there are no signs that this was the case. Rather it seems that the

11

histories offered early Americans a serious dramatic consideration of the problems of government similar to those with which they were personally involved in their daily lives. Three plays that could be so described (*Richard III, King John,* and *Henry IV*) were all on the boards during Boston's first theatrical season in the new postrevolutionary world of 1792. *Richard III* was one of the favorite plays acted in the primitive theatrical conditions that prevailed along the Ohio and the Mississippi during the frontier days, and it was with *Henry IV* that Junius Brutus Booth regaled the mid-century gold-rushers of California. Public men like John Dickinson, John Adams, and John Quincy Adams refer to the histories specifically in their writings as great models of relevant political teaching, and Lincoln not only included *Richard III* and *Henry VIII* among his five favorite plays but, at the height of the Civil War, induced sleepiness in his secretary by selecting *Henry VI* for prebedtime reading aloud.

Nevertheless, despite such widespread acceptance and admiration, there are signs that some Americans found it difficult to reconcile Shakespeare's historical world with the ideals of the new republic. Perhaps Walt Whitman, the most strident and lyrical voice of democracy, may stand appropriately as the "current and index" he claimed to be for all Americans of his time who found themselves with a divided response to these plays. Shakespeare was for the American poet primarily "the artist and singer of feudalism in its sunset" whose great works were "poisonous to the idea of the pride and dignity of the common people, the life blood of democracy." His plays belong "essentially to the buried past" because they

> relate to and rest upon conditions, standards, politics, sociologies, ranges of belief, that have been quite eliminated from the Eastern Hemisphere, and never existed at all in the Western. As authoritative types of song they belong in America just about as much as the persons and institutes they depict.

Nothing apparently could be clearer than these famous pronouncements in the pages of *November Boughs* and *Democratic Vistas.* Yet with regard to the history plays Whitman was willing to contradict himself every bit as much as he does so proudly in his poetry. For just as it was *Richard II* that he spouted in Broadway stagecoaches and *Richard III* which stimulated him to give posterity one of the most vivid accounts of Booth's acting, so it is the history plays generally that he singles out for the highest praise of all: they are not just the products of "as profound and forecasting a brain . . . as ever appeared in literature" but also the most eminent as dramatic performances (my maturest judgment confirming the impressions of my early years, that the distinctiveness and glory of the poet reside not in his vaunted dramas of the passions, but in those founded on the contests of English dynasties and the French Wars). . . . Conceiv'd out of the fullest heat and pulse of European feudalism—personifying in unparallel'd ways the mediæval aristocracy, its towering spirit of ruthless and gigantic caste, . . . works in some respects greater than anything else in recorded literature.

Whitman further adds to this astonishing critical about-face not only the perceptive comment about the political systems they limn (which looks ahead to some mid-twentieth century criticism of the plays) but also poses the question:

> Will it not indeed be strange if the author of "Othello" and "Hamlet" is destin'd to live in America, in a generation or two, less as the cunning draughtsman of the passions, and more as putting on record the first full exposé—and by far the most vivid one, immeasurably ahead of the doctrinaires and economists—of the political theory and results . . . which America has come on earth to abnegate and replace?

However, even though Whitman at the end of his life was able to crown Shakespeare as the poet of democracy, his countrymen generally were not to agree with his judgment of the preeminence of the history plays.

During the first two-thirds of the nineteenth century the study of Shakespeare was a private rather than a professional activity. The Philadelphia edition of the plays of 1795–96 perhaps sums up the nation's general attitude: "An American reader is seldom disposed to wander through the wilderness of verbal criticism"; and the editions of men like Henry Hudson, William Rolfe, and G. C. Verplanck were obviously aimed at a popular audience who would have relished Washington Irving'a amusing spoof of Shakespearean research in his 1819 essay on his search for the Boar's Head tavern.

Still, there were some voiced pleas for professionalism and academic study. Lowell injected Shakespeare into his Harvard lectures in 1863, and before the Edinburgh Institute in 1883 said, "I never open my Shakespeare but what I find myself wishing that there might be professorships established for the study of his works." Specific professorships were not to come, but professionalized Shakespeare scholarship was. It was from

Philadelphia that there came at the beginning of the present century H. H. Furness's Variorum editions of *Richard III* (1908) and *King John* (1919), which represent in detail the attitudes of the previous century to the history plays generally. In these volumes we find heavy stress on the idea of Shakespeare constructing a national epic, which was the nineteenth century's chief contribution to the study of them, and also a good deal of fascination with the characters of dramatic individualists like Richard and Faulconbridge of the Bradleyan kind.

While there has been no lack of treatises during the present century which have remorselessly explored further the previous century's approaches, the main thrust of modern criticism and scholarship has been in three principal areas: (1) textual studies, (2) the nature of the genre of history play, and (3) the relationship between the play's materials and unchanging moral and political values. In all of these fields American scholars have made substantial contributions.

Their labors in textual studies generally are beyond the scope of this paper, but some mention should be made here of examples of the work done on the histories specifically. So far as the early chronicle plays are concerned, it was the question of their origin that most occupied older scholars. J. B. Henneman (*PMLA*, 15 [1900], 290–320) made this century's earliest attempt to separate the layers of composition in Part 1 of the *Henry VI* trilogy, the authorship problems of which were closely studied by C. F. Tucker Brooke (*Transactions of the Connecticut Academy*, 17 [1912], 141–211), H. D. Gray (*PMLA*, 32 [1917], 367–82), and most lengthily by A. Gaw in his monograph, *The Origin and Development of* 1 Henry VI (Los Angeles: Univ. of Southern California Press, 1926), all of whom argued for composite authorship of one kind or another. However, by the time H. T. Price (*Construction in Shakespeare* [Ann Arbor: Univ. of Michigan Press], 1951) and Leo Kirschbaum (*PMLA*, 67 [1952], 809–22) came to reconsider the problem in mid-century, they were able to enunciate the now-prevailing view that Shakespeare was responsible for the whole design.

By far the most influential work on these early plays to come from this country was Madeleine Doran's demonstration ('Henry VI' *Parts 2 and 3* [Ames: Univ. of Iowa Press, 1928]) that *The First Part of the Contention betwixt the Two Famous Houses of York and Lancaster* (1594) and *The True Tragedy of Richard Duke of York* (1595) were not source plays for Parts 2 and 3 of *Henry VI*, but corrupt reported versions of Shakespeare's own plays. Together with Peter Alexander's work published in England the following year, Miss Doran's book has persuaded most scholars to accept this view as orthodoxy, a circumstance which, nevertheless, did not deter C. T.

Prouty ('The Contention' *and* '2 Henry VI' [New Haven: Yale Univ. Press, 1954]) from making a major attack upon it.

Authorship problems were also in the fore in studies of *Henry VIII*. Willard Farnham did some early spadework *(PMLA,* 31 [1916], 326–58), and there were later contributions by A. Oras *(Journal of English and Germanic Philology,* 52 [1953], 198–213) and R. A. Law *(Studies in Philology,* 56 [1959], 471–88). The work of B. Maxwell *(Studies in Beaumont, Fletcher and Massinger,* [1939; rpt. New York: Octagon Boks, 1966]) and Cyrus Hoy *(Studies in Bibliography,* 15 [1962], 71–90) on the characteristics of Fletcher's plays also had an important bearing on any possible division of the play between the two authors. As if to remind us that it is still an open question, Madeleine Doran *(Journal of English and Germanic Philology,* 59 [1960], 287–91) again tried to stave off disintegrators for this late history, though with less success than she had done for the earlier ones.

Henry V and *Richard III* were prominent from the beginning in the deliberations of the "new bibliographers" and there is still no unanimous opinion on the relationship between the Quarto and Folio texts. Neither H. T. Price's arguments for shorthand derived copy for the first quarto of *Henry V (The Text of* Henry V [Newcastle-under-Lyme, 1921]) nor B. Simison's for playhouse origin *(Philological Quarterly,* 11 [1931], 39–56) commanded general agreement, and a measure of the textual uncertainty surrounding the whole play may be indicated by two articles appearing in the same year: W. D. Smith's denial that Shakespeare wrote the Choruses *(Journal of English and Germanic Philology,* 53 [1954], 38–57) and R. A. Law's strong support for his authorship of them *(Texas Studies in English,* 33 [1954], 13–32). Conclusions are even more unsure in the case of *Richard III*. Most scholars agree about the importance of the original work on the relationship between the Folio and Quarto texts done by D. L. Patrick in 1936 *(The Textual History of* Richard III [Stanford: Stanford Univ. Press]), but the issue is still very much alive as the redoubtable Fredson Bowers showed in his review of the European research published on the play *(Shakespeare Quarterly,* 10 [1959], 541–44).

Three history plays were the subject of modern variorum editions. S. B. Hemingway's Part 1 of *Henry IV* appeared in 1936 and was made infinitely more valuable by G. Blakemore Evans' supplement that came out twenty years later. M. A. Shaaber's edition of Part 2 was published in 1940; and M. Black's *Richard II* in 1955. All three of these volumes showed a marked advance in knowledge and technique on the Furness editions in the same series. The other single- and multi-volume Shakespeares originating in America all contain interesting work on the histories, the most im-

portant textually being G. L. Kittredge's (Boston: *Ginn,* 1936), which was
revised by Irving Ribner in the 1960s, and G. Blakemore Evans' Riverside
(Boston: Houghton, 1974) editions. But there is illuminating comment also
to be found in the academic and popular texts such as the Pelican, Signet,
and Craig-Bevington editions.

It was, I suppose, Hemmings and Condell with their First Folio title
"Mr. William Shakespeare's Comedies, Histories, and Tragedies" who first
raised the problem of genre by thus making a group of plays linked by
their subject matter coequal with two long-established types of drama defined by their form and effect. The nineteenth century had been largely
content to accept the plays as a national patriotic epic, but early in the
present century they were seen for the political dramas they are. C. F. Tucker
Brooke *(The Tudor Drama* [New York: Houghton, 1911]) detected in them a
vision of a statecraft founded on the idea of royal responsibility of which
Henry V was the ultimate perfect embodiment; but he also believed, as did
E. E. Stoll *(Shakespeare Studies* [New York: Macmillan, 1927]), that Shakespeare himself was politically neutral and that the cycle demonstrated
no strongly defined convictions.

Later scholars were not so sure on this point, and some set out to
show that Shakespeare was deeply concerned with the political preoccupations of himself and his age. Others, taking their cue from the English
chroniclers, tried to detect topical allusions and contemporary correspondences in and between the lines. For example, Evelyn M. Albright, in a
series of articles in *PMLA* between 1927 and 1932, saw Elizabeth herself
being implicitly discussed in *Richard II* and *King John,* and accepted *Henry V*
as the climax of a Shakespearean propaganda campaign on behalf of the
Earl of Essex. Although such research is less popular now than it used to
be, Alice L. Scoufos *(Shakespeare Studies*, 6 [1970], 355–58) suggests that there
is still life in the allusion-hunting game.

About the same time, other scholars were investigating the influence
of Elizabethan political and historical writings on Shakespeare's mind.
Hall's *Chronicle* was a long-recognized source, and Edleen Begg *(Studies in
Philology,* 32 [1935], 189–96) demonstrated its importance in the composition
of *Richard III,* while Lucille King in some excellent articles did the same
service for *Henry VI (Philological Quarterly,* 13 [1934]; *PMLA,* 50–51 [1935–
36]). The whole subject was superbly brought into focus by W. G. Zeeveld
in *ELH* (3 [1936], 317–53). Once such work as this had shown Shakespeare's reliance on earlier chronicle accounts for his shaping of historical
events into a cyclical unity, it was natural that critics should begin to perceive in the whole sequence a far more profound organizing principle than

that indicated in the studies of the nineteenth century. Thus there came into being a large body of writing which argued that Shakespeare was the spokesman of his own age and the creator of a vast design spread over ten plays, which constitutes the most coherent expression we have of typical Elizabethan political and historical thinking.

The English scholar E. M. W. Tillyard produced the most influential statement of this critical view of the plays in his two books, *The Elizabethan World Picture* (London: Chatto & Windus, 1943) and *Shakespeare's History Plays* (London: Chatto & Windus, 1944). In these he instructed his readers in the main concepts that governed Elizabethan political thinking which he derived from contemporary theorizing about the workings of Divine Providence and the Church of England's Homilies. And he went on to redefine politics to mean a concern with the doctrine of order which implied a reflection in the Commonweal of both God's ordering of the universe and the spiritual order that reigned in the soul of the good man.

American scholars, both before and since the publication of Tillyard's books, made valuable contributions to our knowledge of political and historical theory in Shakespeare's England and to the view that the histories constitute a cyclical design with the "Tudor myth" as its ground and burden. Among books which added significantly to our grasp of the Elizabethan World Picture are H. Craig's brilliant synthesis of ideas (*The Enchanted Glass* [New York: Oxford Univ. Press, 1936]), which shows a widely read man handling complex materials with a fine sense of their interpenetration during the age, and T. Spencer's *Shakespeare and the Nature of Man* (New York: Macmillan, 1943), which studied man in his moral universe and suggested that the movement of all history plays involved the destruction and reestablisment of the all-embracing pattern of order that ruled throughout nature. B. Stirling (*The Populace in Shakespeare* [New York: Columbia Univ. Press, 1949]) reached similar conclusions to those of Spencer and made good use of the antidemocratic pronouncements of Elizabethan writers and preachers to illustrate the horrors of rebellion which are exemplified in the person of Jack Cade.

In a seminal study, *Shakespeare's "Histories"* (San Marino: The Huntington Library, 1947), Lily B. Campbell investigated the degree to which Tudor chroniclers blended moral judgment and factual material to produce examples of God's justice in action and thus used the past to illuminate the present. As she put it, "the Elizabethan expected any work of history to act as a political mirror. The rise of a drama using the materials and subserving the purposes of history was inevitable." The wide-ranging work of two other scholars provided strong support for Miss Campbell's conclusions: L.

B. Wright's unsurpassed analysis of the tastes, ideas, and preoccupations of bourgeois England *(Middle Class Culture in Elizabethan England* [Chapel Hill: Univ. of North Carolina Press, 1935]), and L. F. Dean's scholarly *Tudor Theories of History Writing* (Ann Arbor: Univ. of Michigan Press, 1947).

The official doctrinal beliefs of the period and the theory that seems to lie behind them were not the only context of Shakespeare's histories being explored. The plays were also viewed among contemporary plays of the same kind. I. Ribner *(The English History Play in the Age of Shakespeare* [Princeton: Princeton Univ. Press, 1957]) provided a valuable survey of the whole genre and its factual sources and in general agrees with Tillyard's position, but he does take into account the fact that the Tudor doctrine of passive obedience had its foes whose influence can be traced in some of the plays. Ten years later and casting his net even wider than Ribner, D. Bevington *(Tudor Drama and Politics* [Cambridge: Harvard Univ. Press, 1968]) stressed more heavily this opposition to authority. He demonstrates just how political, religious, and ethical interests of the medieval tradition developed as the reign of Elizabeth progressed, and shows in terms of issues rather than personalities how the political concerns of the time made their appearance on the stage. Shakespeare, for Bevington, is a moderate in whose plays can be found "the impulse for debate and criticism . . . no less than that for official propaganda"; his work, like the best of Tudor political playwriting, "supported Tudor policy in essence while maintaining a noble spirit of free discussion." This view conveys well in miniature one part of the current challenge to the Tillyardian orthodoxy.

No one would deny that the complete rethinking of the history cycle during the 1940s, that may be represented by the work of Tillyard and Campbell, was as important as it was instructive. Yet this approach does lay great stress on the total design and thus sees the ultimate meaning of any one play or even a scene within it as being graspable only by reference to distant consequences or remote antecedents. This being so, the general tendency of such criticism is to force the variegated and plastic materials of very different pieces into a rigid scheme and the differences between them are lost sight of in the search for unifying characteristics. But we know that the basic unit of the Elizabethan theater was the play, and any approach that necessitates keeping the details of the whole cycle in mind implies what G. K. Hunter *(Critical Quarterly,* 1 [1959], 229–36) has called "a coterie audience-response more proper to Bayreuth than the Globe."

There were signs of dissatisfaction with the Tillyard-Campbell view even as it was developing. A. Harbage, for example, the nearest thing we have had to a Johnsonian voice in Shakespeare studies, reminded us in his *As*

They Liked It (New York: Macmillan, 1947) that the basic frame of reference in the plays is "human nature as it still appears," and went on to point out that because there is a dependence in the history play on fact, the genre is therefore susceptible to a formal fragmentariness less suitable for vast moral schemes than are the fabulous kinds of drama. A great deal of the work done on the most monstrous lump of human nature in the plays, Sir John Falstaff, also seemed more intent on setting him in other contexts than that of Tudor orthodoxy. For example, to A. H. Tolman (*PMLA*, 34 [1919], 1–13) and J. W. Spargo and R. A. Law (*Studies in Philology*, 24 [1927], 223–42) he was more significantly a product of the morality play tradition; E. E. Stoll (*Modern Philology*, 12 [1914], 65–108) placed him in the line of stage cowards, and other scholars have pointed out his connections with the clown, jester, Vice, glutton, *miles gloriosus,* figures from festive ritual, and Christian Fool.

However, it was not until the 1960s that a consciously anti-Tillyardian movement developed. Bevington not only perceived the plays' simultaneous advocacy of the status quo and opposition to it, but also detected a shifting of audience attitudes towards the action they see developing on the stage. In a less moderate book than Bevington's, W. Sanders (*The Dramatist and the Received Idea* [Cambridge: Cambridge Univ. Press, 1968]) makes extensive use of recent studies of Machiavelli's influence in England to argue that the driving force of the plays is a dramatizing of doubt and uncertainty rather than the advocation of conformity to the official Tudor position. Greatly influenced by these two studies, M. Manheim (*The Weak King Dilemma in the Shakespearean History Play* [Syracuse, N.Y.: Syracuse Univ. Press, 1973]) also takes Machiavelli to be the chief cultural force in the political life of the age, and he reads the plays as "the chief documents revealing the deeper fears and concerns of one segment of the Elizabethan public"—a conviction which H. M. Richmond also shares in a sometimes brilliant but often erratic book, *Shakespeare's Political Plays* (New York: Random, 1967).

Several books appear to have been written with the explicit purpose of correcting what they take to be Tillyard's overemphasis on the whole design. For example, H. A. Kelly (*Divine Providence in the England of Shakespeare's Histories* [Cambridge: Harvard Univ. Press, 1970]) offers us a fresh reading of the chronicles and a reexamination of their assumptions, but concludes that men like Vergil, Hall, and Holinshed were not so much interested in justifying the legitimacy of the current dynasty as in drawing lessons from the past for their own times. In the light of his studies of these documents and of the plays themselves, he then proceeds to discard

one of the bases of Tillyard's position: "the concept of divine wrath extending for generations over a whole people for a crime committed in the remote past presupposes a kind of avenging God completely foreign to the
piety of historiographers of Mediæval and Renaissance England." What
Kelly sees Shakespeare doing is unscrambling the partisan layers of belief
which had been blended by the Tudor historians, and attributing them to
the appropriate spokesmen for the Lancaster, York, and Tudor myths.

In a book limited to the Henry VI trilogy, David Riggs (*Shakespeare's
Heroical Histories:* Henry VI *and its Literary* [Cambridge: Harvard Univ.
Press, 1971]) provides additional support for Kelly's position. He too queries
the validity of the homiletic approach by doubting the critical method by
which the evidence on which it is based is collected. He notes that most of
the spokesmen in the plays voicing the orthodox Tudor version of events
are choric figures, which neither dramatically nor poetically can hope to
draw the audience's interest away from the concerns and values of the central characters that establish the main angle of vision. The old ideas of the
patriotic epic are also bleakly denied:

> These plays keep saying that the received ideals of heroic greatness
> may be admirable in themselves, but they invariably decay, engender
> destructive violence and deadly rivalries, and, in the process make
> chaos out of history. They lead to anarchy because the notions of
> "honor" that regulate the heroic life can never be securely realized
> within any stable, historical form of national life.

Also rejecting the idea that the plays are vehicles for Tudor ideology are
J. C. Bromley (*The Shakespearean Kings* [Boulder: Colorado Associated Univ.
Press, 1971]) and Robert Ornstein (*A Kingdom for a Stage* [Cambridge: Harvard Univ. Press, 1972]). The former (like Maynard Mack, Jr. in a more
general book, *Killing the King* [New Haven: Yale Univ. Press, 1973]) lays
heavy stress on the destruction of Shakespeare's rulers by the fact and
burdens of royalty, and also on the high personal cost of political success.
Ornstein makes a detailed and penetrating analysis of the plays as dramatic
art and echoes Harbage's earlier conviction that Shakespeare moulded his
narrative material into a vision of political reality that is more dependent
on his insight into human behavior than on Elizabethan political commonplaces:

> He places as great a value on the sanctity of personal relations in the
> History Plays as in the tragedies, because he intuits that order de-

pends, not on concepts of hierarchy and degree, but on the fabric of personal and social relationships which is woven by ties of marriage, kinship, and friendship, by communal interests and ideals of loyalty and trust.

Three other recent works develop aspects of Ornstein's view: D. M. Ricks *(Shakespeare's Emergent Form,* [Logan: Utah State Univ. Press, 1968]) emphasizes the dramatic structure of the early plays, which A. C. Hamilton *(The Early Shakespeare,* [San Marino: The Huntington Library, 1967]) rejects as being didactic and considers as pieces for the stage. R. B. Pierce *(Shakespearean History Plays* [Columbus, Ohio: State Univ. Press, 1971]) concentrates on the family relationships and their analogy with the structure of the state.

In the most magisterial recent book, *The Drama of Power* (Evanston, Ill.: Northwestern Univ. Press, 1973), Moody Prior attempts a massive synthesis of the Tillyardian and modern views. He notes that "even the most original and powerful minds are subject to the limitations of their times," but argues, "when we attempt to reconstruct the age by means of scholarship, what emerges for the most part is the common denominator, a synthesis deeply colored by the contributions of those less creative minds, the official ideologists, the popularizers, the shapers of common opinion, the propagandists." Because of this, "to make notions of the age the primary measure by which the plays are to be understood is not only to make the lesser the measure of the greater; it is to reverse the process of creation and to return to the plays the limited vision . . . from which the complexity of Shakespeare's forms, the richness of his art, the breadth and humanity of his understanding and the transcendent quality of his creative power have freed them." Prior knows that we too are confined to specific attitudes and that we run the risk of making a Shakespeare in our own image. What he would like to see is a reciprocity between the discoveries we make about Shakespeare because of our own experiences as inhabitants of the twentieth century and those we make because of what we learn about the world he lived in. In many ways the whole book is an original commentary on the tensions present in criticism of the history play because of its very nature, and it touches on every critical problem faced during the present century.

While the central critical debate was being carried on, there has been no shortage of work on limited aspects of the plays. No short summary could hope to do justice to the range, variety, and richness of the enormous output, but perhaps a selection of shorter pieces which I consider to rise above

the usual annual level of competence might serve as an indicator. Alvin
Kernan *(Yale Review,* 59 [1969], 3–32) gives a superb exposition of how historical, social, political, psychological, spatial, temporal, mythical, ceremonial, and ritual levels of meaning are interwoven at every point in the second tetralogy. Richard Altick *(PMLA,* 62 [1947], 339–65) makes brilliant use
of the imagery of *Richard II* to show the ways verbal effects can contribute
to dramatic unity. A single poorish scene—the Talbot–Countess of Au-
vergne encounter—provides S. Burckhardt *(Shakespearean Meanings,* [Prince-
ton: Princeton Univ. Press, 1968]) with an opportunity for a display of his
particular virtuosity. M. A. Shaaber *(Joseph Quincy Adams Memorial Studies,*
[Washington, D.C.: Folger Shakespeare Library, 1948]) presents a remarkably clear exposition of the evidence for and against *Henry IV* as a ten-act
play. Most of Ronald Berman's works on the plays contain something
novel; and R. R. Reed *(Richard II: From Mask to Prophet,* [Univ. Park: Pennsylvania State Univ. Press, 1968]) illustrates that psychological criticism
need not be the mental clog it often is. And historical criticism of a different kind from Tillyard's may be found in E. W. Talbert's *Elizabethan Drama
and Shakespeare's Early Plays* (Chapel Hill: Univ. of North Carolina Press,
1963).

   One of the features of recent Shakespearean production in England has
been a demonstration of the extraordinary richness and variety that the histories can have on the boards, whether staged as individual plays or as a
complete cycle. A result of this is that English critics have had their eyes
opened to many dramatic aspects of the plays that they had previously not
observed. In American criticism there has been little reflection of such stage
influence. Naturally, there is an enormous amount of information about
earlier theatrical history in G. C. D. Odell's standard work, *Shakespeare—
From Betterton to Irving* (New York: Scribner's, 1920), but only that inde-
fatigable digger in theatrical records, A. C. Sprague *(Shakespeare's Histories*
[London: Society for Theatre Research, 1964]), has brought the experience
of a lifetime of theatergoing to a thorough viewing of these plays as works
for the stage. Perhaps it is time for one of the numerous successful American Shakespeare festivals to stage the complete cycle in order to fire the
imagination of, say, a Daniel Seltzer (vide. *Reinterpretations of Elizabethan
Drama* [New York: Columbia Univ. Press, 1969], 89–115) or an Irwin Smith
(vide. *Shakespeare's Globe Playhouse,* [New York: Scribner, 1956]), both of
whom have demonstrated that they can use staging knowledge for critical
ends.

   In the very latest book to appear on the history plays we find a curious
echo of that stress on their modern relevance that can be found in the pro-

nouncements of the earliest Americans. Michael Manheim concludes his study of the weak king in this way:

> The only possible conclusion to these chapters is that the plays considered have a deep and immediate significance in our own time. For a recent president of the United States (whom I greatly admired and still admire) to suggest he looked upon Shakespeare's Henry V as a hero and example is to say that the Machiavellian compromise made by Christian nations and their governors in the late sixteenth century is still very much with us.

If sheer amount means anything then Manheim is right. Between 1970 and 1974 eight books have been published with the history plays as their subject, and a complete issue of a learned journal has been devoted to them (*Studies in the Literary Imagination,* 1972). So there are no signs that they will cease to fascinate Americans during the next hundred years of their nation's existence. As indeed why should there be? For if these plays are the profoundest dramatic treatment of politics they are reputed to be, who is more naturally equipped to plumb their depths than the nation which is, after France, the most politically minded that the Western world has yet produced?

American Criticism of Shakespeare's Tragedies

KENNETH MUIR

The debt of Shakespeareans to American criticism is immense, but as there has been a two-way traffic across the Atlantic it is not always easy to isolate it. Some books, too, may easily be passed over as commonplace because one has absorbed the once original ideas. Most of us ignore whether a book is written by an Englishman, a Canadian, or a United States citizen. Some Americans were born in England and one of the best living Shakespeareans in England was born in America. Then again it is particularly difficult to segregate criticism of Shakespeare's tragedies from that which applies to the whole of his work. A few examples will make this clear. The Kittredge annotated editions of Shakespeare, immensely learned and continuously sensible and sensitive, set new standards. He threw light on the meaning and interpretation of sixteen plays, including nearly all the tragedies. Hardin Craig's masterpiece, *The Enchanted Glass* (New York: Oxford Univ. Press, 1936), is one of the most important works on the Elizabethan world picture, more wide-ranging and stimulating than Tillyard's, and Craig also wrote a seminal essay on the tragedies. We shall always feel indebted to Madeleine Doran's *Endeavors of Art* (Madison: Univ. of Wisconsin Press, 1954) and to Virgil K. Whitaker's *Shakespeare's Use of Learning* (San Marino: Huntington Library, 1953). Our reading of the tragedies has been affected by such books as Theodore Spencer's *Shakespeare and the Nature of Man* (New York: Macmillan, 1943)—whether we agree with it or not—Bernard Beckerman's *Shakespeare at the Globe* (New York: Macmillan, 1962), and A. C. Sprague's various books on Shakespeare's plays in performance, which have been valuable trailblazers. Alfred Harbage's *Shakespeare and the Rival Traditions* (New York: Macmillan, 1952) and Robert Ornstein's *The Moral Vision of Jacobean Tragedy* (Madison: Univ. of Wisconsin Press, 1960) have already attained the status of classics, and I find that my British colleagues return to such books, which deal only partly with the tragedies of Shakespeare, more frequently than to works which are more directly concerned with Shakespearean tragedy. Irving Ribner's *Patterns in Shakespearian Tragedy* (London: Methuen, 1960) is an admirable introduction to the subject but contains little that is original.

Some criticism, influential and stimulating as it has been, now seems to have lost its gloss: it has dated because it has been so successful. The voluminous writings of Edgar Elmer Stoll are a case in point. We have all learned from him, directly or indirectly, and we have subsumed the valuable parts of his work, while rejecting his excesses and forgiving him his belligerent style. At his best, in *Art and Artifice in Shakespeare* (Cambridge: Cambridge Univ. Press, 1933), which is a condensation of his previous work, Stoll provided salutary warnings against different kinds of bardolatry—the oversubtle analysis of character, the attempt to gloss over inconsistencies, the turning a blind eye to the conditions of the Elizabethan playhouse, the pretense that all Shakespeare's faults were hidden virtues. Of course Stoll went too far. One gets the impression that he really preferred the naturalistic methods of the modern dramatist to the impressionistic methods of the Elizabethans. He asks us to forgive Shakespeare for his "faults" because he gives us great poetry, although (as later critics have pointed out) these so-called faults are the legitimate devices of a dramatic poet. Yet Stoll has real flashes of insight, as when he quotes Shaw's remark that it is the score and not the libretto which keeps Shakespeare's plays alive and fresh. By contrast with Robert Bridges, another specialist on Shakespeare's faults, Stoll had considerable dramatic sense.

Another "historical" critic, Lily Bess Campbell, has provided us with a splendid edition of *The Mirror for Magistrates* and (together with Ruth L. Anderson and L. Babb) has done much to popularize Elizabethan theories of psychology. Her criticisms of Bradley are, I believe, valid; but, in writing of *Shakespeare's Tragic Heroes* (Cambridge: Cambridge Univ. Press, 1930), she tends to treat them as case histories. This method is most successful with *Hamlet,* which she treats as a tragedy of grief rather than of melancholia; but the chapters on Lear and Macbeth, representing wrath in old age and fear, are not of central importance. There are some valid criticisms of Miss Campbell and Miss Anderson, for taking psychology out of its ideological context, in J. Leeds Barroll's *Artificial Persons* (Columbia: Univ. of South Carolina Press, 1974).

As Coleridge said, "we receive but what we give." We bring to the study of Shakespeare our own political and religious views. Although I can hardly credit the American friend who assured me that it was easy to divide critics into Democrats and Republicans, it seems to be fairly easy to divide them into Christians and Agnostics. Roy Battenhouse's overtly and overly theological book, *Shakespearian Tragedy* (Bloomington: Indiana Univ. Press, 1969), attempts to prove that the tragedies were written in accordance with Augustinian ideas; Paul N. Siegel in *Shakespearean Tragedy and the Elizabethan Compromise* (New York: New York Univ. Press, 1957) is also theologically oriented, assuring us here and elsewhere that Othello seals his damnation by his suicide; and G.R. Elliott in *Scourge and Minister* (Durham: Duke Univ. Press, 1951), *Flaming Minister* (Durham: Duke Univ.

Press, 1953), and *Dramatic Providence in* Macbeth (Princeton: Princeton Univ. Press, 1958) tries to show that all Shakespeare's characters suffer from, and are ruined by, the sin of pride. This tends to have a somewhat reductive effect, notwithstanding valuable comments on scene after scene, and Roland M. Frye's *Shakespeare and Christian Doctrine* (Princeton: Princeton Univ. Press, 1963) has properly warned us against the assumption that Shakespeare was an expert in theology. More recently William Elton, in his exhaustive examination of Shakespeare's religious position in *King Lear and the Gods* (San Marino: Huntington Library, 1966), concludes that it was deeply skeptical. We need not decide between Battenhouse and Elton, and no doubt most readers would adopt a middle position: that the religious views expressed by the characters in the plays are appropriate to their context and do not necessarily correspond to those of the poet, and that perhaps he was a good deal less dogmatic than Battenhouse would have us believe, and generally less skeptical than Elton implies.

The group of critics who have devoted their attention to Shakespeare's imagery have developed and refined the work of Caroline Spurgeon. One of the best books in this field is D. A. Stuaffer's *Shakespeare's World of Images* (New York: Norton, 1949). Cleanth Brooks in a famous essay in *The Well Wrought Urn* (New York: Harcourt, 1949) modified Spurgeon's interpretation of the clothing imagery in *Macbeth* and stressed that the significance of the ill-fitting garments was that they were stolen. He also pointed out the importance of breast-feeding images. On a much broader scale Robert B. Heilman examined the imagery of *King Lear* in *This Great Stage* (Baton Rouge: Louisiana State Univ. Press, 1948) and of *Othello* in *Magic in the Web* (Lexington: Univ. of Kentucky Press, 1956). He demonstrated that the pattern of imagery was much more complex than Caroline Spurgeon had thought; he considered it in relation to the action of the play, and he showed how it could throw light on the characters. His method, I believe, worked better with *King Lear* than with *Othello,* and that his conclusions confirm the traditional interpretation of the two plays is an argument in their favor. Maurice Charney has applied similar methods to the Roman plays and to *Hamlet*, but he incorporates imagistic criticism in wider questions of stylistics and is, perhaps, more concerned with theatrical matters than Heilman had been. Brents Stirling in *Unity in Shakespearian Tragedy* (New York: Columbia Univ. Press, 1956) has essays on most of the great tragedies, but they belie the title of the book by dealing with a narrow range of images. It should be mentioned that none of the imagistic critics has taken sufficient note of Rosemond Tuve's caveats in *Elizabethan and Metaphysical Imagery* (Chicago: Univ. of Chicago Press, 1947).

If one examines the criticism of any of the tragedies, one cannot but be struck by the fact that our view of all of them has been considerably modified by American critics. Reuben A. Brower's *Hero and Saint* (New York: Oxford Univ. Press, 1971) is one of the most stimulating of recent books on the tragedies, especially when he forgets his title. He writes admirably on *Othello, Antony and Cleopatra* and *Coriolanus*. Less original, but impressively judicious, A. C. Hamilton in *The Early Shakespeare* (San Marino: Huntington Library, 1967) has good chapters on *Titus Andronicus* and *Romeo and Juliet*. Eugene Waith's essay on "The Metamorphosis of Violence in *Titus Andronicus*" (*Shakespeare Survey*, 10 [1957], 39–49) is, I believe, the best thing that has been written about that play. Morris Weitz, ostensibly writing on *Hamlet* (*Hamlet and the Philosophy of Literary Criticism*, Chicago: Univ. of Chicago Press, 1965), discussed the whole methodology of Shakespearean criticism; Harry Levin provided us with one of the most profound interpretations of the play in *The Question of Hamlet* (New York: Oxford Univ. Press, 1959); and Maynard Mack's essay on "The World of Hamlet" (Yale Review, 41 [1952], 502–23) was a brilliant analysis of the world of Elsinore to which the hero was opposed. Eleanor Prosser's well-argued book, *Hamlet and Revenge* (Stanford: Stanford Univ. Press, 1967), almost persuades us that the Ghost was luring Hamlet to damnation—until we see the play again in the theatre. Fredson Bowers' several articles on the play reveal how much was lost to literary criticism when he decided to concentrate on textual matters. Mark Rose's *Shakespearean Design* (Cambridge: Harvard Univ. Press, 1972)—a book which has something in common with a British book published about the same time, Emrys Jones' *Shakespeare's Scenic Art*—contains a long section which illuminates the structure of *Hamlet*.

On *Othello* there have been several notable books. Bernard Spivack's *Shakespeare and the Allegory of Evil* (New York: Columbia Univ. Press, 1958) has influenced everyone who has since written on Iago, and it is probably the best demonstration of the continuing influence of the morality tradition on Elizabethan drama, supplementing Farnham's pioneering book, *The Medieval Heritage of Elizabethan Tragedy* (Berkeley: Univ. of California Press, 1936). Spivack accounts for the union in the villain of psychological and theological motives. Stanley E. Hyman in his brilliant posthumous book, *Iago* (New York: Atheneum, 1970), carries the argument a stage further. In successive chapters he shows that without departing from the evidence of the text one can prove that the Ancient is a stage villain, Satan, an artist, a homosexual, and a Machiavel. He might have added, in what he calls "some approaches to the illusion of his motivation," an account of Iago as the sexually jealous man, which to Kittredge and Sprague was the explanation of his conduct, rather than the motiveless malignity described by Coleridge. (Elinor S. Shaffer's "Iago's Malignity Motivated," [*Shakespeare Quarterly*, 19 (1968), 195–203], argued that Coleridge afterwards modified this view.) *The Masks of Othello* (Berkeley: Univ. of California Press, 1961), by

Marvin Rosenberg, and the same author's book on *King Lear* are valuable amalgams of theatrical and critical history. One important article may be mentioned, Ned B. Allen's "The Two Parts of *Othello*" (*Shakespeare Survey*, 21 [1968], 13–29), in which he argued that Shakespeare wrote the last three acts before the first two, which are not so faithfully based on Cinthio's tale. This would account for some of the discrepancies between the two parts of the play.

I have already referred to one notable book on *King Lear* by William Elton, learned, comprehensive, and impressive, though we need not accept all his conclusions. Maynard Mack's *King Lear in Our Time* (Berkeley: Univ. of California Press, 1965), though disappointing on recent stage history, contains the most eloquent and sane appreciation of the play that this generation has seen. More recently there has been a collection of essays entitled *Some Facets of King Lear,* edited by Rosalie Colie and F. T. Flahiff (Toronto: Univ. of Toronto Press, 1974). Some of these "essays in prismatic criticism" take up and develop suggestions thrown out by Mack. Professor Colie died prematurely before the book appeared, and one of her own contributions, on the relation between the play and the crisis of the aristocracy, adds something to our understanding of the play.

When we turn to *Macbeth,* we find that in several respects the standard intrepretation of the play owes a great deal to American scholarship. H. N. Paul's *The Royal Play of Macbeth* (New York: Macmillan, 1950), to take an outstanding example, is a learned and persuasive book. It revealed for the first time the full extent of contemporary pressures on the writing of the play; it shows how diligently Shakespeare studied the taste and prejudices of his royal patron with regard to the length of plays, demonology, his ancestry, and other matters, and it tells us a great deal about Shakespeare's craftsmanship. There is, I presume, no other play of which the genesis and composition could be followed in such detail, and there is perhaps a danger of supposing that Shakespeare would sacrifice his artistic integrity because of his desire to please. It can be shown, indeed, that there are sound dramatic reasons for nearly everything in the play. Although it was necessary, for example, to whitewash James's reputed ancestor, it was also dramatically desirable to contrast his reactions to the prophecies with Macbeth's guilty ones and to substitute the secret murder of a guest for a conspiracy in which Banquo was involved. W. C. Curry's *Shakespeare's Philosophical Patterns* (Baton Rouge: Louisiana State Univ. Press, 1937) has a remarkable essay on the demonology of the play.

Willard Farnham's *Shakespeare's Tragic Frontier* (Berkeley: Univ. of California Press, 1950) deals with the later tragedies, as well as with *Macbeth,* and by a sensitive study of the sources and backgrounds of the plays helps us to interpret them. Mack has essays on Shakespeare's Jacobean

tragedies and, written since I began this survey, on *Antony and Cleopatra.*
Most readers, I believe, will find this a more satisfying interpretation of the
play than the moralistic line taken in Britain by L. C. Knights and in
America by Franklin B. Dickey in *Not Wisely but too Well* (San Marino: Huntington Library, 1957). Even William Rosen in *Shakespeare and the Craft of
Tragedy* (Cambridge: Harvard Univ. Press, 1960), although he is fully sensi-
tive to the poetry of the play, seems to believe that where the moral (of the
destructive effects of sexual passion) seems to conflict with the poetry, we
should discount the poetry. Waith has a fine chapter on *Antony and
Cleopatra* and *Coriolanus* in *The Herculean Hero* (New York: Columbia Univ.
Press, 1962); Brents Stirling deals with *Julius Caesar* and *Coriolanus* in *The
Populace in Shakespeare* (New York: Columbia Press, 1949) and Matthew
Proser is at his best on *Antony and Cleopatra* in *The Heroic Image in Five
Shakespearean Tragedies* (Princeton: Princeton Univ. Press, 1965).

I have said nothing about the well-established *Shakespeare Quarterly,* the
younger *Shakespeare Studies,* and the other learned journals which publish
so many articles on Shakespeare every year, and I have not mentioned the
numerous introductions by well-known scholars to individual plays—
Hubler on *Hamlet,* Harbage on *King Lear* and *Macbeth,* Mack on *Antony and
Cleopatra,* and Levin on *Coriolanus,* to give a few examples.

I have confined my attention to the American Shakespeareans who seem
to have contributed most to our understanding of the tragedies. It is very
much a personal view, and other critics would doubtless wish to add to my
list and subtract from it. Perhaps, in conclusion, I may be allowed to take a
brief glance at the other side of the picture.

The proliferation of criticism of Shakespeare during the last two
generations—and not merely in the western world—has made it more difficult to sift the wheat from the chaff, the original from the commonplace,
the sane from the lunatic fringe. The annual bibliographies, even when
they are selective, are liable to appall the stoutest heart, and editors, receiving ten times as many articles as they can print, survey the hinterland of
the unpublished with even greater alarm. When I tried to make an annual
survey, I came to the conclusion that the commonest weakness, on both
sides of the Atlantic, of books as well as of articles, was that Jaques singled
out as the characteristic neurosis of the scholar—emulation. Authors, who
begin as writers of theses, wish to prove that their predecessors are wrong.
They set out with a theory and try to make the poet's inspiration blow
down their fabricated wind tunnels. It is the wiser critics who have taken
to heart the words of Keats, when he argued for a wise passiveness: "Man
should not dispute or assert but whisper results to his neighbour."

Americans in the Playhouses

HERBERT BERRY

To discuss the contribution of Americans to the study of the Elizabethan stage, as I am about to do, and in honor of the American bicentennial, is to face up to some formidable procedural difficulties. The United States was exactly two hundred years in the future when the first regular Elizabethan playhouse was organized, and one hundred and thirty-four years in the future when the last of them were closed down, and at the nearest three thousand miles beyond the setting sun. Moreover, the American bicentennial is of the *separation* of the United States from the land of the playhouses. The two events ought not to have much in common. Yet they do have a curious relevance together, maybe because of all those years and miles, for distance of time and space has lent more than a touch of enchantment, and the American university system has lent energy and money. Americans have come to work over the old playhouses as diligently as the British, and more diligently for a longer time than the natives of any other country. The study of the old playhouses has been a British and American partnership for many years. Another procedural difficulty: Should one divide the partnership? No, and as we shall see, it is not really possible to do so.

Yet another: The term "American" is in this context an embarrassment. The two nations north of the Rio Grande have the same enthusiasm for the old playhouses, and the border between them was never more undefended. Canadian students of the playhouses have become Americans (Leslie Hotson), and vice versa (D. F. Rowan). Some of the most productive conferences about the playhouses have taken place in Canada—like those at Waterloo, Ontario, and the First World Shakespeare Congress at Vancouver—and many residents of the United States have joined in them. The reverse is also true. Must, therefore, Canadians join at last in tribute to the events of 1776? It seems they must, however deplorable the ironies may be. For "American," then, I silently mean "North American." Finally, which residents of those countries should pass as American? Many of the most influential writers about the old playhouses began elsewhere. Some of them spent many years in North America (C. F. Tucker Brooke, A. M. Nagler), others only a few (W. J. Lawrence, Glynne Wickham, Walter Hodges). I have limited myself to those who have spent the major part of their careers in the United States or Canada. I also limit myself to the playhouse building itself, including theories of stage practice which relate to the shape of the building.

Americans did not always give themselves to the study of the old playhouses. They did not join in the first realization that the shape of the playhouse could help to establish Shakespeare's and his fellows' intentions in their plays. Like so many other awakenings in Shakespearean studies, this one took place in Britain in the last quarter of the eighteenth century under the aegis of George Steevens and Edmund Malone and appeared in the apparatus published with the first three variorums, from 1803 to 1821. The Fortune and Hope contracts were there, and so were the first intimations of Henslowe's diary, because all were part of Edward Alleyn's legacy at Dulwich College, and George Chalmers had been there. (Even before these splendid fruits, that other fruit, the inner stage, had appeared, suggested by Capell in 1774 and Malone in 1780.) Nor did Americans have to do with the growing interest of the 1830s and 1840s. The first attempts to reconstruct the old playhouses were driven on, significantly, by a German, Johann Ludwig Tieck, who urged that old plays be put back on the thrust stage and, coincidentally, in 1836 proposed the ancestor of the stage booths which became fashionable more than a hundred years later. The papers and publications of the Shakespeare Society in the 1840s included J. P. Collier's edition of Henslowe's diary and his discovery that much new information about the playhouses lay among the public documents which were soon to fetch up in the Public Record Office.

In the next generation, it was Collier's younger British contemporary and fellow member of the Shakespeare Society, J. O. Halliwell-Phillipps, who finally demonstrated how useful the material in the Public Record Office and other archives could be, especially in his *Outlines of the Life of Shakespeare,* beginning in the second edition of 1882 and culminating in the seventh of 1887, in which he published the contract by which the Burbages acquired their property in Blackfriars, the sharers' papers, some of the more important documents about the Theatre and Curtain, the Fortune contract, and many other documents of less importance here. He greatly improved on Collier's treatment of such things in accuracy, thoroughness, and judgment, not to say honesty, and he infused his reporting of them with a passion for the old and remote which has ever since been a part of the study of the old stage.

The second edition of Halliwell-Phillipps' book began what might be called the golden age of such studies. For forty years thereafter (1882–1923) people studied and wrote about the playhouses with energy unparalleled before or since. Discoveries among primary documents (mostly at the Public Record Office) came in floods, some of it first published as news in such places as the *Times* and New York *Sun*. Being, however, usually documents about the financial arrangements between those who invested in and used the playhouses, and sometimes about the land on which the playhouses stood, these discoveries contained only hints about the structural aspects of the playhouses and left plenty of room for speculation about that crucial matter, the stage. So there were much greater floods of theorizing about the nature of the stage and hence of the productions on it, some of which appeared in places like *Atlantic* and *Century*. As the period went on, the methods used for both documents and theorizing became increasingly sophisticated. Before the period was over, a great majority of everything we know about the playhouses had been found and argued over, and a rough consensus about the design of the stage and the methods of producing plays on it had been reached which persisted everywhere until some fifteen years ago and still persists in some places.

Apart from British investigators and writers, it was not Americans but Germans who first turned their hands to the work. One of them, Karl Theodor Gaedertz, found and published the DeWitt drawing of the Swan and DeWitt's *Observationes Londiniensis* in *Zur Kenntnis der altenglischen Bühne* of 1888. Gaedertz' discovery gave the enterprise an enormous impetus. Within the year, the three other drawings of the old stage had been announced. Within a year or two, the great surge of theorizing had begun, much of it written also by Germans. These Germans gave themselves vigorously to finding mechanical systems to explain how Shakespeare and his contemporaries had used the stage in DeWitt's drawing. By the turn of the century, they had convinced much of the academic world of the theory of alternation: that the old stage consisted of two main areas—the outer stage, in front of the two pillars shown in the drawing, and the inner stage, behind those pillars; that there was a curtain ("traverse") at the pillars which separated the two areas; that there were props on the inner stage but not on the outer one; and that scenes regularly alternated between the two areas.

These and later theories were almost wholly based on stage directions in old plays and on implications in the action and speeches. A great distinction soon developed between those who did this sort of work and those who searched for evidence in old documents. It was an important aspect of the studies of the time. A person did one or the other, and not infrequently he deliberately divorced himself from the other. Workers among old documents wrote contemptuously of "vain theorists," and theorists scarcely acknowledged the great discoveries of the time. Occasionally they even deprecated them. Many theorists, for example, joined in pronouncing useless the best discovery of their time, the Swan drawing. They usually offered two reasons—that the Swan could not have had walls of flint, as DeWitt said it had, and that it could not have held 3,000 people, as DeWitt said it did. Their real reason was seldom declared—that DeWitt's Swan would not accommodate their theories. This separation of theory and documents was the tragic flaw in much work of the period (echoes exist still). It led to many ideas which to even the casual reader now must seem silly.

Americans joined the work at last about halfway through the period. The first were Brander Matthews,[1] G. F. Reynolds, E. E. Hale, G. P. Baker, and John Corbin, all theorists, between 1903 and 1906. They were soon joined by such people as C. W. Wallace (1906), Felix Schelling (1908), V. E. Albright (1909), C. F. Tucker Brooke (1911), T. S. Graves (1911), J. Q. Adams (1911), and A. H. Thorndike (1916). Though they argued vigorously among themselves (some of them said acrimoniously), they achieved two things. Wallace and, to a much lesser extent, Adams carried the work among documents to a point which Halliwell-Phillipps had not dreamed of, both in method and in the romance which he had attached to it. Wallace must still be the most important person in this kind of work, though he gave himself to it only for about nine years. Reynolds, Schelling, Albright, Thorndike, and others effectually drove the Germans and alternation from the field of theory. Eventually, these Americans had a great deal of help from the first World War, but the process was well underway earlier. Americans made themselves partners of the British within twenty years, perhaps one could say fourteen, and (the Germans not having returned in strength) have remained so. In 1903, alternation was king; by 1917, the theories which another American, John Cranford Adams, brought eventually to fullest flower (in 1942) were accepted almost everywhere. British writers, of course, like W. J. Lawrence, William Archer, Walter Godfrey, and E. K. Chambers, had much to do with it, but this conception of the stage and methods of producing plays on it is to a significant extent American.

In this conception, there was an outer stage consisting of the whole platform of the Swan drawing, not just that part in front of the pillars, and an inner stage behind the stage wall, very much like a modern proscenium arch stage, curtain and all. There was also a similar upper stage above the inner one, and there were doors in the stage wall alongside the inner stage and windows in the stage wall above the doors. While writers had propounded some of the crucial parts of this system as far back as 1774, the theorists of the golden age did not derive the system from them. They invented it afresh as a way of getting rid of alternation. Both systems, however, were at variance with the Swan and other drawings, the newer system, if anything, more than the old. So it was that virtually all theorists found the drawings unreliable.

Wallace has become a legend in both North America and Britain. He was from Hopkins, Missouri, a school teacher, then a school principal, who finished a bachelor's degree at the University of Nebraska in Lincoln when he was thirty-three. He proceeded to the doctorate at Freiburg in Breisgau in 1907, when he was forty-two, and returned to Lincoln as associate professor. Two or three years before, he had taken up document examination at the Public Record Office, where presently he went every year. Through all this, his wife, Hulda, of Wahoo, Nebraska, accompanied him. Though less well-educated than he, she worked furiously and, it seems, accurately at his side over the great table in the Round Room of the P.R.O. year after year. The two of them went through many, many documents (he said over five million), including, apparently, the entire Court of Requests (then uncalendared), until the first World War ended their trips to London. He published his findings, especially the earlier ones, with much flamboyance and even arrogance. He convinced himself that everybody else's work was at best futile in the face of his discoveries. He frequently contributed his findings not to scholarly journals but to *The Times,* for he considered them news of international importance. The speculations which he erected on his findings he thought were ultimate truth, but many of them now seem rather silly and pompously articulated. He asserted that he had invented document work, a claim which might better have been made by Halliwell-Phillipps, or Collier's suppliers of documents, Mr. Monro and Mr. Devon, or even George Chalmers. Stories are still told at the P.R.O. of his and his wife's industry at the great table, and of their feverish struggle with Mrs. C. C. Stopes, who had the misfortune to be competing with them. Each side thought it imperative to hide from the other the documents at which they were at work, and even the tickets which were submitted for documents. As a result of all this, Wallace's work was undervalued in his own time and probably still is. As Adams wrote in 1917, and might write today, ''the extent of'' Wallace's ''services to the study of Tudor-Stuart drama has not yet been generally realized, and has sometimes been grudgingly acknowledged.'' If Wallace was in ways absurd, and if he did not invent document work, he certainly found an astonishing amount of useful information in an astonishingly short time, and he was certainly the first student of the stage really to master document work. Mrs. Stopes assuredly was no match for him, especially at the end of his work, as even a casual glance at his and her books on the Theatre in Shoreditch (1913) will show. When he devoted himself strictly to the search for information and to specialist comment on that information, he could be very good indeed.

He more or less gave up university teaching soon after the war began in favor of lecturing around the United States, and then in 1918 in favor of the oil business in Texas, which he hoped would finance new trips to the P.R.O. It financed instead, however, a personal fortune. He died in 1932 without having returned to London.[2]

Most of the important American theoretical writing of the time is the result of two dissertations, G. F. Reynolds' at Chicago in 1904 and V. E. Albright's at Columbia in 1909. The two men became bitter antagonists, but the drift of their work, at least as seen from this distance, is the same—toward the stage and stage practice which Cranford Adams eventually made his own. Reynolds published his dissertation as two articles in *Modern Philology* in 1904–05, then as a book in 1905. Though he assumed that much of alternation was right, he challenged a good deal of the theoretical writing of his time, and he laid the egg in the nest of alternation which soon destroyed it. He suggested that many of the tenets of alternation would be easier to accept if the inner stage were not on the main stage behind the pillars, but in the tiring house behind the stage wall. Two other Americans, M. L. Spencer and John Corbin, arrived separately and independently at the same idea at much the same time. Reynolds also attacked the alternationists' ideas about props, and he used stage directions more discriminatingly and more rigorously than others had done. Even at this first moment in his career, Reynolds was the best American mind of his time in the theoretical side of stage studies.

In 1906, Corbin wrote a very sensible piece for *Atlantic* defending the Swan drawing as it was almost never defended until our own time. In 1908, in the best of the big surveys of the time, Schelling accepted much of Reynolds' work but hesitated sensibly about the inner and upper stages. He preferred his inner stage as the alternationists' had it, out on the main platform.

Albright's dissertation was the first serious American attempt to arrive at a comprehensive scheme of the old playhouse. Absorbing some of Archer's and Godfrey's 1907 work in Britain, he invented a playhouse and stage practice which were in all the crucial ways identical to that which Cranford Adams was eventually to perfect. He marshalled his evidence, however, with more enthusiasm than discrimination. He unashamedly took for granted that there was a general playhouse which any piece of evidence, whether for the Globe, Fortune, or any other playhouse, could help to establish. He often used stage directions as his theories required. He rather cavalierly dismissed even the contracts and all the drawings except the Messallina, which he accepted only because he convinced himself that some lines under the window above the stage were not a kind of barge board, but a ledge for acting—Cranford Adams' "tarras." He argued backwards from the Restoration stage and even the modern one because he thought that they were developments from the old stage rather than the result of a sharp break from it. Indeed, he often took the evidence of the Restoration stage more seriously than that of the older one. He accepted Reynolds' idea of the inner stage, of course, but he quarreled sharply with him about its use.

Albright's playhouse very soon became standard in North America. Corbin accepted most of it in 1911, as did Tucker Brooke, though rather hesitantly. J. Q. Adams accepted most of it, too, but added a reasoned critique of Albright's methods, especially his use of the drawings and his assumption that the old playhouse was one structure which any piece of evidence could help to reconstruct (Adams designed a playhouse of his own in 1923, based largely on Albright's). Also in 1911, Reynolds returned to the work. Stung, perhaps, by Albright's attack on him, he launched bitterly into Albright's methods, especially his use of stage directions and his assumption that the old playhouse was one structure. Reynolds now worked out rigorous principles for the use of stage directions and the like as evidence, the full import of which was not realized even by Reynolds until much later. They eventually led him to challenge the monster which he had taken a crucial part in creating, the stage behind the stage wall. In 1911, however, he too was content to accept most of Albright's scheme, as was his friend Graves in 1913. Ashley Thorndike, Albright's teacher at Columbia, accepted it wholeheartedly in 1916.[3]

In 1917, J. Q. Adams issued his *Shakespearean Playhouses* as a kind of summary of the historical and documentary side of stage studies. It proved also, and fittingly, to be the last significant American work on the subject of the time. Adams tried to cover all the playhouses, and, as he said, he saw all the documents. It is a sensible, sane, and good book which is still useful.

In 1923, the Englishman Chambers published his famous four volumes, *The Elizabethan Stage,* which are still the main quarry for commentary about the playhouses. The work ended and marmorealized the age which

Halliwell-Phillipps had begun. Chambers did not find, it seems, documents for himself, or even have them in his hands. He presided with great and lasting justice over the fruits of a great age. The work of finding, speculating, and arguing had already been done. Since 1923 one has read Chambers and not Wallace, Brodmeier, Archer, or Albright. The golden age of stage studies is preserved almost wholly as Chambers read it. Yet he would have done better to have taken Adams more seriously than he did. He did not make use of Adams' book because, as he said, it reached him when he had nearly finished his chapter on the public theaters (he also said as much about Graves' book of 1913 on the court theaters). Adams did better with some things, including the Boar's Head, than Chambers did.

I reckon the next age of stage studies as beginning after Chambers' volumes and ending in about 1968, again just over forty years. Chambers' volumes were like a bomb. They left a void in which very little moved for a long time. One of the first signs of life was H. N. Hillebrand's study of the child actors in 1926. Somewhat peripherally to his main purpose, he reviewed all the documents which others had found about the playhouses used by the children, and he offered some fresh ones. One must still turn to him for news about Blackfriars, Paul's, Whitefriars, and Porter's Hall. Eventually, however, it was Cranford Adams in the United States, paralleled to some extent by Lawrence in Britain, who undertook the principal work of the time. He refined, but did not essentially change, Albright's playhouse, and he made the evidence for it much more impressive. Adams wrote a series of articles as he went along, and finally issued a book in 1942, *The Globe Playhouse*, which except for Chambers' must be the most important book in the history of stage studies so far, at least if influence and reaction are the measure of such things. The book presents a very careful and comprehensive reconstruction of the Globe, which by frequent inference was the archetypal playhouse. It is very confident, very convincing, very well written. Yet Adams did not have much new evidence about the Globe or anyplace else, and like Albright before him, he used evidence in a self-indulgent way—though less obviously so—especially that of the plays themselves. The tapering stage, the inner stage ("Study"), doors in walls standing obliquely beside the inner stage, platform ("tarras") above, upper stage behind that, bay windows, and the rest, along with exact measurements for everything—he made it all into solid truth propounded in classrooms everywhere for at least a generation.[4] More and more action was moved to the inner stage and into that like unto it, the upper one, which more and more resembled the proscenium arch stages of modern theatres. Other people, especially his associate, Irwin Smith, set about building models and transferring the scheme to other playhouses, even the private one in the Blackfriars. The Folger asked for and got the chief model, and so truth revealed fell upon the playhouses at last.

Yet the reaction was sharp and prolonged (it went on until the end of the period), and it began two years before Adams had even issued his book. Reynolds had been thinking about his strictures of 1911, and he had been reading Lawrence's works and Adams' early pieces. In 1940, thirty-six years after his first work, he issued a book about the Red Bull playhouse, which is not only one of the most rigorously thoughtful things ever written about the old stage, but the first salvo in the attack on Adams. For a couple of decades, the book had no influence like that of Adams', because it is full of doubts and "negative results" rather than a glittering revelation of the comprehensive playhouse. But it has now become a bench mark for studies of the stage, especially its first fifty-one pages. Reynolds reviewed the way writers had been using evidence, especially of the drawings and the plays themselves. He began by declaring the Swan drawing our best evidence yet, adding that "we have accepted the stage directions as literally true and accurate statements of theatrical fact, when they are demonstrably often as imaginative as the dialogue itself." He concluded what others could not for more than fifteen years: all the Red Bull plays "could be given on a stage structurally like that of the Swan, with the single important addition of a third stage door." He declared that "all theories of staging based on supplying a large number of directions are highly questionable"—an incredible heresy in theoretical writing, even now—and he wrote of the "error which has haunted this study [of the stage] from the beginning, that of reading the present into the past." He admitted his own errors in these things—another innovation—and he cogently attacked the Albright-Adams scheme. The inner stage (which he had been one of the first to promote in 1904–05) and the upper one puzzled him. He was dubious about both and thought seriously of rejecting at least the inner one, an impertinence, he thought, in view of all the writing about the playhouses since the beginning of the century. He proposed the booth stage instead, but in the end he stayed with both inner and upper stages, without enthusiasm and with great limitations on what might go on in them. Adams, of course, took no account of any of this in his book issued two years later.

One of Cranford Adams' strategies was to apply the structural methods and decoration of Tudor wooden buildings to the playhouses. Hence the octagonal shape of his Globe (such methods did not lend themselves to round buildings) and its "black and white" look. To get at the playhouses by seeking out their origins has been an ancient art which Americans have pursued more than anybody else. Malone in 1790 applied the lore of inn yards to the playhouses, and the Americans—Graves, in 1913, that of dramatics at court, Lily Bess Campbell in 1923 that of Continental theatres, and Fletcher Collins in 1931 that of Tudor halls and their screens (as, latterly and more fully, Richard Hosley). Another American, G. R. Kernodle, a student of Reynolds, made the first memorable reply to Adams after the fact by applying in 1944 the lore of Renaissance art and continental theaters to the playhouses. He did this much more thoroughly than Miss Campbell had done. Like Reynolds, Kernodle accepted only rudimentary forms of the inner and upper stages, and he suggested booths on stage to supplement them. Unlike Reynolds, he decked out the old playhouse in the finery of Renaissance art and tried to banish the humble look of Adams' Tudor domestic buildings and the even humbler look of inn yards. The trouble with this method is that ultimately it begs its own question. If one does not have enough direct evidence to know what the playhouses looked like and what the practices used on their stages were, how can he know in which of the available conventions, or in what combination of them, to seek the true origin? No matter how thorough the study of the origin, the point at which the origin joins the playhouses must hang in mere air, and the air about Kernodle's is probably thinner than that about Adams'. Adams' (and in 1952 Irwin Smith's) application to the playhouses of Tudor building methods with wood, if not the decoration which often went along with them, is now taken for granted.

The next replies to Adams carried on some of Kernodle's ideas. In 1953, the Englishman C. Walter Hodges and the American J. Leslie Hotson pushed the booths on stage much further than Reynolds or Kernodle had done, and Hodges decorated his stage in more Renaissance finery more impressively (Hodges being a gifted illustrator as well as student of the playhouses). Hodges had first advanced his views in 1950; Hotson was to advance his more fully in 1958. These booths were a way of getting rid of the inner and upper stages. As the alternationists had done in their time, those who replied to Adams insisted that to argue for those stages was to argue for structures not shown in any of the drawings and for actors doing their work in remote corners a long way from their audiences. Hotson's elaborate booths at the sides, however, have not convinced many, and Hodges' simpler booth at the back has not convinced many more. Hodges and Hotson also argued that the proper shape of the Globe was not that of the angular, polygonal, and badly proportioned structures shown on Visscher's and other early maps but that of the round amphitheatre shown on Wenceslaus Hollar's map of 1647. In this they have convinced much of the readership. Their booths, incidentally, are a kind of return to the divided stage of alternation.

They were presently joined in the attack on Cranford Adams by the American Richard Hosley and such Englishmen as Richard Southern (also a gifted illustrator) and Glynne Wickham. Of these, it must be Hosley who has finally buried Adams. In a series of sharply reasoned articles from 1957 until 1968, he drove all Reynolds' main points farther and harder than Reynolds or others had done: the challenge to Adams' methods, the establishing of the value of the Swan and other drawings, and, above all, the idea that old plays could be played on the stages shown in those drawings. He argued convincingly that the stage of the Swan drawing could accommodate not only the Red Bull plays but nearly all the other extent plays of the time. In effect, he moved out onto the great platform nearly all the action which Adams and his predecessors had put into the inner stage and a great deal of that which they had put onto the upper one. He removed, that is, the need for an inner stage and an elaborate upper one and, coincidentally, for at least the lower part of the various booths. He also drove on Reynolds' strictures about the use of evidence, especially that of the plays themselves. Those who use stage directions these days must heed the precepts of Reynolds and Hosley.

If Hosley resolved the question of the inner stage by abolishing it, he dealt less drastically with the upper one. Again taking Reynolds' suggestions further than Reynolds had, he proposed that there was an upper stage and that it was more or less where Adams had it, in the upper gallery behind the stage, but that actors used it in relatively few plays and not for extensive business, and that when they did not use it, spectators or even musicians did. This idea, like that for the inner stage, has become the consensus. Yet it is prone to the difficulties of Adams' upper stage. It defies the drawings, and it defies the growing evidence that housekeepers, not actors, usually controlled that gallery and derived a considerable income from spectators in it. Moreover, actors would not have been much happier in Hosley's upper stage than in Adams'. We do not have a reliable idea about how actors played scenes marked or otherwise mentioned as "above," and that must now be our most important problem with the playhouses.

Two Americans, A. M. Nagler in 1958 and Bernard Beckerman in 1962, wrote general studies of the playhouses while the attack on Cranford Adams was going on. Beckerman's book is about the Globe, but as it had for so many of his predecessors, the Globe for him easily became the playhouse in general. Both were at least skeptical about Adams' proposals,

yet neither was ready to accept what Beckerman called the "fashion" of following the drawings closely. Nagler looked mainly to Hodges, including
his booth. Beckerman, who had begun as a protégé of Adams, openly
washed his hands of much of Adams' scheme and allowed a booth on his
stage, but in the end he hesitantly offered his readers a rudimentary and
much simplified Adamsian playhouse. He read stage directions much more
literally than Hosley was reading them, and of the Swan drawing he wrote
that its stage "is simply not characteristic of the Renaissance design which
presumably DeWitt sought to catch."

As the previous age of studies had closed with a British summary, this
one closed, perhaps appropriately, with an American one, G. E. Bentley's
seven-volume *Jacobean and Caroline Stage,* the last two volumes of which
concern the playhouse and appeared in 1968. Bentley meant the work to
supplement and finish Chambers'; Chambers had stopped at 1616, Bentley
carried on to 1642. A fair amount of Bentley's volumes is, in fact, Chambers, for Bentley felt that he could not begin at 1616 without a summary
from Chambers of earlier events. The playhouses did not begin a new existence in 1616. Yet Bentley's volumes are different from Chambers'.
Bentley thought that he was writing a work of reference and not an extended study of the old stage. So he listed facts and avoided hypotheses,
especially those about the stage and the productions on it. He has no
treatment of such things, or even of the playhouses in general. Chambers
allotted about a third of a volume to staging and about a third of his whole
work to these and other general matters. Moreover, unlike Chambers,
Bentley tried to verify the evidence he reported and not merely to judge it.
Many of the documents which he mentioned he had had in his hands. His
volumes are more scholarly and less magisterial. Bentley's and Chambers'
work differs mainly, however, in the time which each covers. The events
(and the evidence for them) from 1616 to 1642 are less extensive, less important, and probably less interesting than those up to 1616. Bentley could
report the building of only three new regular playhouses. Chambers reported the building of twelve or thirteen, plus the conversion of five inns.

One should not close a treatment of the period from 1923 to 1968 without a remark about Leslie Hotson. Of all American writers about the
playhouses during the period, he is probably the most widely read and the
most freely criticized. He succeeded C. W. Wallace in the work among
documents, and in some ways he resembled him. He could be as imperious about the value of his findings, as arrogant with people who argued
with him, and as thorough and accurate in his handling of documents. His
proposals about the playhouses were, perhaps, more exotic than Wallace's,
and his accounts of them were surely more fun to read than anything Wal-

lace attempted. His work about the old playhouses is actually less extensive and less important than his work about the Commonwealth and Restoration stage—and less important than Wallace's. But he knew the document business very well, and his handling of documents is always impressive—more thorough and accurate, for example, than that of his British contemporary in the business, C. J. Sisson. If one is to dismiss Hotson's conclusions, one should not also dismiss Hotson's documents. Moreover, some of his conclusions are not so dismissable as they might at first have seemed. It is becoming clear that Hotson was right to describe the old stage practices as theater in the round, with spectators on all four sides, though only a few on one of them.

We should now be at the beginning of the next period of studies, which should end with a vast summary about ten years into the next century. If a silence has followed Bentley's volumes, it is not so profound as that which followed Chambers'. Several important people of the last period are still active in studies: Hosley and Beckerman in North America and Hodges, Southern, and Wickham in Britain. Others have entered the arena since the mid-sixties with impressive studies—Oscar Brownstein, T. J. King, J. A. Lavin, D. F. Rowan, and William Ingram.

These studies have some significant things in common. Cranford Adams' book is now a historical curiosity rather than an imposing thing to be wrestled with. Reynolds' and Hosley's lessons about the use of evidence, especially stage directions, have been accepted, as King's book, *Shakespearean Staging, 1599–1642,* demonstrates. (It takes Hosley's work with stage directions a step further than Hosley had done.) The grand old idea that any piece of evidence about any playhouse might reveal the secrets of the playhouses in general seems dead. We seem to agree at last that one playhouse was not necessarily like any of the others. Writers nowadays— and not a moment too soon—concentrate on one house or one problem, and, occasionally with a nostalgic sigh, they stop there. So Ingram has looked at the Swan and Francis Langley, its builder; Brownstein at bearbaiting, the Bel Savage, and other inns used for various kinds of nonliterary performances; Hosley and I at Blackfriars; I at the Boar's Head, and Rowan at the various possibilities of a set of Jones-Webb drawings which he found.[5] In most of these studies there is new evidence of the hard kind, and in them all there is a determination not to accept unproved assumptions merely because they have echoed from peak to peak. The section devoted to the playhouses at the International Shakespeare Conference in 1976 concentrated on just one playhouse, the Theatre—a significant innovation.

So perhaps for the next thirty years or so we shall pick our way from

playhouse to playhouse with a sharp idea of what evidence is and what it
may be used for. It is a humbler procedure than some of those of the past,
but by the turn of the century it could take us to a more reliable idea about
the playhouses in general than the old studies did.

Notes:

1. Matthews' remarks are slight indeed, but he did suggest the idea of the upper
    stage which is now the usual one: that the balcony above the stage at the back in
    the Swan and other drawings served for both spectators and action "above."
2. His great contemporary at the University of Nebraska, Louise Pound, wrote a fine
    account of him for *D.A.B.* Her final remark is severe, but probably just: "The zeal,
    industry, and the surprising success of the Wallace quests were unmistakable,
    but Wallace's absorption in his work seems to have destroyed his perspective, for
    he anticipated results disproportionate even to what he had already accom-
    plished."
3. He was cautious only about Albright's (and in 1942, Adams') tapering stage. He
    managed to avoid mentioning Reynolds, except where Reynolds was "one of the
    most thorough and acute of recent investigators," but "entirely insufficient."
4. He mentioned Albright some eight times, but never to give him his full due. As
    recently as *The Shakespeare Companion* (1964), Adams' is "the orthodox view," and
    in some places it probably still is.
5. A nice older example of this kind of work by an American is C. T. Prouty's article
    about Trinity Hall (*Shakespeare Survey*, 6 [1953], 64–74). In 1961, Prouty also spon-
    sored a volume of long essays, in one of which James Stinson shrewdly assessed
    the various attempts in this century to reconstruct on paper the old playhouses.
    Lavin published (1970, 1973) two adept cautionary pieces about the use of evi-
    dence.

The Rape in Shakespeare's *Lucrece*

Coppélia Kahn

I

The central problem in Shakespeare's *Lucrece* is rape—a moral, social, and psychological problem which Shakespeare sets before us in all its ambiguities and contradictions, but which criticism has so far failed to confront, for several reasons.[1] In *Venus and Adonis,* traditional sex roles are reversed, with humorous effect; in *Lucrece,* they are taken with deadly seriousness and carried to a logical and bitter extreme, which makes it painful to confront the poem squarely. Furthermore, the rhetorical display-pieces invite critical attention for their own sake, offering readers a happy escape from the poem's insistent concern with the relationship between sex and power. That relationship is established by the terms of marriage in a patriarchal society. The rape is ultimately a means by which Shakespeare can explore the nature of marriage in such a society and the role of women in marriage. Therefore, the poem must be understood in a psycho-social context which takes account of sex roles and cultural attitudes toward sexuality.

In this context, the terms "patriarchal" and "sex role," rather than being modern impositions on a Renaissance sensibility, accurately reflect both the Elizabethan and the Roman reality. Because Shakespeare's own society was patriarchal in the means by which it maintained degree as the basis of the social order, it would be surprising if he had not sensed a strong kinship between Rome and England. As M. W. MacCallum states,

> Thus Shakespeare in his picture of Rome and Romans, does not give the notes that mark off Roman from every other civilization, but rather those that it possessed in common with the rest, and especially with his own.[2]

It is a critical commonplace that Elizabethans regarded Rome as a political mirror of their own times finding in it a series of lessons about the fall of princes, the dangers of mob rule, the horrors of rebellion—lessons which they considered to have more than theoretical value. The story of Lucrece as Shakespeare found it in his Latin sources is also a mirror—a mirror of the patriarchal marriage system obtaining in England, in which matches were arranged so as to insure, through the provision of legitimate male heirs, the proper continuance of wealth and status. In marriage as the propertied classes of the sixteenth century knew it, women were to serve the interests of their fathers' and their husbands' family lines; only in that way could they acquire their own rights and privileges. According to such an authority as Lawrence Stone,

> This sixteenth-century aristocratic family was patrilinear, primogenitural, and patriarchal: patrilinear in that it was the male line whose ancestry was traced so diligently by the genealogists and heralds, and in almost all cases via the male line that titles were inherited; primogenitural in that most of the property went to the eldest son, the younger brothers being dispatched into the world with little more than a modest annuity or life interest in a small estate to keep them afloat; and patriarchal in that the husband and father lorded it over his wife and children with the quasi-absolute authority of a despot. None of these features was new, but the first two became more marked in the later Middle Ages and reached their extreme development in the sixteenth century.[3]

Shakespeare's interest in rape lies in the consequences of the crime for the victim, rather than in the act of committing the crime; hence the poem's original title is simply *Lucrece; The Rape of Lucrece* was an addition by the editor of the 1616 quarto. Shakespeare focuses our attention on the curious fact that Lucrece acquires a moral stigma from *being* raped. Though innocent of the crime, she finds herself disgraced, ruined, an object of shame to herself and the world. In the language of the poem, she is morally "stained" and sexually "tainted." Why should Tarquin's crime pollute Lucrece? Why should she bear, in more than the physical sense, the "load of shame" which he "leaves behind"?

A summary of the plot will help us to place Lucrece's stigma in context. First, a prose argument relates how Collatine, Lucrece's husband, boasted of her "incomparable chastity" to his fellow officers in Tarquin's tent. To verify his and others' claims for the virtue of their wives, the men post to Rome that very night and find all the women save Lucrece "dancing and revelling"; she is spinning with her maids. At this first meeting, Tarquin conceives a lustful passion for Lucrece but hides it. Later he returns to Collatine's house alone; at this point the poem begins. On a pretext he stays the night and, after an agonizing debate with himself (126–356), forces his way into Lucrece's chamber. He threatens to kill her and posthumously slander her as an adulteress if she resists him, but promises not to tell anyone if she submits peaceably to his will. She pleads with him at length (561–666); he rapes her anyway and immediately departs. She then delivers several tirades in the high style of the complaint poem: apostrophes to Night (764 *ff*), to Opportunity (876 *ff*). Attended by her maid, she composes a letter to Collatine summoning him to Rome and bids her groom carry it to him. Then begins the most famous set-piece of the poem, a description of the defeat of Troy as painted on a wall hanging (1366–1568). When Tarquin and other lords arrive, she declares that she has been raped but insists that they swear to avenge her before she names Tarquin as her assailant. Thereupon, she stabs herself to death. Brutus urges the grief-stricken husband and father to their mission of revenge, and in the last stanza we learn that Tarquin has been banished for his crime.

The central metaphor in the poem is that of a stain, which is repeatedly and forcefully attached to Lucrece.[4] The words "stain" or "stained" are mentioned eighteen times in the poem's 1855 lines, and synonyms such as blot, spot, blur, blemish, attaint, scar, and pollution are frequently used. Other words denoting either moral error, social disgrace, or both occur with great frequency: shame, blame, infamy, offence, disgrace, sin, guilt, crime, trespass, defame, fault, and corruption. Tarquin introduces the metaphor as he is contemplating the rape, using it to characterize the effect of the act on her:

> Fair torch, burn out thy light, and lend it not
> To darken her whose light excelleth thine;
> And die, unhallow'd thought, before you blot
> With your uncleanness that which is divine;
> Offer pure incense to so pure a shrine.
>   Let fair humanity abhor the deed
>   That spots and stains love's modest snow-white weed.[5]

He again employs it to describe the disgrace which will follow her death if she resists him:

> Then for thy husband and thy children's sake,
> Tender my suit; bequeath not to their lot
> The shame that from them no device can take,
> The blemish that will never be forgot,
> Worse than a slavish wipe or birth-hour's blot.

(533–37)

After the rape, the idea that she is "stained" becomes the leitmotif of all her laments and the motivation for her suicide.

The poem's major concern is expressed through the metaphor of the stain, but it is expressed ironically. Whatever the stain is, Lucrece believes it to be indelibly hers and tragically lives out the implications of her belief. But Shakespeare has molded the poem so as to examine and question her belief from many angles, as I shall show. First of all, the simple moral facts of the rape impel us to doubt Lucrece's self-indictment. In the poem, as in its sources, Lucrece is wholly innocent of any provocation or complicity in the crime, therefore, the stain cannot indicate her guilt.[6] In fact, it is hard to find any single term or moral category which encompasses Lucrece's conception of how the rape has stained her, as this passage, one of several similar passages, shows:

> He in his speed looks for the morning light,
> She prays she never may behold the day:
> "For day," quoth she, "night's scapes doth open lay,
>   And my true eyes have never practis'd how
>   To cloak offenses with a cunning brow.
>
> They think not but that every eye can see
> The same disgrace which they themselves behold;
> And therefore would they still in darkness be,
> To have their unseen sin remain untold.
> For they their guilt with weeping will unfold,
>   And grave like water that doth eat in steel,
>   Upon my cheeks, what helpless shame I feel."
>
>   (745–56)

On the one hand, she mourns her "disgrace" and "helpless shame," terms which might indicate a fear of social disapproval or loss of prestige but do not necessarily imply that she has done anything to deserve such moral judgments. On the other hand, she refers to "sin" and "guilt" which must, in the rhetorical context, be hers, the result of her own moral failing. To complicate the matter further, she reviles Tarquin as the one who committed the crime but declares herself equally guilty of a crime against Collatine:

> Feast-finding minstrels tuning my defame,
>   Will tie the hearers to attend each line,
>   How Tarquin wronged me, I Collatine.
>
>   (817–19)

Our difficulties in comprehending the basis on which Lucrece judges
herself guilty of such a crime arise from her conception of herself as a
woman in a patriarchal society, a conception which renders irrelevant for
her the questions of moral responsibility and guilt in rape. Though Lucrece
uses moral terms such as sin and guilt, she actually condemns herself according to primitive, nonmoral standards of pollution and uncleanness, in
which only the material circumstances of an act determine its goodness or
evil. In doing so, she embodies the attitudes toward female sexuality underlying Roman marriage. Shakespeare poises these attitudes against
another standard of judgment, radically different from Lucrece's but more
familiar to us. He weaves through the narrator's comments and through
the heroine's speeches suggestions of a Christian ethic which disregards
material circumstances and judges an act wholly according to the motives
and disposition of the agent. His point of view, as a result, is a blend of
ironic distance from Lucrece's materialistic conception of chastity and compassionate respect for her integrity in adhering to chastity as the only value
which gives meaning to her as a Roman wife. What the poem conveys
above all is the tragic cost Lucrece pays for her exquisite awareness of her
Roman duty. She upholds the social order by accepting her stain and
dying for the sake of marriage as an institution.

II

The poem deals with the rape of a *married* woman. Lucrece's chastity is
emphatically that of the wife who has dedicated her body to her husband.
This dedication has so rarified and sanctified her sexuality that she seems
virginal or even unsexual. She is imbued with a modesty so profound as to
make us wonder, perhaps, what sexual satisfactions the marriage bed
could hold for Collatine. The vocabulary of purity and holiness surrounds
her like a halo throughout the poem. In the second stanza, she is

> that sky of his [Collatine's] delight;
> Where mortal stars as bright as heaven's beauties,
> With pure aspects did him peculiar duties.
>
> *(12–14)*

She is called "This earthly saint" (85), a "heavenly image" (288), "the picture of pure piety" (542). In a stanza already quoted, she is "divine," "so
pure a shrine," and her chastity is "love's modest snow-white weed"
(190–96). The wifely chastity of later Shakespearean heroines, such as Desdemona, Imogen, and (to a lesser extent) Hermione, is also depicted in
hyperbolical terms which serve not merely to defend them against slurs on

their sexual honor but to make them seem "enskied and sainted"—above and beyond sexuality.

It is precisely such virginal qualities which make Lucrece the paragon of wives. The sexual act in marriage has not altered the perfect innocence which presumably characterized her before she married, and it has hallowed in Collatine the desire which is evil in Tarquin. The marriage bed which Lucrece shares with Collatine is, before the rape, "clear" (382) and "pure" (684)—free of any carnal sin, and her breasts are "maiden worlds" (408), a phrase which strikingly expresses the anomaly of this conception of woman in marriage. Though she is supposedly her husband's sexual partner, she is also untouched, unchanged by her participation on the sexual act.[7] Marriage has invested sex with a prelapsarian sinlessness, and herein lies its psychological value for man. It is his defense against sexual desire with its risks, perils, and humiliations, and Lucrece is the embodiment of that defense. In her, woman made wife, desire is legitimized; it is made a habit and a right instead of an adventure into the illicit. No longer taboo, desire now is shrouded in the pieties of domestic life.

As Shakespeare would have known from his two main sources, Ovid's *Fasti* and Livy's *The History of Rome,* the National cult of Vesta, goddess of the hearth, virtually institutionalized the virginal wife.[8] This cult duplicated on a national scale the values and rituals of the ancient Roman domestic religion, in which the household altar fire was identified with the ancestral gods of the family and with the earth from which the family drew its sustenance; thus the fire symbolized the continuity of the family itself. When Numa, who according to legend succeeded Romulus as king, founded the temple of Vesta, the tending of the sacred altar fire was entrusted, significantly, to virgins, who enjoyed high public honors. It was believed that catastrophe would befall the state if the vestal fire were ever allowed to go out, and any breach of chastity by the vestals was punished by their being buried alive.[9] The symbolic social value of their chastity is noted by Cicero:

> And since Vesta . . . has taken the city hearth under her protection, virgins should have charge of her worship, so that the care and guardianship of the fire may be the more easily maintained, and other women may perceive by their example that their sex is capable by nature of complete chastity.[10]

At least one Elizabethan saw in the vestals the same kind of social importance. John Florio, in his *First Fruites* (1578), after praising Queen Elizabeth's virginity, declaims on vestal worship in imperial Rome:

O golden worlde . . . then was chastitie knowen in the Temple of Vesta. Then the Emperours dyd frequent the Chappel of Iupiter, then Lust durst not come to the Court of Caesar, then abstinence walked through the markette in euerye Cittye, then the world was chaste, then the world dyd triumph, but nowe euery thyng goeth contrary. Certis it is a lamentable thyng, to consider the state of this world.[11]

Florio might have found this vision of a chaste imperial Rome in Ovid's *Fasti,* in the verses celebrating Augustus' election as pontifex maximus, whose duty it was to preside over the vestals and their temple. In them he pictures the eternal fire of Vesta's hearth next to the "fire" of Augustus' divinity, "the pledges of empire side by side."[12]

The two descriptions of Lucrece's person in the poem, both remarkably nonerotic, elaborate a paradoxical desire to desexualize the woman who, by virtue of her status as wife, is entitled to be sexually possessed. I will discuss them in some detail. The first is the narrator's account of the heroine greeting Tarquin on his arrival at her house in Rome, lines 50–84. This description is so heavily encrusted with heraldic terminology and so burdened with the conceit of a chivalric contest between the lady's beauty and her virtue that nothing of a plausible female face or body survives. Shakespeare is trying to convey the impression that she is surpassingly beautiful without admitting any suggestion that she might be physically desirable—a difficult task. In order to accomplish it, he has recourse to chivalric conventions and to allegory, the battle between red and white representing the parity of beauty and virtue in Lucrece. The result is confusion, in physical reference (is the red and white her habitual complexion, or a succession of blushes?) and in syntax (especially in lines 57–63). But if this contest tells us nothing about Lucrece physically, it does hint at the tension between two conceptions of her, as sexual object and as sexually taboo, that is shortly to explode. It is interesting that she is characterized in terms of two qualities, beauty and virtue, that are necessarily opposed in this context. Insofar as she is beautiful, it is inevitable that men should desire her; but insofar as she is a virtuous wife, she belongs to Collatine and no other man may have her.

As T. W. Baldwin has shown, Shakespeare draws his emphasis on the erotic quality of Lucrece's chastity, as distinct from her beauty, not so much from his sources as from the commentary on Ovid by Paulus Marsus in the edition he used.[13] For instance, the Argument prefacing the poem states, "Collatinus extolled the incomparable chastity of his wife Lucretia." In Livy the terms of Collatine's praise are vague and general; in Ovid, "Each praised his wife" for her "loyalty to the marriage bed." Marsus interprets this phrase to mean *pudicitia* and relates this praise directly to Collatine. To give but one more of many possible examples, Marsus' commentary on Ovid's description of Tarquin's mounting desire,

> verba placent et vox, et quod corrumpere non est,
>   quoque minor spes est, hoc magis ille cupit

> (pleasing, too, her words and voice and virtue incorruptible;
> and the less hope he had, the hotter his desire),

singles out the phrase *quod corrumpere non est,* (*Fasti,* II.765–6) stating *"hoc est ipsa spectata pudicitia."*[14] It is clear that Shakespeare was not the first to discern the peculiar element built into the dramatic situation, the power of chastity to arouse desire. But Shakespeare goes further than Ovid or Marsus in relating this phenomenon to Lucrece's status as the wife of Tarquin's friend.

Shakespeare begins the poem by announcing in the first stanza that Tarquin

> lurks to aspire
> And girdle with embracing flames the waist
> Of *Collatine's fair love, Lucrece the chaste.*

>   (5–7; italics mine)

In the next stanza he suggests that Collatine's praise of his wife's "unmatched red and white" has inspired Tarquin's lust. But it is not only the fact that Lucrece is both beautiful and unavailable which arouses Tarquin; it is the fact that Collatine's proprietorship over Lucrece *makes* her unavailable.

Notice how heavily Shakespeare emphasizes the husband's private possession of his wife:

> For he the night before, in Tarquin's tent
> Unlock'd the treasure of his happy state:
> What priceless wealth the heavens had him lent,
> In the possession of his beauteous mate;
> Reck'ning his fortune at such high proud rate
>   That kings might be espoused to more fame,
>   But king nor peer to such a peerless dame.

>   (15–21)

The strong similarity, in image and in situation, between this boasting contest and that in *Cymbeline,* written some sixteen years later, attests to Shakespeare's enduring perception of the chaste wife as an aspect of her husband's status amongst male rivals. Posthumus, it is said, has asserted Imogen to be "more fair, virtuous, wise, chaste, constant, qualified and less attemptable" than any women in France. Iachimo challenges this claim, contending that one so fair cannot possibly remain chaste against the attempts of other men to possess her: "You may wear her in title yours, but you know strange fowl light upon neighboring ponds," he insinuates.[15] In both works, the chaste wife is seen as a precious jewel which tempts the thief; in both works, the husband's boasts initiate the temptation, in effect challenging his peers to take that jewel.

The conventional metaphor of jewels, treasure, or wealth to represent the value of the lady to her lover has an additional meaning in *Lucrece.* The frequent references throughout the poem to Lucrece as "treasure," "prize," and "spoil," and the comparison of Tarquin to a thief (134–40, 710–11, to cite two of many examples) constitute a running metaphorical commentary on marriage as ownership of women. As the elegiac stanza lamenting the destruction of Collatine's marital happiness tells us,

> Honour and beauty in the *owner's* arms
> Are weakly fortress'd from a world of harms.
>
> > (27–28; italics mine)

Marriage is no fortress against the greedy lust of Tarquin, just as the rich man's coffers cannot prevent his gold from being robbed.[16] If Collatine even speaks of Lucrece to another man, he invites competition for possession of her; Lucrece is "that rich jewel he should keep unknown / From thievish ears, because it is his own" (34–35).

For the husband, his wife's sexuality is both neutralized and protected by marriage; for other men, it is heightened in value because another man, a potential rival, possesses it. When Tarquin considers "his loathsome enterprise" before departing for Lucrece's chamber, he devotes only one stanza to abstract moral arguments against the contemplated rape (the stanza already quoted on p. 4), as an act that would unjustifiably harm the good, as embodied in Lucrece. Otherwise, he thinks of the act as a social disgrace to himself as a nobleman and to his family (196–210), and as one which would place him in a morally disadvantageous position vis-á-vis Collatine:

> If Collatine dream of my intent,
> Will he not wake, and in a desp'rate rage
> Post hither, this vile purpose to prevent?–
> . . . . .
> O what excuse can my invention make
> When thou shalt charge me with so black a deed?
>
> *(218–20; 225–26)*

He then considers hypothetical circumstances which would have justified the deed and made it honorable:

> Had Collatinus kill'd my son or sire,
> Or lain in ambush to betray my life;
> Or were he not my dear friend.
>
> *(232–34)*

That is, he is primarily concerned, not with the absolute moral quality of the rape nor with the harm it will do to Lucrece specifically, but with the possible damage it may cause to his status as a nobleman of honorable reputation. This status, of course, is relative to Collatine's power to accuse him of a dishonorable act and shame him thereby. Tarquin regards Collatine as ultimately the judge of his (Tarquin's) acts, and the only real obstacle to his desire:

> Within his thought her heavenly image sits,
> And in the self-same seat sits Collatine.
> That eye which looks on her confounds his wits;
> That eye which him beholds, as more divine,
> Unto a view so false will not incline. . . .
>
> *(288–92)*

Basically, Tarquin considers the rape a violation not of Lucrece's chastity but of Collatine's honor. It is an affair between men, as the ending of the poem will reveal.

The competition between these two men for possession of Lucrece is exacerbated by the difference in their status, for Tarquin is the king's son and Collatine is merely of a noble family (39–42). But Livy relates that Tarquin's father seized the throne unlawfully, brutally murdering his father-in-law and simply naming himself king without observing the custom of calling on the senate for their approval. *Tel père, tel fils;* both men display a kingly disregard for the legitimate sanction of power, and take power into their own hands. Tarquin's private conduct in seizing his friend's wife is parallel to his father's public conduct in seizing the throne; both actions are inimical to a just and ordered society. Another parallel between the realms of sex and politics is notable; the structure of both is patriarchal, with authority over subordinates designated to certain individual men. But authority cannot withstand the strains exerted against it by rivalry between the men and breaks down in violence and disorder. The rape of Lucrece not only parallels the abuse of kingship in Rome but also precipitates its end. Thus the revenge against Tarquin with which the poem concludes involves (as an educated Elizabethan familiar with Livy would know) not only his banishment but the exile of all the Tarquins, the end of monarchy, and the election of Collatine and his fellow-avenger Brutus as the first consuls of the new republic.

Women in Livy frequently appear as victims of the incessant struggle for political power.[17] For example, in the early days of the monarchy, Amulius deposed his older brother and proclaimed himself king of Alba. To prevent his brother's family from asserting their claim to the throne, he murdered his nephews and made his niece a vestal virgin, "thus, under the pretence of honouring her, depriving her of all hopes of issue" (I.3). Again, in the well-known episode of the rape of the Sabine women, the women rush into the midst of battle, appealing to their fathers on the one side and their husbands on the other to stop the fighting (I.9). In the story of Appius and Verginia (well-known to Elizabethan audiences from Chaucer's version), which is the longest single episode in Book I, the assaulted virgin assumes a symbolic importance quite similar to that of Lucrece; her plight illustrates the patricians' wanton trespass against the legitimate rights of the plebs. When her father stabs her rather than allow Appius to violate her, he declares to his supporters, "In this the only way in which I can, I vindicate my child, thy freedom" (III.48).

Shakespeare also calls attention to male rivalry over the proprietorship of women in a curious episode immediately following Lucrece's suicide, when the heroine's father Lucretius and her husband indulge in a contest of grief:

> Then one doth call her his, the other his,
> Yet neither may possess the claim they lay.
> The father says, "She's mine," "O mine she is,"
> Replies her husband, "do not take away
> My sorrow's interest; let no mourner say

He weeps for her, for she was only mine,
And only must be wail'd by Collatine."

(1793–99)

The egotistic competitiveness of the two male guardians over their lifeless "claim," who now belongs to the ages, is academic. But the metaphors of possessing a "claim" and having "interest" in sorrow remind us of the actual legal position of women in marriage, in Rome as in Shakespeare's England.[18] This "emulation in their woe" between father and husband is checked only by the vigorous efforts of Brutus, who reminds the men that their real task is revenge. Here as in the major conflict of the poem, Shakespeare questions the wisdom and humanity of making property the basis of human relationships.

   The second description of Lucrece raises similar issues concerning marriage and the competition for ownership and power between men. Unlike the first, it portrays Lucrece's body directly, viewed as Tarquin sees her sleeping in her chamber (386–420), but again, it fends off erotic suggestiveness. Since the heroine is being described through Tarquin's lustful eyes, we might expect the titillating detail which the poet handles so deftly in *Venus and Adonis*. Instead, he portrays her as "a virtuous monument" or gravestone effigy, her head "entombed" in her pillow, with a hand like an April daisy and eyes like marigolds, "Showing life's triumph in the map of death, / And death's dim look in life's mortality" (402–403).[19] Even her breasts convey no impression of soft and inviting womanly flesh. They are depicted in legal and political terms, as venerable emblems of her status as Collatine's wife:

Her breasts like ivory globes circled with blue,
A pair of maiden worlds unconquered;
Save of their lord, no bearing yoke they knew,
And him by oath they truly honoured.
These worlds in Tarquin new ambition bred;
   Who like a foul usurper went about,
   From this fair throne to heave the owner out.

(407–13)

But the whole stanza disturbingly portrays Lucrece's sexuality politically, as the colonization of her very flesh by the men who would "lay claim" to her.[20] As at the beginning of the poem, here it is Collatine's proprietorship which provokes Tarquin's desire to rape Lucrece. The last three lines depict his desire in political language; the sight of her naked bosom breeds not new lust but "new ambition." The heroine becomes an image for two fields of political conquest, the expanding Roman empire and the New World (similarly, Virginia is named for a virginal woman), and Tarquin, correspondingly, is a rival power who would snatch the newly won territory from its rightful possessor. In lines 3 and 4, the marriage of Lucrece and Collatine is metaphorically a feudal contract in which she swears fealty to him as her lord. Its awesome legality is sharply contrasted to the lawless "usurpation" of Tarquin's rapine. But both forms of conquest over woman, legal and illegal, involve force. Notice the "bearing yoke" of marriage, an allusion both to the husband's right to subjugate his wife and command, by force if necessary, that she serve him, and to childbearing, the wife's duty to her husband.

In the action of the poem, force is a primary element in both the sexual and political realms, and Tarquin is the primary embodiment of it. I have already discussed the background of political force from which Tarquin emerges (see pp. 12–13). From the beginning he can conceive of taking Lucrece only by force; because of her undoubted chastity and because Collatine would never voluntarily surrender his rights, seduction or persuasion never figure as alternatives:

> His falchion on a flint he softly smiteth,
> That from the cold stone sparks of fire do fly;
> Whereat a waxen torch forthwith he lighteth,
> Which must be lodestar to his lustful eye:
> And to the flame thus speaks advisedly:
>   "As from this cold flint I enforc'd this fire,
>   So Lucrece must I force to my desire."
>
> *(176–82)*

He forces open all the locked doors between his chambers and hers (301–02), and when he places his hand on her breast, it is compared to the invasion of a conquering army (435–39), "a rude ram, to batter such an ivory wall!" (464). He announces his purpose to Lucrece in the language of feudal conquest, saying "Under that colour am I come to scale / Thy never-conquer'd fort" (480–81), a common figure in Renaissance love poetry which regains its martial undertones in this context. He concludes his announcement by shaking "his Roman blade" over the defenseless Lucrece (505–06), a familiar gesture of military victory. In Shakespeare's sources, Tarquin's sword also serves as an emblem of the excessive force by which he frightens an unarmed woman into submission. Livy mentions the sword twice, Ovid four times, in the bedroom scene; both prominently juxtapose the sword with the image of the prone, defenseless Lucrece in her bed.[21] Needless to say, in this context the sword symbolizes phallic as well as military power.

In the end, of course, his victory is hollow, and the "Roman lord" who marched to Lucrece's bed creeps away guiltily, "A captive victor that hath lost in gain" (730). He is vanquished, as he knew from the beginning that he would be, by his own conscience. But in political terms, he is destroyed by Lucrece's avenging guardians. After she kills herself, Brutus ritually legitimizes counter–violence against Tarquin by asking the assembled nobles to swear, by the bloody knife she used, vengeance against Tarquin. On this level, woman is but a pawn in the struggle of the state to maintain its laws (represented by marriage) against the arrogant individual who would seize what he wants in scorn of the law.

Ironically, Tarquin is driven to risk all for Lucrece *because* the law makes her taboo to anyone but her husband. Officially, as a chaste wife, she is desexualized, but to one who desires her despite the law, because she is forbidden she acquires a high erotic potency totally extraneous to her sense of herself as Collatine's wife. Thus the poem suggests that the rape represents in part the failure of marriage as a means of establishing sexual ownership of women. That marriage does not succeed in eradicating illicit desire is conveyed forcefully in Tarquin's tortured debates with himself as he approaches Lucrece's bed. Scrupulously, he enumerates the perils of robbing another man's treasure, then recklessly denies them in frenzied rationalizations (127–441). Honor, piety, reason, and self-respect melt before his desire and bear witness to the destructiveness of this woman's erotic power over him, of which she is wholly unaware.

III

Tarquin, however, can wield a far greater power over Lucrece and does so with great cunning. This power rests not in his "Roman blade" but in the nature of his threat against her, which derives its coercive strength from the conditions of Roman marriage, conditions implied in the threat itself. If she refuses to submit to his lust, he will force her and then kill her. But even worse, he will slander her posthumously by killing a slave, placing him in Lucrece's arms, and claiming that he killed them both for their sexual trespass. This slander will do irreparable damage to Lucrece's reputation as a chaste wife, but that is not its cutting edge. What matters to Lucrece, as Tarquin knows well, is that it will destroy Collatine's honor and his family's:

So thy surviving husband shall remain,
The scornful mark of every open eye;
Thy kinsmen hang their heads at this disdain,
Thy issue blurr'd with nameless bastardy.

(519–22)

In conformity with the patriarchal idea of woman, Lucrece has perfectly identified herself with her husband and sees herself as the seal of his honor. Therefore she cannot forcibly resist Tarquin (though she pleads with him), not because it would result in her death, but because it would dishonor Collatine and all his kin. On the other hand, if she submits to Tarquin, he will say nothing and Collatine's honor will remain unblemished. Neither alternative allows her to remain chaste, if chastity is considered a physical state. The first means death but, more importantly, public dishonor. The second allows her to live, presumably with the secret knowledge of dishonor.

Lucrece's pleas are useless, and she does not struggle when at last the rape occurs. Tacitly, she has chosen the second alternative of not resisting Tarquin and could now simply keep her secret. But because chastity for Lucrece is not merely a matter of social appearance but is a physical reality, she cannot pretend to be the exemplary wife once she is no longer technically chaste.[22] Her extended apostrophe to Night, usually criticized on aesthetic grounds as undramatic and cumbrously rhetorical, has firm psychological justification as an illustration of her profound sense of the reality of chastity and of its loss. She begs Night to conceal her from "the tell-tale day," contending that in the light all would see the evidence of rape (746–56; 806–09). Of course they would not; the topos is only intended to convey her belief in the stain; *she* knows it is there and assumes that everyone else could see it. As she dilates upon her grief, it becomes evident that she thinks of the rape as comprising two crimes, that which Tarquin committed against her and that which she committed against Collatine:

The nurse to still her child will tell my story,
And fright her crying babe with Tarquin's name.
The orator to deck his oratory
Will couple my reproach to Tarquin's shame.
Feast-finding minstrels tuning my defame,
  Will tie the hearers to attend each line,
  How Tarquin wronged me, I Collatine.

> Let my good name, that senseless reputation,
> For Collatine's dear love be kept unspotted.
> If that be made a theme for disputation,
> The branches of another root are rotted,
> *And undeserv'd reproach to him allotted*
>   *That is as clear from this attaint of mine*
> As I ere this was pure to Collatine.

(813–826; italics mine)

Whatever Lucrece believes that she has done to her husband, terms such as "offense" or "crime" do not exactly fit it. Her word "attaint" and the prevailing metaphor of the stain come much closer to describing it. Marriage makes sex, and woman as sexual object, clean; outside of marriage sex is unclean. Once the pure, unsexual wife is brought into contact with sexuality outside of marriage, though it be beyond her powers to avoid that contact, she is a polluted object. According to the anthropologist Mary Dougles, "Pollution rules are unequivocal, [and] do not depend on intention or on rights and duties. The only material question is whether a forbidden contact has taken place or not."[23] "A forbidden contact" is exactly what has taken place, and it is understandable that Lucrece sees it as such and does not take into account what for us would be paramount: the moral questions of intention and responsibility. She is the perfect patriarchal woman, content to be but an accessory to the passage of property and family honor from father to son; she has no sense of herself as an independent moral being apart from this role in marriage. Thus she views her chastity as a material thing, not as a moral attitude transcending circumstances.

In the Rome of *Lucrece,* the social order depends on the institution of marriage as the boundary line between legitimate and illegitimate procreation, another way of defining what is sexually clean or unclean. As Dr. Johnson pointed out, female chastity is of the utmost importance because "upon that all the property in the world depends"; a man trusts that a chaste wife will produce legitimate heirs.[24] Certainly this factor is important in the rape of a married woman. It figures in the first alternative Tarquin offers Lucrece; as a way of coercing her into submission, he threatens that her "issue will be blurr'd with nameless bastardy" (522). It also provides a subsidiary motive for Lucrece's suicide, for she resolves that

> He shall not boast who did thy stock pollute,
> That thou art doting father of his fruit.

(1063–64)

In anthropological terms, place in the caste structure is biologically transmitted through the mother; under a patrilineal system of descent, wives are the door of entry to the group, and the wife's adultery introduces impure blood to the lineage.[25]

As is well-known, the honor of a patrician depended in great measure on the purity of his genealogy, his descent from an unbroken line of patricians with respectable reputations. Honor was collective as well as individual; all in the line shared honor and dishonor. The biological importance of female chastity is thus inseparable from its social importance. Furthermore, whether or not a woman introduced bastards into the line, she could dishonor it by adultery or sexual misconduct. Any alteration in her chastity polluted her permanently and was contagious, passing down through the line from generation to generation, as Tarquin's threat makes clear:[26]

> Then for thy husband and thy children's sake,
> Tender my suit; bequeath not to their lot
> The shame that from them no device can take,
> The blemish that will never be forgot,
> Worse than a slavish wipe or birth-hour's blot.
>
> *(533–37)*

Finally, once a man assumed guardianship of a woman in marriage, the chastity of his wife became a primary component of his honor. He then became vulnerable to dishonor through any threat to his wife's purity, as the many jokes about cuckoldry in Elizabethan drama attest. Since honor was to be gained through competition between individuals and between patrilineal clans, men could dishonor each other by exposing any breach of chastity in their wives. The first alternative Tarquin offers to Lucrece (which involves publicly accusing her of sleeping with a slave) is a way of striking at Collatine through her. Tarquin is well aware that if it is known that he has raped Lucrece, his posterity will also be shamed. But if he can contrive to hide his crime by a lie and publish Lucrece's unchastity by the same lie, only Collatine will lose in the competition for honor.[27] Again, Lucrece's fate as a woman is but incidental to a struggle for power in which only men compete.

Only Lucrece, of all the characters in the poem, fully understands her importance to the Roman social system, possessing an insight which transcends that of an ordinary wife and makes her "a singular patterne of chastity, both to hir tyme, and to all ages following."[28] Lucrece's "singularity"

is most marked when, after revealing the rape to her kinsmen, she rejects
the forgiveness they hasten to offer and plunges the knife into her breast,
on the grounds that

> no dame hereafter living
> Shall claim excuses by my excuse's giving.
>
> *(1714–15)*

They are persuaded by her narration of the particular circumstances surrounding the rape that she is innocent, but she sees herself as a "patterne," a paradigm for all ages of the meaning of female chastity in a patriarchy. In the terms of that paradigm, when a chaste wife is polluted by
sexual contact outside of marriage, no matter what the circumstances, she
is forced across the line between sexuality and innocence which marriage
has drawn for her and becomes a marginal and dangerous person. Furthermore, given Lucrece's total identification with this paradigm, no alternative identity is possible for her once she can no longer call herself a
chaste wife. The tragedy of Lucrece is that only by dying is she able to
escape from marginality and regain her social and personal identity as a
chaste wife.

IV

The suicide of Lucrece was a nexus of controversy long before Shakespeare wrote his poem. In Book I of *The City of God*, Augustine questions
Livy's presentation of her suicide as the proof of her virtue. His way of
articulating the problem is relevant to Shakespeare's Lucrece in two ways.
First, the poet has woven suggestions of the Augustinian viewpoint into
his heroine's speech and into the narrative commentary. Second, these
suggestions form a contrast to Lucrece's attitude, distinguishing it sharply
and enabling us to understand its peculiarities. Augustine's discussion
touches some of the same points of contrast, which fall under the broad
headings of patriarchal versus moral, or pagan versus Christian attitudes
toward chastity.

Augustine's conception of chastity is built on the dichotomy of mind and
body: "In the first place, then, let the principle be stated and affirmed that
the virtue whereby a good life is lived controls the members of the body
from its seat in the mind, and that the body becomes holy through the
exercise of a holy will, and while such a will remains unshaken and steadfast, no matter what anyone else does with the body or in the body that a

person has no power to avoid without sin on his own part, no blame attaches to the one who suffers it."[29] Nothing could be further from the view of chastity represented by Lucrece herself, for whom the only important consideration is material: what Tarquin did with her body. For Augustine, the only important consideration is spiritual: whether Lucrece's will remained steadfast in mental opposition to the rape, or whether she consented to it. If she remained steadfast, then as far as Augustine is concerned, her chastity is intact, and she had no defensible reason for committing suicide. If she inwardly consented to the rape, presumably because she took carnal pleasure in it, then she sinned and added to her guilt by the sin of self-murder. Augustine is not convinced that Lucrece did not consent, but assuming for the sake of the argument that she did not, he concludes that her death was motivated "not by her love of chastity, but her irresolute shame. For she was ashamed of another's foul crime committed on her person, even though not committed with her . . ." (I.xix, p. 89) and declares that she was "a Roman lady, too greedy of praise [who] feared that if she remained alive, she would be thought to have enjoyed suffering the violence that she had suffered while alive" (I.xix, p. 89). The shame and love of praise that he sees in her are in his eyes mere worldliness, for he dwells in the city of God and she in the city of Rome. He regards her as a moral agent whose will is free and whose will determines all; she finds herself trapped by the obligations of her marital role, a role crucially important to the social order. Roman she certainly is, but Augustine is wrong in calling her "too greedy of praise," for she dies not to save her honor but to save Collatine's.[30] Indeed, her honor *is* Collatine's. Thus she declares,

> Let my good name, that senseless reputation,
> For Collatine's dear love be kept unspotted.
>
> *(820–21)*

> If, Collatine, thine honour lay in me,
> From me by strong assault it is bereft.
>
> *(834–35)*

She is not greedy but selfless in terms of the values by which she lives. Though, generally speaking, Shakespeare distrusts honor as a social ideal which is easily perverted, becoming an excuse for political expediency, blind egotism, or vicious rivalry (some of the many forms it takes in the Roman plays), his realistic tolerance impels to him to distinguish between the quality of personal commitment to the ideal and the ideal as shaped by a social milieu. In *Lucrece,* he may deplore the social order which requires dishonored women to martyr themselves or be despised, but he sees in Lucrece's suicide a brilliantly successful attempt to re-create Collatine's honor by symbolically restoring to herself the sexual purity on which it depends.

Lucrece stage-manages her death so as to maximize its social effectiveness for this purpose. She summons her husband cryptically by letter, hinting at some disaster connected with herself but not mentioning the rape (1314–23). First, to tell Collatine she was raped is to risk or invite public knowledge of that fact before she can rally her public to Collatine's cause. Second, she fears that even Collatine would suspect *her* of "gross abuse" were she to tell him plainly that she had been raped. Even to relate the extenuating circumstances, she feels, would be a "stain'd excuse"—stained, perhaps, by his suspicion that she protests too much to cover up her own possible guilt (1314–16). She therefore plans to delay her revelation until she can counteract the social prejudice against her by a histrionic demonstration in which the stain of her rape will be obscured by the stain of her blood in suicide.

When she first resolves on suicide, it is evident that Lucrece understands the blood she will shed as the literal equivalent of the stain which she so laments; she is determined to "let forth my foul defiled blood" (1029). The idea that her moral value and social purpose as a wife have been destroyed is for her as literal as a physical change in her blood and is symbolized for the reader when her blood eerily divides into two streams upon her death, one red and one black, the latter congealing into a black substance and "a watery rigol" (1737–50). The Elizabethans knew from Aristotle that wholesome blood was red, while diseased blood turned black.[31] William Harvey, writing in 1651, attributed the separation of coagulated blood into thick clot and water serum to corruption in the body. Thus, as one critic has suggested, it is possible that the extreme literalism of Lucrece's moral self-analysis seemed quite plausible to Shakespeare's audience, to whom magic and medicine were hardly distinct, and thus escaped that strained, overly schematic quality which may bother a modern reader.[32]

It is significant, though, that the heroine's blood is not *wholly* corrupted, as she believes it to be. The division of her blood into two streams is a detail not found in Livy, Ovid, or any other possible source for the poem. Through it Shakespeare symbolizes a tragic duality in Lucrece which she does not perceive. While she regards herself merely as a polluted object, he sees her as a moral agent whose mind remains pure, whose courage and integrity in taking her own life testify to that purity and make her death tragically ironic. In the final scene Lucrece does distinguish firmly between the staining of her blood, that is, her body consecrated to Collatine, and the purity of her mind:

> Though my gross blood be stain'd with this abuse,
> Immaculate and spotless is my mind;
> That was not forc'd, that never was inclin'd
>   To accessory yieldings, but still pure
>   Doth in her poison'd closet yet endure.
>
> *(1655–59)*

But for her it is a purely intellectual distinction, irrelevant to her vision of herself as a "singular patterne of chastity," whose value does, therefore, reside in her body.

The shedding of Lucrece's "defiled blood" is based on a clearly worked out social rationale. When she submitted to Tarquin instead of resisting, she thereby saved her husband from public disgrace, but only by incurring her private stain. This stain brought upon her an existential crisis in that it deprived her of her raison d'être: being a truly chaste wife. Integrity to the ideal of married chastity prevents her from continuing to be Collatine's loyal wife in name only; thus the sole course of action for her is to re-nounce her role and die. The problem then facing her is how to accomplish this renunciation, which necessarily involves confessing the rape, without bringing disgrace on him and on their families. This problem she solves by contriving her death in such a manner that she symbolically restores her body to its previous sexual purity by the purgation of shedding her blood, thus removing the stain which would dishonor Collatine.

She also wrests from the degradation of rape a considerable moral triumph for herself. Addressing the hand which will wield the dagger, she declares, "For if I die, my honor lives in thee, / But if I live, thou liv'st in my defame" (1032–33), and later adds,

> O that is gone for which I sought to live,
> And therefore now I need not fear to die!
> To clear this spot by death, at least I give
> A badge of fame to slander's livery,
> A dying life to living infamy.
>
> *(1051–55)*

The paradoxes of life and death, honor and "defame," slander and fame
indicate Lucrece's imaginative understanding of the potential in her situation. She sees that the death made necessary by the rape can be the means
of recreating that ideal self which the rape destroyed and of restoring Collatine's honor (implied in "badge" and "livery" in the above lines), which
becomes the theme of the following three stanzas. (1058–78).[33]

On a larger scale, the social rationale for the heroine's death is that she
must sacrifice herself for the survival of marriage as the strongest bulwark
against lust. This aspect of her death is revealed in the last scene, when
Shakespeare makes her step out of character in reversing her previous attitude toward the stain. After describing the circumstances of the rape, she
declares that she will reveal her assailant's name only if the assembled
lords swear to avenge her. They do so, and then she pauses melodramati-
cally to ask:

> "How may this forced stain be wip'd from me?
>
>   What is the quality of my offence,
>   Being constrain'd with dreadful circumstance?
>   May my pure mind with the foul act dispense,
>   My low-declined honour to advance?
>   May any terms acquit me from this chance?
>   The poisoned fountain clears itself again,
>   And why not I from this compelled stain?"
>
> (1701–08)

Her questions are predicated on the Christian idea, voiced by Augustine,
that the "Pure mind" can rule the body and transcend "dreadful circumstance." For nearly a thousand lines previously, Lucrece has seemed
unaware of such a distinction. Furthermore, in referring to the stain as
"forced" and "compelled," she deviates from her previous, amply elabo-
rated belief that it is the inevitable consequence of the rape for her and her
appropriate moral burden. Here Shakespeare simply forsakes consistency
of characterization, as he often does, to clarify an idea which the character
represents. This dramatic last-minute appeal to a moral justice untainted by
sexual prejudice is only the rhetorical prelude, however, to Lucrece's final
enactment of her selflessly patriarchal conception of the role of woman in
marriage.

Not trusting the easy forgiveness of her audience, which immediately follows the above lines, she declares, "No dame hereafter living / By my ex-

cuse shall claim excuse's giving" (1714–15). She hereby rejects any attempt to make married chastity for woman conformable with rational moral standards which take into account the intention of the accused and the circumstances in which the crime occurred. There is simply no excuse for a raped wife, because the social order depends upon pure descent as a mark of status, legitimate heirs as a means of insuring property rights, and the control of male sexual rivalry through the ownership of sexual rights to women in marriage. In addition, as I have argued, marriage enables man to cope with his ambivalence toward his sexual desire by dividing women into two classes, clean and unclean sexual objects. It could be argued that all of these goals, while beneficial to men in particular, are also beneficial to society as a whole. But they all require women to sacrifice themselves, to live or die for the sake of marriage. Lucrece's last words charge Tarquin with guilt for her death as well as for the rape, but her last action, plunging the knife into her breast, indicates her final acceptance of the ultimate female responsibility: to keep herself sexually pure for the sake of her husband and of Rome.

Shakespeare's sensitive understanding of the social constraints which force Lucrece into a tragic role informs the whole poem. But it is made explicit in a passage which I have never seen quoted. In the three stanzas of narrative comment following the pathetic episode in which the heroine and her maid weep together, he clearly blames men for exercising several kinds of unfair advantages over women. I see no reason not to identify the author's point of view with that of his narrator in this passage. The first stanza leans heavily on the traditional conception of woman's physical, moral, and intellectual inferiority to man:

> For men have marble, women waxen, minds,
> And therefore are they form'd as marble will;
> The weak oppress'd, th'impression of strange kinds
> Is form'd in them by force, by fraud, or skill.
> Then call them not the authors of their ill,
>   No more than wax shall be accounted evil,
>   Wherein is stamp'd the semblance of a devil.

(1240–46)

Because woman is so relatively weak, man can mold her to whatever purposes he wishes. In the second stanza, the metaphor changes from the stamping of marble onto wax, male force imposed on female weakness, to open space, smooth surfaces, or clear glass, all of which easily reveal impurities:

> Their smoothness, like a goodly champaign plane,
> Lays open all the little worms that creep;
> In men as in a rough-grown grove remain
> Cave-keeping evils that obscurely sleep;
> Through crystal walls each little mote will peep:
>   Though men can cover them with bold stern looks,
>   Poor women's faces are their own faults' books.

(1247–53)

Women are no more innocent than are men; rather, their simplicity or artlessness prevents them from concealing their faults by a bluff show of strength ("bold stern looks") as men do. The third stanza is a passionate plea that women not be blamed for the abuses perpetrated on them by men. Again Shakespeare stresses, in a very traditional vein, that women are weaker than men:

> No man inveigh against the withered flower,
> But chide rough winter that the flower hath kill'd;
> Not that devour'd, but that which doth devour
> Is worthy blame; O let it not be hild
> Poor women's faults, that they are so fulfill'd
>   With men's abuses! those proud lords to blame
>   Make weak-made women tenants to their shame.

(1254–60)

He imputes a sort of natural inevitability to the relationship between men and women as the relationship between the strong and the weak, through the metaphors of "rough winter" killing the flower, or one beast devouring another. The evil that concerns him is that men not only abuse women but also hold women guilty of those very abuses. The last three and a half lines relate this concern directly to Lucrece. The surname "Superbus" or "proud" applied to Tarquin's father (mentioned in the first line of the Argument), which might fittingly apply to Tarquin as well, is alluded to in the phrase "proud lords." The word "shame," connected with Lucrece so many times in the poem, recalls her predicament. The metaphor of woman being the tenant of man's shame suggests that Lucrece as the chaste wife, subservient to and dependent on patriarchy, suffers for a crime she did not commit.

Notes:

1. J.W. Lever summarizes the issues to which twentieth-century criticism of the poem has directed itself in "The Poems," *Shakespeare Survey*, 15 (1962), 18–30. He lists the relationship of *Lucrece* to *Venus and Adonis,* the function of rhetoric, the problem of whether the poem is "dramatic" or "narrative" in method, Shakespeare's relationship with Southampton at the time it was written, hints of Shakespeare's later work, and the poem as a tragedy. For the purposes of this essay, I will comment only on the few essays which deal with the sexual and moral issues of the rape per se.

    Those critics who do take up these issues find Lucrece in some sense guilty of her own rape. Don Cameron Allen's scholarly examination of sixteenth-century humanistic attitudes toward chastity leads him to characterize Shakespeare's viewpoint as Christian, and to criticize the heroine's suicide on the same grounds as does Augustine (see pp. 62-63 above), as motivated by her "maculate body" and "love of pagan honour" ("Some Observations on *The Rape of Lucrece,*" *Shakespeare Survey,* 15 [1962], 89–98). J. C. Maxwell's Introduction to the new Arden edition of *The Poems* (Cambridge: Cambridge Univ. Press, 1966) concurs in this view. The most thorough and polemical elaboration of the contention that Shakespeare wants us to judge Lucrece by Christian standards is Roy W. Battenhouse's "Shakespeare's Re-Vision of Lucrece" in his *Shakespearean Tragedy: Its Art and Christian Premises* (Bloomington: Indiana Univ. Press, 1969), pp. 3–41. He reads the poem as a critique of Lucrece's typically Roman "inordinate love of glory" (p. 14). Battenhouse finds a contemptuous rejection of Roman moral and social standards in every detail of the poem, and reveals considerable bias against Lucrece, remarking on her "feminine proclivity to self-pity and evasive argument." He finds the sweat on her hand in the bedroom scene evidence of her "subconscious preparation" for Tarquin's visit, and interprets her long plea to Tarquin before the rape as "her way of escaping from calling for help" (p. 16). So far as I am aware, only Kenneth Muir, *"The Rape of Lucrece,"* *Anglica*, 5 (1964), 25–40, explicitly disputes the point of view represented by Allen and Battenhouse, stating, "It was not fear of death that made her give up the struggle, but fear for her reputation after death. . . . When one considers the high value set by the Elizabethans on reputation, and also that this story [Tarquin's threatened slander of Lucrece] would be more damaging to her husband than her actual rape, one can see that in the circumstances Lucrece's duty was not clear. . ." (p. 38). Professor Muir does not develop this argument any further, however.

2. Mungo W. MacCallum, *Shakespeare's Roman Plays and Their Background* (London: MacMillan, 1910), pp. 84–85.

3. Lawrence Stone, *The Crisis of the Aristocracy: 1558–1660* (London: Oxford Univ. Press, 1971), abridged ed., p. 271.

4. It should be noted that the metaphor is also used three times of Tarquin, in lines 221–24, 654–55, and 719–28. Aside from these few instances, the stain is associated with Lucrece.

5. Ll. 190–96. This and all subsequent quotations from *Lucrece* are taken from the New Arden Shakespeare edition, *The Poems*, ed. F. T. Prince (London: Methuen, 1960).

6. For a view completely at variance with mine on this point (and on many others), see Battenhouse, cited in n. 1.

7. Steevens, mischievously attributing his comment to Amner, remarked on the phrase: *"Maiden worlds!* How happeneth this, friend Collatine, when Lucrece hath so long lain by thy side? Verily, it insinuateth thee of coldness." Quoted in *A New Variorum Edition of Shakespeare: The Poems*, ed. Hyder Edward Rollins (Philadelphia: Lippincott, 1938), p. 155. Curiously, Shakespeare employs the same idea, that a chaste wife is in effect a virgin, and uses the same word, "maiden," to express it, near the end of his career. In *Henry VIII*, after the divorce Queen Katherine elegiacally says,

> When I am dead, good wench
> Let me be used with honor. Strew me over
> With maiden flowers, that all the world may know
> I was a chaste wife to my grave.
>
> *(IV.2.167–70)*

8. See Geoffrey Bullough, ed., *Narrative and Dramatic Sources of Shakespeare*, I (New York: Columbia University Press, 1966), 179–80. Relying on previous scholarship by Ewig and Baldwin, he states "Ovid remains the chief source" and "The dramatist seems to have had before him a copy of Titus Livy's *History of Rome*."

9. In Book I, chapter 20 of *The History of Rome*, Livy describes Numa's appointment of virgins as priestesses to Vesta, noting, "He gave them a public stipend so that they might give their whole time to the temple, and made their persons sacred and inviolable by a vow of chastity and other religious sanctions." See Titus Livius, *The History of Rome* (London: J. M. Dent, 1926) I, 24. Shakespeare found the story of Lucrece in chapters 57–60, which conclude Book I.

Ovid's *Fasti* describes the rituals of the first six months of the Roman festive year, drawing upon their origins and on legends surrounding them. Among the observances connected with Vesta are the lighting of a new fire in her shrine on the Kalends of March (III.141–44), and the celebration of her day on the twenty-eighth Kalend of April (IV.949–54). More extensively, he discusses the founding of her worship by Numa, her function as goddess of the hearth, and her virginity and virgin ministers (VI.249–348). The version of the Lucrece story which Shakespeare consulted is found in the *Fasti*, II.721–852. I have used The Loeb Classical Library edition, trans. Sir James George Frazer (London: William Heinemann, 1931).

10. Cicero, *De Legibus*, trans. Clinton Walker Keyes, The Loeb Classical Library (Cambridge, Mass.: Harvard University Press, 1959), II.27.

11. Quoted in Frances Yates, "Queen Elizabeth as Astræa," *Journal of the Warburg and Courtauld Institutes*, 20 (1957), 27–82, esp. p. 73.

12. Ovid, op. cit., III.421–28.

13. T. W. Baldwin, *On the Literary Genetics of Shakespeare's Poems and Sonnets* (Urbana: Univ. of Illinois Press, 1950), pp. 110, 114.

14. I quote from the Paulus Marsus edition of the *Fasti* published in Milan by Antonius Zarotus for Johannes de Legnaro, 1483.

15. *Cym.* I.4.59–61, 88–89.

16. The futility of sexual gain or conquest is likened to the futility of gaining wealth in several passages (127–56; 687–93; 710–11; 855–68).
17. Subsequent quotations in this paragraph are taken from the Everyman edition, cited in n. 9 above.
18. Under Elizabethan marriage laws, when a woman was married she passed from the legal guardianship of her father to that of her husband, as she had under Roman law; thus the claim of Lucrece's father is technically invalid, and he may be understood as referring to an emotional "claim" in her as a father. Nevertheless, the metaphors of legal possession and financial interest recall the marriage portions which Elizabethan fathers settled on their daughters. See Stone, pp. 273–75.
19. We might ask why Tarquin sees no specifically erotic qualities in Lucrece at this rather erotic moment. I would argue that for Tarquin, Lucrece's appeal resides as much in the fact that he must "steal" her from another man to whom she does, in every sense, "belong," as in her physical attributes. Tarquin, like his fellow Romans in Livy, finds women and territory equally exciting fields of conquest.
20. In attending to Ovid's account of the Lucrece story, *Fasti,* II.721–86, Shakespeare could hardly have avoided making this connection between sex and politics. As Tarquin contemplates the possibility of rape, he directly compares it to a previous Roman military conquest:

> Exitus in dubio est: audebimus ultima dixit.
> Viderit: audentes forsque Venusque juvant.
> Cepimus audendo Gabio quoque talia fatus.

> "The issue is in doubt. We'll dare the utmost," said he. "Let her look to it! God and fortune help the daring. By daring we captured Gabii too."
>
> *(II.781–83)*

(Loeb edition, trans. Sir James George Frazer, cited in n. 9 above)
21. Livy, I.58; Ovid, II.784, 793, 795, 802.
22. Somewhat similarly, Richardson's Clarissa refuses to marry Lovelace after he has raped her, though she is advised by all her friends to do so, because she does not subscribe to their "marriage-covers-all" morality. But in contrast to Lucrece, Clarissa asserts that her virtue remains untainted by the rape because her mind never consented to the act. She declares, "Have I not reason, these things considered, to think myself happier without Mr. Lovelace than I could have been with him? *My will too unviolated* [sic]; and very little, nay not anything as to him, to reproach myself with?" (Samuel Richardson, *Clarissa* [London: Chapman and Hall, 1902], VII, 197).
23. Mary Douglas, *Purity and Danger: An Analysis of Concepts of Pollution and Taboo* (New York: Praeger, 1966), p. 130.
24. Quoted in "The Double Standard," by Keith Thomas, *Journal of the History of Ideas,* 20 (1959), 193–216, a learned and most intelligent discussion of the legal and social manifestations of the double standard in England from the Middle Ages through the nineteenth century.
25. Douglas, 126.

26. The rape is also reckoned as a lasting blot on Tarquin's lineage, in ll. 197–98, 204–10, but unlike the dishonor imputed to a raped woman, this dishonor has a clear moral rationale; it results from a crime deliberately committed by Tarquin.

27. Julio Caro Baroja, "Honour and Shame: A Historical Account of Several Conflicts," in *Honour and Shame: The Values of Mediterranean Society,* ed. J. G. Peristiany (Chicago: Univ. of Chicago Press, 1966), 79–137, provides a lucid analysis of this kind of competition for honor in patriarchal society.

28. Quoted from the entry under "Lucretia" in Thomas Cooper's *Thesaurus Lingae Romanae & Britannicae,* first published in 1565. See DeWitt T. Starnes and Ernest W. Talbert, *Classical Myth and Legend in Renaissance Dictionaries* (Chapel Hill: Univ. of North Carolina Press, 1955), pp. 125–34, for a discussion of Shakespeare's use of Cooper, whose phrase "singular patterne" sums up the poet's conception of Lucrece as exemplary, and thus rare, verging on eccentric, in her chastity.

29. St. Augustine, *The City of God Against the Pagans,* trans. George E. McCracken, The Loeb Classics (London: William Heinemann, 1951), I, 75. All subsequent quotations are taken from this edition.

30. Edward Hubler, in the introduction to his edition of *Shakespeare's Songs and Poems* (New York: McGraw-Hill, 1959), maintains that *Lucrece* is a tragedy of honor and reputation, stating, "Lucrece's concern for her good name is Shakespeare's first full statement of this attitude, and it motivates her resolve to die" (xxxi). Like Muir (cited in n. 1), he does not carry the argument further.

31. Aristotle, *The History of Animals,* trans. A. L. Peck, The Loeb Classics, (London: William Heinemann, 1965), I, 67.

32. See Bickford Sylvester, "Natural Mutability and Human Responsibility: Form in Shakespeare's *Lucrece,*" *College English,* 26 (1965), 505–11.

33. Later she also plans that her death will benefit her husband in providing an example of the bloody revenge he should take on Tarquin (1177–83; 1191–97). To insure support for him in that action, she delays the revelation of her assailant's name until the assembled nobles pledge their faith to avenge the rape. Brutus' speech rousing Collatine to move against Tarquin (1818–41) returns the domestic tragedy to a historical context, in which the announcement of Tarquin's offense to the people and the banishment of his family marks the end of the monarchic era in Rome. Thus Lucrece, in effect, provides her husband with a heroic mission.

"To Make a Puppet":
Play and Play-Making in *The Taming of the Shrew*

J. Dennis Huston

It is hardly surprising at a time when critical energies aim insistently at classification that criticism of Shakespearean comedy should play a kind of shell game with *The Taming of the Shrew:* no matter which rubric of classification we look under, *The Shrew* is not likely to be there. It is, we find from a number of recent studies, neither happy, pastoral, nor festive comedy[1]—even though it includes some of Shakespeare's funniest and fun-filled scenes, contains a journey to the country where the heroine, encountering stark images of her own condition, learns to play her way out of that condition, and dramatizes the actions of young men on holiday as presented in play before the drunken unwatch of a lord of misrule. Neither, apparently, is *The Shrew* an early "metadrama,"[2] although it focuses almost as intensively as *A Midsummer Night's Dream* and *Richard II* upon man's actions as play and his identity as player. This critical confidence game of hide-*The-Shrew,* however, finds its most finished form in two recent studies of "early Shakespeare," that ignore the play with barely a word of explanation.[3] Clearly, when we cannot find *The Shrew* under "early Shakespeare," we can hardly expect to find it anywhere,[4] and it is time to cry foul against a critical sleight of hand which has surreptitiously cast our play away among the scraps and leavings under the table.

Critics no doubt have reasons to turn attention aside from *The Shrew.* Criticism is built on text, and this text is suspect. With this play, perhaps more than with any other Shakespearean work, what we have seems hardly a just representation of what Shakespeare meant to write. The biggest problem certainly is the Induction, which first introduces characters who have nothing directly to do with the shrew-taming plot and then abruptly abandons them once the play proper is under way. This problem is then further compounded by the uncertain status of *The Taming of a Shrew,* which may be either a source or a bad quarto of Shakespeare's play and which supplies an ending for the frame of the Induction.[5] Is this ending a part of Shakespeare's source which he strangely chose to ignore? Or is it a version of a lost ending Shakespeare originally wrote, as remembered by the compiler of the quarto? Or, finally, is it, like Baptista's third daughter in *A Shrew,* perhaps merely the invention of a compiler determined to

73

order and improve upon *his* source? Then, as if insoluble problems of beginning and ending were not enough to discourage the critic, difficulties appear in the middle of the play as well. There Tranio's sudden transformation (in his guise as Lucentio) to Petruchio's old friend, Hortensio's precipitous and largely unmotivated decision to visit Petruchio's taming school, and Gremio's lack of interest in how his supposed agent Cambio fares with Bianca suggest more than Shakespeare's occasional oversight of detail. Such inconsistencies suggest incompletion, or the beginnings of radical revision. The play as we have it is almost certainly unfinished.[6]

But the precarious state of its text is not the only reason why Shakespearean critics now so often exclude *The Shrew* from discussions of the comedies. There is another, more obvious reason: the play just does not fit neatly into conventional modes of classification. Shakespeare, Northrop Frye has taught us, wrote essentially romantic New Comedy, works descended from Menander, Plautus, and Terence and distinguished by teleological plots in which an alienated lover moves toward sexual fulfillment, marriage, and a renewed society.[7] In a very general way *The Shrew* follows this pattern. Petruchio, at first alienated from the heroine, devises a plan to win her, endures various trials in the process of securing her love, and ultimately triumphs by bringing forth his "true" wife during a final recognition scene, staged at a wedding banquet. In the process the principal characters discover new identities and settle into new social roles. The only problem with such a general summary of *The Shrew* is that it overlooks nearly everything of importance in the play: the rough outlines of a conventional New Comedy plot in the work serve principally to call attention to its *un*conventionality.

Most obviously, the hero is unconventional. He is a boaster, a brawler, a self-server, whose first action is to beat his servant and whose second is to announce himself intent upon making a moneyed marriage—conduct a little bold-faced for the hero of a New Comedy. His apparent plan for winning the heroine is also a strange departure from convention. First he launches into a courtship that, under cover of conventional lover's praise, is nothing less than psychological rape—as the predominance of sexual puns in the scene emphasizes. Then, having converted the ceremony of courtship to rape, he does the same thing with the ceremony of marriage, declaring his wife, with purposely obscene suggestion, "household stuff" (III.ii.233),[8] tearing her at point of sword from her family, and carrying her off like mere cartable goods. Petruchio, though, is not the only one who perpetrates a kind of rape in this scene. Shakespeare himself also commits sudden and forcing violation here. He rapes convention,[9] for with his comedy barely half over he has married his hero and heroine.

True, they give little promise of living happily ever after, and the whole point of the wedding-rape is that it is hardly a wedding at all. A real marriage, one of true minds without impediment, has yet to be earned, and learned. That Petruchio is to teach Kate in a violently unconventional manner. She is put to the tests common to young lovers—flight from home, deprivation, violence, and threatening madness—but her oppressor is not fate, arbitrary law, or a tyrannous father; it is not even a scornful young man resisting her declarations of love. Instead it is an apparently half-crazed and all-too-solicitous husband. And Petruchio, for his part, suffers trials too—a long and arduous journey, disorder in the home, hunger, sleeplessness, and betrayal by those he loves. Only these trials are all self-made, strange fantasies of an apparently disordered mind.

In this madness there is reason, however, and Petruchio finally imposes his mad vision upon the world: Kate proves herself a loving wife at the final wedding banquet. And where earlier Bianca, the model child and apparently model wife-to-be, replaced Kate in the seat of honor at her marriage feast, now Kate metaphorically replaces Bianca as the center of attention and virtue. Two acts before, the wedding feast of hero and heroine was interrupted before it could begin. Then the hero and author both seemed bent upon rape, but the play has proved them actually law-abiders in disguise: Petruchio has waited for the conclusion of this wedding feast to consummate his marriage—"Come, Kate, we'll to bed" (V.ii.184)—and Shakespeare has led his audience by an unfamiliar route back to the security of the ending it expects. By earlier displacing and disordering the marriage which traditionally concludes New Comedy, he has challenged the tyranny and shallowness of this convention only to return it at last, newly charged with meaning, to its accustomed place at the conclusion of the play. Like Petruchio, he has threatened rape but finally answered to the law's restraint.

Yet even when Petruchio and Shakespeare most obviously seem to rebel against the conventions of New Comedy in this play, they are actually falling back upon another, still older convention. Much that is not New Comedy in *The Shrew* is Old Comedy. Petruchio, for example, would be an almost conventional hero in an Aristophanes play. "In Aristophanes," Cedric Whitman writes,

> the comic hero is a low character who sweeps the world before him, who dominates all society . . . creating the world around him like a god. . . . [T]he comic hero himself is wayward, and abides by no rules

except his own, his heroism consisting largely in his infallible skill in turning everything to his own advantage, often by a mere trick of language. He is a great talker.[10]

Like the heroes of Aristophanes, Petruchio touches upon the "low," the bestial, in man's nature. His language, often scurrilous, repeatedly suggests a life actively dominated by the senses. Eating, drinking, sleeping, kissing, fighting, hawking, hunting, and money-grabbing are everywhere in his talk. Then, to enforce his hero's tie to the bestial, Shakespeare has given Petruchio a servant who is his grotesque shadow figure, a petty tyrant and creature all of appetite. Petruchio is like the heroes of Aristophanes also in being a self-server. Almost as soon as he appears, he announces his self-interested purpose:

> Antonio, my father, is deceased;
> And I have thrust myself into this maze,
> Haply to wive and thrive as best I may: . . .
> I come to wive it wealthily in Padua;
> If wealthily, then happily in Padua.

> (I.ii.54–56,75–76)

Here is a bald-faced fortune hunter sure, and no apparent concern for the niceties of conventional conduct or social decorum will blunt his desire for gain. Even the death of a father serves Petruchio to advantage: it puts money in his purse and frees him to venture for marriageable merchandise abroad. The self-interest is matched only by his enormous ego, which keeps him from ever doubting of success. That is Aristophanic too. But the characteristic which makes Petruchio most like the heroes of Aristophanes is his capacity to carry nearly all before him with the magic of his talk. As he moves through Padua, he talks the world into submission, remaking it according to his desires, almost as if he were a god.

He begins first by imperiously twisting language and Grumio's ears in an argument about the meaning of the word "knock." Then, in announcing his intent to conquer Kate, he reduces her scolding tongue to the mere snapping of a chestnut in a farmer's fire. When next he meets the father of the bride-to-be, he quickly negotiates a self-aggrandizing, no-nonsense business deal and then readies himself for a verbal duel with Kate. The rest of the play catalogues his victories in this extended duel, as he transforms her insults to compliments, her contention to agreement, her rebellion to alliance, and ultimately her hate to love. Here, if anywhere outside of Aristophanes, is the *poneria*[11] of the Old Comic hero.

It is no wonder then that we find many of the distinguishing characteristics of Old Comedy in *The Shrew*. [12] Much of its plot is dialectical rather
than teleological, for the action proceeds by a sequence of encounters, or
agons, between Petruchio and those he sees as impostors to his power. Although these contests are primarily verbal, they are often accompanied by
physical violence: Petruchio wrings Grumio's ears, kicks and strikes his
other servants, hurls food about his house, throws sops in the sexton's
face, beats the tailor with his own yardstick, and generally manhandles
Kate throughout. The looser, dialectical structure of the Old Comic plot
also provides occasion for the long harangue, less suitable to New Comedy
because it interrupts action. Petruchio, as we have already noted, is a great
haranguer: he hardly delivers a speech which is not some kind of public
performance or lecture, whether he is describing his disdain for Kate's
reputation as a shrew, warning a wedding company against the dangers of
stopping his way with his wife, or abusing a terrified tailor. The harangues
in this play, however, do not belong only to Petruchio; Biondello before
the wedding and Kate at the final marriage feast also deliver them.

Perhaps the most obvious way in which *The Shrew* seems indebted to
Old Comedy, however, is in its drive toward fantasy. Critics have long
noted how the world of dream is shadowed forth by many of the play's
particular qualities—physical violence which never really hurts anyone;
sudden changes of dress and motivation; confusion of time sequence,
names, and places; strange comings and goings; curiously repeated actions;
and, finally at the end, sudden and easy satisfaction of desires. So strong,
in fact, is the impression of a dream world in this play that the most interesting critical reading of it argues that Petruchio is really a wish-fulfilling
self dreamed into existence by the sleeping Christopher Sly, who himself
longs to be a shrew-tamer. [13] This interpretation is perhaps farfetched
(mostly because it underestimates the complexity of what Petruchio teaches
and Kate learns), but it testifies to a predominant strain of fantasy in the
play. Here, as in Aristophanic comedy, the hero presides at the end over a
feast celebrating the victory of the impossible over the actual. Here, too, he
is paid reverence, almost like a god: Kate presents her devotions to him.
And then, in the final moment of the play, he is declared a miracle-worker:
"'Tis a wonder, by your leave, she will be tamed so" (V.ii.189).

Yet the outlines of the convention are again misleading; they would reduce the play to a mere shadow of its full-bodied form. For *The Shrew* is
really no more an Old Comedy than a New one. There is, for example,
nothing in the tradition of Aristophanes to account for the Bianca plot—
clearly descended from New Comedy—or for the way it is used throughout
as a balance and complement to the main action. [14] More important, Pe-

truchio's triumph is not as direct and uncomplicated as the pattern of Old Comedy suggests. He may be offered devotion like a god, but the offering, like his own earlier actions as a shrew-tamer, is really a complicated kind of play that his wife has learned from him. Her speech is undoubtedly proof of her pronounced debt to him, for it takes as its model his own harangues—hyperbolic public performances depending for their effect primarily upon the spontaneous generativity of language, both in imagery and sound. Yet the very nature of Kate's performance *as* performance suggests that she is offering herself to Petruchio not as his servant, as she claims, but as his equal in a select society which includes themselves, the playwright, and perhaps a few members of his audience: those who, because they know that man is an actor, freely choose and change their roles in order to avoid the narrow, imprisoning roles society would impose on them. Petruchio, then, is not alone victorious in the final scene. Part of the victory belongs to Kate, as her exalted position as the center of attention suggests. And from a dramatic standpoint at least, it is *her* scene, dominated, and in large measure defined, by her major speech in the play. The conventions of Old Comedy take no notice of Kate, although she demands to be noticed in this play. Again *The Shrew* resists traditional modes of classification, and perhaps it is time to see this resistance as an essential part of Shakespeare's meaning. Like his hero and heroine, the author himself may be rebelling against the limits of convention in this play.[15] That surely is how he begins.

The Induction starts with an enormous explosion of energy. From offstage we hear sounds of a quarrel, and perhaps of glass breaking, and then Sly reels across the stage in drunken flight from the enraged Hostess. He promises violence, and she no doubt inflicts it, as they argue about his bill and trade insults until she realizes she can do nothing to control the drunken rogue and runs off to fetch the law. Sly, too drunk to care about her beatings or threats, hurls a senseless challenge after her and then passes out. The brief episode is a theatrical *tour de force*; there has never been a beginning quite like it on the English stage before,[16] and there will not be one to overgo it in pure physical energy until the spectacular opening scene of *The Alchemist* more than fifteen years later. For here Shakespeare has begun in medias res with a vengeance.

The theater audience, noisily settling into place to watch a comedy, knows what to expect. However, Shakespeare dispels that self-assurance. He presents not traditional dramatic exposition, not a Prologue or an Induction giving a clear and careful summary of problems at hand, but an explosion. And then, almost as suddenly as this episode began—and be-

fore we really know what it is about—it is over, and the stage is quiet
again so that the audience can have the kind of beginning it expected in
the first place: enter a lord and his servants at leisure. After disruption, a
return to normalcy. But now the normalcy does not altogether satisfy us,
because we wonder about the apparently abandoned beginning. Why is
what was so spectacularly begun so quickly over? When is the
thirdborough going to come? Why has Shakespeare left Sly on stage? Is it
so that the Lord can discover him? Why doesn't the Lord notice him? What
will he *do* with Sly if he does see him? The Lord talks on about his
hounds, and we wait impatiently for something to happen.

In the process we may also become vaguely aware of themes from the
earlier episode repeated in different tones. There is talk of money and an
argument which, though it is nothing like Sly's fight with the Hostess, still
provokes an insult: "Thou art a fool" (Ind.i.26). We hear again of "cold,"
but now the reference is to a scent in the hunt. This dramatic world provides a marked contrast to the disordered one we first saw, but something
of that first world lingers here still, not only in the heaped figure at the
edge of the stage but also in the distant echoes of the language. Then the
worlds collide. The Lord stumbles upon Sly, and like the Hostess earlier,
he must decide what to do with him. She tried to beat Sly into shape and
failed, leaving behind her on the stage a mass of indeterminate, subhuman
form. The Lord at first tries his art at shaping this mass into a neatly ordered exemplum: "Grim death, how foul and loathsome is thine image!"
(Ind.i.35). But soon he sees more interesting and complex possibilities for
form in the shapeless mound before him—if he has but art enough. He will
create Sly anew in his own image, raising him up to life as a lord:

> Carry him gently to my fairest chamber
> And hang it round with all my wanton pictures:
> Balm his foul head in warm distilled waters
> And burn sweet wood to make the lodging sweet:
> Procure me music ready when he wakes,
> To make a dulcet and a heavenly sound;
> And if he chance to speak, be ready straight
> And with a low submissive reverence
> Say 'What is it your honour will command?'
> . . . . .
> Some one be ready with a costly suit
> And ask him what apparel he will wear.
>
> (Ind.i.46–54,59–60)

What is happening here is that the creative impulse is taking hold of the Lord and he is becoming a playwright, imagining the details of scene, costume, and even dialogue. What is also happening is that Shakespeare is disorienting his audience again. As we expected, he has brought his Lord and Sly together so that the action of the play can begin, but the action that then begins is the action of imagining the beginning of a play. And that play, its author tells us, is a "jest." We are lost in the funhouse sure. We must, however, get more lost before we can be found. Shakespeare has barely started us on our journey through this dramatic hall of mirrors.

The plot to make a lord of Sly is no sooner begun than it too is interrupted. A trumpet sounds the arrival of someone of note, and the Lord, perhaps still inclining to the role of playwright, imagines an identity and purpose for the visitor: "Belike, some noble gentleman that means, / Travelling some journey, to repose him here" (Ind.i.75–76). The hypothesis is logical enough, and perhaps Shakespeare is just adding a naturalistic detail to his characterization of the Lord; we all fantasize about visitors at our doors. But this fantasy also repeats a pattern we have noted before in the scene: it arouses the audience's expectations about the form Shakespeare's play will take, apparently only to frustrate those expectations. One conventional way to begin the action of a comedy, particularly of a Shakespearean comedy, is with the arrival of an outsider or group of outsiders[17]—the Syracusan Antipholus and Dromio, the Princess of France and her lady-friends, Don Pedro and his victorious soldiers, Viola and Sebastian—who disrupt things as they are. For a fleeting moment Shakespeare here offers us such a beginning and then takes it away. The imagined noble gentleman melts into thin air; the men who enter before us are merely players. Another beginning is forgotten—by everyone except Shakespeare, who eventually will make it serve double duty in his play proper:

> I am arrived for fruitful Lombardy,
> The pleasant garden of great Italy.
>
> (I.i.3–4)

> Verona, for a while I take my leave,
> To see my friends in Padua.
>
> (I.ii.1–2)

The players arouse our interest, not so much because of what they do—the Lord's discussion with them of a play they have acted in the past seems designed, like his earlier talk about the worth of his hounds, to allow us the freedom to pay only casual attention—but because of what they are. Everywhere in this Induction we encounter forms of play and figures of players. Sly, determined to "let the world slide" (Ind.i.5–6), has drunk away the workaday realm of cares and law, and now he can at least play at being someone more important than a beggarly tinker: "the Slys are no rogues; look in the chronicles; we came in with Richard Conqueror" (Ind.i.3–5). The Lord too avoids a world of workaday, passing his days in sport and filling his evening with "pastime passing excellent" (Ind.i.67). He converts his bedchamber into a kind of theater and gives his servants instructions in the art of staging a play. But hardly has he done so when he is interrupted by the fortuitous arrival of "real" players—"real" both by the standards of his world and the audience's, though for the audience this "reality" is double-imaged, since the players are "really" players playing players. In this hall of mirrors that is the Induction we find another hall of mirrors reflecting other halls of mirrors as far as we can see: Shakespeare begins a play, which is then apparently rebegun as a more conventional play, in which a Lord decides to stage a play, but he is interrupted by a group of players, who themselves come to offer service in the form of a play to this Lord, who talks with them about yet another play, which they have acted in the past but which they are not going to present this evening, when a player-lord will observe their performance of a play staged after the "real" Lord and his servants have played out their play with the player-lord, who will sleep through the play which Shakespeare, himself playing through this mind-boggling series of false starts, will ultimately present to *his* audience!

Shakespeare's purposes here are almost as complex as his method. First, he is, like his surrogate figure the Lord, merely playing—recording for his audience the almost unbounded joy of a young man doing something whose possibilities are commensurate with his enormous energies. Such an attitude is also characteristic of Petruchio, whose distinguishing quality is his love of play and essential joie de vivre. This quality of life he is eventually to impart to Kate, who has to learn to direct her own enormous energies outward into varieties of spontaneous play instead of recalcitrantly forcing them into the narrowly confining roles society would impose on her. Of necessity, she will still have to play roles and harness her volatile energies within the compass of forms, some of them tyrannically arbitrary—"be it moon, or sun, or what you please" (IV.v.13)—but she will have learned that since playing roles is an unavoidable consequence of the human condition, the very humanness of that condition is determined by the quality and intensity of the play as play:

> Young budding virgin, fair and fresh and sweet,
> Whither away, or where is thy abode?
> Happy the parents of so fair a child;
> Happier the man, whom favourable stars
> Allot thee for his lovely bed-fellow!
>
> *(IV.v.37–41)*

In short, what Petruchio teaches Kate is his version of a lesson of modern psychoanalysis: man feels "only human when he plays."[18]

Another purpose of the references to playing and play-making in the Induction is to achieve *Verfremdungseffekt:* Shakespeare unconventionally manipulates his audience's response to encourage critical awareness. So often reminded that it is watching a play, an audience cannot help wondering what the reminders are for. Why does Shakespeare keep taking us deeper into the illusive realm of plays within plays? Why does he play such havoc with our expectations about how this play will begin? Gradually we recognize that Shakespeare is wielding over us some of the same powers that the Lord wields over Sly: he is presenting us with a play which upsets our sense of the order of things. But the real purpose of suggesting such a correspondence may be to make us aware of differences. We would hope that we are a more receptive audience than Sly and that Shakespeare is doing more than merely playing a joke on us.[19] Then, too, our consciousness of manipulated response and thwarted expectations may increase our sensitivity to such problems when they become central themes in the shrew-taming plot. There Kate's responses are at first destructively manipulated by a society which judges her—and at least has partly made her—an alien. Baptista's initial exit in Act I, scene i, when he conspicuously leaves Kate behind because he has "more to commune with Bianca" (101) is surely an emblematic statement of Kate's exclusion from the family unit. And a similar condition of isolation from society as a whole is suggested by the way characters talk derisively about Kate in her presence, almost as if she were not there at all (see particularly I.i.55–67). But if society isolates Kate by manipulating her, Petruchio integrates her by manipulation.

The way he manipulates her is to frustrate her expectations continually. He comes courting with praise for her beauty and mildness when everyone else has called her a plain shrew; he stands unshaken, even apparently unnoticing, against her attacks when everyone else has fled her wrath in terror; he announces he will marry her when everyone else has proclaimed her unmarriageable. But when he has won Kate's hand in this madcap manner, Petruchio has only begun to play havoc with her expectations.

Greater violence is to follow—at the wedding, on the journey from home, at his country house, on the road back to Padua, and even at the final wedding feast. By then, however, Kate will have learned her lesson: that society's conventions are imprisoning not so much because they force inchoate human energies and desires into limiting forms—a necessary condition of any social intercourse—but because they can so easily *replace* those energies and desires. Forms may abide where there is no longer feeling, indeed, may even drive out feeling.

Baptista provides a clear case in point. Critics of the play have long argued about whether he really slights Kate, some attacking him because he so obviously favors Bianca, others defending him because he is patient with Kate's unreasonable temper tantrums and concerned for her happiness. In a sense both sets of critics are right, because Baptista *thinks* he loves his daughter and tries to treat her fairly. But in fact he does not. Instead of love he gives Kate only the conventional responses of a loving father. We see him first, in apparent concern for Kate, explaining that he is determined to get her a husband before he will allow Bianca to marry. However pure Baptista's motives here may be, the results are disastrous. He makes a public disgrace of Kate because she has no suitors. And then while nearly everyone in attendance makes jokes about Kate's condition, Baptista keeps returning his attentions to his favorite daughter:

> Bianca, get you in:
> And let it not displease thee, good Bianca,
> For I will love thee ne'er the less, my girl.
> . . . . .
> Go in, Bianca.
> . . . . .
> Schoolmasters will I keep within my house,
> Fit to instruct her youth.
> . . . . .
> For I have more to commune with Bianca.
>
> *(I.i.75–101)*

Later when he talks of a possible marriage for Kate, Baptista sounds again like a loving father. When Petruchio calls for contracts to be drawn up, Baptista resists: "Ay, when the special thing is well obtain'd, / That is, her love; for that is all in all" (II.i.129–30). But after Petruchio has met Kate and, to all apparent circumstances, *failed* to obtain her love, Baptista still proceeds with the match, and to Gremio's joking, but probing, inquiry,

"Was ever match clapp'd up so suddenly?" (II.i.327) he answers in a language which makes his motives plain: "now I play a merchant's part, / And venture madly on a desperate mart" (II.i.328–29). He is clearly marrying his daughter off for money.

That Baptista would also marry off Bianca with the same unconcern for her feelings[20] does not alter the fact that his world is one in which conventions replace feeling. Those conventions have many forms. Love may be reduced to solicitous public concern or to patently possessive favoritism, as it is with Baptista for his daughters. Or it may become tantalizing flirtation, as with Bianca; or self-generated fantasizing, as with Lucentio; or plain and practical self-interest, as with Hortensio. It may even appear as comically misshapen greed, as with Gremio. What matters is not the form to which it has been reduced but the act of reduction itself. For in a world ruled, not served, by convention, energies once spontaneously felt either dissolve into cliché—Baptista talking like a loving father about his daughters, Lucentio pining after Bianca in the language of a Renaissance sonneteer, Hortensio fitting his love poetry to the formula of a gamut—or lock themselves into obsessive, repetitious behavior—Grumio's recurrent concern for food and sex, Gremio's instinctive twitch toward his money bag, Kate's repeated attempts to beat others into submission. In such a world man is threatened ultimately by dehumanization: he can act either formulaically in cliché or mechanically in obsession, but he cannot *act* in the true philosophical or theatrical sense of the word because he can no longer feel. All spontaneity, all play disappears.

"Belike you mean to make a puppet of me" (IV.iii.103), Kate cries in frustration when Petruchio will not let her have the gown the tailor has delivered.[21] In this judgment of Petruchio's purposes Kate is both right and wrong. Yes, Petruchio is here playing puppet-master with Kate, making her do exactly what he wants. But he makes a puppet of her so that she may be delivered from her woodenness of response, from her imprisonment (to borrow an image from *The Tempest*) in a tree: in nonhuman nature. When she first meets Petruchio, Kate is a kind of puppet—hard, grotesquely limited both in feeling and action, manipulated by a force she cannot control. But she does not realize she is puppetlike. In fact, she obstinately argues to the contrary:

> Why, and I trust I may go too, may I not?
> What, shall I be appointed hours; as though, belike,
> I knew not what to take, and what to leave, ha?
>
> *(I.i.102–104)*

Manipulated by society, family, and her own uncontrollable emotions, Kate cannot see what she is. Petruchio, however, makes his manipulation of Kate obvious; he makes her **see** that she has become a puppet so that, recognizing her condition, she may alter it, may escape from the bondage of a mechanical existence into the freedom of human form and play. That freedom is, it is important to note, not absolute. All man's world is but a stage and he is merely a player, an actor fleshing out a variety of roles. But compared to a puppet, he is a full and fine thing indeed. Petruchio calls Kate out of the woodenness of the puppet show into the human theater of play. Her answer is, shortly, to command stage-center.[22]

And what Petruchio does to Kate, Shakespeare does to his audience in the Induction. He writes as if he means to make a puppet out of this audience, manipulating its responses in sudden and arbitrary ways, jerking it first one way and then another. But also like Petruchio, he calls attention to his actions by carrying them to extremes. In the process he wakens the audience to perception. He shows it that the theater it sits in, where actors play parts assigned to them, is just another form of the theater it daily lives in: "do I dream? or have I dream'd till now?" (Ind.ii.71). And then he invites the audience to join with him in the act of playing: its role will be, of course—audience. The role is not to be taken lightly. Mere polite attention will not serve, for that is not *playing* the role of audience; it is slipping woodenly into convention, which for Shakespeare is little better behavior at a play than nodding drunkenly into sleep. "My lord, you nod; you do not mind the play" (Ind.i.254), a servingman tells Sly, but the words are addressed also to the audience of Shakespeare's play. For if this audience does not "mind" the play, does not bring to it all energies and faculties of mind in an effort to join with the author in **his** play of mind, then it is no better an audience than Sly, and perhaps in the theater of its world awaits no better fate than he—unaccountably cast into oblivion by the playwright who first breathed the magic of life into him.

Notes:

1. The studies I refer to are John Dover Wilson, *Shakespeare's Happy Comedies* (Evanston: Northwestern Univ. Press, 1962); Thomas McFarland, *Shakespeare's Pastoral Comedy* (Chapel Hill: Univ. of North Carolina Press, 1972); and C. L. Barber, *Shakespeare's Festive Comedy* (Princeton: Princeton Univ. Press, 1959). Wilson actually makes a passing admission that *The Shrew* belongs in his category but then ignores it anyway, as "only Shakespeare's in part" (p. 37).
2. James L. Calderwood, *Shakespearean Metadrama* (Minneapolis: Univ. of Minnesota

Press, 1971). Although Calderwood does not discuss *The Shrew,* his analysis of the metadramatic elements of Shakespeare's early plays has significantly influenced my interpretation of this work; I am much in his debt.

3. A. C. Hamilton, *The Early Shakespeare* (San Marino: Huntington Library Press, 1967) and *Early Shakespeare,* Stratford-upon-Avon Studies 3, ed. John Russell Brown and Bernard Harris (New York: St. Martin's, 1962). Hamilton briefly explains his omission: "I exclude *The Taming of the Shrew* because the other comedies sufficiently show the pattern set up by these early plays" (p. 7). Brown and Harris deal implicitly with the exclusion of *The Shrew* by explaining that the central focus of their collection is three plays "written around 1595 and 1597" (p. 7).

4. The classification which most often does include *The Shrew* is romantic comedy: Peter G. Phialas in *Shakespeare's Romantic Comedies* (Chapel Hill: Univ. of North Carolina Press, 1966) and Hugh Richmond in *Shakespeare's Sexual Comedy* (Indianapolis: Bobbs-Merrill, 1971) both discuss the play. But even in this category the status of *The Shrew* is uncertain. It is not, for instance, included in *Discussions of Shakespeare's Romantic Comedy,* ed. Herbert Weil, Jr. (Boston: Heath, 1966) or in John Vyvyan, *Shakespeare and the Rose of Love* (London: Chatto & Windus, 1960).

5. For a full discussion of this problem see Peter Alexander, "The Original Ending of *The Taming of the Shrew,*" *Shakespeare Quarterly,* 20 (1969), 111–16; Richard Hosley, "Sources and Analogues of *The Taming of the Shrew,*" *Huntington Library Quarterly,* 27 (1964), 289–308; and "Was there a 'Dramatic Epilogue' to *The Taming of the Shrew?*" *Studies in English Literature,* I (1961), 17–34.

6. See John Dover Wilson, "The Copy for *The Taming of the Shrew,*" *The Taming of the Shrew,* ed. Sir Arthur Quiller-Couch and J. D. Wilson (Cambridge: Cambridge Univ. Press, 1928), pp. 97–126, particularly pp. 124–26.

7. This argument first appeared in "The Argument of Comedy," *English Institute Essays for 1948,* ed. D. A. Robertson, Jr. (New York: Columbia Univ. Press, 1949), pp. 58–73.

8. All quotations from the play are from *The Complete Works of Shakespeare,* ed. Hardin Craig (Chicago: Scott, Foresman, 1951).

9. I am borrowing an image here from Eugene Paul Nassar, *The Rape of Cinderella* (Bloomington: Univ. of Indiana Press, 1970). Nassar's arguments about Shakespeare's manipulation of his audience and about the problems of discontinuity in literature—though they are sometimes opposed to what I say here—have significantly influenced my interpretation of *The Shrew.*

10. *Aristophanes and the Comic Hero* (Cambridge: Harvard Univ. Press, 1964), p. 51.

11. The term is Whitman's, and he uses this modern Greek word to describe the essential qualities of Aristophanes' comic hero: *"Poneria* in modern Greek indicates not wickedness, but the ability to get advantage of somebody or some situation by virtue of an unscrupulous, but thoroughly enjoyable exercise of craft. Its aim is simple—to come out on top; its methods are devious, and the more intricate, the more delightful. . . . [F]or though the word may be translated simply 'cleverness,' it also connotes high skill in handling those challenging aspects of life in which the agonistic tendencies of Greek psychology find a field of enterprise. It connotes further the qualities of protean resourcefulness and tenacity of purpose, and with all the world to gain, it can afford to dispense with any superfluous high-mindedness" (p. 30).

12. The defining characteristics of Old, as differentiated from New, Comedy are identified by Northrop Frye in "Old and New Comedy," *Shakespeare Survey,* 22 (1969), 1–5.

13. Sears Jayne, "The Dreaming of *The Shrew,*" *Shakespeare Quarterly,* 17 (1966), 41–56.

14. For a careful analysis of this pattern see Cecil C. Seronsy, " 'Supposes' as the Unifying Theme in *The Taming of the Shrew,*" *Shakespeare Quarterly,* 14 (1963), 15–30.

15. This argument was first proposed, in a somewhat different way, by H. B. Charlton in *Shakespearian Comedy* (London: Methuen, 1938): *"The Taming of the Shrew* is literally Shakespeare's recoil from romance" (p. 45).

16. There have been, of course, Inductions on the English stage before this one, but they have been concerned with introducing a theme or situation that will be directly explored in the play proper. This Induction, in contrast, generates its own autonomous dramatic world, and although it shares themes in common with the main play—uncertain and imposed identity, change of dress, violence, and war between the sexes—it is essentially independent of that play. Thelma N. Greenfield in *The Induction in Elizabethan Drama* (Eugene: Univ. of Oregon Press, 1969) identifies such an Induction as a "frame" and classifies *The Shrew* with such works as *The Old Wives Tale, James IV,* and *Four Plays or Moral Representations in One,* which also have "frames" for Inductions: "With the frame, the actual stage holds two imaginative realms simultaneously. . . . While one play envelops the other each has its own time, place, situation, and series of unfolding events" (p. 98). The Induction to *The Shrew* is, however, only vaguely like the other "frames," since it has a uniquely explosive beginning, no ending, and an extended series of false starts, as I hope to show.

17. See Sherman Hawkins, "The Two Worlds of Shakespearean Comedy," *Shakespeare Studies,* 3 (1967), 62–80, an essay hardly noticed and yet perhaps the finest ever written about Shakespearean comedy.

18. Erik Erikson, *Childhood and Society* (New York: Norton, 1950), p. 214.

19. This idea and the concomitant importance of Sly's falling asleep are more fully discussed by Thelma N. Greenfield in "The Transformation of Christopher Sly," *Philological Quarterly,* 33 (1954), 34–42.

20. See Irving Ribner, "The Morality of Farce: *The Taming of the Shrew,*" *Essays in American and English Literature Presented to Bruce Robert McElderry, Jr.,* ed. Max F. Schultz (Athens: Ohio Univ. Press, 1967), pp. 165–76, particularly p. 171.

21. Robert Heilman in "The *Taming* Untamed, or, the Return of the Shrew," *Modern Language Quarterly,* 27 (1966), 147–61 argues that this quotation is indicative of "what farce does to all characters" (p. 155). Although he sees a different kind of symbolic meaning in the line than I do, his analysis first drew my attention to its importance.

22. Richard Henze in "Role Playing in *The Taming of the Shrew,*" *Southern Humanities Review,* 4 (1970), 231–40, makes a corroborating argument: "What Petruchio does, then, both during the wooing of Kate and the taming of Kate, is, like the Lord with Sly, to place his subject in a pageant where she will need an actor's ability to assess her role and decide how to play it. Unlike Sly, who remains a simple tinker because he lacks that ability, Kate finally learns, under the direction of Petruchio, to alter her role as the pageant of marriage and life requires" (p. 234).

The Mutilated Garden in *Titus Andronicus*

ALBERT H. TRICOMI

A significant critical reexamination of *Titus Andronicus* has begun. Whereas earlier critics used to dismiss this early tragedy with memorably derisive strictures or else involved themselves in lengthy extra-literary disputes of authorship and authorial indebtedness,[1] a new and more dispassionate regard for the play itself has begun to produce greater knowledge of its meaning. Most recently, in *Shakespeare's Early Tragedies*, Nicholas Brooke has examined the emblematic structure of the play as well as the choric function of many of its otherwise inappropriately elaborate poetic descriptions.[2] Also, Alan Sommers, in an important article, has opened the way toward a thematic understanding of the dialectic antagonism between barbarism and civilization in the tragedy. In the unprincipled machinations of Aaron the Blackamoor and of Tamora, the revengeful Queen of Goths, Sommers finds the assault of a barbaric primitivism against the traditional Roman values of "virtue," "justice," and "piety."[3] In their own way, each of these analyses provides an answer to the critical question of taste in *Titus Andronicus* and to Shakespeare's widely misunderstood mixture of decorous poetry and Senecan horror. In my judgment this attention to the functions of the poetry in *Titus Andronicus,* while not providing the only legitimate approach, is most constructive and is critically necessary if *Titus Andronicus* is to be genuinely reintegrated into the Shakespeare canon.[4] In keeping with the spirit of this recent critical development, my own approach will be to examine the thematic functions of the central image patterns in the play.

Customary though it has been to highlight the ornamentality and decorativeness of the poetry in *Titus Andronicus,* its images create a thematic matrix that is impressive considering the early date of the tragedy. This thematic matrix, which governs the imagistic structure of the play, culminates in a dialectic contrast between the play's predatory animal images and its cardinal emblem of the enduring but mutilated garden. Through these central image patterns, the play reveals the tragic efforts of the Andronici to preserve a world of civilized virtues from the onslaught of a demonic barbarism. Oddly enough then, the very qualities of language in *Titus Andronicus* that once excited critical contumely hold the potential for revealing the play's thematic integrity and imaginative power.

I

Wolfgang Clemen observes of *Titus Andronicus* that the images lack "internal and external connection" with the structure of the tragedy; they appear to be "tacked on."[5] The focal point of his strictures, as well as those of Miss Bradbrook and a host of other reputable critics, is the prettified Ovidian monologue in Act II, scene iv, in which Marcus Andronicus discovers that his niece, Lavinia, has been raped and mutilated.[6] Clemen's excoriation of the passage, "It is not only the idea that a human being at sight of such atrocities can burst forth into a long speech full of images and comparisons which appears so unsuitable and inorganic; but it is rather the . . . almost wanton playfulness [of these images] which reveals the incongruity,"[7] is characteristic of many; however, it goes too far, for when on a broader level of generalization Clemen declares, "The images 'run wild,' they are not yet organically related to the framework of the play . . . ,"[8] his devastating judgment blinds us to the imagistic achievements of the play. The thematic integrity of the play's pastoral images, although couched in a context of Senecan horror, is not so very ludicrous at all. In fact, the same monologue that has become a cynosure of derision establishes the principal images of the garden setting that are basic to the thematic structure of the tragedy.

In this passage Marcus responds to the sight of Lavinia's mutilation by likening her to a denuded shade tree:

> Speak, gentle niece, what stern ungentle hands
> Hath lopp'd and hew'd and made thy body bare
> Of her two branches, those sweet ornaments,
> Whose circling shadows kings have sought to sleep in.
>
> (II.iv.16–20)[9]

Having made this elaborate arboreal comparison, Marcus soon compares Lavinia's bleeding body, in a notorious simile, to a bubbling fountain:

> Alas, a crimson river of warm blood,
> Like to a bubbling fountain stirr'd with wind,
> Doth rise and fall between thy rosed lips,
> Coming and going with thy honey breath.
> But, sure, some Tereus hath deflow'red thee,
> And, lest thou should'st detect him, cut thy tongue.
> Ah, now thou turn'st away thy face for shame,

> And, notwithstanding all this loss of blood,
> As from a conduit with three issuing spouts,
> Yet do thy cheeks look red as Titan's face
> Blushing to be encount'red with a cloud.
>
> *(II.iv.23–32)*

In perusing this speech, we must notice that its central images of the denuded shade tree and the bubbling fountain are integrally related to one another, both being drawn from a pastoral setting, and are by no means ornamental. They also bear considerable symbolic weight in supporting the imagistic framework of the play. Let us consider the merits of each point in its turn.

Milton's description of Eden in the fourth book of *Paradise Lost,* Bacon's essay "On Gardens," as well as other less important works of the Renaissance reveal the fountain to be a traditional fixture in the pastoral setting.[10] As a matter of fact, Shakespeare's only pastoral poem, "Venus and Adonis," which was written during the same early period as *Titus Andronicus,* unites these same images of the fountain and the park.

> She [i.e. Venus] locks her lily fingers one in one.
> "Fondling," she saith, "since I have hemm'd thee here
> Within the circuit of this ivory pale,
> I'll be a park, and thou shalt be my deer:
> Feed where thou wilt, on mountain or in dale;
> Grace on my lips, and if those hills be dry,
> Stray lower, where the pleasant fountains lie."[11]

For all its double entendre, the image of the fountains appears in a recognizably pastoral context that illustrates its pertinence to the pastoral imagery of Marcus' own speech. Moreover, it is important to recognize that while the vivid pictorial images in Venus' speech—the lily and the deer as well as the fountains and the park—are all integrally related to the pastoral setting in that poem, they all reappear in *Titus Andronicus* as part of *its* pastoral setting—the lily (II.iv.44), the deer (III.i.88–90), the fountain (II.iv.23–30), and the park (III.i.88).[12] They too are integrally related to one another. Even more notably, these pastoral similes, which may appear to function as mere poetic ornament, are all associated with Lavinia and are made to bear unusual symbolic weight, for Lavinia and the forest in *Titus Andronicus* are imagined as one or nearly one throughout the play. Through this association, which becomes manifest by degrees, Shakespeare both defines and magnifies the significance of Lavinia's violation.

Before the forest is ever explicitly identified with Lavinia, that is before Marcus' speech at II.iv.11, it begins to assume increasingly symbolic importance. As the title of Sommers' article, "Wilderness of Tigers," suggests, the forest in *Titus Andronicus* eventually becomes synonymous with barbarism and chaos, but in the early acts, we must remember, it is often depicted as lovely and attractive. For Titus and for Saturninus the forest is initially an appealing, fit place to celebrate an Emperor's marriage with a recreational hunt. Possessing also "wide and spacious" private walks (II.i.114) as well as many unfrequented bowers, it is much more like an English park than a wild forest, and at one point Marcus calls it just that, "a park" (III.i.88). Thus perceived, the forest is not unlike Sidney's estate at Penshurst as Jonson depicts it with its deer and private "walks for health as well as sport."[13]

Through most of the second act Shakespeare delineates the forest as a pastoral haven so that even Tamora's illicit tryst with Aaron in the secluded bower bears the earmarks of an idyllic retreat or demi-paradise. In this wooded retreat "The birds chant melody on every bush" (II.iii.12; cf. 22) and the green leaves "quiver with the cooling wind" while offering a pleasing shade (ll.14–15). Here, Tamora observes, lovers may enjoy "a golden slumber" while the "sweet melodious birds" act as "a nurse's song / Of lullaby to bring her babe asleep" (II.iii.28–29). We do well to savor the luxurious details of Tamora's pastoral description, for in the scenes immediately following, these very pastoral images reappear in Marcus' delineations of his niece Lavinia. However inappropriate his poeticizing otherwise appears, Marcus establishes the visual and aural correspondences between Lavinia and this idyllic retreat. In phrases that cannot help but recall Tamora's pastoral narration, Marcus describes Lavinia as "a sweet melodious bird" (III.i.85; cf. II.iii.12), as a tree under "Whose circling shadows kings have sought to sleep in" (II.iv.19; cf. II.iii.28–29), as a deer "straying in the park" (III.i.88; cf. II.i.117), and as one whose hands are "like aspen-leaves" (II.iv.45; cf. II.iii.14)—all of which suggests not only that Lavinia is associated with this pastoral demi-paradise but that her person appears to embody it.

Were this idyllic view of the forest unqualified throughout the play, we could indeed conclude that the images associated with it are part of a largely ornamental, albeit integrated, display. But there is dramatic tension in our perception of the forest from the outset. Aaron alone amongst the principal characters believes the forest to be "ruthless, dreadful, deaf, and dull" (II.i.128), "Fitted by kind for rape and villainy"(II.i.116). Tamora's oafish sons, who are the henchmen of Aaron's thoughts, enter the forest in eager expectation of a rape; "Chiron, we hunt not, we, with horse nor hound, / But hope to pluck a dainty doe to ground" (II.iii.25–26). If we attend as well to the pastoral landscape that presides over Tamora's adulterous liaison with her black paramour, we will find in it a cause for eerie fascination and alarm, for in the midst of this paradisic haven we find that the coiled snake lies motionless in the cheerful sun (II.iii.13).

As the symbol of the forest unfolds, then, we see in it a pastoral haven ominously threatened by an impending act of doom, the rape of Lavinia. That the forest and Lavinia are intimately associated with one another and that they share the same fate is made clear by Tamora's elaborate dissimulation that Lavinia's husband Bassianus intends to rape her. In creating this false witness, Tamora paints a new picture of the forest that inadvertently prophesies what it actually becomes:

> A barren detested vale you see it is;
> The trees, though summer, yet forlorn and lean,
> Overcome with moss and baleful mistletoe:
> Here never shines the sun: here nothing breeds,
> Unless the nightly owl or fatal raven:
> And when they show'd me this abhorred pit,
> They told me, here, at dead time of the night,
> A thousand fiends, a thousand hissing snakes,
> Ten thousand swelling toads, as many urchins,
> Would make such fearful and confused cries,
> As any mortal body hearing it
> Should straight fall mad, or else die suddenly.
>
> *(II.iii.93–104)*

As if in ghoulish anticipation of the rape scene that is immediately to follow, Tamora's dissembling narration presents us with a metamorphosis of the pastoral garden she had previously portrayed. That the idyllic pastoral world always contained the possibility of becoming its opposite is, as I have said, strongly implied by the coiled snake within it and also by the satanic image of the adulterous lovers "wreathed in each other's arms" (II.iii.25). We begin to understand that the sounds of the forest out of which the miscegenous lovers create their bliss—"the babbling echo [which] mocks the hounds, / . . . / As if a double hunt were heard at once" (II.iii.17–19, but also, 27–29)—are imagistic foreshadowings of the hunt that will cost Lavinia her tongue (cf. III.i.83–84) and her chastity. Thus, in strik-

ing contradiction to Tamora's earlier account, the pastoral haven now reveals itself to be the pit of hell; the sleeping snake in the first account now
hisses and is in its diabolism multiplied a thousandfold as the idyllic setting, now transfigured, is about to preside over Lavinia's own disfigura-
tion. The metamorphosis of the pastoral forest *is* the metamorphosis of
Lavinia writ large; the dual transfiguration is part of the same symbolic
event.

II

At the center of these images that identify Lavinia with this pastoral setting and with the violation of its gardenlike condition stands the symbol of
the bubbling fountain. As the most vividly developed metaphor in Marcus'
ode to Lavinia's lost beauty, the image only appears to suffer from ornamentality and to disassociate itself from the pastoral imagery that otherwise
dominates the speech. Not only is the fountain a proverbial fixture in the
Renaissance pastoral, but it is also conventionally associated with the
female sexual organs. Shakespeare's own poetic practice demonstrates its
venereal associations when in "Venus and Adonis" Venus encourages her
reluctant lover to "Stray lower, where the pleasant fountains lie" (l.234).
Moreover, ever since the *Song of Songs* the image of the stopped fountain,
especially in a garden setting, has possessed symbolic associations with
virginity and the virtue of chastity.[14] The groom in the *Songs* praises his
intended bride, with these words—"My sister, my spouse, *is as* a garden
inclosed, as a spring shut vp, *and* a fountain seled vp . . . O fountaine of
the gardens, ô well of the living waters and the springs of Lebanôn."[15]
Given this cultural context, Marcus' comparison of Lavinia to a bubbling
fountain and his earlier identification of Lavinia with the pastoral image of
the shade tree reveals itself to be anything but decorative. The delineation
of Lavinia as a bubbling fountain—that is, as an opened fountain whose
seals have been broken—is an appropriate, tasteful, and almost conventional image of lost virginity and consequent shame.[16]

In the mutilated form of her body as well, with tongue and hands cut
out, Lavinia becomes just what Marcus says of her, "a conduit with three
issuing spouts" (II.iv.30). In the seemingly endless streams of blood that
spurt from her body, Lavinia becomes an emblem of ceaseless suffering
and loss. She *is*, indeed, the fountain of sorrowful life; her maimed body
has been sculpted in its image.

In all the important details of its imagined construction, in fact, the foun-

tain image in *Titus Andronicus* reflects the tragedy that has befallen the Andronici. Not long after her mutilation, Marcus brings Lavinia to her father
Titus who, although unaware of Marcus' earlier speech, employs a second
figure of the fountain.[17] This time the image functions explicitly as an
emblem of irremediable sorrow:

> And thou [Lavinia], and I, sit round about some fountain,
> Looking all downwards to behold our cheeks
> How they are stain'd, like meadows yet not dry,
> With miry slime left on them by a flood?
> And in the fountain shall we gaze so long
> Till the fresh taste be taken from that clearness.
> And made a brine-pit with our bitter tears?
>
> *(III.i.123–29)*

If the bubbling fountain waters as Marcus imagines them symbolize
Lavinia's violated chastity and the mutilated condition of her limbs as well,
the fountain basin as Titus imagines it is transfigured into "a brine-pit."
This pit of brine evokes a memory of the pit into which Aaron craftily lures
two of Lavinia's brothers so that they are later executed for the murder of
Bassianus. At the same time, the waters in the fountain basin reflect the
disconsolate faces of Titus and Lavinia. In this way the image of the fountain, which originates in the specific symbolism of Lavinia's violation, soon
embraces as emblem all the suffering Andronici.

Because the fountain image iterates the metamorphosis of Lavinia and of
the Andronici fortunes in general, it becomes a locus for the metaphysical
anxiety that underlies the tragedy. As Titus gazes tearfully into the fountain basin, he finds not only the disfigured reflection of Lavinia but the sul-
lied remains of a once verdant world. In Titus' imagination the salt drops
from his eyes transform the clear waters of the fountain into a briny sea.
This briny sea, fed by a flood of grief, overwhelms the earthen world and
mires with slime its meadows. Through this image we discover once more
the metamorphosis of the green landscape, but, even more importantly, we
find the transfiguration of Titus' inner world. The same grief that mires
with slime the weeping cheeks of Titus and Lavinia so mires their spirits
with thirst for vengeance that they can never again regain the humanity
they lose. In this inward transformation of Titus and Lavinia, the fountain
water, now imagined as brinish with tears, reveals itself to be a symbol of
the broken-bodied, broken-spirited, Andronici. Far from functioning as
ornamental brocade, the image of the fountain, as Marcus employs it and

as Titus later develops it, is fully integrated into the pastoral imagery in the play. Moreover, as Marcus delineates it, the spurting fountain embodies by the very details of its construction the most pervasive features of the tragedy, the maimed and bleeding human body. In this latter regard, the fountain with seals unstopped richly symbolizes Lavinia's violation, the violation of the pastoral garden, and the emergence of that power of blackness whose malignity the forest had always latently contained.

III

The hyperbolic events of plotting—the rape and disfigurement of Lavinia, the emperor's scornful rejection of the "gift" of Titus' right hand, and the heartless executions of Quintus and Martius—flamboyantly raise in theatrical terms the ontological issue of whether civilized men can withstand the enormity of evil that the world contains and still retain their humanity. The issue is visualized concretely in the literal opposition between Aaron's blackness of person and character and Lavinia's assailed whiteness of body and spirit. Through these emblematic characterizations, which beget a rich web of associative images, Shakespeare endeavors to explore the power of blackness in its eternal antagonism to its opposite. So many of the play's events, seemingly more sensational than meaningful, function as what we may call "images-in-action"[18] that define and deepen the characteristic oppositions of the play.

On the day of the fateful forest hunt, we hear that Titus and the court have prepared to hunt the panther and the deer. The hunted deer, we ironically discover, is to be Lavinia herself; but even more ironically, the panther, whom we never really see, begins to hunt his hunters and soon reveals itself to be identified with Aaron. The identification is established in the second act as Aaron draws two of the Andronici to their dooms by leading them to a pit into which a panther is said to have been trapped. As the two brothers draw near, first one and then the other tumbles into its malevolent darkness, whose hellish powers are then immediately illuminated:

> *Mart.* Lord Bassianus lies beray'd in blood,
>   All on a heap, like to a slaughtered lamb,
>   In this detested, dark, blood-drinking pit.
>
> *Quint.* If it be dark, how dost thou know 'tis he?

Mart.   Upon his bloody finger he doth wear
          A precious ring, that lightens all this hole,
          Which, like a taper in some monument,
          Doth shine upon the dead man's earthy cheeks,
          And shows the ragged entrails of this pit:
          So pale did shine the moon on Pyramus
          When he by night lay bath'd in maiden blood.

                                            (II.iii.222–32)

The "abhorred pit" that Tamora had imagined earlier in the fecundity of her malediction is in this scene with Aaron objectified and given life, which is to say that the unseen power of malevolence that Tamora first delineates is now rendered visible and real. At the same time we also recognize that while no real panther lies at the bottom of the pit, only the imagined pretence of one, Aaron's fraudulence is a genuine manifestation of his own fiendish imagination—and that power of blackness Martius and Quintus do discover at the bottom of the pit. Aaron is indeed the black panther of the tragedy, and it is the reality of that diabolism that Martius and Quintus discover when they find the decapitated body of their brother Bassianus and are subsequently charged with perpetrating the bloody deed.

By contrast, it would seem that Titus' swatting of a fly is in the total scheme of the tragedy so trivial as to be ludicrous and so ludicrous as to invite disavowals of Shakespeare's responsibility for the episode in which it occurs. Occurring after Titus has witnessed the effects of his daughter's mutilation and undergone the lopping off of his right hand in a futile attempt to stay the executions of his two imprisoned sons, Marcus's squashing of the fly brings the disheartened Titus to the brink of madness. As theater the event is next to impossible to enact convincingly and is in danger of appearing absurdly silly rather than profound in its seeming absurdity; yet, for all of its dramatic implausibility, the incident possesses a poetic logic worth admiring. Initially, Titus empathizes with the threatened insect because he sees in its extermination the same wanton disregard for innocent life that threatens to destroy him and his family, but in the metaphoric logic of the play Titus has been deceived since the seemingly harmless fly, as it turns out, is Aaron himself, the fiend who can indeed bring men to madness. And the image sticks. Marcus describes the fly in this well-known incident as "a black ill-favour'd" thing (III.ii.66), while Titus, fooled by its seeming innocuousness, speaks of its ". . . lamenting doings in the air! / Poor harmless fly, / That, with his pretty melody came here to make us merry . . ." (III.ii.62–65). It is a fine line that gently recalls Aaron's luxurious liaison with Tamora in the forest and the deceptively pleasing music of that pastoral episode.

Significantly, the deceptive music of Aaron's speech finds its thematic antithesis in the genuine music that Lavinia creates. Oddly enough, the source of the contrast is the speech Marcus makes in the forest. Having just witnessed his niece's mutilated body, Marcus pauses to consider how Lavinia's hands, now completely severed, "could have sewed better than Philomel," and how they once could "Tremble like aspen-leaves upon a lute, / And make the silken strings delight to kiss them" (II.iv.45–46). No doubt the cultured allusion to Philomel's pretty hands sounds in context like so much adolescent humor, but while I make no defense for the dramatic plausibility of Marcus' learned memory, the conceit, itself a leitmotif, possesses a poetic resonance that we ought not to ignore. Whether created by her delicate fingers upon the lute or by the pleasing song of her voice, Lavinia's music is a source of heavenly beauty. By lopping off her hands and tearing out her tongue, Demetrius and Chiron literally deprive the world of the source of that music. Hence, in the next scene, when Marcus, still the play's irrepressible poet, speaks of Lavinia's shorn tongue, he declares:

> O, that delightful engine of her thoughts,
> That blabb'd them with such pleasing eloquence,
> Is torn from forth that pretty hollow cage,
> Where like a sweet melodious bird it sung
> Sweet varied notes, enchanting every ear.
>
> *(III.i.82–86)*

Again, were it not for our more immediate judgment that the comparison of a vibrating tongue to a bird's song is inescapably offensive, we would notice that Shakespeare is establishing an effective aural contrast between Lavinia's ethereal song and its demonic counterpart in Aaron, whose music of joy prompts a beguiled Titus to exclaim, ". . . O gentle Aaron! / Did ever ever raven sing so like a lark" (III.i.158). These polarities of gain and loss imaginatively heard through the ear thus accompany in a demonstrably rich way the visual polarities that Shakespeare imagines with respect to the forest setting. In the silencing of Lavinia we thus find both the mutilation of the pastoral garden and the loss of a heavenly music which once the world could hear.

Whatever the faultiness in the manner of their dramatic presentation, the arresting musical leitmotifs in the play and its vivid images in the action of the panther and the fly demonstrate the imaginative coherence of the tragedy. Knit in a fine web of association, these images in *Titus Andronicus* certainly reveal something more than "wanton playfulness."[19]

IV

Stated imagistically, the dialectic clash between dark and light, black and white, barbarism and civilization is subsumed in the play's two great imagistic clusters—its animal imagery and its mutilated plant imagery. Through these two great clusters of images, the play's poetic dialectic takes on dramatic life. According to the terms of this tragedy, Lavinia and the Andronici, depicted as mutilated trees and flora, are piece by piece literally torn apart by the savage animal principals of the play and cannot ever flourish until the latter are themselves destroyed.

The animal symbolism that identifies Aaron and Tamora and their scions is exuberant and unsurprising—Aaron is characteristically identified with the dark creatures of the earth: the adder (II.iii.35), the panther (II.iii, explained above), the raven (III.i.158; cf. II.iii.153) and the black fly (III.ii.66–67); his mistress Tamora with the feline predators: the lion (II.iii.151), and the tigress (II.iii.142; V.iii.195)—and appropriately so, for she, like her sister in vengeance Margaret of Anjou, is possessed of a "tiger's heart wrapp'd in a woman's hide."[20] The adulterous and miscegenous coition between Tamora and her crafty blackamoor, whose fleecy hair suggestively "uncurls / Even as an adder" (II.iii.34–35), is depicted as a "wreathed" coupling (II.iii.25), which further intimates the movements of the uncoiling snake. Similarly, the black babe subsequently born of this copulation is referred to variously as a black-legged swan (IV.ii.102), a "tadpole" (IV.ii.85), and a "sorrowful issue: / . . . as loathsome as a toad" (IV.ii.67; cf. II.iii.101–03). Likewise, Tamora's barbarous sons, Chiron and Demetrius, paternity undeclared, are characteristically referred to as the empress' tiger cubs (II.iii.142–47) and "bear-whelps" (IV.i.96). Through such blazoned images as these, Tamora and her brood are depicted as savage carnivores preying upon the Andronici, who are the flesh and blood of civilized Rome.

At the same time that the Andronici are depicted as the anguished human victims of an animal barbarism, they are also depicted emblematically as plants cut down or stunted in their growth. That is to say, when Marcus discovers Lavinia wandering in the woods and likens her to a shade tree hewed and lopped of its branches, he establishes the central emblem of the tragedy and the second of its irreducible imagistic terms. From this perspective, the opposition between the animal and the plant imagery ought not, strictly speaking, to be viewed in terms of the predator's relation to its victim since by definition the carnivore is not herbivorous and the metaphor is mixed in any case; rather, the relationship between the two great emblems of the tragedy functions as an affective device that underscores the helplessness of the Andronici and the initially unlike natures of the two opposing principals. More particularly, these antithetic emblems delineate the antagonism between a powerful, predatory principle of malevolence embodied in Tamora and Aaron and a vegetative principal of creative, civilized life, originally embodied in Lavinia and the other Andronici.

The meaning of this tragic conflict between the animal and the plant principles returns inevitably to the destruction of the pastoral world in Act II, scene iv, for once the panther and the tigress with her whelps overrun the forest and rape Lavinia, the park then loses its pastoral identity and becomes indeed in Titus' famous phrase, "a wilderness of tigers" (III.i.54). And the onslaught against the Andronici, both literal and imagistic, is relentless. Demetrius, one of Lavinia's rapists, resolves to "thrash the corn" of Lavinia's body and "then after burn the straw" (II.iii.123). Later in the play Lavinia, the living emblem of the tragedy that befalls the Andronici, becomes the great tree "trimm'd" and deprived of its shade-making powers. Finally, as Titus informs us, she is "a gath'red lily almost withered" (III.i.113). From this point on the Andronici men are also perceived in terms of trees and herbs. Titus' boy is a "tender sapling . . . made of tears" (III.ii.50), Titus' own hands are "with'red herbs . . . / . . . meet for plucking up" (III.i.177–78) and Bassianus' corpse is depicted as a "dead trunk" (II.iii.130), as is the body of Titus at the end of the play (V.iii.152). Speaking of his own decimated family, Titus sums up the benighted powers of justice-loving men when he remarks, "Marcus, we are but shrubs, no cedars we" (IV.iii.45).

Because of this relentless "trimming" of the Andronici, their hands, formerly victorious and able, are, like Lavinia's, rendered useless one by one. In the first act, Lavinia's request that Titus bless her "with thy victorious hand" (I.i.163) proves, in view of her unhappy fate, utterly futile, as does Quintus' brotherly offer of a helping hand to Martius in the second act and as does Titus' unavailing gift of his hand to ransom the lives of his two sons from Saturninus in the third act. As Titus explains in the scene of his greatest grief,

For they [Titus' hands] have fought for Rome, and all in vain;
And they have nurs'd this woe, in feeding life;
In bootless prayer have they been held up,
And they have serv'd me to effectless use.

. . . . .

'Tis well, Lavinia, that thou hast no hands,
For hands to do Rome service is but vain.

(III.i.73–80)

In the mutilation of the Andronici, we witness the visual image of Rome's own mutilation, for in this tragedy the fortunes of the patriotic Andronici become synonymous with the destiny of the Roman state and civilization in general.

V

Tied to the political tragedy and expressed by the same imagery of mutilation is a large religious issue concerning the nature of life. Behind Titus' allusions to the uselessness of hands there stands the haunting emblem of the trimmed tree of Lavinia's body and the fundamental question of God's ultimate providence in reconstituting the garden of life. The hands of the Andronici, we are told explicitly, once possessed the creative power of feeding life, but now they have been rendered useless. Even their outstretched hands calling for the aid of Providence have gone unheeded.

Marcus' question to Titus, "Oh, why should nature build so foul a den, / Unless the gods delight in tragedies?" (IV.i.59–60), explicitly voices this ontological concern. The answer in terms of *The Tragedy of Titus Andronicus* is that the gods are just but the justice they mete out does not preclude human tragedy. Lavinia and Titus, who at first helplessly endure the barbarian onslaught, begin to enact a retributive justice of their own. Albeit deprived of hands and tongue, Lavinia most providentially identifies her assailants by writing their names with a pole held between her stumps.[21] In the absence of all civil justice, Titus, who has endured the mutilation of his own right hand, is thus able to undertake his own terrible revenge. No longer the mere object of Aaron's animal cunning, no longer a mere withered herb, Titus becomes in vengeance another carnivore in the wilderness of tigers. Thus, he dismembers the bodies of Lavinia's assailants and serves them to their mother Tamora in a baked pie. And because the revenge is accomplished in dumb show—Tamora, Chiron, and Demetrius are dis-

guised respectively as Revenge, Rapine, and Murder—the allegorical significance of the event is played out fully before us.

Truly the gods delight in justice, but whether they do not delight in
Titus' tragedy and Lavinia's is problematical. The potential for human sacrifice, which we first witnessed in the pious dismemberment of Alarbus,
now finds its grotesquely inhuman fulfillment in Titus' barbaric retribution.
The same man who had blanched at the swatting of a fly is now able to slit
the throats of Chiron and Demetrius while Lavinia, her humanity consumed by what she has suffered, ghoulishly catches up the blood in a
basin that she holds between her stumped arms.

The gods are just, but they are not kind. Transformed by the horrors
they have undergone, Titus and Lavinia cannot restore the processes of
creative life, nor can they ever emerge humanely whole again. Titus' slaying of his own dishonored daughter out of pity before he is himself slain is
tacit recognition that this world which has made a mangled ruin of their
bodies has also transformed them utterly in spirit. With their thirst for revenge sated, there is nothing left for either Lavinia or the maddened Titus
but the surcease of sorrow in death.

Yet, whatever the cost in body and spirit, Titus' retribution successfully
extirpates the Gothic tigress and whelps from Rome. This accomplished,
the state can be knit together again by others and the mutilated garden can
once more grow healthily. This image of the fractured and dismembered
state being knit together again is the play's resolving metaphor. With
hands and heads and trunks of bodies the Andronici have fed throughout
the tragedy the heartless beasts of Rome. The voracious tigers and the
cunning vipers who have overrun the city have literally torn the body politic apart, for with each mutilation of the patriotic Andronici, Rome has lost
a part of itself.[22] Never can that body politic, that tree of civilized life, grow
healthily again until these beasts (Aaron and Tamora) have been extermi-
nated. This Titus' last remaining son accomplishes when he becomes
"planted"[23] on the throne. In Lucius, the dismembered state will be sewn
together again. Marcus expounds upon this future prospect, saying:

> You sad-fac'd men, people and sons of Rome,
> . . . . .
> O, let me teach you how to knit again
> This scattered corn into one mutual sheaf,
> These broken limbs again into one body.

> (V.iii.67–72)

All brought together in Marcus' oration to the citizens of Rome, the central images of the mutilated body, now united and whole, and the dismembered plant, healthy once more, demonstrate the metaphoric and imaginative integrity of the tragedy. Joined "hand in hand" (V.iii.132,136), the only surviving Andronici, Marcus and Lucius, will meet whatever fate is theirs. Under Lucius' leadership, the Andronicii, who have been cut down like so many stalks of wheat, will harvest at last the staff of life.

Such a sustained dialectic of imagistic ideas demonstrates Shakespeare's ability, even at this early stage of his career, to thrust seemingly ornamental images into a coherent poetic matrix. There is, of course, no point in denying that the play often suffers from a manifest discontinuity between its poetic conception and its dramatic realization. For this reason alone *Titus Andronicus* will surely remain one of Shakespeare's minor tragedies, but even so we need not be ashamed of it. Through its synthesizing emblem of the mutilated garden and all the images attendant upon its transformation, *Titus Andronicus* reveals the integrity of its imagistic structure and the authenticity of its tragic idea.

Notes:

1. Some of the most significant scholarship on *Titus Andronicus* has been done in the areas of authorship and source study, especially in response to the disintegrationist theories of J. M. Robertson, *An Introduction to the Study of the Shakespeare Canon* (London: Routledge, 1924). On these matters see Hereward T. Price, "The Authorship of 'Titus Andronicus'," *Journal of English and Germanic Philology*, 42 (1943), 55–81; J. C. Maxwell, ed., *Titus Andronicus* (Cambridge: Harvard Univ. Press, 1953), pp. xxiv–xxxiv, and R. F. Hill, "The Composition of *Titus Andronicus*," *Shakespeare Survey*, 10 (1957), 60–70. On the question of Shakespeare's sources see the indispensible Ralph M. Sargent, "The Source of *Titus Andronicus*," *Studies in Philology*, 46 (1949), 167–84, as well as Geoffrey Bullough, *Narrative and Dramatic Sources of Shakespeare*, VI (New York: Columbia Univ. Press, 1966), 6–13.

    Flamboyant derogations of *Titus Andronicus* have never lacked color, and this for three hundred years. In his revision of *Titus Andronicus* (1686; rpt London: Corn–market, 1969), sig. A2, Edward Ravenscroft derides Shakespeare's play as "a heap of rubbish." Johnson remarks that "The barbarity of the spectacles . . . can scarcely be conceived tolerable to any audience . . . ," Arthur Sherbo, ed., *Johnson on Shakespeare* (New Haven: Yale Univ. Press, 1968), p. 750. Dover Wilson, ed., *Titus Andronicus* (Cambridge: Cambridge Univ. Press, 1948), p. xii, compares the play to a "broken-down cart, laden with bleeding corpses." Eliot lambasts the tragedy as "one of the stupidest and most uninspired plays ever written" in *Selected Essays: 1917–1932* (London: Faber, 1932), p. 82. Mark Van Doren, in *Shakespeare* (Garden City: Doubleday, 1939), p. 30, judges the style to be "as coarse as burlap."

2. *Shakespeare's Early Tragedies* (London: Methuen, 1968), 13–47.

3. " 'Wilderness of Tigers': Structure and Symbolism in *Titus Andronicus*," *Essays in Criticism*, 10 (1960), 276. There can be no doubt that the critical turn in recent criticism of *Titus Andronicus* owes much of its impetus to Eugene M. Waith, "The Metamorphosis of Violence in *Titus Andronicus*," *Shakespeare Survey*, 10 (1957), 39–49.

4. Except for the writing of the first act, which is sometimes attributed to Peele, there is now little question that Shakespeare composed *Titus Andronicus*. With the question of authorship largely resolved, the more difficult task will be to reintegrate the play into the mainstream of Shakespearean criticism.

5. *The Development of Shakespeare's Imagery* (New York: Hill & Wang, 1951), p. 24.

6. Muriel C. Bradbrook's criticism in *Themes and Conventions of Elizabethan Tragedy* (Cambridge: Cambridge Univ. Press, 1935), pp. 98–99 is representative. Sensitive observations on the emblematic groupings of the characters and on the discontinuity between the poetic and dramatic impulse in *Titus Andronicus* will be found in her more recent study, *Shakespeare and Elizabethan Poetry* (New York: Oxford Univ. Press, 1952), pp. 104–10.

7. P. 26.

8. P. 22.

9. Citations to the text of *Titus Andronicus* are from J. C. Maxwell's New Arden edition (London: Methuen, 1953).

10. The prototype of all gardens, the Garden of Eden, is watered, as Milton envisions it, by natural fountains (Merritt Y. Hughes, ed., *John Milton: Complete Poems and Major Prose* [New York: Odyssey, 1957], IV, 222–47). See also Francis Bacon, "Of Gardens" in *Essays or Counsels Civil and Moral* (1625) (*The Works of Francis Bacon*, ed. James Spedding, Robert Leslie Ellis, and Douglas Denon Heath [Cambridge, Eng.: Riverside Press, 1872], XII, 241–42). The word "garden" must be taken in the Renaissance sense of a wooded area of many acres. In "Of Gardens" (p.239) Bacon suggests a minimum of thirty acres as sufficient to comprise the garden grounds.

11. F. T. Prince, ed., The New Arden edition of *The Poems* (Cambridge: Harvard Univ. Press, 1960), ll. 228–34.

12. The imagistic similitude between the above passage in "Venus and Adonis" and Marcus' pastoral descriptions of Lavinia and "the park" in II,iv and III,i is close enough to suggest that one passage depends upon the other, but the direction of the dependence is in doubt. F. T. Prince dates "Venus and Adonis" around 1592–93, (p. xxvi). A likely date for *Titus Andronicus* is 1593–94, although the tragedy could, according to Maxwell (pp.xxiv-xxxiv), have been composed as early as 1590.

13. Ben Jonson, "To Penshurst," l.9, *Ben Jonson*, ed. C. H. Herford and Percy Simpson, VIII (Oxford: Clarendon Press, 1947), 93. The detail of the private forest walks in *Titus Andronicus* becomes the occasion of a cruel joke later in the play. After Lavinia's tongue has been ripped out, Demetrius suggests to Chiron, in what appears to be a cynical travesty of humanistic contemplation, that they "leave . . . [Lavinia] to her silent walks" (II.iv.8). A good example

of the humanistic values associated with the pastoral garden setting and with its opportunities for private thought may be found in Erasmus, "The Godly Feast" (1592), *The Colloquies of Erasmus,* trans. Craig R. Thompson (Chicago: Univ. of Chicago Press, 1965), p. 48.

14. See D. W. Robertson, Jr., "The Doctrine of Charity in Medieval Literary Gardens," *Speculum,* 26 (1951), 24-49.

15. *The Geneva Bible* (1560 edition; rpt. Madison: Univ. of Wisconsin Press, 1969), iv.12,15.

16. The garden metaphor in the word "de-flowering" appears to be deliberate and occurs in *Titus Andronicus* with respect to Lavinia's violation on three occasions, at II.iii.191, II.iv.26, and V.iii.38. The point is an arresting one since Lavinia is married to Bassianus and is presumably no longer a virgin even before her rape. However, it is clear that Shakespeare wishes to delineate Lavinia's extreme purity and chastity, which is at the least "virginal" in the terms of the tragedy.

17. Related although they are, the two fountains are not identical. Marcus imagines a fountain with a centerpiece that shoots out streams of water; the fountain that Titus envisions appears to be more of a font with a pool of water in its basin.

18. The phrase belongs to Hereward T. Price in "The Function of Imagery in Webster," reprinted in *Elizabethan Drama: Modern Essays in Criticism,* ed. Ralph J. Kaufman (New York: Oxford Univ. Press, 1961), p. 242.

19. Clemen, p. 26.

20. *III Henry VI,* I.iv.137, in *The Riverside Shakespeare,* ed. G. Blakemore Evans (Boston: Houghton Mifflin, 1974).

21. For a discussion of this point and of the witty literalism of the play see Tricomi's "The Aesthetics of Mutilation in *Titus Andronicus,* in *Shakespeare Survey,* 27 (1974), 11-20.

22. Shakespeare characteristically describes the state in terms analogous to the human body. See, for example, the famous simile in *Coriolanus* (ed. Evans), I.i.96-155.

23. The specific phrase refers to I.i.444, in which the emperor Saturninus is "planted" on the throne.

Jessica's Morals: A Theological View

AUSTIN C. DOBBINS AND ROY W. BATTENHOUSE

Capping a century of romantic interpretation of Shylock, Sir Arthur Quiller-Couch in 1926 termed Jessica "bad and disloyal, unfilial, a thief; frivolous, greedy, without any more conscience than a cat."[1] Such an estimate, though it may appeal to readers swayed by Shylock's view of her as "damned," clearly is not that of the play as a whole. The father's moral imagination is comically undercut by his absurd love of gold more than daughter, and Jessica's elopement not only secures Lorenzo's friends as sponsors but also a welcome by Portia at Belmont. Indeed, the play ends with Jessica as the prospective heiress of all of Shylock's property—an outcome which, unless we wish to quarrel with the justice of the whole play, implies a hearty approval of the marriage. Most theatregoers therefore feel no qualms about Jessica's morals; they accept her actions as wholesome and right.

Is this favorable judgment merely instinctive, or can it be justified also in terms of traditional theology? The question seems worth asking since some commentators would defend Jessica, as does J. Middleton Murry, by arguing that characters in a fairy tale "cannot be judged by realistic moral standards."[2] Jessica, says Murry, if "taken out of the play and exposed to the cold light of moral analysis, may be a wicked little thing; but in the play, wherein alone she has her being, she is nothing of the kind—she is charming." Can we be satisfied with Murry's suggested dichotomy between what the play-world reveals and what moral analysis might reveal? Granted that *The Merchant of Venice* has a fairy-tale quality, must we say with Murry that the drama's coherence is "not intellectual or psychological" but only that of an unrealistic story in which Jessica wins our approval because she is portrayed as "a princess held captive by an ogre"? Why disown intellectual coherence in arguing for artistic integrity? It may be well to recall a remark of S. L. Bethell about Shakespeare in general, that his world is that of "folk legend more profoundly understood—a development, in fact, of Medieval Christianity."[3] Moral sanction for Jessica's behavior can in fact be found within that tradition.

Jessica's sense of values is not unrealistic. It has roots, rather, in those aspects of ancient Hebrew tradition which foreshadow Christian ethics. Her very name, as has been noted by Israel Gollancz and by Barbara

107

Lewalski, is a form of Hebrew *Iscah* (Gen. 11:29), which Elizabethan commentators glossed as meaning "she that looketh out"; and this meaning is reflected in her looking "out at window" for Lorenzo's coming. In doing so, Jessica disobeys the repressive decree of Shylock (whose name probably derives from *shalach,* translated "cormorant" in Deut. 14:17), but her action may be likened to that of Daniel, who prayed at his window (Dan. 6:10) despite a decree forbidding such piety. Jessica's readiness to venture by faith in a "promise" is an attitude characteristic of the Hebrew patriarchs and prophets. Her departure with Lorenzo the Christian, therefore, as Professor Lewalski suggests, can be attributed to an Israelite righteousness of faith, which by obeying spirit over letter anticipates the New Law's superseding of Old Law.[4]

Strictly speaking, Old Law is represented by Shylock only distortedly and out of context. When he cries out for "Justice" and interprets Jessica's act of taking treasure as stealing, he is ignoring a paradigm of justice set by Moses which Shakespeare very likely had in mind. In Exodus 3:21–22 (a text which Shylock as a Jew ought to know and respect), God instructed Moses that "when ye go [out of Egypt], ye shall not go empty: But every woman shall borrow of her neighbour, and of her that sojourneth in her house, jewels of silver, and jewels of gold, and raiment: and ye shall put them upon your sons, and upon your daughters; and ye shall spoil the Egyptians." Shylock seems to have forgotten Israel's own practice in leaving Pharaoh's house. For if this charter event in the history of Judaism justified a spoiling of Egyptian wealth, how can Shylock logically object to Jessica's taking ducats and jewels in fleeing his own house, which has become, as Jessica says, a hell? The irony of course is that Shylock has no logic except that of greed since he is, as Lorenzo rightly remarks, a "faithless" Jew. He is no true son of the Jewish worthies he invokes—Jacob, Abraham, and Daniel. On the contrary, when Shylock raises his knife in the courtyard scene, Shakespeare is emblematizing a parody of Abraham's "sacrifice"; and earlier, when Shylock terms Antonio a "fawning publican," audiences could be expected to recognize that Shylock unwittingly is describing himself since usury is an extortionist taxing like that for which biblical Jews ostracized publicans.

Exodus 3:21–22 (along with 11:2 and 12:35) was a text well known in Christian commentary. Augustine had applied it, in a broad sense, to the general problem of how Christians should treat pagan arts and letters. These Egyptian treasures, he said, are to be taken from idolators who misuse them: "When the Christian separates himself in spirit from their miserable society," he should take, hold, and "convert" their treasure to Christian uses (*De Doctrina*, II.40). This interpretation was quoted with approval by Elizabethan moralists such as William Baldwin and Thomas Bowes.[5] The text, moreover, furnished a standard instance for illustrating the difference between seeming theft and real theft. Tertullian, for example, justified the Israelites by explaining that their depriving the Egyptians of gold and silver was no fraudulent act but rather "compensation for their hire, which they were unable in any other way to exact from their masters."[6] And Aquinas, similarly, declared the Israelite taking of the spoils of the Egyptians to be "no theft," because God ordered it "on account of the ill-treatment accorded [the Israelites] by the Egyptians without any cause" (*Summa Theologica*, II–II.66.5). According to Aquinas,

> when a man's property is taken from him, if it be due that he should lose it, this is not theft or robbery as forbidden by the decalogue. Consequently, when the children of Israel, by God's command, took away the spoils of the Egyptians, this was not theft, since it was due to them by the sentence of God.
>
> (S.T. *II–I.100.8*)

Echoing the medieval view, Reformation theologians also commended the action of the Israelites. They tended to make its ethics somewhat more baffling, however, by retaining the word "theft" in their descriptions. Thus the Lutheran Wolfgang Musculus, stretching paradox to the point of apparent contradiction, commented on the spoiling of the Egyptians:

> What was that other than theft? And yet it is not onely excused by Gods commaundemente, whereof we reade Exod. xi. But it deserueth also cōmendation of obedience. For they did (sayeth Moyses) as the Lord commaunded, and to do that which the Lord commaundeth, is the praise of true obedience.[7]

A similar view appears in the note added by Tyndale to the conclusion of Genesis in his translation of the Pentateuch (1530):

> Jacob robbed Laban his uncle: Moses robbed the Egyptians: And Abraham is about to slay and burn his own son: And all are holy works, because they are wrought in faith at God's commandment. To steal, rob and murder are no holy works before worldly people: but unto them that have their trust in God: they are holy when God commandeth them.

Commentary of this kind tends to reduce the moral issue to the single extenuating circumstance of God's commanding without explaining why God might so command. Commentators who followed Aquinas were more reasonable in that they sought to explain God's command on the grounds of natural law and justice. Auditors of Shakespeare's *The Merchant of Venice*, therefore, might have been more ready to approve Jessica's so-called "theft" if their orientation was to the Old Faith than if their orientation was of Protestant vintage.

Yet the paradigm itself, to any Elizabethan who remembered it, would suggest justification for Jessica's action. Moreover, as the quotation from Tyndale suggests, justification for Jessica's "theft" also might be found in Genesis 31, in the episode of Jacob's spoiling Laban of his sheep and other possessions (an incident which immediately follows the rod-peeling incident with which Shylock was familiar). Did Jacob commit theft? The Anglican Andrew Willet thought not. Jacob (Israel) did no more than recover what was rightly his. Willet's commentary reads:

> who knoweth not, that God beeing Lord of all, may transferre the right of things from one to another, where no other inferior title or propertie is challenged: as God gave the land of the Canaanites the auncient possessors thereof, to the Israelites [Ex. 3:8] . . . . Iacob by this meanes doeth recouer but his owne, which was due vnto him in a double right both in respect of his 20. yeares seruice, all which time he serued without wages.
>
> [Gen. 29–31][8]

This paradigm, as well as the one from Exodus, ought to have given Shylock pause before denoucing Jessica as a thief, for, again ironically, it is he who is behaving like a Laban or a Pharaoh. In this context Shylock's outcry over "my Christian ducats" doubles the irony since in fact the ducats have been wrongfully extorted from Christians (through usury) and now are being rightfully "used" by Christians.

Unlike her father, Jessica remains faithful to the paradigms of historic Judaism. Like the Israelites of old, she seeks to escape from Shylock's all-too-Egyptian house of bondage to a land of promise. Like Jacob, she takes with her property to which she has a natural right.[9] And like Rachel (of whom Ambrose remarked "Happy was Rachel who concealed the false idols"[10]), Jessica carries off, concealed under her clothes, her father's household gods, his barren metal. Although she has no more intention than her forebears had of returning "borrowed" property, only to worldly eyes will her action seem theft (the employment of an evil means). Instead, leaving her father to cleave to her husband, Jessica uses worldly wealth for nature's increase, that of happiness through marriage. Shylock, misapplying Jacob's example, uses his wealth for unnatural increase, that of making money breed money.

Like the Egyptians, Shylock is an extortioner—a usurer. In terms of traditional theology he is a thief. Indeed, he is more than a thief. According to Anglican Bishop Robert Sanderson, a usurer

> sinneth against the *sixt Commandement* [that against killing], by distempering his *body;* he sinneth against *the seventh* [that against adultery], by enflaming his *lust;* he sinneth against *the eighth* [that against stealing], by making waste of the good *Creatures of God.*[11]

Properly classified, maintained Phillip Caesar, usurers are "wasters, pollers, stealers of holie thynges, Theeues, Murtherers, Idolaters...."[12] Similarly, wrote Leonard Wright, a usurer is "worse than Judas.... There is no more mean in this vice, than is in thefte, adulterie, and murther."[13] As a usurer Shylock has no moral right to his stolen riches. It is a property which, as a gloss on Proverbs 28:6 in the Geneva Bible states, "God will take awaye ... & giue ... to him that shal bestowe them wel."

But if Jessica is not a thief, can she be guilty of the other charges Quiller-Couch would lay on her—for instance, that of "unfilial" behavior? Renaissance canon law (Church of England) forbade clandestine marriages.[14] But whether this canon would apply to a "convert" situation is uncertain. Jessica, we need to recall, eloped not only because she was "ashamed to be my father's child" but because she had determined to become a Christian. These are extenuating circumstances which even Desdemona in *Othello* does not have; yet in *Othello* the Venetian Senate accepts Desdemona's marriage after hearing her testify that she acted of her own free will. Would Elizabethan moralists have judged more severely?

There is some ground for guessing that Protestants in Shakespeare's audience may have been more hesitant than Catholics to approve Jessica's elopement. It was customary among the Reformers to interpret the marriage contract as a matter restricted by the commandment to honor one's father and mother. Peter Martyr, for instance, writes:

> *Paule* saith to the Ephesians; *Children obeie your parents in all things.* He excepteth nothing, when he writeth so: but saith, *In all things:* Namelie, which they command not against the word of God. And in

his first epistle to the Corinthians, the seuenth chapter, is most mani-
festlie declared, that it belongeth to the parents to giue their
daughters in marriage to husbands.

. . . So then it seemeth maruellous, that christians at this daie determine, that marriages are lawfull, without consent of the parents.[15]

Henry Bullinger and Edwin Sandys echo this Protestant view.[16] If children
cast aside their parents, says Bullinger, the parents may refuse and disan-
nul the children's promise. Citing Colossians 3:20 as his proof text, Sandys
calls marriage without parental consent a fault not only "most heinous in
the sight of God" but condemned also by "the law of nature, the law civil,
the law canon, and the opinion of the best writers."

But Bullinger indicates an awareness (as does Martyr in his final sentence
cited above) that some Christians (Catholics) hold a view differing from his
own:

I wonder what the papisticall bokes & learned men dyd meane, whan
they taught that the consent only of both the parties doth fastē the
matter, & coupleth thē togither in marriage: the cōsent of ye parētes
also, say they [the papists] is good with all, but whan two [the lovers]
haue cōsented, and one hath taken the other, ye knot can not be
vnknyt, neyther maye the parentes seperate thē from a sunder.[17]

The opinion which Bullinger questions is well expounded by Aquinas. St.
Thomas gives the Colossians text a somewhat different interpretation. He
explains (S.T. II–II.104.5) that when the Apostle says (Col. 3:20), "Children,
obey your parents in all things," he is referring to matters within the
sphere of a father's or master's authority but not to matters in which a person is subject immediately under God, by whose higher authority each
person is taught "either by the natural or by the written law." And on the
specific matter of contracting marriage, Aquinas says:

The maid is in her father's power, not as a female slave without
power over her own body, but as a daughter, for the purpose of education. Hence, in so far as she is free, she can give herself into
another's power without her father's consent, even as a son or daughter, since they are free, may enter religion without their parents' consent.

(S.T. Suppl. 45.5)

Note how, for Aquinas, freedom to marry is a right parallel to that of taking a religious vow. This is quite evident in his discussion elsewhere (*S.T.* III.68.10) of "Whether Children of Jews or Other Unbelievers Should be Baptized Against the Will of their Parents." He replies:

> The children of unbelievers either have the use of reason or they have not. If they have, then they already begin to control their own actions, in things that are of Divine or natural law. And therefore of their own accord, and against the will of their parents, they can receive Baptism, just as they can contract marriage.

Aquinas allows a validity even to secret marriage since all that is essentially necessary to a true marriage are "words of the present expressive of consent" by the two contracting parties (*S.T.* Suppl. 45.5). All else, he explains, belongs to the "fittingness" of the sacrament rather than to its essence. Yes, he says, the Church's canon law does forbid clandestine marriages, but simply as a safeguard because secret marriages are often liable to fraud by one of the parties, or to hasty unions later repented of, and because also there is something "disgraceful" about them. Secret marriage is therefore a sin *unless* the lovers have a lawful motive for being excused.

Aquinas' view upholds a concept which Protestant commentators questioned. Yet, so far as Jessica is concerned, the disagreement is more apparent than real. For in eloping with Lorenzo, Jessica, a Jew, agreed to become a Christian. To Christians, whether Protestant or Catholic, this was a commendable action. Jessica's motive was the lawful one of becoming a Christian and a true wife. Rightly then she answers Launcelot Gobbo's teasing, in a comic scene, that she is damned by her heredity to Shylock and without hope unless not "got" of her father. "I shall be sav'd by my husband," she replies (cf. Eph. 5:23), "he hath made me a Christian." Fleshly fatherhood cannot determine Jessica's moral choice. True, the Fifth Commandment requires children to honor their parents (Deut. 5:16). But the New Testament adds a stipulation: ". . . in the Lord" (Eph. 6:1–2). Rightly speaking, then, only by disobeying Shylock could Jessica obey the Lord. The logic of this statement may sound harsh. But it is fundamentally both Christian and Hebraic. "Children ought not to obey their parents," wrote Henry Bullinger,

> if they command any thing contrary to God, or preiudicall to his law. Jonathan obeyed not his father Sauls commandemět who charged him

to persecute Dauid: and therfore is he worthily cõmended in ye holy Scriptures. The 3. companions of Daniel obeyed Nabuchodnozor in al that he said, they loued him, & reuerenced him as a most mightie, puissant, & bountifull king, but so soone once as he charged them to fall to idolatrie, they set not a button by his commaundement. And *S.* Peter, who taught vs the honor & obediĕce y^t wee owe to our parents & magistrates, whĕ he was commãded by ye princes & fathers of ye people, not to preach Christ crucified to ye people any more, did answere them, that we *ought to obey God more thã men.* [18]

Obeying God rather than man, Jessica marries Lorenzo. At the same time she takes precaution against fraud and rashness. A *seeming* disgracefulness, it is true, is present and acknowledged by Jessica—in her reference, for example, to the "shame" of her boy's clothing (a matter which Puritan theory judged sinful but which Aquinas would have excused);[19] and a *guise* of impropriety is acknowledged by Lorenzo likewise, in his saying that he is *playing* thief. But of genuine disgracefulness there is none. Jessica's exchange of vows with Lorenzo is, in fact, not wholly secret, since it is spoken in the presence of Lorenzo's friends as witnesses, while Lorenzo calls on "Heaven and thy thoughts" as witness. To mere "seeming" can be attributed whatever aura of scandal the elopement involves; unfilialness and disloyalty are not its moral substance.

But if we can thus clear Jessica of unfilialness as well as thievishness, what shall we say to a third and related charge that she is guilty of deceit and dissimulation? She does of course dissimulate her sex when she dresses as a boy, an action to which surely no auditor who approves Portia's similar disguising can morally object. But what of Jessica's verbal deception when asked by Shylock regarding what Launcelot Gobbo has been whispering in her ear? Is she telling a lie when she replies: "His words were 'Farewell mistress,' nothing else"? In her defense let us note that "Farewell" can have a double meaning: there is no lie in her reporting that the substance was that she *fare well.* One can also note that no lie is involved in simply holding back the amplifying details of what was said. An audience familiar with moral theology would have no difficulty in approving Jessica's reply.

Both Catholic and Protestant theologians distinguished between lying and dissimulating. Liars, said William Perkins, are guilty of three things: first, of saying what is false indeed; second, of doing so willingly, knowing it to be false; and third, of doing so with a motive of malice.[20] Dissimulation, on the other hand, is of two kinds, according to Peter Martyr:

One, which hath respect onelie to deceiue; the which, seeing it dif-
fereth not much from a lie, vndoubtedlie it is sin. If one, being
wicked, doo faine himselfe to be honest and godlie, the same is an
hypocrite; & in that he dissembleth, he sinneth greeuouslie. . . . But
there is an other kind of dissimulation, which tendeth not to the de-
ceiuing of anie man; but serueth onlie to keepe counsell secret, least
they should be hindered: and this dissimulation is not to be refused,
or condemned as sinne, seeing (as we haue alreadie declared) it is not
alwaies required that we should open whatsoeuer truth we doo
knowe.[21]

Similarly, wrote Andrew Willett, dissimulation is commendable

I. When it is done for deliuerance out of daunger, without the hurt of
an other, as Dauid by faining himselfe madde, escaped, . . .
II. When one dissembleth to profit his brother, as . . . [when] our
Sauiour made shewe, as though he would haue gone further [Lk.
24:28], to trie the humanitie of the two disciples.[22]

In Shakespeare's play, do we not recognize the first of these kinds of dissimulation (wicked hypocrisy) in Shylock's bargain with Antonio but the
second kind (permissible deception) in Jessica? Jessica dissimulates; that is,
she conceals the truth, yet her dissimulation is not evil. Indeed, for her action she is more to be praised than blamed.

Discussions of lying and dissimulation by medieval theologians present
much the same point of view. "To pretend is not always a lie," said
Aquinas, "but only when the pretense has no signification" (*S.T.* II–
II.111.1, quoting Augustine). It is necessary to get at the sense. Abraham,
when he said Sara was his sister, wished to hide the truth, not to tell a lie,
for she was in fact his half-sister (Gen. 20:12); and Jacob's assertion that he
was Esau was spoken in a mystical sense, because Esau's birthright was
due Jacob by right, and Jacob spoke moved by a spirit of prophecy to sig-
nify a mystery, namely, that the younger should supplant the firstborn.
Sometimes, Aquinas insisted, words contain truth in a figurative or
prophetic sense; and sometimes truth may be kept prudently hidden. No
lie is involved in such cases. Moreover, although lying in itself is always a
sin, its gravity is diminished when it is intended to help another person, or
to save him from being injured; and the greater the good intended, the
more the sin of lying is diminished. No mortal sin is involved in an "offi-
cious" lie or a "jocose" lie where its end is not contrary to charity (*S.T.* II–

II.110–11). In the light of such analysis, surely Jessica's deception of her father should be judged as at most no more than a venial fault, and probably not even that.

Indeed, the more Jessica's dissimulation is examined, the more it seems prophetic and a prefiguring of later events in the play. Jessica's masking as a page and torchbearer foreshadows, as Theodore Weiss has noted, the later action of Portia, when as a masked lawyer-page she is a torchbearer to Bassanio, by bringing light to bear against Shylock ("So shines a good deed in a naughty world"[23]). Shakespeare links Jessica and Portia by involving both in a secret departure from home—in the one case, with resulting dismay by a father; in the other, with resulting bafflement (in Act V) by a husband. Both of these plotted surprises have as their lesson the theme that a duty-to-save transcends conventional submissiveness. Also, in the play's structure, Jessica's bringing news to Portia of Shylock's villainy provides Portia the impetus for her own decision to undertake a pilgrimage—whose benefits, mysteriously, redound to everyone, including Jessica and Lorenzo. Portia, acting as Balthazar-Daniel, in a sense completes the exodus from pharaonic Judaism begun by Jessica. For Portia's Daniel role, figuratively, effects and fulfills the promise to Abraham that by his "seed" *all* families of the earth would be blessed.

"If e'er the Jew her father come to Heaven," Lorenzo had remarked in Act II, "It will be for his gentle daughter's sake." The gentle daughter's sake, in the trial scene in Act IV, is no doubt chiefly what inspires Antonio's proposal for Shylock's baptism and his deeding of property as an inheritance for Jessica. Note how this "deed" makes the Lorenzo marriage fully legal by imputing parental consent and also how it opens up a hope of rebinding father to daughter by providing both the conditions and the means. Are you contented? Portia asks Shylock, and he replies: "I am content." Within the context of the play there is now for him a meaningful future—a future which would not have been possible had he succeeded in his earlier wish to have Jessica married to a Barabbas. Thus Jessica's dissimulation, far from injuring her father, actually has forwarded his only hope of *faring well*—in this respect like the benefit which young Jacob bestowed on the dim-sighted Isaac of biblical story.

Considering all the ways in which traditional theology would sanction Jessica's actions, what flaw in Jessica can critics allege? We have answered Quiller-Couch's catalogue of accusations—except perhaps for the charge of frivolity. Conceivably Sir Arthur might cite as evidence Jessica's honeymoon lark of trading off for a monkey the turquoise ring Shylock was given by Leah, or Jessica's spending fourscore ducats during a night of festivity in Genoa. But is frivolity a sin on festive occasions? If so, we would have to fault equally the frivolity of Portia in Act V, including her "monkey-business" jesting about her ring. Surely, however, mockery is appropriate to festival. And as for extraordinary spending, this was deemed unthrifty only by a Shylock who despised parties. Moreover, Shylock's anguish over the Leah-ring is suspect. Why had he ceased wearing the ring if he still valued Leah? If we consider that on the night of his daughter's flight his dreams were not of Leah but of money bags (an ironic contrast to Jacob's dream of a ladder-to-heaven), we may infer that Shylock's sentiment for Leah was no more than afterthought to justify self-pity and indignation. And if, nevertheless, we yet wonder why Jessica could treat the Leah-ring so cavalierly, perhaps the answer is that both in Scripture and in tradition Leah (the "blear-eyed" wife who symbolizes mere practicality) is less valued than Rachel, symbol of the contemplative life and of Israel's and mankind's higher hope. St. Ambrose, in the treatise we cited earlier, associates Leah with the letter-of-the-law and Rachel with grace, a spirit which supersedes the weak vision of the synagogue. Such a Rachel is Jessica.

A conjoining of playfulness and insight wraps up the play's action. Act V begins and ends on this note. In the finale a harmonizing of jest and deeper truth sounds its music from the moment Lorenzo and Jessica come on stage pretending in themselves a likeness to Troilus and Cressida, Pyramus and Thisbe, Aeneas and Dido, or Jason and Medea. The jest depends on the fact that the love story of Lorenzo and Jessica has only a surface likeness to these instances of pagan dotage. Jessica's "stealing" from home has not been like Thisbe's, benightedly rash and accompanied by the solitary music of fearful sighs and weeping moans; nor has Lorenzo "stolen" Jessica's soul with Troilus-like sighs. Their love has been neither willowy nor unthrift nor dismayed by shadows. All such comparisons "slander" their love, as Lorenzo wittily concludes, and can easily be "outnighted," as Jessica says. For their own venture in love has not been one of tragic miscarriage; it has brought them, rather, to Belmont and the care of its beautiful mountain. And as they await the return of Belmont's pilgrim-mistress, there creeps into their ears, as Lorenzo says, the melody of the music of the spheres:

> Sit, Jessica. Look how the floor of heaven
> Is thick inlaid with patens of bright gold.
> There's not the smallest orb which thou behold'st
> But in his motion like an angel sings,
> Still quiring to the young–ey'd cherubins.

(V.i.58–62)

Here the word *patens* suggests, as scholars such as Malone and others long ago noted, an allusion by Shakespeare to the metal plates upon which the bread of the sacrament customarily was placed in Catholic Eucharists.[24] If we follow this suggestion, the orbs are both singing and offering themselves up to God, thus celebrating a cosmic Eucharist. It is the grandest liturgical image in all of Shakespeare. Lorenzo pauses over it long enough to regret that our "muddy vesture of decay" hampers our hearing the music.

The observation is apt. For although the lovers have transcended Shylock's dislike of music, they can be granted only a momentary sense of heaven's music before returning to their earthly duty of striking up a Belmont music to welcome Portia's homecoming. She then, as a little candle come home, will reveal through jesting riddle a human and more-than-human mystery of wedlock's ring: it is a double bond in which doctor or physician is the hidden meaning behind and within that of wife. "By this ring," says Portia, "the Doctor lay with me." This paradox of a love secretly remedial while also wifely is the truth of the play as a whole. Human duty is most truly moral when grace and gratitude overarch obedience to mere literal code. In the subplot, Jessica's escaping from legalism into the freedom of a true but seemingly disgraceful marriage has paralleled, anticipatively, this same theme. Jessica, like Portia, transcends run-of-the-mill codes for the sake of what is most fundamentally moral, a pilgrimage of salvation. Shakespeare intends auditors of his play to be enlightened by this paradox and to receive its "increase" as Lorenzo and Jessica do the comforting manna of Shylock's deed at the play's end. Manna, in John 6 and in medieval interpretation, is a figure for the Eucharist. Toward that symbol the play and its world of comedy have been moving.

Notes:

1. Introduction to the New Cambridge *Merchant of Venice* (Cambridge: Cambridge Univ. Press, 1926), p. xx.
2. *Shakespeare* (London: J. Cape, 1936), pp. 192–94.
3. *Shakespeare and the Popular Dramatic Tradition* (Westminster: P. S. King and Staples, 1944), p. 82.
4. "Biblical Allusion and Allegory in *The Merchant of Venice*," *Shakespeare Quarterly*, 13 (1962), 327–43.
5. See Baldwin's "Prologue to the Reader," in his *A Treatise of Morall Phylosophye* (London, 1547), and the Bowes "Epistle Dedicatorie" to a translation of *The French Academie* (London, 1586).
6. "Against Marcion," IV.24, in *Ante-Nicene Fathers*, trans. Roberts and

Donaldson (Buffalo, 1885), III, 387. Long before Tertullian, the Jewish philosopher Philo had advanced this interpretation. The action of the Hebrews was right, he explained, because in the spoil they took "they were but receiving a bare wage for all their time of service," a payment long held back. See "On the Life of Moses, " in *Philo,* trans. F. H. Colson and G. H. Whitaker (Cambridge: Harvard Univ. Press. 1961), I.xxv.

7. *Common Places of Christian Religion,* trans. John Man (London, 1578), p. 219. The Reformers tended to argue, however, that the special privileges of the patriarchs were not in the present day to be normally revived; see Bainton's essay in *The Cambridge History Of The Bible,* ed. S. L. Greenslade (Cambridge: Cambridge Univ. Press, 1963), III, 14. England's King James reflects this Protestant view when, in his *Trewe Law* (1598), p. 60 in McIlwain edition (New York: Russell and Russell, 1965), he questions whether Israelite "theft" on coming out of Egypt and Jacob's "lying" to his parent are not "extraordinary examples" inapplicable under modern conditions.

8. *Hexapla in Genesin* (London, 1608), p. 194. Similarly, Calvin writes in *Commentaries on . . . Genesis,* trans. John King (Grand Rapids: Eerdmans, 1948), II, 156, that God "purposed to connect his grace with the labour and diligence of Jacob, that he might openly repay to him those wages of which he had been so long defrauded."

9. Among today's commentators on Jessica, several have defended her taking of Shylock's ducats as being a marriage portion rightfully owed her by Shylock. See, e.g., Bernard Grebanier, *The Truth About Shylock* (New York: Random House, 1962), pp. 201–02, and Warren Smith, "Shakespeare's Shylock," *Shakespeare Quarterly,* 15 (1964), 197. This view, in fact, was the fifteenth-century Masuccio's in the tale Shakespeare probably used as his source (see Bullough, *Sources,* I, 497–505); Masuccio sees the miser-father as getting his due.

10. "Jacob and the Happy Life," 5.25, trans. M. P. McHugh, *Fathers of the Church* (Washington: McGrath, 1972), pp. 160–61.

11. *XXXIV Sermons,* 5th ed. (London, 1671), p. 203.

12. *A general Discovrse Against . . . Vsurers* (London, 1578), sig. 3ᵛ.

13. *A Summons For Sleepers* (London, 1589), p. 9. See also John Jewell, *An Exposition Vpon . . . Thessalonians* (1583), *Works,* ed. John Ayre, Parker Society (Cambridge, 1867) pp. 853–54; and C. T. Wright, "The Usurer's Sin in Elizabethan Literature," *Studies in Philology,* 35 (1938), 178–94.

14. *Constitutions and Canons Ecclesiasticall, 1604,* ed. H. A. Wilson (Oxford: Clarendon Press, 1923), Canon C; also (in Canon LXII) a publication of marriage banns was required unless dispensed for special reason (as of course was done in the case of Shakespeare's own marriage).

15. *The Common Places . . . ,* trans. Anthonie Marten (London, 1583), II, 432.

16. Bullinger, *The goldē boke of cristen matrimonye,* trans. Theodore Basille (London, 1543), fols. x–xii; Sandys, *Sermons* (1585), ed. John Ayre, Parker Society (Cambridge, 1842), p. 281. See also Louis B. Wright, *Middle-Class Culture in Elizabethan England* (Chapel Hill: Univ. of North Carolina Press, 1935), pp. 205–11.

17. *The goldē boke,* fol. x.

18. *Godly and learned Sermons,* trans. H. I. (London, 1584), I, 146.

19. Citing Deut. 22:5, Puritan treatises are full of objections to women who "un-sex" themselves. Phillip Stubbes, in his *Anatomy of Abuses* (1583), ed. F. J. Furnival, New Shakespeare Society, Series VI (London, 1879), I, 73, insisted that women who wear men's clothes "may not improperly be called Hermaphroditi, that is, Monsters of bothe kindes, half women, half men." Aquinas, on the other hand, judged that although it is in itself sinful for a woman to wear men's clothes, "Nevertheless this may be done sometimes without sin on account of some necessity, either in order to hide oneself from enemies, or through lack of other clothes, or for some similar motive *(S.T.* II–II.169.2). Shakespeare obviously shared this view, as his whole theater-practice makes evident.

20. *Workes,* 3rd ed. (Cambridge, 1631), III, 266.

21. *The Common Places,* II, 541. Nurses and physicians, Martyr has explained, use good guile and a profitable feigning toward the sick.

22. *Hexapla,* p. 291. See also John Marbeck, *A Booke Of Notes and Common places* (London, 1581), p. 628; and John Downame, *A Treatise Against Lying* (London: 1636), pp. 15–16, 41–45, 69–74.

23. *The Breath of Clowns and Kings* (New York: Atheneum, 1971), p. 130.

24. See the Furness Variorum *Merchant of Venice* (1888), pp. 246–47; and J. H. De Groot, *The Shakespeares and the Old Faith* (New York: King's Crown Press, 1946), p. 176. Quotations from Shakespeare follow Russell Brown's text in the Arden edition (1964).

Lucan—Daniel—Shakespeare:
New Light on the
Relation Between *The Civil Wars* and *Richard II*

GEORGE M. LOGAN

Numerous parallels in action, atmosphere, political and historical interpretative perspective, and language exist between the first edition (1595) of Samuel Daniel's *Civil Wars* and Shakespeare's *Richard II*.[1] Several of the parallels are not found in other treatments of Richard's history. Charles Knight, who first called attention to these similarities in his Pictorial Edition of Shakespeare (1838–44), offered the explanation that Shakespeare had borrowed material of Daniel's invention. R. G. White, in his edition of Shakespeare's *Works* (1859), argued that the debt lay on Daniel's side, basing this conclusion on a comparison of the first edition of Daniel's poem with a mythical second edition of 1595, which contained Shakespearean parallels (and those the significant ones) not present in the first edition. E. K. Chambers, in *William Shakespeare* (1930), was the most influential twentieth-century spokesman of this view, which dominated opinion on the question until J. Dover Wilson, in his edition of *Richard II* (1939), destroyed its foundation by showing that there was no second edition of Daniel's poem in 1595, but merely a second printing differing from the first only in its title page, and that the changes that White had noted first occurred in the 1609 edition (where Daniel was indeed influenced by Shakespeare's play). Since the appearance of Wilson's edition, almost all writers on the matter, including M. W. Black, Peter Ure, and Laurence Michel, editors of recent standard editions of the two works, and Geoffrey Bullough, the judicious commentator on Shakespeare's sources, have acknowledged that there is a direct connection between the works and have inclined to the view that Shakespeare is the debtor.

Nevertheless, this view, based as it is entirely on internal evidence, is not held with great confidence. Black, to be sure, takes it for granted that Shakespeare is the debtor,[2] but Ure says that it is "by no means . . . impossible" to think that Daniel is the borrower, although it is "simpler and easier to believe" that the influence was in the other direction. Michel, though more strongly convinced of Shakespeare's indebtedness than Ure, admits that the case rests only on "broad probabilities." Bullough also confines himself to a cautious statement of probabilities.[3] Recently, Guy Lambrechts has reopened the whole question, pointing out how flimsy most of the parallels are and arguing—though on no firmer basis than a subjective view of the psychology of creativity—that those passages where a direct connection seems certain are best explained if we assume that Daniel is the debtor.[4]

The question of the relation of the works is worth arguing about for two reasons. First, the relationship of Shakespeare's political and historical thought to the thought of a contemporary who is generally acknowledged to be among the most learned and profound students of history that the Elizabethan period affords is a matter of considerable interest. Second, the establishment of a debt on one side or the other would make it possible to assign a date (either a *terminus a quo* or a *terminus ad quem,* depending on the direction of indebtedness) for the composition of Shakespeare's play. *The Civil Wars* was entered on October 11, 1594, and printed with the date 1595, presumably at the end of 1594 or early in 1595. Dating evidence for *Richard II* is scanty.[5] There are links between the play and *Woodstock,* but the date of *Woodstock* is itself uncertain.[6] The only additional piece of evidence usually cited (apart from the date of publication, 1597) is Sir Edward Hoby's letter to Sir Robert Cecil on December 7, 1595, inviting him to supper on the ninth, where "K. Richard [will] present him selfe to your vewe."[7] As has often been pointed out, not much can be inferred from this item.[8]

The present paper aims to strengthen the case for assuming Shakespeare's indebtedness to Daniel by arguments based on the nature of the relationship among the two works and Lucan's *Pharsalia.* Daniel was heavily indebted to the *Pharsalia.*[9] Numerous passages of *The Civil Wars* are based on passages of Lucan's epic, and Daniel imposed, sometimes at the cost of distorting material from his chronicle sources, a Lucanic pattern on his poem as a whole. Several of the passages where Daniel and Shakespeare are closest come at points where Daniel is following Lucan and where Daniel's passages are integral to his overall Lucanic patterning. Shakespeare appears to have known and cared relatively little about Lucan.[10] The only passages of *Richard II* that include Lucanic reminiscences come at places where Shakespeare is close to Daniel, and there is nothing in these passages to suggest that Shakespeare is drawing from Lucan rather than from Daniel. The conclusion is that in these passages Daniel is following Lucan and Shakespeare is following Daniel. It is barely possible to argue for the opposite explanation. Some of the Lucanic resemblances in Shakespeare's play may be coincidental; Shakespeare may have drawn some bits directly from Lucan; the other passages could be explained by saying that Daniel's Lucanic inspirations were here and there reinforced and complemented by exposure to Shakespeare's play. But, as I hope will become clear, it requires a good deal of dedication or perversity to argue for this kind of explanation.

The most substantial link between Daniel and Shakespeare is that found in their episodes of the final meeting of Richard and Isabel. Ure summarizes the parallels in situation and atmosphere:

> . . . it is especially in the fifth Act [Scenes i and ii] of the play that Shakespeare and Daniel come closest together. The treatment of the processional ride of Richard and Bolingbroke into London; the grief of Queen Isabel, looking on from a window at her lord's disgrace; and the final meeting of Richard and Isabel—these are episodes which in their general mood resemble a passage in Daniel's second Book, stanzas 66–98. Although Daniel's and Shakespeare's treatments differ, they have a grand design in common, which rests on the unhistorical conception of Isabel as a mature woman, not a girl of eleven.[11]

These situational parallels are embodied in language that exhibits verbal parallels of varying degrees of closeness. Shakespeare's Isabel stations herself along the processional route because she has prior knowledge of that route: "This way the king will come; this is the way / To Julius Caesar's ill-erected tower" (V.i.1–2).[12] Similarly, Daniel's Isabel "Had plac'd her selfe, hearing her Lord should passe / That way where shee vnseene in secret was" (II.71.7–8).[13] Shakespeare's Isabel is torn between a desire to look at her husband and a desire not to see his disgrace: "But soft, but see, or rather do not see, / My fair rose wither" (V.i.7–8). In Daniel, this ambivalence is worked for two stanzas:

> Let me not see him, but himselfe, a king;
> For so he left me, so he did remove.
>
> Thus as shee stoode assur'd and yet in doubt,
> Wishing to see, what seene she grieud to see.
>
> *(II.82.1–2, 83.1–2)*

In both passages, this ambivalence is connected with a momentary denial that the wretched object can be Richard: "Thou map of honour, thou King Richard's tomb, / And not King Richard" (V.i.12–13); "This is not he" (II.82.3; cf. above ll. 1–2 of the same stanza). Shakespeare's Richard recommends a brief and silent parting:

> Come, come, in wooing sorrow let's be brief,
> Since, wedding it, there is such length in grief:
> One kiss shall stop our mouths, and dumbly part.
>
> *(V.i.93–95)*

Daniel's similar silent leavetaking is conducted in terms of a somewhat distasteful metaphor of unsuccessful labor (perhaps derived from *Astrophel and Stella* 1):

> Thus both stood silent and confused so,
> Their eies relating how their harts did morne
> Both bigge with sorrow, and both great with woe
> In labour with what was not to be borne:
> This mighty burthen wherewithall they goe
> Dies vndeliuered, perishes vnborne;
> Sorrow makes silence her best oratore
> Where words may make it lesse not shew it more.
>
> *(II.97)*

The closest parallels, however, are those between Richard's melancholy prognostication of the stories Isabel will tell of him and a passage from Daniel's third book in which Richard soliloquizes in Pomfret prison on the differences between his condition and that of a peasant whom he sees through "a little grate." The passages have in common verbal details, an atmosphere of wistful self-pity, and the general situation of comfortable small people gossiping about the misfortunes of the great:

In winter's tedious nights sit by the fire	Thou sit'st at home safe by thy quiet fire
With good old folks, and let them tell thee tales	And hear'st of others harmes, but feelst none;
Of woeful ages long ago betid;	And there thou telst of kinges and who aspire,
And ere thou bid good night, to quite their griefs	Who fall, who rise, who triumphs, who doe mone:
Tell thou the lamentable tale of me,	Perhappes thou talkst of mee, and dost inquire
And send the hearers weeping to their beds;	Of my restraint, why here I liue alone,
For why, the senseless brands will sympathize	O know tis others sin not my desart,
The heavy accent of thy moving tongue,	

And in compassion weep the fire
    out,
And some will mourn in ashes,
    some coal-black,
For the deposing of a rightful king.
       (V.i.40–50)

And I could wish I were but as thou
    art.[14]

                       (III.65)

Among treatments of Richard's reign, only Daniel and Shakespeare portray Isabel as a mature woman, and only Daniel and Shakespeare have a last meeting between Richard and Isabel after Richard's fall.[15] Nor is there much authority in the chronicles for the entry of Bolingbroke and Richard into London "tandem-style, the one triumphantly in the lead, the other following unnoticed or reviled"[16] in Act V, scene ii, and the beginning of Daniel's passage about Richard and Isabel (II.66–70).

Now let us consider the parallels between Daniel's episode and passages in the *Pharsalia.* The most important point here is that Daniel's episode is an integral part of the modeling of his poem on Lucan's epic. The *Pharsalia* was, for the Middle Ages and the Renaissance, a major work, a principal source of information on the last days of the Roman Republic and on Caesar, Pompey, and Cato Uticensis. In addition, it was regarded as the *locus classicus* for the treatment of the subject of civil war. It was natural, then, for Daniel, writing a history of the Wars of the Roses, to take the *Pharsalia* as a model. Lucan could provide terse Stoic maxims on civil war and human conduct and precedents for turning military incident into poetry. Beyond these local benefits, he could provide for an English poet an interpretative pattern to impose order and dignity on the squalid panorama of the fifteenth-century wars and a measure of prestige by the association of the poet and his subject with a major account of the cataclysmic struggle of figures of enormous historical and imaginative importance, Caesar and Pompey. That Daniel means to use the *Pharsalia* for these purposes is clear from his opening stanzas, which are simply a close paraphrase, with the necessary adaptations to English circumstances, of Lucan's opening. Daniel is here inviting the reader to rethink the Wars of the Roses in terms of the war between Caesar and Pompey, and throughout the eight books of his long, unfinished poem, we find maxims, images, descriptions of battles, and interpretations of character and motive and of political and historical process borrowed from or developed in response to passages in Lucan.

In Books I–IV of *The Civil Wars,* the most important aspect of this modeling is the interpretation, sanctioned by some genuine historical parallels, of the opposition between Bolingbroke and Richard in terms of the opposition between Lucan's Caesar and Pompey. Caesar is by far the most interesting character in the *Pharsalia*. Lucan, a staunch republican writing a century after the event and thus free to indulge himself in the creation of a villain of the magnitude of (and sometimes resembling) Milton's Satan,[17] makes Caesar ruthless, fantastically dynamic, unerringly practical and precise in his judgments, untouched by sentiment for man or *patria*. Daniel evidently perceived similarities between this character and Bolingbroke, and he makes several tacit identifications between the two. A conspicuous case is found in Daniel's episode of the Genius of England, an apparition who appears to Bolingbroke on the night of his return from exile:

> A fearefull vision doth his thoughts molest,
> Seeming to see in wofull forme appeare
> A naked goodly woman all distrest,
> Which with ful-weeping eies and rent-white haire,
> Wringing her hands as one that grieud and praid,
> With sighes commixt, with words it seem'd shee said,
>
> O whither dost thou tend my vnkind sonne?
> . . . . .
> Stay here thy foote, thy yet vnguilty foote,
> That canst not stay when thou art farther in.
>
> *(I.88.3–8, 89.1, 90.1–2)*

The passage is based directly on the vision of Roma that Caesar encounters at the Rubicon. Lucan writes:

> Ingens visa duci patriae trepidantis imago
> Clara per obscuram voltu maestissima noctem,
> Turrigero canos effundens vertice crines,
> Caesarie lacera nudisque adstare lacertis
> Et gemitu permixta loqui: "Quo tenditis ultra?
> Quo fertis mea signa, viri? si iure venitis,
> Si cives, huc usque licet."[18]
>
> *(I.186–92)*

(The general saw a vision of his distressed country. Her mighty image was clearly seen in the darkness of night; her face expressed deep sorrow, and from her head, crowned with towers, the white hair streamed abroad; she stood beside him with tresses torn and arms bare, and her speech was broken by sobs: "Whither do ye march further? and whither do ye bear my standards, ye warriors? If ye come as law-abiding citizens, here must ye stop.")

One sees in what follows that the use of Lucan goes beyond mere classicizing decoration to the interpretation of character and the causes of events. The responses of both rebels to these apparitions—and thus the interpretation of their motives or excuses in launching rebellion—are quite similar:

Roma, fave coeptis; non te
    furialibus armis
Persequor; en adsum victor
    terraque marique
Caesar, ubique tuus—liceat modo,
    nunc quoque—miles.
Ille erit, ille nocens, qui me
    tibi fecerit hostem.

(I.200–203)

(Rome, . . . smile on my enterprise; I do not attack thee in frantic warfare; behold me here, me Caesar, a conqueror by land and sea and everywhere thy champion, as I would be now also, were it possible. His, his shall be the guilt, who has made me thine enemy.)

Deare Country ô I haue not
    hither brought
These Armes to spoile but for
    thy liberties:
The sinne be on their head
    that this haue wrought
Who wrongd me first, and thee
    doe tyrannise;
I am thy Champion and I seeke
    my right,
Prouokt I am to this by others
    spight.

(I.91.3–8)

To a less conspicuous degree, Daniel's Richard is interpreted in the light of Lucan's Pompey. Like Pompey, Richard is weak, vacillating, rendered unfit for war by years of luxurious peace. At the same time, the very unfitness of each man for the role he is forced into, coupled with sensitiveness of perception and an introspective habit, renders him a sympathetic, even a tragic, figure.

These characteristics, in the case of Richard, have varying degrees of support in the chronicles. One trait that is almost absent from the chronicles is Richard's attachment to his wife.[19] Scenes between Pompey and his wife Cornelia, however, punctuate Lucan's military narrative. Cornelia is one of the few women in the *Pharsalia* and easily the most attractive, as the popularity, in Middle Ages and Renaissance, of Lucan's episodes between

Pompey and Cornelia attests.[20] In view of the consistent parallelism between Caesar and Bolingbroke and Pompey and Richard and in view of
Daniel's well-known weakness for pathetic scenes involving star-crossed
lovers, it seems likely that Daniel raised the age of Isabel and developed
his scene of reunion and final parting in order to continue the historical
parallels in an area that especially tempted him.[21]

In constructing the passage, Daniel seems to have drawn material from
two episodes of the *Pharsalia*. First, the overall conception of a melancholy
reunion after Richard's defeat (a meeting not found in the chronicles) was
probably inspired by Lucan's account of the reunion of Pompey and Cornelia after Pompey's defeat at Pharsalia. There are a number of situational
parallels between Lucan's passage and Daniel's, as well as a similarity of
mood and some similar language. At the beginning of Daniel's passage,
Isabel stands at a window watching for Richard. Near the beginning of Lucan's eighth book, following the climactic account of Pharsalia in Book VII,
Cornelia watches (from a cliff on Lesbos) for Pompey's return. Neither wife
has been fully informed of what has befallen her husband (*Phars.* VIII.49–
53; *CW* II.72.3–8). Both husbands come into view downcast and disheveled;
their appearances confirm the wives' worst suspicions (*Phars.* VIII.54–57;
CW II.79–84). Both wives swoon, and Isabel's swoon resembles Cornelia's
unusually severe attack:[22]

Obvia nox miserae caelum
    lucemque tenebris
Abstulit, atque animam clausit
    dolor; omnia nervis
Membra relicta labant,
    riguerunt corda, diuque
Spe mortis decepta iacet.
                (VIII.58–61)

(Darkness closed upon her
grief and robbed her of the
light of heaven; sorrow stopped
her breath; betrayed by the
muscles, all her limbs relaxed,
her heart ceased to beat, and
long she lay deceived by the
hope that this was death.)

Sorrow keepes full possession
    in her soule,
Lockes him within, laies vp
    the key of breath,
Raignes all alone a *Lord*
    without controule
So long till greater horror
    threatneth:
And euen in daunger brought,
    to loose the whole
H'is forst come forth or else
    to stay with death.
                (II.85.1–6)

Reviving, both wives protest their faithfulness *(Phars.* VIII.86–105; *CW* II.86–92). From a hint in Lucan—"incipe Magnum / Sola sequi" (VIII.80–81: "from this time be the sole follower of Magnus")—Daniel develops two graceful stanzas (II. 89–90) of Isabel's speech:

> And yet deare Lord though thy vngratefull land
> Hath left thee thus, yet I will take thy part,
> I do remaine the same vnder thy hand,
> Thou still dost rule the kingdome of my hart;
> If all be lost, that gouernment doth stand
> And that shall neuer from thy rule depart.
>
> *(II.89.1–6)*

For the second part of the passage, which narrates Richard and Isabel's last night together, Daniel drew upon an earlier scene between Pompey and Cornelia. Preparing for Pharsalia, Pompey sends Cornelia away from the danger of battle. Similarly, Richard urges Isabel to sail for France. In both scenes, the lovers find themselves struck dumb by sorrow:

> Shee that was come with a resolued hart
> And with a mouth full stoor'd, with words wel chose,
> Thinking this comfort will I first impart
> Vnto my Lord, and thus my speech dispose:
> . . . . .
> When being come all this prou'd nought but winde,
> Teares, lookes, and sighes doe only tell her minde.
>
> Thus both stood silent and confused so,
> Their eies relating how their harts did morne
> Both bigge with sorrow, and both great with woe
> In labour with what was not to be borne:
> This mighty burthen wherewithall they goe
> Dies vndeliuered, perishes vnborne.
>
> *(II.96.1–4, 7–8, 97.1–6)*

Lucan's episode is closer in setting and atmosphere than in language:

> Mentem iam verba paratam
> Destituunt, blandaeque iuvat ventura trahentem

Indulgere morae et tempus subducere fatis.
Nocte sub extrema pulso torpore quietis,
Dum fovet amplexu gravidum Cornelia curis
Pectus et aversi petit oscula grata mariti,
Umentes mirata genas percussaque caeco
Volnere non audet flentem deprendere Magnum. . . .
Exiluit stratis amens tormentaque nulla
Vult differre mora. Non maesti pectora Magni
Sustinet amplexu dulci, non colla tenere,
Extremusque perit tam longi fructus amoris,
Praecipitantque suos luctus, neuterque recedens
Sustinuit dixisse "vale"; vitamque per omnem
Nulla fuit tam maesta dies.

(V.731–38, 791–97)

(Though his mind was made up already, words failed him: he preferred to postpone what must come, to yield to the allurements of delay, and to steal a reprieve from destiny. Night was ending and the drowsiness of sleep was banished, when Cornelia clasped in her arms the care-laden breast of her husband and sought the dear lips of him who turned from her; wondering at his wet cheeks and smitten by a trouble she could not understand, she was abashed to discover Magnus in tears. . . . She sprang forth from the bed in frenzy, refusing to put off her agony for a moment. She cannot bear to clasp in her dear arms the breast or head of her sorrowing husband, and the last chance of enjoying their long and faithful love was thrown away. They hurry their grief to an end, and neither had the heart to say a parting farewell. Of their whole lives this was the saddest day.)

The scene is quite powerful, representative of Lucan's metallic and hyperbolic mode at its best, and it is not surprising that it seems to have inspired what is usually regarded as the most moving episode in Daniel's poem.

We can, then, find an inspiration for the raising of Isabel's age and the fabrication of a final reunion between Richard and Isabel, as well as a source for several details, some of them shared by Daniel and Shakespeare, in Lucan.[23] There appears to be a direct connection between Shakespeare's episode and two passages in Daniel (Daniel's episode of Richard and Isabel and Richard's soliloquy in Pomfret), and between Daniel's episode and two passages in Lucan. Daniel and Shakespeare have, as Ure says, "a grand design in common"; they also share such (apocryphal) details as Isabel's prior knowledge of the route of the procession, her momentary denial of Richard's identity, and the close verbal and situational parallels between Richard's prognostication in Shakespeare and his soliloquy in Daniel's third book. None of these details is in Lucan. In the same way, Daniel and Lucan share such details as the wives' incomplete information, the nearly fatal swoon, the elaborate protestation of faithfulness (including the detail that each wife will henceforth be her husband's "sole follower"), and a last night together, none of which is in Shakespeare. Moreover, Shakespeare's episode shares nothing with Lucan that is not also in Daniel. Daniel knew Lucan thoroughly and was certainly intent on patterning at least some episodes of his poem on the *Pharsalia*. Shakespeare, on the other hand, nowhere gives evidence of knowing more of Lucan than a few passages from Book I and the outline of the work as a whole.[24] When one takes all these circumstances into account, it is natural, though not mandatory, to assume that Daniel developed this episode out of Lucan and perhaps the hint in the *Traïson* chronicle[25] and that Shakespeare recognized and appropriated, with judicious modifications, a good thing when he saw it in Daniel.

This argument can be reinforced by the examination of two other passages where Shakespeare and Daniel are close at points and where Daniel is following Lucan. It has often been noted that Carlyle's prophecy is close to Daniel's opening stanzas:[26]

> And if you crown him, let me prophesy—
> The *blood* of English shall manure the ground,
> And future ages groan for this foul act,
> Peace shall go sleep with Turks and infidels,
> And, in this seat of peace, *tumultous wars*
> *Shall kin with kin, and kind with kind, confound.*
> Disorder, horror, fear, and mutiny,
> Shall here inhabit, and this land be call'd
> The field of Golgotha and dead men's skulls—
> O, if you raise *this house against this house,*
> It will the woefullest *division* prove
> That ever fell upon this cursed earth.
> Prevent it, resist it, let it not be so,
> Lest child, child's children, cry against you woe.
>
> (*IV.i.136–49*; italics mine)

Daniel's passage, like Shakespeare's, deals with impending blood and chaos, and there are a number of close verbal parallels:

> I Sing the ciuil *warrs, tumultuous broyles,*
> And *blowdy factions* of a mighty land:
> Whose people hauty, proud with forain spoyles
> Vpon themselues, turne back their conquering hand:
> *Whilst Kin their Kin, brother the brother foyles,*
> Like Ensignes all against like Ensignes band:
> Bowes against bowes, *The Crowne against the crowne,*
> Whil'st all pretending right, all right throwen downe.
>
> What furie, ô what madnes held you so
> Deare people to too prodigall of *bloud?*
> To wast so much and warre without a foe,
> Whilst France to see your spoyles, at pleasure stood;
> How much might you haue purchasd with lesse wo?
> T'haue done you honor and your Nephewes good,
> Yours might haue been what euer lies betweene
> The Perenei and Alps, Aquitayne, and Rheine.
>
>   (I.1–2; italics mine)

Daniel's idea that glorious foreign conquests would have been preferable by far to the impiety of civil war also finds parallels in Shakespeare's play.[27] But if it be granted that there is any direct connection between the play and these opening, thematic stanzas of Daniel's poem, then it is certain that Shakespeare is the debtor, since Daniel (as I pointed out above) is here simply paraphrasing, almost translating, Lucan's opening:

> Bella per Emathios plus quam civilia campos,
> Iusque datum sceleri canimus, populumque potentem
> In sua victrici conversum viscera dextra,
> Cognatasque acies, et rupto foedere regni
> Certatum totis concussi viribus orbis
> In commune nefas, infestisque obvia signis
> Signa, pares aquilas et pila minantia pilis.
>   Quis furor, o cives, quae tanta licentia ferri?
> Gentibus invisis Latium praebere cruorem,
> Cumque superba foret Babylon spolianda tropaeis
> Ausoniis umbraque erraret Crassus inulta,

Bella geri placuit nullos habitura triumphos?
Heu, quantum terrae potuit pelagique parari
Hoc quem civiles hauserunt sanguine dextrae,
Unde venit Titan, et nox ubi sidera condit.

                                                                    (I.1–15)

(Of war I sing, war worse than civil, waged over the plains of
Emathia, and of legality conferred on crime; I tell how an imperial
people turned their victorious right hands against their own vitals;
how kindred fought against kindred; how, when the compact of
tyranny was shattered, all the forces of the shaken world contended
to make mankind guilty; how standards confronted hostile standards,
eagles were matched against each other, and pilum threatened pilum.
What madness was this, my countrymen, what fierce orgy of slaugh-
ter? While the ghost of Crassus still wandered unavenged, and it was
your duty to rob proud Babylon of her trophies over Italy, did you
choose to give to hated nations the spectacle of Roman bloodshed,
and to wage wars that could win no triumphs? Ah! with that blood
shed by Roman hands how much of earth and sea might have been
bought—where the sun rises and where night hides the stars.)

The close parallel between Shakespeare's "Shall kin with kin . . . con-
found" and Daniel's "Whilst Kin their Kin . . . foyles" is especially interesting, since Daniel's phrase is a careful and intelligent rendering of Lucan's
characteristically difficult and witty "Cognatasque acies," a translation influenced by the parallelism of "signis / Signa, pares aquilas et pila minantia
pilis," with "brother the brother foyles" replacing the irrelevant "rupto
foedere regni" (Lucan's allusion to the disintegration of the First Triumvirate). Thus we have Daniel, in the middle of a close paraphrase of Lucan,
producing an idiosyncratic translation of Lucan's line, and Shakespeare
close to Daniel, not the Lucanic original. Similarly, "tumultuous wars" and
"this house against this house" resemble Daniel ("warrs, tumultuous
broyles," "the Crowne against the crowne"), not Lucan, in whose passage
there is nothing that quite corresponds to these phrases.

To me it seems certain that Shakespeare has Daniel's passage in mind. In
this major thematic speech, he thinks naturally of the thematic opening of
an interesting, newly published poem on his subject: as usual, not only
ideas but also words and phrases and rhythms stick in his mind and echo
in his verse. Against this argument one can of course say that formulas of
the "brother kills brother," "son kills father" kind had long been

commonplaces—ultimately deriving from Lucan's opening (and from natural reflection on the horrifying nature of civil war)—of the literature of civil war.[28] Shakespeare himself invokes these formulas in passages in *Henry VI, Part 3* and *Richard III*.[29] But none of these passages employs the word "kin" found here. Indeed, while "brother," "father," and "son" abound in passages of this kind in late medieval and Renaissance English literature on civil war, the use of "kin" in these formulas is infrequent, and the word appears in Daniel's passage only as a specific response to Lucan's "Cognatas." Moreover, the closest parallels to Shakespeare's passage are certainly found in Daniel's passage, not in any other treatment of this material.

Carlyle's speech also contains a parallel to the prophecy spoken—likewise to Bolingbroke—by Daniel's Genius of England:

And if you crown him, let me prophesy—	What bloudshed, ô what broyles dost thou commence
The blood of English shall manure the ground,	To last for many wofull ages hence?
And future ages groan for this foul act.	. . . . .
	The babes vnborne, shall ô be borne to bleed
	In this thy quarrell if thou doe proceede.[30]

(I.89.7–8, 90.7–8)

Carlyle's remark near the end of the same scene also appears to echo this passage: "The woe's to come: the children yet unborn / Shall feel this day as sharp to them as thorn" (IV.i.322–23).[31] But Daniel's speech, and in fact the whole episode of the Genius' appearance, is, as I demonstrated above, based directly on Lucan's episode of Caesar's vision of Roma. Again the argument is weakened somewhat by the fact that statements of this kind about the effects of civil war are commonplace.

Gaunt's prophecy (II.i.31–68) offers one further case. The speech contains fairly close parallels with Daniel's passage on the murder of Duke Humphrey by Margaret of Anjou:

This fortress built by Nature for herself	*Neptune* keepe out from thy imbraced Ile
Against infection and the hand of war	This foule contagion of iniquitie;
. . . . .	Drowne all corruptions comming to defile

England, bound in with the
    triumphant sea,
Whose rocky shore beats back
    the envious siege
Of wat'ry Neptune, is now
    bound in with shame,
With inky blots and rotten
    parchment bonds;
That England, that was wont
    to conquer others,
Hath made a shameful conquest
    of itself.[32]

(II.i.43–44, 61–66)

Our faire proceedings ordred
    formally;
Keepe vs mere *English*.[33]
. . . . .
But by this impious meanes
    that worthy man
Is brought vnto this lamentable
    end,
And now that current with maine
    fury ran
(The stop remou'd that did the
    course defend)
Vnto the full of mischiefe that
    began
T'a vniuersall ruine to extend,
That *Isthmus* failing which the
    land did keepe
From the intire possession of
    the deepe.

(IV.90.1–5, 91)

Dover Wilson quotes both stanzas from Daniel and is sure that there is a direct connection between the two passages. "The 'infection' Gaunt means is a moral one, that of bloody-mindedness and civil strife. But as his meaning is not fully clear until Daniel's text is in front of us, it follows, I think, that Shakespeare is the debtor."[34] Indeed, as in the case of Carlyle's prophecy, if we accept that there *is* a direct connection between Shakespeare's passage and the second stanza of Daniel's passage, the conclusion that Shakespeare is the debtor follows inescapably, since one image shared by Shakespeare and Daniel—that of a small piece of land besieged by an envious sea—comes directly from Lucan. Shakespeare applies the image to England itself. Daniel applies it to Humphrey, who stands as an isthmus holding back the opposed tides of civil war. Daniel is simply paraphrasing Lucan, who uses the image to describe Crassus' role and the effect of his death:

Temporis angusti mansit concordia discors,
Paxque fuit non sponte ducum; nam sola futuri
Crassus erat belli medius mora. Qualiter undas
Qui secat et geminum gracilis mare separat Isthmos

Nec patitur conferre fretum, si terra recedat,
Ionium Aegaeo frangat mare.[35]

(I.98–103)

(For a brief space the jarring harmony was maintained, and there was peace despite the will of the chiefs; for Crassus, who stood between, was the only check on imminent war. So the Isthmus of Corinth divides the main and parts two seas with its slender line, forbidding them to mingle their waters, but if its soil were withdrawn, it would dash the Ionian sea against the Aegean.)

Let us recapitulate the arguments. Shakespeare is close to Daniel in a number of places for which no source can be found in the chronicles. (A few of these passages, including one case which, as Dover Wilson points out, provides a seemingly indisputable link between the two works, are unrelated to Lucan and are therefore not discussed in this paper.[36]) It is generally accepted that there is some direct connection between the two works. Daniel, in turn, is heavily indebted to Lucan. In one major episode, and in at least two passages with good verbal parallels, Shakespeare is close to Daniel at points where Daniel is following Lucan. The episode of Richard and Isabel provides the most interesting case. Shakespeare's episode seems almost certainly to be directly related to Daniel's. Situational parallels are reinforced by strong verbal parallels. But whereas there is no inspiration for the episode in Shakespeare's known sources, there *is* an inspiration in Daniel's principal model, the *Pharsalia*. Daniel's episode has much in common with Lucan's scenes involving Pompey and Cornelia, including some fairly persuasive verbal parallels. In the case of Carlyle's prophecy, there are excellent verbal parallels between this thematic speech and Daniel's thematically parallel opening stanzas, and here Daniel is certainly following Lucan, with a closeness that admits of no other inspiration. If there is a direct connection here, Shakespeare is certainly the debtor. The case of Gaunt's prophecy is similar, though not as strong. Daniel's metaphor of Duke Humphrey as an isthmus is clearly from Lucan, but the resemblance between Daniel's passage and Shakespeare's could be coincidental. The fact that there seem to be direct connections between the two works at other points, however, increases the likelihood that there is a direct connection here.

It is possible to dismiss most of the parallels between the works as coincidental. But the instances of Carlyle's prophecy and the episode of Richard and Isabel (as well as a few close parallels without Lucanic antecedents) surely indicate a direct connection between them. Who is the debtor in these instances? In the case of Carlyle's prophecy, it is impossible, in view of the connection of Daniel's passage with Lucan, to argue that Daniel is following Shakespeare. In the case of the episode of Richard and Isabel, one could offer the explanation that Daniel, already at work on a Lucanic poem, saw Shakespeare's play, realized that it contained elements compatible with his Lucanic conception, and carried away not only ideas for episodes but also some individual lines for incorporation into his poem. One who would choose this explanation has also to cope with the fact that Daniel *did* echo *Richard II* in the 1609 revision of his poem,[37] so that he must have returned more than a decade later to consideration of the play, been inspired by it a second time, and modified details of his poem in ways that did not seem appropriate to him in 1594. It is necessary only to state this alternative to reveal its weakness. None of the arguments for assuming Daniel's indebtedness to Shakespeare rests on more than subjective evaluations of the psychologically likelier order of composition of similar passages. The best way, and the only satisfactory way, then, to account for the parallels is to assume that Shakespeare is the debtor. Having arrived at this conclusion, we can return with more confidence to the remarks of Dover Wilson and others on Shakespeare's poetic and philosophic indebtedness to Daniel, and we can assign a *terminus a quo* of late 1594 or early 1595 for the composition of *Richard II*.

Notes:

1. In the New Arden edition, Peter Ure writes: "There are about thirty places where the language and ideas of the poem resemble those of the play. Not all these can confidently be ascribed to borrowing by one writer from the other. . . . None the less, there are enough places left [i.e., when those possibly coincidental or from common sources are excluded] to make the connexion a probability, if not a certainty." *King Richard II*, 5th ed. (Cambridge: Harvard Univ. Press, 1961), pp. xlii–xliii. In the New Variorum Edition, Matthew W. Black lists seventy parallels of one kind and another. See *The Life and Death of King Richard the Second* (Philadelphia: Lippincott, 1955), pp. 478–99. See also J. Dover Wilson, ed., *King Richard II* (Cambridge: Cambridge Univ. Press, 1939; rpt. 1951), pp. xxxviii–xliv, and notes, passim; Geoffrey Bullough, ed., *Narrative and Dramatic Sources of Shakespeare*, III (London: Routledge and Kegan Paul, 1960), 353, 373–79; and Samuel Daniel, *The Civil Wars*, ed. Laurence Michel (New Haven: Yale Univ. Press, 1958), pp. 8–21. The information in this paragraph about the history of the question of the relationship between Daniel and Shakespeare is drawn from these works.
2. See "The Sources of Shakespeare's *Richard II*," in *Joseph Quincy Adams Memo-*

rial Studies, ed. James G. McManaway, G. E. Dawson, and E. E. Willoughby (Washington: The Folger Shakespeare Library, 1948), pp. 199–216, and Variorum, p. 477.

3. Ure, p. xliv; Michel, pp. 7–8, 21; Bullough, III, 353, 375.

4. "Sur deux prétendues sources de *Richard II,*" *Études anglaises,* 20 (1967), 118–39. Lambrechts' assessment of the significance of the various parallels is judicious. I shall not attempt to reply to his involved arguments about the comparative likelihood of Shakespeare's version of a particular episode having preceded or followed Daniel's. It seems to me that one of the attractions of my own approach is that it removes us from the endless spiral of ingenious arguments of the kind Lambrechts advances.

    C. A. Greer denies, "assez sommairement," as Lambrechts says (p. 128*n*), that there is any connection between the two works. See "Did Shakespeare Use Daniel's 'Civile Warres'?" *Notes and Queries,* 196 (1951), 53–54.

5. See Wilson, pp. vii–x; Variorum, pp. 393–95; Ure, pp. xxix–xxx; and Greer, "The Date of *Richard II,*" *Notes and Queries,* 195 (1950), 402–404.

6. See, most recently, Lambrechts, pp. 120–25.

7. Quoted by Ure, p. xxx.

8. See I. A. Shapiro, "*Richard II* or *Richard III* or . . . ?" *Shakespeare Quarterly,* 9 (1958), 204–06.

9. For a detailed examination of the relation between Daniel and Lucan, see my article, "Daniel's *Civil Wars* and Lucan's *Pharsalia,*" *Studies in English Literature,* 11 (1971), 53–68.

10. This is a matter that I investigated in painful detail in my unpublished doctoral dissertation, "Lucan in England: The Influence of the *Pharsalia* on English Letters from the Beginnings through the Sixteenth Century," Diss. Harvard 1967, pp. 175–83. Failing this work, see T. W. Baldwin, *William Shakspere's Small Latine & Lesse Greeke* (Urbana: Univ. of Illinois Press, 1944), II, 549–51; Bullough, V, 10–12, 36; Kenneth Muir, *Shakespeare's Sources* (London: Methuen, 1957), I, 199–200; J. A. K. Thomson, *Shakespeare and the Classics* (London: George Allen and Unwin, 1952), p. 90 et passim.

11. Ure, p. xliii. Cf. Michel, pp. 11–12; Bullough, III, 375–77; Lambrechts, p. 136. Ure also says, without elaborating, that Shakespeare's treatment in this episode "is dramatic, not, like Daniel's, modelled on Lucan and the *Heroides*" (p. 145*n*).

12. Citations from *Richard II* are to Ure's edition.

13. Citations from Daniel are to *The First Fowre Bookes of the ciuile wars between the two houses of* Lancaster *and* Yorke (London, 1595).

14. If this parallel to *CW* III and/or those between Gaunt's prophecy and two passages in *CW* IV (discussed below) involve a direct connection between the two works, and if Shakespeare is the debtor, then the debt is to the 1595 edition of *CW* and not to the MS of Books I and II that Cecil Seronsy has shown to be the earliest surviving form of Daniel's poem. See Seronsy's article, "Daniel's Manuscript *Civil Wars* with Some Previously Unpublished Stanzas," *Journal of English and Germanic Philology,* 52 (1953), 153–60.

    O. A. W. Dilke has recently pointed out that Daniel's speech "is somewhat akin to Lucan's envy of the poor fisherman, Amyclas" *(Phars.* V.527 ff.). See "Lucan and English Literature," in *Neronians and Flavians: Silver Latin I,* ed.

D. R. Dudley, *Greek and Latin Studies: Classical Literature and Its Influence* (London: Routledge and Kegan Paul, 1972), p. 90. The resemblance is tantalizing but not very close.

15. Ure, p. 145*n*; Michel, pp. 11–12.

16. Michel, p. 12 (cf. p. 348*n*); cf. Ure, p. 152*n*.

17. William Blissett calls attention to the resemblances and argues a direct connection. See "Caesar and Satan," *Journal of the History of Ideas,* 18 (1957), 221–32.

18. Quotations and translations of Lucan are from *The Civil War,* ed. J. D. Duff (Cambridge: Harvard University Press, 1928). Duff's text is based on A. E. Housman's standard edition (Oxford: Blackwell, 1926).

19. Michel, pp. 11-12; Wilson, pp. lix-lx, 215*n*. *La Chronicque de la Traïson et Mort de Richart Deux,* which Daniel knew and Shakespeare may have known, contains an impressive passage (translated by Wilson, p. lx) on Richard's affectionate farewell to Isabel on his departure for Ireland.

20. See, for example, Jessie Crosland, "Lucan in the Middle Ages: With Special Reference to the Old French Epic," *Modern Language Reivew,* 25 (1930), 43–46; Eva Matthews Sanford, "Quotations from Lucan in Medieval Latin Authors," *American Journal of Philology,* 55 (1934), 3–4; and Dom David Knowles, "The Humanism of the Twelfth Century," in *"The Historian and Character" and Other Essays* (Cambridge: Cambridge Univ. Press, 1963), pp. 22–23. Robert Garnier wrote a tragedy *Cornélie* (1574), a play translated by Thomas Kyd (1594). The characterization of Cornelia in Chapman's *Caesar and Pompey* (ca. 1605) is indebted to Lucan in several particulars.

21. Daniel may have felt that the passage in the *Traïson* chronicle referred to above (n. 19) provided some justification for his fiction.

22. Dilke (loc. cit.) has concluded independently that Isabel's faint comes from Cornelia's.

    Isabel's mixed feelings about looking at her husband (discussed above in the account of parallels between Daniel's episode and Shakespeare's) may have been developed from a detail in a later scene in Lucan, where Cornelia witnesses Pompey going to his death: "Attonitoque metu nec quoquam avertere visus / Nec Magnum spectare potest" (VIII.591–92: "and panic fear prevented her either from turning her eyes away or from looking steadily at Magnus"). Note that Shakespeare's Isabel, unlike Daniel's, has detailed information (III.iv.81–91, V.i.1–4) about Richard's misfortune before she sees him.

23. This fact undercuts Lambrechts' argument that Daniel is not clever enough to have invented the episode: "Quand bien même l'on serait disposé à prêter à Daniel beaucoup plus de hardiesse et d'imagination qu'il n'a coutume d'en témoigner, il serait beaucoup plus difficile d'imaginer qu'il s'est éloigné d'un coup des chroniqueurs pour créer un épisode complexe et admirablement construit" (p. 138).

24. This is about what we would expect a graduate of the Stratford Grammar School to know of Lucan. See Baldwin, loc. cit.

25. See above, n. 19.

26. Wilson (p. 206*n*), Ure (p. 133*n*), Michel (pp. 17–18), and Bullough (III, 375) all comment on this resemblance. Bullough writes: "Many of the similar details

which critics have discussed could be due to common sources or a shared attitude; but a few suggest that particular turns of thought and phrase were suggested by Daniel's poem, notably in Gaunt's panegyric on England and the Bishop of Carlyle's protest."

27. Michel, p. 20. Cf. *R2* II.i.65–66, 171–83.
28. Cf., for example, the Tudor homily against rebellion: "countrymen to disturb the public peace and quietness of their country . . . the brother to seek, and often to work the death of his brother; the son of the father, the father to seek or procure the death of his sons . . . and by their faults to disinherit their innocent children and kinsmen their heirs for ever." Quoted by Ure, p. 133*n*.
29. Cf. *3H6* II.v.55 ff.; *R3* II.iv.61–63, V.v.23–26.
30. Lucan speaks repeatedly of the harm the war between Caesar and Pompey will do to future generations. See, for example, *Phars.* I.24–32, VII.638–45.
31. Michel (p. 19) points out this resemblance, as well as a parallel between Daniel's lines (and *CW* III.53.3–6) and *R2* III.iii.85–88, 95–97.
32. With the last two lines here, cf. *CW* I.1.3–4 and *Phars.* 1.2–3 (both quoted above). But this phrase from Lucan's opening— "populumque potentem / In sua victrici conversum viscera dextra"—had long since become a commonplace, and Shakespeare could have picked it up anywhere.
33. Cf. also *CW* IV.43.1–4, which is close to ll. 43–44 and 65–66 in Shakespeare's passage.
34. Wilson, p. 157*n*. Cf. Bullough (above, note 26), and Ure's strictures against Wilson's argument (p. xliv*n*). Lambrechts (p. 129) argues that the passages are not connected.
35. One other passage in *R2* may show obligation to Daniel where Daniel is following Lucan. The portents that forerun civil war in *R2* and in *CW* are similar in some details (cf. II.iv.8–10 with *CW* I.114.3–8, 115.1–2). Michel correctly notes that the occurrence of portents is in the chronicles and that "what . . . [Shakespeare and Daniel] have in common, 'Meteors' and 'Stars,' is common indeed" (p. 12). But that Shakespeare has Daniel in mind is perhaps suggested by the lines immediately following (II.iv.11–15), which seem to echo *CW* I.81–82, forming a sort of simplified, reactionary version of Daniel's analysis of the social conditions that lead to civil war. But in this analysis of the causes of the war, with its division into public causes and personal causes, and throughout the account of generalized panic and despair that closes Book I (sts. 108–21) and that includes his list of portents, Daniel is following the parallel episodes of Lucan's poem (*Phars.* I.120–82, 466–695, II.1–66). At some points the imitation is quite close (cf., e.g., *CW* I.81–82 with *Phars.* I.158–63, 174–76, 181–82). And Daniel's list of portents, though shorter and less sensational than Lucan's, follows the Roman poet's list both in the particular marvels included and in their order. See "Daniel's *Civil Wars* and Lucan's *Pharsalia*," pp. 59–60.
36. Cf. *CW* III.57 with *R2* V.iv. See Wilson, pp. xl–xlii. Lambrechts (pp. 135–36) provides a detailed summary of the close connections between the deposition scenes in the two works.
37. See Wilson (pp. xliii, 119*n*, 235–36*n*), who quotes the relevant passages from *CW*.

Valor's Better Parts: Backgrounds and Meanings of Shakespeare's Most Difficult Proverb

PAUL A. JORGENSEN

Probably no Shakespearean line has given more comfort to craven mankind, notably academics, than Falstaff's "The better part of valor is discretion."[1] And probably no Shakespearean proverb of such importance has been less understood. It is a disarmingly simple line. We have yielded gladly to its genial permissiveness, but we have not inquired what it means; we have not appreciated its most important proverbial features, its metaphor and its enigma; we have not admired its logical form; and we have not lewdly enjoyed the covert meanings of its three connotative nouns.

Much of the subdued rhetorical potency of the line resides in the Shakespearean manner of densely connotative expression, celebrated by William Empson as ambiguity. The line is like "To be, or not to be" in that it would appeal to us but not deeply haunt us if it were as easy in meaning as it seems, as swift and momentary in comprehension as it is in utterance. Although Empson remarks about one line of a Shakespearean sonnet that a word can be "effective in several ways at once" (in this case ten ways), perhaps the "at once" does not do justice to the prolonged, subterranean period of comprehension that goes on.[2]

The complexity of Falstaff's line, and the justification for an explication of it, is increased by its acceptance as a proverb. Even the puristic academic mind, for whom caution means so much, has accepted its standard form recorded by Morris Palmer Tilley as "Discretion is the better part of valor." Putting "discretion" first is an indication of what we have found most delightful and reassuring about the statement. As a good proverb should, this one pleases us by surprise, even though, impatient with Shakespeare's more climactic structure, we have chosen not to wait to be surprised but to come immediately to the debased form of "discretion" that liberates us from the age-old tyranny of the ethic of courage. The resultant expression reflects what Archer Taylor has found in most proverbs: "the adherence to the middle way, and indeed their reason for existence lies in that fact." "Proverbs," he adds, "will not champion martyrdom or villainy."[3]

The proverbial nature of the line and the justification for a thorough explication are supported by other universal features. Since Aristotle, Cicero,

141

and Quintillian, a proverb has been recognized as metaphoric, condensed, deceptive, enigmatic, and leading to an acquisition of knowledge. In the Renaissance, particularly, it provided an acknowledged challenge to the solution of what Puttenham described as its "covert and darke termes."[4] As Rudolph Habenicht has said, "The solution to the enigma, or 'dark saying,' became a challenge to the ingenuity of the interpreter, and sometimes this explanation was a thousandfold longer than the proverb itself."[5] Particularly because this seems to be a Shakespearean proverb, unusually difficult and connotatively rich, I have found no simple "solution" to the line but mainly an Empsonian appreciation of its complex structure. The proverb will continue to mean to each of us according to our individual need to temper courage with discretion.

In turning to editions of 1 Henry IV I have found more academic discretion, sometimes as inglorious as Falstaff's own, than courage. Of some fifteen modern texts consulted, at least one-third make no annotation at all. And, for all practical purposes, most of the others contribute no more than silent (a euphemism for plagiaristic) uses of the one thoughtful annotation supplied by George Lyman Kittredge. From my previous experience with editorial glosses, I had expected no more. Annotations tend to vary from shamelessly exact to a more criminally rephrased form of plagiarism. Although I have been amused by editorial discretion, I have from my own limited experience with the art become sympathetic with it. Most editors, having no leisure for philological work, have been plagiarists upon compulsion rather than instinct.

Kittredge, perhaps the last philologist to edit Shakespeare, recognized that the line was a problem, and he tried, as was his custom, to make clear sense of it.[6] His mind first balked at "better part." Probably to remedy the infelicity of an imperfect comparison, he provided the gloss: "*Part* is 'quality'—not 'portion.' " Admittedly the line makes an easier, if more unenigmatic and trivial sense, when so read; but there are difficulties. The comparison makes stronger sense if "part" is quantitative rather than (or as well as) qualitative. Further, to justify his gloss, Kittredge had to reckon with the continuation of the line: "in the which better part I have saved my life," and was compelled to do what he hated to do, rephrase it with an addition: "in the exercise of which better part." Furthermore, both the OED and Schmidt's *Lexicon* agree that "part" was used "almost always" in the plural in this sense of attribute, and even this comes, in the OED, under the rubric of "Portion allotted, share." Nevertheless, subsequent editors have, invariably without justification or attribution, been grateful for Kittredge's simple gloss, and eight have used it, usually without further comment. Maynard Mack dropped it from his Signet Classic Shakespeare (1965), but he took the pains to give it what is probably the best paraphrase of the line based upon it: "Falstaff willfully misinterprets the maxim that valor is the better for being accompanied by discretion." This reading departs from Shakespeare, however, by having discretion accompanying valor rather than being the better part of it. Kittredge's equation is dropped totally by A. R. Humphreys in the New Arden edition (1960). Nevertheless it has resurgently appeared in later editions; and, in 1974, when I turned eagerly to the Harvard–centered Riverside edition, heralded for its explanatory notes, I found the following: *"part:* quality." Harvard, after searching elsewhere, had again found its best man at home.

A few editors have added individual paraphrases of another, more questionable, interpretation made by Kittredge. His paraphrase of the line is: "Bravery that is not directed by good judgment is not true valor: it is mere foolhardiness." "Such," he concludes, "is the serious meaning of the maxim that Falstaff applies in witty defense of his stratagem." I suspect that it is the serious meaning because it is the wrong meaning. Perhaps Kittredge was misled by an earlier gloss supplied by R. P. Cowl in the original Arden edition (1914). Cowl quotes from *Vincentio Saviolo his Practise* (London, 1595) in a context of what weapons are suitable for gentlemen in duelling:

> The wisdome and discretion of man is as great a virtue as his magnanimitie and courage, which are so much the greater vertues, by how much they are accompanied with wisdome: for without them a man is not to be accounted valiant, but rather furious.
>
> *(sig. Bb1ʳ)*

This does suggest Falstaff's line, even though Falstaff is not warning against being "furious" and even though, again, Falstaff's statement does not have courage being "accompanied" by discretion, but being rather the better part of it. But the quotation may have suggested to Kittredge that Falstaff was "applying" a "maxim." A maxim, according to the *OED* and in Shakespeare's own usage,[7] is characterized by "aphoristic or sententious form." It is not a sober, prosaic platitude. J. Dover Wilson's spirited edition remedies this semantic difficulty by quoting Saviolo, under an incorrect title, so as to make the passage sound proverbial. To do so, he not only abridges but misquotes: "Without wisdome and discretion . . . a man is not to be accounted valiant but rather furious." He is thus able to exclaim: "Falstaff's cynical misinterpretation of a wise maxim is now generally accepted as its true meaning!"[8] Later editors, misled by either Kittredge or Wilson, but not inhibited in their own phraseology, continue to lament the "wise maxim" that Falstaff has "willfully misinterpreted" or "distorted its bearing." The realization soon struck me that Kittredge at least, and probably the others, thought that Shakespeare was employing a proverb. Kittredge, in fact, does refer to it as a proverb in his note to Shakespeare's earlier use of valor and discretion in *A Midsummer Night's Dream* (V.i.236, 237: "the proverb quoted by Falstaff.")

Thus began my conscientious search for the maxim that Falstaff misapplies, a search that became so fascinating that I have come to know it as the case of the missing maxim. What I discovered was no maxim at all, but rather long, inconclusive, diverse expositions upon one of the most important literary and philosophical subjects in human history. What emerged was a *topos* rather than a maxim, a *topos* which Ernst Robert Curtius has briefly discussed as *fortitudo et sapienta* and which R. E. Kaske has found to be basic to *Beowulf*.[9] In Greek literature it took the form of wise counsel versus brave deeds, learned age versus impetuous youth. In Homer, according to Curtius, "we are confronted with something primal" (p. 171). Virgil, on the other hand, "created a new ideal of the hero, based upon moral strength," with virtue taking the place of wisdom (p. 173). In the Renaissance the *topos* appeared in didactic writings on courtly ideals, as in Castiglione, and it took especially the form of "arms and letters" or "pen and sword" (pp. 178–79). So diverse were the contexts that no single maxim seemed to suffice or to have been sought.

Among the philosophers few *topoi* engaged the best minds so much as the relationship of courage and wisdom. The Renaissance, to judge mainly by encyclopedic works like La Primaudaye's *The French Academie*, found the *topos* in Isocrates, Plato, Aristotle, Cicero, Plutarch, and Lactantius. Plato in particular was cited, though it is questionable how directly Renaissance writers knew the works which they roughly paraphrased. What is important was that Plato served as a primary authority. In the *Laws, The Republic, Laches,* and *Protagoras* he returned again and again to the relationship between the virtues of man, trying to reconcile courage, seemingly a unique character trait, with more thoughtful virtues. In *Protagoras,* for example, the question which begins the discussion on courage is, "Are wisdom and temperance and courage and justice and holiness five names of the same thing? or has each of the names a separate underlying essence and corresponding thing having a peculiar function, no one of them being like any other of them?"[10] Protagoras takes the view that four of these qualities are parts of virtue, but that courage "is very different from the other four."

Socrates questions this position, and obviously Plato never made up his mind on the subject, for in Book IV of *The Republic* he argues that temperance is unlike courage and wisdom, which reside in a part only, whereas temperance runs through all the notes of the scale. And in *Laches,* the most central document, the dialogue ends without a conclusion. One encounters expressions like "thoughtful courage," but there is no assertion so confident or so crisp as discretion being the better part of valor. A statement found in the *Laws* is perhaps most characteristic: that "justice and temperance and wisdom, when united to courage, are better than courage alone" (V.7). This is substantially the "accompanied by" formula which modern editors favor in giving a lucid meaning to Falstaff's line, but not a meaning which would have the shock, the puzzle, of a proverb. Aristotle, with his carefully phrased formula about fortitude, comes somewhat closer to a maxim, but on the whole the philosophers did not use or seek this kind of statement. In the Renaissance we may find the popular philosopher Pierre Charron writing pithily and wittily (much like his master Montaigne) that "Humane valour is a wise cowardlinesse."[11] But the history of the subject from the Greeks to the early seventeenth century is stated, as it must have appeared to more than one Renaissance reader, by Thomas Milles in 1613:

> Many Authors, both Anchient and Modern, have delivered their judgments concerning Man-hood or Valor: but yet so weakely, and without any true validitie, as nothing can be collected from such enstructions. . . . The French, Germaines, English, Italians, and Spaniards, have (like Fresh-men) discoursed on this Argument, using so many words, and little grace; as if they were deprived of all means to write on such a subject.[12]

Despite Milles' gloomy view of the prevalence of "so many words, and little grace," there was assuredly in philosophy adequate wisdom and eloquence to create a proverb that would catch the essence of the age-old anxiety about manhood and caution. One proverbial view of the proverb is that it is the wisdom of many and the wit of one.[13] There may be closer individual approximations to the ultimate form in literatures which I have not surveyed. But it is more likely that, if such were the case, we should find something like the ultimate form in English writings before Shakespeare. The only approximation before Shakespeare recorded by Tilley is Caxton's "Than as wyse and discrete he withdrewe him saying that more is worth a good retreayte than a folisshe abydinge" (1477), a line that was not taken up by others, doubtless because it lacks the literary qualities of the proverb. I would conclude that Shakespeare, with much folk wisdom behind him, was the wit who created, and gave to his amplest spokesman for imperfect humanity, the proverb that editors say he was quoting. He did not achieve this feat entirely alone. Earlier English writers, themselves the imperfect beneficiaries of classical wisdom, had been giving the *topos* a form that was distinctively English both in its intellectual auspices and in its phrasing. It is only rarely, as Archer Taylor has said, that we can "see a proverb actually in the making" (p. 3). In this case, I think, we can come tantalizingly close to doing so.

In the Renaissance, and particularly Renaissance England, the tyranny of an ethic of courage was especially strong. Curtis Brown Watson perhaps puts it too sweepingly when he seeks to "provide evidence that for the man of the Renaissance, including Shakespeare, a resonant sense of honor is in every respect excellent and never questioned."[14] Nevertheless, again and again in Shakespeare we find statements like the following: "Of all base passions, fear is most accursed" (*1H6* V.ii.18) and "True nobility is exempt from fear" (*2H6* VI.i.129). The English had the reputation, according to a Hollander, of being "bold, courageous, ardent, and cruel in war, fiery in attack *(vyerlich int aegrijpen)*, and having little fear of death."[15] Another wrote of them: "They contemne all dangers, and death it selfe, with more courage than judgment."[16]

The superiority of courage over judgment lay deep in English pride as well as in military practice. But the pride was a costly one to maintain, and the effort to do so may have contributed, in a way impossible for another age or nation, to the folk rebellion against it and acquiescence in a fat coward and skeptical proverb. The stiff military stance was as difficult to maintain as the psychological one. The English had prided themselves on plain force rather than strategy. An apprentice in Heywood's *Edward II* expresses the staunch attitude toward martial discretion:

> We have no trickes nor policies of warre,
> But by the antient custom of our fathers,
> We'll soundly lay it on.[17]

It is chiefly in military writings, often "Englished" from classical historians and authorities on war, urging a more intelligent view of strategy, that we find the developing cynical and ultimately witty questioning of this chauvinistic stance and, accordingly, the preparation for Falstaff, who in strategy as in recruiting is an exponent of the enlightened view. English adaptations of classical precepts on strategy tend to be rough approximations of the originals and contribute to the development of the proverb mainly sententious, oversimplified statements of long, complex passages. They are especially helpful if viewed in chronological order, for thereby we can see the vocabulary of Shakespeare's line coming slowly, hesitantly into being.

Much of this preparatory material is the work of military alarmists who, for patriotic reasons, sought to educate a tactlessly valiant English army to the value of policy in war. In dedicating to Henry VIII his translation of Frontinus' *The Strategems, Sleyghts, and Policies of Warre* (London, 1539), Richard Morison states the creed for most of the subsequent books on the subject: "Many mo fields have been lost for lacke of polycie, then for want of strength" (sig. A4ᵛ). Barnaby Rich similarly cites Sallust for his purposes. What is interesting about his allusion is that, following the English manner of quoting the classics, he gives epigrammatic simplicity to a longer passage in Sallust's *The War with Catiline*. Rich states it like a maxim: "Sallust sayth, that wytt and wyll joyned togeather, maketh a man valiant."[18] Of further interest in the passage are, first, the dull, unpromising tendency merely to "joyne togeather" valor and strategy and, second, the vocabulary, typical of most of the early works, in which "wit" and "will" are used as the complementary agents.

Gradually the citations of the classical authorities on war take an all-important step by selecting or modifying their texts so as to make not a balanced ideal but a preference for policy over force—a step crucial to Falstaff's point of view. Peter Whitehorne's version of Onosander, for example, affirms that the captain "ought to be much valianter with prudence of mynde, then with the force and lustines of bodye."[19] One of the most interesting writers to adapt classical authority in this manner is William Baldwin, who gave a summary form to the general gist of Xenophon's *Hipparchicus* or *The Cavalry Commander*. Typical of Xenophon's counsel is the sentence, "A prudent commander will never take risks unnecessarily, except when it is clear beforehand that he will have the advantage of the enemy."[20] Baldwin gives this kind of cautious and specific philosophy an unwarrantedly generalized expression:

> Yf that it chaunce the in warre for to fyght,
> More than to wyt, trust not to thy myght.
> For wyt wythout strength much more doth avayle,
> Than strength wythout wit, to conquer in battayle.[21]

This example is also the closest I have found to a proverbial form before Shakespeare, and indeed Baldwin lists it under "Of proverbs & adages." I am convinced, however, since Baldwin gives the same versified condensation to other authors, that he is the sole fabricator of the doggerel. I am equally convinced that he had no influence on Shakespeare, though he does show the Elizabethan fondness for giving complex wisdom a simplified, epigrammatic form.

In most early paraphrases of military classics, we have not only the terms "wit" and "will" in the translation but also a tendency to favor wit over will. New tendencies are also visible in a key work that Shakespeare probably had read, Sir Thomas North's translation of Plutarch's Alexander the Great: "But Alexander setting upon them [Greeks in the service of Darius], more of will then discretion, had his horse killed under him."[22] Thus in 1579 appears the first use of "discretion" which I have found in this context. Equally important, the "will" is not bluntly deplored; rather, there is the faint beginning of a tendency to allow the ironic humor implicit in the contrast to speak for itself. And also important is the strong possibility that "discretion" is taking on the meaning of strategy and not merely caution. It is, after all, a replacement for "wit," which in military context implied intelligent policy.

Turning momentarily to native English literature, we find in Spenser a use of "discretion" that in the context must mean strategy:

> Daunger without discretion to attempt,
> Inglorious and beastlike is: therefore Sir knight,
> Aread what course of you is safest dempt,
> And how we with our foe may come to fight.[23]

A more important example from creative literature, likewise almost surely read by Shakespeare, occurs in Sidney's 1590 *Arcadia* (probably composed in 1584). Palladius, first ascertaining knowledge of his own forces and those of the enemy, tells Kalender "that by playne force there was small apparaunce of helping Clitophon: but some device was to be taken in hand, wherein no lesse discretion then valour was to be used."[24] This, first of all, is the earliest instance I have found using both "discretion" and "valor." Second, "discretion" clearly means a strategy. Third, the whole passage is set in a humorous context which ridicules plain courage. The enemy, for example (pp. 38–39), are "more determinate to doo, then skilfull how to do: lusty bodies, and brave arrows: with such courage, as rather grew of despising their enemies, whom they knew not, then of any confidence for any thing, which in them selves they knew."

Thereafter, "discretion" and "valor" appear as almost standard terms. Shakespeare had his vocabulary. More, he had a meaning for "discretion" and a tendency, often witty, to make discretion the better part. In a journal of a siege of 1591, for example (which is interesting additionally for the "cowardlye crueltie" of some soldiers who gloried in thrusting their sword into dead bodies), it is recorded that there was shot through the thigh "a tall Irish soldier who did excellent well, but yet his valure to be praised more than his discretions."[25] Still another report of an actual engagement tells of a Colonel Randall who was praised for his courage because, without allowing "the footmen to give their volley of shot as reason did require, . . . presently put the spurs to his horse, and ran into the thickst of the enemies." The chronicler, a military man, observes: "I have heard some of good account say that his dooinges in the same was valorous: I am not of that minde, but it is for the most parte holden for valour with such as doo not understand what true valour is: when in troth it is but very foolish hardines, without any discretion at all."[26]

It is surely significant that the valor-discretion dichotomy had become before 1597 a standard part of military vocabulary, and that it was beginning to lend itself to aphoristic statements and occasionally to witty deprecation of plain valor. Shakespeare could confidently make his fraudulently learned military professional take an heroic pose as a master of the newest science of war and as a strategist rather than a foolish fighter. Much, alas, of the comfort that subsequent readers have derived from their own craven interpretation of "discretion" was probably not Falstaff's primary and proud meaning. The *OED* does not list until 1720 the deteriorated version of "Discretion, a species of lower prudence" (Swift, *Fates of Clergymen*).

It is not only as a soldier that Falstaff is a logician. We must now come to the difficult "part" aspect of his line, in which he demonstrates himself to be a triumphant fraud as a formal logician. Logician is one of the many roles that Falstaff plays, and in this instance it helps to give epigrammatic form and a mock precision to what so far we have seen as a rather casual conjunction of valor and discretion. From the evidence so far viewed, we can say that Falstaff was not distorting a proverb. Discretion was indeed, in late Elizabethan England, coming to be viewed as more important than mere courage. But for "the better part of valor" we must turn to formal logic.

As Hardin Craig has shown, "formal logic is to Shakespeare, for the most part, a subject of jest," and Craig finds some of this in the dialogue between Sir John and the Prince.[27] An early example is Falstaff's "I deny

your major" (II.iv.544). In the very speech in which "valor" and "discretion" appear, moreover, S. L. Bethell has exposed the sophistical logic beneath Falstaff's use of "counterfeit," concluding that Falstaff is triumphant:
"Thus a false argument transfers the opprobrium of forgery and deceit
from the living coward to the guiltless corpse."[28]

Falstaff gives structure to his proverb, and much of its plausibility, by
putting it into the form of a definition. Logicians, classical and Renaissance, looked upon division into parts as a basic step in definition. Cicero
stated that "definitions are made partly by enumeration and partly by
analysis; by enumeration when the thing which has been set up for definition is divided into its members as it were."[29] In the Renaissance, division
into parts is discussed at length by Thomas Wilson in *The Rule of Reason*
(London, 1551), with the justification that "he that doth well divide, doth
teache well" (sig. D8ʳ). Besides contributing to definition, *partitio* was a
"maner of handling a single Question" (sig. E4ᵛ), a procedure which Hamlet knew well in dividing his "question" of "To be or not to be" into essentially two parts. The formula for division proposed by Ramus is especially
relevant to the logical success of Falstaff's line:

> The distribution ryseth of argumentes, whiche dothe agree with the
> whole, but amonge them selves doth disagree. And therfore however
> muche the whole with the parts agreeth, and the partes amonge them
> selves disagreeth: so much is the distribution the more accurate.[30]

The formula is rhetorically congenial to the proverb, which characteristically achieves some of its metaphorical strength by finding similarity
in dissimilarity, discretion in valor. This formula is related to the tradition
of dividing parts, when they are faculties of man, into the two kinds most
sharply opposed, the ireful (or bold) and the intellective (or patient). Fortitude, according to Nicholas Caussin, "hath two arms, one to undertake,
the other to suffer: Aristotle assigneth it four parts, that is, confidence, patience, love of labour, and valour."[31] Here again we may note the structural basis of Hamlet's soliloquy: whether it is nobler to suffer or to do (or
be). Thomas Rogers cites Chrisoppus to the effect that "Fortitude was
either a science teaching how to suffer things: or it was a vertue of the
minde, obeying unto reason without all fear, either in patient bering, or ad-
venturing anything."[32]

In making this important *partitio*, Rogers was following the almost invar-
iable procedure for defining fortitude. Aristotle, as we have seen, divided it
on one occasion into four parts. Cicero similarly defines it as follows:

"Courage is the quality by which one undertakes dangerous tasks and endures hardships. Its parts are highmindedness, confidence, patience, perseverance."[33] Almost without exception Renaissance writers who define this virtue do so by *partitio*. Elyot in *The Governor* (1531) divides fortitude into five parts, one of which is "magnanimitie" or "valyaun courage" and most of the others are intellective faculties involving control or patience.[34] Jaques Hurault separates "Prowesse" into six parts.[35] So traditional was the practice that Renaissance books often have, as does Thomas Rogers (fol. 139^v), a caption called "The partes of fortitude." And equally traditional was the practice, regardless of the number of parts prescribed, of representing both the "valyaun courage" and the intellective virtues of fortitude. Falstaff's "better part" would seem, in this tradition, to be one or all of the intellective virtues, perhaps with some emphasis upon heroic patience. He is of course without any sound basis in logic for choosing this better part (Hamlet with equal reason could say that conscience, or an intellective faculty, makes cowards of us all). Logic alone offers only the division between the parts. Military doctrine supplied the gratifying clue to the better part.

One should not, in the discussion of parts, overlook Aristotle's tripartite system for defining a virtue. In one of his key expressions on the subject he wrote:

> Of every continuous entity that is divisible into parts it is possible to take the larger, the smaller, or the equal part, and these parts may be the larger, smaller, or equal either in relation to the entity itself, or in relation to us. The "equal" part is something median between excess and deficiency.[36]

This passage has been frequently applied to the concept of honor in the play as a whole, but it leaves something to be desired in application to the proverb. What is the "equal" part? The entity being defined by Falstaff is of course valor, but then the other parts must be excesses, and discretion could scarcely be an excess. Elsewhere, to be sure, Aristotle observes that sometimes one excess is to be preferred to another. In the case of valor, unfortunately, "it is not the excess, recklessness, which is more opposed to courage, but the deficiency, cowardice" (p. 49). Falstaff cannot then afford to be an Aristotelian. But we cannot rule out the possibility that he is slyly upgrading the deficiency into discretion.

It is at any rate interesting that "discretion" had a sufficiently favorable denotation to permit using it propitiously in the "parts" interpretation. It still kept popularly its Latin meaning of discrimination, discernment, parting—all intellective and involving choice. Elyot's Latin *Dictionary* (1538) defines *discretus* as "severed or parted. Valla sayth, that it is he that discerneth the qualyties of men, and value of thinges." Cawdrey's dictionary of 1604 defines it as "a wise choice of one for another."[37] The *partitio* is more evident in Henry Peacham's longer definition:

> Discretion is so called of *Discerno,* which properly is to sever or part one thing from another, . . . a quintessence from Elementary parts. So that Metaphorically it is applyed to our judgements in severing or dividing virtue from vice . . . the necessary from the superfluous, a freend from a foe &c. and indeede it is the hyest pitch of understanding and judgement, which the most men seem to have, but fall short off, yea in their weightiest actions: . . . without discretion the whole course of our lives, is nothing else but folly, or rashnesse.[38]

What Falstaff is doing in his whole soliloquy, and throughout the play, is making "a wise choice of one for another," choosing "the necessary from the superfluous," the life-saving from folly or rashness. Again, we must not underestimate the true meaning and worth of the "better part." It does not, in the agile brain of this skillful logician and master of devious language, mean too palpable an espousal of the ignoble but an election of that part of valor which will sustain life: "Give me life, which if I can save, so; if not, honor comes unlook'd for, and there's an end" (V.iii.63–65).

One of the reasons for the difficulty of precisely defining "better part" is that Shakespeare wished, or was impelled, to give it multiple meanings. It is as rich in ambiguity as Falstaff in the roles he plays. Falstaff is here more than a military strategist or logician. He is the actor[39] who is now threatened in the "part" of Valor which has been his principal role and sustenance in the play. It sustains his swagger in the Tavern Scene, even when he is cornered in his sophistical logic as a "valiant lion" (II.iii.302) and a little later when he acknowledges himself to be "as valiant as Hercules" (II.iv.298); it reaches a mock-pathetic eloquence in "valiant Jack Falstaff, therefore more valiant, being, as he is, old Jack Falstaff" (II.iv.523–25); and it becomes personified in himself in the complaint, "Let them that should reward valor bear the sin upon their own heads" (V.iv:153). The clearest personification of all, however, is in the proverbial line. In the Folio text, in Rowe, and in Pope, but not in modern editions, "Valor" is capitalized, probably suggesting the name of a character. "Valor" is personified elsewhere in Shakespeare (*Mac.* I.ii.19; *Tro.* I.iii.176;

and *Cor.* V.v.134), and in these instances editors usually retain the original editions' capitals. They have not done so for Falstaff, despite the fact that he is, as Bernard Spivack has seen, similar to Iago in being essentially "a set of cognate personifications."[40] Thomas Fuller, little more than half a century after the play, wrote of Sir John Fastolfe: "the stage hath been over bold with his memory, making him a Thrasonicall Puff, & emblem of Mock-valour."[41] And the *OED* recognizes that "Valor" can be "used as a personal name or (with possessives) as a quasi-title; also, a person of courage." "Part," furthermore, is used twenty-two times in Shakespeare to mean a role.

Indeed, if there is a single, primary meaning for the whole line, it may well lie in this stage metaphor. Falstaff now recognizes that in his present predicament, with its threat to his persona as Valor, his better role will have to be Discretion (also capitalized in Folio). Such an interpretation, now silent in editorial annotations and obviously so in the popular mind, has died in the proverb also, despite the fact that, according to Archer Taylor, "simple metaphors which verge on personification are of course common to proverbs in all lands" (p. 142). But the subsequent history of this proverb would show that it has lost much of its verbal sophistication, and indeed dramatic accuracy, and no longer requires the Renaissance fascination in the enigma for its satisfying meaning.

This atrophy in the semantic richness of the line is especially evident in a loss that Shakespeare might have regretted above all others: its indecency. This indecency can be shown, like the actor metaphor, to be not just a casual excrescence but basic to the defense of threatened manhood in the passage and in Falstaff's entire career. It has been overlooked by editors and by usually sensitive pornographers like Eric Partridge[42] partly because two of its major words, valor and discretion, are usually only obliquely bawdy and can be discerned as such only if we examine Shakespeare's habit of embodying a moral or temperamental quality in a localized region. "Part," however, to any alert Shakespearean should have aroused interest, especially in a poet who in the matter of bawdy must always be assumed guilty if he is not proved innocent. In *The Comedy of Errors,* the use of "part" is grossly topographical. Of the wench Luce it is asked, "In what part of her body stands Ireland?" Dromio replies: "Marry, sir, in her buttocks; I found it out by the bogs" (III.ii.119–21). Peter Brook's scandalous interpretation for the part of Wall in *A Midsummer Night's Dream* was convincing. The wall's crucial part, as Clifford Leech and others have suggested,[43] is its "chink," which the actor should prominently display, commenting as he leaves, "Thus have I, Wall, my part discharged so"

(V.i.207), and drawing the plaudits of the gentle spectators, "It is the wittiest partition that ever I heard discourse, my lord" (V.i.168–69). Falstaff's declining manhood, which we shall see as basic to his valor speech, is referred to by the Chief Justice in his cruel remark, "every part about you blasted with antiquity" (2H4 I.ii.207–208).

For "valor" and "discretion," particularly the latter, there are few grossly overt sexual identifications elsewhere in Shakespeare. The parts they represent are suggested by what the words mean morally. "Valor," standing for the male principle of prowess and potency, is localized in the penis, and it is interesting that there is a proverb, "Penis erectus non habet conscientiam" (Taylor, 171). "Discretion," in the meaning which the OED exemplifies by a quotation from Tyndale, "To be discrete, chast, huswifly," and equated by Elyot (p. 106) with modesty, is optimistically localized in the primary female part. Shakespeare gets greater venereal effect by subtlety than by explicitness. The obliquity of his typical kind of allusion, having only a functional relationship to the sexual member, is deftly comic in Mercutio's "for I was come to the whole depth of my tale, and meant, indeed, to occupy the argument no longer" (Rom. II.iv.104–106), where a more clinical term than "argument" would have been humorless. The same strategy is evident in Shakespeare's tireless exploitation of "wit," even in respectable girls like Rosalind, for pudendum.[44] "Wit" is very close in its intellectual denotation to "discretion," and both are suggestively localized in the female region which, like "argument," expresses a temperamental as well as an erotic feminine trait. "Pudendum" comparably derives from the word for "shame." The strategy is, at bottom, a synecdoche, in which the part stands for the whole.

A convincing case for genital meanings of valor and discretion could be made from the elaborate play on these words in A Midsummer Night's Dream (V.i.232–59). But to make such a clarification would take an entire essay. I will instead cite only a few isolated instances of suggestive meaning. When Orleans in Henry V (III.vii.118–22) refers to the Dauphin's valor as "no hidden virtue in him," the Constable replies: "By my faith, sir, but it is; never anybody saw it but his lackey. 'Tis a hooded valor, and when it appears, it will bate." Even the austere lexicographer Schmidt acknowledges a "quibble" on "bate," for the meaning is that the Dauphin's "valor" will prove inoperative upon appearance or proof. The dependable malapropist Mistress Quickly in the same play (II.i.45–46) likewise suggests both the weapon and the function when she urges Nym to "show thy valor, and put up your sword." The fall of valor is intended in Ulysses' reference to Achilles responding to his "male whore's" jest: "and at this sport / Sir

Valor dies" *(Tro.* I.iii.175–76). And potency is almost too obvious in the servant Gregory's observation in *Romeo and Juliet:* "To move is to stir, and to be valiant is to stand" (I.i.11–12).[45]

For "discretion" as pudendum we are again indebted partly to a malapropist. Evans, describing Mistress Page's assets, says, " 'Tis one of the best discretions of a 'oman as ever I did look upon" *(Wiv.* IV.iv.1–2). In *Love's Labor's Lost,* a play in which almost every line is suspect, Armado acknowledges his error in a typical military-sexual metaphor: "I have seen the day of wrong through the little hole of discretion, and I will right myself like a soldier" (V.ii.732–35), where "right" has the *OED* meaning of "To set up . . . ; to raise, rear, erect, set upright."

This is, in effect, what Falstaff does. The most triumphant meaning of his proverb is "Falstaff erectus," essentially a happy outcome to his most basic fear of "dying." Earlier Falstaff had experienced a fear in a military metaphor involving a sexual pun: "Well, 'tis no matter; honor pricks me on. Yea, but how if honor prick me off when I come on?" (V.i.130–32). In the subsequent soliloquy which contains the proverb, he explains his "counterfeiting." This word is possibly a more outrageous pun than Partridge recognizes, for it contains, besides "feit" or "fit," the fundamental word which Princess Katherine has immortalized in *Henry V:* "coun" (III.iv.47–53), a "mauvais" word. Falstaff describes dying as a counterfeiting:

> To die is to be a counterfeit, for he is but the counterfeit of a man who hath not the life of a man; but to counterfeit dying, when a man thereby liveth, is to be no counterfeit, but the true and perfect image of life indeed. The better part of valor is discretion; in the which better part I have saved my life.
>
> *(V.iv.116–22)*

If "Falstaff" can be taken as a pun on Fall-staff,[46] the passage takes on a beautifully sexual meaning, though the syntax is difficult because it has had to carry other meanings as well. Falstaff, who has chosen for his "valor" its better part, will, in that discreet part, only counterfeit dying. I must confess that this meaning, though beautiful, is not so simple as one might wish; it will be admired by the prurient rather than the voyeuristic. For me it is as with poor Malvolio's M, O, A, I: "there is no consequency in the sequel. That suffers under probation. A should follow, but O does" *(TN* II.v.141–43). One might equally well expect Falstaff to "die" in the better part. But he does not, whether or not it is the result of counterfeiting or whether or not the better part is taken to be genuine female discretion. At any rate, perhaps the finest symbol of Falstaff erectus is the stage direction, printed boldly as a line in the early texts but not in most modern editions: "Falstalffe riseth up" (1598 quarto).

In all of its parts, then, the proverbial line, now as blasted in its parts as Falstaff, could if revived minister to one of mankind's, and particularly man's, basic needs. It provides relief for an anxiety that requires a comic answer as much as Hamlet's equally basic question requires a serious answer. Falstaff, in rising up, assures the uneasy male that valor—ethical, military, and sexual—has a better part.

Notes:

1. *1 Henry IV* V.iv.20–21. All Shakespearean citations, unless otherwise indicated, are to *The Complete Plays and Poems of William Shakespeare,* ed. William Allan Neilson and Charles Jarvis Hill (Cambridge, Mass.: Houghton, 1942). I have, however, preferred the modern American and frequent Elizabethan spelling of "valor."

2. *Seven Types of Ambiguity* (New York: Noonday, 1955), p. 5. Like Empson's, the researches of C. S. Lewis justify the most complex study of a Shakespearean word or line. In *Studies in Words* (Cambridge: Cambridge Univ. Press, 1960), Lewis, while acknowledging that "prolonged thought *about* the words we ordinarily think *with* can produce a momentary aphasia," argues that this kind of thought should be welcomed in order that we may feel the full potency of the words (p. 6).

3. *The Proverb and an Index to the Proverb* (Cambridge: Harvard Univ. Press, 1931), p. 168.

4. George Puttenham, *The Arte of English Poesie* (London, 1589), p. 155.

5. John Heywood, *A Dialogue of Proverbs*, ed. Rudolph E. Habenicht (Berkeley: Univ. of California Press, 1963), p. 3. As late as 1670, the anonymous editor of John Ray's *A Collection of Proverbs* said of the proverb that it is "frequently beholden to the propriety or the ambiguity of a word, for its singularity and approbation." Quoted by B. J. Whiting, "The Nature of the Proverb," *Harvard Studies and Notes in Philology and Literature,* 14 (1932), 298. And U. R. Burke remarked that "there are very few proverbs which do not convey a meaning beyond that primarily expressed, which have not in fact a secondary signification." *Sancho Panza's Proverbs* (London: Pickering and Chatto, 1892), p. xi.

6. I have used the edition in *Sixteen Plays of Shakespeare* (Boston: Ginn, 1946). An earlier edition appeared in 1940.

7. "Therefore this maxim out of love I teach; / Achievement is command, ungain'd beseech." *(Tro.* I.ii.318–19)

8. The New Shakespeare edition (Cambridge: Cambridge Univ. Press, 1946). Humphreys duly quotes Wilson in his New Arden edition.

9. Curtius, *European Literature and the Latin Middle Ages,* trans. Willard R. Trask (New York: Harper, 1963); Kaske, "*Sapienta et Fortitudo* as the Controlling Theme in *Beowulf,*" *Studies in Philology,* 55 (1958), 423–57.

10. *Protagoras, in The Dialogues of Plato,* trans. B. Jowett (London: Oxford Univ. Press, 1892), I, 186.

11. *Of Wisdome* (London: for E. Blount and W. Aspley, ca. 1611), p. 500.

12. *The Treasurie of Auncient and Modern Times* (London, 1613), pp. 259–60.

13. Cited by B. J. Whiting, p. 300.

14. *Shakespeare and the Renaissance Concept of Honor* (Princeton: Princeton Univ. Press, 1960), pp. 10–11.

15. Emanuel van Meteren, *History of the Netherlands* (1599), in W. B. Rye, *England as Seen by Foreigners* (London: John Russell Smith, 1865), p. 70.

16. John Barclay, *Icon Animorum* (1614), Englished by Thomas May (London, 1631), p. 81.

17. *1 Edward II, in Dramatic Works of Thomas Heywood,* ed. R. H. Shepherd (London: J. Pearson, 1874), I, 17.

18. *A right Excelent and Pleasant Dialogue, Betwene Mercury and an English Souldier* (London, 1574), sig. C4^r. The plundered passage in Catiline may be found in the translation by Thomas Heywood (1608), in The Tudor Translations, 2nd ser., ed. Charles Whibley (London: Constable, 1924), Ch. I, The Proeme, p. 56. In the Loeb edition it appears on p. 2.

19. *Onosandro Platonico, of the Generall Captaine, and of His Office* (London, 1563), fol. 99^r.

20. In *Xenophon. Scripta Minora* with an English translation by E. C. Marchant (London: W. Heinemann, 1925) Bk, IV, p. 13.

21. *A Treatise of Morall Philosophie* (London, [1547]), sig. P8^v.

22. *The Lives of the Noble Grecians and Romanes* (Oxford: B. Blackwell, 1928), V, 184. Amyot has "cholère" for "will" and "sain jugement" for "discretion."

23. *The Faerie Queene* III.xi.23.1–2, in *The Poetical Works of Edmund Spenser,* ed. J. C. Smith and E. De Selincourt (London: Oxford Univ. Press, 1950).

24. *The Countess of Pembrokes Arcadia* (1590), ed. Albert Feuillerat (Cambridge: Cambridge Univ. Press, 1939), p. 39.

25. Sir Thomas Coningsby, *Journal of the Siege of Rouen,* ed. John Gough Nichols (London: Camden Society, 1847), pp. 45, 50.

26. Humphrey Barwick, *A Breefe Discourse, Concerning the Force of All Manuall Weapons of Fire* (London, ca. 1594), sig. D1. For other examples of military uses of "valor" and "discretion," with the latter meaning "strategy," see a 1588 item from the *Calendar of State Papers* (Foreign), XXI, 417, Lord Willoughby to Walsingham; also a statement about his own strategic discretion, as opposed to courage, by Essex in the *Calendar of State Papers* (Domestic), April 5, 1596, p. 200.

27. "Shakespeare and Formal Logic," in *Studies in English Philology, a Miscellany in Honor of Frederick Klaeber,* ed. Kemp Malone and Martin B. Ruud (Minneapolis: Univ. of Minnesota Press, 1929), pp. 280–96.

28. "The Comic Element in Shakespeare's Histories," *Anglia,* 71, (1952), 96–97.

29. *Topica* with an English Translation by H. M. Hubbell (London: William Heinemann, 1949) V. 28, p. 401.

30. *The Logicke of the Most Excellent Philosopher P. Ramus Martyr*, trans. Roland MacIlmaine (1574), ed. Catherine M. Dunn (Northridge, Calif.: San Fernando Valley State College, 1969), Ch. XXIIII, "Of the distribution," p. 31.
31. *The Holy Court*, trans. T. Hawkins (n.p., 1638), Bk. I, p. 468.
32. *A Philosophical Discourse Entituled, The Anatomie of the Minde* (London, 1576), fol. 139ʳ.
33. *De Inventione*, with an English translation by H. M. Hubbell (London: William Heinemann, 1949), II.liv.163; p. 331.
34. Everyman ed. (London: Dent, 1937), pp. 229–52.
35. *Politicke, Moral and Martial Discourses*, trans. Arthur Golding (London, 1595), p. 276.
36. *Nichomachean Ethics*, trans. Martin Ostwald (New York: Bobbs-Merrill, 1962), p. 42.
37. Robert Cawdrey, *A Table Alphabeticall* (London, 1604), sig. D3ᵛ.
38. *The Truth of Our Times* (London, 1638), pp. 160–61.
39. Dover Wilson correctly sees his principal activity in "the untiring 'play extempore' with which he keeps the Prince, and us, and himself entertained from beginning to end of the drama." *The Fortunes of Falstaff* (Cambridge: Cambridge Univ. Press, 1944), p. 3. And Mark Van Doren observes that "the essence of Falstaff is that he is a comic actor, most of whose roles are assumed without announcement." *Shakespeare* (New York: Henry Holt, 1939), p. 330.
40. "Falstaff and the Psychomachia," *Shakespeare Quarterly*, 8 (1957), 458.
41. *The History of the Worthies of England* (London, 1662), II, 253.
42. Besides being absent from *Shakespeare's Bawdy*, it is unnoticed by Hilda Hulme's *Exploration in Shakespeare's Language* (London: Longman) and by E. A. M. Colman's *The Dramatic Use of Bawdy in Shakespeare* (New York: Longman, 1974).
43. Clifford Leech, *Times Literary Supplement* (Dec. 25, 1970), p. 1516; G. B. Shand, *TLS* (Jan. 29, 1972), p. 1266; Thomas Clayton, *TLS* (March 19, 1971), p. 325; and, at length, in Clayton's article " 'Fie What a Question's That If Thou Were Near a Lewd Interpreter': The Wall Scene in *A Midsummer Night's Dream*," *Shakespeare Studies*, 7 (1974), 101–13.
44. Cf. *AYL* IV.i.82–86; *Rom.* I.iii.41–42 and II.iv.87–88; *Oth.* II.i.132–35; *Tro.* I.ii.282–86.
45. Further examples may be found in *TN* III.ii.19–22; *Rom.* III.i.118–20.
46. I owe this suggestion to Janette Lewis, but it has been noticed by Robert F. Willson, Jr., *Shakespeare Quarterly*, 27 (1976), 200.

Comic Theory and the Rejection of Falstaff

MOODY E. PRIOR

Recent commentaries sometimes leave the impression that disapprobation of Prince Hal and his rejection of Falstaff is a product of modern sensibilities. In fact, it entered criticism at least as early as 1709 when Rowe asked, rhetorically, "whether some people have not in remembrance of the diversion he afforded 'em, been sorry to see his friend use him so scurvily when he comes to the crown in the end of the Second Part of *Henry IV.*" This is a damaging question, for it undermines the Prince at the very moment when he has put on the crown which he is to carry to such glory at Agincourt in *Henry V.* Samuel Johnson supplied a common sense answer to such doubts in his note on the rejection: "if it be considered, that the fat knight has never uttered one sentiment of generosity, and with all his power of exciting mirth, has nothing in him that can be esteemed, no great pain will be suffered from the reflection that he is compelled to live honestly, and maintained by the king, with a promise of advancement when he shall deserve it." The two statements represent the opposing terms of a debate that has come to occupy an important position in the conflicting interpretations of *1* and *2 Henry IV* and *Henry V,* and that has had the effect of polarizing the criticism of these plays. Those who feel strongly that the Prince has indeed used his old friend scurvily find support in this response for the view that Hal and his father are cold, unscrupulous political opportunists and that Falstaff is the ironic foil to their political and heroic pretensions. Those, on the other hand, who are convinced that the dramatic strategy of these plays calls for a favorable attitude toward the Prince, approval of his reformation, and admiration for his conduct as a hero king feel obliged to demonstrate that the rejection is a proper action for the Prince, and that indignation at Falstaff's humiliation at the end of *2 Henry IV* is misplaced.

In recent years, while the essential opposition in attitudes has remained the same, a shift in interest has occurred from the preoccupation with Falstaff as a complex, unique character to a concern for Falstaff as a special variant of some original prototype who plays out an assigned role and then is dismissed without any waste of sympathy. The argument runs, that because of a similarity between Falstaff and a particular prototype, Shakespeare's audience would have responded predictably to an established pattern of comic enjoyment followed by rejection. Dramatic tradition offers models for such characters, notably the braggart soldier, with a lineage that goes back to Plautus, and the Vice of the medieval morality play. Folk figures from traditional games and customs still observed in Shakespeare's day have also been proposed, notably the Lord of Misrule, who reigned for a brief Saturnalian holiday and was dethroned and expelled at the end of the festival. Freudian psychology has provided a prototype that transcends historical associations: Falstaff becomes the surrogate father (a relationship pointedly suggested by the play scene) who must inevitably be the victim of the Oedipal wish of the adopted son (Hal) to destroy him. All of these researches contribute to an appreciation of the complexity of Falstaff and his universal appeal, but if any one of them constituted a completely persuasive explanation of our feelings at the rejection scene the others would be redundant. It is a line of argument that fails, in part, because it is reductive. No one appears, for example, ever to have been saddened by the routing of a Vice, or a braggart soldier, and the similarities between Falstaff and such types does not account for the differences which produce dismay in those who disapprove of the Prince's action. It is, after all, the uniqueness and originality of Falstaff that has impressed audiences and critics, and it is therefore not very persuasive to argue from any one of these possible analogues that what is true of one possible constituent part is true of the whole, any more than it is to suppose that by putting together all of these components we can reconstitute Falstaff. The appeal to prototypes and conditioned patterns of response fails because it does not give sufficient weight to the dramatist's control over the effects produced by his play. It is his art which determines the direction of our sympathies and antipathies while we are looking at his play—how otherwise would we know whether, say, the rejection of a lover or the killing of a father is to be tragic, comic, melodramatic, or absurd? All the arguments about the rightness of the rejection of Falstaff, whether new or old, aim to demonstrate why no one should be offended; they do not explain why many are.

Throughout the entire inconclusive debate over the rejection scene one common note of agreement emerges. Virtually all critics of whatever persuasion are in accord that Falstaff is one of the great comic characters of literature. It is a judgment of long standing. "The best of all comic characters," Dryden says of Falstaff in *An Essay of Dramatic Poesy*. In the General Observations which conclude his notes on *Henry IV* Johnson writes, "But Falstaff, unimitated, inimitable Falstaff, how shall I describe thee?"—and how often do we find the great Doctor in an enthusiastic vein? The problem of our response to the final scene of the play resolves itself finally into the question of the conditions which govern a comic rather than a serious response. To propose this approach, however, is to invite at once all the reservations and confusions which arise at the mere suggestion of comic theory, and one can sympathize with those who are impatient with the seeming irrelevance of most discussions of the comic when applied to a triumph of comic creation such as Falstaff. A great deal of comic theory is preoccupied with laughter: what is laughter? why do we laugh? what is a joke? These are interesting questions, but investigations into the nature of laughter seem to have little bearing on the understanding and appreciation of comedy. Theories of tragedy do not start out by asking, what are tears? why do we cry? what is a calamity? Theories of the comic, moreover, usually endeavor to approach complete comprehensiveness such as we associate with a generalization in science, to embrace in a single formula the entire range of comic experience, whether the conventional paradigms of the dignified man slipping on a banana peel or having his hat knocked off by snowballs thrown by mischievous boys (when was the last time anyone actually saw either of these exempla outside of a treatise on comic theory?) or *As You Like It,* or *Duck Soup,* or an exchange of witticisms, or any other experience which can arouse amusement.

Extreme diversity is one of the impressions which extensive reading of comic theory leaves initially, yet most discussions of the comic do not go very far in basic ideas beyond the limits set by a few early theorists. The classic idea of comedy placed the source of the comic in some deformity or perversity whose exposure creates amusement under certain conditions; for instance, one must feel a sense of superiority over the victim, the discovery of the discrepancy between the deformity and the norm must be sudden and unexpected, and the like. The comic experience is presumed to serve the useful purpose of providing a corrective for the victim, and at the same time for the society which perceives his deformity as a source of amusement. The variations of this basic formula are numerous, and a good deal of comic theory consists of refinements, amplifications, and modernizations of these terms. The limitations of this approach to comedy can be seen if we try to apply it to Falstaff and his rejection by Hal: he represents certain physical and moral defects which are derided by laughter, and he is finally exposed and corrected! What the tradition of the punitive and corrective theory of comedy has generally failed to take into account is the kind of comedy in which the source of amusement and laughter is not a comic butt or victim but a comic character which, whatever its flaws, frailties, and oddities, arouses affection and even admiration as well as amusement, and is triumphant, or at least unbowed, at the end—e.g., Benedick and Beatrice, Tanner and Anne, Chaplin in most of his roles.

The theoretical distinction between these two aspects of the comic situation can be illustrated by two modern treatises, those of Henri Bergson and Susanne Langer. Bergson's widely admired and influential treatise, *Le Rire. Essai sur la Signification du Comique* (Paris: Alcan, 1900), is an original and subtle development of the punitive, corrective idea of the comic in terms of his idea of the creative force in nature, the *élan vital*. The essential requirement for survival in nature and society is, according to Bergson, elasticity of mind and body, and the defect or abnormality out of which the comic arises is, in consequence, rigidity and inflexibility. A comic situation exists when the mechanical is encrusted upon the living ("du mécanique plaqué sur la vivant"): we laugh when a human being gives the impression of being an object, a thing—a man walking down the street suddenly stumbles and falls, an unsociable person fails to respond flexibly to the demands of society. Hence the corrective function of laughter: the comic exposure of rigidity of mind, body, and character encourages the elasticity and sociability which nature and society require. But laughter, Bergson notes, is never absolutely just because its function is to intimidate by humiliation, and so laughter is possible only when there is a momentary anesthesia of the heart ("une anesthèse momentanée du coeur"). In comedy, Bergon believes, these conditions for laughter can best be met not with individualized characters but with types, and he finds his most admired examples in the comedies of Molière.

Bergson remarks that he has no wish to imprison the comic spirit in a definition, and it is perhaps in the spirit of his enquiry to note that his theory, like that of others in the same tradition, is surrounded beyond its applicable limits with uncertainties and disturbing exceptions. A man falling suddenly in the street in not invariably funny even when we are assured that he is not injured. The rigidity of old age can be made to seem funny on the stage, but what corrective purpose can it serve since the defect is not a consequence of character or will? Not all rigidity is a sign of inflexibility of mind or insociability; it can be created by the application of power, and the more ruthless the power the more rigidity of response it exacts of its victims. A military drill is a common form of rigidity since it requires all the soldiers to act as identical machines, but it usually does not arouse humor, except for the goose step, which outside the old Germany was generally thought comical. The art of bullying is also the art of reducing the victim to an object. There are film clips showing storm troopers pushing their bewildered victims around the streets, and some of the troopers appear to be laughing. Their hearts are completely anesthetized, but the rigidity and automatism of their victims are not the result of any inherent physical defect or insociability but something imposed on them by the exercise of power designed to deprive them of their humanity. More to the present point, like other punitive corrective theories, Bergson's does not prepare us to explore a wide range of comic effects which arise from a determined resistance on the part of an individual to those forces which are bent on thwarting and upsetting his adaptability and his affirmation of life. It can be funny when a man falls, but it can be funnier still when, finding himself slipping on ice, he manages after wild gyrations to recover his balance and walk away as though nothing had happened. Chaplin's films are full of this kind of comedy. Whether the force that threatens him is a blizzard, or the disapproval of respectable society, or the machines in "Modern Times," in the end he walks away as though ready to face another bout with society and chance. Such comic figures produce sympathy at the same time that they afford amusement, because their resistance to the forces that threaten their vitality and individuality is a sign of their indomitable humanness.

It is this area of the comic that Susanne Langer attempts to explain in *Feeling and Form: A Theory of Art* (New York: Scribners, 1953). The underlying feeling of comedy is, in her phrase, "the pure sense of life". It arises out of the organism's vitality and its adaptation to a continually threatening or frustrating environment. "To maintain the pattern of vitality in a nonliving universe is the most elementary instinctual purpose," she writes, "but the impulse to survive is not spent only in defense and accommodation; it appears also in the varying power of organisms to seize opportunities. . . . All creatures live by opportunities in a world fraught with disasters." In this complicated and menacing world man survives by a "brainy opportunism in the face of an essentially dreadful universe." But brainy opportunism is not enough; survival also calls for luck. That is why Langer, in a statement that seems to echo Schlegel, emphasizes the element of chance in comedy: "destiny in the guise of Fortune is the fabric of comedy; it is developed by comic action, which is the upset and recovery of the protagonist's equilibrium with the world and his triumph by his wit, luck, personal power, or even humorous, or ironical, or philosophical acceptance of mischance." For Langer, the almost perfect embodiment of this desperate but lively game is the buffoon, common to many literatures and especially popular in folk drama, because he represents "the indomitable living creature fending for itself, tumbling and stumbling (as the clown physically illustrates) from one situation to another, getting into scrape after scrape and getting out again, with or without a thrashing. He is the personified élan vital."

There is an echo of Bergson in the last phrase, and in fact the two start out from strikingly similar premises, but then move in opposite directions. Langer's buffoon is the "personified élan vital," whereas for Bergson the source of the comic is the loss of vitality. Bergson's comic figure is the dupe, the butt, the victim; Langer's is, for want of a better term, the comic hero. Bergson finds the comic figure in the failure, Langer in the success. For Bergson the function of laughter is punitive and corrective, and the norm is society; for Langer it is a celebration of the "life-feeling," and the norm is the individual. And whereas for Bergson anesthesia of the heart is an essential prerequisite for a comic response, for Langer a degree of warmth and sympathy is aroused by the comic figure at its best. It is not a matter of right and wrong but of looking at two different aspects of the comic situation and the comic response. The comic writer prepares differently for each. For the comedy that arises directly from the exposure of defects, the butt must not greatly engage our sympathies, and those who expose and judge him should be characters who leave a neutral impression, or who elicit our good will, or who represent such qualities as prudence, reasonableness, and humanity in an agreeable form. It has to be the opposite with the comic hero. Our sympathies must finally be with him and not with those who oppose him, even when his conduct is neither particularly virtuous nor respectable, and if he has victims they must not engage our concern.

Langer selects Falstaff as the "perfect example of the buffoon raised to a human 'character' in comedy," and though the label, buffoon, typecasts him, Falstaff could, in fact, be used to illustrate many of the features of the comic figure as she presents it—"the pattern of vitality," "brainy opportunism," "the indomitable living creature fending for itself." "Give me life," he says as he eschews the honor of dying gallantly in battle. One of his chief qualities is his resilience, his capacity to recover from a potential humiliation or disaster. The dramatic strategy here is ingenious, since some of the memorable instances of his brilliance in recovery arise from situations contrived by the Prince to place him in an embarrassing position. If this were a simple standard comic situation, Falstaff would be a comic butt whose failings are exposed, and superficially this is exactly what Poins and the Prince appear to be contriving: they will pretend to engage in the robbery only to rob Falstaff and the others for the purpose of exposing Falstaff's cowardice and enjoying "the incomprehensible lies that this same fat rogue will tell us when we meet at supper." Falstaff does not disappoint them—he does tell incomprehensible lies, though with such imagination and gusto that one wonders how much of it Falstaff thinks anyone will believe; but the comic climax comes when he is confronted with his lies and all await to see how he will wriggle out of his predicament—and he does not disappoint them in this either. The trap was set not, ultimately, to humiliate him but to provide him with an opportunity to display his wit, his virtuosity, his capacity to bounce back. It is the same with the practical joke of picking his pockets while he is lying asleep behind the arras in the tavern. What in a fairly conventional comic design would be the comic exposure of the failings of a dupe is in Falstaff's case the preparation for an opportunity to see a brilliant humorist recover.

The kind of comedy which depends on the triumph of the life force is usually associated with youth. Some theorists relate it to fertility myths, the replacing of the dying king, the rejuvenation of spring, the return to the green world, and the like. But Falstaff is not young. The coming on of age is an irreversible handicap threatening his determination to survive and to enjoy life, but he staves off age by a transparent pretense that his "Allhallow summer," as the Prince calls it, will last indefinitely. "They hate us youth," he exclaims as he robs the "bacon fed knaves." His other disabilities, notably his corpulence and his chronic lack of money, also become matter for a humor that temporarily translates them into assets. There is an element of desperation as well as absurdity in his defiance of time and adversity, but it only enhances the comic triumph of his moments of self-justification and affirmation, and of evasion and recovery. He must, literally, live by his wits. As the play opens he is in rare luck. His friend is the Prince and heir to the throne, and Falstaff has not only a lively companion and appreciative audience but also a source of funds and protection in adversity—he can afford to take a nap when the sheriff comes to the inn to inquire about the robbery because Hal will take care of that small hanging matter. The Prince is his lucky piece which can be depended on to provide him with means, salvation from the consequences of misbehavior, and self-esteem. He is like a man whom fortune has placed in just the right situation to exercise his calling and enjoy the flourishing of his talents, and he is unwilling to question his good fortune or consider the possibility that his good luck charm will not exercise its potency forever. For the Prince, however, good fortune will mean that his father has succeeded in preserving the title and passing it on to his son, and the Prince will then cease to be Hal and will be crowned Henry V and repudiate his past. We know this early on from the Prince's soliloquy, and his declaration that he will some day leave his companions and the carefree life is a cloud no bigger than a man's hand which we put out of our mind to enjoy the brightness of Falstaff's ebullient and irreverent humor. When we come to Part II, it is evidences of this "inimitable Falstaff" that we continue to look for, and we are reluctant to observe any of those changes which undermine or dull the extraordinary comic achievement of Part I or threaten its original comic genius.

We tend, in consequence, to give scant notice, except upon reflection, to Shakespeare's careful management of the role of Falstaff in Part II, a play more sombre in tone, more serious in content than Part I. In Part I, Falstaff's first scene is with Hal, and the two are closely associated throughout; in Part II, Falstaff's first scene is with the Chief Justice, and he is seen with the Prince in only one brief portion of one scene. Lacking the opportunities for lively banter, Falstaff at times turns monologist. What is particularly striking in Part II is an occasional undisguised drop in the vitality and resilience which animates much of the comedy in Part I. Falstaff may seem the very symbol of the life force in comparison with the dessicated Shallow, but in a depressed mood after beating Pistol he responds to Doll's admonition to "begin patching thine old body for heaven" with "Peace, good Doll, do not speak like a death's head, do not bid me remember mine end." In the midst of amorous play with Doll he can say, "I am old, I am old." In Part I, when the Prince trips him up by revealing the truth about the robbery, Falstaff lies cheerfully, "By the Lord, I knew thee as well as he that made ye"; but in a similar scene in Part II, when the Prince puts off his disguise as a drawer and reveals himself with a direct allusion to the earlier episode, "Yea, and you knew me, as you did when you ran away by Gad's Hill," Falstaff seems merely cresfallen: "No, no, no, not so; I did not think thou wast within hearing." These signs of change and decline do not, however, eclipse continuing evidences of vitality and comic power, and so the Falstaff who is rejected seems to be, for anyone who has experienced both plays, the one firmly engraved on our minds by the remarkable achievement of Part I. The rejection amounts, in consequence, to the crushing of a comic figure whose natural fate is not to go down in defeat but to triumph. The comic hero who defies time, contingency, respectability, and caution, who uses his wit and resilience to beat the odds against him is created to win or at least to survive to try again. To respond to him as a comic we must be on his side. Falstaff dominates every scene in which he appears and is a primary source of amusement in it, and he manages, even in Part II, to make some kind of recovery from every difficulty, embarrassment, and momentary dejection, except for the last. Henry V's "I know thee not old man, fall to thy prayers" destroys

Falstaff as an engaging, resilient, irreverent source of gaiety and humor. The rejection is a sudden reversal whose effect is the very opposite of comic. It is as though instead of walking down the road unscathed and ready for the next encounter with society and the laws of gravity, Chaplin were to be crushed to earth by the fierce looking waiter; as though the sheriff had finally caught up with Groucho's shady practices and we see him, dejected, being led away to jail; as though W. C. Fields, after his assaults on every decent sentiment, ended up not rich or heading for the Grampian Hills but instead in a D. T. ward; or as though the Good Soldier Schweik finished his brilliant career at the end of a halter. Such magnificent comic heros were not created for such ends. No matter by what critical avenues the rejection of Falstaff is approached, the unpleasantness of which so many have complained cannot be argued away.

One source of the complexity of feeling in this final scene is the special relationship of Falstaff and Hal. What degree of friendship or affection is supposed to exist between the two has been a matter of some critical debate, but whatever the case may be thought to be, this relationship is the motive power behind most of the comedy in Part I and provides the circumstances through which we come to know Falstaff himself. In this sense, Hal helps to create the Falstaff we know, and his amused sympathy with Falstaff is one of the things we share with him. In his public rejection of Falstaff Hal proclaims him "the tutor and the feeder of my riots," and in retrospect we can reflect that Falstaff is not really a fit companion for a Prince and future king (this is one preoccupation of his father's that we can respond to); but from what we hear and see of their association we are more readily inclined to think of Falstaff as the inciter of the Prince to wit, in which he never equals Falstaff, and merriment, in which the Prince indulges with reservations. The most serious defection presented in the play is Hal's participation in a robbery. Certainly, robbery is a crime and a social evil, but that is not the way the episode is presented. It is an escapade for the Prince; and the victims, who never really touch us, get their money back. From beginning to end the episode of the robbery is a hilarious business and that is how we view it, and the Prince's participation in it is one of the principal means by which Falstaff's power to beguile, surprise, and entertain is brought out. When Hal turns on his former companion, he destroys something in the discovery of which he is seen to have played a big part, and in that context it is the repudiation not of his tempter and evil genius that we are witnessing but of his collaborator in high comedy. In spite of the insolence of Falstaff at the coronation procession, it is impossible not to feel that something is not right. It is not a scene of comic exposure in which the dupe or butt is humiliated and made a laughing stock. The Falstaff of *Henry IV* cannot be dismissed easily in this way because, throughout, the Falstaff scenes are managed so that he remains, however precariously, the object of our interest and sympathy. When a sympathetic character is humiliated the result is not comic denouement or poetic justice but pathos, and so it is the former Prince that seems suddenly to have been exposed, not Falstaff.

These disturbing complexities of response arise because the world of *Henry IV* is not that of pure comedy but of history and political power, and given the circumstances both the rejection and the unpleasantness are inevitable. The center of the action is not Falstaff but the beleaguered Henry IV and his son. What is a disaster from the point of view of our comic involvement and response is a necessity from the point of view of the political action. From the start of Part I there are clues that the Prince must eventually become king and is fully aware of the difference between a private man, or even a prince, and a king. The transformation from one to the other poses special problems in Hal's case. He enters the office with a flawed title and the reputation of a flawed character. As a new king he has an obligation to reassure his country that in his hands the questionable title will not be a handicap and that his wantonness is a thing of the past. Falstaff's behavior at the coronation procession forces upon him the first occasion to show publicly that he is a new man to whom the task of governing the nation can be entrusted. He speaks to Falstaff, therefore, not as a former companion and reformed friend but as a king facing an unpleasant political necessity. No matter that the penalties imposed on Falstaff are not as harsh as they appear. The comic balance is shattered, and is replaced by a stern note, a cold, forbidding act of authority and power, sudden and imperious.

Falstaff's first speech after Hal has finished is, "Master Shallow, I owe you a thousand pound"—momentarily a flash of the old brilliance breaks out. But however it may be interpreted, the speech is not free of pathos, any more than are his feeble reassurances to his companions that "there that you have heard was but a color," and "I shall be sent for soon at night." We last see him being led away to the Fleet, remonstrating to the Chief Justice, "My lord, my lord—." The great master of the quick recovery is reduced to impotence. But that is exactly how power works when it is exerted in such a way as to deprive an individual of everything that makes him what he is and leaves him with no recourse. The only one who might possibly laugh at this sudden turn from vitality to helplessness is Prince John; he had demonstrated at Gaultree Forest his capacity to anesthetize the heart. Instead, however, he, along with the Chief Justice, gives expression to the official reaction to the rejection, that the separation of the king from Falstaff is for the good of the realm. There is no arguing against their sensible, prudent view; but they have not had the experience of witnessing those remarkable episodes in which Shakespeare shows the great irreverent comic genius flowering in the Prince's company. The political soundness of their sentiments does not alter the dismay of those who have.

It is always risky to theorize, as occasionally some have in support of particular interpretations of plays of Shakespeare's age, that its inhabitants were deficient in qualities which experience leads us to suppose are fairly common in ourselves. There is no reason in nature to suppose that the question which Rowe raised would not have occurred to at least some of those who attended performances of *Henry IV* a century earlier. This conjecture receives support from *Henry V*. The Epilogue to *2 Henry IV* contains a half promise: "If you be not too much cloyed with fat meat, our humble author will continue the story, with Sir John in it, and make you merry with fair Katharine of France; where for anything I know, Falstaff will die of a sweat, unless a be killed with your hard opinions." Falstaff did not die of their hard opinions, for the indications are that he was an immediate success (note the top billing in the Epilogue). But what characteristic role could Falstaff play in the heroic day at Agincourt that would not humiliate him more than the last scene in *Henry IV* had done? Of the references to him in *Henry V*, all relate to that dramatic moment. He does die, but not, in the opinion of his former cronies, of a sweat: *Hostess.* "The King has killed his heart." *Nym.* "The King hath run bad humors on the knight." *Pistol.* "His heart is fracted and corroborate." These comments would seem to argue for the possibility of some similar public response. At the same time, there is also an apology for the King: Nym says, "The King is a good king, but it must be as it may: he passes some humors and careers." The most elaborate apology for the King is provided by Fluellen, and it occurs, oddly enough, in the midst of the battle of Agincourt, an episode which even the harshest critics of the character find it hard to interpret to Henry's discredit. Fluellen winds up a rambling comparison of Alexander and Henry V to the latter's advantage, because "as Alexander killed his friend Cleitus, being in his ales and cups, so Harry Monmouth, being in his right wits and good judgments, turned away the fat knight with the great-belly doublet: he was full of jests, and gipes, and knaveries, and mocks; I have forgot his name." All these references, it should be noted, would be meaningless to anyone who had not seen or heard about the two *Henry IV* plays, and the attempt to justify the king would be redundant if there had been no reason to provide a defense. The allusions in *Henry V* produce a mixed effect. They arouse sympathy for Falstaff, yet express support for the king. They offer glimpses that recall the troubled effect, the ambiguity, of the rejection scene, and they pointedly imply that one factor in the dual feeling is the sense of dismay at the King's action—necessary but nonetheless offensive. They make it reasonable to suppose that the offense of which many have complained was there from the very beginning.

It has been argued that Shakespeare miscalculated the effect of the rejection, and the allusions to the scene in *Henry V* could be cited in support of the view that the scene did not come off quite as planned. We need not conclude, however, that Shakespeare did not anticipate some conflict of feelings from the King's stern dismissal of Falstaff. The strategy of Part II not only separates Falstaff from the Prince, but occasionally introduces a passing cloud over the comic scenes, until in the scene immediately preceding the rejection, we see the hostess and Doll being led to prison by beadles because "the man is dead that you and Pistol beat amongst you." There are also signs of hubris in Falstaff—he preens himself on his wit ("I am not only witty in myself, but the cause that wit is in other men"), he presumes on the Prince's friendship the nature of which he misunderstands, and in a final abdication of his native shrewdness he hurries off to the coronation with, "Let us take any man's horses—the laws of England are at my commandment." Immediately before this episode, in a scene analogous to Hal's reconciliation with his father and the recapturing of his lost honor in the fight with Hotspur, the young king is reconciled to the Chief Justice and adopts him as "the father of my youth," and in so doing identifies himself with something nobler than the honor he gained from Hotspur when he praises the Justice for punishing him for having once disgraced the king's court of justice, a courageous act which the Chief Justice performed "in honor, / Led by the impartial judgment of my soul." This is not the kind of strategy which provides appropriate preparation for the triumph or survival of the comic hero. Under the demands of the principal action, Shakespeare gradually but certainly modifies and ultimately abandons the conditions for pure comedy. The progress of Falstaff is from felicity to failure and defeat—a fall of princes story which turns out to be contrary to our original expectations and our wishes and which we see unfold with misgivings because the fall is that of the Prince of Comics.

In the course of dramatizing English history from the abdication of Richard II to the coming of the Tudors, Shakespeare represented many facets of politics and political man and revealed in a variety of ways how the assumption of power sets a man apart and sometimes calls for acts which may be necessary and justified on political grounds but are nevertheless distressing when judged by the standards of genial humanity. The moment arrives in the narrative when Hal becomes Henry V, pledged to act in the best interests of the nation and ready not only to reject his past but to demonstrate that he has done so. At that very moment, Falstaff, misreading the signs, addresses his sovereign as though he was still a wayward prince. When he wrote that scene, Shakespeare had become a master of comedy as well as of historical and political drama. He could hardly have been oblivious to the highly charged potential in the meeting between Falstaff and the King, a confrontation of irreconcileable claims which must end in the triumph of the embodiment of power over the embodiment of the free spirit of comedy. The shock leaves the atmosphere at the end of the play troubled, and has continued to reverberate in criticism ever since.

The Text of *2 Henry IV*: Facts and Problems*

George Walton Williams

In a paper delivered in 1952, Professor Fredson Bowers described *Henry IV, Part 2*, as the text which, "with *Othello*, seems to present the most difficult problem about the nature of the printer's copy for the Folio, that crucial question which prevents any form of accurate editing until it is answered."[1] I have found that the text is not lacking in difficult problems of other sorts, but it is true that the nature of the Folio copy is the essential crux. In this study I propose to notice four aspects of the text: the printing of the single quarto of 1600; one of the distinctive features of that quarto, a cancel sheet; the problems of the copy for the quarto; and the problems of the copy for the Folio. Many of these remarks will be no more than a general survey, but there will be perhaps a few novelties here and there.

The first fact about the quarto of 1600 is the entry in the Stationers' Register of August 23, 1600, where Andrew Wise and William Aspley "Entred for their copies under the handes of the wardens Two bookes. the one called *Muche a Doo about nothinge*. Thother *the second parte of the history of kinge HENRY the iiii*[th] *with the humours of Sir IOHN FFALLSTAFF:* Wrytten by master Shakespere." A perfectly normal entry, though of particular note because of the connection here established between *2 Henry IV* and *Much Ado*, a connection that will be of substantial interest later. The two plays were printed in 1600, both by Valentine Simmes. The composition of the quartos has been carefully studied by W. Craig Ferguson; he has determined that they are the work of a single compositor, Compositor A, as he is called.[2] Subsequent inquiry by other scholars has confirmed this attribution and has found his hand in other work as well. The compositor is solely responsible for the first editions of *2 Henry IV* and *Much Ado*, and of *Hamlet* (Q1, 1603), and partly responsible for *Richard II* (Q1, 1597), *Richard III* (Q1, 1597), and *The First Part of the Contention* (Q2, 1600). Passing out of the Shakespeare canon, we find him also in *A Warning for Fair Women* (Q1, 1599), Dekker's *Shoemakers' Holiday* (Q1, 1600), Marston's *Malcontent* (Q1, 1604), and Marlowe's *Faustus* (1604).[3] Compositor A is thus a man of no little importance in the history of English dramatic literature, and he is wholly or in part responsible for five substantive Shakespeare texts, some of them set from holograph.

The compositor is recognized chiefly by his tendency to omit the period

173

following a speech-prefix which is unabbreviated, but he has another characteristic, about which we may be less happy: he is careless. Professor Alan
E. Craven has analyzed the work of this Compositor in reprinting *Richard II*
in 1598.[4] In this second quarto of the play, Compositor A as the sole compositor reprints the edition of the preceding year; examination of his work
here is rather discouraging. Professor Craven has shown that the compositor is careless—carefree, one might almost say—and that he tends to
vary the text of *Richard II* substantively as it passes through his hands once
in every seventeen lines. On the basis of this record, we may extrapolate
his achievement in setting *2 Henry IV*: he is probably responsible for introducing nearly two hundred corruptions by varying from his copy in setting
this quarto.

Compositor A's corruptions, as Mr. Craven tells us, "reflect errors of a
memorial nature. Compositor A seems characteristically to have taken more
material into his head than he could deal with accurately. Thus he frequently substituted one word for another, interpolated [a word,] or omitted
a word. The words thus affected are not usually nouns and verbs but instead are connectives and qualifiers (conjunctions, prepositions, articles,
pronouns, and, less frequently, adjectives and adverbs): . . . Compositor A
corrupted his text in an especially damaging way. For the corrupted lines
almost always make tolerably good sense and seldom, of themselves, reveal that a reading has suffered corruption."[5]

Compositor A set all the type for *2 Henry IV* and for *Much Ado,* as we
have seen. The closeness of the relationship between the two quartos Greg
has established by noticing that the title pages of the two quartos are
printed from the same setting of type. It is demonstrable, therefore, that
they were both being set at the same time, and Greg has argued that *2
Henry IV* was the earlier twin.[6] Professor John Hazel Smith in a paper read
before the Bibliographical Evidence Group of the MLA in 1961 has argued
on the basis of type analysis that *Much Ado* was set by formes.[7] Professor
Hinman on the basis of what seems to have been a fresh scrutiny of the
evidence has been convinced "that the hypothesis of setting by formes is
not really tenable." He thinks that Professor Smith would be convinced
too.[8] I tentatively suggest that the printing of *2 Henry IV* was *seriatim.* I
reach this conclusion on the basis of type shortages of capital italic "F,"
italic "D," italic "S," and of capital roman "W" and of distribution patterns. No single type shortage can be traced meaningfully through the
sheets, but the coming and going of various sorts and the pattern of distribution (which suggests that the compositor was consistently moving
more slowly than his press) combine to argue for *seriatim* setting.[9]

We may turn now to the second aspect of this quarto—the cancel. About half of the extant copies of this quarto contain a cancel. The cancel, replacing two leaves of one sheet (E3–4), consists itself of four leaves (E3–6), i.e., a full quarto sheet in imposition. The cancellans adds to the text the whole of III.i (107 lines in Globe counting; 115 lines of type and 3 blank lines in the quarto). The cancellans also reprints in a new setting of type the sections of the scenes on either side of the added matter, i.e., the last 52 lines of II.iv and the first 114 lines of III.ii, a total of 166 lines. On the basis of these facts, three problems rise for consideration: the relationship between the original settings and the reprintings of the sections of the two scenes, the nature of the new scene, and the history behind the cancel.

As we have noted, the quarto is the work of a single compositor throughout. As it happens, the cancel is the work of the same man. We have examined already the degree of inaccuracy exhibited by this man, Compositor A, in his reprinting of the quarto of *Richard II,* and I have intimated that the same degree of inaccuracy is likely to be found in his work of setting *2 Henry IV* from manuscript. We cannot verify that intimation until we recover the manuscript, but we can make a test of it by observing in the cancel how carefully Compositor A reset his own work in this play. In the reset lines, totalling 165, there are nine substantive variants.[10] (None of these can be said to correct a manifest error.) Nine variants in 165 lines gives a figure of one variant every 18 lines, or, as the reprinted 165 lines constitute exactly 1/20th of the entire text (3349 by TLN), twenty times nine corruptions, 180 in the entire quarto. This figure is close enough to that derived from the analysis of the setting of *Richard II* to assure us that the intimation of inaccuracy is correct.

The second problem is the nature of the new scene, III.i. The scene includes the king's soliloquy on sleep and his discussions with Warwick and Surrey on the sickness of the kingdom, on the cyclical theory of history, on the double treachery of Northumberland to both kings, and on the deposition of Richard. Critics have suggested that the scene was omitted (a) because of excessive censorship or (b) in error. The argument of censorship—of which, as we shall see, there appears to be enough in this quarto—requires an additional hypothesis to account for the omission of Richard's name elsewhere in the quarto and the inclusion of it here. The argument of omission by human failure—surely an argument of sufficient weight to account for a trifle like this—seems on balance the more tenable argument.

Such an argument receives support when we turn to the third problem of the cancel, its history. Following Dr. McManaway's exploratory study in

1946,[11] John Hazel Smith has in 1964 revisited the cancel, finding that it was very likely printed soon after the printing of the complete quarto (perhaps two weeks after) and that it was printed while *Much Ado* was being printed in the same shop by the same compositor.[12] He has discovered evidences of damaged types and of comparable type shortages and distributions that persuade him that the cancel was printed between sheets G and H of *Much Ado*. He explains the need for the cancel by imagining that one leaf of the holograph of *Henry IV* was misplaced amid the leaves of *Much Ado* and that the compositor, discovering the error while setting *Much Ado*, saw to it that the cancel was prepared immediately and added to the unbound sheets of *Henry IV* (about half of the edition, as we have supposed).[13] This is an attractive hypothesis, consonant with the facts of the matter and uniquely linking two of Shakespeare's quartos.

In recent years there has been little controversy as to our third question, the nature of the copy for the quarto; critics are generally agreed that it was a manuscript in the author's hand. Professor Shaaber in his Variorum edition has made abundantly clear the various kinds of technical evidence that support this assumption: "stage-directions describing costume, character, and locality, generic speech-prefixes, indeterminate stage-directions, and the omission of directions for the entry of certain characters seem to agree with Shakespeare's working habits as revealed in other plays."[14] Professor Shaaber illustrates each of these types of evidence thoroughly, and one can add only a few details to the fullness of his findings. The phenomenon of generic speech prefixes, for example, was first analyzed by McKerrow in 1935; his interpretation has been generally accepted, though, if literally applied, it leads to some absurdities.[15] (The same can, of course, be said of most theories of Shakespeare; some, indeed, begin with absurdities.) The Lord Chief Justice is given the prefix *"Justice."* twenty times in Act I, scene ii; after line 200 his prefix changes to *"Lord"* for twenty-one times in the rest of the scene and in his next scene (II.i); in Act V he is once more *"Justice."* This shifting can scarcely be explained by McKerrow's theory, but it reveals clearly Shakespeare's lack of concern for the detail of this name. The same quality obtains for the name of the fat Knight. It is well known that the original name of this character was Sir John Oldcastle and that the name was changed at the insistence of Oldcastle's descendants. At some point, certainly after Act II and probably after the entire play had been written, great command o'erswayed the author; the company was required to change the name of the character called *Oldcastle*. Within the spirit of this command, we may suppose, Shakespeare decided that he was under no compulsion to change the knighthood or the Christian name of his character (with its nickname and puns). The "old lad of the castle," now given a new family name, remained "Jack with [his] familiars, John with [his] brothers and sisters, and Sir John with all Europe." When the corrector (more likely the bookkeeper than Shakespeare personally) undertook to change the name of the character in dialogue, directions, and speech prefixes his aim was at the offensive *Oldcastle* only. He replaced it with Shakespeare's new invention, a name descriptive of the character already created, a name which responded to the character's fundamental dishonesty and to the waning of his powers erotic and military. We are blessed in the change. In the dialogue, 76 Christian Johns or Jacks could remain, but 22 *Oldcastle* forms were now to be changed to *Falstaff* (all but one of them spelled in the quarto exactly *Falstaffe*).[16] In the directions, 5 Johns or Sir Johns remained, but 5 *Oldcastle* forms were changed to *Falstaffe*.[17] In the prefixes, 20 Johns or Sir Johns remained, but 156 *Oldcastle* forms or the abbreviation *Old.* were changed—all but one—to *Fa.* (3), *Fal.* (64), *Falst.* (85), or *Falstaffe* (3).[18] That one, the prefix *Old.* (I.ii.137), the corrector missed, and by that miss gives us sure proof that Oldcastle was the man.[19]

The generic variations between *Justice* and *Lord* and the nominal variations between *Sir John* and *Oldcastle/Falstaff* demonstrate Shakespeare's rapid composition and casual attitude.

A comparison of the quarto text and the Folio text of *2 Henry IV* provides one more piece of information about the copy for the quarto: it has been abridged. Eight passages in Acts I, II, and IV, totalling 170 lines, are lacking in the quarto. Four of these passages (about 63 lines) contain lines amplifying what has been said before. They could well have been excised as a means of sharpening four long speeches, but why anyone should have troubled to remove 60 lines from a play of 3300 remains a mystery. The other four of the passages contain references to the deposition and death of Richard II; their omission from the published form of a play that had already been in trouble with the authorities can be readily understood. It is worth a note in passing that the cancel supplies the only reference to Richard in the quarto, and it does so only because the leaf containing the reference was misplaced at the time the political cuts were made in the quarto.

With the mention of the Folio text of the play, we have arrived at our final inquiry, the nature of the printer's copy for the Folio. The Folio text differs markedly in character from the quarto text. As we have seen, the Folio includes some 160 lines that the quarto lacks. In addition, it lacks a few lines and a few passages that the quarto includes. Furthermore, and perhaps most notably, the Folio bowdlerizes all of the profanity and some of the indecencies found in the quarto, and it modernizes "a great number of Q's colloquialisms, archaisms, rusticisms, and apparent solecisms."[20] The Folio also varies from the quarto "in many words and phrases, by insertions, omissions, transpositions," and substitutions (its readings are generally inferior); its punctuation is substantially heavier than the quarto's. In staging matters, the Folio varies from the quarto in all but the simplest directions; in speech prefixes and directions its characters are more accurately and uniformly named; its stage-sense is generally superior to that of the quarto.

The two texts are, in short, substantive. It is argued that a source other than the quarto was used to prepare the copy for the Folio, and the superiority of the Folio text in theatrical matters suggests that stage practice lies somewhere behind it. Professor Shaaber has advanced the hypothesis that the copy was a scribal transcript of the prompt-book.[21] It is also argued that the quarto was used to prepare the copy, for there are many similarities in accidentals, in lining, and in typographical peculiarities between Folio and quarto. Dr. Alice Walker has advanced the hypothesis that the copy was a quarto annotated for the printing of the Folio.[22] Since neither of these hypotheses is really convincing, Professor Bowers has proposed a *tertium quid,* a scribal transcript of the quarto which had been annotated and used as the prompt book.[23] Professor Humphreys refines this hypothesis: "The ingredients [of the Folio copy] must . . . have been a quarto and a virtually full MS showing some cognizance of stage practice . . . combined in a transcript made . . . from a Q and a MS concurrently, the scribe keeping his eye on both in varying degrees."[24] Professor Humphreys is the first to object to the complexity of this hypothesis; but nothing else so far advanced is better, and every hypothesis has its antithesis.

But I am upon compulsion, and, as hypotheses are as plentiful as blackberries, I will give you another. The most striking features of the copy used for the Folio are its propriety and its literary formality. Greg reminds us that the act against profanity concerned words spoken on stage and not words put into print;[25] there is no necessity therefore to suppose that 2 *Henry IV* was cleaned up specifically in preparation for the Folio publication. The literary formality of the text is similarly no criterion for publication in the Folio. We are dealing, then, conceivably with a manuscript which might have been prepared without any intention of its being used as copy for the Folio. Secondly, the manuscript shows an awareness of stage practice, yet it contains still too many errors and oversights ever to have been used as the prompt book or to be considered as any kind of appropriate transcript of that book. Again, it is a manuscript which might have been prepared without regard to copy for the Folio.

Dr. Walker has indeed postulated just such a manuscript, "a fair copy of the foul papers made ca. 1598."[26] She supposes that this fair copy was used as the basis from which to correct and annotate the quarto; I suggest that this fair copy was used as the printer's copy for the Folio.

Why should there have been a fair copy of the foul papers that was made neither for the Folio nor for a prompt book? Fortunately, no one is required to answer that question. Yet Professor Humphreys recognizes that such a "polished 'literary' text" could have been provided for a "patron with refined tastes."[27] Such a "prettified" manuscript might also have been provided to satisfy the requirements of an irate, influential, and puritanical antagonist.[28] Miss Walker has suggested that the literary polish of the Folio text of *2 Henry IV* is to be found also in the quarto text of *1 Henry IV.* She concludes that the manuscript behind Folio *2 Henry IV* "was a companion piece to the manuscript from which the *1 Henry IV* quarto was printed, the work of the same hand and roughly of the same date.[29] It was [she thinks] a fair copy of the foul papers."[30] Why should there have been fair copies of two sets of foul papers that were made neither for the Folio nor for a prompt book? Fortunately, an answer for the two *Henry IV* plays and for them only is available: the fair copy of both parts might have been prepared to prove to Oldcastle's angry posterity that their ancestor had been removed from both plays. *Henry IV, Part 1,* was promptly printed (in 1598) in order to demonstrate the submission of the actors, and it was printed from the fair copy that had been offered to the objectors and that had been returned to the company, having accomplished its purpose.[31]

There is one detail that offers some corroboration to this thesis. Earlier in this paper, I noted that, in the foul papers of Part Two, speech-prefixes for the fat knight were indifferently *John, Sir John,* and *Oldcastle.*[32] I should suppose that in the foul papers of Part One, the speech prefixes for the fat knight were similarly *John, Sir John,* and *Oldcastle.* In the presumed fair copy lying behind the Folio of Part Two these variant prefixes have all been changed to some form of *Falstaffe.* In the presumed fair copy lying behind the quarto of Part One these variant prefixes have all been changed to some form of *Falstaffe.*[33] In other words, the copyist of the two sets of foul papers was determined that the name Falstaff should be prominent, and accordingly in the prefixes he not only revised all the *Oldcastle* forms but he also replaced all the *John* and *Sir John* forms as well. The character should have no name but Falstaff, and as that was an invented name, it could give offense to no one.

But could such a fair copy made from the foul papers of Part Two re-

semble in its Folio printing the accidentals that appear in the quarto printing of those foul papers? I think it could. Among the arguments advanced
by Miss Walker, Sir Walter, and Professor Humphreys for the direct tran-
scription of the Folio from the quarto, I find none that is bibliographically
compelling, and the aggregate of all does not convince.[34]

I submit, then, that this latest—probably not last—hypothesis is not demonstrably impossible, solves the problem posed by conflicting evidence,
is economical, and in all is reasonable bibliographically. Insofar as it
touches on the historical background of the text, it is consonant with the
facts as they are known or imagined. The conclusion is that the quarto and
the Folio derive alike from Shakespeare's foul papers, the Folio through an
intervening transcript prepared specifically to satisfy objections raised by
Oldcastle's descendants.

Notes:

*This paper was delivered before the meeting of the Shakespeare Association of
America in Pasadena, March 29, 1974. It was designed solely for oral presentation and not for print, but at the suggestion of the then Associate Editor
it is here submitted to a more permanent form of publication. It stands as it
was presented, with most of its imperfections still on its head, but I have
supplied in the footnotes some of the many thoughtful and beneficial suggestions made by the scholars attending the session. If the paper has any merit,
it lies in the quality of their responses to it.

1. Fredson Bowers, "A Definitive Text of Shakespeare" in *Studies in Shakespeare*
   (Coral Gables: Univ. of Miami Press, 1953), p. 25.
2. W. Craig Ferguson, "The Compositors of *Henry IV, Part 2* . . . ," *Studies in
   Bibliography,* 13 (1960), 19–29.
3. Charlton Hinman, *Richard the Second 1597* [Shakespeare Quarto Facsimiles,
   No. 13] (Oxford: Clarendon Press, 1966), pp. xiv–xvi; Alan E. Craven, "Simmes' Compositor A and Five Shakespeare Quartos," *Studies in Bibliography,* 26
   (1973), 37–60.
4. Craven, pp. 49–60.
5. Ibid., p. 56.
6. W. W. Greg, *Bibliography of the English Printed Drama,* I (London: Bibliographical Society, 1939), 167.
7. John Hazel Smith, "The Composition of the Quarto of *Much Ado About Nothing,*" *Studies in Bibliography* 16 (1963), 9–26.
8. Charlton Hinman, *Much Ado about Nothing* [Shakespeare Quarto Facsimiles,
   No. 15] (Oxford: Clarendon Press, 1971), p. xvn. He suggests (p. xiv) that
   special treatment was given to the handling of the italic "B" sorts and of
   these sorts only, and that the recurrence of other types proves that the
   quarto was set *seriatim.* Professor Smith has, privately, agreed.

9. This analysis receives some support from Mr. Hinman's argument that *Much Ado* was also so set, for it is more likely than not that the two quartos were set in the same manner.

10. Charlton Hinman, "Shakespeare's Text—Then, Now and Tomorrow," *Shakespeare Survey,* 18 (1965), 27 and 23–33.

11. James G. McManaway, "The Cancel in the Quarto of *2 Henry IV*," *Studies in Honor of A. H. R. Fairchild* (Columbia: Univ. of Missouri Press, 1946), pp. 67–80.

12. John Hazel Smith, "The Cancel in the Quarto of *2 Henry IV* Revisited," *Shakespeare Quarterly,* 15 (1964), 173–78.

13. The leaf contained, as it chanced, the whole of III.i and nothing else; hence, its loss was not readily noticeable. Critics accept the assumption that Shakespeare wrote about 50 lines to the page, a figure when doubled close enough to account for the 107 lines of the scene.

   In *Shakespeare and the Homilies* (Melbourne: Melbourne Univ. Press, 1934), Alfred Hart considered the appropriateness of the location of the inserted scene, since the detached nature of the scene allowed it to fit anywhere in the play between I.iii and IV.i. He is certainly correct in raising this question, but there is a propriety in the present location that has been generally accepted. The MS contained presumably no act or scene numbers, but it was probably paginated.

14. Matthias A. Shaaber, ed., *The Second Part of Henry the Fourth* [New Variorum] (Philadelphia: Lippincott, 1940), p. 489.

15. R. B. McKerrow, "A Suggestion Regarding Shakespeare's Manuscripts," *Review of English Studies,* 11 (1935), 459–65.

16. The figure of 22 does not include one appearance in the Epilogue which is omitted in the count as perhaps constituting a special case, but the spelling is the same as in the other examples. The exception noted is the spelling "Falstalfe" (the preferred spelling of Part One) at V.iv.97 (Glove line). (Attributable perhaps to the orthographic influence of "the Fleet"?)

17. Did the five directions now reading in the quarto *Sir John* originally read *Sir John Oldcastle*—was the surname simply deleted?

18. These statistics I derive—with much gratitude—from Professor Howard-Hill's *Oxford Shakespeare Concordance: Henry IV Part II* (Oxford: Clarendon Press, 1971).

19. Professor Richard Hosley questioned whether there might not be another explanation for this *Old.* form, that it might have been a short prefix for *Old Knight* or *Old Man*. He was thinking, I believe, of an analogy with *Romeo and Juliet* (a play in which we both have a vested interest), but there is no support for this conjecture.

20. A. R. Humphreys, ed. *The Second Part of King Henry IV* [New Arden Edition] (London: Methuen, 1967; rpt. 1970), pp. lxxvi; lxxiv–lxxvii.

21. Shaaber, pp. 507–15, and "The Folio Text of *2 Henry IV, Shakespeare Quarterly,* 6 (1955), 135–44.

22. Alice Walker, *Textual Problems of the First Folio* (Cambridge: Cambridge Univ. Press, 1953), pp. 98–107.

23. Bowers, p. 26.

24. Humphreys, pp. lxxxi–lxxxii.

25. W. W. Greg, *The Shakespeare First Folio* (Oxford: Clarendon Press, 1955), p. 151.
26. Walker, p. 109.
27. Humphreys, p. lxxvi.
28. Professor Hinman has intimated something of this sort in *Henry the Fourth Part I* [Shakespeare Quarto Facsimiles, No. 14] (Oxford: Clarendon Press, 1966), p. x.
29. Professor Trevor Howard-Hill observed that if the fair copies were made in 1598–1600, the suggestion that Ralph Crane was the scribe of the MS behind Folio Part Two is rendered invalid. He supposed that if Heminge and Condell troubled themselves to find this MS when the quarto lay before them, they must have known that the MS contained passages omitted in the quarto. It was agreed that the MS might have contained a notation to that effect.
30. Walker, p. 111.
31. In response to the question of where the fair copy of Part Two might have been between 1600 and 1623, Professor Alice Scoufos noted that it was most unlikely that the MS had remained with the Cobham family, for the line in fact died out very shortly after the celebrated protest was made. There was no "library" in which the MS could have been preserved. Professor John Freehafer suggested that the fair copy might have been submitted not to the Cobhams but to the Master of the Revels, and it might have been preserved by him. He noted also, however, that the Masters did not generally possess copies of the plays they licensed.
32. When the foul papers reached print, all the *Oldcastle* forms had been changed—with one exception.
33. In Part One (Q1): *Fa.* 2; *Fal.* 55; *Falst.* 95. In Part Two (F1): *Fal.* 117; *Falst.* 57; *Falstaffe* 3. I disregard here the fact that Part One regularly spells the second syllable -*stalffe;* my point is that the Falstaff name is made more prominent than it needs to be. As neither of the fair copies derives from a prompt book, the argument that this consistency results from theatrical necessity does not weigh heavily.
34. The only parallel that may be considered to have the weight of a bibliographical link (i.e., a peculiarity of the original necessitated by a phenomenon of the printing process which is reproduced in the reprint where the phenomenon is anomalous) is the spelling "maner" (II.i. 120; TLN 711). This spelling is used in the quarto to justify a line; it is found also at the same place in the Folio, a unique spelling among five other examples of the word in the play and among 130 other examples throughout the Folio. Strange as this parallel may seem, it may be coincidental. In the first place, the spelling "maner" in the Folio may also have been used to justify a line. In the second place, the normal spelling in the quarto of Part One is "maner(s)" (five times); if the same hand provided the fair copy of both Parts, as has been suggested, it would follow that the fair copy spelling for both plays was "maner," copied regularly in Part One (Q), copied once in Part Two (F).

The Reform of a Malcontent:
Jaques and the Meaning of *As You Like It*

ROBERT B. BENNETT

I

Shakespeare's portrayal of Jaques in *As You Like It* is one of the earliest significant studies in Elizabethan drama of the malcontent, that age's version of the social dropout or alienated intellectual. Moreover, Shakespeare is the only playwright to subject the malcontent to a pastoral experience, to make him more an object of social criticism and romantic correction than an authorial mouthpiece for anatomizing the ills of society. Jaques' kinship with the Italianate Englishman and with the behavioral patterns which are typical of the figure commonly labeled malcontent by Elizabethans has been the subject of a number of critical studies and will receive further attention later in this essay. My chief concern, however, is not Jaques' literary heritage but Shakespeare's dramatic intentions and achievements in including a malcontent in the romantic world of Arden Forest.

In a catalogue of Elizabethan character types, Jaques shares the label *malcontent* with such major figures as Hamlet, Malevole, Bussy, Vindice, Flamineo, and Bosola, but their common traits are mostly superficial. Even more important, the exigencies of a romantic milieu differ radically from those of a tragic or darkly satiric one and necessarily alter the role which a malcontent can play. The contrasts between Jaques and these other malcontents, however, are instructive of Shakespeare's special achievement, and it is helpful to understand first how the malcontent typically functions in his more common environment of the satiric drama of court intrigue. The following observations about Jaques' serious counterparts are made with the characters Hamlet, Malevole, Bussy, Vindice, Flamineo, and Bosola especially in mind. Obviously, no single point can apply with equal validity to all of the characters, and a number of generalizations will apply only to most of them; but these characters do possess a similarity in dramatic function based upon their common conception as genuine malcontents that will be evident when they are viewed in contrast with their nominal kin, Jaques.

Behind all of the malcontents lies an unfulfilled potential for greatness, particularly for being a model of the complete Renaissance man, "the courtier's, soldier's, scholar's eye, tongue, sword." The malcontents are intelligent men, deprived of a world governed by reason and virtue in which their talents might have been nurtured and exercised to full expression. They are able both to abstract experience into moral philosophy and to make immediate judgments about character and situation in the course of conversation and action. In other words, they are effective as both thinkers and doers. The two activities are frequently incompatible, however, and the necessity to be either a thinker or a doer forms a central tension in the character of the malcontent. John Webster is careful to alert us early in both *The White Devil* and *The Duchess of Malfi* that Flamineo and Bosola are at heart men of quality. Only because they have found no market in their worlds for virtuous counsel have they chosen to be doers, which for them means a life of villainy. Their choice has not been one of preference, as it would have been for a machiavel, but rather one of constitutional necessity. As men of energy and ability in human affairs, they find especially galling the poverty, idleness, and exclusion from positions of influence that inevitably attend men who govern their actions by rules of honor and morality. Their choice of villainy grows out of despair, not innate evil. Concerning Bosola of *The Duchess of Malfi,* the honest Antonio comments:

> 'Tis great pitty
> He should be thus neglected—I have heard
> He's very valiant: This foule mellancholly
> Will poyson all his goodnesse.
> . . . . .
> want of action
> Breeds all blacke male-contents.
>
> *(I.i.77–82)*[1]

The bleaker world of *The White Devil* affords Flamineo no such sympathic spokesman, but he tells us of his scholarly background in the very process of denouncing it to his mother as degrading, debilitating, and, by inference, useless in attaining the position of authority for which it supposedly was training him.

> You brought me up,
> At *Padua* I confesse, where I protest
> For want of meanes, the University judge me,
> I have bene faine to heele my Tutors stockings
> At least seven yeares.
>
> *(I.ii.312–16)*

In a similarly ironic way we hear of Vindice's scholarly nature at the point where he finds it an undesirable virtue. Having, after nine years of idleness, his first opportunity to avenge the death of his betrothed, Gloriana, by becoming a "child o' the court," he chooses to repress moral sensibilities, invoking Impudence:

> Strike thou my forehead into dauntless marble,
> Mine eyes to steady sapphires; turn my visage,
> And if I must needs glow, let me blush inward,
> That this immodest season may not spy
> That scholar in my cheeks.
>
> (I.iii.8–12)[2]

Since one might conclude, judging only from their actions, that these three characters bear closer resemblance to machiavels like Lorenzo (*The Spanish Tragedy*), Iago, and Edmund than to the free-spirited malcontents Hamlet, Malevole, and Bussy, it is important for an understanding of their dramatic function as malcontents to recognize their kinship with these latter characters in their reflective habits of mind, their inherent moral sensibility, and their high-spirited refusal to accept idleness as the lot of the virtuous man.

The multi-sided and high-spirited intellect is the malcontent's most significant dramatic characteristic. Because of it he provides the playwright with a natural means for integrating tragic vision and tragic action. The malcontent's scholarly bent makes him a proper exponent of the moral and philosophical matter that in other tragedies is usually relegated to a character on the periphery of the action: a chorus, a fool, or a sententious counselor. Because the malcontent is himself centrally involved in the plot of the play, his discourses do not intrude on the dramatic action but rather become a part of it, helping to shape his own feelings and actions. We find an interesting example of this process in Hamlet's speech beginning "What a piece of work is a man!" In addition to its intrinsic poetic appeal, this meditation, or *consolatio philosophiae*, aids Hamlet in coping with his frustration and disappointment over his friends' disloyalty while at the same time diverting them from the specific cause of his melancholy.

Through the actions and fates of the free-spirited malcontents Malevole, Hamlet, and Bussy the playwrights explore ways in which virtue is able to assert itself or is defeated in a world dominated by evil. Of central interest is how the malcontent can participate in his world without becoming tainted by it. The tension resulting from this dual responsibility is a shaping force in the malcontent's condition. His spirited sense of honor and moral responsibility impels him to enter the world and brave its corrupting influences in order to reform it, even though he despises the task. Thus it is wrong, for example, to say that sheer desire for power lies behind Malevole's disguising and plotting to win back his place as Duke of Genoa. He himself persuades Pietro of the folly of such desires by likening the court to a bawdy-house and the world to a dung heap upon which the cosmic elements cast their excrement,[3] and his admonitions to Pietro must be taken seriously. Through them we perceive the conflict in Malevole between a sense of his obligation to regain his rightful position and a contempt for his world which inclines him away from action and involvement. The conflict is developed to its highest point in *Hamlet,* where the Prince is placed in precisely this dilemma by the Ghost's charge: "But, howsoever thou pursuest this act, / Taint not thy mind. . . ." (I.v.84–85).[4] Hamlet accepts the responsibility to revenge with anguish because he knows the moral dangers involved: "The time is out of joint;—O cursed spite, / That ever I was born to set it right!" Bussy, like Hamlet, involves himself in the court world he despises out of a sense of obligation to reform it: "I am for honest actions, not for great: / If I may bring up a new fashion, / And rise in Court with virtue, speed his plough" (I.i.124–26).[5] The strong odds against virtue's succeeding in such a world are dramatized not only by the malcontent's relative isolation in court—Malevole can trust only Celso; Hamlet, only Horatio—but also by the subverting effect of the malcontent's own wasted and unsettled condition. The sheer intensity of his vision of evil is itself corroding, and his outrage exhausts his energies in frustration. Poverty, idleness, and neglect, typically suffered by the malcontent, warp his spirit as they waste his body.

The effort to avoid the taint of a corrupt world is not a dramatic issue in the roles of Vindice, Flamineo, and Bosola. They have repressed the stirrings of conscience and chosen to engage in villainous intrigue rather than imprison their high spirits in useless poverty and idleness. But just as we wonder with the free-spirited malcontents how far they can sustain their virtue, we wonder with these whether they can prevent their schooled and natural sensibilities and self-respect from surfacing. For example, in *The White Devil* Flamineo violates the rules of his assumed role as tool villain when he refuses to cower before his patron Brachiano's abuse at their meeting before the house of convertites (IV.ii.45–71). Later when Flamineo is brought before Brachiano for murdering his brother Marcello, the Duke grants him no pardon but only a lease on his life to be renewed daily "or be hang'd," and he explains his sentence: "You once did brave mee in your sisters lodging; / I'le now keepe you in awe for't" (V.ii.77–78). Ironically Flamineo is brought low because of his one overt show of personal integrity. A similar tension marks Bosola's deeds of villainy and explains his later reform. With Vindice there is less a sense of tension than of exquisite irony in his constant flow of moral commentary as he gleefully sets about his plot to torture and murder the Duke.

Despite the seeming pleasure with which, at times, these villainous malcontents engage in spying, pandering, and murder, all voice, just as the free-spirited malcontents do, sentiments of *contemptus mundi* that counterpoint their active participation in the intrigues of court life. The true malcontent is a reservoir of unresolved tensions and contradictions. His philosophical bent, his social alienation, and his psychological instability serve vitally the dramatic interests of theme, plot, and characterization. Because the malcontent shares his musings and satiric vision with us and sometimes preaches to us, we typically view the action and the other characters through his eyes. This is absolutely true of Hamlet and in varying degrees true of the others. We generally respect the malcontent's view of the world even if we cannot condone his actions.

Now, the image of a man standing defiantly against the current of a society that seeks to wash away his integrity and independence stirs our romantic sensibilities; and commentaries indicate that many romantic young men of Shakespeare's time displayed the malcontent's marks of noble suffering—his dishevelled appearance and blunt, unmannerly speech—in hopes of persuading others and themselves that they possessed an innate greatness of spirit. In most the manner must have been mere affectation, for it takes, after all, the rare combination of a morally sensitive and self-reliant person living in an unusually decadent environment to generate these forms of behavior naturally. When a malcontent's environment is not really evil, his display of cynicism and melancholy is evidence of either a corrupt nature or a foolish fashion. But except for Shakespeare, whom John Davies of Hereford distinguished as having "no rayling, but, a raigning Wit,"[6] Jacobean playwrights could not free their attention enough from the ills of society to concentrate on its redeeming qualities and to portray, in what might even appear self-parody, the potential absurdity in malcontent posturings. Jaques is Shakespeare's and Elizabethan drama's only fully conceived comic malcontent.[7]

Jaques cannot, like his tragic counterparts, be a confidant of the audience, because his expressed view of his world is not consonant with the one we see. The incongruity, in fact, alerts us that his manner derives not from experience but from a romanticized image of himself. Jaques has no serious personal dilemma; Arden is remarkably free from the kind of conditions that usually induce the malcontent state. And he, far from having the tragic malcontent's acute sensitivity to the nature of his surroundings, is notably lacking in awareness. The comic action of the play anatomizes the folly of Jaques' malcontent for the viewer's edification and, within the context of the play, for Jaques' own reformation.

To understand Jaques' role in *As You Like It*, we need first to define what in the nature of Arden makes it an ideal community for spiritual instruction and to realize why Jaques' nature is basically compatible with this benign human environment. Such an inquiry leads us to view Jaques' nature and the reasons for his malcontent manner in more positive terms than they have generally been accorded and consequently enables us to see how he contributes to and benefits from the lessons of the forest and at the end is cleansed of his malcontent.

II

The concept of nature that operates in the romantic worlds of Shakespeare's comedies derives from the principle that God created the world out of love. Love is by definition the ultimate source of order and of physical and spiritual generation in nature. It is also the strongest force in nature, superior to the powers of fortune, evil, custom, and time. Accordingly, if a man chooses not to act out of love, he chooses to be unnatural and thereby destroys the harmony of his own spirit and of the social unit within his sphere of influence. His world then becomes subject to the unstable and capricious rule of those lesser orders of power in nature whose prevalence calls forth genuine malcontent.

In *As You Like It* fortune rules in the self-seeking world of Duke Frederick's court. There Celia bids Rosalind, "Let us sit and mock the good housewife Fortune from her wheel, that her gifts may henceforth be bestowed equally," to which Rosalind agrees that "[Fortune's] benefits are mightily misplaced" (I.ii.34–38). Their ensuing conversation foreshadows the change of ruling powers that is about to occur in their experience. Celia says of Fortune, "those that she makes fair she scarce makes honest, and those that she makes honest she makes very ill-favouredly," to which Rosalind corrects, "Nay, now thou goest from Fortune's office to Nature's. Fortune reigns in gifts of the world, not in the lineaments of Nature" (I.ii.40–45).

By contrast to the world of Duke Frederick's court, the society in Arden is in harmony with nature because it originates in and grows through love, manifest in selfless giving and spiritual instruction. Jaques is a contributor to as well as a beneficiary of this creative environment. The society in Arden as we know it has really begun when Jaques, together with other loyal courtiers, has voluntarily forfeited his lands to help the Duke survive in the wilderness. He may compose a verse (II.v.52–59) proclaiming himself and others fools for leaving their wealth and ease to please a stubborn will, but the act itself speaks for a generous and kind nature beneath the cynical veneer. This pattern of service is repeated and the society grows as new-comers banished from civilization arrive at the forest physically spent and are brought relief by other human beings already there. Corin provides for Rosalind, Celia, and Touchstone; the Duke aids Orlando and Adam; Orlando saves Oliver from the lioness. This last instance, as Oliver recounts it, is particularly instructive of how love overrules fortune and custom in an ordered nature:

> Twice did he turn his back and purpos'd so [to leave];
> But kindness, nobler ever than revenge,
> And nature, stronger than his just occasion,
> Made him give battle to the lioness.

(IV.iii.128–31)

In allowing kindness and mercy to overrule his own baser inclination for revenge, Orlando acts in time to prevent fortune from taking its course with the lioness' victim; moreover, in saving Oliver's life he also moves him to a spiritual conversion and reconciliation. In thus deciding the fate of his older brother, Orlando has shown nature ("kindness") to be a truer authority than the custom of primogeniture by which he earlier had been misruled.

These deeds of physical service indicate the spiritual readiness of the persons in Arden, including Jaques, for the kind of education that the forest experience can provide. Those whom we see in Arden are not perfect; otherwise, there would be no point to all the discussion in the play. But from the start they have manifested by their actions the kind of selflessness that will make them receptive to the lessons of the forest. The elemental lesson that the winter wilderness has taught its inhabitants is that love, shown in mutual service, is the human faculty most essential to survival. All having learned this basic rule are ready for the instruction that each can provide the other in their various encounters in the forest. In the perfectly free forum of the forest persons converse and criticize and in the process refine themselves and the audience. No idea is left unqualified, and nearly every idea has some measure of truth. Each person contributes to the spirit of the forest; but, being less than the whole, each individual nature is made better by it.

In light of this dramatic structure, it is easier to explain why Jaques is so important to the play despite his irrelevance to the plot. His predisposition to moralizing and philosophizing is not simply to provide entertaining embellishment; it perfectly fits the conversational design of the play. Shakespeare's addition of Touchstone and Jaques to the company he found in Lodge's romantic narrative provides *As You like It* with two characters expressing explicitly cultivated court views. Thus, as Eugene Waith has nicely phrased it, Touchstone and Jaques are critics of romantic behavior through whom Shakespeare is able to balance "one convention against another, the romantic against the satiric."[8] They represent man's art through their court wit, and they represent textbook education in juxtaposition to Corin's natural philosophy and to the refined aristocratic natures of the Duke, Orlando, and Rosalind. Moreover, just as Jaques' "matter" helps balance the debates, so his cynicism brings a needed tartness to an otherwise too sweet scene, even though it is precisely this cynicism which must be purged from Jaques himself. Finally, his easily satirized eccentricity makes him conducive rather than offensive to the comic spirit.

III

While the broad lines of Jaques' dramatic function are hardly in dispute, there remains considerable disagreement over the more specific matters of how seriously and exactly in what way we are to judge Jaques for his melancholy malcontent. Since Zera Fink's important article, "Jaques and the Malcontent Traveller," the idea has been generally aired that Jaques both puts on a melancholy fashion of the age and is genuinely melancholic.[9] But Jaques' melancholy fashion is part of a larger pose of intellectualism. His preoccupation with bookish matters appears frequently. He is anxious to know from Amiens whether he has properly described the verses of his song by the term *stanzos* (II.v.17–19). He is thrilled by Touchstone's ability to rail in set terms, and his own defense of satire and his discourse on the seven ages of man sound like exercises learned and recited by rote. His melancholy is similarly practiced if we may judge from the care and pride with which he distinguishes it from other forms of melancholy in his conversation with Rosalind (IV.i.1–26).

Jaques is a would-be intellectual, not a misanthrope, though he confuses the two; and his melancholy is donned to impress others with his wisdom. In *The Merchant of Venice,* Shakespeare referred briefly to this type, who dons a melancholy pose to convey an impression of philosophical preoccupation and wisdom. There Gratiano berates his friend Antonio for acting melancholy:

There are a sort of men whose visages
Do cream and mantle like a standing pond,
And do a wilful stillness entertain,
With purpose to be dress'd in an opinion
Of wisdom, gravity, profound conceit

. . . . .
             I do know of these
That therefore only are reputed wise
For saying nothing, when, I am very sure,
If they should speak, would almost damn those ears
Which, hearing them, would call their brothers fools.

(I.i.88–99)

Ben Jonson's satiric persona Asper describes the same assumed posture to Mitis in the conversational preface to *Every Man out of His Humour*:

And MITIS, note me, if in all this front,
You can espy a gallant of this marke,
Who (to be thought one of the iudicious)
Sits with his armes thus wreath'd,
          his hat pull'd here,
Cryes meaw, and nods, then shakes his empty head.

(ll.158–62)[10]

We should see Jaques in this company and recognize that in affecting a melancholy disposition he is really trying to appear and to be the malcontent philosopher. Jaques, however, is not a vacuous simpleton putting on airs of intellectual refinement but rather a seriously motivated intellectual whose efforts have in part been perverted by a misunderstanding of what constitutes true wisdom.

The degree to which we can attribute genuine melancholy to Jaques is less certain. To discount the presence of melancholy altogether we must discount the Duke's references to Jaques' "sullen fits," which before we even see him incline us to regard him as a melancholy man even though he seldom, if ever, appears genuinely melancholy on stage. To credit him at such times as the seven-ages-of-man speech with a measure of genuine intellectual melancholy and not simply affectation is to give Jaques and the play moments of sober reflection which nicely vary the predominantly light mood without disrupting the overall comic effect. But here a distinction should be made between the sober meditation of the melancholy scholar and the cynicism of the malcontent. If we say that Jaques is genuinely· malcontent—that is, if we say that his cynicism is ingrained as well as practiced—then I believe we have mistaken fashion for nature. If Jaques not only behaves cynically but is a real cynic, then we must not simply criticize him for being foolishly captivated by current fashion but denounce him as damnable for his lack of compassion, an indictment which is altogether too harsh in relation to his behavior or to the spirit of the play.

Helen Gardner takes his cynicism as genuine. Jaques is "the cynic, the person who prefers the pleasures of superiority, cold-eyed and cold-hearted. The tyrannical Duke Frederick and the cruel Oliver can be converted; but not Jaques. He likes himself as he is." She concludes: "Jaques arrogates to himself the divine role. He has opted out from the human condition."[11] This judgment requires us to take Jaques' cynicism seriously throughout and not view it as merely a fashionable pose. It also denies that any sense of conversion is implicit in the kind tone of his final speech to the Duke and the lovers.

By contrast we have Erwin Panofsky's somewhat startling evaluation: "A climax of refinement [of intellectual melancholy] is reached in Shakespeare's Jaques who uses the mask of a melancholic by fashion and snobbery to hide the fact that he is a genuine one."[12] To accept Panofsky's interpretation, we would have to view the constant satirizing to which Jaques is subjected as misdirected, inasmuch as Jaques would be as aware as his critics are that his melancholy manner is put on and in addition would be conscious of a need for it which they do not perceive. Panofsky's position exaggerates Jaques' intellectual awareness and rules out the possibility of a final conversion. Michael Jamieson interprets Jaques' melancholy less literally: "The fact that Jaques' melancholy is shown to be a carefully cultivated state makes him an appropriate figure for comedy, not an authoritative philosopher."[13] If not his melancholy, his pose of cynicism certainly makes him foolish, not vile or noble. For understanding Jaques this perspective must be kept in mind; fashion must not be confused with reality.

We should be warned by Jaques' dramatic, social, and literary antecedents from taking too literally the misanthropic manner that he parades. In dramatic function Jaques is not of a kind with Timon, who is a genuine misanthrope and a subject for tragedy; nor is he like the malcontents of humours comedy, Macilente (Jonson's *Every Man out of His Humour*) and Dowsecer (Chapman's *An Humourous Day's Mirth*). These serve as moral spokesmen for their authors because they are the rare voices of sanity in a society ruled by unnatural custom and fashion. Jaques, by contrast, is the most artificial character in Arden, with the possible exception of Phoebe.

Dramatically he is the descendant of the fantastical melancholy Spaniard, Don Adriano de Armado, though with Jaques the fashion of the intellectual traveler has changed in important ways. Jaques, like Armado, presumes himself a great wit, is a meticulous observer of form, and is welcomed into the courtly company for the entertainment he will provide. As described by the King of Navarre, Armado is

> a refined traveller of Spain;
> A man in all the world's new fashion planted,
> That hath a mint of phrases in his brain;
> One who the music of his own vain tongue
> Doth ravish like enchanting harmony.
>
> *(Love's Labour's Lost, I.i.164–68)*

Longaville welcomes the news of this knight's presence: "Costard the swain and he shall be our sport" (I.i.180). The roles of Touchstone and Jaques are, in a general sense, dramatically parallel to those of this earlier pair. But by 1600 the Spanish Armada was no longer topical, and the traveler's fashion of malcontent was well established. Jaques' resemblance to the malcontent traveler has been accurately described by Zera S. Fink, and Fink's description needs only to be quickly recalled and slightly refined here.[14] Jaques mirrors the contemporary self-conscious gentleman who must travel, preferably to Italy, and return appearing melancholy to prove to others that his experiences have made him wise. He cultivates the image of Diogenes or Juvenal, not Machiavelli, and he is a philosophical, not a political, Italianate Englishman. Fink relates Jaques to the description of the malcontent in William Rankin's *The English Ape* (1588) and to Marston's Bruto in *Certaine Satyres* (1598), as distinct from Lodge's sketch in *Wits Miserie* (1596) of the machiavellian malcontent Scandal-Detraction. Equally valid analogues of intellectual malcontents are Nashe's Pierce Penilesse (1591) and Robert Greene's self-description in *The Repentaunce of Robert Greene* (1592).[15]

Jaques is also properly to be linked with the then current mode of railing satire. His stock satirist's defense against the accusation of libel (II.vii.70–87) and such railing phrases as "I will through and through / Cleanse the foul body of th' infected world" (II.vii.59–60) place him unquestionably in the company of contemporary Juvenalians. The controversial and highly popular satiric style of coarse rhetoric which Marston affected in his satires of 1598 and 1599 was easily and appropriately incorporated into the manner of the melancholy intellectual, completing his appearance as a malcontent.

The malcontent traits of moral seriousness and satiric manner, which distinguish Jaques from Armado, give greater depth to his character and greater flexibility to his role as a fashionable intellectual in the more mature comedy. Whereas the King of Navarre expects only laughable elocution from Armado, the Duke enjoys Jaques because he is a philosopher, "full of matter." Perhaps Sir John Harington's irreverent satirical manner, which at various times delighted and annoyed the Queen, encouraged around the turn of the century the frequent dramatization of princes welcoming moralizing railers.[16] At any rate, we may agree with the Duke that while the malcontent manner distorts learning by casting everything in a negative light, it does not preclude a sincere intellectual disposition and a measure of profitable knowledge. Thus Jaques is not limited to the role of unwitting entertainer but can contribute to the philosophical dialogue in Arden. In addition, the malcontent fashion itself dictates a life of austerity, moral propriety, and meditation, thus lending a degree of dignity to a believer in it like Jaques. For example, admitting the comedy of the situation, there is credit due Jaques for his moral scruples in persuading Touchstone not to carry through the improper marriage ceremony that the clown has arranged with the hedge-priest Sir Oliver Martext. Jaques also deserves credit for his refusal to be intimidated by Orlando's uncivil intrusion into the Duke's company (II.vii.88–101). Although he may not be skillful in recognizing virtue in these early scenes, Jaques does respond appropriately to impropriety.

Censure of the malcontent fashion and of Jaques' devotion to it is too absolute if it fails to acknowledge these virtues, but Jaques needs the help of the Arden community to see the flaw in the fashion's premise that melancholy and cynicism are indispensable partners of intelligence and virtue. Jaques does not hate man; rather he is infatuated with the attitude of cynical melancholy. "I do love it better than laughing," he tells Rosalind (IV.i.4). The implication of such a belief, were it truly understood and pursued, is self-destructive despair; and Rosalind, who recognizes that excessive sobriety no less than excessive laughter is a sign of an unhealthy state of mind, rebukes Jaques sharply:

> Those that are in extremity of either are abominable fellows, and betray themselves to every modern censure worse than drunkards.
>
> (IV.i.5–7)

And indeed the genuine misanthrope, one like Timon, is literally abominable, apart from humanity.

Despite Jaques' pretence of misanthropy, nature working both from without and from within him is continually undercutting the cynical front which he tries to maintain. The powers of benevolence in Arden operate in both direct and oblique ways to alert us to what is extreme or absurd in Jaques' three major displays of cynicism: his moralizing on the deer, his oration on the seven ages of man, and his wish to wear motley. Jaques' moral and philosophical lament upon the wounded deer has enough truth in it that Arden can expose the inadequacy of the position only gradually and subtly. It is difficult both at the time the scene is reported to the Duke by one of his lords and later, when Jaques' character has become more clearly ridiculous and openly satirized, to make an outright judgment. In his introductory description of Jaques, one lord relates how he overheard the solitary malcontent first accuse the Duke and his courtier of usurping the deer's "assign'd and native dwelling-place" and then rail upon the indifference of the herd to the plight of its wounded member, calling the healthy deer the "fat and greasy citizens" of the wood whose action proves the general rule "thus misery doth part / The flux of company" (II.i.21–64). Shakespeare has numerous ways of preventing us from regarding this as simple misanthropy in Jaques. The scene is not shown, but is related to the Duke by a lord, so that we never see an occasion when Jaques actually sits alone and lashes out at "country, city, court." Then, too, the lord prefaces his narrative of Jaques' moralizing with his own account of the wounded deer, an account that rivals that of an eighteenth-century man of feeling in its abundance of sentiment. The Duke, whom Charles the wrestler has prepared us to accept as a Robin Hood-like folk hero, anticipates Jaques' charge of intrusion by confessing a sense of guilt for shooting "the poor dappled fools, / Being native burghers of this desert city" (II.i.22–23). If Jaques is overly sentimental toward the deer, he is no more so than the Duke and the lord, and there is no evidence that the Duke regards Jaques' charge as unwarranted or especially excessive. On the contrary, the Duke obviously enjoys Jaques' critical moralizing, just as he enjoys finding honest counsellors in the winter's wind and cold (II.i.1–10).

Only in retrospect, when Jaques' cynicism shows itself to be a stubborn pose distorting his intellectual disposition and when the benevolence of the forest company becomes evident, do the untenable aspects of Jaques' initial moralizing become clear. Where the indifference of the herd to its wounded members is proof to Jaques that nature is cruel, Orlando reminds us of nature's kindness by likening his service to Adam to that of a doe caring for its young (II.vii.127–28). Looked at from another perspective, Jaques' likening the deer to greasy citizens may be rejected as a comparison of unlikes which does injustice to the deer. Amiens' song "Blow, blow, thou winter wind" excuses the harsh winter elements as "not so unkind / As man's ingratitude" (II.vii.175–76). Like the elements, the deer do not possess moral reason and free will as man does; hence, Jaques mistakes their nature when he measures their actions by a standard of responsibility that is properly demanded only of humans. Jaques is also in error when he judges man's rule over the deer in societal terms of tyranny and usurpation. The absurdity of holding that man should obey in his relationship with animals the same laws that bind him with members of his own kind becomes clear in the city-versus-country debate between Corin and Touchstone. When Corin concludes his glowing picture of the plain honest country life—"and the greatest of my pride is to see my ewes graze and my lambs suck"—Touchstone, with "too courtly a wit," deflates the idyllic vision:

> That is another simple sin in you, to bring the ewes and the rams together, and to offer to get your living by the copulation of cattle; to be bawd to a bell-wether, and to betray a she-lamb of a twelvemonth to a crooked-pated, old, cuckoldly ram, out of all reasonable match.
>
> *(III.ii.77–87)*

If we agree that to call a shepherd a bawd for breeding sheep is mere fooling, then we must likewise discard the less obvious but equally distorted notion that men can tyrannize deer.

Later scenes reveal more clearly how Jaques is unwittingly denying himself the chance to respond sensitively to events because of his effort to relate all experience to stock themes of injustice and decay. His speech on the seven ages of man anticipates the arrival of the starving aged Adam; and, as does the commentary on the deer, it develops the Duke's own thoughts about life's unpleasantness. The speech views man's life in the context of historical time, that is, as a simple progression from birth to death; and the vision conveys a sense of life's tediousness, an effect achieved both by the content of each stage described and by the inevitable progression to decay and death. This abstract overview of life was probably, as T. W. Baldwin suggests, common moral feed to Elizabethan schoolboys, for which Palingenius' *The Zodiak of Life* was a likely source, though recent scholarship has uncovered a great number of other ancient and contemporary analogues.[17] Jaques' speech is thus a moral and rhetorical commonplace. He has a theoretical but not a personal commitment to the substance of the speech. And immediately, the spirit of Arden points to errors in the speech's conception of old age and time. The entry of Adam carried by Orlando confirms the unpleasant truth of enfeebling age but adds the elements of compassion and veneration which a good man in his old age calls forth from others. Orlando's devotion to Adam is a virtue inspired by Adam's own goodness. On the issue of time, Jaques' encompassing vision of a lifetime is a purely abstract feat which in no way reflects the way human beings actually experience time. By defining man solely in terms of the physiological restrictions of a life span, the vision fails to distinguish man from other living creatures, since all creatures are similarly bound. Touchstone parodies such philosophy when he moralizes to Jaques on the time, "And so, from hour to hour, we ripe and ripe, / And then, from hour to hour, we rot and rot" (II.vii.26–27). Rosalind shows the ineffectiveness of describing human experience in terms of historical time by pointing out that one's given situation and disposition determine the only sense in which he experiences time. She lectures Orlando:

> Time travels in divers paces with divers persons. I'll tell you who Time ambles withal, who Time trots withal, who Time gallops withal, and who he stands still withal.
>
> *(III.ii.326–29)*

By defining time in relation to persons rather than persons in relation to time, she comically but accurately establishes human nature's capacity to govern time.

Jaques' abstract philosophy comes into conflict with the actualities of Arden for a third time in his petition to the Duke to wear motley. His request for motley is based upon the commonplace cynical beliefs that court society is corrupt, that only flattery holds the ruler's ear, and that only the fool, who has no stake in the system, may speak his mind freely. Such "wise" court fools as Henry VIII's Will Summers enjoyed by their peculiar status a special privilege to criticize and satirize court conditions, and the Elizabethan malcontent as represented in drama had through his eccentric behavior won this same privilege. The malcontents Dowsecer and Malevole, for instance, are favored by royal patrons because their unbridled manners balance the predictable flattery of the other courtiers.[18] The notion that the malcontent has supplanted, or at least joined, the fool as a privileged spokesman at court is directly suggested in the Chapman play *Bussy D'Ambois*, where the steward Maffé, who is jealous of Bussy's rise to favor, comments:

> it seems my Lord
> Will have him for his jester; and believe it,
> Such men are now no fools, 'tis a Knight's place.
>
> (I.i.193–95)

But Jaques' request for motley is absurd because in Arden the social order is not diseased but rather is in tune with nature. Counsel is freely welcomed and flattery is nonexistent. The Duke, who revels in the physical hardship of winter because "This is no flattery: these are counsellors / That feelingly persuade me what I am" (II.i.10–11), is pleased to listen to Jaques' moral matter; and to Jaques' exclamation, "I am ambitious for a motley coat," he replies, "Thou shalt have one" (II.vii.43–44). But Jaques is not thinking of Arden when he requests motley and seems not even to hear the Duke's reply. He is contemplating an image of himself as the lone honest man in a world of corruption, whose special calling is to purge that world with railing. Within the context of Arden, his vision is a private one that reflects the unhealthy preoccupation of the speaker rather than any flaw in the society he is addressing. The Duke appropriately applies the satirist's physic to Jaques by rehearsing to his face unsavory aspects of his past:

> Most mischievous foul sin, in chiding sin.
> For thou thyself hast been a libertine,
> As sensual as the brutish sting itself;
> And all th' embossed sores and headed evils
> That thou with license of free foot hast caught,
> Wouldst thou disgorge into the general world.
>
> (II.vii.64–69)

Rosalind administers the same harsh antidote in a later scene (IV.i.1–41), where she satirizes the fetishes of the fashionable traveler. By his example Orlando instructs Jaques to look at his own folly before judging the world's; to Jaques' invitation to rail on the world, he replies, "I will chide no breather in the world but myself, against whom I know most faults" (III.ii.297–98). It is crucial that Jaques understand this lesson in humility because unless he can acknowledge that he is a son of Adam, he will lack the self-knowledge he needs to convert his fashionable wisdom into true wisdom and to see the world around him freshly and directly. Orlando accuses him of deriving his knowledge from "painted cloth," that is, from the moral clichés which were commonly illustrated on canvas wallhangings. He tells Jaques that he finds his borrowed knowledge and fashion tedious. Thus both by satiric rebuke and by personal example the three most spiritually refined members of Arden press Jaques to look to his own nature.

Besides the continual external counters to Jaques' professed beliefs, his own nature regularly contradicts his malcontent rules. The frequent failure of his actions to match the cynicism of his words should win our sympathies since it prevents us from taking his misanthropy literally and since it reveals beneath the pose a benign spirit. He plays the role of the malcontent in the first place as much out of a sense of moral obligation as out of a desire to parade intellect. He openly avows the moral worth of unsociability, satire, and melancholy, three cardinal virtues of the malcontent manner. He would thank Amiens for singing to satisfy him except that he would not flatter:

> Well then, if ever I thank any man, I'll thank you; but that they call compliment is like the encounter of two dog-apes; and when a man thanks me heartily, methinks I have given him a penny and he renders me the beggarly thanks.
>
> *(II.v.25–30)*

The attitude is not far removed from John Webster's belligerent manner of thanking his patrons in his dedications to *The Duchess of Malfi* and *The Devil's Law-Case*,[19] and it is very much in the manner of the malcontent in its refusal to express gratitude for fear of appearing a flatterer.[20] And just as Jaques' malcontent code refuses to draw the line between virtuous thanks and selfish flattery, so it also categorically condemns civil conversation as frivolous. Jaques replies with strained incivility to Amiens' message that the Duke wishes to talk with him:

> He is too disputable for my company. I think of as many matters as he; but I give heaven thanks, and make no boast of them.
>
> *(II.v.36–38)*

Set satire, on the other hand, is virtuous according to his rule book. When the Duke is suddenly angered by Jaques' saying he would cleanse "th' infected world," Jaques asks in ingenuous bewilderment, "What, for a counter, would I do but good?" The Duke's reply that he would spew out his own corruption on the world quite escapes Jaques, who proceeds mechanically to the next rule in his philosophy, that the satirist only rails upon the general evil. Ultimately Jaques' commitment to melancholy is based, he thinks, upon moral grounds. He tells Rosalind quite seriously, "Why, 'tis good to be sad and to say nothing" (IV.i.8).

Happily, Jaques himself often violates these rules of his malcontent catechism. His need to explain to Amiens why he cannot thank him in itself shows his nature surfacing and having to be restrained. He is, despite his unsociable phrases, the most ubiquitous and social character in Arden. He converses during the play with Amiens, the Duke, Touchstone, Orlando, Rosalind, and the lords and foresters—more people than any other character. He tells Amiens that he does not wish to talk with the Duke, but having seen Touchstone rail on fortune in good set terms, he rushes with abandon to tell the Duke that he has found a kindred spirit in a fool. This ingenuous enthusiasm is quite becoming to Jaques, but we should observe that it is quite uncharacteristic of a malcontent.

Orlando draws out Jaques' nature much in the way that Touchstone does. To Jaques' unsociable remarks, Orlando replies in the most fashionable and polite unsociability, thus winning Jaques' admiration.

Jaques. I thank you for your company; but, good faith, I had as lief have been myself alone.
Orlando. And so had I; but yet, for fashion sake, I thank you too for your society.
Jaques. God buy you; let's meet as little as we can.
Orlando. I do desire we may be better strangers.

(III.ii.269–75)

From this beginning Jaques is forced to invent insulting conversation to prolong his acquaintance with this charming fellow until, running out of insults, he surrenders his pretence and suggests that together they sit and rail on their miserable world. Orlando dismisses Jaques at this point with a wittily contrived insult that forces Jaques to see himself as a fool.

To blot his malcontent record further, Jaques twice calls for music to be played (II.v.10 and IV.ii.6). He is quick to profess no desire for pleasure or harmony, but the inconsistency between rhetoric and action remains. The Duke, hearing that Jaques was "merry, hearing of a song," comments ironically on his offense to his fashion: "If he, compact of jars, grow musical, /

We shall have shortly discord in the spheres'' (II.vii.5–6). Moreover, one reason Jaques presses Amiens to play is that he has composed a verse which he wishes to sing. Again, the fact that the verse is predictably belligerent in no way alters the fact that he has entered into a courtly game of wit which his philosophy, strictly taken, would not excuse.

To this point we have seen the limitations and flaws in Jaques' manner exposed by the natural forces of the forest, one component of which is Jaques' own nature. The question remaining is, does this exposure have any effect on Jaques, or is it merely for the audience's edification while Jaques remains a pawn to his ill-formed philosophy? His refusal to join the marriage celebration and his intention to join Duke Frederick in self-imposed exile rather than return with the company to court have drawn varying responses in recent studies of the play. Harold Jenkins, Jay Halio, and Helen Gardner deny any change in Jaques and maintain that his cynicism is confirmed by his departure at the end.[21] Jamieson says that Jaques' departure from the marriage celebration is consistent with his character; however, he adds, "his predictions for the future lives of the others have perception and even authority."[22] He does not mention that the balanced tone and vision of this speech is unprecedented in Jaques' behavior to this point. John Russell Brown states that a change has taken place:

> Jaques cannot join the dance which celebrates the new order of the lovers; unappeased, he must seek more matter for his contemplation. But having seen them all endure "shrewd days and nights" (V.iv.179), he accepts this as testimony of their inward virtues, and, for the first time in the play, sees promise of order, not of disorder.[23]

I agree with Brown's argument, but it still leaves unanswered the question, why is Jaques "unappeased"? The general confusion over Jaques' position in the final scene rests, I believe, on the failure to keep in mind the distinction between practiced fashionable melancholy and genuine intellectual melancholy. The conversion that one must expect, or hope, for Jaques is not one from cynical philosopher to reveler but one from fashionable intellectual to true intellectual—and it takes place. As cynicism lies at the core of the fashion, its absence in the final scene is a crucial indication of Jaques' change. Jaques' pleasures, not unlike the Duke's, are intellectual. He is entertained in this last scene by Touchstone's account of dueling just as he was entertained earlier by his moralizing on time, and the Duke here as before joins in Jaques' pleasure: "By my faith, he is very swift and sententious"; "I like him very well" (V.iv.66, 55). And so do we. It would be wrong to censure Jaques' pleasure in moral matter as either unnatural or unprofitable. We might as well condemn the concept of the contemplative life. His intention to join the repentant Duke Frederick because "Out of these convertites / There is much matter to be heard and learn'd" (V.iv.190–91) echoes the good Duke's stated pleasure in disputing with Jaques.

The significant change, then, is not in his interests but in his vision. He has come to see the natures of the Arden inhabitants, including his own, and has replaced rancor with measure. The following speech could not be that of a malcontent or would-be malcontent:

> (To Duke Senior)   You to your former honour I bequeath;
> Your patience and your virtue well deserves it:
> (To Orlando)   You to a love, that your true faith doth merit:
> (To Oliver)   You to your land, and love, and great allies:
> (To Silvius)   You to a long and well-deserved bed.
> (To Touchstone)   And you to wrangling; for thy loving voyage
> Is but for two months victuall'd. So to
>   your pleasures;
> I am for other than for dancing measures.
>
> *(V.iv.192–99)*

As this is the last major speech in the play, it would be strange indeed if we were not to respect the speaker. It is still Jaques speaking. He still enjoys passing judgments, but the vision now is personal, not abstract. His judgments here fit the conditions, whereas formerly conditions were fitted to his preformed judgments. Were he like Malvolio, he would merely have left the scene with a few harsh words for the Duke, Rosalind, and Orlando, who purged his humor with rather harsh physic; but his misanthropy was never convincing and finally has been abandoned. Jaques' former practiced unsociability in telling Amiens "I have been all this day to avoid him [the Duke]" (II.v.35) contrasts with his departing statement to the Duke, "What you would have / I'll stay to know at your abandon'd cave" (V.iv.201–2). He no longer plays the malcontent by such actions as calling for music and then saying that he dislikes it. He does not disdain the dancing and pastime. He only sees that in choosing the sober intellectual and religious life, he is choosing not to participate in the pleasures allied to court and marriage.[24] His departure is not absurd, as his former poses of unsociability had seemed, but is fitting and calls for reluctant acceptance, not censure, from those who like his company but respect his choice.

Notes:

1. Quotations of Webster are from *The Complete Works of John Webster*, ed. F. L. Lucas, 4 vols. (London: Chatto & Windus, 1927).
2. *The Revenger's Tragedy*, ed. R. A. Foakes (Cambridge: Harvard Univ. Press, 1966).
3. See I.iii.48–60 and IV.v.105–18 in *The Malcontent*, ed. M. L. Wine (Lincoln: Univ. of Nebraska Press, 1964). All quotations are from this edition.
4. Quotations of Shakespeare are from *The Complete Plays and Poems of William Shakespeare*, ed. William Allen Neilson and Charles Jarvis Hill (Cambridge, Mass.: Houghton, 1942).
5. *Bussy D'Ambois*, ed. Nicholas Brooke (Cambridge: Harvard Univ. Press, 1964).
6. "To our English Terence, Mr. Will. Shake-speare," *The Scourge of Folly*, included in E. K. Chambers and Charles Williams, *A Short Life of Shakespeare with the Sources* (Oxford: Clarendon Press, 1933), p. 208.
7. One expects that Jonson's Macilente *(Every Man out of His Humour)* will be developed as a comic humorous malcontent type from the playwright's character sketch of him in the dramatis personae: "A Man well parted, a sufficient Scholler, and trauail'd . . . wanting that place in the worlds account, which he thinks his merit capable of" *(Works,* ed. C. H. Herford and Percy Simpson [Oxford: Clarendon Press, 1927], III, 423). However, Jonson does not really concern himself with setting up a malcontent for satiric examination and exposure but rather places Macilente outside the malcontent's customary environment of the educated aristocracy and amidst the common folk where, like Jack Juggler or the witty servant of Roman comedy, he brings out the follies of all around him through a clever plot. The malcontent background of the prefatory sketch is thus a poorly integrated trapping on an old dramatic type.
8. Eugene Waith, *The Pattern of Tragicomedy in Beaumont and Fletcher* (New Haven: Yale Univ. Press, 1952), p. 82.
9. *Philological Quarterly,* 14 (1935), 237–52, esp. 250.
10. For the definitive study of the Aristotelian and Renaissance idea that melancholy was the natural condition of the intellectual, see Raymond Klibansky, Erwin Panofsky, and Fritz Saxl, *Saturn and Melancholy* (London: Thomas Nelson & Sons, 1964).
11. "As You Like It," in *Twentieth Century Interpretations of "As You Like It,"* ed. Jay L. Halio (Englewood Cliffs, N.J.: Prentice-Hall, 1968), pp. 66–67. Miss Gardner's article originally appeared in *More Talking of Shakespeare,* ed. John Garrett (London: Longmans, 1959; rpt. New York: Theater Arts Books, 1959), pp. 17–32.
12. *Albrecht Dürer* (Princeton: Princeton Univ. Press, 1948), I, 166.
13. *As You Like It,* ed. Michael Jamieson (London: Edward Arnold, 1965), p. 17.
14. *Op. cit.*
15. *The Life and Complete Works in Prose and Verse of Robert Greene,* ed. A. B. Grossart (1881–86; rpt. New York: Russell & Russell, 1964), XII, 172. *The Works of Thomas Nashe,* ed. R. B. McKerrow (London: Sidgwick & Jackson, 1910), I, 169–70.
16. See, for example, Robert Markham's letter to Harington regarding the Queen's reaction to his satirical discourse on privies, *The Metamorphosis of Ajax* in *Nugae Antiquae,* ed. T. Park (1804; rpt. New York: AMS, 1966), I, 239–40.
17. T. W. Baldwin, *William Shakspere's Small Latine & Lesse Greeke* (Urbana: Univ. of Illinois Press, 1944), I, 652–73. Other articles on Jaques' seven-ages-of-man

speech include William E. Miller, "All the World's a Stage," *Notes and Queries,* 208 (1963), 99–101; Cecil C. Seronsy, "The Seven Ages of Man Again," *Shakespeare Quarterly,* 4 (1953), 364–65; and John W. Draper, "Jaques' 'Seven Ages' and Bartholomaeus Anglicus," *Modern Language Notes,* 54 (1939), 273–76.

18. See *An Humourous Day's Mirth* in *The Plays and Poems of George Chapman,* ed. Thomas Marc Parrott (London: George Routledge and Sons, 1914) II, 71–72; and *The Malcontent,* I.ii.24–28.

19. See Lucas, II, 33 and 235.

20. For Shakespeare's attention, in general, to the vice of ingratitude see Curtis Watson, *Shakespeare and the Renaissance Concept of Honor* (Princeton: Princeton Univ. Press, 1960), pp. 222–23.

21. All three of the following articles are included in *Twentieth Century Interpretations of "As You Like It"*: Jenkins, *"As You Like It,"* p. 36; Halio, " 'No Clock in the Forest': Time in *As You Like It,"* p. 92, n. 6; and Gardner, *"As You Like It,"* p. 67. Jenkins' article originally appeared in *Shakespeare Survey,* 8 (1955), 40–51, and Halio's in *Studies in English Literature,* 2 (1962), 197–207.

22. Jamieson, p. 19.

23. *Shakespeare and his Comedies* (London: Methuen, 1957), p. 156.

24. Compare Shakespeare's distinguishing the life and the world of the courtier and the scholar in *Hamlet,* where, in careful juxtaposition, he has Laertes and Hamlet request Claudius' permission to return to Paris and Wittenberg respectively.

"After Their Fashion":
Cicero and Brutus in *Julius Caesar*

MARVIN L. VAWTER

For a fuller recognition of Shakespeare's symbolic artistry in *Julius Caesar*, Cicero's few lines exchanged with Casca in Act I, scene iii provide a point of view. After listening skeptically to Casca's awesome account of the supernatural events supposedly occurring during the terrible thunder storm and to what Casca thinks they portend, Cicero simply replies,

> Indeed, it is a strange-disposed time:
> But men may construe things, after their fashion,
> Clean from the purpose of the things themselves.
>
> *(I.iii.33–35)*

This characterization of Cicero—albeit brief—is historically precise, suggesting once again Shakespeare's familiarity with Cicero's works. The historical Cicero was fundamentally a skeptic and Shakespeare's concise portrait of him emphasizes this trait. But more relevant to *Caesar* may be Cicero's treatise attacking the widespread supersitions in Rome called *De Divinatione*.[1] Cicero did not believe in divination and augury and thought such superstitious practices were extremely stupid, even dangerous. Singling out the Stoics as the most notorious defenders and practicers of divination throughout the work, he uses them as his chief opponent, saying, for example:

> I wish (God) had made the Stoics wise, so that they would not be so pitiably and distressingly superstitious and so prone to believe everything they hear!
>
> *(II.xli.)*[2]

One by one, Cicero refutes the Stoics for their belief in divination through searching sacrificial entrails, soothsaying, portentous lightning and thunder, the flights of birds, astrological signs, dreams, and ghostly apparitions. "Superstition," says Cicero in summary,

> has taken advantage of human weakness to cast its spell over the mind of . . . man. We must tear this superstition up by the roots

205

. . . . For superstition is ever at your heels to urge you on. . . . It is
with you when you listen to a prophet, or an omen; when you offer
sacrifices or watch the flight of birds; when it thunders or light-
ens . . . or when some so-called prodigy is born or is made; . . . no
one who believes in them can ever remain in a tranquil state of mind.

(II.lxxii)

I am convinced that Shakespeare knew *De Divinatione* and used it to help
shape the point of view in *Caesar*. Not only does Shakespeare have Cicero
appear and speak lines only during the discussion of portents—and speak
perfectly in character—but Cicero's catalogue of portents and practices of
divination is much closer in detail and completeness to those in *Caesar* than
is Plutarch's account.[3] More important, Cicero's work offered Shakespeare
extended commentary on and psychological insight into the fatalistic personalities of Roman Stoics, particularly the distorted, even perverse syllogisms with which Stoics rationalized events—events they may only have
imagined—as signs of Fate and "reasoned" about the future. To be able to
prophesy the future, argues Cicero, the Stoics

take propositions for granted which are not conceded at all; yet a
chain of reasoning, to be valid, should proceed from premises which
are not doubtful to the conclusion which is in dispute . . . your Stoic
friends assume as certain what is the subject of doubt and discussion.

(II.xlix–l)

Throughout *De Divinatione,* therefore, Cicero refutes Stoic epistemology,
because men may simply not see and hear what they think they do, and
Stoic fatalism, because equivocal events may lead to imprudent action or
total resignation.[4]

Now all of this is directly relevant to *Caesar*. As I have shown elsewhere,
Stoic philosophy is very much a part of the play's focus.[5] Particularly, the
Stoic veneration of reason and their reliance on sense perception for the
accumulation of knowledge is examined in *Caesar* in microscopic detail.
Time after time, men relying on their reason to interpret events which they
have seen or heard "construe things, after their fashion, / Clean from the
purpose of the things themselves." The "construing" (which in the sixteenth century could mean constructing or shaping as well as interpreting)
occurs at two different levels: literally, events are "construed"; and, symbolically, human beings are reshaped into something else. In both cases, a
fundamental belief in the inexorable power of Fate motivates the construer.

The first instance of "construing" the meteorological phenomena occurs as soon as Cicero exits. Cassius enters and Casca repeats his fears about the strange events. Cassius, on the other hand, believes it is a "very pleasing night to honest men" (I.iii.43) and goes on to explain his view of the night's unusual happenings:

> if you would consider the true cause
>
> . . . . .
>
> Why all these things change from their ordinance,
> Their natures, and pre-formed faculties,
> To monstrous quality, why, you shall find
> That heaven hath infus'd them with these spirits
> To make them instruments of fear and warning
> Unto some monstrous state.
>
> *(I.iii.62,66–71)*

The notable aspect of Cassius' words here is their ambiguity. Though Cassius is speaking about the supposed portents, clearly Shakespeare means for us to apply the words to the men in this world who have repudiated God's "ordinance" by changing "Their natures, and pre-formed faculties, / To monstrous quality;" and the "monstrous state" is both the politic soul and the human soul. The conspiracy, we remember, has a "monstrous visage," and Cassius himself draws an analogy between the events and the "prodigious" Caesar (I.iii.77). Later Caesar echoes Cassius' words again when he warns that flattery may "turn pre-ordinance and first decree / Into the law of children" (III.i.38–39).

The most obvious example of divination as a symbolic method of characterization is Caesar's attitude toward the portents. Given an interpretation of Calphurnia's dream by Decius that contradicts hers, Caesar, construing things after his fashion, chooses to believe the one that most agrees with his conception of himself: "And this way have you well expounded it," says Caesar to Decius after having heard himself portrayed as a god in Decius' interpretation (II.ii.91). When told that the priests, in their "sacrifice" of an animal in order to search its entrails for omens, "could not find a heart within the beast," Caesar immediately shapes this to his own liking:

> The gods do this in shame of cowardice:
> Caesar should be a beast without a heart
> If he should stay at home to-day for fear.
>
> *(II.ii.41–43)*

Thus ignoring his own best instincts and those of Calphurnia, Caesar goes off to the Capitol to have his head literally severed from his heart and body.

Cicero's *De Divinatione* discusses at some length the implications of the same beast without a heart—in much greater detail than Plutarch's account. To Cicero, Caesar's death was his own fault and had no relation to Fate. His pride and vanity blinded him to the obvious signs of discontent and plotting among the nobles. When Cicero comments on the beast with no heart, he therefore treats the whole episode as a symbolic reflection of Caesar's ego:

> How does it happen that you understand . . . that the bull could not have lived without a heart and do not realize . . . that the heart could not suddenly have vanished I know not where? . . . I suspect that the bull's heart, as a result of a disease, became much wasted and shrunken and lost its resemblance to a heart. But, assuming that only a little while before the heart was in the sacrificial bull, why do you think it suddenly disappeared at the very moment of immolation? Don't you think, rather, that the bull lost his heart when he saw that Caesar in his purple robe had lost his head?
>
> *(II.xvi.)*

The passage rings with the same images that Shakespeare uses throughout *Caesar* as unifying symbols: disease—heart—head. Shakespeare's interest in recounting the omen is also the same as Cicero's: he is much less concerned with the validity of the omen than he is in how Caesar reacts to it and what that reaction demonstrates about his character. Shakespeare's Caesar is not the victim of Fate; indeed, he has many opportunities to perceive the dangers and avoid them. Had he listened to his own fears about Cassius, read Artemidorus' letter, listened to the Soothsayer's prophecy,[6] or been able to see through Decius' obvious sycophancy, he would not have died. Rather, Caesar is his own worst enemy, dividing his mind from his heart, his rational soul from his sensitive soul. The Soothsayer hoped to "beseech him to befriend himself" (II.iv.30), but Caesar, like Brutus with himself at war, ignores anything that "touches us ourself." Caesar *is* a beast without a heart, not because he feels fear but because he ignores the emotion. But other Stoic Romans in the play have also lost contact with their hearts, and Shakespeare has them reenact the sacrifice of the beast in desperate and maniacal efforts to search their own entrails for a heart no longer there. As he commits suicide, Cassius commands Pindarus to help him: "with this good sword, / That ran through Caesar's bowels, search this bosom" (V.iii.41–42). Upon seeing Cassius' body, Titinius picks up the same sword and says, "Come, Cassius' sword and find Titinius' heart" (V.iii.90). Finally, Brutus, shortly before he plunges his sword into his own chest, looks down at the bodies of Cassius and Titinius and says,

> O Julius Caesar, thou art mighty yet!
> Thy spirit walks abroad, and turns our swords
> In our own proper entrails.
>
> *(V.iii.94–96)*

But Caesar's spirit has had nothing to do with Cassius' death; Cassius dies, like Caesar, because of his corrupted senses and judgment. His own "pre-formed faculties" are miserably weak and mislead him. The Stoics believed that knowledge and wisdom are the results of sense impressions—particularly sight and sound—being received by the mind and judged true by the reason; the senses they deemed trustworthy. The anti-Stoics, how-ever, ridiculed this belief because of daily proof that the senses are limited, the mind feeble, and they warned of the dangers of acting only in accor-dance with such data.

At significant intervals throughout *Caesar,* we are reminded of "infirm" faculties. Caesar is deaf in one ear, Caius Ligarius has an unhealthy ear, and Brutus' inadequate vision is the subject of his first interchange with Cassius. Now these early suggestions of feeble senses become central to the action and to the play's thematic statement. Seeing what he thinks is a "fire" near his tents, Cassius sends Titinius to investigate. He then sends Pindarus up to a hill to see and report what happens to Titinius, because, says Cassius, "My sight was ever thick" (V.iii.21). Pindarus' narration of what he sees and hears is a crucial echo of Brutus' mistaken interpretation of the shouts in I.ii:[7]

> *Pindarus.*   Now, Titinius! now some light. O, he lights too!
> He's ta'en!
>   And, hark! they shout for joy.
> *Cassius.*   Come down; behold no more.
> O, coward that I am, to live so long,
> To see my best friend ta'en before my face!
>
> *(V.iii.31–35)*

The manifold irony, of course, is that not only do the shouts not mean what Cassius thinks they do, but Cassius has not *seen* anything! Pindarus is the only one who views what happens. Yet Cassius says he has seen his "best friend ta'en before my face!" After Cassius has killed himself, Titinius and Messala return, see the dead Cassius, and cry out in grief at the gruesome mistake. Messala underscores the significance of Cicero's original comment:

> Mistrust of good success hath done this deed.
> O hateful Error, Melancholy's child,
> Why dost thou show to the apt thoughts of men
> The things that are not?
>
> *(V.iii.66–69)*

In words that remind us of Cicero's speech, Titinius adds his own lament: "thou has misconstrued everything" (V.iii.84). Thus the man who was once "a great observer" and who could see "through the deeds of men" (I.ii.199–200) now lies dead as the result of his own blind judgment which made him see the "things that are not."

The question then must be why did Cassius have "apt thoughts"; why was he so ready to believe that Titinius had been captured? In fact, the larger and more significant question must be why is Cassius of Act V not the same self-assured, skeptical independent Cassius that we have seen in Act I? Implied in the structure of the fourth act is the answer to these questions.

At the beginning of Act IV, Shakespeare shows us the new triumvirate—Antony, Octavius, and Lepidus—cavalierly trading human lives. What we are to make of this short scene in terms of understanding Octavius and Lepidus is difficult to say. But when Lepidus exits (IV.i.11.s.d.), we do get an important perspective on the noble Antony. Antony ridicules Lepidus as "a slight unmeritable man" (IV.i.12), but Octavius defends him as "a tried and valiant soldier" (IV.i.28). Antony retorts,

> So is my horse, Octavius, and for that
> I do appoint him store of provender.
> It is a creature that I teach to fight,
> To wind, to stop, to run directly on,
> His corporal motion govern'd by my spirit.
>
> *(IV.i.29–33)*

To conclude his characterization of Lepidus as a mere mindless body, Antony calls him a "barren-spirited fellow" (IV.i.36).

As much as this brief interchange may give us a perspective on Antony, we should also realize that Antony's treatment of Lepidus is but another mirror of Brutus' attitude towards his own body and the bodies of human beings all around him. Immediately after this scene, Shakespeare stages the quarrel between Brutus and Cassius. Precisely the same disdain Antony shows for Lepidus can be seen in Brutus for Cassius. Before Cassius enters, Brutus describes him as one of the "hollow men" that are "like horses hot at hand," full of "gallant show" but unable to endure (IV.ii.23–25). Obviously, Brutus' view of Cassius at this moment parallels Antony's view of Lepidus: Brutus also conceives of Cassius as little more than a horse and a "barren-spirited" man. To enforce this fact, Shakespeare adds the quarrel scene in which Brutus brutally destroys the spirit of Cassius. In further echo of Antony, Brutus calls Cassius a "slight man" (IV.iii.37); he berates, degrades, and finally dictates to Cassius, who ends by calling himself a "bondman" (IV.iii.96) to Brutus. "O, I could weep / My spirit from mine eyes" (IV.iii.98–99), cries Cassius. Just as the Stoic Brutus had destroyed part of his own spirit and had gone on to eliminate the independent souls of Caius Ligarius and Portia, culminating in what he thought was the destruction of Caesar's spirit, so he now obliterates the spirit of Cassius. With the same disdain that Antony had shown for Lepidus' skill as a soldier, Brutus refuses to listen to Cassius' battle strategy. "Hear me good brother" (IV.iii.211), pleads Cassius, but Brutus—always the man of "reason"—ignores him and gives "reasons" (IV.iii.202) to refute Cassius' plan: their armies must attack first, Brutus says, because

> We, at the height, are ready to decline.
> There is a tide in the affairs of men,
> Which, taken at the flood, leads on to fortune;
> Omitted, all the voyages of their life
> Is bound in shallows and in miseries.
>
> *(IV.iii.216–19)*

Brutus' analogy, an argument to Nature typical of the Stoics, is stretched beyond validity. Essentially a piece of fatalism, the analogy fails to recognize the possibility of another tide and another opportune moment for the battle. Nonetheless, even though Cassius knows full well that Brutus' plan is a mistake, he answers submissively, "Then, with your will, go on"

(IV.iii.223). Wholly under the rule of Brutus, Cassius becomes a man void of his own will, a "hollow" creature whose "corporal motion" is governed by 'Brutus' already divided and decaying soul. Cassius' parting words to Brutus symbolically describe what has happened to all these "virtuous" men:

> This was an ill beginning of the night.
> Never come such division 'tween our souls!
>
> *(IV.iii.235–36)*

From the literal level of political and social turmoil to the symbolic depths of the human soul, Shakespeare shows us the ravages of division and, in the last act especially, the utter desperation and inevitable failure to which it leads.

Students of Shakespeare have frequently noted the change of attitude toward omens manifested by Cassius during the course of *Caesar*. At first convinced that extraordinary phenomena have little significance and that "Men at some time are masters of their fates: / The fault . . . is not in our stars, / But in ourselves" (I.ii.137–39), Cassius grows progressively fatalistic. Just before the climactic battle, Cassius evinces a complete resignation to the power of Fate:

> This is my birth-day; as this very day
> Was Cassius born. Give me thy hand, Messala:
> Be thou my witness that against my will
> (As Pompey was) am I compell'd to set
> Upon one battle all our liberties.
> You know that I held Epicurus strong,[8]
> And his opinion; now I change my mind
> And partly credit things that do presage.
>
> *(V.i.72–79)*

After describing the eagles who once sat on their ensign and are now replaced by carrion birds, Cassius relates what he thinks this omen signifies. The ravenous birds, he says,

> downward look on us,
> As we were sickly prey; their shadows seem
> A canopy most fatal, under which
> Our army lies, ready to give up the ghost.
>
> *(V.i.86–89)*

Cassius' change of mind reveals to what extent Brutus' mind dominates Cassius' spirit. In decision after decision, Brutus has imposed his will on Cassius; yet Brutus has "rul'd" (V.i.47) without serious objection from Cassius. Nonetheless, as if he is compelled to rationalize his own impassivity to Brutus' tyranny, Cassius construes the birds as a fatal omen of their defeat. But it is clear—even from the way Cassius has yoked together Brutus' despotism and the fatal omens—that Brutus is Cassius' Fate and that he has indeed given "up the ghost"—his soul—to make his body one of the "mortal instruments" to Brutus' "genius." Brutus the "exorcist" has once again "conjur'd" the "mortified spirit" (II.i.323–24) out of a human being, turning him into "sickly prey." Significantly, Cassius closes his rumination on Fate with words that sound as if they came from the Stoic mind of Brutus:

> I am fresh of spirit, and resolv'd
> To meet all perils very constantly.
>
> *(V.i.93)*

There thus emerges a different Cassius; the same man who had scoffed at the notion that men could be constant (I.ii.309) is now possessed of the disease that consumed Portia. And just as Portia's tongue, cut off from her sickened heart, sent a lie to Brutus, so Cassius turns to Brutus to speak in contradiction to his pessimistic feelings:

> Now, most noble Brutus,
> The gods to-day stand friendly, that we may,
> Lovers in peace, lead on our days to age!
>
> *(V.i.93–95)*

Cassius is lying, for the will to fight and hope of success have been sucked out of him. His pretended optimism, in fact, is betrayed as he goes on to say,

> But since the affairs of men rest still incertain,
> Let's reason with the worst that may befall.
>
> *(V.i.96–97)*

With these extremely important words, Cassius brings the events of *Caesar* full circle. At this point, two central facets of the tragedy are apparent: first of all, Brutus has "misconstrued" or reshaped everyone he has touched into an imitation of himself—"after his fashion," in other words, and "clean from the purpose" for which human beings were originally created. The words of Cicero's warning resound in Brutus' speeches throughout the play. He says of Caius Ligarius, "Send him hither, and I'll fashion him" (II.i.220), and shortly thereafter he changes Ligarius into a "heart new fir'd." To Portia, just before he infects her with his sickness, Brutus promises,

> by and by thy bosom shall partake
> The secrets of my heart.
> All my engagements I will *construe* to thee,
> All the charactery of my sad brows.
>
> *(II.i.305–308;* italics mine)

The result is that Portia is made over into a hideous parody of Brutus' Stoicism. Now, Cassius has been reconstructed as a puppetlike image of Brutus. Second, fundamental to the plot of *Caesar* is Brutus' Stoic epistemology and fatalism, for the conspiracy began with the greatest misconstruction of them all when Brutus began to "reason with the worst that may befall" about Caesar.

Earlier Brutus had misconstrued the meaning of the shouts he heard coming from the festival. Twice the shouts occur (I.ii.77.s.d. and 130.s.d.) and each time he mistakes their significance. In support of this distorted reasoning about the shouts, Brutus finds the letter, actually written by Cassius, which he believes must be from the people (II.i.46ff); again, he mistakes an appearance for a fact and interprets the sketchy letter after his fashion—that is, he seizes upon the slightest evidence to bolster his own attitude. The misinterpretations of sounds and appearances, therefore, initiate the conspiracy just as they bring about its disastrous end.

With these facts as background, we can approach Brutus' now famous syllogism on Caesar's ambition with a fresh perspective. Actually the formal argument only appears to be a logical syllogism but is in reality a monstrous piece of rationalization, a tissue of words built to cover over a subjective conclusion that Brutus has already drawn. The psuedo-syllogism begins and ends with the same resolution, thereby betraying its circularity: "It must be by his death" (II.i.10), Brutus begins, and the termination of the argument merely restates the original hypothesis: "therefore . . . kill him" (II.i.32,34). But the middle terms of the syllogism form the epitome of Cicero's prediction on how men "construe things, after their fashion, / Clean from the purpose of the things themselves." The first movement of the argument requires Brutus to reshape Caesar:

He would be crown'd:
How that might change his nature, there's the question.
It is the bright day that brings forth the adder,
And that craves wary walking.

(II.i.12–14)

Notice how Brutus admits that Caesar has not changed his nature yet; instead, Brutus himself changes the nature of Caesar by first making him into an "adder" in order to proceed to the conclusion that Caesar must be killed:

And since the quarrel
Will bear no colour for the *thing* he is,
Fashion it thus: that what he is, augmented,
Will run to these and these extremities;
And therefore think him as a serpent's egg,
Which, hatch'd, would, as his kind, grow mischievous,
And kill him in the shell.

(II.i.28–34; italics mine)

Nothing more clearly illustrates the historical Cicero's charge against the Stoics that they construct false syllogisms and practice "verbal legerdemain." To make his syllogism fit his previously announced verdict, Brutus has "fashioned" Caesar into a venomous "thing," gone on to argue blithely according to the nature of the "kind," and neatly arrived at his predetermined goal. But Brutus has not only "reasoned with the worst that may befall"; he has "reasoned" the impossible.

Furthermore, within the terms of his argument, Brutus lays the foundation for his own moral condemnation. Reasoning according to a "common proof" (II.i.21) that men climbing the ladder of ambition eventually turn vicious, Brutus concludes that the same viciousness, though there is no sign of it yet, will no doubt appear in Caesar and he will become dangerous: "So Caesar *may*; / Then lest he *may, prevent*" (II.i.27–28; italics mine). Later, however, when Cassius says that he and Brutus should "reason with the worst," Brutus applies a different standard to himself:

Even by the rule of that philosophy
By which I did blame Cato for the death
Which he did give himself, I know not how,
But I do find it cowardly and vile,

> For fear of *what might fall, so to prevent*
> The time of life.
>
> (*V.i.101–106,* italics mine)

In other words, Brutus did not consider Cato's suicide a reasonable departure in line with Stoicism's limited approval of self-slaughter because Cato
killed himself "to prevent" what might have happened if he were captured; but on precisely the same basis—to prevent what might have happened to Caesar *if* he were crowned—he generates a plot to murder him, a
plot that we must therefore conclude is "cowardly and vile." The whole
specious chain of reasoning is but one more example of the Stoic Wise
Man's continual application of a double standard to himself and others.

There must also be significance in the fact that Brutus' twisted
argument—which becomes a visionary's dream and prophecy—occurs in
the middle of the night when everyone else is asleep. Calling to Lucius to
"Awake" (II.i.5), Brutus remarks that he would like to sleep as soundly as
his servant. Portia later mentions his inability to sleep (II.i.252). Inserted in
the letter he receives, however, is a challenge to him to "awake, and see
thyself" (II.i.46). Then, in his funeral address, Brutus adheres to Stoic epistemology when he says to the crowd, "Censure me in your wisdom, and
awake your senses, that you may the better judge" (III.ii.16–18). These
many allusions to sleeping come to a symbolic climax in Act IV when
Brutus confronts a second vision of Caesar for which he had not bargained.
In a sense, however, Shakespeare has prepared his audience for the coming of Caesar's ghost by placing the episode within a symbolic setting. Following the quarrel scene, in which Brutus has several times illustrated his
corrupted judgment, Brutus tells Cassius to go to bed because

> The deep of night is crept upon our talk,
> And nature must obey necessity,
> Which we will niggard with a little rest.
>
> (*IV.iii.225–27*)

This is really a false division characteristic of the Stoic Brutus throughout
the play: nature and necessity are mutually dependent and must be in
harmonious balance, but Brutus divides them and makes one the slave of
the other. Seven lines later, Cassius laments the "division 'tween our
souls" (IV.iii.234). These lines from Brutus and Cassius act as a preliminary
orchestration for the next movement. Instead of going to sleep as he had
said he must do, Brutus discovers the book in "the pocket of my gown"

which he had accused Lucius of losing (IV.iii.251–54)—another instance of Brutus' faulty judgment. He then asks Lucius to "touch thy instrument a strain or two" (IV.iii.256).

Clearly, if we have been sensitive to the many indications of Brutus' perversion of his soul, we are prepared to see this scene as a dramatic image of spiritual disharmony. As Lucius plays "a sleepy tune" (IV.iii.266) upon his "instrument," the gentle servant boy slowly falls asleep, but Brutus resists what he calls "murd'rous slumber" (IV.iii.266), thereby ignoring his bodily needs as he has all along. Rather than sleep, Brutus picks up his book (of "philosophy," no doubt) and begins to read. As he does, he calls attention to his sense of sight again—just as Cassius emphasizes his poor eyesight prior to "seeing" what he thought was the capture of Titinius. "Let me see" (IV.iii.272), murmurs Brutus as he begins reading. At this symbolic moment, with Lucius, Varro and Claudius asleep, the "instrument" no longer playing, and Brutus reading rather than taking his much-needed rest in the "wholesome" (II.i.264) bed with Portia, the Ghost of Caesar enters (IV.iii.273.s.d.). Once more, Brutus underscores the inadequacy of his sight:

> How ill this taper burns! Ha! who comes here?
> I think it is the weakness of mine eyes
> That shapes this monstrous apparition.
>
> *(IV.iii.274–76)*

When he questions the identity of the ghost, the apparition replies, "Thy evil spirit, Brutus" (IV.iii.281). As soon as the ghost has vanished, Brutus calls to his servants to "awake" so as to verify what he has seen. Lucius, thinking that he is still playing his instrument, drowsily answers, "The strings, my lord, are false" (IV.iii.290). What we have watched in this brief scene, it seems to me, is an extremely concise but crucial dramatic symbol of Brutus' moral decay. As Brutus reads rather than sleeps, he testifies to the enforced division he has created between his rational and sensitive soul. Attempting to live solely in the mind, Brutus' Stoic soul no longer enjoys the spiritual harmony that obtains through the mutual interchange of mind and body. His body should be as much the "instrument" of the soul as is the mind, two chords of spiritual being that when sounded together bring harmony into the life of a man. With one of those chords unused, "The strings . . . are false"; and Brutus, like Cassius, sees the "things that are not."

Sir John Davies, in his elegy entitled "The Soul of Man," a part of *Nosce*

Teipsum published early in the same year (1599) in which *Caesar* seems to have appeared, speaks of the necessary harmony between mind and body, both of which are "instruments" of the soul, that must occur before man achieves spiritual wholeness. If the "brain" tries to act without the cooperation of the "heart," the partial man, bereft of the "Motive Virtue . . . in the heart below," is powerless to find moral goodness:

> The mutual love, the kind intelligence
>   'Twixt heart and brain, this Sympathy doth bring.
> From the kind heat, which in the heart doth reign,
>   The spirits of Life do their beginning take!
>   . . . . .
> Thus the Soul tunes the Body's instrument;
>   These harmonies She makes with Life and Sense:
>   The organs fit, are by the Body lent;
>   But th'actions flow from the Soul's influence.[9]

Shakespeare's rendering of spiritual harmony, whether or not derived from Davies, takes its authority from Elizabethan commonplaces concerning the body as an "instrument" of the soul. Clearly then, the appearance of Brutus' "evil spirit" in the shape of Caesar at the moment when the instrument is silent symbolizes Brutus' spiritual somnambulism; Brutus' moral soul is asleep and his "evil spirit" is thereby unleashed from his body, "exorcised" out of him as it was out of Ligarius, Portia, and Cassius. That spirit takes the shape of Caesar because the Stoic Brutus *is* Caesar "augmented," as Cassius has said he is, and now the "prodigious grown" Caesar in Brutus "Would run to these and these extremities." Brutus, cut off from "the kind heat" of the heart and inflamed with the devouring fire of the mind,[10] has seen not the "spirits of Life" but a mirror of death in himself that will shortly make him literally destroy his physical body because, to use his own words, "He bears too great a mind" (V.i.113). "The evil that men do lives after them" (III.ii.77); so let it be with Brutus.

Notes:

1. Trans. William Armistead Falconer (Cambridge, Mass: Loeb Classics, 1964). It has been argued elsewhere that Shakespeare was familiar with *De Divinatione* in connection with *2 Henry VI*. See Karl Schmidt, *Margareta von Anjou vor und bei Shakespeare, Palaestra,* LIV (1906), p. 286. No one seems to have investigated the work in reference to *JC*. All citations from *Julius Caesar* are from the New Arden

Shakespeare, ed. T. S. Dorsch (Cambridge: Harvard Univ. Press, 1955).

2. I find it extremely curious that Joseph Chang, in an otherwise thorough study of Stoicism ("Shakespeare and Stoic Ethics," 2 vols., Diss. Univ. of Wisconsin 1965), should say that the Stoics believed that "there is no point in augury" (p. 274) and "omens reveal nothing of consequence to man" (p. 275). Chang is completely wrong here. On the contrary, it was because the Stoics revered Fate that they tried to divine Fate's will through all forms of divination and augury. Cicero tells us that the "stoics . . . defended nearly every sort of divination" and he lists the many treatises on divination written by famous Stoics: *De Divinatione,* I.iii.

3. It would require a separate study to document the point, but I hope it will be granted that Cicero's list of superstitious practices is remarkably close to the events in *JC.* The most interesting fact is that while Plutarch simply recounts the events in terse detail without commentary, Cicero discusses the contradictions, fallacies, and absurdities in such beliefs. Furthermore, he examines the kind of personality and moral character involved in such practices, especially in reference to Caesar, as I will show below.

4. With the exception of the entrance of Caesar's ghost (IV.iii.s.d.), which I shall shortly discuss, nothing supernatural occurs in *JC.* Many things, of course, are *said* to have happened, but these are in large part repeated secondhand. All we see, like Lear's Fool, is a very bad thunderstorm. The presence of cosmic Fate, in other words, is at best ambiguous.

5. " 'Division 'tween our souls': Shakespeare's Stoic Brutus," *Shakespeare Studies,* 7 (1974), 173–95. There I also discuss Brutus' misinterpretation of the shouts coming from the forum and his view of himself as a minister of Stoic Fate.

6. I think it significant that the Soothsayer tells Portia that he does not "know" of any danger to Caesar, only "much that I fear may chance" (II.iv.32). That is, the Soothsayer is working on instinct and/or common sense, not divination.

7. Brutus assumes the shouts which occur at I.ii.77.s.d. and 130.s.d. indicate that "the people / Choose Caesar for their king," and upon that assumption rests Brutus' argument for killing Caesar. But the shouts, Casca later explains, were not for that at all. Instead, the crowd shouted—and hissed—"according as he pleas'd and displeas'd them" (I.ii.256). The shouts of approval, in fact, occurred because "the common herd was glad he refus'd the crown" (I.ii.260–61).

8. The reference to Epicurus' disbelief in omens is another indication that Shakespeare, perhaps from *De Divinatione,* knew of the chief defenders of the omens—the Stoics—as well as the chief detractors—the Epicureans.

9. *Silver Poets of the 16th Century,* ed. and intro. Gerald Bullett (London: E. P. Dutton, 1947), pp. 377–78.

10. That we are to view Brutus as an obsessively cerebral character is clear from the many references in the play to his "mind," to his reliance on "reason," and to his ignoring of his bodily and emotional needs as evidence of his Stoic "constancy." Portia sums up the cerebral imagery surrounding Brutus when she says to him, "You have some sick offence within your mind" (II.i.268). As I have argued in the earlier article (see above, n.5), the imagery ultimately portrays Brutus as a disembodied mind in much the same way that the historical Cicero characterized the Stoic Wise Man.

Hamlet's Dream of Innocence

W. L. GODSHALK

Laurence Michel writes that "tragedy is consumated when the dream of innocence is confronted by the fact of guilt, and acquiesces therein."[1] Although Michel's "working formula," as he calls it, allows a rather wide variety of works to be called tragic, the formula conveniently indicates a fundamental approach to *Hamlet*; for the prince, though thirty, begins the play dreaming of innocence and personal integrity, and in the course of the action, this innocence and integrity are severely compromised. The play is essentially about this compromise and Hamlet's continuing adjustment to a world of seeming, a world in which pretense and artifice are used to cover the fact of guilt. Indeed the pretense and artifice become inextricably linked with the guilt which they cover, and by engaging in the strategies of pretense, Hamlet, in effect, acquiesces in the fact of guilt.

In Hamlet's first scene, Gertrude asks him why he allows the "common" occurrence of a father's death to seem "so particular" with him (I.ii.72, 75),[2] and his answer to his mother's probing is important in that it gives us an insight into the prince's initial attitude toward himself and toward the court:

> Seems, madam? Nay, it *is*. I know not "seems."
> 'Tis not alone my inky cloak, good mother,
> Nor customary suits of solemn black,
> Nor windy suspiration of forced breath,
> No, nor the fruitful river in the eye,
> Nor the dejected havior of the visage,
> Together with all forms, moods, shapes of grief,
> That can denote me truly. These indeed seem,
> For they are actions that a man might play,
> But I have that within which passes show;
> These but the trappings and the suits of woe.
>
> (I.ii.76–86; italics mine)

Hamlet sees himself as a complete rather than a fragmented man: he knows not "seems." In the sartorial context with the emphasis on clothes, he is probably punning that he knows not "seams," and the very pun as-

221

serts the coherence and the integrity of the inner and the outer man. Although he implies that his "inky cloak" is a true index to his inner feelings, he does so invertedly by insisting that outward actions—wearing black, sighing, weeping, those "shapes of grief"—cannot in truth characterize his grief. Outward manifestations of grief may be acted, and this observation brings us to the heart of "seems." Acting, in the sense of theatrical pretense, becomes one of the central symbols for the guilty facade of the court. In contrast, Hamlet insists that his inward feelings surpass anything that might be acted. Rather pedantically, he eschews pretense, and we may certainly catch a glimmer of pride in his declaration of integrity.

Indirectly he is drawing a contrast between himself and the court which surrounds him. The audience is already visually aware of the contrast, for Hamlet's black stands out somberly against the gaudy velvet of Claudius' court. Filled with theatrical pretense, Claudius' opening speech is spoken with a jocular familiarity:

> Though yet of Hamlet our dear brother's death
> The memory be green, and that it us befitted
> To bear our hearts in grief, and our whole kingdom
> To be contracted in one brow of woe,
> Yet so far hath discretion fought with nature
> That we with wisest sorrow think on him
> Together with remembrance of ourselves.
> Therefore our sometime sister, now our queen,
> Th' imperial jointress to this warlike state,
> Have we, as 'twere, with a defeated joy,
> With an auspicious and a dropping eye,
> With mirth in funeral, and with dirge in marriage,
> In equal scale weighing delight and dole,
> Taken to wife.

(I.ii.1–14)

Although Claudius' rhetoric ostensibly covers his offense against both the legal and the natural practice of marrying his brother's wife, the paradoxical phrasing—"defeated joy," "mirth in funeral," "Dirge in marriage"—unintentionally suggests the emotive fragmentation of the court world; and Hamlet's assertion of emotional integrity stands as an implied criticism. Claudius's speech is a mask; it only *seems*. The confidence he exudes is used to hide the fact that Denmark is "disjoint and out of frame" (l.20). Dressed uniformly in black, Hamlet proudly desires to be seen as a symbol of completeness and reality against which the duplicity and the seeming of the court may be measured.

His reaction, we may feel, is immature if not childish. Maturity allows us to accept death with a certain degree of equanimity, or at least to dissemble the depth of our feelings so as not to embarrass others. In Michel's phrase, Hamlet still lives in a "dream of innocence." At thirty, he still remains a student, and as Norman Holland has puckishly observed, "you can see him as a recognizable type that you might find around, say, New Haven or Harvard Square: the perpetual graduate student."[3] Holland's observation carries a good deal of critical weight, for it underlines the essential naiveté of the prince. While Laertes seeks Claudius' leave to return to Paris and the worldly joys of that city, Hamlet sues to return to his academic studies at Wittenberg, to scholarly seclusion. The contrast is meant to emphasize Hamlet's retiring nature, and we may imagine him speaking with the accents of the Viennese duke: "I have ever loved the life removed" (*MM*, I.iii.8). Hamlet's assertion that he knows not "seems" can then carry the additional meaning that, as a kind of Renaissance Santayana, he lacks insight into the world beyond the University walls, a world which sadly enough is filled with masks. O. B. Hardison suggests that *hamartia* may be glossed as "ignorance," and accepting that definition, we can see that Hamlet's *hamartia* is his ignorance of seeming.[4] He must learn how to live in a world of hidden motives, desires, and guilts, a world of actors where clothes do not reveal but cover the essential man.

In this context, the ghost may be seen as the supernatural aspect of seeming. What kind of ghost is it? "The spirit that I have seen / May be a devil, and the devil hath power / T'assume a pleasing shape," Hamlet theorizes (II.ii.605–607) some two months after hearing the ghost's story. Though some critics have been quick to dismiss this theory as Hamlet's insubstantial excuse to delay killing Claudius, we should think carefully before we reject Hamlet's suspicions as mere excuses. In the first scene, where the ghost appears for the second time to Barnardo and Marcellus, the apparition is never called "King Hamlet." It is "like the king" (I.i.43, 58, 110); and the similitude is emphasized. It is "this thing" (21), "this dreaded sight" (25); the ghost is always an "it" (143 ff.). The whole of the first scene indicates the similarity of the ghost to the dead king, but the equation is never made. The ghost *seems,* but *is* not. When Hamlet confronts the ghost, he will no longer be able to assert so confidently that he knows not seems.

Meeting the ghost, Hamlet must learn to deal with the subtle metaphysics of seeming, and to begin he does so bluntly, as befits a man who knows not seems. "Thou com'st in such a questionable shape / That I will speak to thee" (I.iv.43–44), he says, and while the shape may be dubious, worthy of question, he immediately decides on identification: "I'll call thee Hamlet, / King, father, royal Dane" (44–45). His response is indicative of a man who is not accustomed to dealing with the dubiety of reality, and he here without thought asserts identity in a situation where identity should be questioned and investigated. It is an index to Hamlet's awakening from his dream of innocence that, by the end of the second act, the ghost's identity is no longer taken for granted and his story is open to question. Hamlet has learned that the academic world of Wittenberg is not the dubious world of the Danish court.

It is significant that after his conference with the ghost, Hamlet himself turns to the arts of seeming, for if Hamlet's father has been literally poisoned through the ear, so figuratively has been Hamlet. Like Othello, Hamlet is poisoned with words. Hamlet *père*'s revelation of guilt poisons and corrupts the dream of innocence that his son is still partially able to keep. Hamlet's family has had, in his uncorrupted vision, an idyllic relationship:

> So excellent a king . . .
> . . . so loving to my mother
> That he might not beteem the winds of heaven
> Visit her face too roughly. . . .
> Why, she would hang on him
> As if increase of appetite had grown
> By what it fed on.
>
> *(I.ii.139–45)*

And now he learns from the ghost that Claudius has "won to his shameful lust / The will of my most seeming–virtuous queen" (I.v.45–46). The ghost's injunction, "Taint not thy mind" (85), is rendered impossible, ironically by the ghost itself. Hamlet's psyche has been tainted; his dream has been compromised; and he promises "from the table of my memory / I'll wipe away all trivial fond records" (98–99). Like his "reflector" Laertes,[5] Hamlet has not lacked a talebearer "to infect his ear / With pestilent speeches of his father's death" (IV.v.91–92). His family relationship has only *seemed* idyllic.

Immediately after the supernatural confrontation, Hamlet rejects his absolute "I know not 'seems'." If our interpretation is correct, Hamlet's change is initiated by the ghost's revelation of evil beneath the seeming good of the family relationship. Things are far less clear cut, and Hamlet now realizes emotively what before he had perhaps suspected intellectually: "one may smile, and smile, and be a villain" (I.v.108). Concomitantly Hamlet acknowledges a split in his own integrity between the outward action and the inward idea. Without revealing his reasoning, he decides to espouse his own brand of pretense: "I perchance hereafter shall think meet / To put an antic disposition on" (171–72), and the direct action he had promised the ghost—"Haste me to know't, that I, with wings as swift / As meditation or the thoughts of love, / May sweep to my revenge" (I.v.29–31)—is indefinitely deferred.

Why he decides to "put an antic disposition on" has been the subject of a good deal of scholarly inquiry, and lacking a clear statement from Hamlet, we are unlikely to reach a conclusive answer. Peter Alexander has suggested that Hamlet uses his seeming madness to tell Claudius that his guilt has been discovered. "Hamlet's victim must know what is coming to him. Hamlet cannot tell the King in so many words what to prepare for . . . but [he] can create a thundery atmosphere that threatens a stormy sequel."[6] The answer is an attractive one, and perhaps the desire to indicate to Claudius that he knows the truth as it has been revealed to him by the ghost does lie behind Hamlet's mask. But the point to be made here is that the ruse, if it is a ruse, fails, and Hamlet in his soliloquies never justifies his false seeming.

When Rosencrantz and Guildenstern question him, Hamlet informs them that "Denmark's a prison" (II.ii.247) and that he is "most dreadfully attended," i.e., carefully spied upon (274).[7] The remarks may be passed over as comments made to mislead two inept inquisitors, but there is a kernel of truth. Claudius murmurs, "Madness in great ones must not unwatched go" (III.i.189), indicating that by his pretended madness Hamlet has inhibited the scope of his action. At the beginning of the play, Claudius is more than willing to let bygones be bygones, "Be as ourself in Denmark" (I.ii.122), which may be interpreted as an invitation to Hamlet to assume the pretenses of the court. When the invitation is rejected, Claudius is determined that Hamlet "shall with speed to England" (III.i.170). Hamlet's madness, his initial attempt to act within the realm of "seems," has backfired. In his journey toward revenge, it is a false start.

In fact, Claudius counters Hamlet's antic pretense with his own pretenders: Rosencrantz and Guildenstern, and Ophelia. The first pair Hamlet sees through with a quickness that underlines their ineptitude: "Were you not sent for?" (II.ii.280), and after a muttered conference they admit that they are the king's spies. The rapidity with which they are disposed of as serious threats indicates not only their inconsequence as pretenders but also Hamlet's growing awareness of "seems." On the other hand, when Ophelia enters to act out her role as the forsaken lover, Hamlet is presented with a situation of deep emotional potential. Rosencrantz and Guildenstern are former friends; Ophelia is his present lover. The play which she acts is Claudius' equivalent to Hamlet's *Murder of Gonzago,* and, like Horatio and Hamlet at the latter, Claudius and Polonius are an attentive audience. And though he does see Polonius behind the arras—"Where's your father?" (III.i.130)—Hamlet is caught in the trap. Claudius has seen through the pretense: "Love? His affections do not that way tend, / Nor what he spake, though it lacked form a little, / Was not like madness" (163–65). Hamlet's mask disintegrates in the strong emotions generated by Ophelia's pretense.

Ironically, Claudius' amateur actors, Rosencrantz and Guildenstern, announce the expected arrival of the legitimate players, an arrival which leads to Hamlet's second attempt at seeming, a simile of his father's death: "I'll have these players / Play something like the murder of my father / Before mine uncle" (II.ii.601–603). If the ghost is the supernatural embodiment of Hamlet's problem, the players are the conventional symbols of seeming, for they create a world which is only virtually real: these are the actions that a man might play. As Aeneas (II.ii.453), the player assumes the role of a disinherited prince with a supernaturally imposed mission, the founding of Rome, while at the same time he describes to Dido the revenge of Pyrrhus, a prince who is exacting a grim vengeance for a dead father. Hamlet requests this speech because, of course, it recalls his basic situation, and, at the same time, also reflects his delay: Pyrrhus' sword "seemed i'th' air to stick. / So as a painted tyrant Pyrrhus stood, / And like a neutral to his will and matter / Did nothing" (II.ii.486–89). The final, incomplete line emphasizes his inaction, but after this moment's pause, Pyrrhus immediately kills Priam; momentary delay is followed instantly by precipitous action. In contrast, Hamlet rejects direct action for the seeming action of a play "like the murder." Compared to the heroic actions of Aeneas and Pyrrhus, Hamlet's actions are more closely allied to the virtually real actions of the player. Like the player whose rhetoric affects him so deeply, Hamlet has so far in the play acted only in the realm of words, the symbols of act and action.

Moreover, the evidence gathered at *The Murder of Gonzago* is far from conclusive. Horatio is strangely reticent about Claudius' supposedly guilty reaction to the play. "Didst perceive?" Hamlet asks him, and Horatio responds: "Very well, my lord. . . . I did very well note him" (III.ii.291–92, 294). Surely this is no strong confirmation of Hamlet's assertion, "I'll take the ghost's word for a thousand pound" (290–91). Why is Horatio so unwilling to commit himself? For one thing, the play is not simply a conjectural reenactment of the primal murder; it is an implied threat. The murderer in the play is not the king's brother but "Lucianus, nephew to the king" (248), and Hamlet punctuates the theatrical murder with a wild fury of words.[8] The king naturally enough calls for light and leaves hurriedly. No one in the court questions his hasty removal, and because of Hamlet's lack of subtlety, the reason for his leaving is never made clear. Is he afraid of Hamlet, or is he oppressed with guilt? The fact that the dumb show does not seem to embarrass the king suggests that the former is the most legitimate answer. He has been able to weather the reenactment of his crime, but Hamlet's threat of violence frightens him. Like Hamlet's antic disposition, the play is a failure at determining guilt. The built-in ambiguities, built-in because Hamlet essentially lacks the ability to deal in seeming, prohibit a final judgment, and only Hamlet's enthusiasm can blind him to the fact that the evidence is inconclusive. Hamlet has not caught the conscience of the king, and the skeptical Horatio can validly reserve his opinion.

In the scenes which immediately follow, Hamlet further reveals his inability to evaluate and deal with a world of seeming. As Claudius kneels in an attempt at prayer, he seems to be in a state of grace, and Hamlet believes that to kill him at this point would be "hire and salary" (III.iii.79), for Claudius would go, seemingly, to his heavenly reward. Meditating savagely and hubristically on a future vengeance which will damn Claudius' soul irretrievably to hell, Hamlet puts up his sword and walks on, while Claudius rises from his futile prayer: "My words fly up, my thoughts remain below. / Words without thoughts never to heaven go" (97–98). Hamlet is completely deluded by the apparent piety of the king, but he is even more tragically deluded in the following scene by the voice of Polonius from behind the arras. "Is it the king?" (III.iv.27), he asks after he has killed the old spy. Polonius' murder, no matter how Hamlet may justify it, is another manifestation of his inability to discriminate in a world of false or confusing appearances. Again Hamlet has found Polonius behind the arras—that symbol of veiled reality—but this time, with much the same kind of dangerous impetuosity he exhibited when he rashly assumed the ghost to be his dead father, he has taken the surrogate for the king himself. Here the mistake will, in the end, cost him his life.

The death of the surrogate king marks the passing of certain restraints from the play's action. Polonius has stood for the indirect method of handling problems. He is the lover of words and the chief of spies:

> Your bait of falsehood [will] take this carp of truth,
> And thus do we of wisdom and of reach,
> With windlasses and with assays of bias,
> By indirections find directions out.
>
> *(II.i.63–66)*

Polonius is totally committed to the world of similitude, and we may believe that there is something of the theatrical director in him as he coaches his daughter in her approach to Hamlet: "Read on this book / That show of such an exercise may color / Your loneliness" (III.i.44–46). Underneath his rhetoric is a shrewd politician, but violence is not his tool. With his death, political intrigue gives way to direct violence. Claudius orders "the present death of Hamlet" in England (IV.iii.66), and Hamlet vows "from this time forth, / My thoughts be bloody, or be nothing worth!" (IV.iv.65–66). The tone of the play changes. The mockery of Hamlet's antic disposition becomes the reality of Ophelia's madness, and Hamlet's game of seeming develops, for him, into a desperate attempt to keep alive. To save his neck from the axe, he must forge the document which sends Rosencrantz and Guildenstern to their deaths.

However, though violence has entered the play, the consequences of Hamlet's actions hardly disturb the king. Laertes' direct action is far more dangerous for Claudius. At this point in the play, Hamlet's suicidal leap onto the pirates' ship is placed in contrast to Laertes' successful storming of the king's palace. Laertes makes his point with a good deal of energy; Hamlet is captured by the pirates, and only his status as heir apparent, we assume, wins him his life and his freedom. Again, Hamlet's ineffectuality is underlined. His thoughts may be bloody, but he has not been able to strike through the arras, the tragic mask, to kill the real king.

In the graveyard scene, Hamlet achieves a more mature vision through his contemplation of mortality and consequently his own human limitations. His present attitude has grown through his experiences and failures in the world of seeming, and this play is not sprinkled with those glib assurances "that death, a necessary end, / Will come when it will come" which we find scattered throughout *Julius Caesar* (II.ii.36–37). To begin, Hamlet sees death as the solution to his inexplicable and naive despair:

> O that this too too sullied flesh would melt,
> Thaw, and resolve itself into a dew,
> Or that the Everlasting had not fixed
> His canon 'gainst self-slaughter.
>
> *(I.ii.129–32)*

By Act III, however, death becomes for Hamlet the fearful unknown which is an impediment to meaningful action: "the dread of something after death . . . puzzles the will" (III.i.78, 80). Now in the graveyard, amid the black humor of the clowns and with Yorick's skull in his hand, he realizes that death is not an undiscovered country but rather a means to enlightenment, a way to clarification. It is an answer to the mask of seeming: "Now get you to my lady's chamber," he says pointing to the skull, "and tell her, let her paint an inch thick, to this favor she must come" (V.i.192–94). The passage imaginatively takes us back to Claudius' aside: "The harlot's cheek, beautied with plast'ring art, / Is not more ugly to the thing that helps it / Than is my most painted word" (III.i.51–53).[9] The metaphor of cosmetics with which the king defines his own deceit, his own seeming goodness, is made reality in the graveyard. The passages thus juxtaposed suggest that death which reveals the bare bone under the cosmetic will also uncover hidden evil in man.

One aspect of Hamlet's ignorance, his "dream of innocence," his *hamartia,* is overcome. He has now reached a true understanding of death and its proper place in the scheme of things. His leap into Ophelia's grave—if indeed this action is implied by the lines—is not a relapse into juvenile theatrics but a genuine overflowing of emotion and a symbolic confirmation of his new insight. At the same time as he asserts his royal identity—"This is I, Hamlet the Dane" (V.i.257–58)—he accepts death and its consequences. In death there is no seeming. The way is now prepared for his complete enlightenment.

The last step in his development is the religious quietism of the final scene. "Our indiscretion sometime serves us well," he tells Horatio:

> When our deep plots do pall, and that should learn us
> There's a divinity that shapes our ends,
> Rough-hew them how we will.
>
> *(V.ii.8–11)*

The OED points out that "indiscretion" here is more likely to suggest "want of discernment" than "want of judgement." Hamlet has, as we have abundantly seen, lacked the ability to discern reality in a world of masks, and Alfred Harbage has cogently argued that "it was an artistic necessity of the case that Hamlet should be so fertile in ideas, so sterile in actions, that upon his intrigues should be graciously conferred a soul-saving futility."[10] In the cases of Iago, Vindice, and Bosola, to cite three examples, successful intrigue leads inexorably to the damnation of the intriguer. Hamlet's inept-ness is ironically his salvation; he is more victim than victimizer.

In the quiet moments before his duel with Laertes, Hamlet appears to recognize his personal failures in action, and though he has outwitted the witless duo, Rosencrantz and Guildenstern, he attributes his success to Providence: "in that was heaven ordinant" (V.ii.48). He no longer has a plot, but simply waits: "There is special providence in the fall of a sparrow. If it be now, 'tis not to come; if it be not to come, it will be now; if it be not now, yet it will come. The readiness is all" (V.ii.221–24). From the frenetic "scourge and minister" at the play's center (III.iv.176), Hamlet has become the quite tool of a just divinity whom he serves by standing and waiting.

And, as far as the completion of his mission is concerned, his confidence in the workings of Providence is rewarded. Laertes and Claudius are al-most as unsuccessful as Hamlet in their intrigue, and as Laertes points out before his death, they are caught in their "own springe" (V.ii.308). Nevertheless, Hamlet is also caught by the seemingly innocuous fencing match. Although he tells Horatio "thou wouldst not think how ill all's here about my heart" (214–15), he insists on going through with the match, and he is thus finally destroyed by the seeming of the court. In his attempt to espouse the ways of false seeming, he has acquiesced to "the fact of guilt" and has inadvertently killed Polonius behind the arras. He has brought Laertes back to Denmark seeking revenge, and he has left himself vulner-able to this final trap. His vulnerability notwithstanding, Hamlet completes his mission and through his experiences achieves a unity of character which he had naively proclaimed at the play's beginning: "I know not 'seems.' " This unity is subtly suggested in his killing of Claudius with both sword and cup, the emblems of male and female, active and pas-sive.[11] Forcing Claudius to drink from the poisoned cup—a cup seemingly dedicated to Hamlet's success—Hamlet punningly asks: "Is thy union here?" (328), and the question reflects Claudius' unsuccessful attempts to unify the fragmented society over which he has been ruler. Because of his evil, he has metaphorically poisoned the society just as he has actually poisoned his brother, and he appropriately finds his "union" in death from poison. And it is because of death that the guilt of the king is finally re-vealed. The dying Laertes confesses, "The king, the king's to blame" (322).

As Hamlet realizes in the graveyard, death strips away the cosmetics of seeming. At the end of the play, the skeptical Horatio and the hard-headed Fortinbras occupy the center of the stage.

Hamlet's tragedy is that of a man who knows not "seems," who does not understand the artifice of his society. With words and actions, he is unable to penetrate the tragic mask of seeming. After the concatenation of failure which makes up a major part of the action, Hamlet finds truth inextricably linked with death. For him, death is the tool of truth, and he must wait for that tragic moment for an answer. And, of course, for the audience, the heart of his mystery remains. "You would play upon me; you would seem to know my stops; you would pluck out the heart of my mystery; you would sound me from my lowest note to the top of my compass" (III.ii.372–75). That Hamlet's character remains an unsolved mystery is central to the play. For if Hamlet cannot wipe away the cosmetics to find the simple face of truth beneath, if he cannot pierce the arras to find the real king, neither can the audience come to a final answer using the strategies of similitude. Our passion for certitude cannot be satisfied in the seeming world of drama nor yet in the customary world we all inhabit. It is only at the very verge of existence that we may possibly grasp some tragic insight, some recognition of truth. This possibility is the ultimate hope extended by Hamlet's tragedy.

Notes:

1. Laurence Michel, *The Thing Contained: Theory of the Tragic* (Bloomington: Indiana Univ. Press, 1970), p. 12.
2. The text used throughout is *The Tragedy of Hamlet, Prince of Denmark,* ed. Edward Hubler, in *The Complete Signet Classic Shakespeare,* ed. Sylvan Barnet (New York: Harcourt, 1972).
3. Norman N. Holland, *The Shakespearean Imagination* (Bloomington: Indiana Univ. Press, 1968), p. 158.
4. Leon Golden and O. B. Hardison, Jr., *Aristotle's Poetics: A Translation and Commentary for Students of Literature* (Englewood Cliffs, N.J.: Prentice-Hall, 1968), pp. 183–84.
5. See Francis Fergusson, *The Idea of a Theater* (Garden City, N.Y.: Doubleday, 1953), p. 115; and Holland, pp. 163, 165.
6. Peter Alexander, *Hamlet: Father and Son* (Oxford: Clarendon, 1955), p. 180.
7. The phrase, of course, may be interpreted as a pun, in which Hamlet suggests he is accompanied by dread, i.e., by his knowledge of the murder, or by the ghost, i.e., a figure of dread. The phrase may also allude to the quality of Polonius' service and/or to his general treatment as a prince, i.e., poor.
8. Harold Goddard's elaborate analysis of this scene, *The Meaning of Shakespeare*

(Chicago: Univ. of Chicago Press, 1951), pp. 362–68, emphasizes the irony of Hamlet's lack of control seen in the light of his advice to the players. Goddard also sees the "mouse trap" as a relative failure.

9. That Claudius and Polonius are going to hide behind the arras may lead to the king's cosmetic metaphor. Arras is not only a hanging but also "orris," a powder used as a cosmetic. The visual pun unites the two methods of deception.

10. Alfred Harbage, "Intrigue in Elizabethan Tragedy," in *Essays on Shakespeare and Elizabethan Drama in Honor of Hardin Craig,* ed. Richard Hosley (Columbia: Univ. of Missouri, 1962), p. 43.

11. Cf. Michael C. Andrews, "The Double-Death of Claudius in *Hamlet," Renaissance Papers 1970,* ed. Dennis Donovan (Durham, N.C.: Southeastern Renaissance Conference, 1971), pp. 21–27.

Shakespeare's Desdemona

S. N. GARNER

I

As Desdemona prepares to go do bed with Othello in Act IV, scene iii of Shakespeare's *Othello,* the following conversation occurs between her and Emilia:

Emilia.	Shall I go fetch your nightgown?
Desdemona.	No, unpin me here.
	This Lodovico is a proper man.
Emilia.	A very handsome man.
Desdemona.	He speaks well.
Emilia.	I know a lady in Venice would have walked barefoot to Palestine for a touch of his nether lip.

(ll. 36–42)[1]

Surely this is startling dialogue coming as it does between the brothel scene and the moment when Desdemona will go to her wedding with death. An actress or director would certainly have to think a great deal about how these lines are to be spoken and what they are to reveal of Desdemona's character. But a reader or critic is not so hard pressed, and he may, if it suits him, simply skip over them. This is precisely what most critics do.

Robert Heilman is representative. In his lengthy book on the play, *Magic in the Web,*[2] he does not discuss the passage. One reason for this omission, of course, is that he, like most critics, is mainly interested in Othello and Iago. Nevertheless, since he uses the New Critics' method of close reading—underscoring images, habits of diction, and grammatical structure—it is peculiar that when he treats Desdemona's character, dealing in two instances with Act IV, scene iii specifically (pp. 189–90, 208–10), he fails to notice these lines. A partial explanation for this failure is that he sustains his interpretation of Othello and Iago and the theme of the play by insisting on Desdemona's relative simplicity and diverges from other critics who make her "overintricate" (p. 209). More significantly, however, the passage is difficult to square with his contention that in the last act Desdemona "becomes . . . the saint" (p. 215), a representation of "the world of spirit" (p. 218).

233

Other critics whose method, if nothing else, will scarcely allow them to ignore the passage cancel it out as best they can. G. R. Elliott, for example, in his line-by-line commentary, *Flaming Minister,* remarks that here Desdemona "speaks *listlessly* [italics mine]; and she pays no heed to the vivid tale begun by her woman of the Venetian lady. . . . She herself would make a hard pilgrimage for a 'touch' of Othello's love."[3] In other words, she does not mean what she says about Lodovico, her mind is really on Othello, and when Emilia talks about touching Lodovico's "nether lip," Desdemona *must,* Elliott implies, think of Othello. Similarly, M. R. Ridley, editor of the Arden edition, is evidently bothered by the lines and can only hope they somehow do not belong to Desdemona: "What did Shakespeare intend by this sudden transition to Lodovico? Is Desdemona for a moment 'matching Othello with her country forms'? One is tempted to wonder whether there has not been a misattribution of speeches, so that this line [38] as well as the next should be Emilia's."[4] It is unusual, to say the least, that an editor who has argued so carefully for his preference of the quarto to the folio edition for his copy-text should speculate so carelessly here. He wishes to attribute to Emilia a line that both editions give to Desdemona, make Emilia's lines repetitious (as they would be since "proper" and "handsome" are synonymous), and destroy the rhythm of the dialogue, rather than let Desdemona have the line Shakespeare evidently gave her.[5]

The reason for these efforts to get rid of Desdemona's lines about Lodovico seems obvious. Many critics and scholars come to Shakespeare's play with the idea that Desdemona ought to be pure and virtuous and, above all, unwavering in her faithfulness and loyalty to Othello. The notion is so tenacious that when Desdemona even appears to threaten it, they cannot contemplate her character with their usual care and imagination.

At what appears to be the other extreme is such a critic as W. H. Auden, one of the few who notices the passage and sees it as a significant revelation of Desdemona's character. Viewing her cynically partly on account of it, he remarks: "It is worth noting that, in the willow-song scene with Emilia, she speaks with admiration of Ludovico [sic] and then turns to the topic of adultery. . . . It is as if she had suddenly realized that she had made a *mésalliance* and that the sort of man she ought to have married was someone of her own class and colour like Ludovico. Given a few more years of Othello and of Emilia's influence and she might well, one feels, have taken a lover."[6] But isn't Auden finally making the same assumption as the others? Doesn't his cynical and easy dismissal of Desdemona imply that he has expected her to be perfect? If she is not, then she must be corrupt. Isn't this Othello's mistake exactly? Either Desdemona is pure or she is the "cunning whore of Venice" (IV.ii.88).

The poles of critical opinion are exactly those presented in the play.[7] On the one hand is the view of Desdemona the "good" characters have; on the other is the negative vision of her that Iago persuades Othello to accept. At a time when we have become especially careful about adopting any single perspective of a character as the dramatist's or the "right" perspective, why do many critics now simply accept one extreme view of Desdemona or the other? I can only assume that they share a vision Shakespeare presents as limited.

Desdemona's character is neither simple nor any more easily defined than Iago's or Othello's. Any effort to describe it must take into account all of what she says and does as well as what other characters say about her and how their views are limited by their own personalities and values. Though Shakespeare does not give Desdemona center stage with Othello, as he gives Juliet with Romeo and Cleopatra with Antony, he does not keep her in the wings for most of the play, as he does Cordelia or Hermione. She is often present so that we must witness her joy, fear, bewilderment, and pain. What happens to her matters because we see how it affects her as well as Othello. The meaning of the tragedy depends, then, on a clear vision of her character and experience as well as those of Othello and Iago.

II

That Desdemona is neither goddess nor slut Shakespeare makes very clear. He evidently realized that he would have to defend his characterization of her more against the idealization of the essentially good characters than the denigration of the villain. Consequently, though he undermines both extremes, he expends his main efforts in disarming Desdemona's champions rather than her enemy. In her first two appearances, Shakespeare establishes her character and thus holds in balance the diverging views, but he goes out of his way to make her human rather than divine.

He carefully shapes Othello's account of Desdemona to counter Brabantio's initial description of her as "A maiden never bold, / Of spirit so still and quiet that her motion / Blushed at herself" (I.iii.94–96). Because Brabantio is unwilling to believe that Desdemona's "perfection so could err" (l. 100) that she would elope with Othello, he accuses him of seducing her by witchcraft or drugs. In Othello's eloquent defense (ll. 127–69), he shows not only that Brabantio's accusations are false but also that it was

Desdemona who invited his courtship. His description of her coming with "greedy ear" to "devour" his tales of cannibals, anthropophagi, and his own exploits suggests that she is starved for excitement and fascinated by Othello because his life has been filled with adventure. She loved him, he says, for the dangers he had passed. So far is Desdemona from being Brabantio's "maiden never bold" that she gave Othello "a world of kisses"[8] for his pains and clearly indicated that she would welcome his suit:

> She wished
> That heaven had made her such a man. She thanked me,
> And bade me, if I had a friend that loved her,
> I should but teach him how to tell my story,
> And that would woo her. Upon this hint I spake.
>
> (ll. 161–65)

The scene is carefully managed so as to create sympathy for both Othello and Desdemona. Because Desdemona initiates the courtship, Othello is absolutely exonerated of Brabantio's charge. His cautiousness acknowledges the tenuousness of his position as a black man in Venetian society and is appropriate and even admirable. The Moor cannot be confident of Desdemona's attraction to him, and he undoubtedly knows that marrying him would isolate her from her countrymen. Recognizing Othello's reticence and undoubtedly its causes, Desdemona makes it clear she loves him but, at the same time, maintains a degree of indirection. Shakespeare does not wish to make her seem either shy or overly forward.

When Desdemona finally appears, she strengthens the image Othello has presented. Before the senators, she answers her father's charges forcefully and persuasively, without shyness or reticence. More significantly, it is she, and not Othello, who first raises the possibility of her going to Cyprus. Othello asks only that the senators give his wife "fit disposition" (I.iii.233), but when the Duke asks her preference, Desdemona pleads:

> If I be left behind,
> A moth of peace, and he go to the war,
> The rites for why I love him are bereft me,
> And I a heavy interim shall support
> By his dear absence. Let me go with him.
>
> (ll. 250–54)

Her wish not to be left behind as a "moth of peace" is a desire not to be treated as someone too fragile to share the intensity of Othello's military life. As though she might have overheard Brabantio tell Othello that she would not have run to his "sooty bosom" (I.ii.69), she confirms her sexual attraction to him as well as her own sexuality by insisting that she wants the full "rites" of her marriage.[9]

Shakespeare must have wanted to make doubly sure of establishing Desdemona's sensuality, for he underscores it the next time she appears. At the beginning of Act II, while she awaits Othello on the shore of Cyprus, her jesting with Iago displays the kind of sexual playfulness that we might have anticipated from Othello's description of their courtship.

As soon as Desdemona arrives at Cyprus, together with Emilia, Iago, and Roderigo, and is greeted by Cassio, she asks about Othello. Immediately a ship is sighted, and someone goes to the harbor to see whether it is Othello's. Anxious about her husband, Desdemona plays a game with Iago to pass the time; in an aside, she remarks, "I am not merry; but I do beguile / The thing I am by seeming otherwise" (II.i.120–21). Their repartee grows out of a debate that Iago begins by accusing Emilia of talking too much. A practiced slanderer of women, he chides both his wife and Desdemona. Although Desdemona rebukes him, "O, fie upon thee, slanderer!" (l. 111), she asks him to write her praise. Instead he comments on general types of women:

Iago.	If she be fair and wise: fairness and wit,
	The one's for use, the other useth it.
Desdemona.	Well praised. How if she be black and witty?
Iago.	If she be black, and thereto have a wit,
	She'll find a white that shall her blackness fit.
Desdemona.	Worse and worse!

(ll.127–32)

Iago's "praises" commend women for what he might expect Desdemona to regard as faults, and none are without sexual overtones. Though Desdemona remarks that they "are old fond paradoxes to make fools laugh i' th' alehouse" (ll. 136–37), they do not offend her and serve her well enough as a pastime for fifty-five lines, until Othello arrives.

Critics who take an extreme view of Desdemona see her pleasure in this exchange with Iago as a failure of Shakespeare's art. Ridley, for example, comments: "This is to many readers, and I think rightly, one of the most unsatisfactory passages in Shakespeare. To begin with it is unnatural. Desdemona's natural instinct must surely be to go herself to the harbour, instead of asking parenthetically whether someone has gone. Then, it is distasteful to watch her engaged in a long piece of cheap backchat with Iago, and so adept at it that one wonders how much time on the voyage was spent in the same way. All we gain from it is some further unneeded light on Iago's vulgarity" (p. 54 *n*).[10] But this scene is unnatural for Ridley's Desdemona, not Shakespeare's. What the dramatist gives us here is an extension of the spirited and sensual Desdemona that has been revealed in the first act. Her scene with Iago shows her to be the same woman who could initiate Othello's courtship and complain before the senators about the "rites" she would lose in Othello's absence. Her stance is similar to the one she will take later when she tries to coax Othello into reinstating Cassio. That the scene impedes the dramatic movement too long and that its humor is weak are perhaps legitimate criticisms; to suggest that it distorts Desdemona's character is surely to misunderstand her character.

Shakespeare makes a special effort to maintain the balance of the scene. He keeps Desdemona off a pedestal and shows her to have a full range of human feelings and capacities. Yet he is careful not to allow her to fail in feeling or propriety. The point of her aside is to affirm her concern for Othello as well as to show her personal need to contain anxiety and distance pain and fear. As we see how Desdemona acts under stress later in the play, it seems consistent with her character that she should want a distraction to divert her attention in this extremity. Shakespeare brings the exchange between Desdemona and Iago to a brilliant close as Othello enters and greets his "fair warrior."[11] The sensual import of this moment and his address is surely heightened by what we have seen of Desdemona shortly before.

Shakespeare's delicately poised portrayal of Desdemona to this point prepares us for the splendid antithesis between Iago and Cassio in the middle of the second act:

Iago.	Our general cast us thus early for the love of his Desdemona; who let us not therefore blame. He hath not yet made wanton the night with her, and she is sport for Jove.
Cassio.	She's a most exquisite lady.
Iago.	And, I'll warrant her, full of game.
Cassio.	Indeed, she's a most fresh and delicate creature.
Iago.	What an eye she has! Methinks it sounds a parley to provocation.
Cassio.	An inviting eye; and yet methinks right modest.
Iago.	And when she speaks, is it not an alarum to love?
Cassio.	She is indeed perfection.

(II.iii.14–28)

Such a carefully counterpointed exchange invites us to adjust both views.

Iago distorts Desdemona's character by suppressing the side of it that Cassio insists on and emphasizing her sensuality. His suggestions that she is "full of game" and that her eye "sounds a parley to provocation" call up an image of a flirtatious and inconstant woman. Iago's view is clearly limited by his devious purpose and also by his cynical notions about human nature in general and women in particular.

But Cassio's view is limited as well. He idealizes Desdemona as much as her father did. It is evidently clear to Iago that his efforts to persuade Cassio of his vision will fail when he pronounces Desdemona "perfection," as had Brabantio before him (I.iii.100). The extravagance of language Cassio uses earlier in describing Desdemona must also make his view suspect. For example, he tells Montano that Othello

> hath achieved a maid
> That paragons description and wild fame;
> One that excels the quirks of blazoning pens,
> And in th' essential vesture of creation
> Does tire the ingener.
>
> *(II.i.61–65)*

After the safe arrival of Desdemona and her companion in Cyprus, Cassio rhapsodizes:

> Tempests themselves, high seas, and howling winds,
> The guttered rocks and congregated sands,
> Traitors ensteeped to enclog the guiltless keel,
> As having sense of beauty, do omit
> Their moral natures, letting go safely by
> The *divine* Desdemona.
>
> *(II.i.68–73; italics mine)*

This idealization gives as false a picture of Desdemona as Iago's denigration of her. Cassio's lines in fact comment more on his character than on Desdemona's. To accept his view of Desdemona, as many have done, is as grievous a critical mistake as to accept Iago's.

III

Desdemona's liveliness, assertiveness, and sensuality are corroborated in her marrying Othello. The crucial fact of her marriage is not that she elopes but that she, a white woman, weds a black man. Though many critics focus on the universality of experience in *Othello*,[12] we cannot forget the play's racial context. Othello's blackness is as important as Shylock's Jewishness, and indeed the play dwells relentlessly upon it.[13]

It is underscored heavily from the beginning. The first references to Othello, made by Iago to Roderigo, are to "the Moor" (I.i.37, 54). Roderigo immediately refers to him as "the thick-lips" (I.i.63). He is not called by name until he appears before the senators in scene ii when the Duke of Venice addresses him. He has been referred to as "the Moor" nine times before that moment.

Iago and Roderigo know they may depend on Brabantio's fears of black sexuality and miscegenation. When he appears at his window to answer their summons, Iago immediately cries up to him, "Even now, now, very now, an old black ram / Is tupping your white ewe" (I.i.85–86) and urges him to arise lest "the devil" (l. 88) make a grandfather of him. The tone intensifies as Iago harps on Othello's bestial sexuality. To the uncomprehending and reticent Brabantio he urges impatiently:

> You'll have
> your daughter covered with a Barbary horse, you'll
> have your nephews neigh to you, you'll have coursers
> for cousins, and gennets for germans.
>
> *(ll. 107–10)*

Mercilessly, he draws a final image: "Your daughter and the Moor are making the beast with two blacks" (ll. 112–14). The unimaginative and literal Roderigo adds that Desdemona has gone to the "gross clasps of a lascivious Moor" (l. 123).

Brabantio had "loved" Othello, invited him often to his home, and encouraged him to tell the stories that captivated Desdemona (I.iii.127–31); yet he has the prejudices that Iago and Roderigo expect. Although he had objected earlier to Roderigo as Desdemona's suitor (I.i.92–95), he now commiserates with him, "O, would you had had her!" (I.i.172). Brabantio obviously never imagined that Desdemona could be attracted to Othello because he is black. When Othello appears, he tells him that only if his daughter was enchanted or drugged would she have "run from her guardage to the sooty bosom / Of such a thing as thou—to fear, not to delight" (I.ii.69–70). He cannot believe that she fell in love with what he assumes "she feared to look on!" (I.iii.98).

But even to the other characters who do not have reason to malign

Othello as do Iago, Roderigo, and Brabantio, black is not beautiful. Othello is accepted because he is like white men or in spite of his blackness. The Duke tells Brabantio, "Your son-in-law is far more fair than black" (I.iii.285). When Desdemona affirms her love for Othello, she explains, "I saw Othello's visage in his mind" (I.iii.247). More importantly, Othello himself sees his blackness as a defect. When Iago first tries to raise doubts about Desdemona's fidelity, Othello reassures himself, "She had eyes, and chose me" (III.iii.189); that is, she married him *despite* his blackness. Later, as he begins to believe Iago's insinuations about Desdemona, he laments:

> My name, that was as fresh
> As Dian's visage, is now begrimed and black
> As mine own face.
>
> *(III.iii.383–85)*

Iago knows that he may appeal to Othello's sense that his blackness is a liability to undermine his faith in Desdemona. He warns him that Desdemona's "will, recoiling to her better judgment," may begin to "match" him "with her country forms, / And happily repent" (III.iii.236–38).

Othello's blackness is further associated with a lack of grace, particularly with a lack of manners and eloquence. Mistakenly imagining that he speaks ineloquently, Othello apologizes to the senators before he addresses them, "Rude am I in my speech, / And little blessed with the soft phrase of peace" (I.iii.81–82). Later when he finds causes in himself for Desdemona's supposed infidelity, he considers one possibility, "Haply for I am black / And have not those soft parts of conversation / That chamberers have" (III.iii.262–64). Iago will, of course, take advantage of Othello's superficial deficiencies; he tries to persuade Roderigo that Desdemona will tire of Othello because the Moor lacks "loveliness in favor, sympathy in years, manners, and beauties" (II.i.227–28). It is probable that Othello takes Cassio with him when he courts Desdemona to compensate for what he considers his own insufficiency. The Florentine aristocrat is distinguished for his handsomeness, grace, and eloquence.

Critics speculate about what Othello's marriage to Desdemona means for him but usually fail to consider what it means for her to marry someone so completely an outsider. What are we to make of Desdemona's choosing Othello rather than one of her own countrymen? Brabantio tells Othello that Desdemona has "shunned / The wealthy, curlèd darlings of our nation" (I.ii.66–67). It seems incredible to him that, having done so, she should then choose Othello. But Shakespeare intends to suggest that the "curlèd darlings" of Italy leave something to be desired; the image implies preciousness and perhaps effeminacy. He expects us to find her choice understandable and even admirable.

Of all Desdemona's reputed suitors, we see only Roderigo. The easy gull of Iago and mawkishly lovesick, he is obviously not worthy of Desdemona. When Othello and Desdemona leave for Cyprus, Roderigo tells Iago, "I will incontinently drown myself" (I.iii.300), and we cannot help but assent to Iago's estimation of him as a "silly gentleman" (I.iii.302). Even Brabantio agrees that he is unsuitable, for he tells him, "My daughter is not for thee" (I.i.95). Only by comparing him to Othello does he find him acceptable.

The only other character who might be a suitor for Desdemona is Cassio. But it occurs to neither Cassio nor Desdemona that he should court her. Shakespeare makes him a foil to Othello and characterizes him so as to suggest what Desdemona might have found wanting in her countrymen. He is evidently handsome and sexually attractive. In soliloquy, where he may be trusted, Iago remarks that "Cassio's a proper man" (I.iii.381) and that "he hath a person and a smooth dispose / To be suspected—framed to make women false" (ll. 386–87). Drawing Cassio as one who is "handsome, young, and hath all those requisites in him that folly and green minds look after" (II.i.244–45), Iago persuades Roderigo that Cassio is most likely to be second after Othello in Desdemona's affections. In soliloquy again, Iago makes clear that he thinks Cassio loves Desdemona: "That Cassio loves her, I do well believe 't" (II.i.285).

Though he is handsome and has all the surface graces, Cassio is wanting in manliness. Shakespeare certainly intends Cassio's inability to hold his liquor to undermine his character. He gives this trait mainly to comic figures, such as Sir Toby Belch, or villains, like Claudius. Once drunk, the mild-mannered Cassio is "full of quarrel and offense" (II.iii.50). His knowledge of his weakness (II.iii.39–42) might mitigate it, but even aware of it, he succumbs easily. Though at first he refuses Iago's invitation to drink with the Cypriots, he gives in later with only a little hesitation to Iago's exclamation, "What, man! 'Tis a night of revels, the gallants desire it" (II.iii.43–44). His lack of discipline here and his subsequent behavior that disgraces him lend some credence to Iago's objections to Othello's preferring him as lieutenant.

Cassio's relationship with Bianca also calls his masculinity in question. Nowhere else does Shakespeare show a man of Cassio's rank keeping company with prostitutes. His affair with Bianca tends to reduce him to the level of Touchstone, though Bianca is far superior to Audrey. Yet his friendship with Bianca in itself does not discredit him as much as his behavior towards her. He makes fun of her behind her back; Iago tells us,

"He, when he hears of her, cannot restrain / From the excess of laughter" (IV.i.99–100). Yet when she confronts him, angry because she believes he is unfaithful to her, and threatens to stop seeing him, he anxiously follows after her for fear "she'll rail in the streets" (IV.i.162).

Cassio is, then, as Auden has described him, something of a "ladies' man" (p. 10), who idealizes women of his own social class and spends his time with prostitutes. He serves ideally to help Othello woo Desdemona because he has no interest in her sexually; he would keep her "divine" Desdemona. The embodiment of style, Cassio is hollow at the core. But just as he knows that he has a tendency toward drunkenness, so he recognizes his own impotence. As he awaits Othello's ship on Cyprus, he prays that "Great Jove" will guard it so that Othello can "Make love's quick pants in Desdemona's arms, / Give renewed fire to our extinct spirits" (II.i.80–81). In this last line he recognizes a potency in Othello that he finds wanting in himself and those around him. Desdemona enters immediately, and Cassio's striking address, following his anticipation of Othello's and Desdemona's sexual union, underscores his sexual failing:

> O, behold! The riches of the ship is come on shore!
> You men of Cyprus, let her have your knees.
> *Kneeling.*
> Hail to thee, lady! and the grace of heaven,
> Before, behind thee, and on every hand,
> Enwheel thee round.
>
> *(II.i.82–86)*

As Alfred Harbage has remarked, his greeting suggests "a prayer to the Virgin";[14] the extravagance of these lines and others that describe Desdemona point up Cassio's tendency to idealize her.

Desdemona's marrying a man different from Roderigo, Cassio, and the other "curlèd darlings" of Italy is to her credit. She must recognize in Othello a dignity, energy, excitement, and power that all around her lack. Since these qualities are attributable to his heritage, she may be said to choose him because he is African, black, an outsider. When she says she saw Othello's visage in his mind, she suggests that she saw beneath the surface to those realities that seemed to offer more promise of life. If the myth of black sexuality (which Othello's character denies at every turn) operates for Desdemona, as it does for some of the other characters,[15] it can only enhance Othello's attractiveness for her as she compares him with the pale men around her.

Desdemona shows courage and a capacity for risk in choosing Othello, for it puts her in an extreme position, cutting her off from her father and countrymen. Brabantio in effect disowns her since he would not have allowed her to live with him after her marriage (I.iii.237) if she had not been permitted to go with Othello to Cyprus. His last words are not to her, but to Othello, and they cut deep: "Look to her, Moor, if thou hast eyes to see: / She has deceived her father, and may thee" (I.iii.287–88). Later we learn that Brabantio died of grief over the marriage (V.ii.204–206). We are to disapprove of Desdemona's deception no more than we are to disapprove of Juliet's similar deception of Capulet, or Hermia's of Egeus. Shakespeare gives Brabantio's character a comic tinge so that our sympathies do not shift from Desdemona to him.

That her marriage separates her from society is implied because of the attitudes we hear expressed toward Othello, but it is also made explicit. Brabantio does not believe that Desdemona would have married Othello unless she had been charmed partially because of his sense that she will "incur a general mock" (I.ii.68). After Othello has insulted Desdemona, Emilia's question of Iago makes clear what lines have been drawn: "Hath she forsook . . . Her father and her country, and her friends, / To be called whore?" (IV.ii.124–26). Desdemona does not marry Othello ignorant of the consequences; when she pleads with the Duke to allow her to go to Cyprus, she proclaims:

> That I love the Moor to live with him,
> My downright violence, and storm of fortunes,
> May trumpet to the world.
>
> *(I.iii.243–45)*

She knows her action is a "storm of fortunes." Her willingness to risk the censure of her father and society is some measure of her capacity for love, even though her love is not based on complete knowledge. She does not see Othello clearly and cannot anticipate any of the difficulties that must necessarily attend his spirited life. Her elopement is more surely a measure of her determination to have a life that seems to offer the promise of excitement and adventure denied her as a sheltered Venetian senator's daughter.

IV

Because Desdemona cuts herself off from her father and friends and marries someone from a vastly different culture, she is even more alone on

Cyprus than she would ordinarily have been in a strange place and as a woman in a military camp besides. These circumstances, as well as her character and experience, account in part for the turn the tragedy takes.

At the beginning she unwittingly plays into Iago's hands by insisting that Othello reinstate Cassio immediately. On the one hand, she cannot know what web of evil Iago is weaving to trap her. On the other, her behavior in this matter is not entirely without fault. It is only natural that Desdemona should wish Cassio reinstated since he is her old friend and, except for Emilia, her only close friend on Cyprus. But her insistence is excessive. She assures Cassio that Othello "shall never rest" (III.iii.22) until he promises to restore the lieutenant's position, and indeed, she makes sure that he never does. Yet her persistence does not seem necessary, for Emilia has assured Cassio earlier:

> All will sure be well.
> The general and his wife are talking of it,
> And she speaks for you stoutly. The Moor replies
> That he you hurt is of great fame in Cyprus
> And great affinity, and that in wholesome wisdom
> He might not but refuse you. But he protests he loves you,
> And needs no other suitor but his likings
> To bring you in again.
>
> *(III.i.41–48)*

Desdemona harps on her single theme playfully, teasingly. Her manner is no different from that which she took when she courted Othello or jested with Iago. Her vision seems not to extend beyond the range that allowed her to manage domestic life in Brabantio's quiet household.

As soon as Othello's jealousy and rage begin to manifest themselves, Desdemona's forthrightness and courage start to desert her. She can no longer summon up those resources that might help her. She is not as fragile as Ophelia; she will not go mad. But neither is she as resilient or as alert to possibilities as Juliet, who was probably younger and no more experienced than she. Before Juliet takes the potion the Friar has prepared to make her appear dead, she considers whether he might have mixed a poison instead, since he would be dishonored if it were known he had married her to Romeo (IV.iii.24–27). She confronts the possibility of evil, weighs her own position, and takes the risk she feels she must. There is never such a moment for Desdemona.

Under the pressure of Othello's anger, Desdemona lies to him, by denying she has lost the handkerchief he gave her, and makes herself appear guilty. Her action is perfectly understandable. To begin with, she feels guilty about losing it, for she has told Emilia earlier that if Othello were given to jealousy, "it were enough / To put him to ill thinking" (III.iv.28–29). But more important, she lies out of fear, as her initial response to Othello indicates:

	Why do you speak so startingly and rash?
Othello.	Is't lost? Is't gone? Speak, is it out o' th' way?
Desdemona.	Heaven bless us!

(III.iv.79–81)

Then she becomes defensive: "It is not lost. But what an if it were?" At this point Othello's demeanor must be incredibly frightening. Shortly before this moment he has knelt with Iago to vow vengeance against Desdemona if she proves unfaithful, and moments later, he is so enraged that he "falls in a trance" (IV.i.44). In this sudden crisis, latent fears of Othello that are inevitably part of Desdemona's cultural experience must be called into play. Her compounded terror destroys her capacity for addressing him with the courage and dignity that she had summoned in facing her father and the senators when they called her actions in question.

If Desdemona has wanted the heights of passion, she finds its depths instead. That she is simply bewildered and unable to respond more forcefully to Othello's subsequent fury is attributable to several causes. To begin with, his change is sudden and extreme. When Lodovico arrives from Venice and meets the raging Othello, he asks incredulously:

> Is this the noble Moor whom our full Senate
> Call all in all sufficient? Is this the nature
> Whom passion could not shake? whose solid virtue
> The shot of accident nor dart of chance
> Could neither graze nor pierce?

(IV.i.262–66)

Noble Othello is like the flower that festers and smells far worse than weeds. Only Iago anticipates the full possibilities of his corruption.

But the most important causes of Desdemona's powerlessness lie within herself. She idealizes Othello and cannot recognize that he is as susceptible to irrationality and evil as other men. She tells Emilia that her "noble Moor / Is true of mind, and made of no such baseness / As jealous creatures are."

Evidently surprised, Emilia asks if he is not jealous, and Desdemona replies as though the suggestion were preposterous: "Who? He? I think the sun where he was born / Drew all such humors from him" (III.iv.26–31). Though Emilia immediately suspects that Othello is jealous (III.iv.98), Desdemona does not credit her suspicions since she "never gave him cause" (l. 156). Emilia tries to explain that jealousy is not rational and does not need a cause:

> But jealous souls will not be answered so;
> They are not ever jealous for the cause,
> But jealous for they're jealous. It is a monster
> Begot upon itself, born on itself.

(ll. 157–60)

Though Iago provokes Othello, his jealousy, as Emilia says, arises out of his own susceptibility. He has romanticized Desdemona, as she has him. Forced to confront the fact that she is human and therefore capable of treachery, he is threatened by his own vulnerability to her. If he cannot keep himself invulnerable by idealizing her, then he will do so by degrading her. His fears are heightened because he thinks his blackness, age, and lack of elegance make him less attractive sexually than Cassio.

Despite the worsening crisis, Desdemona will not be instructed by Emilia, nor will she alter her view of Othello so that she might understand and possibly confront what is happening. Her only defense is to maintain an appalling innocence. The more she must struggle to keep her innocence in the face of the overwhelming events of the last two acts, the more passive and less able to cope she becomes.[16] She must hold on to it for two reasons. First, nothing of her life in the rarefied atmosphere of Brabantio's home and society could have anticipated this moment, and nothing in her being can rise to meet it now. Therefore, she must close it out. Second, if she is deserted by her husband, there is nowhere for her to turn. Rather than suffer the terror and pain of her isolation, she must deny that it exists.

Shakespeare's portrayal of Desdemona from the beginning of Act IV until her death illustrates how finely and clearly he had conceived her character and how well he understood the psychology of a mind under pressure. As Iago's poison works and Othello becomes more convinced of Desdemona's guilt and increasingly madder with rage, Desdemona will become gradually more passive and continually frame means of escape in her imagination.

After the brothel scene, when Othello leaves calling Desdemona the "cunning whore of Venice" (IV.ii.88) and throwing money to Emilia as to a madam, Desdemona is stunned. Emilia asks, "Alas, what does this gentleman conceive? / How do you, madam? How do you, my good lady?"; Desdemona replies, "Faith, half asleep" (IV.ii.94–96). The action is too quick for her to be literally asleep; Othello has just that moment left. Rather, she is dazed;[17] her mind simply cannot take in what it encounters. Almost at once she begins to look for ways out. Directing Emilia to put her wedding sheets on the bed (IV.ii.104), she hopes to be able to go back in time, to recover the brief happiness and harmony she and Othello shared when they were newly married. Though she will subsequently assert that she approves of Othello's behavior (IV.ii.106; iii.20–22), part of her will not approve and will continue to create fantasies to save herself.

Next, Desdemona begins to anticipate her death, directing Emilia to shroud her in her wedding sheets if she should die (IV.iii.26–27) and singing the willow song. She not only foreshadows her death but also expresses an unconscious desire for it. Her preface to the song makes her wish clear:

> My mother had a maid called Barbary.
> She was in love; and he she loved proved mad
> And did forsake her. She had a song of "Willow";
> An old thing 'twas, but it expressed her fortune,
> And she died singing it. That song tonight
> Will not go from my mind; I have much to do
> But to go hang my head all at one side
> And sing it like poor Barbary.
>
> (IV.iii.28–35)

That the song will not go from her mind and that she has "much to do" to keep from hanging her head and singing it suggest the insistence of a death wish. To express a desire for death here and to plead with Othello later to let her live is not inconsistent. Death wishes are more often hopes of finding peace and escape rather than real wishes to die. The song itself—quiet, soporific—promises calm in contrast to Othello's raging.

Just before Desdemona sings, she starts the conversation about Lodovico quoted at the beginning. That she thinks of Lodovico when she is undressing to go to bed with Othello suggests that she is still trying to find a way around the emergency of the moment. She admires Lodovico as "a proper man"—precisely the phrase Iago used to describe Cassio (I.iii.381)—and as one who "speaks well," calling up those qualities that Cassio has and Othello lacks. Since the man Desdemona has loved, married, and risked her social position for has turned into a barbarian and a madman, she unconsciously longs for a man like Lodovico—a handsome, white man, with those attributes she recognizes as civilized.[18] In her heart she must feel she has made a mistake.

Desdemona does not know the world, or herself, for that matter. Like Lear, she has been led to believe she is "ague-proof." At the end of Act IV Shakespeare makes it certain, if he has not before, that she is self-deceived and that there is a great discrepancy between what she unconsciously feels and what she consciously acknowledges. When Desdemona asks Emilia whether she would cuckold her husband "for all the world," Emilia plays with the question, answering, "The world's a huge thing; it is a great price for a small vice" (IV.iii.71–73). Desdemona finally says she does not think "there is any such woman" who would (IV.iii.88). Her comment underscores her need to close out knowledge that might threaten her. Coming as it does after the passage about Lodovico, her remark can only emphasize her pitiable need to maintain an innocence that must inevitably court ruin.

Like Sleeping Beauty waiting for the prince's kiss, Desdemona is asleep when Othello comes. When he threatens her, the most she can do is plead for her life. Desdemona is not Hermione, who has the wisdom to know that if Leontes doubts her fidelity, she cannot convince him of her chastity by insisting on it. And unlike Hermione, Desdemona merely asserts her innocence rather than reproaches her husband, with whom the final blame must lie. She can only lament that she is "undone" (V.ii.76) and beg for time. She acts differently from the heroine of *The Winter's Tale* not only because she is more fragile and less wise but also because her accuser is not a white man following at least the forms of justice in a court. Othello is a black man with rolling eyes (V.ii.38) coming to do "justice" in her bedroom at night.

When Desdemona revives for a moment after Othello has stifled her, she affirms her guiltlessness (V.ii.122) and to Emilia's asking who has "done this deed," she answers, "Nobody—I myself. Farewell. / Commend me to my kind lord" (V.ii.123–25). Her answer is often thought of as an effort to protect Othello. Had Othello stabbed Desdemona, then the notion is plausible that she might pretend to have killed herself to save him. But Desdemona could not have smothered or strangled herself. I think her answer acknowledges instead her full responsibility for her marriage and its consequences. What her implied forgiveness of Othello means is unclear. Her remark of a moment before, "A guiltless death I die," must be rendered with pain or anger, so her forgiveness may merely follow her old pattern of denying what she feels and acknowledging what she must; in other words, it may be unfelt. If her forgiveness is genuinely felt, however, it might suggest that Desdemona has come to see Othello with the prejudices of her countrymen and to regard him as acting according to a barbarian nature that will not allow him to act otherwise.[19] She forgives him, then, as she would a child. Or at its best, her pardoning Othello means that she is finally capable of an ideal love, one that does not alter "when it alteration finds" or bend "with the remover to remove." But even if we see Desdemona as acting out of pure love, as most critics do, her triumph is undercut because she never confronts the full and unyielding knowledge in the face of which true love and forgiveness must maintain themselves. Furthermore, there is no ritual of reconciliation between Desdemona and Othello. Though Othello is by Desdemona's side when she forgives him, she uses the third person and speaks to Emilia.

Othello learns that he is wrong, that Iago, whom he trusted, has deceived him heartlesstly, monstrously. But he never understands what in himself allowed him to become prey to Iago. The final truth for him is that he has thrown a pearl away. His suicide is a despairing act. He finally sees himself as unblessed and bestial—beyond mercy. Paradoxically, his only redemption must come through self-execution.

Othello is surely one of Shakespeare's bleakest tragedies. Given their characters and experience, both personal and cultural, Desdemona and Othello must fail. They do not know themselves, and they cannot know each other. Further, they never understand the way the world fosters their misperceptions. We must watch as Othello is reduced from a heroic general, with dignity, assurance, and power to a raging, jealous husband and murderer, out of control and duped by Iago. We see Desdemona lose her energy, vitality, and courage for living to become fearful and passive. Both suffer the pains of deception, real or supposed loss of love, final powerlessness, and death. Tragedy never allows its protagonists to escape suffering and death, but it often graces them with the knowledge of life, without which they cannot have lived in the fullest sense. Yet for all their terrible suffering, Desdemona and Othello are finally denied even that knowledge.

Notes:

1. William Shakespeare, *The Complete Signet Classic Shakespeare,* ed. Sylvan Barnet (New York: Harcourt, 1972). All quotations from Shakespeare are from this edition.

2. *Magic in the Web* (Lexington: Univ. of Kentucky Press, 1956).

3. *Flaming Minister* (Durham, N.C.: Duke Univ. Press, 1953), p. 203.

4. *Othello* (1958; rpt. New York: Random, 1967), p. 166n.

5. In *The Stranger in Shakespeare* (New York: Stein and Day, 1972), Leslie Fiedler forgets that it is Desdemona who begins the conversation about Lodovico when he comments that Emilia "appears to be tempting poor Desdemona by evoking the charms of . . . Lodovico" (p. 166).

6. "The Alienated City: Reflections on 'Othello,'" *Encounter,* 17 (1961), 13.

7. Most critics, too many to cite, see Desdemona as wholly good and virtuous, even saintly. Those not mentioned elsewhere in this paper who have a negative or mixed view of her are: Richard Flatter, *The Moor of Venice* (London: William Heineman, 1950); L. A. G. Strong, "Shakespeare and the Psychologists," *Literature and Psychology,* 14 (1964), 56–61; Robert Dickes, "Desdemona: An Innocent Victim?," *American Imago,* 27 (1970), 279–97; Stephen Reid, "Desdemona's Guilt," *American Imago,* 27 (1970), 245–62; and Janet Overmyer, "Shakespeare's Desdemona: A Twentieth Century View," *The University Review,* 37 (1971), 304–305.

8. Though using the Folio edition, which reads "kisses," as copy-text, editors adopt the quarto's "sighs" more often than not; Alvin Kernan, editor of the Signet *Othello,* is a pleasing exception. Though most offer no explanation for the gratuitous change, "kisses" evidently violates their sense of Desdemona's character and the dramatic situation. The differences in the Folio and quarto texts prompt some of Ridley's most unpromising speculation: "Perhaps the compositor had recently been setting a passage in which 'world of kisses' occurred, and it stuck in his mind." He finds it "hard to imagine anyone making the alteration deliberately" (p. 30n). Ridley, of course, is justified in retaining "sighs" since his copy-text is the quarto edition.

9. Ridley (p. 36n) compares Shakespeare's use of "rites" here to *Romeo and Juliet,* III.ii.8–9: " 'Lovers can see to do their amorous rites / By their own beauties.' "

10. So strong are Ridley's objections to this passage that he even calls Thomas Rymer to his aid; he quotes from *A Short View of Tragedy* (1693): " 'Now follows a long rabble of Jack-pudding farce [i.e. stuffing, padding] between Jago and Desdemona, that runs on with all the little plays, jingle, and trash below the patience of any Country Kitchenmaid with her Sweetheart . . . and when every moment she might expect to hear her Lord (as she calls him) that she runs so mad after, is arrived or lost' " (p. 54n).

11. Desdemona is obviously Othello's "warrior" because she has come to battle along with him, but his address has sexual implications as well. It recalls the opening line of Spenser's "Sonnett LVII" in the *Amoretti:* "Sweet warriour when shall I have peace with you?"

12. Heilman sees the play as "a drama about Everyman" (p. 139); Leo Kirschbaum ("The Modern Othello," *ELH,* 11 [1944]) regards Othello as a "romantic idealist" (p. 289); R. N. Hallstead ("Idolatrous Love: A New Approach to *Othello,*" *Shakespeare Quarterly,* 19 [1968]) finds in him the pattern of "idolatrous love" (p. 107); Wilson Knight (*The Wheel of Fire,* 5th ed. [1930; rev. New York: Meridian Books, 1958]) sees in Desdemona and Othello "essential" man and woman (p. 111).

13. Studies by Eldred D. Jones (*Othello's Countrymen* [London: Oxford Univ. Press, 1965] and *The Elizabethan Image of Africa* [Charlottesville: The Univ. Press of

Virginia, 1971]) and G. K. Hunter ("Othello and Colour Prejudice," *Proceedings of the British Academy,* 8 [1967], 139–63) deal with Elizabethan attitudes toward blacks and affirm that they were not generally regarded with tolerance. Two articles that examine the way racial attitudes work in *Othello* are Miriam Halevy's "The Racial Problem in Shakespeare" in *The Jewish Quarterly,* 14, No. 2 (1966), 3–9; and K. W. Evans's "The Racial Factor in *Othello*" in *Shakespeare Studies,* 5 (1969), 124–40.

14. *William Shakespeare: A Reader's Guide* (1963; rpt. New York: Farrar, 1970), p. 351.

15. The myth is apparent in Iago's and Roderigo's efforts to incite Brabantio (see pp. 240-41 above) and in Iago's absurd suspicions that Othello has slept with Emilia as well as in the rumors that give fuel to those suspicions (I.iii.375–77; II.i.294–95; IV.ii.144–46).

16. Many have commented on Desdemona's passiveness, but there is no indication that Shakespeare means us to see it with the condescension of Fiedler, who describes her as becoming a "passive, whimpering Griselda" (p. 142), or Allardyce Nicoll, who sees her as becoming "a mere slave" to Othello *(Studies in Shakespeare* [London: Hogarth, 1927], p. 88).

17. Compare Nicoll, p. 92.

18. Though my view differs from his, Harley Granville-Barker, in *Prefaces to Shakespeare* (Princeton: Princeton Univ. Press, 1947), is the only critic who sees Lodovico as having a significant function in the play (II, 57–60).

19. The play, of course, does not support such a view of Othello; G. K. Hunter comments: "The fact that the darkness of 'Hell and night' spreads from Iago and then takes over Othello—this fact at least should prevent us from supposing that the blackness is inherent in Othello's barbarian nature" (p. 159).

The End of *Lear*
and a Shape for Shakespearean Tragedy

Duncan S. Harris

In a series of lectures at Bryn Mawr,[1] Frank Kermode approached the study of narrative by, as he said, "discussing fictions of the End— about ways in which, under varying existential pressures, we have imagined the ends of the world." Mr. Kermode proposed that an analysis of these endings "will provide clues to the ways in which fictions, whose ends are consonant with origins, and in concord, however unexpected, with their precedents, satisfy our needs."[2] I think that we can usefully apply his method to the experience of the *Tragedy of King Lear*. If we can isolate the fiction of the end which best describes the horrors of blood and sentiment in which *King Lear* concludes, we will have begun to encompass the play, to understand that construction of language and event which shakes us so deeply. I will argue that the fiction of the end employed in *King Lear* is basically Christian—an assertion which, on the face of it, is not terribly surprising, considering the cultural context out of which the play came, but one which, nonetheless, has been ignored or disputed by many critics.[3]

Before I begin my argument, I want to make clear that I use the term "Christian" only in the sense that the end of *King Lear* depends for its astonishing effect on those ideas usually associated with the Christian conception of man's place in the world and with the Christian understanding of death.[4] This is not to say that the play is narrowly doctrinaire or that a true appreciation of the play hinges upon the finer points of Christian dogma. I will argue instead that the play presents a vision of cosmos—not chaos—and that its cosmos is Christian.

According to the Christian notion of the fallen world, man's estate stretches from the gates of hell to the portals of heaven; in this fallen world, man lives between the doors of certainty, in hope of an apocalyptic understanding which can redeem him from present confusion. His life is a journey toward one of those doors, and his death not only ends this journey but brings down judgment upon it. Death relieves man of the obscurity of the flesh, and God's judgment gives value to what has passed. Shakespeare follows the paradigm of a Christian's life—progression through time to the certainty of death—in his four great tragedies: beginning in the semblance of order, the tragedies progress into deeper and deeper confusion and then resolve themselves in death and final clarity.[5] The progression through mutability to the end of time, to death, judgment, and understanding, is the form of Shakespearean tragedy.

Shakespeare's characters as well as his plots repeatedly testify to a belief in a final clarity. In the dark comedy *Measure for Measure* Isabella asks for the patience to out-wait the reign of error when the Duke will not believe her charges against Angelo:

> Keep me in patience, and with ripened time
> Unfold the evil which is here wrapp'd up.
>
> *(V.i.116–17)*[6]

In *King Lear* this affirmation is thrice repeated. The repentant Edmund gives us one text:

> What you have charg'd me with, that have I done,
> And more, much more; the time will bring it out.
>
> *(V.iii.162–63)*

Edgar too places his faith in time:

> Mark the high noises, and thyself bewray
> When false opinion, whose wrong thoughts defile thee,
> In thy just proof repeals and reconciles thee.
>
> *(III.vi.114–16)*

Cordelia simply affirms, "Time shall unfold what plighted cunning hides" (I.i.280). As Caroline Spurgeon points out, "We find that one of the most important of time's functions is as a revealer and disentangler of truth."[7]

J. V. Cunningham appears to ignore this function of time when he argues that the form of Shakespeare's tragedies belongs to the Donatan tradition of an action leading from order to disorder. However, he so qualifies his statement that he presents instead the Christian formulation:

The greater part of a Shakespearean tragedy does, it is true, consist of a progression toward deeper and deeper disorder, but a) the beginning is not tranquil since there is already some disorder (as in the opening scenes of *Romeo, Hamlet,* and *Othello*), and b) the end always involves (with the curious exception of *Troilus* whose literary form is still a matter of dispute) the restoration of order and tranquility.[8]

Cunningham's qualifications are just; however, when he concludes that the Donatan "principle is clearly operative,"[9] he overlooks a more economical explanation. Cunningham's first qualification, the presence of disorder in the exposition, accords less with the Donatan formulation than with what I have called the Christian: the Donatan tradition demands initial order; the Christian places man in a fallen world where chaos constantly threatens the balance he has constructed out of his limited knowledge.

Cunningham's second qualification of the Donatan formulation does more than simply temper the tradition: it flatly contradicts it. Donatus would have tragedy end in disorder; but, as Cunningham points out, Shakespeare's tragedies conclude with the "restoration of order and tranquility." In turn, Cunningham's qualification misleadingly simplifies what actually occurs. True, there is a restoration of order, but the renewed order is a little different from the initial condition out of which the tragedy came. The survivors of the tragic catastrophe may have grown in knowledge and stature by their experience. Still, the possibility of tragedy remains so long as Adam's curse holds. Yet there is another kind of order, another resolution, present at the end of the great Shakespearean tragedies—the order which fully understood and wholly completed past experience possesses. There is nothing left to explain. This particular sort of order, which we rarely or never see in life outside of art, permits us to experience a final clarity and affirms, if only metaphorically, the possibility of complete understanding. The restoration of provisional order, the resolution of the personal and political difficulties, is temporal and, as such, is susceptible to further disruption; the order of clarity, of understanding, belongs to the sphere of permanence and finitude, available in its secular version only through imagination. Both kinds of order, both resolutions, exist at the end of tragedy; both are significant.

But these resolutions do not completely encompass the experience of the end of *King Lear*; actually, four different sorts of resolutions—not one or two—occur in the final act of the play. One is the resolution of justice, meting out reward and punishment according to merit. The second sort of resolution negates the first, providing in the suffering deaths of Cordelia, Lear, and Gloucester vicious hurt in place of deserved solace. The third resolution, for those who survive the catastrophe, presents the return to perilous balance in which the tragedy began. And the fourth resolution, in which the theater audience and the surviviors share, is the catharsis of clarity. These resolutions are distinct, but they are also interdependent: no one of them alone will account for the totality of our reaction to the incidents which close the play, and all of them together are essential to a complete presentation of man's place in a Christian cosmos. Let us examine more carefully these four resolutions.

I

Justice is a positive ideal to which men look for assurance of order. Laws—human, natural, divine—describe the order in which men live, and justice gives force to those laws. Justice in *King Lear* takes a particular form which emphasizes its function as an instrument of order. Paul Siegel takes note of the "poetic fitness of the retribution that overtakes villainy" in Shakespeare's tragedies, and he quotes Miles Coverdale, the sixteenth-century priest and translator, who found God's hand in the execution of poetic justice: "God tempereth and frameth the punishment even like unto the sin."[10] Justice in *King Lear* is often particularly fitting. Edgar sees the relationship between Edmund's illegitimate birth and Gloucester's blinding:

> The Gods are just, and of our pleasant vices
> Make instruments to plague us;
> The dark and vicious place where thee he got
> Cost him his eyes.
>
> *(V.iii.170–73)*

Edgar discovers the justice of his father's blinding when he connects the darkness of Gloucester's sightless world with the darkness—both physical and moral—of the adulterous bed in which Gloucester begot his betrayer. In another instance of the execution of poetic justice no explicit moral is drawn, for the circumstances make it plain. Cornwall, a guest in Gloucester's home, blinds his host and is in turn killed by one of his own servants. The trangressor of the social order dies at the hand of a servant who opposes his master. No lesson of the schoolroom could be clearer.

But justice in *King Lear* is something less than an ideal, even though the didactic links between crime and punishment emphasize the sense of order and suggest divine providence. After Coverdale says that crime and punishment "do agree together . . . in form and likeness," he adds that they also complement each other "in proportion and quality."[11] Our modern sense of the seriousness of adultery may have eroded, but the play itself suggests that blinding is a disproportionate penalty for Gloucester's "pleasant vices." The Gods may be just, but they also create "instruments to *plague* us" (italics mine). This justice seems harsh, bitter, brutal. Other instances of justice in the play also call into question its ideal quality. When Lear acts as judge of his daughters' protestations of love, we see justice fail: here justice rewards imposture and punishes truth. Later, when Lear in his madness sits as judge of the joint-stool, his pathetic confusion and his evident powerlessness mock our illusions about the efficacy and the ideality of justice.

Justice in *King Lear* is not only harsh and didactic but also limited. In order for justice to sustain order, it must not only punish crime but also reward virtue and relieve unmerited suffering. By the end of *King Lear,* however, we have seen only the punitive aspect of justice. Although Albany promises that "All friends shall taste / The wages of their virtue" (V.iii.302–303), neither Lear nor Cordelia collects those wages. Albany offers Lear "comfort to this great decay" and declares, using the royal plural, "We will resign, / During the life of this old Majesty, / To him our absolute power" (V.iii.297–300). But Lear never recovers sufficiently to enjoy his comfort or to exercise his restored dominion. Cordelia, too, is beyond any temporal ministrations; if we are to find any mitigation of the brutality which Lear's innocent daughter is made to suffer, we must look elsewhere.

Shakespeare was not content to allow his audience to enjoy the simplistic affirmations of order presented in the deaths of Edmund, Cornwall, Regan, and Goneril, nor was he willing to provide so literary a solution to the problem of guiltless suffering as would be suggested by a happy ending in which Lear is restored and Cordelia saved. Albany, who saw in the deaths of Edmund, Regan, and Goneril a "judgment of the heavens" (V.iii.231), offers no transcendent reading of the cruel and tortured passing of Lear and Cordelia. The justice which ends the lives of the three evil children and which holds the audience's attention during the first part of the play's last scene utterly dissolves with the entrance of Lear holding the dead Cordelia in his arms. Shakespeare knew that the resolution of justice is not the ultimate resolution of tragedy; Albany specifically warns us against it:

> This judgment of the heavens, that makes us tremble,
> Touches us not with pity.
>
> *(V.iii.231–32)*

We may find the second part of the Aristotelian definition of the emotional effect of tragedy—fear and pity—only when we come to examples of injustice. The fates of the victims of villainy, not those of the villains themselves, complete the formula for tragedy.

So we move from the incomplete resolution offered by justice to the unjust and tragic death of Cordelia. Lear and Gloucester belong as well in this category, although they do not share Cordelia's perfect innocence. Gloucester is the victim of his own sensuality, and Lear does the ultimate penance for being a proud, foolish, fond old man. However, their suffering is so much greater than their crimes that the radical disproportion between guilt and punishment makes them martyrs, sharing with Cordelia the curse of mutability.

Tragedy is, in part, the victory of man's fallen state over his attempts to order his environment by reason and purpose. Man's hope of dealing successfully with his condition is represented in literature by poetic justice; his failure to do so, by tragedy. G. Wilson Knight so assesses the power of tragedy:

> Tragedy is most poignant in that it is purposeless, unreasonable. It is the most fearless artistic facing of the ultimate cruelty of things.[12]

This ultimate cruelty of things leaves man ultimately defenseless.

This cruelty, at one point in *King Lear*, takes the form of unreconcilable knowledge. Gloucester, confronted by his son's self-revelation and greatly weakened by his trials, cannot sustain the knowledge of Edgar's virtue and of his suffering. When Edgar confesses his identity to his father, hoping to gain his blessing, Gloucester's

> flaw'd heart,
> Alack, too weak the conflict to support!
> 'Twixt two extremes of passion, joy and grief,
> Burst smilingly.
>
> *(V.iii.196–99)*

Lear too dies in a state of radical conflict. But he dies not precisely from the ultimate cruelty of unreconcilable knowledge; instead he succumbs to the cruelty of being stretched between the opposite poles of reality and illusion. He knows that Cordelia is dead:

> She's gone for ever.
> I know when one is dead, and when one lives;
> She's dead as earth.
>
> *(V.iii.259–61)*

Yet he will not believe what he knows; he tries repeatedly to prove she lives, but even when his imagination momentarily persuades him that there yet is life in the quiet body, even when he thinks that he sees a movement of the feather placed on her lips, his doubt makes his statement conditional:

> This feather stirs; she lives! *if it be so,*
> It is a chance which does redeem all sorrows
> That ever I have felt.
>
> (V.iii.265–67; italics mine)

When his mind can no longer sustain the tension, he dies, with the ambiguous command which is the product of his illusionary hope and his final knowledge:

> Look on her, look, her lips,
> Look there, look there!
>
> (V.iii.310–11)

Neither Gloucester nor Lear can be saved by human intervention; justice can offer them nothing.

Lear and Gloucester die in the most radical states of emotional confusion. Cordelia dies not because of an inability to reconcile various knowledges and feelings but because of an external confusion which keeps her would-be saviors from their task. Seconds after Albany discovers Edmund's plot on the lives of Lear and Cordelia, he sends an officer to rescind Edmund's order, but the message is moments too late, for Lear enters, cradling the dead Cordelia, crying, "I might have sav'd her; now she's gone for ever! / . . . I kill'd the slave that was a-hanging thee" (V.iii.270, 274). The ultimate cruelty of things demands Cordelia's life, despite the two attempts to save it. Her death, like Lear's and Gloucester's, offers no solace to the human intellect; our attempts to recreate the order lost in Eden constantly fail.

For those who survive the senseless cruelty and the workings of a harsh and limited justice, there is a third sort of resolution. During the major part of the play, Kent and Edgar have been forced to appear in disguise, to hide their identities, if not their natures. The discarding of their masks represents this third resolution. Here there is a return to the condition of perilous balance between the ever-threatening chaos beneath temporal order and the power of man's intellect to sustain this order, to keep chaos confined. When provisional order returns, men like Kent and Edgar can return to the identities of which disorder robbed them. In addition, those who survive often have learned from their experience and are better able to deal with what the world presents to them.

Edgar is the most active in the resolution. After the death of his father, he claims from his brother the identity which Edmund took from him. Now the Earl of Gloucester, Edgar takes his place with Kent and Albany to form the chorus which guides us through the final scene. Edgar is no longer the

> brother noble,
> Whose nature is so far from doing harms
> That he suspects none.
>
> (I.ii.186–88)

In fact, his new knowledge of the way of the world allows him to assume two new disguises in the resolution: he first pretends to be a humble messenger when he delivers to Albany the letter from Goneril and his offer to challenge Edmund, and then he becomes the vizored knight, the nameless challenger, who dispatches Edmund. These new disguises are initiated by Edgar to serve his own purposes; they are not forced upon him by circumstances, as was the mask of Poor Tom. When provisional order returns, Edgar's experience makes him better able to sustain it.

The banished Kent, having reunited Lear with Cordelia, also resumes the position he has cast off. His last act in the play is to confess his masquerade to the distracted Lear, although the saddened king cannot understand it. Kent,

> who in disguise
> Follow'd his enemy king, and did him service
> Improper for a slave,
>
> (V.iii.219–21)

will perform one last act of loyalty: he who followed his banished king in his tortured wanderings will attend him one final time.

> I have a journey, sir, shortly to go;
> My master calls me, I must not say no.
>
> (V.iii.321–22)

He returns to the perilous balance, but, in doing so, he underlines its temporary quality and looks ahead to that conclusion—the final resolution—which will surpass all others.

Both Edgar and Kent, in discarding disguise and returning to a condition of provisional order, do not actually resume what were their previous identities; their recent experiences have annealed them. Kent argued vehemently with Lear in the first scene and again when Lear would not believe that Regan treated his messenger disrespectfully; now he is no longer willing to cause Lear to suffer in the interest of truth:

> Vex not his ghost: O! let him pass; he hates him
> That would upon the rack of this tough world
> Stretch him out longer.
>
> *(V.iii.313–15)*

Edgar, too, has undergone a change: he who was "far from doing harms" (I.ii.187) has killed his brother; he, who at the beginning of this series of events saw no evil, "shall never see so much" (V.iii.326) again. But it is Albany who, in the end, has grown most. Lear divided his kingdom because he feared "future strife" (I.i.44) among his sons-in-law; but he misjudged: Goneril, not her husband, ruled and threatened conflict between the new principalities. Leo Kirschbaum persuasively describes Albany's growth from a weak husband to a sensitive and forceful leader.[13] Albany directs our feelings at the deaths of Goneril, Regan, and Edmund: this sight of their bodies "touches us not with pity" (V.iii.232). He manages the stage: "Produce the bodies, be they alive or dead" (V.iii.230). He promises to Lear comfort and to Edgar and Kent reward for their services. Deep in his wife's shadow during most of the play, Albany at last shines with the strength and knowledge that the tragedy has allowed him to acquire. He finally proves himself to be his wife's master and master of his realm. When order returns, he strengthens it by becoming what he never was.

Although a strengthened order has returned, although Edgar tells us that "we that are young shall never see so much" again, there is no assurance that what has passed can prevent future tragedy. Chaos is always imminent, no matter what quantity of greatness or knowledge can be ranged against it. The resolution offered in Kent, Edgar, and Albany is wholly in the realm of provisional order. Shakespeare is to offer greater recompense for the sufferings of Lear, Gloucester, and Cordelia than the growth of Kent, Edgar, and Albany, and he gives us greater solace for the irremediable crimes of Goneril, Regan, and Edmund than the deaths of criminals.

II

The three resolutions we have just examined are all in some way incomplete, limited, or unsatisfying. The resolution of justice fails to fulfill our hopes of seeing Cordelia's virtue rewarded, and it exceeds our expectations of the extent of Lear's and Gloucester's punishment. The resolution provided by a return to provisional order is limited. No one can right the wrong Cordelia suffers; provisional order will always be subject to such catastrophe. In no way can the return to order or the operation of justice prevent future disorder, future tragedy. The last of the incomplete resolutions illustrates this realization; the resolution of unjust death negates the previous two and offers only anguish. William R. Elton makes of this resolution the final statement of the direction which Lear's tragedy has taken us:

> In conclusion, I have indicated . . . an implicit direction of the tragedy: annihilation of faith in poetic justice, and, within the confines of a grim, pagan universe, annihilation of faith in divine justice. In this dark world, the last choruses tell us, we find the promised end, or the image of that horror, in which man's chief joy is to be removed from the rack of this tough world and in which man's pathetic solace is—ultimate irony—the illusion that that which he has most loved still breathes: "Look on her, look, her lips, Look there, look there!" No redemption stirs at this world's end; only suffering, tears, pity, and loss—*and* illusion.[14]

This sort of resolution resolves nothing: it denies order; it leaves the audience shaken, bewildered. I will argue that the play moves beyond such despair, but the final vision is scarcely less shocking than this penultimate one described by Elton.

Elton's reading of the ending of *King Lear* contradicts radically the kind of ending which literary theorists have repeatedly found in tragedy. F. R. Leavis, in describing the experience of tragedy in general, gives no support to Elton's vision of *King Lear:*

> We have contemplated a painful action, involving death and the destruction of the good, admirable, and sympathetic, and yet instead of being depressed we enjoy a sense of enhanced vitality.[15]

Joseph Wood Krutch finds that the tragic author "seizes upon suffering and uses it only as a means by which joy may be wrung out of existence"; tragedy does "what all religions do, for it gives a rationality, a meaning, and a justification to the universe."[16] Elton clearly found no such affirmation in *King Lear.*

Because most of the critical readings of the tragedy of *King Lear* which reveal some sort of affirmation fail to account for Lear's horrible death, racked by illusory hope and unacceptable knowledge, they leave the reader or theater-goer as Elton left him, without a convincing affirmation of coherence. L. C. Knights picks out the single note of joy in the conclusion and points to it as the good which justifies all pain:

> In the successive stripping away of the layers of appearance, what remains to discover is the most fundamental reality of all. In the play it takes the form of the love and forgiveness of Cordelia.[17]

But the reconciliation of Lear and Cordelia is only one part joy mixed with many parts sorrow. I think that the recognition of affirmation which caused Knights to point to Cordelia's love and forgiveness is generally right, but the road taken stops far short of the goal. He gives us only an unequal balance, not a conclusion which encompasses all we have experienced.

How, then, can we justify Leavis' sense of enhanced vitality? How can we substantiate Aristotle's metaphor of catharsis? I have suggested that Shakespeare's tragedies move from provisional order to chaos and then to a clarifying resolution, that Shakespearean tragedy manifests the Christian conception of time which will make all things plain. All things *are* plain at the end of *King Lear:* the tragedy is over, and the characters who participated in it, with the exception of Edgar and Albany, are gone. A moment of clarity is the objective of tragedy. That moment of clarity comes when the tale ends, when the world ends. When the veil which the curse of Eden has cast over the lives of Lear, his knights, kinsmen, and countrymen, is briefly lifted, we can glimpse finitude and permanence.

In the last act of *King Lear,* the motives and the actions of all the characters are seen wholly and unambiguously. Edmund and Goneril confess; Kent and Edgar discard their disguises; Albany finally fills out his role as the first noble of the kingdom. The language which Goneril and Regan, Kent and Edgar, the good as well as the evil, have used to obfuscate reality is now used to make clear all relationships, motives, meanings. The audience has seen a completed action, and there is no longer any thread of plot or motive left tangled.

This final untangling of the web of *Lear* is cathartic. The dramatic confusions in which the audience has been immersed are relieved at the end of the play, and a momentary clarity prevails. Clarity is characteristic of most narrative closures, and the sense of satisfaction resulting from a well-told story in which all the incidents lead to an orderly and comprehensive conclusion is one of the primary techniques in a writer's repertory. However, when Fielding brings together the separate strands of his tale in the conclusion of *Tom Jones,* we appreciate the magician's facility, we are pleased with the fates accorded to the characters, but we are not invited to look on clarity itself. Shakespeare might have ended King Lear as Tate did; he had the authority of his source for such an ending,[18] and he could write at least as good a line as Tate's concluding "Truth and Vertue shall at last succeed."[19] But he chose instead to look into the heart of light and not at what moral that light might produce. Our gaze in the last scene is unrelentingly fixed on the final horror in which the preceding course of events culminates. That vision is apocalyptic in its clarity, its terror, and its hope.

When Kent, Edgar, and Albany are confronted with the howling father Lear bearing his dead child, the three see a vision of the earth's end:

> *Kent.*   Is this the promis'd end?
> *Edgar.*   Or image of that horror?
> *Albany.*   Fall and cease.
>
> *(V.iii.263–64)*

Where in this "image of that horror" can we find an affirmation of order, a joy, a renewed sense of vitality? We find it in that fearful yet all-justifying "promis'd end," of which the last scene of *King Lear* is an image. We find it in the knowledge that all things will be made plain, can be made plain. At the final judgment man will be relieved of the fallibility of flesh, and he will share in God's complete understanding; at the end of *King Lear* we see the end of a particular group of experiences, and we are made to comprehend all.

Edgar's last words, the last words in the play, instruct us in the nature of the events we have seen, in the radical character of tragedy, and in the condition in which it leaves us:

> The weight of this sad time we must obey;
> Speak what we feel, not what we ought to say.
> The oldest hath borne most: we that are young
> Shall never see so much, nor live so long.
>
> *(V.iii.323–26)*

What we have just seen allows us, while we bear the very bitter "weight of this sad time," to "speak what we feel, not what we ought to say," to command language to express fully what has occurred. The limitations of language and the limitations of man for which they stand are momentarily rescinded through art.[20] Edgar never expects to see another version of "this sad time." *King Lear* is only a metaphor and it offers only a vision, but it does affirm a terrible clarity, a "promis'd end."

III

Although it is beyond the scope of this paper to do more than suggest the application of the paradigm developed here to other Shakespearean tragedies, I do want to affirm that *King Lear* is not alone in its embodiment of the form I have outlined. The conclusions of the great tragedies—*Hamlet, Othello, Lear,* and *Macbeth*—all incorporate the four resolutions discussed above. The resolution of justice is manifested in the deaths of Claudius and of Macbeth and his lady and in the certain punishment of Iago. The counter-resolution of the unrelieved suffering of innocence is offered in the putative suicide of Ophelia, in the murders of Desdemona and of Lady Macduff and her children, and in Young Siward's death in battle. The third resolution, the restoration of temporal order, is accomplished by the transfer of power to Fortinbras, Cassio, and Malcolm. The catharsis of clarity, the great sense of the lifting of the weight of obscurity, is underlined by the injunctions of Hamlet and Othello to tell their stories, stories which at the ends of these two plays are complete and which only then can be told because only then are they understood. In *Macbeth* Macduff proclaims that at last "The time is free" (V.vii.55). The witches' prophecies have been fulfilled, the tale is done. These common elements allow us to see through their particular realizations to the Christian vision of human experience which stands behind them.

Cunningham's paradigm of Shakespearean tragedy shows the hero moving from order through disorder to order again. But this model does not fit the facts. Tragedy occurs only in a world where there is always present the potentiality for tragedy; this is not a world of order, but rather one of perilous balance. True tragedy is a rarity, but it is a rarity no further away than a misdirected word or an apparently innocuous act. Further, the course of tragedy does not merely return us to order, does not improve our condition so much as to render a second tragedy impossible. It is not a disease which immunizes us against further attacks. To ask this sort of immunization is to expect emancipation from mortality. Tragedy, successfully conducted, can do only one thing, and that one thing, for almost all practical purposes, is gratuitous. Although tragedy can demonstrate no strategy to lead us out of the worldly labyrinth we inhabit, it can give us a sense of what it is to be free of obscurity, to touch a final reality. Just as man has been able to create out of the powers of his imagination a metaphoric explanation for his limited nature in the myth of the Fall and the curse of Babel, so has he found in tragedy an image by which he can momentarily reach beyond his limitations to the clarity he has lost. After this fugitive resolution, we return to the perilous balance. But we have been able, if only for a moment, to speak what we feel.[21]

Notes:

1. Published under the title, *The Sense of an Ending: Studies in the Theory of Fiction* (New York: Oxford Univ. Press, 1967).
2. Kermode, p. 5.
3. For a recent, brief summary of both Christian and nihilist interpretations of *King Lear,* see Marvin Rosenberg, *The Masks of Lear* (Berkeley: Univ. of California Press, 1972), pp. 323–26.
4. Mary Lascelles (*"King Lear* and Doomsday," *Shakespeare Survey,* 26 [1973], 69–79) has suggested that *King Lear* is "burdened with a vision of Doomsday" (70) and argues convincingly certain parallels between the play and the numerous church mural paintings of the Last Judgment.
5. For a significant reinterpretation of the Aristotelian "catharsis" as clarification, see Leon Golden, "Catharsis," *Transactions and Proceedings of the American Philological Association,* 93 (1962), 51–60. O. B. Hardison, with Golden in view, finds this sort of cathartic clarification in *Hamlet.* See his "Three Types of Renaissance Catharsis," *Renaissance Drama,* NS 2 (1969), 3–22.
6. Citations from *Lear* refer to the New Arden text, ed. Kenneth Muir, 8th ed. (London: Methuen, 1952). References to Shakespeare's other plays are to *The Riverside Shakespeare,* ed. G. Blakemore Evans (Boston: Houghton, 1974).
7. Caroline F. E. Spurgeon, *Shakespeare's Imagery and What It Tells Us* (Boston: Beacon, 1958), p. 172. The idea that time reveals truth was proverbial. See Morris Palmer Tilley, *A Dictionary of the Proverbs in the Sixteenth and Seventeenth Centuries* (Ann Arbor: Univ. of Michigan Press, 1950), T 580. For a discussion of the history of this concept, see Fritz Saxl, "Veritas Filia Temporis," *Philosophy and History: Essays Presented to Ernst Cassirer,* ed. Raymond Klibansky and H. J. Paton (New York: Harper Row, 1963), pp. 197–222.
8. *Woe or Wonder: The Emotional Effect of Shakespearean Tragedy* (Denver: Swallow, 1964), p. 39.
9. Cunningham, p. 39.
10. Quoted in *Shakespearean Tragedy and the Elizabethan Compromise* (New York: New York Univ. Press, 1957), p. 85 and pp. 213–14.
11. Siegel, p. 214.
12. "Lear and the Comedy of the Grotesque," in his *Wheel of Fire* (Oxford: Oxford Univ. Press, 1930), p. 191.
13. "Albany," *Shakespeare Survey,* 13 (1969), 20–29.

14. *King Lear and the Gods* (San Marino: Huntington Library, 1966), p. 334.
15. "Tragedy and the 'Medium,' " in *The Importance of Scrutiny,* ed. Eric Bentley (New York: New York Univ. Press, 1964), p. 219.
16. "The Tragic Fallacy," in *A Krutch Omnibus* (New York: Morrow, 1970), p. 20.
17. *Some Shakespearean Themes* (London: Chatto and Windus, 1960), p. 99.
18. In Holinshed and *The True Chronicle History of King Leir,* Lear regains his kingdom and Cordelia survives her father's restoration.
19. N. Tate, *The History of King Lear* (1681; facsimile rpt. London: Cornmarket Press, 1969), p. 67.
20. My argument here ultimately runs counter to the perceptive analysis of Anne Barton ("Shakespeare and the Limits of Language," *Shakespeare Survey,* 24 [1971], 19–30). I do agree with her central contention that Shakespeare often shows the inability of language fully to render meaning and feeling, but I disagree that such is his final position, as I argue below.
21. I wish to acknowledge two works which have generally influenced this study: Roger L. Cox's *Between Earth and Heaven: Shakespeare, Dostoevsky, and the Meaning of Christian Tragedy* (New York: Holt, Rinehart, 1969) describes the numerous parallels between *King Lear* and Paul's letters to the Corinthians and emphasizes the difficulty of calling the effect of the tragedy either affirmative or pessimistic, and H. D. F. Kitto's *Form and Meaning in Drama: A Study of Six Greek Plays and of Hamlet* (London: Methuen, 1956) and its seminal definition of religious drama have everywhere influenced my reading of *King Lear.* Work on this article was made possible by a Summer Research Fellowship granted by the Graduate School of the University of Wyoming.

Macbeth at Stratford-upon-Avon, 1955

MICHAEL MULLIN

T he 1955 *Macbeth* at the Shakespeare Memorial Theatre, Stratford-upon-Avon, has become a standard of excellence by which stage historians judge twentieth-century productions of the play.[1] From reviews we know a good deal about how Laurence Olivier and Vivien Leigh interpreted the main roles. Yet our knowledge of the production as a whole is fragmentary—its overall design is lost in the conflicting impressions of different reviewers. That there was a design is certain, however, for the director Glen Byam Shaw made a unique record of his work—a promptbook and two notebooks.[2] His promptbook shows how he staged the play, with cues for effects and with detailed stage maps for blocking and stage business. His notebooks analyze each scene and each character. Together with reviews and photographs, these manuscripts give us a fascinating, detailed blueprint of the play's nonverbal dimension: the actions, sights, and sounds implicit in the text, which come to life only in performance. I shall first look briefly at the script, costumes and sets, and then examine the play's formal rhythms and dramatic imagery as Shaw mapped them.

I

Of course a nonverbal dimension of the play appears in every performance. Yet it seldom appears with the clarity it had in 1955. What makes Shaw's work especially valuable is that it was exceptionally successful in the theater and exceptionally well documented, altogether a rare combination. The play is difficult. Actors and directors from Davenant onwards have revised it outright or dressed it up in the newest theatrical fad—flying and dancing Witches in Davenant's time, modern dress in our own century.[3] Yet, update it how they might, success has been so elusive that the play is well known as a theatrical jinx. Shaw reconciled the conflicting demands of an old play and a modern audience. He kept the text nearly intact, omitting the spurious Hecate scene (III.v) and the scene following between Lennox and Another Lord (III.vi), elsewhere only cutting a line here and there which would be obscure to today's audience.[4] Costumes were appropriately "medieval"—not crude and simple, however, but elegant, appealing directly to the modern audience's sensibilities. *Punch* (June 15,

269

1955) said pointedly that Olivier's Macbeth goes "to a good barber and is not hung about with old rugs." Vivien Leigh, "serpent-green" (*Daily Mail,* June 8, 1955) wore a "slinky gown and off-red wig" (*Daily Sketch,* June 8, 1955). The costumes for the rest of the cast followed the same fashions, Malcolm standing out in his white tunic and Lady Macduff in her light blue gown.

The settings by Roger Furse blended traditional medieval architecture with modern expressionism. Rough stone steps in wide halls under arches and vaulting dated the scene, and surrealistic distortions of these familiar shapes gave an emotional tone to the settings, so that, said the *Birmingham Mail* (June 8, 1955), they "were in thorough keeping with the mood and spirit of the play, offering as they did the impression of rude and massive halls and storm-racked wastes in which the gloomy and lurid story unfolded itself with perfect propriety." Others sensed this too. "To the eye it is harsh and charmless," said the *News Chronicle* (June 8, 1955), "the castle is jagged and barbaric, with pointed arches and not so much as a claymore to adorn its gaunt walls"; and the *Birmingham Gazette* (June 8, 1955) called it "stark in a Teutonic way."

The director and designer ingeniously maintained continuous action. To avoid interruptions, they used multiple acting areas—the apron stage, upper levels, and an inner stage—within the full stage sets, and for scene changes they alternated action between forestage and full stage. "Tabs" or inner curtains would be drawn behind the action, and the set would be changed while the action continued on the forestage. Thus each of the three "Parts" into which Shaw divided the play ran without pause. In Part I (I.i to II.iv), for example, the setting for the first three scenes (I.i–iii) was a mountain-filled backdrop with a prop tree and three "crags" placed further downstage. Then, for I.iv (set in "Forres," the promptbook says) the tabs were closed, and while action continued downstage, stagehands set the courtyard of Macbeth's Inverness where the next scenes (I.v, through II.iv) were acted without a break when the tabs opened. The overall result was a staging which was at once "modern" in appearance and still continuous in rhythm.

II

Continuity did not mean uniformity. Because Shaw's sets made concrete much that Shakespeare left to the imagination, they marked out patterns within the uninterrupted flow of action. The production's atmosphere was not constant; rather, it modulated from one kind of environment—a place in time and space—to another, and, in turn, to others. In sequence, these changes formed a kind of scenic rhythm. From Shaw's notebook, where he carefully worked out the location and time of day for each scene, the scene plot traces both temporal and spatial rhythms which structure the play's action and meaning.[5] He divided the action into three Parts: Part I (Acts I and II) from the beginning to the discovery of Duncan's murder; Part II (Act III) the banquet scene and events leading up to it; and Part III (Acts IV and V) from the cauldron scene to the end of the play, each Part thus forming a "movement" in the play's rhythmic structure.

While Shaw's time scheme occasionally makes specific what Shakespeare left purposefully vague, it nonetheless marks quite clearly the play's alternating rhythm of day and night, an opposition which, as everyone knows, is also expressed in the imagery. The first Part begins in early evening and ends in dark night, the second Part repeats this movement. In Part III the pattern is reversed, and the play emerges from Macbeth's night to Malcolm's new day. Running parallel to the temporal rhythm in Shaw's scheme is a spatial rhythm. Just as the play modulates between day and night, it also moves in- and out-of-doors. The interior, "an angular, cavernous background that stands slightly askew as if warped by all the treachery it beholds" (Daily Mail, June 8, 1955), set the tone for Shaw's production, as did night and darkness. Yet, just as daylight makes night darker, so the scenes outdoors gave a glimpse of a world outside Macbeth's and made his all the blacker by contrast. This contrast could be muted when the tabs gave a merely neutral background, as they did for I.iv, "Forres." Or it could be heightened, as it was for the scene in England (IV.iii), enclosed by trees and looking out on a picturesque backdrop. Taken in sequence, these locales form a pattern of movement from the open places of heath and camp into the confines of Macbeth's castle in the middle of the play, to end finally "outside Dunsinane Castle." The changes in lighting and setting which the text demands thus form patterns of meaning as full of imaginative power as is the imagery in the text.

III

They also shape the action. When Shaw marked out these movements in time and space, like a conductor marking a musical score, he delineated the play's form. Next, he followed Shakespeare in the subtler effects of stagecraft: the movement of the actors, their number, the volume and intensity of sound and light, and everything else that controls what Granville-Barker called the play's "music"—its pace and tempo. The result

Richard David called a "meditative pace," meaning that the pace was at times hesitant and slow, and then, like the mind's own kindling in its thought processes, it would flash forward in a dazzling burst.[6] Again and again the reviewers insist on this effect: "Macbeth grew in stature throughout the evening;"[7] "grows steadily as he wades through his sea of blood towards doom;"[8] "steadily gathers terrific momentum."[9]

> Macbeth came in at Stratford-upon-Avon in thunder, lightning and in rain. It thundered and flashed too, in our imaginations, though the storm did not begin at once. That is as it should be. The idea must grow. . . . Macbeth, for many people, must strike twelve at once. For them he must be all sound and fury that, as we know on good authority, signify nothing. That has so often been the cause of disaster. A Macbeth has not been able to sustain his frenzy, and the play has sagged fatally to its end.[10]

The production did not so much eliminate violence from the opening as modulate it. The reviewer for *Truth* (June 15, 1955) said: "The pace of the first two scenes, hastened by the stormy music of Anthony Hopkins, is very exciting. The play rushes towards the first entrance of Macbeth. When it reaches him, it suddenly slows down." The real artistry of Shaw's direction lay in his skillful alternation of brisk and slow tempos, each crisis wound up a little tighter than the one before and the whole rhythm derived from his sensitive scrutiny of the text. "The rhythm," Shaw wrote, "is extraordinary. There is a feeling of tremendous speed." To convey that speed to the audience, Shakespeare requires changes in pace, not rapidity alone.

Bursts of action and voices raised in alarm punctuate the play. The discovery of Duncan's murder (II.iii), Macbeth's defiant terror at the solemn supper (III.iv), and, last, his desperate swordfight with Macduff are three points of intensity which mark out the great rhythm of the play. At each peak, Shaw set off a dazzling theatrical explosion. When Macduff goes to Duncan's room, "There are a few agonising moments of suspense which should seem like an eternity and then the appalling crime is discovered," Shaw wrote in his notebook. Then, after the crime is told, "the whole castle is in an uproar. The Alarum bell crashes out and half-naked figures stand about in the Courtyard confused and terrified." The promptbook calls for more than a score of actors to fill the stage from every entrance and at every level. When Banquo's ghost appears, "Macbeth turns and sees it and practically goes off his head in terror," wrote Shaw. At this point, Olivier leapt on the table and outfaced the ghost amidst the clatter of flying tableware and the shocked stares of the guests.[11] And, finally, when Macbeth is cornered in Dunsinane, the stage rings with the sounds of steel on steel, shouts, and trumpets. Attack is met with counterattack. Young Siward falls. "Macduff meets Macbeth. . . . For a moment Macbeth despairs" upon hearing of Macduff's untimely birth, "but when Macduff orders him to yield and calls him a coward his courage comes back and he fights it out to the end," wrote Shaw. "The battle is won and retreat is sounded." The promptbook records blow-by-blow the long and violent battle between Macbeth and Macduff—the two men fighting from one level to another until, with his knife at Macbeth's throat, "Macduff pushes Macbeth off [stage]."

Between these high points there are relatively quieter stretches, each of which serves to prepare the audience for the violence to come. In these stretches Shaw carefully checked the pace. Some of the reviewers complained that it was too "restrained."[12] Yet, seen as part of the play's larger rhythms, that restraint had a purpose, even when it violated stage traditions. The dagger speech has usually been a "big" scene in which great actors were expected to pull out all the stops and exhibit fits of terror.[13] Olivier underplayed it. "Lady Macbeth has gone to drug the grooms," Richard David writes:

> Macbeth is giving last instructions to the servant. The man is still beside him when he sees the spectral dagger and checks at it like a pointer. With a terrible effort he withdraws his gaze for a moment and dismisses the servant; then with a swift and horrid compulsion swings round again. The first part of the dagger speech was spoken with a sort of broken quiet, only the sudden shrillness of "Mine eyes are made the fools o' th' other senses" and "There's no such thing" revealing the intolerable tension that strains the speaker. . . . Olivier dismissed the influence of evil in its physical manifestation only to be more strongly seized by it in his mind. The second part of the speech sank to a drugged whisper and, speaking, Macbeth moved, as in a dream, towards Duncan's room, but with his face turned away from it. Tarquin's strides were only dimly reflected in his dragging pace, and it was the already trodden stones behind him that Macbeth, with deprecating hand, implored to silence. It was this scene above all that brought the audience under enchantment.[14]

The promptbook, which repeatedly calls for "a step" this way and that, shows a sort of slow motion circling before he finally goes the way the dagger points. In short, Shaw followed the play's extraordinary rhythm, even when it meant that stage traditions would be shattered, and his spectators' expectations would be disappointed.

Within the great rhythms, there are of course smaller ones. Consider, for example, the scene in which Lady Macduff and her young son meet their fate, a scene which builds towards the climax in which Macbeth himself is slain. Shaw's staging brought out its internal rhythm. It begins quietly with the anxious mother (Maxine Audley) consulting a nobleman. In Shaw's production, she was accompanied by three children, one, the promptbook says, a baby. They are a family at peace. The nobleman is close kin. "He kisses her," says the promptbook, and as they speak of the children, "he goes back to the baby, saying 'My pretty cousin, Blessing upon you!' " (IV.ii.25b–26a). Lady Macduff banters with her child. She sits in a chair: one of the boys lies down; the other, wearing a toy sword, "looks at the baby and kneels." All are at rest. Then a threat materializes in the form of an old Shepherd telling of dangers, who "is frightened himself and leaves as soon as he has given his warning." The tableau breaks: "Audley rises, moves DS a little. Almost immediately, the two terrible brutes who murdered Banquo appear." One boy "takes a step . . . drops his sword" then turns to his mother, "puts his arms around her; hides his face." The other boy "runs to LC top of steps. Haddrick [the murderer] grabs [him] hits him on head with R hand. . . . John falls on his knees." Warning his mother to run away, "John falls down dead," and Lady Macduff flees shrieking; "Audley screams twice, runs off P perch [exit] with Philip."[15]

Itself a step in the acceleration which reaches top speed in the final combat between Macbeth and Macduff, this scene repeats in miniature that greater movement. The same movement—from still moments at a scene's beginning to violent climax at its end—occurs again and again: Duncan's murder proceeds from a stillness where the owl's shriek and the cricket's cry are the loudest things to the knocking on the gate and thence to alarums and the tumult which greet the crime's discovery. Banquo's uninvited appearance at the banquet comes after a calm, ceremonial seating of the guests and the proposing of a toast. Macduff's conference with Malcolm in England (IV.iii) leads to the shocking news of the murdered family. And, of course, as the fifth act draws to a conclusion, armies gather strength, Dunsinane is fortified, all in preparation for the final hand-to-hand struggle between the tyrant and the avenger. Thus, Shaw's promptbook shows how each gesture and movement of the actors modulates the rhythms, great and small, which shape the play onstage.

IV

Movements and gestures not only control the play's rhythms; they also shape its meaning. Just as the text calls forth a stream of images in the mind when read or spoken, it calls forth dramatic images when performed. Shaw's notebooks and promptbook suggest that, as with verbal imagery, underlying patterns also structure the play's dramatic imagery.[16] The stage business, for instance, contains recurrent dramatic images. Blood colors the play onstage: the wounded sergeant, Macbeth twice bloody-handed, Banquo blood-boltered, the murderer with blood on his face, the bloody babe rising from the cauldron, Macbeth's bloody head on a pike. In another kind of dramatic image, costumes can indicate changes in Macbeth's and Lady Macbeth's state of mind: the dissembling nightgowns at the end of Act II, the royal robes in Act III, a nightgown again for Lady Macbeth in Act IV, and Macbeth's armor in Act V.

The blocking, or placement of actors onstage, reveals a substructure of dramatic imagery. As with the play's scenic rhythm and pace, there are distinct patterns of form and meaning in the way the text requires the actors to move.[17] Shaw's flexible staging permitted him to follow those patterns. The setting framed the action; the text directed it. It specified what the actors did, their relationships to each other, and hence the physical relationships among them. Shaw's stage directions, maps, and notes thus made explicit what the text otherwise only implies.

Two major patterns control the blocking throughout *Macbeth*. On the one hand, blocking consistently isolates Macbeth and Lady Macbeth and, on the other, it unites—or tries to unite—those around them. Consider isolation first. Every time Macbeth comes onstage, a pattern of isolation is enacted. His first appearance sets the pattern. Banquo's query "Good Sir, why do you start, and seem to fear" (I.iii.143) points to Macbeth's physical isolation. The promptbook insists on this, having Macbeth enter before Banquo and stand atop a rock downstage center, then move towards each of the Witches as Banquo stands still; after Ross and Angus come with their news, the stage map separates him from the others by the depth of the stage as he stands downstage OP to consider the supernatural soliciting.

This pattern of isolation recurs with striking regularity. In the Forres scene (I.iv) Macbeth greets Duncan, kneeling in obeisance to his king, only to leave "backing down steps OP" to end up, once again, "OP forestage," physically distant from Duncan and his entourage as he bids the stars hide their fires (I.iv.48–53). When Duncan comes to Inverness (I.vii), Macbeth is absent from the feast, an absence emphasized by the Sewers' dumbshow (which Shaw used to localize the banquet at OP), by Lady Macbeth's chiding, as she enters from OP, and by Macbeth's troubled retreat away from the "banquet" side of the stage as he begs his wife for peace. The murder scene (II.i–ii) opens with an enactment of the estrangement between Macbeth and his friend Banquo, then depicts the stages by which he is cut off from objective reality (the air-drawn dagger), from God and nature (the voice crying "Sleep no more"), and from his wife, who hears only an owl and crickets and thinks him merely foolish. This isolation Shaw brought out by restricting Macbeth's movements, thus setting him in contrast to Lady Macbeth, who circles around him until she finally seizes the daggers. Then, returning from Duncan, she sets him moving "Pushing him towards PS steps" away from the death room. The pattern culminates in the discovery of the murder. Shaw saw the moment vividly and described it in his notebook. When Macbeth reenters, bloody-handed from the slaying of the grooms, "Suddenly Macbeth comes back from the King's apartment & the white faces staring out of the darkness are focused on him. Everyone is completely silent. The Alarum bell stops." Macbeth speaks to the assembly; then, with a grim irony,

> His wife cannot stand the strain & she loses consciousness. Immediately the focus, if not the suspicion, centre on her. Her husband goes to her at once & as she recovers they are face to face with the knowledge of their guilt & surrounded by those strained, white faces peering at them out of the darkness.

Macbeth kneels over his fallen wife downstage; they stare in horror at each other, and the assembled company watch as "she recovers slowly." Thus, the blocking creates a kind of *tableau vivant* onstage which eloquently portrays the isolation that crime and kingship will bring to Macbeth and Lady Macbeth.

As the play proceeds, the pattern recurs again and again, and Shaw's blocking continues to stress it in every detail. In Act III, Lady Macbeth asks her husband why he keeps alone (III.ii.3); in the palace scenes (III.i and ii) Shaw keeps Macbeth apart, at first stepping forward to question Banquo. Then, when the murderers have come, he becomes active, "restless," the promptbook says, to stand out vividly. As Richard David recalled,

> The murderers, half-scared, half-fascinated by the now evil magnetism of the King, shrank back each time he approached them in a

swirl of robes, while he, pacing the stage between and around them, continuously spun a web of bewildering words about their understandings.[18]

The banquet scene is the climax, in which at every turn Macbeth's attempts to overcome his isolation are thwarted. While Lady Macbeth keeps her state, he leaves his throne to play the humble host, only to be called away by the murderers. Then, as he again tries to join the company, he springs in terror from Banquo's ghost. He flees from it, rushing around the table; Lady Macbeth rises from her throne and follows him to the forestage, where they stand together as Macbeth speaks of "the time has been, / That, when the brains were out, the man would die" (III.iv.78–79), Lady Macbeth watching "with her eye on Lords," as they "turn and look at him." Again Shaw stages the *tableau vivant,* husband and wife isolated in terror under the gaze of all. And again, there is another attempt to break from everything that keeps him "cabin'd, cribb'd, and confin'd," another toast to the absent guest, and once again isolation enforced by the ghost with even greater force, Macbeth leaping on the table, running amok, until the guests depart, leaving Macbeth and Lady Macbeth alone at the deserted banquet table.

In Part III (Acts IV and V) isolation becomes absolute. In the cauldron scene we see Macbeth cut off even from his infernal allies by the vision of Banquo and his heirs. He stands DS OP "tortured and driven into a state of fury by what he is shown," says the promptbook, as the kings pass silently over the stage. Lady Macbeth, trapped in her nightmarish reenactment of the crime, comes from US C, down "the great long corridor leading to the Queen's apartments," according to the notebook, while the Doctor and Waiting Gentlewoman look on. Her futile expiation performed, she goes back the way she came, to be seen no more. Macbeth's final scenes enact ultimate isolation: "the Thanes fly from me" (V.iii.49), and even those he commands desert him. He abuses and spurns his servants. The "cream fac'd loon" he dismisses, "pushing him away" with "take thy face hence" (V.iii.19a); the Birnam wood sentry he "seizes" then "throws down," says the promptbook. Cut off from those who serve him only in fear, his meditations—"My way of life is fallen into the sere, the yellow leaf" (V.iii.22–28); "Tomorrow, and tomorrow, and tomorrow" (V.v.19–29)—are spoken as a man apart, downstage, where he has stood many times before to speak his mind. And in the final scene with Macduff, we see isolation become absolute in his last, desperate attempt to challenge Fate.

As the blocking consistently isolates Macbeth and Lady Macbeth, it
brings those who surround them together, creating images of unity, fellowship, and mutual trust. The pattern is set early in the play. Then, after
Duncan's murder, it slowly re-forms as the play goes on. The Bloody
Sergeant scene (I.ii) is the first of three enactments of social unity. Shaw
began it with an assembly: Duncan and his sons enter PS with a "Royal
Standard Bearer" and two soldiers carrying banners; then come Lennox,
Menteith, Caithness, and three more soldiers with banners, then an officer
and two more soldiers. The King and his assembled entourage form a picture of an ordered society, a dramatic image PS balanced by the excited
entry of the wounded Sergeant OP. Where Macbeth will find himself
thrust from that society, the Sergeant, another bloody man, is drawn into
it and given succor: Lennox and Malcolm "help him," as "D[uncan] moves
forward to PS front steps followed by S[tandard] B[earer] & D[onalbain]."
After Angus and Ross enter OP, there is a greeting and "general movement in [wards]" of the assemblage, implying a sense of community which
is made explicit when they "cheer" at news of the victory and "exeunt
cheering" at the end of the scene.

The Forres scene follows the same pattern. First, the court assembles; as
the scene goes on, the king stands flanked by his nobles and two chamber-
lains bearing candelabra, next to him the Standard Bearer with a coronet
on a cushion. As men come in from the field, ceremony makes the blocking significant. Macbeth first kneels in greeting until "D[uncan] raises
him." Banquo repeats the ceremony. Then another subject does homage to
the King: "Mal[colm] kneels. S[tandard] Bearer moves forward. D[uncan]
takes Coronet from cushion & puts it on Mal's head & kisses his forehead.
Mal rises, & D[uncan] turns to M[acbeth]." The investiture over, Macbeth
comes downstage, speaks, and exits, Duncan and the rest following in
stately procession. The blocking and the ceremonial stage business thus
reinforce the sense of community embodied in the courtly language and in
the common cause which unites the King and his loyal retainers. So too
does the blocking and stage business for Duncan's entry into Inverness,
when "the King greets his hostess with great courtesy and charm" before
he and his company go in through the center arch. And the sounds of
feasting in the scene that comes next (I.vii) continues the sense of a thriv-
ing society.

Having been firmly established at the play's opening, this dramatic
image of an ordered society becomes the model towards which group
scenes move in the acts that follow Duncan's murder, culminating at last in
Malcolm's restoration of order at the play's end. Immediately after the

murder, only fear unites them—"those strained white faces peering" at Macbeth and Lady Macbeth; then, at the banquet, alarm and suspicion replace confusion, and only in the last act does purposeful reunion bring them together. Viewed in this context, Shaw's blocking and stage business take on added significance. The nobles who rush from the banquet through every available exit are a living representation of the community in disarray. Macbeth's attempts to play the humble host (which on Shaw's set required an actual physical descent from the royal dais) become improprieties when compared to Duncan's constancy in dignity and courtesy. The scene thus illustrates not only Macbeth's derangement but also society's loss of the ceremonies of community and all they represent.

Even as the group scenes depict society's disorder, there are other smaller scenes which depict remedy to come. These choric scenes—II.iv (the Old Man, Ross, and Macduff) and III.vi (Lennox and Another Lord)—anticipate the long scene in England with Malcolm, Macduff, and Ross, which is often said to be unplayable and hence is cut. Yet Keith Michell (who played Macduff) and Trader Faulkner (who played Malcolm) both attest to its power in the theater.[19] As the third in a sequence of dramatic images that depict the reforming of society, part of the scene's power is cumulative, and Shaw's blocking and stage business bring this out. The two men are at first cautious with each other; the dissembling Malcolm sits, feigning indifference, to test Macduff, who kneels as he pleads with Malcolm (IV.iii.70ff.) until, the testing nearly over, he rises and turns from Malcolm in disgust, and Malcolm goes to keep him from leaving. He succeeds, and they are now friends. Ross comes then, greetings are exchanged, the news of Macduff's slain family told, and, following Shakespeare literally, Shaw says, "Mac[duff] pulls his cap over his eyes." Malcolm offers comfort: he "gently pulls Mac[duff's] right arm away from his face." "Malcolm & Macduff now trust each other completely," and, along with the words of testing, grief, and comfort, gestures and movement onstage have enacted the making of that trust.

In the last act, the blocking for Malcolm and his followers repeats the pattern of greeting and alliance. In V.ii, Shaw had Menteith, Angus, and Lennox enter OP, as Caithness and a Scots soldier enter PS. The two groups meet center stage, declare their common cause, and then leave together. So too, the Birnam Wood scene (V.iv) enacted a meeting and an alliance between Malcolm's party and the Scots rebels from V.ii. As they had done for Duncan, trumpets and drums sound, Malcolm and his English allies enter OP, the Scots PS, and, meeting center stage, Malcolm "shakes hands with Ang[us] & Len[nox], then with Men[teith] & Caith-

[ness]." Their plans concluded, they leave together, marching to "Drums and trumpets." To the same music in V.vi, they enter as a group, now grown to twenty, with their leafy screens, and then disperse in several directions to hunt out Macbeth. Finally, in the last scene, they reassemble around Malcolm, whose position at the center of the tableau marks him as Duncan's successor as surely as do his white robes, the trumpets, and the cheers of his subjects.

V

Shaw's notebooks and promptbooks thus trace formal rhythms that structure *Macbeth* and give us a staging of the play uncluttered by the gimmicks and self-conscious "interpretation" which many theatergoers have come to loathe in modern Shakespearean productions. Shaw simply made himself aware of the distance between Macbeth's quiet meditations and his frenzied ecstasies, and by his arrangement of the action he emphasized that distance. The blocking continually thrust Macbeth forward—literally downstage—and kept the audience's attention centered on him and on the workings of his mind. When others were onstage, they were witnesses of Macbeth's derangement, allies against him, not individuals speaking of private doubts and fears. Thus Shaw has given us an interpretation of the play in which Macbeth is at once at the center of the action and outside it, as if somehow, as in dreams, the events are projections from deep within his diseased mind.

Notes:

1. Richard David ("The Tragic Curve" *Shakespeare Survey,* 9 [1956], pp. 122–31) wrote that "Byam Shaw gave us Shakespeare's tragedy in all its balanced perfection." Dennis Bartholomeusz *(Macbeth and the Players* [Cambridge: Cambridge University Press, 1969], p. 254) judged it "the most successful interpretation of *Macbeth* in this century."

2. I wish to thank Glen Byam Shaw for allowing me to examine his promptbook and his notebooks. Shaw came to Stratford as codirector (with Anthony Quayle) in 1953, after two decades in the London theatre. At that time, he was perhaps best known for his work with Sir John Gielgud at the New Theatre before World War II and for his work as Director of the Old Vic Dramatic School after the war. He has been Director of Productions for Sadler's Wells Opera at the London Coliseum since 1962. The 1955 production was his first *Macbeth.* See *Who's Who in the Theatre,* 15th ed. (London: Pitman, 1972), pp. 1400–401, and *l'Enciclopedia dello spettacolo* (Rome: le Maschere, 1961), VIII, 1933. See also my *"Macbeth" Onstage: An Annotated Facsimile of Glyn Byam Shaw's 1955 Promptbook* (Columbia: Univ. of Missouri Press, 1976).

Besides Shaw's manuscript promptbook and notebooks, the production is documented by a promptbook made by the stage management (described in Charles Shattuck's *The Shakespeare Promptbooks* [Urbana: Univ. of Illinois Press, 1965], p. 267) and kept at the Shakespeare Centre Library, Stratford-upon-Avon. For permission to examine that promptbook I wish to thank Dr. Levi Fox, Director of the Shakespeare Centre Library, and the Governors of the Shakespeare Birthplace Trust. Unless otherwise noted, I quote from Shaw's MS for stage directions and commentary; the quotations from the text follow the New Arden Edition, ed. Kenneth Muir (Cambridge: Harvard Univ. Press, 1972).

3. Sir Barry Jackson's modern-dress *Macbeth* was staged at the Royal Court Theatre, 1928. For Davenant's revisions, see Christopher Spencer, *Davenant's Macbeth from the Yale Manuscript* (New Haven: Yale Univ. Press, 1961). For a short stage history of the play, see C. B. Young's essay in the New Cambridge ed. (Cambridge: Cambridge Univ. Press, 1947), pp. lxix–lxxxii. For a detailed history of the actors' interpretations of the title roles, see Bartholomeusz, *Macbeth and the Players*.

4. The complete cuts on the text: I.ii.25–28a, 47–48a, 60–64; iii.93–97a; III.i.21, 131b–132a; iv.14; v and vi *in toto;* IV.i.37–43, 125–132; ii.38b–43; iii.27, 53b–55a, 63b–65a, 70b–72, 82b–85a, 125b–131a; V.vi.6b–8; vii.12–29; viii.32b–33a; ix.16b–19.

5. Shaw's scene plot assigns a time and a place to each scene:

Part I

Scene 1	Opening Scene	No time	In space
Scene 2	Bloody Sgt Scene	5 P.M.	The heath
Scene 3	Witches Scene	6 P.M.	The heath
Scene 4	Forres Scene	9 P.M.	The Royal Palace
Scene 5	Murder Scene	Next day from 5 P.M. till morning	The Courtyard of Macbeth's Castle

Part II (Three Months later)

Scene 1	Palace Scene	5 P.M.	Royal Palace
Scene 2	Banquo Murder Scene	7 P.M.	Park of the Palace
Scene 3	Banquet Scene	8 P.M.	Royal Palace

Part III (Next day)

Scene 1	Cauldron Scene	2 A.M.	Witches Cavern
Scene 2	Lady Macduff Scene	5 P.M. (next day)	Macduff's Castle
Scene 3	England Scene	12 noon (week later)	English Country
Scene 4	Sleep Walking Scene	2 A.M. (week later)	Dunsinane Castle
Scene 5	Revolt Scene	4 A.M.	Dunsinane Castle
Scene 6	Cream Fac'd Loon Scer	6 A.M.	Dunsinane Castle
Scene 7	Birnam Wood Scene	5 P.M.	Birnam Wood
Scene 8	Last Scene	6 P.M. – 4 A.M.	Outside Dunsinane Castle

6. *Shakespeare Survey,* 9 (1956), p. 123.

7. *Birmingham Gazette,* June 8, 1955.

8.   *Birmingham Evening Dispatch,* June 8, 1955.

9.   *Morning Advertiser,* June 15, 1955.

10. *Birmingham Post,* June 9, 1955.

11. Bartholomeusz, who describes this scene in detail (262–64) also reproduces the pages in Shaw's promptbook which refer to it (Appendix II, 284–85). See also Richard David, p. 130.

12. Milton Shulman of the *London Evening Standard* (June 8, 1955) decried "restraint run amok"; the reviewer for *Time and Tide* (June 18, 1955), while admitting that the "play gains power," thought it was set "at well below the necessary imaginative pressure." Stephen Williams of the *London Evening News* (June 8, 1955) called it "noble and intelligent" but lacking in a "vast spaciousness of gesture"; and Desmond Pratt of the *Yorkshire Post* (June 8, 1955) felt it "missed the great flood."

13. Thus, for example, from Bartholomeusz we learn that Garrick, who "started" at the vision, seemed a man possessed (57–58); after a "start dramatic," John Kemble put his hand over his eyes, then uncovered them slowly (128–29); Macready did not start but went slowly from tones of majesty to terror, ending with his famous pose, his body itself offstage, but his leg still in sight, trembling (163–64); Irving spoke as if in a trance until awakened by the bell (202). In 1911, Beerbohm Tree had something like an epileptic seizure (Tree promptbook, Theatre Library, Bristol University, England).

14. Pp. 128–29.

15. I here conflate Shaw's promptbook with the stage management's, which names actors, not parts; where needed, the part follows in square brackets. The promptbook uses the following abbreviations: "P" = "Promptside" (stage left), "OP" = "Opposite Promptside" (stage right), "DS" = "Downstage," "US" = "Upstage," and "C" = "Center."

16. Criticism has been largely silent about dramatic imagery, perhaps in part because it is difficult to discuss rigorously without the firm evidence of actual performance. See Alan C. Dessen, "Hamlet's Poisoned Sword: A Study in Dramatic Imagery," *Shakespeare Studies,* 5 (1970), pp. 53–69, esp. pp. 53–55; Clifford Lyons, "Stage Imagery in Shakespeare's Plays," in *Essays on Shakespearean and Elizabethan Drama in Honor of Hardin Craig,* ed. Richard Hosley (Columbia: Univ. of Missouri Press, 1962), pp. 261–74; Maurice Charney, *Shakespeare's Roman Plays: The Function of Imagery in the Drama* (Cambridge: Harvard Univ. Press, 1961), pp. 4–5, 7–9; and R. A. Foakes, "Suggestions for a New Approach to Shakespeare's Imagery," *Shakespeare Survey,* 5 (1952), pp. 85–86.

17. Unlike many directors, Shaw made the promptbook first, before rehearsals, and stayed close to it during them. Lee Montague, who played Seyton, has told me that Shaw worked out the blocking with the aid of chessmen on a model of the set and that, once the blocking was set down in the promptbook, the actors followed it "to the inch." A comparison of Shaw's promptbook with the stage management's (which controlled actual performance) bears this out, for there are virtually no differences, although Shaw's is more detailed.

18. P. 130.

19. Trader Faulkner (Malcolm) said that the actors were afraid of the scene: "Everyone said it's such a deadly scene, I hope it will be cut." In rehearsals and in performance its importance became clear, and Keith Michell (Macduff) said that it was "a fantastically moving scene" (in interviews with the present author, August, 1973).

Timon, Cupid, and the Amazons

Robert C. Fulton, III

The masque of Cupid and Amazons in Shakespeare's *Timon of Athens* enjoys a high degree of resonance with the play which incorporates it. As in the case of contemporary masques produced at the court of James I, the significance of this show is determined by a body of interpretive tradition founded on the classical literature which invigorates the antique gods and heroes in the Renaissance. Unlike the shows at court, of course, the masque at Timon's house exists within a context created by the playwright and therefore represents part of a carefully controlled whole. My aim in this essay is to describe the nature and extent of the resonance between masque and play by taking account of Shakespeare's use of the interpretive conventions associated with his masque figures.

Cupid and the Amazons possess an iconographic doubleness common to many Renaissance mythological representations. The ambiguous quality of such classical figures is well illustrated by Edgar Wind in his discussion of the significance attached to Virgil's Venus, the deceitful mother-goddess who hides her identity from her son Aeneas in *Aeneid* I by disguising herself as Diana:

> In her the Renaissance Platonists thought they had found a fine poetical confirmation for their doctrine of the union of Chastity and Love. While it is doubtful Virgil intended the image to convey any mystery of that kind, they expanded it into a semi-chaste, semi-voluptuous cult of Venus, in which her double nature could be refined to the highest points of either reverence or frivolity or both. . . . The emblem acquired a new courtly twist in France and England, where its potentialities were developed more fully than in Italy itself. . . .
>
> In view of the Italian sources of English imagery perhaps the question is not unjustified whether the worship of Queen Elizabeth as Diana was not also a cult of Venus in disguise.[1]

The doubleness that Wind ponders in the Venus-Virgo image is also present in the Renaissance conception of Cupid, as well as the Amazons whom he introduces in Shakespeare's play. These masque figures are apt symbols for the radically broken world of Timon's Athens, in which, we might re-

283

call, splendor and magnificence give way to the jockeying of Timon's creditors and associates, in which the sense of elation experienced in the
celebrations of friendship at the play's beginning rapidly dissipates in the
hedging and hypocrisy depicted thereafter, and in which Timon's bitter,
lashing cries against man and city in Acts IV and V counterpoint the sweet
airs heard in Act I.

And yet at first view, there is not much about the masque to awaken
curiosity:

> *Sound Tucket. Enter the Maskers of Amazons, with Lutes in their hands,*
> *dauncing and playing.*
> Tim.   What meanes that Trumpe? How now?
> *Enter Seruant.*
> Ser.   Please you my Lord, there are certaine Ladies
>   Most desirous of admittance.
> Tim.   Ladies? what are their wils?
> Ser.   There comes with them a fore-runner my Lord,
>   which beares that office, to signifie their
>   pleasures.
> Tim.   I pray let them be admitted.
> *Enter Cupid with the Maske of Ladies.*
> Cup.   Haile to thee worthy *Timon* and to all that of
>   his Bounties taste: the fiue best Sences acknowledge
>   thee their Patron, and come freely to gratulate
>   thy plentious bosome.
>   There tast, touch all, pleas'd from thy Table rise:
>   They onely now come but to Feast thine eies.
> Timo.   They're welcome all, let 'em haue kind admittance.
>   Musicke make their welcome.
> Luc.   You see my Lord, how ample y'are belou'd.

> [Apemantus' speech, *ll. 137–50*]

> *The Lords rise from Table, with much adoring of Timon, and to shew*
> *their loues, each single out an Amazon, and all Dance, men with women,*
> *a loftie straine or two to the Hoboyes, and cease.*[2]

This is thoroughly conventional in form and device, as numerous
Elizabethan and Jacobean examples demonstrate. In *Romeo and Juliet* Shakespeare makes fun of this kind of announced processional masque. In Ben-

volio's judgment, "The date is out of such prolixity."[3] For Romeo's cousin, Eros-as-presenter is a pretty tired gambit:

> We'll have no Cupid hoodwinked with a scarf,
> Bearing a Tartar's bow of lath,
> Scaring the ladies like a crow-keeper.
>
> *(I.iv.3–6)*

E. K. Chambers concurs, noting that in this period "the child dressed as . . . Cupid became rather *banal* through much repetition."[4] Nevertheless, Cupid continued to appear regularly long after Benvolio's censure, as many Stuart masques attest. Amazons are also familiar stuff. They appear frequently in sixteenth-century entertainments and are evidently still considered modish in 1609, when they are a central part of the fiction in Jonson's *Masque of Queens.* Although Penthesilea is the only literal Amazon masquer, all the others except "Bel-Anna" (Queen Anne) are described in military and warlike terms which suggest a strong Amazonian streak.[5] In short, Shakespeare's masque is not in the least recherché, although, as I will show, it introduces figures who incarnate a unifying imagery within the play's polar movement.

Cupid's costume is not indicated in the text of Shakespeare's play; yet he probably would have appeared blindfolded, with bow and arrows, as he regularly does in the English Renaissance, whether in a masque or in a sonnet. Here he is, for example, in Beaumont's *Masque of the Inner Temple* (1613): *"Enter four Cupids . . . attired in flame-coloured taffeta close to their body like naked boys, with bows, arrows, and wings of gold, chaplets of flowers on their heads, hoodwinked with tiffany scarfs. . . ."*[6] The properties of bow, arrows, and blindfold are tiresomely reiterated in love poetry of the period. Nevertheless, Cupid's hoodwinking calls for a few remarks at this point, since it offers the first clue to an understanding of the masque's doubleness. The antique love god did not acquire his blindfold until the thirteenth century, but the feature was soon seized on as an iconographically significant detail. Moralists explain that Cupid is blind because he deprives man of his good sense and wisdom; painters show his eyes bandaged to stress the fact that those in love are ignorant of their own destination and misguided by passion. The blindfold is never regarded as a playful item of dress for a quaint deity. Instead, it designates the basic immorality of erotic experience. Thus, in discussing the medieval tradition, Erwin Panofsky has noted that blind Cupid "came into existence as a little monster, created for admonitory purposes."[7]

In the Renaissance blind Cupid's origins are not forgotten. English poets as disparate as Spenser and Jonson are sensitive to the malevolent potential of the love god. The destructive force of Eros is felt equally in Shakespeare's and Sidney's sonnets. It is Cupid who blights creativity in *The Shepheardes Calendar,* driving Colin Cloute to break his pipe in the January eclogue. In the larger view of Spenserean epic Cupid has become, in the House of Busyrane, a sadistic overseer in the grim processional masque celebrating the tortures of Amoret:

> His blindfold eyes he bad a while vnbind,
> That his proud spoyle of that same dolorous
> Faire Dame he might behold in perfect kind:
> Which seene, he much reioyced in his cruell mind.[8]

Ben Jonson is quite specific about the figure described in *The Haddington Masque* (1608) as

> Love, a little boy
> Almost naked, wanton, blind;
> Cruel now, and then as kind.

> (ll. 75–77)

"I express Cupid, as he is *Venus' son,* and owner of the following qualities ascribed him by the antique and later poets," explains Jonson marginally (p. 524), while the Graces expound on his playfulness and treachery, his delicacy and might (ll. 74–133). Biron, in *Love's Labour's Lost,* humorously underscores just these aspects when he realizes that he has actually come under the power of Eros, characterizing him as "This wimpled, whining, purblind, wayward boy; / This senior-junior, giant-dwarf, Dan Cupid. . . ." (III.i.181–82). Nor are the negative connotations of the blindfold confined to loss of reason. As Rosaline reminds Katherine in *Love's Labour's Lost,* Cupid can be lethal:

> You'll ne'er be friends with him; 'a kill'd your
> sister.
> *Kath.*   He made her melancholy, sad, and heavy,
> And so she died.

> (V.ii.13–15)

The lethalness is visually forecast by Andrea Alciati when he depicts Death, a sinister skeleton, leaning over a blindfolded Cupid who sleeps securely with his bow next to him on the ground. Death already clutches the boy's arrows. Soon all the properties of Cupid will belong to this thief.[9]

This widely shared mythographical understanding is testimony to the strength and pervasiveness of the iconographic tradition of the hood-winked Cupid. Nevertheless he remains for many merely a conventional ornament to embellish those courtly entertainments "when love was free and Venus seized all men's eyes."[10] The fact that Ben Jonson finds it necessary to explain the difference between "good" and "bad" Cupids suggests that blind Eros is frequently viewed as no more than an ornament. Jonson, who conceived of his masques as serious moral vehicles, tries to counteract this tendency of the audience to lose sight of iconographically significant details by resorting to various aids and helps in the printed texts of the entertainments. For example, in *The Masque of Beauty* (1608) a treble intones, "If all these Cupids now were blind, / As is their wanton brother," while Jonson glosses, "I make these different from him which they *feign blind with desire* or *wanton* . . . these being chaste Loves. . . ." (p. 514).[11] But unless the audience at Timon's banquet is alert to the fine moral shades of meaning conveyed by mythological figures, there is no reason to suppose they sense anything special in the Cupid they see before them. He is, after all, an ordinary occurrence at shows of this kind. And furthermore, the masque which the god of love presents is intended by its producer as a compliment for Timon, not as an admonition. As Inga-Stina Ewbank has observed, this show "gathers into itself symbolically all the elements of Timon's earlier life: lavish expenditure, social grace, ceremony and ostentation."[12] For the guests at Timon's banquet Cupid is a fine decoration, used with a graciousness those around Timon exhibit in the play's first act. "You see how ample y'are belou'd," says Lucullus, and Timon is gratified by the scene of harmony and pleasure.

Yet Ewbank's description is only a fair one when maintained from within the world of the play. For us, beyond that world, judgment of Cupid is disentangled from the persuasions of the occasional moment. We share the perspective of Apemantus, who is distanced from the event, a nonparticipatory observer. His running commentary throughout this scene forms an effective contrast to the demonstration of love and harmony at which the banquet aims. And although they are for the most part ignored by the others on stage, his acerb remarks help us remain aware of the darkness implicit from the beginning in the figure of blind Eros.

In the case of the Amazons there is no single iconographic detail which provides a clue as to their moral tone. The doubleness of the female warrior inheres in the whole figure, whose significance cannot be altered by the addition or subtraction of some item of costume. On the one hand,

Amazons seem to have carried strong positive associations on the masquing stage and must have provided ample opportunity for magnificent display with their costumes.[13] Although Ben Jonson is not explicit about what the Queen's ladies wore when they masqued as Amazons in 1609, he reassures his readers that Inigo Jones had satisfactorily executed their costumes, which *"had in them the excellency of all devices and riches, and were worthily varied by his invention to the nations whereof they were queens"* (ll. 463–65). Whatever the details of costume Shakespeare had in mind, the overall impression was surely meant to be glittering and grand. These imposing female warriors suggest several gratulatory meanings. As Cupid's speech indicates, the Amazons are a "feast" for the eyes of the revellers, perhaps reminding them of the greatness of Athens, the magnificent master city, in part made so by Timon's bounty. They might have recalled the triumph of Theseus, the wise and exemplary ruler of Athens, over the Amazonian nation, and his taming of Hippolyta in marriage. She herself is addressed in *The Two Noble Kinsmen* as "Most dreaded Amazonian," "soldieress, / That equally canst poise sternness with pity," and "dear glass of ladies."[14] Of Penthesilea, another of their queens, Jonson writes, "She lived and was present at the war of Troy, on their part against the Greeks, where, as Justin . . . gives her testimony, 'among the bravest men great proofs of her valor were conspicuous.' She is nowhere mentioned but with the preface of honor and virtue and is always advanced in the head of the worthiest women" *(Masque of Queens,* p. 542). As I have already suggested, eleven of the masquers in this work are for all intents and purposes Amazons. Jonson is careful to stress their nobility, thus insuring the reader's respect for them: ". . . it was my first and special regard to see that the nobility of the invention should be answerable to the dignity of their persons" (ll. 3–5). Spenser found the female warrior an apt figure for militant chastity, and Britomart's deeds in *The Faerie Queene,* Book III, are a pattern for valiant action. Seen from this angle, the Amazons in Timon's masque are symbolic of heroic virtue.

On the other hand, there is a strong bias in the Renaissance against Amazons. Celeste T. Wright, in her study of the subject, has amply documented this sentiment, showing how they were singled out in literature of the period as much for their cruelty, ferocity and inhospitality as for their positive qualities.[15] Behind the barbarity of the type was an emblem of chaos, since the Amazon represented an inversion of male and female roles extending from the personal through the political sphere. It was surely Spenser's sensitivity to this attitude which caused him to cast Radigund as the only literal Amazon in his epic, thereby freeing Britomart and Belphoebe from any suspicion. Radigund is specifically identified as an Amazon and exhibits all the bad qualities of the type. She is merciless in victory, starving and effeminizing her victims by making them spin and card for their diet of bread and water (V.iv.31). She is by nature ferocious and unforgiving: having seen a former victim of hers set free, "Her heart for rage did grate, and teeth did grin" (V.iv.37). Once having overcome her opponent, as in the case of Artegall,

> the warlike Amazon,
> Whose wandring fancie after lust did raunge,
> Gan cast a secret liking to this captive strange.[16]
>
> *(V.v.26)*

Amazonian ferocity and unconstrained passion are the results, Spenser explains, of living in a disordered and unnatural state of freedom:

> Such is the crueltie of womenkynd,
> When they haue shaken off the shamefast band,
> With which wise Nature did them strongly bynd,
> T'obay the heasts of mans well ruling hand,
> That then all rule and reason they withstand,
> To purchase a licentious libertie.
>
> *(V.v.25)*

It is true that Theseus is able to prevent such an inversion by marrying his Amazon opponent, Hippolyta. In *A Midsummer Night's Dream* there is not a trace of tension in the royal union about to take place, although the Duke hints at the discordant beginnings of his courtship:

> Hippolyta, I woo'd thee with my sword,
> And won thy love doing thee injuries.
>
> *(I.i.16–17)*

And in *The Two Noble Kinsmen* the attributes of the newly wedded Amazonian queen are seen as a heterodox mixture of fierce and mild qualities, of female supremacy tempered by marriage with Theseus—she "ow'st his strength / And his love too" (see I.i.77–101). Of this characterization Paul Olson observes: "The meaning of the rulers' marriage is here explicit: it is even directly related to the prelapsarian relationship in which man and woman, or the analogous inner faculties, were rightly oriented. . . ."[17] But, as we have seen in the case of Spenser, when freed from the stabilizing institution of marriage, Amazons tend to take on alarmingly negative qualities.

Timon's entertainment, of course, has nothing to do with marriage, and the Amazons in it seem anything but fierce and lustful, although Apemantus' remarks will certainly encourage us to regard the figures ambivalently:

> They dance? they are mad women.
> Like madness is the glory of this life,
> As this pomp shows to a little oil and root.
> We make ourselves fools to disport ourselves,
> And spend our flatteries to drink those men
> Upon whose age we void it up again
> With poisonous spite and envy.
> Who lives that's not depraved or depraves?
> Who dies that bears not one spurn to their graves
> Of their friends' gift?
> I should fear those that dance before me now
> Would one day stamp upon me; 't has been done;
> Men shut their doors against a setting sun.[18]
>
>   (I.ii.138–50)

The speech is clearly choric and predictive. Apemantus' remarks, as I have already suggested, also help to make us aware of the ambiguity of the show. Its charm and sweetness are blasted by the cynic's words, and any graciousness is wilted. "My lord, you take us even at the best," curtsies an Amazonian masquer in response to a compliment, and Apemantus snarls: "Faith, for the worst is filthy, and would not hold taking, I doubt me" (ll. 157–59). In his observations, then, can be glimpsed the negative connotations associated with these dancing ladies—ferocity and cruelty and the disease which signals destructive lust.

Not only does the philosopher's commentary underscore the show's doubleness, but the very words Cupid uses to introduce the Amazons ought to render the whole affair suspect. The directness of the presenter is startling: Cupid is the spokesman for a banquet of sense, not a celebration of love and social harmony. Timon is the patron of the five senses, which come in joy to his plenteous bosom.[19] At Timon's bosom (a metonym, perhaps, for his bountiful table) one may please the senses which have gathered; and, having tasted and touched what Timon has laid out, one may then feast the eyes on the approaching Amazons. The idea of the carnal banquet is reinforced by the sensuality which the Amazons represent as they dance with their Athenian partners.[20] But the fact that the god of love presides at the entertainment hides from Timon any darkness inherent in the show. From the host's perspective the banquet is a communion of friendship whose genius is, quite appropriately, Cupid. Timon is overwhelmed by his sense of the occasion, exclaiming to his companions: "O joy, e'en made away ere't can be born! Mine eyes cannot hold out water, methinks; to forget their faults, I drink to you" (ll. 109–12). And Timon's friends also treat the banquet as a celebration of love, properly climaxed when *"The Lords rise from Table, with much adoring of Timon, and to shew their loues, each single out an Amazon, and all Dance. . . ."*

The banquet scene suggests in visual terms the imagery which the play will develop as it dramatizes the relationship between Timon and his city. Central to this imagery is the metaphor of whoring. Consider, for instance, the speech of the Senator in the scene following Timon's masque, in which Timon's house is linked with the brothel:

> No porter at his gate,
> But rather one that smiles and still invites
> All that pass by.
>
> *(II.i.10–12)*

The metaphoric implication that Timon's is a house of prostitution is strengthened in the next scene, in Apemantus' exchange with Caphis and the servants of Isidore and Varro. There the philosopher observes of those who have come to collect their masters' debts from Timon, "Poor rogues, and usurers' men! bawds between gold and want!" (II.ii.60–61). Shakespeare had already imaged usury as whoredom in *Measure for Measure,* where Mistress Overdone's pimp is heard to lament on the way to court, " 'Twas never merry world since, of two usuries, the merriest was put down, and the worser allowed by order of law . . ." (III.ii.6–8). His counterpart in *Timon of Athens,* the Fool accompanying Apemantus in II.ii (he is, like Pompey in *Measure for Measure,* employed in a brothel), observes to the creditors whom the cynic has been abusing: "I think no usurer but has a fool to his servant; my mistress is one, and I am her fool. When men come to borrow of your masters, they approach sadly, but go away merry; but they enter my [mistress'] house merrily, and go away sadly" (ll.103–107). In Athens Timon has come to fulfill the function of both usurer and bawd: in I.i, men come to his house sadly and go away merrily (the messenger from Ventidius and an Old Athenian); in III.vi, men enter his house merrily but go away sadly (the Lords who come to a banquet and are served water and stones). Timon even has his fool for a servant, as Lucullus callously observes of Flaminius when the latter refuses a bribe (III.i.41–53).

Late in the play, in Act IV, scene iii, Timon, the metaphorical whore and bawd of Athens, comes face to face with two literal prostitutes, Phyrnia and Timandra, who are marching with Alcibiades' troops. The confrontation is charged with bitterness, filled with vile and scathing language. "This fell whore of thine," says Timon to the Captain, "Hath in her more destruction than thy sword, / For all her cherubin look," to which Phyrnia hisses, "Thy lips rot off!" (ll. 61–63). But when Timon learns that the army is marching against Athens, he comes to look on this rebel force as a means of revenge and incites them to destroy the city, giving heaps of gold. "There's gold to pay thy soldiers, / Make large confusion . . ." (ll. 126–27). The pitiless destruction he urges is not, however, confined to the work of Alcibiades and his men. He envisions Phyrnia and Timandra as instrumental in the downfall of Athens. By making them a part of the military encounter he imagines will take place, he is in effect bestowing Amazonian qualities on them. Indeed, "Amazon" appears to have been Elizabethan cant for a prostitute.[21] Appropriately, then, these Amazons will conquer by lust instead of the sword.

> Be whores still;
> And he whose pious breath seeks to convert you,
> Be strong in whore, allure him, burn him up;
> Let your close fire predominate his smoke,
> And be no turncoats; yet may your pains, six months,
> Be quite contrary: and thatch your poor thin roofs
> With burthens of the dead—some that were hang'd,
> No matter;—wear them, betray with them. Whore still;
> Paint till a horse may mire upon your face;
> A pox of wrinkles!
> . . . . .
> Consumptions sow
> In hollow bones of man; strike their sharp shins,
> And mar men's spurring. Crack the lawyer's voice,
> That he may never more false title plead,
> Nor sound his quillets shrilly; hoar the flamen,
> That scolds against the quality of flesh
> And not believes himself. Down with the nose,
> Down with it flat, take the bridge quite away

Of him that, his particular to foresee,
Smells from the general weal. Make curl'd-pate ruffians bald;
And let the unscarr'd braggarts of the war
Derive some pain from you. Plague all,
That your activity may defeat and quell
The source of all erection.

(ll. 139–64)

Timon's invoking of disease presents a sickeningly vivid picture of rampant venereal plague battening on the city, eating Athenian flesh and bone. This terrifying charge to the prostitutes provides a crucial metaphoric reversal which fuses the play's broken halves. For the first three acts Timon has been food for Athens.[22] The metaphor, like that of whoring, is occasioned by the masque scene. Apemantus introduces the image of Timon as food. Timon invites him to the banquet about to occur—"Wilt dine with me, Apemantus?"—and he snaps, "No; I eat not lords" (I.i.206–207). Timon is characteristically unaware of the significance of the remark, but Apemantus' meaning is fairly clear: dining *with* Timon is equivalent to dining *on* Timon.[23] Alcibiades' greeting to his host refines the cynic's downright image: "Sir, you have sav'd my longing, and I feed / Most hungerly on your sight" (ll. 261–62). In a phrase which directly anticipates Cupid's speech of presentation, one lord, about to enter the banquet, says to a fellow guest, "shall we in / And taste Lord Timon's bounty?" (I.i.284–85). Then, at the banquet itself, before the masque takes place, Apemantus breaks out—"O you gods, what a number of men eats Timon, and he sees 'em not! It grieves me to see so many dip their meat in one man's blood; and all the madness is, he cheers them up too" (I.ii.39–43). Apemantus' bitter insight forces us to question whether "bosom" is a figure of speech at all. Seen through his eyes the banquet is a cannibals' feast; from our perspective it suggests a grotesque parody of the Last Supper.[24] The image of Timon as sustenance is echoed later in the play, after his friends have begun to refuse his requests for money. In III.ii, three Strangers have been observing Lucius, an associate of Timon, put off Servilius, one of Timon's servants, with patently hollow excuses. The Strangers comment disgustedly on the state of affairs in Athens, one prefacing his observations to another by saying, "For mine own part, / I never tasted Timon in my life" (ll. 83–84). The image comes naturally, even to the lips of outsiders, almost as if there were no other way to speak of the man.[25] We are encouraged to think of the relationship between Timon and Athens in the terms these metaphors have suggested: Timon is the feast which Athens eats. The

mock banquet of III.vi, at which Timon serves his guests water and then
drives them out of his house in a rage, signals the end of this feast. And
with Timon's speech to Phyrnia and Timandra the metaphoric terms are
reversed. Now it will be Timon who eats Athens. In a scene which clearly
echoes the once bounteous Timon's encounters with a prickly Apemantus,
the recently transformed misanthrope howls at the philosopher, fiercely
grasping a root:

> That the whole life of Athens were in this!
> Thus would I eat it.

(IV.iii.281–82)

The mastic ferocity and even the food itself—the root—recall Apemantus at
Timon's banquet of I.ii. Yet this is only a wish, however vehemently ex-
pressed. For Timon has already engaged his surrogate whores to devour
Athens.

The sight of Alcibiades' troop seems to galvanize Timon's imagination.
"Enter ALCIBIADES, *with fife and drum, in warlike manner;* PHYRNIA *and*
TIMANDRA" (IV.iii.47.s.d.). The masque of Act I, scene ii, has undergone a
total metamorphosis. The bright shapes and sparkling figures of that first
banquet have given way to images of chaos and destruction. Cupid has become the presiding genius at a feast of death. The brave habits of the dancing ladies have fallen away to reveal a pair of poxy Amazons. What Timon
sees is a reflection of the inversions he has experienced. In response to this
negative harmony he pours out the corrosive, metaphorically dense
speeches which follow, his newly acquired hate having achieved a focus in
this show of destruction.[26]

Notes:

1. *Pagan Mysteries in the Renaissance,* rev. ed. (New York: Norton, 1968), p. 77.
2. *The First Folio of Shakespeare: The Norton Facsimile,* ed. Charlton Hinman (New
    York: Norton, 1968), pp. 697–98; the text contains three printing errors *(Bount es,
    Sencesa cknowledge* and *wecome),* which I have corrected, and two light commas
    (there tast, touch all,), which I have retained. With the exception of the masque,
    quotations from Shakespeare's plays, unless otherwise noted, are uniform with
    the edition of William A. Neilson and Charles J. Hill (Cambridge, Mass.: River-
    side, 1942). I have retained the F1 text of the masque because I think it is basically
    sound as it stands. The editorial practice of breaking up the calls for entry and
    sending Cupid off stage to fetch the Amazons (following Timon's "Musicke make
    their welcome") tends to confuse rather than clarify this scene, and obscures the

fact that the text as we have it is at some remove from production, closer to Shakespeare's conception of what would happen on the stage than to what actually did happen (see W. W. Greg, *The Shakespeare First Folio* [Oxford: Clarendon, 1955], p. 410). H. J. Oliver gives several examples of authorial stage directions, e.g., "Ventigius which Timon redeem'd from prison" (Shakespeare reminding himself of a character's place in the plot when he calls for the entry) and "Then comes dropping after all Apemantus discontentedly like himselfe" (Shakespeare visualizing the entrance), *Timon of Athens* (London: Methuen, 1959), p. xviii (see pp. xiii–xxii for Oliver's discussion of textual and bibliographical problems, to which this note is indebted). If the initial entry—*"Enter the Maskers of Amazons, with Lutes in their hands, dauncing and playing"*—is regarded as a descriptive note rather than a call for entry, which, in fact, is succinctly accomplished in the direction *"Enter Cupid with the Maske of Ladies,"* then the F1 stage directions for the masque are sensible. Furthermore, as editorially emended, Shakespeare's masque is quite unlike other contemporary processional masques, in which the masque figures are in view of the audience while they are being presented: Cupid, in the emended versions of Shakespeare's masque, is made to present the Amazons first, then go off stage to get them. As for his speech of presentation, it is comprehensible in its F1 form and needs no tampering for clarity.

As far as I know, the only scholars to argue directly that *Timon* could have been staged are M. C. Bradbrook and E. A. J. Honigmann. Bradbrook feels that the play was finished and produced. "What we have is based on the author's manuscript, 'rough work' indeed, but not corrupt—partly recopied, and set up, as Hinman tells us, by the wicked Compositor *B,* while the boy prentice distributed the type. Part being recopied by the company's scrivener accounts for some inconsistencies." The character of the stage directions themselves was determined by the fact that Shakespeare did not know, as he wrote, under what stage conditions the play would be produced. Perceiving several clear scenic indications in the dialogue and action, Bradbrook views the work as "an experimental scenario for an indoor dramatic pageant," a response to the court masques being produced 1603–1609. (See *The Tragic Pageant of "Timon of Athens"* [Cambridge: Cambridge Univ. Press, 1966].) Honigmann sees the strong possibility of an Inns of Court production and finds no indication in the F1 text that Shakespeare gave up the play as unworkable: "the view that *Timon* would never have been performed because the only text that happens to survive looks like a rough draft ignores all the decisive factors—the printers' dilemma, the craftsmanship of Shakespeare, the possibility of a special design for a special audience, and the state of the play as we have it." (See *"Timon of Athens," Shakespeare Quarterly,* 12 [1961], 3–20.) There is, of course, sharp scholarly debate over the play, centered not so much on the issue of *Timon*'s fitness for the stage as on its state of artistic completeness. Can we see in the only direct evidence we have, the F1 text, a fragmentary or a whole conception, a false start or a play essentially finished?

3. Thus J. W. Cunliffe describes *Timon*'s entertainment as a typical earlier Elizabethan masque ("The masque in Shakspere's plays," *Archiv für das Studium der Neueren Sprachen und Literaturen,* 135 [1910], 79).

4. *The Elizabethan Stage* (Oxford: Clarendon, 1923), I, 191. A good indication of the

popularity of the device is the illustration of a masque in the Unton memorial portrait, reproduced as the frontispiece to Vol. I of *The Elizabethan Stage*—there we see ten Cupids being led in by a presenter. (See J. C. Maxwell's ed. of *Timon of Athens* [Cambridge: Cambridge Univ. Press, 1957], where this masque is also reproduced as the frontispiece.)

5.   For the poet's description of their genealogy and the classical sources he has drawn on, see *Ben Jonson: The Complete Masques,* ed. Stephen Orgel (New Haven: Yale Univ. Press, 1969), pp. 542–47; quotations from Jonson's masques are uniform with this edition. There are records of Amazon masques occurring in 1551 and 1579—see respectively *Documents Relating to the Revels at Court in the Time of King Edward IV and Queen Mary* (Louvain: A. Uystpryst, 1914), p. 85, and *Documents Relating to the Office of the Revels in the Time of Queen Elizabeth* (Louvain: A. Uystpryst, 1908), pp. 286–87, both edited by Albert Feuillerat. Amazons make a part as well in an entertainment celebrating the baptism of Henry, son of James VI of Scotland, in 1594—recorded in *A True Accompt of the . . . Baptism of . . . Prince Henry Frederick* (London, 1603); rpt. in John Nichols, *The Progresses in the Reign of Queen Elizabeth,* 2nd ed. (London, 1823), III, 353–69. The device continued in popularity after Jonson's *Masque of Queens.* John Chamberlain informs a friend in 1618, "There was a maske of nine Ladies in hand at theyre owne coste, whereof the principall was the Ladye Haye as Quene of the Amazons . . . whatsoever the cause was, neither the Quene nor King did like or allow of yt and so all is dasht" *(The Letters of John Chamberlain,* ed. N. E. McClure [Philadelphia: American Philosophical Society, 1939], II, 125–26). Finally, in Jones's and Davenant's *Salmacida Spolia* (1640), Henrietta Maria and her ladies are cloud-borne to the stage *"in Amazonian habits of carnation, embroidered with silver, with plumed helms, baldrics with antique swords hanging by their sides. . . ."* (ll. 365–80 in the edition of T. J. B. Spencer, in *A Book of Masques in Honour of Allardyce Nicoll,* ed. T. J. B. Spencer and Stanley Wells [Cambridge: Cambridge Univ. Press, 1967]).

6.   Ll. 191–94 in the edition of Philip Edwards, in *A Book of Masques in Honour of Allardyce Nicoll.*

7.   *Studies in Iconology: Humanistic Themes in the Art of the Renaissance,* rev. ed. (New York: Harper, 1962), p. 121; see pp. 95–169 and plates for Panofsky's treatment of the whole topic, on which my discussion of Cupid is based.

8.   *The Faerie Queene,* III.xii.22, in *The Poetical Works of Edmund Spenser,* ed. J. C. Smith and E. de Selincourt (London: Oxford Univ. Press, 1912); quotations from Spenser are uniform with this edition.

9.   Cf. James Shirley's treatment of the idea in his masque, *Cupid and Death* (1653), ed. B. A. Harris, in *A Book of Masques in Honour of Allardyce Nicoll,* where Alciati's emblem (from *Emblematum Libellus* [Basel, 1534], p. 70) is reproduced on pl. 48; Harris summarizes the tradition of Cupid as Death, pp. 373–75.

10.   Allardyce Nicoll, *Stuart Masques and the Renaissance Stage* (1938; rpt. New York: Benjamin Blom, 1963), p. 174.

11.   Cf. Panofsky's discussion of Titian's *Education of Cupid* in *Studies in Iconology,* pp. 165–69; Panofsky's interpretation could well have served for Jonson's note, excepting, of course, a gap of more than three centuries. Panofsky says of the clear-sighted Cupid in Titian's painting, the one who appears to be advising the woman bandaging the other Eros (Jonson's "wanton brother"): "he foresees

trouble if the dangerous weapons should be handed over to a blind little fellow who shoots his arrows at random so as to cause short-lived and disillusioning passions" (p. 165). Edgar Wind, it should be noted, takes issue with Panofsky's interpretation: "While [the central figure of the painting] listens to the advice of the seeing cupid, she herself puts a blinding band over the eyes of his restive brother so that he may bring knowledge to fruition in joy. . . . Titian's picture shows . . . how intellectual love is not an end in itself but must find its fruition in passion *(voluptas)"* *(Pagan Mysteries in the Renaissance,* pp. 79–80). In Ch. IV— "Orpheus in Praise of Blind Love"—Wind qualifies Panofsky's assessment of blind Cupid as a negative symbol in the Renaissance, detailing the Neoplatonic theory that supreme love is blind, a supraintellectual experience which, far from participating in the bestial, represents man's closest approach to the divine: "Like *acedia* and *ira,* the vice of *luxuria* continued to be classed as a deadly sin, and the vulgar *voluptas,* that is incontinence, was pictured in her image. And yet, on the authority of Plotinus, sustained in this instance by Epicurus, a noble *voluptas* was introduced as the *summum bonum* of Neoplatonists" (p. 69). The argument is taken up by Panofsky in *Problems in Titian, Mostly Iconographic* (New York: New York Univ. Press, 1969), pp. 129–37, where the author identifies the two Cupids in Titian's painting as direct descendants of Alciati's emblems depicting the rival Loves, Eros and Anteros, and suggests: "The 'seeing' Anteros . . . may wish to claim the weapons for himself; he may be enjoining Venus to unblind the 'other Cupid' so as to raise him to a higher level . . . or he may be suggesting to share the use of the weapons with his rival once the latter has regained his sight. But however we may interpret the purpose of his action, it always amounts to the establishment of a *modus vivendi* between what still must be called 'celestial' and 'terrestrial' love." I refer the reader to Panofsky's study for full discussion of issues raised by Wind in *Pagan Mysteries in the Renaissance.* Whatever may be said about the blindfolding of the one Cupid in Titian's painting, the fact remains that Jonson, in a gloss to *The Masque of Beauty,* makes a clear distinction between clear-sighted "chaste Loves" and their hoodwinked brother, who is *"blind with desire* or *wanton."* The significance is twofold: 1) for the early Jacobean masque writer blind Cupid could carry definitely negative connotations, and 2) English audiences of the period apparently had to be reminded that Cupids were more than mere decoration, that they carried meaning according to the details of their costumes.

12.   " 'These pretty devices': A Study of Masques in Plays," in *A Book of Masques in Honour of Allardyce Nicoll,* p. 418. Ewbank is wrong when she says that "Apemantus is in this scene in the most literal sense an anti-masquer" (p. 418). *Timon*'s masque has no antimasque, and, in any event, Apemantus is not a participant of any kind in the entertainment. Ewbank's assertion implies that we are the only audience of the show, whereas it is obvious that Shakespeare has represented a masque *and* its audience on stage, each of which we see as separate and distinct from the other.

13.   Consider their appearance in a masque of 1579 (already mentioned in n. 5, above) in which the warrior women presented themselves "in all Armore compleate parcell gilte . . . with Counterfett Murryons silvered ouer and parcell guylte . . . and Laied with silver Lace and frindge with pendauntes of golde

Tassells. . . ." (*Documents: Elizabeth,* pp. 286–87); my discussion of Amazons is based in part on Celeste T. Wright's essay, "The Amazons in Elizabethan Literature," *Studies in Philology,* 37 (1940), 433–56.

14. I.i.78, 85–86, 90 in the edition of Clifford Leech (New York: New American Library, 1966); quotations from *The Two Noble Kinsmen* are uniform with this edition.

15. *Studies in Philology,* 37, 449–54.

16. On this episode, see Mark Rose, "Sidney's Womanish Man," *Review of English Studies,* 15 (1964), 358–59.

17. "*A Midsummer Night's Dream* and the Meaning of Court Marriage," *ELH,* 24 (1957), 103. See also D. W. Robertson, who suggests that by overcoming the Amazons Theseus has symbolically conquered "figures for rampant sensuality or effeminacy." By taking their leader in marriage he has prevented "the inversion [typically] achieved by these ferocious ladies," a disordering which "may be thought of as a triumph of the flesh" (*A Preface to Chaucer: Studies in Medieval Perspectives* [Princeton: Princeton Univ. Press, 1962], p. 265).

18. I have altered the punctuation of l. 138 (Neilson/Hill ed.: *They dance!*) to retain F1's question mark.

19. Or, alternatively, which come to congratulate, show gratitude for, pay back and gratify (*OED,* s.v. "gratulate")—all meanings seem possible. Frank Kermode compares Shakespeare's scene with the banquet Satan gets up to tempt Christ in *Paradise Regained* II—"Milton's Hero," *Review of English Studies,* 4 (1953), 324–25—and notes that the Renaissance Neoplatonists conceived of the sensual banquet as the "antitype of the celestial banquet of the *Symposium* as Ficino explained it" (p. 324).

20. The sensual thrust would have been underscored by the widely held Renaissance view of the Greek as "a voluptuary or a crook" (see T. J. B. Spencer, " 'Greeks' and 'Merrygreeks': A Background to *Timon of Athens* and *Troilus and Cressida,*" in *Essays on Shakespeare and Elizabethan Drama in Honor of Hardin Craig,* ed. Richard Hosley [Columbia: Univ. of Missouri Press, 1962], pp. 223–33).

21. See *3 Henry VI,* where York accuses Margaret of behaving like "an Amazonian trull" (I.iv.114) and Brome's *The Weeding of Covent-Garden,* where in Act IV, scene i, Bettie and Frank, "Two Punks" about to attack each other with swords, are also called "Amazonian Trulls" (*The Dramatic Works of Richard Brome,* II [London, 1873])—both examples are cited by Wright, *Studies in Philogy,* 37, 449. There is an extended example in "*Another Letter from Sea, directed to the Lord Admiral*" (part of the elaborately silly apparatus of the Gray's Inn festivities of 1594–95), in which the writer informs the Court of Purpoole that shipping is being severely hindered in Clerkenwell, Newington, and Bankside due to "an huge *Armado* of *French Amazons. . . .* To conclude, they burn all those Vessels that transport any dry Wares into the *Low-Countries.*" Once the reader catches the bawdy tone, the letter is seen as an extended sexual double entendre. There is a description of a battle between the flagship of the French Amazons ("the Rowse-Flower," whose cargo consisted of "Cochanella, Musk, Guaiacum, Tabaco and *La grand Vezolle*" [i.e., *vérole:* pox, syphilis]) and an English merchantman, during the course of which fire from the Amazon spreads to other ships: "and had not one *Barbara de Chirurgia* been ready with his Syringe, to have cast on Water, Milk, Lotium, and

such like cooling liquors, and there quenched the Wild-fire betimes," the combatants would have been burned to ashes. As it is, they are "shrewdly scorched" (*Gesta Grayorum . . . 1594*, ed. Desmond Bland, English Reprints Series No. 22 [Liverpool: Liverpool Univ. Press, 1968], pp. 65–67); I am indebted to Winfried Schleiner for calling this passage to my attention.

22. On this system of images see Oliver, ed., *Timon*, p. 22*n*, and W. H. Clemen, *The Development of Shakespeare's Imagery* (London: Methuen, 1951), pp. 169–70.

23. Oliver, ed., *Timon*, p. 16*n*.

24. For a full development of this idea see Jarold W. Ramsey, "Timon's Imitation of Christ," *Shakespeare Studies*, 2 (1966), 162–73.

25. Cf. Clemen, *The Development of Shakespeare's Imagery*: "he, too, unconsciously identifies Timon's food with Timon himself" (p. 170).

26. In an essay on the play's conclusion, Richard D. Fly suggests a way of understanding the disparity between Timon's misanthropic end and Alcibiades' willingness to lay down the sword ("The Ending of *Timon of Athens:* A Reconsideration," *Criticism*, 15 [1973], 242–52). Although Fly does not deal with the masque of Cupid and Amazons, his reading of the play helps to illuminate the structural significance of the entertainment within the whole movement of the drama. He argues that Act V functions on two levels, "the ethical absolute and the historical" (p. 248). Timon, in his rejection of Athens and mankind, lodges himself beyond history in a world of absolutes; Alcibiades, in his peaceful entrance through the city's gates at the end of the play, accepts the primacy of social order and the "need for historical continuity." When considered in light of the play's conclusion, the masque of Act I, scene ii is seen to perform a double function. Not only does it help to establish the duplicity and hollowness of Athens and the metaphoric terms for Timon's swing from love to hate, but as a celebration of community, the masque also points to the social reordering which brings the play to a close. This reordering, as well as Timon's powerfully expressed desire for the city's destruction, is put in perspective by Alcibiades at the end of the play:

> Bring me into your city,
> And I will use the olive with my sword,
> Make war breed peace, make peace stint war, make each
> Prescribe to other as each other's leech.
>
> *(V.iv.81–84)*

The masque of Cupid and Amazons establishes the grounds for this complexly balanced conclusion, although the onlookers at that show could never have guessed at the potential inherent in what they saw.

REVIEWS

Artificial Persons: The Formation of Character in the Tragedies of Shakespeare by J. Leeds Barroll. University of South Carolina Press, 1974. Pp. x + 267. $14.95

Reviewer: Norman Sanders

During the long years of reaction against A. C. Bradley's criticism of the tragedies, the numerous thematic, symbolic, theatrical, and historical studies that have appeared have not managed to produce any agreed replacement for the primacy that "character" had in his readings. While most subsequent interpretations deny the validity of the character approach or offer some alternative to it, perhaps only Lily B. Campbell's *Shakespeare's Tragic Heroes* (1930) challenged Bradley by questioning his assumptions rather than his methods and conclusions. In his recent book, Mr. Barroll seeks to repeat Miss Campbell's challenge in a work which is far less narrowing and far more suggestive than hers proved to be. By means of detailed historical research, Mr. Barroll wishes to make explicit "some protocol, some theory of characterization . . . that the tragedies of William Shakespeare seem to require us to hold." His case is based on the belief that, although obviously Shakespeare detected at first hand human traits that modern psychology accepts as a part of human nature, "the structure of ideas by which he sought to account for such phenomena would have been quite importantly different from ours."

In the first part of his study Mr. Barroll attempts to define this "structure of ideas" which he believes Shakespeare and his contemporaries would have absorbed, if only from early childhood teachings. With a formidable array of evidence and a display of enormous knowledge of the relevant documents, he proceeds to derive this structure from the implications of Renaissance transcendentalism:

> . . . men are never satisfied . . . because they have continued to desire Absolute Being and cannot ever be content with less. Men's strivings after goals are all, as it were, subconscious strivings after that Absoluteness of Being realized only in God. Their emotions reflect

their transcendental aspirations, and even if they do not know "God," they nevertheless strive for an undefined Supremacy of Being without understanding why.

The effect of this for the playwright bent on the creation of dramatic character is, for Mr. Barroll, inevitable:

> . . . human personality was not, in itself, an objectively recognised entity. Divorced from participation in a concept of suprahumanity and its attendant value systems, the human party to this divine contract was nothing. The proposition which accordingly faced the dramatist was that all facets of a purely human personality were equivalent, finally, to mere aberrations.

Thus we find structured into Shakespeare's characterizations some tendency "to pit those abilities which are used to define the self against objects of desire which may not only be illusory in strictly transcendental terms but are also not necessarily to be gained by the particular abilities in question." The resultant confusions of this spiritual state are seen to be a major portion of the tragic creations. It is in his important fourth chapter, "The Shakespearean Approach," that Mr. Barroll examines his theory in relationship to individual characters: Othello, Macbeth, Hamlet, Brutus, Lear. In very different ways, all these figures are seen to gather their sense of what they "are" not from the degree to which they conform to transcendental exemplars but from their decisions to define themselves in terms of what they are capable of in a purely earthly context.

In the second part of the book four types of character process are explored. The first comprises figures who define the self through unity with material things, who lack a grasp of abstractions and mistake sign and symbol for reality, who are pleasure-hating hypocrites, and whose lives are governed by fixed notions of desert and deserving; e.g., John of Lancaster, Malvolio, and Angelo. The second group are the pseudo-transcendentalists: Romeo, Othello, Hal, Troilus. All these are capable of conceiving something outside or above themselves, but all aspire not to the ideal personality but to a hypothetical one manufactured by their own desires for a woman, love, honour, success, or power. With Hamlet, perhaps the most complex of this class, we may usefully equate his "portraits of people whom he admires with his wishes for himself, with his quest for a version of both mental and physical perfection, a quest which is challenged when circumstances force him into specific definition." The third type of characters possess "the kind of mind for which the sense of identity was not satisfied by merging but by remaining self-sufficient." These men are the stage descendants of the Herods of the Mysteries (a figure which Mr. Barroll discusses brilliantly), and they are also connected with the idea of role-playing and thus with theater itself. For they are the ones who must assume a new part when an old one no longer provides the necessary evidence for them to retain their conviction of the validity of the superiority of self. The final grouping comprises Shakespeare's villains, characters who are unable to have confidence in any particular conceptualization. Their sense of their own value depends upon being esteemed by others, upon pretending the intensity of love they seem to long for: they are the self-conscious materialists who ultimately despise themselves.

A summary such as this may convey the impression that this book is dogmatic and rigidly schematized. In fact, just the opposite is true. The reader is struck by the lack of pretentiousness, the desire to suggest a strategy for the future discussion of Shakespeare's characters rather than any claim to have plucked out the heart of their mystery. Mr. Barroll is consistently aware that any theory of characterization "can never be a close description of specific figures in a given drama. It is only the basis upon which structures are built." However, it should be said that the book does contain much thoughtful comment on individual characters and plays.

In sum, I think this is a book which everyone interested in Shakespeare should read. I would like to have said "will want to read," but the style in which it is written makes no concessions to readability. There are too many sentences which seem designed to stand between at least the general reader and the idea like a kind of verbal smokescreen. For example, "And in such a cultural context, the translation of psychological assumption into the mimesis of dramatic causation and process will espouse the redundancies of an appeal to the root concept of original sin or its idealogical synonyms." This is the sort of phrasing which will prevent Mr. Barroll's ideas from playing the part in critical discussion that they should.

Shakespeare's Comedies: Explorations in Form by Ralph Berry. Princeton University Press, 1972. Pp. 214. $10.00.

Reviewer: Kent van den Berg.

Professor Berry offers a sober, unsentimental reading of Shakespeare's comedies. He is an intelligent critic; nearly everyone will find something to value in his book. I am grateful for his insights about Adriana's possessiveness (in *The Comedy of Errors*) and the relationship of Touchstone and Jaques. His chapters on *Love's Labour's Lost* and *Much Ado About Nothing*, while abstract and schematic, provide conceptual frameworks useful in organizing a fuller response to the challenging diversity of these plays. But the book as a whole is disappointing. Much of its logic seems to me superficial and its style glib; it is marred by a pervasive cynicism that rests on ill-founded assumptions about Shakespeare's comedies.

Berry presents his ten chapters—one for each comedy through *Twelfth Night*—as brisk and incisive studies which will accomplish their purpose with maximum efficiency. Many begin by sweeping aside unwanted material, as though the remarkable copiousness of Shakespearean drama were a mere nuisance: "The subject matter . . . is of no interest here whatsoever" (p. 25); "I propose here to say no more of the farce elements" (p. 54); "The romantic elements need no recapitulation here" (p. 175). As soon as these irrelevancies are cleared away, central themes are singled out and the mechanisms of interpretation put in gear: "*A Midsummer Night's Dream* is, in effect, nothing but two dramatized symbols: the dream and the play. . . . The lovers declare illusion to be reality; the actors declare reality to be illusion" (pp. 89, 106); *Twelfth Night* "can usefully be analyzed in terms of fantasy (or illusion) and reality. . . . We can begin by classifying the principals. Orsino is a fantasist, and music is the symbol of his fantasy. His vein is auto-erotic, clear from the opening line. . . . It is *simpliste* to speak of him as being prey to illusions. For Orsino, illusion is the only reality. He is contrasted with Viola, who is a reality figure. . . . Olivia is in part under the sway of illusion, but is more poseuse than fantasist" (pp. 199, 200). The elegant diction of these statements does not conceal their crudely categorical distinctions. The critical machinery clanks loudly beneath its highly polished covering, especially when it drops into the low gear of academic bombast: "The men [Demetrius and Lysander], in brief, are subjectivists who advance their retinal impressions as objective and rational justifications for their conduct" (p. 98).

Some of the machinery seems to have a mostly decorative function. Berry proposes, for example, to approach *The Merchant of Venice* "as a conjugation of the verb *to gain*" (p. 113). But he does not really mean to do so and quickly replaces his grammatical metaphor with another (which seems to be Darwinian): "The formal principle . . . I take to be a series of mutations of 'venture' " (p. 114). As he proceeds, his deft allusions to economics and psychology combine to produce a contradiction: Antonio is contemptible because, like all capitalists, he wants to gain secure profits, despite his predictable cant about the risks he is willing to assume (pp. 118–21); yet, being a neurotic gambler, he wants to lose so that he may indulge "self-pity, and the enjoyment of unconscious psychic masochistic pleasure" (p. 128). Berry often alludes to the possibility that Shakespeare's plays, taken serially, manifest a coherent development of dramatic art, but he invokes the idea less for its conceptual importance than for its rhetorical appeal: "Nothing is more interesting in *The Comedy of Errors* than to see the dark wind from the horizon of Shakespeare's future, blowing toward him" (p. 39); "*Much Ado* is a base camp that secures the approaches to the peak [viz., to *Hamlet* and *Othello*]" (p. 174); *Twelfth Night* "is a conclusive, magisterial exposition of techniques and tonalities; it recapitulates and restates the themes that have engaged its author since *The Comedy of Errors*. It is a terminus of evolution, a work whose concerns and mastery openly prohibit a successor. . . . [It] points unmistakably toward *King Lear*" (pp. 196, 212).

In his Introduction, Berry promises to limit his survey to those serious and ironic elements of the comedies which he believes other critics have slighted: "I judge it unnecessary to elaborate to my readers the romantic qualities . . . [or the] explicit treatment of love and its values. That is essentially an aspect of the plays' subject matter, and it has been admirably charted by John Russell Brown in *Shakespeare and His Comedies* [London: Methuen, 1957]. The emphasis in these studies is on the 'other' play, the serious and at times somber presence that the comedies contain" (p. 22). His justification for this admittedly one-sided approach vacillates among several different and contradictory assumptions, none of which is fully developed in his "studies." I fail to see how his book can pass for a complement or corrective to Brown's. Even a brief comparison of the two will suggest their irreconcilable differences. Brown affirms that *As You Like It* "culminates in the fullest celebration of the ideal of love's order" (p. 141); the characters in Arden find content "in terms of the gentleness, service or order which has been neglected in the world outside" (p. 150); "In the circumscribed steps of the dance, the abundance of their joy finds full expression" (p. 144); "The play's generosity and confidence spring chiefly from the characterization of Rosalind" (p. 158). Berry insists to the contrary that "Virtually all the relationships [in *As You Like It*] manifest a sense of unease, of latent or open hostility. There is little true accord in Arden" (p. 195); Rosalind "is motivated above all by a will to dominate" (p. 184); "The play . . . focuses on the mating dance of a masterful female round her captive male" (p. 194). Berry and Brown are not complementary critics; one of them is dreadfully wrong.

Berry would deny this, arguing that Shakespeare, in many of his comedies, constructs "two distinct plays within one frame," so that "*Much Ado About Nothing* can be regarded as a jolly elaboration of its title, or a serious analysis of modes of knowing (and naturally, a draft of *Othello*). *As You Like It* is an idyll, or a fairly perturbed pastoral. *Twelfth Night* is a warm-hearted defense of cakes and ale, or an inventory of illusions" (p. 21). If Shakespeare really does construct two plays in a single frame, we cannot fully interpret one in complete isolation from the other, whichever one we choose to emphasize—especially if Shakespeare (as Berry often says) "synthesized" them (pp. 22, 25, 42, 53, 54, 145, 175). Despite his concern for "organic form" and "principle of organization" (p. 6), he has no time for the "jolly," idyllic, or "warm-hearted" plays. Although he says they are half of Shakespeare's achievement in comedy, he dismisses them as mere "subject matter" (pp. 22, 155), "nominal activity" (p. 114), and "plot" (p. 175), not worthy of serious consideration. Berry does not in fact allow the duality to exist; invariably the "other" play turns out to be the *only* play.

Apparently to mitigate his rigor, Berry proposes that a Shakespeare comedy "is open to diversity of interpretation" (p. 193*n*), so that "the audience has some warrant, if it wishes, for classifying the comedy under Plays Pleasant or Plays Unpleasant" (p. 21). However, his generous concession that we may take the plays as we like them is entirely at odds with the harsh verdicts he thrusts upon us as the inevitable results of cold, unsentimental scrutiny: "The best epigraph, perhaps, [for *A Midsummer Night's Dream*] is H. L. Mencken's. 'Love: the illusion that one woman is any different from another' " (p. 101). In *The Merchant of Venice*, "Bassanio is the type of aristocrat who exploits his charm to ensure that he is never on the losing side. What he risks is other people's money. Bassanio is one of life's winners; no wonder Antonio admires him" (p. 132), Antonio being a "passive-feminine male gambler" (p. 131) who plays to lose. *Merry Wives* is "a markedly unpleasant play," an "account of ignorant stereotypes clashing by night" (p. 153); worse yet, its "revenge motif unleashes much sadism in the audience" (p. 148). In *As You Like It*, "Shakespeare pre-

sents . . . a struggle for mastery between two human beings" (p. 176), while
"The main business of *Twelfth Night* is illusion, error, and deceit" (p. 199).
These statements seek specious validity from their exaggerated cynicism:
they must be true because they are so contrary to what we prefer. Berry
terms this prejudice "the reality principle" and recommends it "as the proper criterion . . . of the comedy as a whole" because "it upholds no systems of values whatsoever" (pp. 14–15). To avoid self-deception, we must
take the plays as we *dis*like them.

Berry's two-play theory and his appeal to relativism are inconsistent with
his assumption that the comedies offer a single action which "refutes" the
romantic idealism of the main characters, exposing their "follies of fantasy
and self-deception" (p. 10). The burden of refutation is carried mostly by
the clowns and fools whose parody and deflating commentary—"If the cat
will after kind, / So be sure will Rosalind"—Berry takes at face value. He
ignores the consensus that parody and satire function in Shakespeare's
comedies to protect romantic ideals from both extravagance and cynicism:
"the illusions thrown up by feeling are mastered by laughter, and so love
is reconciled to judgment."[1] Perhaps this consensus needs revision, but
Berry offers little reason for thinking so. In one place, he does make large
claims for the wisdom of clowns, arguing that Dogberry and the Watch
have an "impeccable logic" for detection: "In their system, a hypothesis
must be checked against a sufficient body of confirmatory data" (p. 165).
But most of his remarks about clowns and fools are brief and unexcep-
tional: "It is a safe generalization that Shakespeare's clowns are never
merely funny; they always provide some form of commentary on or parody
of their social betters" (p. 33). He often quotes their commentary not to
analyze it but to express his own views: "Shakespeare's predilection for
locating the common-sense viewpoint among clowns, boobies, and servants is already marked; and we should take, as the final internal criticism
of the action [in *Two Gentlemen*], the words of Thurio: 'I hold him but a fool
that will endanger / His body for a girl that loves him not' " (p. 51). Thurio
is a "reality-figure." When Berry gets down to cases, he has less than most
other critics to say about that interaction of perspectives which might qualify romantic ideals; his own "ironic" perspective excludes from view any
value worthy of qualification. An example is his response to the episode in
Twelfth Night where Feste's fooling moderates Olivia's grief for her dead
brother. This would seem a good example of a fool's wisdom countering
noble folly, but Berry says: "When we first meet [Olivia], her self-chosen
role of grief-prostrated sister is clearly becoming irksome. She is ready to
be delivered from her ennui by the clown" (p. 200). It does not occur to

Berry that Olivia's grief, however self-indulgent, might be a tribute to her instinctive generosity of spirit. She is merely a "poseuse," and Orsino, who sees in her mourning "a heart of that fine frame / To pay this debt of love," is hopelessly deluded by "the unabashed auto-eroticism of his humor" (p. 209). Neither Feste nor Viola, for all their wit and wisdom, can redeem such shallow persons. In fact, Berry concludes, as he must, that the play ends ambivalently by seeming to condone the illusions of Orsino and Olivia: "The cynicism of *Twelfth Night* lies in its acceptance of the truths that fantasy need not bring unhappiness, nor exposure to reality happiness" (pp. 211–12). Not all lovers are unhappy; some are blind.

Berry argues that all the comedies, except *The Comedy of Errors*, have "ambivalent, question begging conclusions" (p. 13). He suggests that Shakespeare deceives the spectator with the illusion that his comedies end happily by suppressing their ambivalence at the close, "so that the emotions generated by the final festivities will not be marred" (p. 12); as a result, "the playgoer is entitled to yield to the agreeable emotions of the final dance" (p. 15). If Berry is correct, it is difficult to avoid the further conclusion that the comedies are artistic failures, even if we accept his proposal that they were "a means of preparation for the tragedies" (p. 23). By implying that the immediacy and affective power of performance becloud critical judgment, Berry seems to rest his case on antitheatrical prejudice: "Generally, the critic who attends a Shakespearean revel (I say nothing of the playgoer) would, I feel, be well advised to follow a simple precept: to stay sober" (pp. 15–16)—despite Shakespeare's effort to intoxicate him.

The sober critic will ask: "How festive is this feast?" (p. 13). Is sobriety really the best response to Shakespeare's comedies? If we regard his men and women with "ironic detachment" (p. 100), we may in fact wonder at them for thinking so well of themselves and might even speak of their hypocrisy and self-deluding folly. But at its logical extreme, our detachment might stifle imagination altogether, preventing us from responding to dramatic fiction by degrading the characters to what they are in fact, "merely players," and by reducing both court and forest to an "unworthy scaffold." As soon as we begin to make believe, we cease to be entirely "sober" and wish to credit the "illusions" of the characters, knowing from our own imaginative participation what value they can claim. This knowledge need not be discredited by whatever critical scrutiny we subsequently bring to bear on the play or our responses to it. Critical scrutiny should reveal that Shakespeare gives our capacity to pretend cognitive and moral value. The point is admirably made by John Russell Brown:

[*A Midsummer Night's Dream*] suggests that lovers, like actors, need, and sometimes ask for, our belief, and that this belief can only be given if we have the generosity and imagination to think "no worse of them than they of themselves." The play's greatest triumph is the manner in which our wavering acceptance of the illusion of drama is used as a kind of flesh-and-blood image of the acceptance which is appropriate to the strange and private "truth" of those who enact the play of love. By using this living image, Shakespeare has gone beyond direct statement in words or action and has presented his judgement in terms of a mode of being, a relationship, in which we, the audience, are actually involved.

(p. 90)

Surely Berry has let himself become involved in the way; he even professes to have "laughed inordinately" (p. 18) at all of Shakespeare's comedies in performance. I wish he had allowed this response to mitigate his sobriety a little.

Note:

1. C. L. Barber, *Shakespeare's Festive Comedy* (Princeton: Princeton Univ. Press, 1959), p. 236. See also John Bayley, *The Characters of Love* (London: Constable, 1960), pp. 185–94 and Dean Frye, "The Question of Shakespearean 'Parody'," *Essays in Criticism*, 15 (1965), 22–26.

Shakespeare's Grammatical Style: A Computer-Assisted Analysis of "Richard II" and "Antony and Cleopatra" by Dolores M. Burton. University of Texas Press, 1973. Pp. 364. $13.75.

Reviewer: Mary P. Hiatt.

A *New Yorker* cartoon (June 24, 1974) depicts a young man and a young lady of about nine or ten standing before a bust of William Shakespeare. The young man is explaining: "He was a very, very, very, very, very, very, very, very, very, very, very, very, very, very, very important writer." One cannot help but wonder whether a similar awe accounts for the periodically apologetic and defensive stance of Dolores Burton's book. There are problems enough involved in stylistic research, and there are problems enough involved in computational research. Studies of style which employ the computer might therefore be considered especially fraught with problems without the additional burden of magnified modesty. Being overwhelmed by the object of study should have been firmly resisted, for the tone of Burton's book unfortunately calls into question her considerable competence and skill, as well as the importance of her contribution. Her seeming lapses of self-confidence, such as predicting that some of her results will be considered trivial and pointing out that her study has restated stylistic features observed by others, only serve to undercut her handling of the real problems.

The book, originally her dissertation, needs no apologia. It grapples effectively with such difficult matters as the many-headed hydra of stylistic theory and those aspects of literary style which are found in syntax. Less perceptive is her grasp of the ways in which a computer can be useful, if avoidance of the topic is any indication. Her book is therefore of value primarily to Shakespeareans and stylisticians.

The Preface should not be overlooked, for it contains the author's general intentions. She points out that the study of the two tragedies *Richard II* and *Antony and Cleopatra*, since it is based on a selective computerized concordance, is confined to *formal* linguistic features and cannot be concerned with imagery, vocabulary, and rhetorical figures. Her intention is also to formulate a theory of style.

To this second task she addresses herself in the first chapter. A chapter section, entitled "The Problem of Style" (there are very few books on style which do not begin with precisely that title), offers the definition of style most widely accepted by American linguists: the "way of doing it." Burton wishes to avoid "falling into a form-content dichotomy" (p. 11); yet her approach is essentially dualistic. The chapter includes a detailed and somewhat obscure description of the "style function," as well as a review of the theoretical work of several major linguists and stylisticians. It might usefully have been expanded to include reference to the work of G. N. Leech, Louis T. Milic, Jan Mukarovský, and Viktor Sklovskij, since their theories have a definite bearing on Burton's study.

Chapter II, "Locating Style in Literature," deals with methodological preliminaries and offers three methods of "locating" style in text. "Locating" style is, of course, a matter of theory: Is style a deviation from some linguistic norm? Is it more simply a matter of grammatical options? Citing Michael Riffaterre's theory that stylistic analysis begins with a reader's response to a passage, Burton suggests three methods: (1) a study of sentence mood, (2) an analysis of those passages within each play "thought to be" stylistically representative, and (3) an examination of passages from each play that have similar content and different styles. The author's references to Riffaterre, incidentally, should have been updated. His expanded and revised essays were published as *Essais de stylistique structurale* (Paris: Flammarion, 1971).

Sentence mood as a stylistic feature is examined through the occurrence of exclamatory, interrogative, and imperative sentences. Burton finds, for example, that the number of exclamatory sentences in *Richard II* decreases by 25% in *Antony and Cleopatra*. (The decrease is actually closer to 50%; the author overlooks a difference in sample sizes.) Frequency of interrogatives does not differ significantly between the two plays, though there are differences in types of interrogatives. Imperatives increase significantly in *Antony and Cleopatra*. Burton observes that within that play, Cleopatra's commands are "only one percentage point fewer than Antony's" (p. 38). This particular comment might indicate a degree of surprise on the part of its author. It would seem that women, even queens, are not supposed to give many commands. At any rate, the detailed discussion of these three sentence moods, plus the findings of the author's earlier study of conditionals in *1 Henry IV*, demonstrates that such data can be useful in revelation of style and that style in turn may to some extent reveal the personality of one or another character. Method 1 is useful.

Somewhat disturbing, however, is Method 2, "locating" stylistic differences in passages "felt to be representative of each text" (p. 42). The circularity of this method cannot be ignored. One cannot contrast styles which have already been deemed somehow stylistically typical. Burton justifies the method as a way of "exploring intuitive feelings" about stylistic variation. However, any semblance of objectivity is tossed to the winds when styles are impressionistically described—before analysis—as "loose" and "Roman," as well as being representative of, respectively, *Richard II* and *Antony and Cleopatra*. One ultimately gathers that left-branching sentences are periodic sentences, hence "Roman." Involved in her conclusions is a careful analysis of hypotactic structures in both plays. One can only wish such analysis had been based on impartially-chosen passages.

By Method 3, Burton chooses "constant" topics and observes stylistic differences by reducing passages to kernel sentences, her main concern being the frequency, type, and function of certain adjectives. There is again a tendency to make impressionistic judgments, e.g., the polysyllabic adjective base in *Antony and Cleopatra* makes the diction of that play more "interesting" than the diction of *Richard II*. But the method is a cogent one; it reveals significant differences in the adjective-noun patterns of the two plays.

In the third chapter, theoretical problems are raised which might better have been presented earlier in the book. The rapid change of the English language during the thirteen years between the two plays suggests that some type of broad-based stylistic study might be necessary to serve as a background and hence as a solution to some of the questions Burton discusses. Nontheoretical material of the chapter is largely quantitative, with many clear and easily grasped tables having to do with word order and sentence complexity. One might question the implication that "loose" construction indicates simplicity of style (p. 109), but in general the findings are thoroughly researched and statistically sound. As is often the case in this type of work, however, the amount of detail tends to blur emphasis. And there are occasional lapses into impressionistic statements: a "stylistically best" passage, for example, and "flatulent and self-conscious clauses."

The fourth chapter, "Grammar as Meaning," is by far the best in the book. Here Burton's comments on the homophoric nature of the definite article and its significance in both plays are entirely persuasive. For example, the definite article modifies the word "world" more than three times as often in *Antony and Cleopatra* as it does in *Richard II*. Thus, in *Antony and Cleopatra*, "the individual is measured against the backdrop of the world," and the world is "at once a source of higher status and greater anxiety in *Antony and Cleopatra* than it was in *Richard II*" (p. 153). Her analysis of the use of determiners in general and the manner in which they "control" nominal groups is original and refreshing. She notes, for instance, the appearance in Richard's language of the words "a king," contrasting with the previous use of the definite article; Richard's increasing use of the nonspecific determiner reflects "his growing awareness of the split between role and person and of the fact that he is not 'the King,' but 'a king' " (p. 174).

There are several good suggestions for further study offered in the fifth chapter, such as ways of determining sentence complexity and rarity of vocabulary. Foregrounding (*aktualisace*) of the Prague School is, curiously, mentioned only in a footnote; paradigmatic foregrounding is not mentioned at all. Yet these two aspects of stylistic theory are central to the facets of Shakespeare's style which Burton feels should be investigated. After some rather elaborately defensive comments, Burton does strike a blow for broad-based stylistic research using the computer.

The book concludes with an attempt to make the leap from stylistics to poetics. This is not altogether successful; explication is not style analysis.

For this reader, the word "computer" was foregrounded only three times in the entire book. This count is quite likely to be inaccurate; the frequency of the word "computer" can only be ascertained reliably by a computer.

But the impression of such an infrequent occurrence means, of course, that the work of the computer in the study is deemphasized. More's the pity. In the Preface, as previously noted, Burton takes pains to point out that because the study is based on a computerized concordance, it is confined to formal linguistic features and cannot be concerned with imagery, vocabulary, and rhetorical figures. While it is true that a computer can only scan for formal elements, it is also true that it is a serendipitous instrument, a fact overlooked by Burton. In several chapters and despite Burton's disclaimer, many nonformal aspects of the two works are both revealed and discussed.

Also, she repetitively argues that the main function of quantitative analysis is to "support" intuitive criticism. The fact of the matter is quite the opposite. Not infrequently literary criticism is based on false perception. Far from the computer functioning as a confirmatory agent for critical judgment, it should instead be utilized as a basis for such judgment.

Beyond these seeming denigrations of the computer lies the fact that, for those of us interested in the specifics of computer-assisted research, the unanswered questions abound: What programming language was used? Who did the programming? Was the use of the computer limited to establishing the "selective" concordance? Was the concordance on cards or tape or disc? What computer was used? And so forth. Some of the answers can be found in *Shakespeare Newsletter*, 15 (December 1965), 55, if the brief description of procedures therein was the one actually followed. But in any case, the information should have been included in the book. A sample computer program would also have been helpful.

In general, however, this is a useful book and certainly worthy of membership in the ever-growing critical oeuvre concerning "a very, very, very . . . important writer."

Shakespearean Romance by Howard Felperin. Princeton University Press, 1972. Pp. 319. $11.00.

Reviewer: Joan Hartwig.

The publication of at least five major books on Shakespeare's last plays since 1972 attests to a revaluation. Obviously, many of Shakespeare's readers have wanted to find an approach and a vocabulary adequate for a just criticism of these special plays, so long neglected or slighted when noticed. Reading Howard Felperin's book two years after the flood of last-plays criticism reminds me that all too often illuminating insights each of us has had individually and independently are but the common ground of under-standing. Felperin's book is in general ways sound, but its point of view is not new, except perhaps in its consideration of the "so-called problem plays" and the tragedies. My primary dissatisfaction with his study is that, aside from adding little to what has often been said about the last plays, it does not allow for the life—the magic vitality—of these plays as perfor-mances to emerge.

This failure is due, I think, to Felperin's almost exclusive focus on the formulas of romance literature applied to the plays without consideration of the dramaturgical complexities and multiple conventions, other than those of romance, which feed into the dramatic effect of any specific scene. Abstracted, Felperin's romance formulas seem to apply, but they make the plays which use them appear to be simpler and less exciting than they are.

To see Pericles as a conventional hero of a miracle play and Marina as "the human embodiment of Diana's divine grace" (p. 161) may lead us in an appropriate direction. Yet Felperin's patterned view does not allow for the complex qualifications of both Pericles' martyrlike suffering and Mari-na's saintlike virtue that specific dramaturgical choices, made by the play-wright, require an audience to notice: for examples, the comic touches in the presentations of Pericles' recovery on the shores of Pentapolis and of Mari-na's reformation of Mytilene's citizenry. In other words, I do not so much disagree with Felperin's interesting observations that *Pericles'* action closely parallels that of the medieval miracle and morality plays as I object to the narrowness of the vision toward which he leads me.

A similar case in point is the discussion of the recognition scene in *Cym-beline* (pp. 183–85). Felperin argues that the offstage action of Christ's in-carnation informs the characters' actions, as each awakens from stoic apathy to "a resurrected life. . . . Even Iachimo is caught up in the new spirit of the final scene and undergoes an otherwise unmotivated, morality-like reformation." Interesting as this interpretation is, it fails to ac-count for the stop-and-go method of presentation, the comically deflation-ary merging of revelations, that shapes audience response to the content of the scene.

A third instance of an unnecessarily narrow reading of a scene occurs in the discussion of Gonzalo's speech on the commonwealth. Though Felpe-rin says that "the jibes of Antonio and Sebastian that frame Gonzalo's monologue no doubt damage their speakers more than their target" (p.

260), he does not consider the fact that Gonzalo himself qualifies the idealism of his speech, admitting that it is a fiction he created in order to comfort the grieving Alonso. The points Felperin makes about the limitations of the romantic vision are important ones, but he distorts Gonzalo into a Polonian figure by ignoring the full dramatic context of the speech.

Felperin says that "one of the aims of this study is to demonstrate the pervasive presence of romance within Shakespeare's entire work" (p. 58), and his demonstration of the fundamental ambivalence toward romance in Shakespeare's problem comedies is perhaps the most innovative and rewarding section of the book. Neither the ideal of Troilus (valuing faith over expediency) nor of Ulysses (valuing order and degree) "is set up solely to be knocked down" (p. 77); their exhortations are not invalidated but negatively borne out by the play's action. Cressida, like the morality protagonist, wavers between the best and the worst in her nature and in her world, combining romantic and antiromantic attitudes; but she is unable to reconcile these attitudes as heroines of earlier romantic comedies have done, and she is divided by them. A crucial feature of *Troilus* and of the other problem comedies, Felperin argues, is "that they contain no fully realized second world where the romantic imagination has room to maneuver, is free to create constructs that rival and rehabilitate the first" (p. 82). In *All's Well* and in *Measure for Measure*, Helena and Isabella adopt morality roles that are inappropriate for the secular dramas in which they appear. Rather than healing the divisions between body and spirit, both women widen the division. The art which each of these plays needs is the art of a Prospero, an art which does not ignore or despise the imperfections of this old world but which repairs them. Even so, Prospero's triumph is that he recognizes the limits of his art and acknowledges life's resistance to being transmuted into art at all, especially into romance. The problem plays lack such figures of vision and resourcefulness: instead of Prospero, there is Pandarus, or at best Duke Vincentio, who fails to know the limits of his role.

Shakespearean Romance opens with a chapter on background and theory, which oddly enough omits any reference to such a substantial book as E. C. Pettet's *Shakespeare and the Romance Tradition* (London: Staples, 1949). The task of defining romance precisely is admittedly difficult, since, according to Felperin, "all literature is fundamentally romantic" (p. 7). He distinguishes three historical developments which converge in Shakespearean romance: the classical romance of the Greeks, the chivalric romance of the Middle Ages, and the religious drama (particularly the miracle and morality plays) of the later Middle Ages. Shakespeare's romance, Felperin says, ventures out onto the high seas, whereas his contemporaries in the great tradition of English comedy stop at the seashore (p. 17). What Shakespeare does in the romances "is to take an older romance model and show its inadequacy to contain and comprehend the experience of his play, to expose the dangers inherent in the mode he uses by testing it against a reality it cannot cope with, to avoid escapism by making his plays about escapism. . . . The moral and mimetic dimension of Shakespearean romance comes into being through its stubborn refusal to accept and repeat the conventions of romance without revaluating them" (pp. 53–54).

The second section's three chapters describe Shakespeare's movement toward romance. This section contains useful distinctions between the romantic comedies and the later romances, the discussion of the problem plays, and a view of the mature tragedies as antiromantic structures. Felperin employs Bacon's view of the world—"a hard, unyielding, brazen reality whose one certainty is flux and where human affairs are subject to the ceaseless roll of Fortune's wheel" (p. 136)—to define this kind of tragedy. His major point is that Shakespeare worked with romance as a mode of perceiving the world not only at the beginning and at the end of his career but throughout. The tragedies and the romances are related in their antiromantic structures, but the tragic heroes "persist in expecting romance and get tragedy; the romantic protagonists are disabused of all romantic expectations and get romance" (p. 63). I am not convinced, however, that these formulas are adequate to account for the hugeness of *King Lear*. When Felperin says that "Lear reveals in the last act a capacity for self-deception—'This feather stirs; she lives!' . . . —reminiscent of that which characterized him in the first" (p. 104), I am left with a simplicity of perception that does not begin to match my sense of the magnitude of values and attitudes being exposed in this scene. On the other hand, I am intrigued by the discussion of the Gloucester subplot, pp. 113–16, which finds the Gloucester universe to be morally transparent and unappealing in contrast to the complexities of the universe that Lear inhabits.

The third section of the study examines five of the last plays in individual chapters, and it is here that I find my expectations most thwarted. The discussion of *Pericles* is right in its attempt to retrieve a beautiful play from calumny by reporting on its heritage, but it does not do justice to this play's complex dramatic experience, possibly because Felperin depends much too heavily upon the formulas of morality structure to explain and inform the later play's action.

Both *Cymbeline* and *Henry VIII* fail to bridge the gap between reality and romance, according to Felperin—*Cymbeline* because of its dependence upon topical reference and *Henry VIII* because its circle of redemption is too all-inclusive to be true. Although I cannot quite agree that *"Cymbeline* is finally the victim of its own romantic unity, a unity of design so tight that it effectively seals off the play from the world we know" (p. 196), I can agree that *Henry VIII's* "golden age represents not creation out of nothing but the distortion of something, a gilded age passed off as a golden" (p. 209).

The chapter on *The Winter's Tale* contains a very good section (which the author is willing to discount too easily) on Shakespeare's method for making conventional figures out of an older drama come alive (pp. 218–19), on Autolycus' art as parody of the high art of the play itself, and on the restorative relationship between art and life. Still, there are two points with which I must take issue. First is the statement that neither Desdemona nor Cordelia has the flesh-and-blood vitality of Hermione because neither of the tragic figures expresses her sense of wrong as does Hermione. This argument is attached to one equally puzzling: romance figures are not supposed to have the lifelike characterization that Hermione has. Felperin considers this to be a breakthrough in characterization which is unprecedented in romantic drama to this point (p. 220). I would be negligent not to suggest that this example displays the limitations of applying only romantic formulae to Shakespeare's conventions and intentions in the last plays.

A second objection which is perhaps negligible, but which I consider important in that it applies to the book as a whole, is to Felperin's asseveration that "in *The Winter's Tale* ripeness, and the whole process of birth, growth, death, and rebirth that it implies, really is all. . . . When we hear in the opening scene of a projected visit to Bohemia 'this coming summer,' and see the action shift to that place and season with the fourth act, we learn that the seasons change in the world of this play just as they do in the real world" (pp. 225, 227). These statements, which are not false concerning the dominant metaphors operating in the play, nonetheless do not consider Shakespeare's carefully announced anachronism about the natural seasons which occurs in Perdita's speeches to Polixenes and Camillo. The sheepshearing festival is taking place, not at the normal time in the spring, but while, "the year growing ancient, / Not yet on summer's death nor on the birth / Of trembling winter, the fairest flowers o' th' season / Are our carnation and streaked gillivors, / Which some call nature's bastards" (IV.iv.79–83). Later she says, "These are flowers / Of middle summer" (106–107), and still later, "I would I had some flowers o' th' spring" (113). It seems to me that in order to make the kind of statements that Felperin wishes to make about these plays, one must also consider the conscious dramaturgical choices on Shakespeare's part to force his audience to reconsider its "natural" assumptions.

Clearly, it is not Felperin's intention to suggest a thorough review of scholarship that has been presented on the plays; yet, in some cases, and especially with individual plays, he seems unaware of much significant criticism that precedes him. The Bibliographical Appendix on "The Fortunes of Romance" provides a limited overview of the reception of Shakespeare's romances from an anonymous critic of 1609 through Northrop Frye of 1965. The three-page index is not full enough to be really helpful.

In the final analysis, I have to say that for a serious work of scholarship, this books seems too casual. Intelligence and superficiality coexist: there are valuable insights, but too frequently their implications remain unexplored.

The Stranger in Shakespeare by Leslie A. Fiedler. Stein and Day, 1973, Pp. 263. $8.50.

Reviewer: Morse Peckham.

Whoever likes psychoanalytic and archetypal literary interpretation will probably like this book, and whoever enjoys the criticism of Professor Fiedler will almost certainly like it. On the other hand, anyone interested in Shakespearean scholarship can almost certainly neglect it with safety. The book gives me the impression that Professor Fiedler is depending upon the Shakespearean scholarship he learned in graduate school, or even in an undergraduate course; otherwise he has depended upon the odder among contemporary Shakespearean critics. He mentions them on page ten, but I prefer not to. His scholarly care—and his intellectual bias—is indicated in the following passage, in which he is talking about what fascinates him, the playing of women's parts by boys.

> Then he-she curtsies with that strange perfection of grace possible only to a male playing the idea of femininity and sets throbbing—we are free to imagine—more than one male heart in that largely homosexual circle of gallants, which, sitting on stage rather than standing in the pit, must have felt itself sometimes more actor or chorus than audience.

How does he know that that circle of gallants was largely homosexual? And as for the first part of the sentence, if he means that women do not play the idea of femininity, I can scarcely agree with him. Femininity is not a biological determinant but a social role. Like masculinity, it is an "idea." Professor Fiedler compares seeing in Shakespeare's time one of his plays to going to a performance by female impersonators today. But surely there is a difference between a commonplace convention and a rarely seen and very special kind of show.

By "stranger" Professor Fiedler means women, Jews, blacks, and American Indians. And since he is an intelligent, and frequently brilliant, but self-indulgent, writer, what he has to say about these figures is at times of considerable interest, though he does not reveal that he is forcing the issue a bit when he admits that Caliban is a strange blend of African and Indian. Certainly throughout his career Professor Fiedler has always been fashionable, but he has rarely been so fashionable as he is here, so extremely au courant with the preoccupations of the media and the media's fellow-travelling intellectuals, though to be sure bringing in anti-Semitism is a little old hat. However, he begins, and is preoccupied throughout, with Shakespeare's alleged homosexuality. Whether Shakespeare actually engaged in sexual relations with men is unrecorded. He himself says, if the Sonnets are to be trusted (and the reasons for trusting them seem to be as good as the reasons for not trusting them; that is, there are no good reasons for either position), that he engaged in sexual relations with at least one woman. He also, it certainly seems, had sexual relations with his wife. But I am not concerned with whether Shakespeare had sexual relations with men or not but rather with what Professor Fiedler does with his conviction that Shakespeare was homosexual or at least bothered by the possibility. There has been an enormous amount of writing about homosexuality, but the only solid information on the subject is to be found in the works of the researchers at the Sex Research Institute, founded by Alfred Kinsey at Indiana University. What appears to be a preliminary report on homosexuality has now been published (M. S. Weinberg and C. J. Williams, *Male Homosexuals* [New York: Oxford Univ. Press, 1974]). From that book I, at least, arose with the conviction that homosexuality is a subject on which it is not possible to say anything of interest. What I mean is that from the proposition that a particular individual is homosexual it is impossible to move to any other propositions. Or to put it differently, the attribute of homosexual behavior does not entail or permit the prediction of any other attibutes of behavior. What Professor Fiedler does with Shakespeare, however, does not recognize this, for Professor Fiedler is a Freudian. Thus what he does with Shakespeare's homosexuality is very much what you would expect, for what a Freudian can do with homosexuality is very limited, and Professor Fiedler does not transgress those limits.

The trouble with Freudianism is that Freud did not study or even ob-

serve human behavior. He studied verbal behavior in situations of extraordinary permissiveness, and he studied individuals who were deeply troubled by their own behavior, especially their sexual behavior. Freud, insofar
as he told them anything, like any psychiatrist, the moral policeman of a
secular society, told them that they ought to be troubled. Professor Fiedler,
like all Freudians, therefore assumes that all homosexuals are troubled by
their homosexuality, and therefore Shakespeare must have been. But in the
Sonnets he seems to have been troubled only by his heterosexuality. The
Kinsey researchers report that a third of full-time homosexuals, not to
speak of bisexuals, are not troubled in the least by their sexual preference
and never have been. Freud merely confirmed his patients' judgments of
their own behavior—judgments derived from their culture. He merely confirmed the incoherence of their attitudes. It is not surprising that he felt
psychoanalysis could benefit only a very tiny number of people.

But this is not the only difficulty with Freud for critics like Professor Fiedler. Freud, like Jung—with whom he engaged in a correspondence frequently marked by childish petulance and from whom he parted in the
same spirit—read too many books, and too many of the books that he read
were literature. Now literature, at any cultural level, is made up of a limited number of verbal patterns which are repeated with slight variations
over and over and over. The literature of any culture is thus very much
like its cooking or the way it fights its wars. Literature differs from these
and similar behavioral groupings in that the same patterns can be used to
exemplify quite different ideologies. The task of the scholar is to discover,
if he can, what ideology that particular work exemplifies, or, more interest-
ingly, is engaged in undermining. I myself do not see that Shakespeare
was very interested in the second possibility or even, as that great poet-
thinker, Edmund Spenser, interested in clarifying and making coherent
certain incoherencies in the predominating ideology of his time. On the
contrary, my most recent reading of Shakespeare has left with me two attitudes: first, a sense that his work is extraordinarily surefire, reeking of
commercial theater; and second, a sympathy with a Shakespearean scholar
who, were it financially possible, would abandon the study of Shakespeare
and take up astronomy. Freud, and after him Jung, mistook the recurrent
and platitudinous patterns of literature for reflections of the actual behavior
of human beings.

One such pattern is that of incest, which is presented in literature as a
very dreadful affair. Literature is thus one of the important means whereby
the incest taboo is transmitted. Consequently it is theatrically surefire, and
Professor Fiedler finds it inexhaustibly fascinating. Now it is true that vir-

tually all cultures have an incest taboo, but two things need to be observed: first, that what is considered to be incest varies from culture to culture, and second, that there is little point in having a taboo against a kind of behavior that does not occur. Actually incest is quite common, as the examination of the police records in any city will reveal. To be sure, such records reveal it as taking place almost entirely in the lower classes, but it is mostly the lower classes that get arrested. The middle and upper classes are not necessarily different in their behavior; they are merely far less likely to be involved with the police for any reason. On the contrary, there is good reason to think that incest is one of the most useful as well as a not particularly uncommon way to resolve intra-familial discord. A lot of incest is between siblings, and a great deal of it is between siblings of the same sex. In short, literature, like most sociology, psychology, and psychiatry, that is, like virtually all culture—in the anthropological sense—does not aid us to observe the world around us and the human beings in it; it prevents us from such observation by normatively directing our attention to a very limited set of behaviors. Freud and Jung are not exceptions to the operation of this general law, nor is Professor Fiedler. Freud and Jung were superb humanists, that is, victims of literature and of high-level culture in general. It is not surprising that numerous—far too numerous—literary critics have found that the ideas of Freud and Jung made a wonderful fit with literature. Of course; that is where most of their ideas came from.

Let me make, merely for the sake of a workable vocabulary, a distinction between the scholar and the critic. The first, as I have suggested, is concerned with discovering the ideology which controls the literary work in question. The critic, however, is concerned with using the literary work to exemplify an ideology of his own culture. Most literary hermeneutics belong to the latter school. I have no objection to this; I merely wish to point out that the one should not be confused with the other. Actually, the use of an existing work of literature to exemplify a current or emerging ideology is one of the most interesting things people do with literature. But clearly its interest lies not in what it contributes to an understanding of the literary work but rather in the exemplified ideology. Just as clearly, *The Stranger in Shakespeare* belongs to the latter school. The discouraging thing about Professor Fiedler's work, whether critical or his own original fiction, is that he has, so far as I know, never exemplified an emerging ideology but only a rather commonplace and mostly Freudian ideology which has been fashionable in the course of his career but, unfortunately for Professor Fiedler, is becoming less fashionable as the years go by.

The interesting matter, however, is why it is that the works that go under Shakespeare's name, no doubt quite correctly, are so peculiarly suitable for what I have called criticism. Shakespeare has been called infinitely various, universal, vast, all-encompassing. Put more coolly, such assertions amount to a statement that the information in Shakespeare is characterized by an extraordinary randomness. This is why he presents such a glorious opportunity for the disintegrators and the antiStratfordians. It is also why he is the perfect subject for anyone who wants to get something off his chest about anything at all. And for the most part that has been the history of Shakespearean interpretation. An eminent Shakespearean has indeed told me that less scholarship has been done on Shakespeare than on any important English author. Shakespeare would lose the world for a theatrical effect—and thereby gained it, or at least, it would seem, very considerable commercial success. He was indeed a magpie, an Autolycus, who could manufacture the flashiest theatrical success from the most inconsidered trifles. No matter what ideology you wish to exemplify, you can find materials in Shakespeare. Hence Shakespeare criticism has itself become an enormous literature which does not study Shakespeare but is part of that ideological and exemplificatory redundancy which is the warp and woof of any society's culture, which, indeed, is the society.

Nevertheless this randomness, which permits every Tom, Dick, and Harry of a critic to have his way with him, is precisely Shakespeare's greatness. To him the personality was not a coherent structure but an incoherent package. That is why no coherent explanation of his major characters ever holds up and why those characters are always useful for exemplifying any ideology one pleases. One need only select, governed in the observation of recurrent patterns by one's own ideology, as Professor Fiedler has been. Shakespeare seemed to know, or at least intuited, that the human mind is fundamentally and incurably insane and that in creating an imaginary world on the stage he was doing exactly what every human being does offstage in his daily life. No wonder he retired when he could afford to. Like all of his predecessors, Professor Fiedler has attempted to create a coherent structure, a marvelous—and sinister— peacock's tail out of the feathers of this disillusioned magpie. It cannot be done, or, rather, with no author is it easier to do than with Shakespeare.

Patterning in Shakespearean Drama: Essays in Criticism by William
Leigh Godshalk. Mouton, 1973. Pp. 199. 50.00 DG.

Reviewer: S. K. Heninger, Jr.

At best, a reviewer's lot is not a happy one. And when confronted with
a dust jacket like that on Professor Godshalk's book, his heart (as well as
his good humour) is likely to sink. For there we are told that "Shakespeare
used the same techniques of patterning in his early comedies and tragedies
as he did in his final romances." Furthermore, "it is the chief purpose of
the present study to . . . [argue] that the dramatist did not undergo a per-
ceptible change in his ability to mold the images and actions of his plays
into meaningful patterns." We may well despair of a scholar/critic who can
see no difference between the technique of *Titus Andronicus* (the subject of
Professor Godshalk's first chapter) and of *The Tempest* (the subject of his
last). However, this argument is laid on top rather than forming the substance of the book, and despite its prominence on the dust jacket little is
done with it until a final two pages set apart from the rest and entitled "To
Conclude." The body of Professor Godshalk's study is given over to a
reading of ten plays spanning Shakespeare's career, a reading that looks
for "patterning" in the plays.

   To look for patterns in Shakespeare's plays is undeniably a worthwhile
endeavor, especially if one wishes to relate Shakespeare to the esthetics of
his age. Although Professor Godshalk makes no mention of the fact, in
London of the 1580s there was increased attention to form in literature.
Spenser was hailed as "the new poet" because, as E. K. notes in the dedi-
catory epistle of *The Shepheardes Calender*, "What in most English wryters
useth to be loose, and as it were ungyrt, in this Authour is well grounded,
finely framed, and strongly trussed up together." No longer did formless
narratives such as those in *A Mirrour for Magistrates* please the sophisticated. They now expected poems to be "strongly trussed up." Furthermore, the new rage for form affected not only the narrative but also
the mechanics, so that there was wholesale experimentation with meter,
even attempts at reviving quantitative verse. The rising interest in form
both in narrative and in metrics appears most evidently, perhaps, in the
sudden efflorescence of the sonnet sequence. In 1582 Thomas Watson published his *Hekatompathia*, exactly one hundred "passions" that run the
gamut of emotional and metrical variety, and about the same time Philip
Sidney composed *Astrophel and Stella*, carefully adumbrating the diverse

experiences of a lover and interlacing sonnets with songs in a beautifully modulated medley of metrical variations. With such an emphasis on form in literary London, it is no wonder that the drama too should be "patterned."

Having recognized the validity and importance of its subject, we return to the book in hand. It begins with an introductory essay that has the chief aim of explaining its method, which consists wholly of identifying "patterns" in the plays. Such a method, of course, depends upon what is meant by the word "pattern." Professor Godshalk construes it in the broadest possible terms: "Patterns are inclusive rather than exclusive; for as we are using the word, a pattern may include image and theme and action; it may be part of the characterization and the scenic layout. In theory, there is no limitation to the elements which may be included in an identifiable pattern, for the pattern is an intellectual construct" (p. 13). Since definition of "pattern" is the crux of the matter, we must examine this statement in close detail.

"A pattern," Professor Godshalk tells us, "may include image and theme and action." We see immediately that it may comprise not only a number of things but a number of disparate things. It may include "image," a term not defined here but which in practice means both the kind of Shakespearean imagery that Caroline Spurgeon catalogued for us forty years ago and also the nonverbal imagery of stage groupings and stage business that has occupied some more recent critics. "Image," in sum, can mean anything that the critic perceives, either in reading the play or in imagining a performance of it in his mind's eye. "Image," we must conclude, is in some way a sense datum, what is apprehended through sense experience, though of a secondary or vicarious (as opposed to direct) sort.

A pattern may also include "theme," again a loose term left undefined here but apparently meaning something like "thought" or "idea" or "motif." At one time or another, Professor Godshalk uses each of these words. Theme presumably transpires at some level of experience different from the sense experience of an image; it is abstract rather than concrete.

Finally, a pattern may include "action," and this term pertains to the larger areas of sequential development in the play, what actually takes place on stage. It covers such things as the arrangement of scenes to point up similarities or contrasts and the arrangement of characters in sympathetic or antagonistic alignments. It is what the percipient sees, again presumably in the performance which he stages for himself in his mind's eye, though possibly also during an actual performance in a theater.

Despite the incongruities of image and theme and action as modes of experience, they somehow coalesce to produce "an intellectual construct." Whether the percipient is the agent or the patient in this mysterious process Professor Godshalk leaves unexamined. But it is clear that in his method the patterns are indeed inclusive—so much so that it is difficult to ascertain what they might exclude. Anything can contribute to a pattern, whatever strikes the critic's fancy. But a method that includes everything is no method at all. It is license rather than discipline. In practice, of course, the critic starts with a preconceived notion of what the play is about—the chapter titles in this book serve as examples—and then without much difficulty he finds in the text sufficient evidence of some sort to contrive a pattern to support his foregone conclusion. The result is no more "an intellectual construct," however, than is the response to a Rorschach test.

In his honesty, Professor Godshalk admits to the difficulty: "There is no foolproof method of finding and describing a play's dominant patterns. Unfortunately, what seems of the utmost significance to one critic is of only minor importance to another. . . . The critical procedure is, at very bottom, subjective" (pp. 14–15). Unfortunately, indeed, candor cannot take the place of discriminating rigor. So Professor Godshalk's method dissolves into critical anarchy. Each interpreter must be left to his own devices. Antony, though in a different mood, puts the problem rather nicely:

> Sometime we see a cloud that's dragonish,
> A vapor sometime like a bear or lion,
> A tower'd citadel, a pendant rock,
> A forked mountain, or blue promontory
> With trees upon't that nod unto the world,
> And mock our eyes with air.

As readers of Professor Godshalk's book, we can do no more than tag along beside him like Polonius humouring Hamlet and murmur: "By th'mass and 'tis, like a camel indeed," or "Very like a whale." Apart from our willingness to agree, he provides no criteria by which we can test his interpretation of the plays.

We must conclude that Professor Godshalk's method is not valid—or rather, that it is no method at all. So what we are left with are readings of ten plays stretching from the beginning of the Shakespearean canon to its end. Although these readings are far from being comprehensive and equally far from being focused, they do not suffer from over-subtlety. Often, in fact, by his schematic approach Professor Godshalk can highlight an image or theme or action that might not otherwise receive its due.

We will not be surprised to learn that *Titus Andronicus* contains patterns of conflict, dismemberment, pleas, kneelings, and cannibalism and that *Two Gentlemen of Verona* contains patterns of mythological allusion, love letters, and journeys. The patterning of *Love's Labour's Lost*, in contrast, derives from character relationships ("The king and his three courtiers are perfectly matched by the princess and her three ladies-in-waiting," p. 55) and from the arrangement of scenes ("Scenes one, three, five, and seven—the odd scenes—are given in the main to the king, the princess, and their groups. Scenes two, four, six, and eight—the even—are given to Armado, Holofernes, and the characters of the subplot," pp. 56–57); furthermore, "The play moves . . . from illusion to reality" (p. 66).

For *Richard II* Professor Godshalk makes the familiar point that Richard's world is comprised of empty ceremony, broken bonds, and ambiguous oaths. But within this insubstantial and unstable world, "both Richard and Bolingbroke must seek their identities, try to ascertain their roles" (p. 76), thereby producing an "identity pattern" (p. 85). Professor Godshalk fails to mention, however, the most obvious pattern in the play: the symbiotic relationship between Richard and Bolingbroke. It is emblematized for us when the Duke of York's gardener explains to the Queen that both men have been weighed in the great scale of justice and Richard has been found light (III.iv.84–89), and again by Richard himself in the deposition scene when he insists that Bolingbroke take one side of the crown while he holds the other, thereby making it a deep well with the two men like buckets rising and falling within it (IV.i.181–89).

The Merchant of Venice, we are told, is based upon the opposition between bondage and choice, while *As You Like It* "builds a pattern of contrasting versions of pastoral" (p. 101), with also patterns of family relationships, pairs of lovers, exile and apprehension, suddenness, time, broken promises, cockold's horns, *nosce teipsum*, etc. Perhaps the most perceptive reading is that of *Macbeth*, which delineates a geometric pattern, a circle: "The past returns to haunt the present; time is curved and comes back upon itself. In form, the play simulates this circle of recurrent time" (p. 117). In *Measure for Measure* we have no trouble recognizing the patterns evolving from opposing forces ("mercy and justice, appearance and reality, chastity and sexual license," p. 135), though we may not wish to be so doctrinaire as to argue that "their final resolution [lies] in the acceptance of Original Sin" (p. 135). In *Antony and Cleopatra* the moral coordinates are not so clear: "The pattern of instability and insecurity is basic, and encompasses all elements of the play" (p. 150), though "the movement of the play is from initial flux to final stasis" (p. 151). The last chapter deals with *The*

Tempest, which with some novelty is seen "as patterned around ideas of governing, of the master-servant situation in its multiple aspects" (p. 166).

There follow the two pages "To Conclude." And to pick up our opening comments, Professor Godshalk's overriding thesis—"that, in its essentials, Shakespeare's dramatic technique did not significantly change from *Love's Labour's Lost* to *The Tempest*" (p. 167)—is inane. It is facile to argue that because Shakespeare used patterning in his plays from first to last, his technique remained static. Even if Professor Godshalk successfully demonstrated that "patterning is a constant factor in Shakespeare's art" (p. 179), there would still be development of the playwright's dramaturgy as he improved his artistry in projecting these patterns into dramatic action. The patterns of *Love's Labour's Lost*, for example, are much more nearly bareboned than the full-fleshed patterns of *Antony and Cleopatra*, even though both plays deal with the same motif: the sexual relationship between men and women. And this is true whether one talks of scene arrangement, character alignments, or strands of poetic imagery.

Finally, a point to suggest a larger dimension for this study. In his preface Professor Godshalk announces a secondary purpose, to which he returns in the last paragraph of the book. He confides, "As my work continued, one major motif emerged from the plays—the idea of the social bond" (p. 9). And he amplifies, "It became more and more apparent to me that Shakespeare was recurrently interested in man's relationship to society and in what his duties within that society consisted." Professor Godshalk brings this theme to the fore in his reading of *The Merchant of Venice*, and it culminates in his reading of *The Tempest*. It is not a new thesis in Shakespearean studies, and of course it is inherent in a study that seeks to reveal patterns in Shakespeare's plays. The notion of patterning assumes that the playwright sees his play as an integrated structure, a whole composed of interrelated parts. In the Renaissance he would undoubtedly look to the cosmos as a *typus* and in his dramatic structure would attempt to reproduce the proportions and symmetries that supposedly exist in the universe. He would consider his play to be a *speculum mundi*, a microcosm, the great world's stage. Consequently, the consonance between the various parts of the cosmos would be echoed in the relationships between the various characters that comprise the world constructed by the dramatist. The resultant social harmony, a strain which contributes to the universal harmony, is manifested in the multiple marriages that conclude most of the comedies, for example, and also in the marriage that Cleopatra looks forward to at the end of her triumphantly tragic affair with Antony. The point to make is that the form of the play—what Professor Godshalk calls "patterning"—is a mode of discourse available to the playwright. The form itself conveys meaning, which in the case of a symmetrically patterned play implies the social bond.

Perhaps the concept can best be put as a question. Why would a playwright such as Shakespeare work so meticulously to achieve these patterns? Was it to satisfy some esthetics based upon proportion and symmetry? Was it to reflect a principle of natural order, a belief in universal harmony, a recognition of cosmic or archetypal patterns? Are the last two questions the same question? These are the mandatory concerns of the structural critic. And even though he may not wish to align himself with any particular school of structuralism or formalism, he cannot afford to ignore their urgency.

The Art of Thomas Middleton: A Critical Study by David M. Holmes. The Clarendon Press, 1970. Pp. xix + 235. 55s.

Reviewer: Joel H. Kaplan.

On the dust jacket of Mr. Holmes's book Thomas Middleton is described as "the greatest of Shakespeare's playwright-contemporaries". The point is well taken. Middleton alone among Shakespeare's fellow dramatists seems equally at home in comedy and tragedy, and his best plays in either genre can hold their own with almost anything in the period. In fact it is surprising that a new book on Middleton has been so long in coming. Back in the 1950s when the studies by Messrs. Schoenbaum and Barker first appeared a "case" still needed to be made for the dramatist. In the few years that have intervened Middleton has been the subject of some excellent short articles, a half-dozen or so of his plays have appeared in paperbound editions, and producers on both sides of the Atlantic have decided that at his best Middleton may be a dramatist worth staging. (Most recently Mr. Peter Barnes has talked about the possibility of a Middleton festival!) At this time, then, a book that sets out to provide a comprehensive view of Middleton's achievement, or as Mr. Holmes puts it, "an appreciation of his art and of the point of view and feeling that underlie it" (p. xv) ought to be welcome indeed. Unfortunately, in spite of some intriguing comments on individual works and a refreshing willingness to talk about pieces that have not attracted much critical attention in the past, *The Art of Thomas Middleton* does not really rise to its subject. The problem in part lies with Mr. Holmes's decision to give us a Middleton in isolation—isolated from the literary and dramatic conventions of his time, from the various kinds of theaters and companies for which he wrote, and finally from his fellow playwrights (many of them his collaborators) and the light that their work might be able to shed upon his. In its own right such a dogged determination to "stick to the text" has its appeal; all too often we find ourselves at the other extreme, confounded by an overplus of background material that ends up obscuring the literature it means to elucidate. Yet if knowing the context of an author's work cannot by itself save us from errors of judgment, it can at least prevent us from making errors of a certain order. And it is here that Mr. Holmes's approach finds its severest limitation.

This is most apparent in a brief opening chapter on Middleton's poetry, especially in Holmes's discussion of *Micro-Cynicon*, or *Six Snarling Satires* (pp. 5–7). Holmes attaches more importance to the early poems than have any of Middleton's previous critics, seeing in them "an implicit introduction and explicit credo for [Middleton's] literary career." In *Micro-Cynicon* he finds in germinal form many of the themes and motifs that occupy its author's attention as a mature dramatist. The piece is cited as a promising sign of "intellectual courage and honesty," and used to support generalizations about Middleton's personality, esthetic sensibilities, and moral awareness. Yet nowhere in the course of all this are we told that, whatever else it may be, *Micro-Cynicon*, published when Middleton was still an undergraduate at Oxford, is a thoroughly conventional and predictable exercise in the vein of Juvenalian satire made fashionable a few years earlier by Hall and Marston and that those very qualities singled out for comment in Middleton's poem—its defiant tone, its tendency to focus upon "particular sins," even the self-critical posturing of Wise Innocent in Satire Six—are common to the genre as a whole. This is not to say, of course, that the outrage of *Micro-Cynicon* might not have been deeply felt but merely that if Mr. Holmes wishes to place so much weight upon this poem, attributing to Middleton himself the qualities of its satiric commentator, he owes it to his readers to set the work within its wider context. He must let us know, in short, that other young men were writing much the same kind of thing at the same time, and that the shift in tone and style that separates this piece from Middleton's earlier *Wisdom of Solomon Paraphrased* is just as likely to be due to a change of genre as to the jolted sensibilities of a youth on the verge of discovering sin.

The poems, though, are a minor concern. Any study of Middleton's art must stand or fall on the quality of its discussion of the plays. Mr. Holmes, however, seems so taken with the notion of Middleton's juvenilia as "credo"—the later works are "promises fulfilled"—that the greater part of his book becomes an application to the plays of the personality that he postulates for Middleton on the basis of the early poems and prose pieces. The image of the dramatist that emerges is that of a crabbed and not slightly ludicrous figure stalking the London stews, notebook in hand, to transcribe the time's deformities. A comparison with Zola is drawn at one point, but the general impression smacks as much of Justice Overdo. One of the dangers of such an approach is the oversolemnity it is likely to encourage in a critic who, like the Middleton of his mind's eye, attempts to tally up the plays in terms of enormities and "moral progresses." As we might expect, Holmes finds initial support for this view in an autobiographical reading of *The Phoenix*, identifying the young prince who sets out to uncover vice with Middleton himself (again we are not told that such "dukes in disguise" were the commonest of common property). But things go very far awry as soon as the pattern is applied to some of Middleton's more exuberant works. It is strange indeed to hear young Witgood, the enterprising cheat of *A Trick to Catch the Old One*, praised for his "infant-like ability to respond to wholesome influence" (p. 82). This is, it seems, because he finally agrees to help his ex-whore to a fortune and a foolish husband. Or to be told that *Michaelmas Term* shows us "how it is possible to emerge from the school of experience either morally unscathed or utterly corrupted" (p. 32). Are the fantastical plots and counterplots of Quomodo and his associates reducible to this? And if so, is it to Middleton's credit? In *A Chaste Maid in Cheapside* we find that, on the evidence of his fifth act repentance, Sir Walter Whorehound has become the play's "moral spokesman" (p. 96). To be sure, Sir Walter does suffer a fit of conscience after his duel with Touchwood Jr., but to speak here as Holmes does is to ignore the episode's larger spectacle of rogue against rogue, as the initiative for self-righteous posturing passes back and forth between Sir Walter and the equally unsavory Allwits. One sympathizes with Holmes's conviction that these city plays are ultimately moral in their overall design, but at the same time senses that this morality is far too complex to be dealt with by the clichés and platitudes of Middleton's undergraduate poetry.

A variety of the same problem confronts us in Holmes's section on the tragedies and tragicomedies, and here it might be best to look in some detail at a single familiar work. The discussion of *The Changeling* on pages 172–84 once more takes its cue from Holmes's reading of the verse satires.

The central action of the play is seen to follow that of *Micro-Cynicon* (false-seeming exposed by an abrasive but painfully honest moralist), as Middleton demonstrates the ways in which "the 'brutal reluctations' of a hypocrite place him in a class apart from, and below, the individual whose brutishness is manifest as such" (p. 183). The arch-hypocrite of the piece, however, turns out to be the much duped and betrayed Alsemero. Beatrice-Joanna is passed over lightly—she is "tragically unprepared for life"—while De Flores is transformed into another of Middleton's moral spokesmen. This is, to say the least, an odd reading of the play, and Holmes's argument is forced to take some curious turns to support it. Thus Alsemero's "hopes" on first seeing Beatrice-Joanna in church become his "hopes that [she] is a virgin," an observation that is then used to reinforce Holmes's claim that Alsemero is from the outset a dissembling lecher with "a pharisaical distaste for 'toucht' women." His interest in Beatrice-Joanna, we are told, is the same as De Flores', only less honorable because disguised, and he is justly punished in the end. No matter that Alsemero talks of wedlock, the church, and holy intent. For Holmes this only redoubles the charge of hypocrisy against one willing to use marriage as "a veil of propriety" for his lust (p. 178). The effect of this blackening of Alsemero is most telling on De Flores, who, stripped of his villain's cloak, dwindles to little more than "a datum from which the superficiality of Alsemero's character might be judged" (p. 179). The mystery of evil evaporates before us, and we find ourselves back on square one working out trite distinctions between seeming and being. The moral categories of verse satire turn out to be crude instruments for probing so complicated an organism, and we can only regret that Holmes chose to limit himself to such tools.

At the same time it is strange that Holmes, in his search for a unifying "credo" or central core for Middleton's work, makes so little use of what we actually know of the dramatist's life and professional career. Thus we are given much vague speculation about "youthful susceptibilities" and their relationship to art, but next to nothing is said about Middleton's early entanglement in his family's legal wranglings with Thomas Harvey or the effect that this protracted and rather nasty episode might have had on his portrayal of Jacobean London. (And what of J. B. Brooks's identification of Harvey as the notorious Captain in *The Phoenix*?) Likewise, Holmes is fond of telling us that Middleton's plays, the city comedies in particular, are precise transcripts of contemporary manners and events. Yet when a historical model for one of these works presents itself, as the Howe trial of 1596 does for *Michaelmas Term*, it too is passed over in silence. One would like to have seen some discussion of the ways in which Middleton transformed such raw material into the stuff of drama. The collaborations with Dekker are given scant attention in spite of what they might tell us about the mutual influence of both playwrights (nothing is said of the late Peter Ure's excellent article on just this point), nor is any notice taken of the peculiar nature of the boys' companies for which Middleton did much of his best work. The whole question of rival repertories and acting styles is admittedly a vexed one but must at least be raised in any study of a dramatist like Middleton who wrote so extensively for the private theaters. One also queries the complete absence of *The Revenger's Tragedy* from Holmes's book. While the case for Middleton's authorship is far from conclusive, it is surely strong enough to warrant a passing mention.

More serious is Holmes's omission of Middleton's considerable career as a writer of pageants, masques, and civic entertainments. We know that Middleton was involved in such activity as early as 1603, when he contributed the speech of Zeal to Dekker's *Magnificent Entertainment*, and, more important, that the type of emblematic representation he found in these productions was to play a central role in his work for the professional stage. A consideration of this side of Middleton's art might have saved Holmes from the oversimplified notions of realism that he brings to the comedies and tragedies. There is, no doubt, a harsh and unblinking view of contemporary life that underlies much of Middleton's work. But from the very beginning Middleton chose to temper this local habitation with devices borrowed from a tradition of symbolic and allegorical theatre that found its fullest expression in the morality play and civic pageant. The fantastical quality of Middleton's best work owes much to such a union—the induction to *Michaelmas Term*, the Dampit scenes in *A Trick to Catch the Old One*, and the succubus of *A Mad World, My Masters* come immediately to mind, as do the symbolic chess matches of *Women Beware Women* and, of course, *A Game at Chess*—and one is sorry to see it prove so intractable to Holmes's approach. To miss this complexity and richness is, after all, to miss a major aspect of Middleton's genius and to overlook just those qualities that make him an important figure in his own right and not simply an inferior Ben Jonson. Middleton may well be, as Holmes calls him, "the greatest of Shakespeare's playwright-contemporaries." But the book that demonstrates this not inconsiderable claim will have to be a far more inclusive and expansive work than Mr. Holmes has given us.

Ralph Crane and Some Shakespeare First Folio Comedies by T. H.
Howard-Hill. The University Press of Virginia for the Bibliographical Society of the University of Virginia, 1972. Pp. xvi +
190. $7.50.

Reviewer: Christopher Spencer.

Ralph Crane (ca. 1560–ca. 1632), Scrivener (according to his own account)
to City, Country, Court, Church, Law, and Stage, transcribed sixteen surviving manuscripts. Of eight nondramatic manuscripts, six were described
by F. P. Wilson in his seminal article on Crane (*The Library*, 7 [1926], 194–
215), and the other two are noted by T. H. Howard-Hill in *Ralph Crane and
Some Shakespeare First Folio Comedies*. The eight dramatic manuscripts, six of
which were described by Wilson, are one manuscript each of Jonson's
masque *Pleasure Reconciled to Virtue*, Fletcher and Massinger's *Barnavelt*,
Middleton's *Song in Several Parts* and *The Witch*, and Fletcher's *Demetrius
and Enanthe* (i.e., *The Humorous Lieutenant*); there are three manuscripts of
Middleton's *Game at Chess*. In his edition of *The Winter's Tale* (1931), John
Dover Wilson suggested that the first four plays in the Shakespeare First
Folio (*The Tempest, The Two Gentlemen of Verona, The Merry Wives of Windsor*,
and *Measure for Measure*), as well as the last play in the Folio comedies, *The
Winter's Tale*, were printed from manuscripts transcribed by Crane. His
suggestion has been regarded favorably—by the editors of the five plays in
the Arden edition, for example, and by W. W. Greg in *The Shakespeare First
Folio* (Oxford: Oxford Univ. Press, 1955). Crane has also been identified as
the scribe for the copy behind the first quarto of Webster's *Duchess of Malfi*
(1623) and several plays in the Beaumont and Fletcher Folio (1647). Finally,
it has been suggested that Shakespeare's *King John, Timon of Athens*, and *2
Henry IV* in the Folio may have been printed from Crane manuscripts.

After examining Crane's habits in his extant dramatic manuscripts,
Howard-Hill discusses the indications of his influence on the five Folio
comedies, especially in orthography and spelling. He has a major help and
a major hindrance to drawing evidence of Crane's habits for use in studying the Shakespeare First Folio. The major help is the existence of five
manuscripts of Middleton's *Game at Chess*, including the three by Crane
and one apparently in Middleton's hand (a sixth manuscript is noted by J.
W. Harper, ed., *A Game at Chess* [London: Ernest Benn, 1966], p. xxv);
these provide an unusual opportunity for study of probable errors in trans-
cription. The major hindrance is that with the minor exception of *A Song in*

Several Parts (1622), Crane's extant dramatic manuscripts were done in 1618–19 and 1624–25, not during the years when he would have been working for the Folio; since Crane's habits appear to have changed and since he also seems to have prepared his manuscripts in somewhat different ways depending on their purposes (such as prompt book or private transcript), there is a gap between the non-Shakespearean evidence and the application to Shakespeare.

Nevertheless, Howard-Hill leaves little room for doubt that Crane was responsible for the copy of the five Shakespeare comedies, and his general conclusions and particular examples should be helpful in at least three ways. First, the Folio histories and tragedies can be more readily examined for evidence of Crane's influence. Second, editors of Crane plays can have more assurance in explaining several peculiarities of their texts; the Arden editors, especially Frank Kermode of *The Tempest* (p. xci) and J. W. Lever of *Measure for Measure* (pp. xi–xiii), give some indication of possible consequences. Third, to the extent that we can isolate characteristics of a scribe, we are better able to isolate characteristics of the printing house compositor on the one hand and the kind of manuscript the scribe used to work from on the other. Howard-Hill has used the evidence for these purposes in several articles. In "The Compositors of Shakespeare's Folio Comedies" (*Studies in Bibliography*, 26 [1973], 86), he points out that in pages usually assigned to Jaggard's Compositor A and printed from a Crane manuscript there are spellings not used by Compositor A in other plays and not used by Crane, and he is thus able to argue that there must have been another compositor involved. In articles in *Notes and Queries* (210 [1965], 334–40, and 211 [1966], 139–40), he argues that the much higher number of parentheses in *Winter's Tale*, which corresponds with the number in two manuscripts of *A Game at Chess* that seem to have been copied by Crane from his own previous transcripts, suggests that *Winter's Tale* too was a Crane transcript of a Crane transcript (and so more likely to contain typical Crane alterations and errors).

Howard-Hill dissents from the fairly widespread view that *The Tempest* was supposed to serve as a model for editing. He notes that the next plays, *Two Gentlemen of Verona* and *Merry Wives of Windsor*, "have significantly different styles of stage-directions" and prefers Pollard's suggestion that "the publishers chose a clean manuscript of an unpublished play to introduce the Folio" (pp. 107–108). He suggests tentatively that the order in which Crane prepared the manuscripts was *Measure for Measure, Two Gentlemen, Merry Wives, Tempest*, and *Winter's Tale* (p. 138).

One is certainly entitled to limit himself rather tightly to his subject, as

Howard-Hill has done. But it is unfortunate that the only book on Crane should not have a brief account of what we know of his life and his non-dramatic manuscripts. The information is available in Wilson's 1926 article, but it would have been convenient to have it here. In addition to Howard-Hill's articles in *Notes and Queries* referred to above, the serious student of Crane will also wish to consult J. R. Brown's comments on *The Duchess of Malfi* (*Studies in Bibliography*, 6 [1954], 134–37 and 8 [1956], 126–27) and J. M. Nosworthy's appendix on the songs that appear in *The Witch* and *Macbeth* (*Shakespeare's Occasional Plays*, [London: Arnold, 1965], pp. 227–31). Milton A. Buettner has a recent dissertation, "*A Game at Chess* by Thomas Middleton: A Textual Edition Based on the Manuscripts Written by Ralph Crane" (Michigan State, 1972; *Dissertation Abstracts International*, 33 [1972], 2317A–18A).

Shakespearean Staging, 1599–1642 by T. J. King. Harvard University Press, 1971. Pp. xiv + 163. $6.75.

Reviewer: John Freehafer.

Professor King's *Shakespearean Staging, 1599–1642* is designed to shed new light on physical staging in the playhouses of the age of Shakespeare by analyzing stage directions from acted plays and pictures of early stages. King concludes that the plays of the age of Shakespeare required no more than two stage doorways, an unlocalized facade and placeless stage, sometimes a discovery space or acting areas above or below stage, virtually no machines, and no scenes of any kind. Vague as it is, however, King's claim to have proved "that the stage equipment needed was much simpler than has been thought" must be rejected, because much the same concept has already been set forth by others who insist, despite evidence to the contrary, that the Shakespearean stage had no scenes, machines, or other courtly or neoclassical features. King's book, like earlier attempts to prove that the Shakespearean stage was invariably bare and simple, ends up with what may be described as a "least common denominator" of staging in such early unroofed public playhouses as the Swan, the first Globe, and the first Fortune. For various reasons, King's conclusions cannot be accepted. First, his evidence is arbitrarily chosen; in every category of data he includes much that is irrelevant and excludes much that is relevant. Second, his evidence is rarely accompanied by sufficient argument or independent commentary, even when the predecessors that he cites disagree sharply. Third, my own check of the kinds of evidence King says he has considered shows that he has repeatedly omitted or minimized such evidence when it conflicts with his concept of Shakespearean staging. Fourth, King has virtually omitted whole categories of relevant evidence, such as prologues, epilogues, inductions, academic plays, the courtly drama, and older plays, by Shakespeare and others, that were revived after 1599.

This is a difficult book, because it largely consists of statistics which are not shown to have significance and tabulations of raw data which are scattered and unfocused. For example, bits of evidence about stage doorways, or large properties, are distributed throughout the book but never brought together for adequate discussion or analysis. Indeed, the reader's difficulties begin at once, with King's Pickwickian title, in which he uses the magic word "Shakespearean" to describe a book which excludes most of Shakespeare's works—including all the pre-Globe plays and four of later date as well. In this title the word "staging" is also used in an oddly constricted sense, which excludes not only the physical dispositions of actors with respect to one another and the audience, but even the placement of the music, which, King assures us, was "not dependent on the structure of the stage or playhouse." (Was all Shakespearean stage music evoked out of thin air by the likes of Owen Glendower and Ariel?) As his title suggests, King begins his book in the fall of 1599, when the Globe opened, but he provides no acceptable reason for this awkward choice of date. Beginning in 1599 causes special difficulties, because there are five plays by Shakespeare and about two dozen acted plays by Jonson, Marston, Heywood, Dekker, Chapman, and others which cannot be certainly dated before or after the fall of 1599. Of these plays, King includes eight and omits twenty-one, virtually without explanation of his choices. A more inconvenient and imprecise date for dividing a study of the older drama could scarcely have been found. And why should a study of such a continuous body of drama and stage history be so divided at all? Many drawbacks of this study, such as the amputation of the majority of Shakespeare's plays, could have been avoided by beginning it at an appropriate date, such as 1576.

Furthermore, King repeatedly disregards his own limits of 1599–1642. Of his nine stage pictures, only three or four—two by Jones, the *Messalina* vignette, and possibly the *Roxana* vignette—can be dated between 1599 and 1642. Therefore, the other five or six are at variance with his announced aim of seeking "positive correlations between the external evidence, as provided by contemporary architecture and pictures of early English stages, and the internal evidence, as provided by the texts of plays first performed in the years 1599–1642." King is also inconsistent in reprinting a picture from an academic play (*Roxana*), because he silently excludes the stage directions of all academic plays from his main text. Furthermore, the three pictures out of his nine that can be probably dated between 1599 and 1642 do not support King's concept of a stage with two doorways and no scenes, because the Jones stages have three and five doorways respectively; they may have featured scenic vistas copied from those that Jones had studied at the Teatro Olimpico in Vicenza, and even the *Messalina* stage reveals a neoclassic scene on its hangings. Furthermore, while King objects to his predecessors' rejection of some "extant pictorial evidence," he omits many relevant stage pictures that fall between 1599 and 1642, such as the interior designs of the Jacobean Banqueting Houses by Smythson and Jones, Jones's designs for Davenant's proposed Fleet Street Theater of 1639, Jones's designs for the staging of plays and masques, and Fludd's "memory theatres." These numerous omitted pictures sharply conflict with King's concept of Shakespearean staging.

King claims to include in his main text all acted plays first produced between 1599 and 1642, but he omits many plays for which there is abundant evidence of production, such as *Eastward Ho, Bartholomew Fair, The Queen of Aragon, Aglaura, The Royal Slave*, and *Microcosmus*—none of which, it may be noted, could have been fully staged on King's bare, simple platform. King's assumption that a play for which there is no external record of performance cannot be supposed to "depend on playhouse copy" is a curious non sequitur, since it is obvious that printers generally strove to expunge all direct evidence of playhouse use from the play texts that they published. By omitting hundreds of plays that were almost certainly acted simply because the meager existing records of licenses and performances do not specifically include them, King attaches unwarranted importance to the accidents of the historical record and omits a vast body of relevant data which must be scrutinized and evaluated, not excluded. The absence of a specific external record for such a play as *Antony and Cleopatra* is readily explained and does not justify King's omission of that play. *Antony and Cleopatra* apparently was produced in a season for which very few records of play licenses or performances exist, and it had no separate title page on which its stage history might have been disclosed, because it was published only in the Folios. In any case, even unacted plays (such as Jonson's *Sad Shepherd*) can be important sources of information about Shakespearean

staging. Furthermore, King presents unsatisfactory summaries of stage histories of plays that he includes. His statements of their performance and
publication records are so incomplete, compressed, and unqualified that
they are often misleading or erroneous. Improbable statements are set
down as if they were established fact, and puzzling or seemingly contradictory statements are listed without any attempt to reconcile them. No usable
summaries of the complex and revealing theatrical and publishing histories
of *Bussy D'Ambois* and *Rollo, Duke of Normandy* will be found here. King
says flatly that *Troilus and Cressida* was acted by "King's men at the Globe"
on the basis of *the* title page, but of course the quarto has *two* variant title
pages and an epistle to the reader which casts serious doubt upon King's
flat assertion of performance at the Globe. King assumes that *Henry V* was
produced at the Globe and presents an inconclusive and unconvincing argument that *Julius Caesar* was first acted there.

   King's great contribution is supposed to be his discussion of promptbook
evidence of staging, but here too he assembles his evidence inaccurately
and without adequate discussion. He lists eighteen texts under the heading
of "promptbooks, manuscripts dependent on prompt copy, and printed
texts with manuscript prompter's markings, for plays first acted by profes-
sionals in the years 1599–1642." As this protean heading suggests, even
this small group of texts is far from consisting entirely of authenticated
promptbooks. What is more, three of the texts listed by King—*Hengist* and
the so-called Padua promptbooks of *Measure for Measure* and *Macbeth*—
probably date after 1642. Although King lists only about eight authenticated promptbooks (in a period for which hundreds of printed play texts
exist), he omits three manuscripts that appear to be genuine promptbooks
of 1599–1642—namely, *Charlemagne, The Captives*, and *Timon*. His choice of
1599 as a starting date also obliges him to omit several early promptbooks,
including the most important Shakespearean promptbook of all, *Sir Thomas
More*. Moreover, the evidence that King presents from promptbooks does
not support his claim that they are uniquely important sources of staging
evidence, because the promptbook stage directions that he lists are few in
number and differ in no substantial or fundamental way from the more
familiar and much more numerous authorial stage directions. In any case,
it is necessary to reject King's extraordinary contention that an obscure
play manuscript with a few commonplace markings by an anonymous
prompter must be accepted as a prime source of stage evidence, whereas
the authorial texts of *All's Well That Ends Well, Coriolanus, Timon of Athens*,
and *Antony and Cleopatra* are, according to King, of "no primary value as
evidence for the study of staging." King's evidence on the textual nature of

promptbooks and texts that may be based on promptbooks consists of brief quotations from his predecessors, and he does not comment on these even when they are contradictory—for example, as to whether prompt copy was used in printing *Cymbeline, The Two Noble Kinsmen*, or the Folio *Othello*. Perhaps a case can be made for the extant promptbooks as especially significant sources of staging evidence, but King has not made it. In part, this is due to the fact that he has not presented independent evidence on the nature of promptbooks, their relationship to staging, or the scope of a prompter's work and markings. For example, no significance can be attached to a lack of prompter's markings relating to scenes and machines, because the prompter was not responsible for scenes and machines, and he was not charged with compiling a complete record of all physical aspects of a production.

King devotes one chapter to a "staging plot" of *Twelfth Night* to show that it could be acted on his simple, bare Shakespearean stage. Yet he does not comment on the one supposed problem in the staging of *Twelfth Night*—the representation (if any) of the dark "house" in which Malvolio was confined. The choice of *Twelfth Night* for a showpiece is inappropriate, because no contemporary promptbook for it exists, and the very simple and basic staging of the play provides no test of the limits of King's concept of Shakespearean staging. If King wished to show that his staging would suffice for Shakespeare's plays, he ought, at the least, to have prepared a stage plot for a Shakespeare play with fairly complex staging, such as *Cymbeline, The Tempest*, or *The Two Noble Kinsmen*. It is notable that King's attempts to confine some entrances, exits, and large properties in *The Second Maiden's Tragedy* (for which a promptbook exists) to a stage with two doorways are awkward and unconvincing.

Perhaps the most disturbing aspect of King's book, however, is the manner in which he has minimized or omitted plays which call for a more spectacular staging than he is willing to allow. At least fifty plays acted between 1599 and 1642 could not have been fully produced on King's bare stage, because they require scenes or machines or more than two stage doorways. King excludes six spectacular plays by Heywood because they are "classical legends," but he never explains why plays based on classical legends should be omitted from a study of staging. *Cymbeline* and *The Tempest* are stumbling blocks for King. Following Chambers, he suggests that the descent and ascent of Jupiter may be an "interpolation"; but Jupiter's flight appears in the earliest text, and therefore the use of flying machinery in *Cymbeline* by 1623 is a fact that conflicts with King's concept of Shakespearean staging. King goes on to make the astonishing suggestion that

Ariel did not use a flying machine but vanished "in Thunder" (in the guise
of a winged Harpy) by sinking below the stage (into Caliban's element)
through a trapdoor! King also tries to explain away the use of "post-
medieval" scenic properties in *A Game at Chess*. To avoid the evidence that
the King's Men used a hell-mouth ("bag") at the close of that play, King
rejects all the complete texts of it and cites instead an incomplete manuscript which omits "the bag business with which other texts end the play."
Even this truncated text, however, shows that there were physical scenic
"houses" for the two chess teams on stage throughout Middleton's play.
King attempts to explain away these houses by dubbing them the "White
doorway" and "Black doorway"! Middleton, however, calls them the
"White-house" and "Black-house." Elsewhere King asserts that "canvas
houses for performances at Court" were used "for the precisely localized
plays of Plautus and Terence or their Renaissance imitators," but the use of
such houses was confined neither to the Court nor to such plays. The use
of "mansions" and hell-mouths on the Shakespearean stage conflicts with
King's concept of Shakespearean staging. In addition, such large properties
as beds, tombs, altars, thrones, bars of justice, trees, and prison equipment
served as scene-setting devices and refute the notion that Shakespearean
staging was always "unlocalized" and "placeless." King also errs in stating
that the conventionalized neo-Vitruvian scenes of Serlio and his followers
represented "specific locales" and were confined to "the Italian stage." Of
seventeen pre-Restoration plays that are known to have been acted with
painted scenery, King omits eight, lists four without any reference to this
remarkable aspect of their staging, and confines five others to a single
footnote in which he erroneously suggests that such scenery was mounted
only at Court. King emphasizes that "the Globe" may not have been
equipped to handle scenes and machines, but this applies only to the first
Globe. The second Globe had a large machine room, which suggests that it
had more elaborate stage equipment than the first Globe. Furthermore,
both Blackfriars playhouses and both Cockpits accommodated changeable
scenery, while scenic properties were mounted at many playhouses. In
general, King mistakes the routine, everyday staging of plays at several
early roofless public playhouses for the entirety of Shakespearean staging.

For two centuries able scholars have been finding and interpreting information about Shakespearean staging. The fact that much of this information is hard to evaluate does not justify the use of rules of thumb that
omit most of the relevant evidence. As John Cranford Adams has noted,
the real need is for a study in which "as far as possible *all* the evidence
should be taken into account." Such a book would show that, on quite a

few occasions, Shakespearean staging was more complex and elaborate
than King will allow. Fortunately, such a book may now be in preparation.
Pending its appearance, usable and substantial information on the topics
touched upon by King may be found in the works of Chambers, Greg,
Bentley, W. J. Lawrence, Lily Bess Campbell, Nicoll, Bald, Reynolds, the
Adamses, Harbage, Hodges, Irwin Smith, Wickham, Southern, Schoenbaum, Hosley, and other commentators who have shown at least a pass-
able ability to gather valid evidence, analyze it logically, and discuss it per-
ceptively.

The Weak King Dilemma in the Shakespearean History Play by
Michael Manheim. Syracuse University Press, 1973. Pp. 198.
$8.00

Reviewer: David M. Bergeron.

   Michael Manheim offers a slightly different approach to the histories, for
he focuses on a dramatic fact of most of these plays, namely, the presence
of a weak king. Such a king provokes problems for his subjects and creates
difficulties for us as audience. Basically the question is, how should he be
viewed? Does his weakness justify rebellion or deposition? Manheim argues that Shakespeare consciously raised this problem and offered a solution that not only responded to the political facts of life at the end of the
sixteenth century but also has its relevance for our political world.
   The solution lies in coming to terms with a brand of Machiavellianism,
which Manheim deliberately leaves broadly and vaguely defined. What we
need instead of the weak and wanton Richard II or the weak and meek
Henry VI is the strong Machiavellian (of a sort) Henry V; that is Shakespeare's answer, as Manheim sees it. To oversimplify, the answer to weakness is strength, and therein lies one of the problems with the argument of
the book. Shakespeare presumably worked his way through the two kings
who epitomize weakness, Richard II and Henry VI, through the transi-
tional figure of the Bastard in *King John* and through the ambiguous portrait of Henry IV, finally to arrive at Henry V, a practical, strong sovereign.
It is all too neat. Manheim skips over a rather strong king named Richard

III, who in this thematic scale is surely better than his predecessor Henry VI. While no one could possibly argue that there are not weak kings in these plays, I believe that in the final analysis Manheim's approach fails.

For one thing, an implicit assumption on which this book hinges is that Shakespeare in a rather self-conscious manner set out to offer us his political program, a kind of "mirror for magistrates"—that he was responding to an immediate political problem and this was his answer. Manheim in a sense simply substitutes his own pattern for Tillyard's; we now have a weak-king dilemma giving design and shape to the tetralogies instead of a morality or providential structure offered by Tillyard. In both cases the critics impose a consistent pattern that the plays do not themselves sustain. So eager is he for political statement that Manheim runs the risk of forgetting that these are plays. I find it very difficult to entertain the vision of Shakespeare sitting down to map out his strategy, to create, as Manheim says, "a model for most Western political leaders to follow. . . ."

A crucial point which I think Manheim largely ignores throughout is the relationship of Shakespeare's sources to his historical drama. This does not mean that the author should have presented some sort of source study but only that he should have remembered that in historical drama one's limits are set by historical fact. Try as he might, there is no way, except to violate historical truth entirely, that Shakespeare can make Richard II or Henry VI strong, or Henry V weak, any more than he can present Richard III as saint. While all this is very obvious, it gets lost in the shuffle in this book.

There are some problems of focus. Both in the opening and in the conclusion of the book the author emphasizes how his discussion pertains to the twentieth century. He decries the decline in public and political morality, the difficulties with modern-day leaders, etc. But though all this might be true and needed, it seems unduly polemical and out of keeping with the presumed purpose of the book. He presses his conclusions to the breaking point as he alludes to "a true example of the weak king . . . waiting in Edinburgh" to replace Elizabeth. Shakespeare knew all this, of course, as he also knew that "To the sixteenth century, monarchy in and of itself was doomed to failure." Elizabeth and a few others would have been surprised to learn this. The weak king from Edinburgh certainly did not agree in the early seventeenth century as he told his parliament: "The state of monarchy is the supremest thing upon earth. For kings are not only God's lieutenants upon earth and sit upon God's throne, but even by God himself they are called gods."

In the chapter on *Richard II* Manheim also includes discussion of *Woodstock* and *Edward II*, which exemplify the problem of the weak king. I find, however, a number of things about the analysis of *Richard II* puzzling, if not misleading. Manheim cannot seem to decide what he thinks of Richard, other than the obvious—that the king is weak. He calls him "frivolous, whimsical," "indecorous," but in the next breath, "the most sensitive and intelligent" of the kings considered in this particular chapter. And repeatedly he refers to Richard as "lazy," which does not strike me as one of his more emphasized traits, though he may not be obsessed with the Puritan work ethic. At the tournament scene he finds Richard whimsical, cutting off the combat and thereby deeply offending "not only the combatants but also the elders, to whom the trial by combat is richly satisfying." It is a sign of the weakness of kings "who resolve their problems superficially, on the spur of the moment, without bothering to give even the appearance of wisdom and considered judgment." But to examine carefully the text of the play gives a different impression as Richard withdraws to consult his advisers and then returns to render his judgment: "Draw near / And list what with our council we have done" (I.iii.123–24). The "long flourish" of the trumpets is meant to indicate the passage of time, which we know from Holinshed was some two hours.

Manheim comments that Richard "has his drinking and jesting companions, but he dominates them rather than they him." I, for one, do not know who these people are in the play, and Richard seems some kind of harbinger for Prince Hal. Further, if Richard dominates them, that sounds vaguely like strength. Richard's making York Lord Governor of England after seizing Gaunt's titles and lands Manheim views as a flippant act. But there is a perfectly good argument for seeing it as a sign of Richard's political shrewdness. Manheim exaggerates the Queen's dramatic function of generating sympathy for Richard, and he offers this curious comment: "Childless, the queen has only Richard, and his absence can breed only sadness, not children."

In the discussion of *Richard II*, as throughout, Manheim refers to the audience's reaction to the events of the drama. Noting the excess of Richard's speeches in III.iii, the author comments: "The audience needs every bit he can provide to help purge them of their own emotions, their extreme fear and pity at the fall of the weak king." Elsewhere he refers to the "guilt" that the audience feels. These ideas seem foreign to our actual response to the play; it is certainly less than proved that we come away purged of those extreme emotions or that we had them in the first place.

It is a painfully shallow conclusion to draw from Richard's only soliloquy that "Had he his reign to live again, he would try not to waste time." This is insensitive both to the form and substance of that speech. Manheim re-

minds us that Richard has been "terribly weak as a monarch and probably
would always be"—whatever that final phrase means. But, Manheim says,
we do feel compassion for him, "and our sense of guilt at having hated
him earlier makes us vindictive toward his enemies." I personally feel no
guilt, no hatred for Richard, no vindictiveness toward his enemies.

Manheim rightly comments on Bolingbroke's strength, but some of the
comments about the deposition scene leave one puzzled. To cite a minor
problem, Manheim says that this state function is attended "by all the important lords of the realm, both secular and ecclesiastical"; but the number
in the play is relatively small, and only the Bishop of Carlisle and Abbot of
Westminster represent the clergy—again Manheim seems to have a somewhat dim recollection of the text. He says that Carlisle's long speech "un-
nerves Bolingbroke and directly precipitates the deposition ritual which follows." If Bolingbroke is unnerved, he doesn't show it in the text. Finally
Bolingbroke must cut short Northumberland's badgering of Richard "less
from sympathy than from fear that, out of control, Richard may mar an
otherwise perfect *coup*." This is simply wrong-headed and perverse, if one
is supposed to be arguing that Richard is weak and Bolingbroke strong.

Not to belabor the point, but there are similar problems of interpretation
in the discussion of *Henry VI*. Manheim says: "The qualities of the true
Machiavel may be learned, but Henry shows little aptitude." This tinge of
regret is misplaced, since how could Shakespeare do otherwise with the
historical Henry? We find out later that it is not so much a matter of Henry's being weak as that everybody else is too strong. Manheim gets carried
away: Henry "alone believes in justice and the triumph of truth. . . . He
alone believes in the natural dignity of man." But Manheim observes a few
pages later that Duke Humphrey is the ideal protector, "as honest and
eminently courageous to the end as he is outspoken about the envy and
deceit of his enemies." Again the author exaggerates with no basis in the
text: "Henry's hard lot is to know not a single moment of earthly pleasure." Commenting on Henry's detached role, Manheim suggests that
Henry watches the action "as from above, like an angel in an Italian Renaissance painting. His position on the molehill suggests this." How on
earth Henry's *sitting* on a molehill gives rise to the image of an angel in an
Italian painting I do not know. And four pages later we learn surprisingly
that "Henry is far from a uniformly ideal figure of wisdom and detachment." Surprise follows surprise as we find out that in his death Henry,
"True to form, . . . is strong and heroic." True to form? So much for our
weak Henry! Manheim finds Henry's words of forgiveness for Richard "in
character" but "surprising," since the dying York did not forgive Margaret,

or the dying Clifford or Warwick forgive Richard. No comment is needed on the logic of this argument. Finally we may find Richard's murder of Henry "refreshing" because Richard is a true-blue Machiavel, no facade, no hypocrisy. I find this an insidious argument and symptomatic of the book's faulty thesis: strength equals Machiavellianism, which is good.

The book is seriously flawed. I am not sure that the topic warrants book-length treatment, or at least not as Manheim has done it. It is a confused book that offers us little illumination. A few pages from the end we come upon a statement which tellingly reveals a weakness of both style and substance in this book: "Death ultimately renders all kings weak. . . ."

Shakespeare's God: The Role of Religion in the Tragedies by Ivor Morris. George Allen & Unwin, 1972. Pp. 496. $15.95.

Reviewer: R. W. Dent.

According to Helen Gardner's *The Business of Criticism*, "A critic's attitude to works of art must depend ultimately on his conception of the nature of man." To an extraordinary degree, *Shakespeare's God* illustrates the truth of this statement, so much so that I remain baffled by the appearance of Shakespeare's name in the title.

After a research degree in Elizabethan studies at Oxford and several years of teaching at Göteborg University, Sweden, and Mount Alison University (United Church of Canada), New Brunswick, Mr. Morris returned to England to study for the ministry. He was ordained a minister of the Congregational Church in 1968. By then the present study must have been virtually completed. His bibliography implies he was actively engaged in the study of Shakespeare criticism only during the decade ending about 1962, and Frye's 1963 *Shakespeare and Christian Doctrine* appears a kind of watershed; he cites it frequently, usually with unqualified approval, in making his own assessment of Shakespeare's "religious" interpreters. But of the thirty-plus articles pertinent to his subject in the following quatercentenary year—by Battenhouse, Myrick, Ribner, Weisinger, and West, for example—he refers to none, and except for Henn, Merchant, and Sewall in 1965–66 the rest is silence. Inevitably, one thinks of a score of studies from the late '60s one wishes he had at least confronted and attempted to answer—Elton's *King Lear and the Gods*, West's *Shakespeare and the Outer Mystery*, to name but two—especially if he thought his title a genuinely defensible one.

But this is part of the difficulty. The present title, perhaps modestly revised to something like *Shakespeare's Tragic Vision: the role of religion in the major tragedies*, might well have fitted the book as initially conceived. As early as 1961, apparently, Morris had well underway what he believed a long-needed supplement to Bradley. Convinced that Shakespeare's major tragedies imply an "essentially Christian and basically world-forsaking" vision akin to that "apparent and explicit" in the tragedies of Greville, he felt Bradley verged on perceiving this truth but failed to pursue it, "due partly to the limited [explicit] expression it finds in Shakespeare, partly to its intangibility and the perilous degree of subjectivity needed for its apprehension, and mainly to the realization that these thoughts are utterly opposed to the tragic mood, and are tending outside the province of the play" ("The Tragic Vision of Fulke Greville," *Shakespeare Survey*, 14 [1961] 66–75). Even then, however, Morris was concerned not merely with revealing what vision Shakespeare's tragedies may share with one another but also with what seems to me a radically different topic: what vision they share with all great tragedy.

Thus in *Shakespeare's God* Morris has endeavored to do even more than transcend Bradley. By admitting what Bradley excluded, "a spiritual level of being and good above and beyond the evident good of creaturely being," he hopes to "reconcile or resolve the anomalies that tragedy [not merely Shakespearean tragedy] brings into prominence." For a nonreligious conception of whatever "order" transcends man

> . . . can offer no explanation of the order's yielding a place to evil while being essentially averse to it. It is aghast at the order's destruction and waste of its own good in the tragic paroxysm. It must leave as absurdity the beholder's being neither crushed nor rebellious as the order exercises its devastating prerogatives, and lets fall its "horrible pleasures" upon subject humanity. It knows no means whereby men's lives, which appear diminutive and puny in comparison to the order, can yet appear as significant within it. It cannot account for the transformation of tragic man's intention and act into the opposite of itself, and the apparent disproprotion between what is thought or done and its effect in the tragic world. It can see no reason why a man's virtues should help to destroy him—and is not at all inclined to search for one. And that the order should determine men's actions

which at the same time safeguarding their freedom of choice it would not believe if it could escape from its own observations.

(pp. 266f.)

To achieve his purpose, Morris divides his work into four sections, the first an extremely readable, thought–provoking, and suspensefully promising critique of previous attempts to provide a "theological interpretation of Shakespeare's tragedies." His concluding paragraph (p. 83) briefly summarizes his basic objection to his predecessors and his plans for the remaining three sections:

Tragedy is eloquent of man's state in the world. The conditions of its creation [about which Morris is inexplicably far more certain than I] ensure an incongruity with conceptual thought. And a true criticism must therefore be as close as possible to the dramatic immediacies of thought, impression and event. For all these reasons, the bringing of theological concepts into the detailed interpretation of [a?] tragedy must be held in general to be precluded. But if experience arising from the contemplation of [a?] tragedy, rather than formulations within it, be regarded as the proper ground in the search for religious significance—if, from the phenomenon itself, in its devoted rendering of the secular condition of man, some revelation of further meaning may be gained—a basis is found for bringing theological concepts into relation with tragedy. What tragedy has to say about the human condition [III], in fact, may be brought into comparison with what theology has to say about it [II]. If tragedy, from a religious point of view, can be said to deal with the state of affairs above which the man of faith is empowered to rise [III], theology, in the process of defining the principles of faith, and of applying them, cannot but make reference to the conditions of human existence in which faith takes root [II]. It is therefore not accidental that in the greatest of Christian philosophers are to be discerned the widest of human sympathies: the truths of theology which they formulate are intimately associated with the realities of their experience as men. The attempt will therefore be made to see whether the human condition as it has appeared in Christian thinking [II] can approximate to the experience of life which the greatest tragedies have shared [III], and Shakespearian tragedy reveals [IV].

(In II, the authorities for "Christian thinking" are almost exclusively Augustine, Aquinas, Luther, and Calvin; in III and IV these are supplemented extensively, primarily by Kierkegaard and Reinhold Niebuhr. To the latter's memory *Shakespeare's God* is appropriately dedicated.)

What follows, accordingly, is Section II, "The Human Condition: Theology's Assessment of the Medium of Tragedy," with Augustine-dominated and fairly predictable chapters on man as a creature, the created universe, the human will, the human intellect, the grace of God, the justice of God, the tragedy of man, and the uses of adversity (pp. 85–165); then Section III, "The Tragic Phenomenon: Literary Tragedy as the Secular Enactment of Theological Principle," interpreting in the light of Section II the implications of some familiar experiential responses to tragedy: the sense of necessity, of paradox (e.g., truth from confusion, joy in sorrow, greatness in failure, reality in transcience), of tragic flaw (a crucially untraditional chapter), dread, destiny, and constraining (pp. 167–299); then Section IV, "A Theological Interpretation of Shakespearian Tragedy: The Heroic Predicament as the Operation of the Apostate Will Beneath Providential Ordinance"—four unchronological chapters of increasing length: *"Macbeth"* (pp. 310–22), *"Othello"* (pp. 323–43), *"King Lear"* (pp. 342–68), and *"Hamlet"* (pp. 369–430). A brief "Conclusion," summarizing what Morris has hoped to achieve (pp. 433–36), is followed by three well-worth-reading appendices, perhaps responses to late criticism of the manuscript which might better have been worked into earlier sections. The first, Max Scheler-based, defends overcryptically the use of modern theologians and philosophers (pp. 439–46); the next two defend, scarcely for the first time, approach through character rather than concept (pp. 447–60) or image (pp. 461–77).

For me, *Shakespeare's God* is badly muddled by Section III's effort to embrace "all great tragedy" and its ultimate "function" for mankind. These broader concerns operate to the serious detriment of the aim implied in the title, and all the more so because—despite the inordinate length of the book—Morris makes no clear attempt to explain how they are related to one another. It may well be true, from a religious point of view, that "the high duty of tragedy . . . is to present the situation that faith must overcome" (p. 180), that those "who are not prepared to limit significance to the bounds of a mortal existence are able to discern in literary tragedy something of what Augustine called 'the benefit of affliction' " (p. 183), even that "the tragic [presumably embracing the real-life experience of all mankind, the experience of at least some tragic protagonists, the conviction of at least some dramatists, and the experience of qualified audiences; on such distinctions and their possible relevance Morris is often unclear] is . . . an instrument in the hands of a God who teaches by sorrow, and wounds men in order to heal them" (p. 295). Thus, according to the conclusion of Morris' chapter on "The Tragic Constraining,"

> Tragedy . . . directs attention to certain necessary means or conditions for transcendence—but only in the process of revealing the human world to which it is bound. That world is seen to have no power to transcend itself, and the conclusion of literary tragedy must therefore be "general woe." But even in its conclusion, tragedy makes clear what Christian experience affirms: that for the true completion both of the principle of goodness in man and of the significance of his own spirit, the working and grace of a higher order is necessary. And those to whom faith is present may find in tragedy's brief history of perturbation, mischance and defeat in the mortal undertakings of man's spirit the confirmation of its loftier need and potentiality: the truth that [in Augustine's words] "Thou madest us for Thyself, and our heart is restless, until it repose in thee."
>
> *(p. 299)*

This might well be the subject of a book: to what degree, and in what sense, does all tragedy worthy the name "make clear" even to a predisposed reader "what Christian experience affirms"? Morris attempts nothing of the kind. His few brief references to Greek tragedy or tragedies scarcely warrant as much as is claimed above (cf. pp. 180, 185, 216, 227, 290). *Dr. Faustus* is the only non-Greville Elizabethan tragedy to which he even alludes (pp. 21, 213), mainly to contrast its explicit and simple morality play didacticism with Shakespeare. (Symptomatically, his bibliography includes only four dramatists: Shakespeare, Anouilh, Greville, and Marlowe [for Part I of *Tamburlaine*, from which he makes three out-of-context quotations; pp. 92, 201, 243]). One wonders in vain how Morris might approach a Webster or Middleton, whether he would credit either with having written legitimate tragedy and if so whether their God could even conceivably be unlike "Shakespeare's."

Indeed, I am by no means certain which of Shakespeare's own plays Morris regards as legitimate tragedies. Frustratingly, he appears so bound by his commitment to Bradley that he limits his discussion almost entirely to the four plays in *Shakespearean Tragedy*. Many of the tragedies he does not even mention. *Antony and Cleopatra* he does, while condemning a previous critic's efforts to impose a Christian ethic upon the play: "there can be few tragedies with so triumphant an ending. No audience would have

Cleopatra other than she is. . . . Her ending of her own life is effected as an achievement, and with a sense of rejoicing in which the audience shares . . ." (p. 45). Will so triumphant an ending, scarcely one of "general woe," encourage Morris to go one step beyond Bradley and disqualify the play from true tragedy? Or will he somehow reconcile what he says on p. 45 with such later generic assertions as that from p. 299 above? and with such "Shakespearean" formulations as the following?

> . . . there is evident in criticism [and in audiences, he notes earlier] a marked reluctance to reject the virtues for which the hero is admired . . . The love of Shakespeare's tragic heroes is earthly and selfish; and they are therefore to be numbered among the ungodly who, trusting in their own powers rather than in the power of God, can see only ruin when their hopes are ruined.
>
> (p. 238)

We never learn. Two subsequent undeveloped references to Cleopatra (the first of which seems to me seriously misleading, pp. 365, 451) probably imply that in some sense, thanks to apostate(?) Cleopatra, *Antony and Cleopatra* fulfills Morris' criteria for tragedy, but how it "makes clear what Christian experience affirms" I am too worldly a critic to understand: "If the world's gladnesses are tokens of a wickedness unpunished, and its miseries are proof of its guilt—if, in fact, literary tragedy declares the spiritual condition of mankind—the worldly critic is in little better position to recognize it than the tragic hero" (p. 395; cf. p. 175). One wishes—at least I do, most sincerely—that Morris had clarified his views on both tragedy and "Shakespeare's God" by devoting a chapter to *Antony and Cleopatra*, which seems to resist his Augustinian generalizations, rather than to *Macbeth* (on which, as he knows, he has very little to say that has not been repeatedly said already). And one wishes, too, that somewhere he had said at least a word about comedy as a genre, and about the relevance, if any, of "spiritual discernment" in responding to Shakespeare's comedies and final romances.

If Section III frustrates by trying to do too much, Section IV does so most of all by not attempting enough, even with the four tragedies to which it restricts itself. The initial chapters of *Shakespeare's God*, in criticizing previous religious interpreters, endlessly emphasize what Morris again stresses at the close of that first section: theological meaning, if any, "must come from the impact of the play as a whole" and from a beholder "exposed to the full effect of the tragedy" (p. 81). In turn, many passages in Section III (most of all, perhaps, pp. 182–85 on the insensitivity of "secular criticism" to the "positive intimations" in *King Lear*'s conclusion) make the reader genuinely anxious to reach the concluding section and discover what Morris will there reveal. One scarcely expects a twenty-six-page essay that spends two-thirds of its length analyzing Lear's spiritual condition in I.i, concludes with Lear's spiritual state in IV.vi (badly misread, in my opinion), and says nothing about Lear's reunion with Cordelia, or any of Act V, or the entire Gloucester action, or even the non-Christian setting. In short, to express things rather unfairly, one scarcely expects four chapters on Macbeth, Othello, Lear, and Hamlet entitled *Macbeth, Othello, King Lear*, and *Hamlet*. Even a rereading of "The Tragic Flaw" and "The Tragic Constraining" cannot prepare us for so limited a scope. Yet the only explicit statement of any rationale for what seems an abandonment of previous promises lies half hidden in the "Introduction" to this concluding section. The entire passage is worth quoting, especially for its implication that what one seeks one will find:

> The correspondence that has been shown to exist between a theological estimate of the human condition and the course of literary tragedy . . . indicates the need for a degree of theological awareness in any thorough criticism of Shakespeare's tragedies, or of any great tragedy; and the need is at its greatest where consideration is given to the nature of the hero's failing and its consequences within his personality. A theological interpretation of Shakespeare's main tragedies—if it be possible, and if it is to be successful—must devote itself in particular to the profoundest possible analysis of the state of will and quality of motive in the tragic hero. Beneath the secular or prudential level of his awareness, which manifests the operation of ambition or jealousy, or the workings of passion, or the grip of obsession, it must be able to distinguish an underlying state of radical guilt, "some form of inordinate self-interest," a pride or a *hubris* of gross and baleful aspect which must corrupt the purposes played out on the tragic state. It must be able, in short, to show that the hero's error, and his disordered affections, are the symptoms of a disease of personality which a secular criticism lacks the means to diagnose. In the studies of Shakespeare's tragedies which follow, the attempt will be made to reach the heart of tragedy, and to test the correspondence that has been indicated at a more theoretical level, by determining whether there may be detected—through a literary approach that is undivorced from religious awareness—a kind of significance within mortal thoughts which cannot be bordered within mortal considerations, and which in itself is inimical to humanity: a desire in the tragic

hero for that depravity of existence comprised in the choice of the city
of man in contempt of God.

(pp. 308–309)

On the chapters that follow, taken within their own limits, there is
scarcely room here for much discussion. Those on *Macbeth* and *Lear* I have
already discussed enough. That for *Hamlet* seems to me far too long and
too labored for what it has to say (partly because it redoes too much of
what II and III have already done), but some may find it satisfying. For me
it seems objectionable mainly for building too heavily on a definition of repentance no Elizabethan would recognize (see especially pp. 414f.), for
simply ignoring as if nonexistent well-known arguments on how the
prayer-scene may be essential to the structure of the play (surely relevant
to a book on "Shakespeare's God"), and for treating with too little real
thought or respect the incompatible views of Battenhouse (scarcely an unqualified secular critic).

As for *Othello*: one can predict from Sections II and III that Morris will
inevitably take a view in the Leavis tradition, minimizing—with Augustine's help—Iago's importance as a "cause" of the tragedy. And one may
find intriguing, even if ultimately unacceptable, the argument that "Iago's
sinister presence in the play, and the inscrutability of his motives, may
stem at the deepest level from his being the dramatic representation of the
true nature of Othello's ideal, if not of the ulterior condition of his soul"
(p. 336). But who can be long intrigued by a "theological" interpretation
which then appears equally to dismiss innocent Desdemona? According to
the chapter's conclusion, predictably cross-referenced to Sections II and III,
"Othello has tried to gain life from a world that has no true life within itself; after a manner, he has sought a unity and an omnipotence, but in the
realm of the temporal, where all things are transient like a shadow; he has
looked for sublimities in creatures, and fallen into confusion and error"; his
whole life has been "a feverish search for beatitude amongst things imperfect and perishing" (pp. 340f.). Obviously, Morris does not mean to imply
that Shakespeare should have made Desdemona guilty—but he probably
does imply that Shakespeare might have done so without altering the essential nature of the tragedy (or at least of the protagonist's tragedy, to
which IV confines itself).

Few readers, even among those who most share Mr. Morris' particular
religious convictions, will think *Shakespeare's God* predominantly a success.
Yet portions surely deserve attention which the work's flaws will discourage. It is excessively long and repetitious on its key theses, yet (whether
consciously or not) unduly silent or evasive on questions crucial to

adequate understanding or evaluation. Because Morris so often does not
mean quite what he appears to say, especially when he tries to make universally applicable generalizations about tragedy, I have perhaps done him
an injustice by quotations out of context (the context, in this case, being
almost five hundred large pages). If so, I may have verged on a kind of
unintentional misrepresentation akin to that which recurs endlessly in the
book itself. With no intention whatever of misrepresenting his sources and
with perhaps an excessive desire to acknowledge all species of indebtedness, including extensive verbal indebtedness approximating quotation, he
often imperceptibly merges his own views with those of others. Footnotes
should not mislead one into thinking, for example, that Oscar Mandel
meant what Morris does by "death is not necessarily an evil" (pp. 296f.),
or that W. Macneile Dixon ever claimed "the wisdom of paganism is
summed up in Aristotle's saying, that 'Death is a dreadful thing, for it is the
end' " (p. 297), or that Niebuhr necessarily claimed that "tragedy is to be
regarded as the consequence of a creaturely self-centredness and perverse
will to predominance which disturbs the harmony of existence" (p. 251).
Niebuhr might well have approved such an assertion, which derives in
large part from his own views on the nature of man, but his immediate
subject on p. 166 of *Beyond Tragedy* (a title, incidentally, Morris might well
have used rather than *Shakespeare's God*) is not tragedy but sin: "It does indeed accompany every creative act; but the evil is not part of the creativity.
It is the consequence of man's self-centredness and egotism by which he
destroys the harmony of existence."

English Schools in the Middle Ages by Nicholas Orme. Methuen
and Company, 1973. Pp. xiv + 369. $30.50.

Reviewer: Erika Lindemann.

Nicholas Orme's *English Schools in the Middle Ages* is a thorough survey
of a topic which has not been treated in such depth since the turn of the
century, when A. F. Leach debunked the myth that medieval schooling
had been largely in the hands of the monks. The author confines his study
to English schools, not universities or Inns of Court, detailing changes in
their administration, curriculum, and constituency from the twelfth century
to the accession of Elizabeth (1558). Following a brief introduction which

surveys previous investigations of the topic, the first chapter sketches the extent of literacy in each class of medieval society. Chapters 2–5 treat public, secular schools, staffed and attended by secular clerks and laymen, "which constituted the main source of literary education in medieval times" (p. 8). Chapters 6–8 trace the historical development of schools— their numbers, endowments, and influence—from the twelfth to the sixteenth century and explain the contributions of the religious orders to English education during the same period. Chapters 9–10 discuss the changes in education from 1534–60, changes in curricula prompted by the new learning of the Renaissance and constitutional changes effected by the Reformation, which extinguished the schools of the religious orders and modified the schools of cathedrals, secular colleges, and chantries.

Chapters 3, 4, and 5, the most informative section of the book, describe the curriculum, daily life, and administration of medieval schools. Ernst Curtius' *European Literature and the Latin Middle Ages*, which Professor Orme does not cite, remains the best discussion of the school texts summarized in Chapter 3. On the other hand, Chapters 4 and 5 permit us an entertaining and instructive glimpse inside the medieval schoolroom. There we observe the schoolmaster, earning an annual wage of ten pounds and teaching sixty to one hundred and fifty students for eight or nine and a half hours a day, as he presides, cane in hand, from his high chair under the awesome image of God the Father speaking the words "Ipsum audite." We meet several delightful, albeit atypical, dedicated teachers—John Ree, for example, a Worcestershire octogenarian whose career spanned twenty-five years in one school—and roguish masters arrested for poaching, rioting, threatening priests, and beating monks. Since life in the schools receives scant attention in medieval manuscripts, Professor Orme is to be commended for his carefully assembled description of the recreations and misdemeanors of schoolboys, holidays, school fees and supplies, and class discipline.

The major weakness of the book may be noted in Chapters 6–10, which survey the historical development of medieval schools from the twelfth to the sixteenth centuries. The organizational scheme of these chapters is chronological, whereas in Chapters 1–5 it is topical. Thus, the first half of the book comprises, broadly speaking, a description of life in the schools; the second half, a historical narrative. As a result, each half repeats material belonging to the other. In Chapter 6, pp. 172–73, for example, the author reminds us again of the shortcomings of medieval historical records, redefines "schools," and repeats a discussion of the secular cathedral's schoolmaster's duties, material already treated in Chapters 1 (p. 11) and 2 (pp. 59 and 80) respectively. Conversely, the broad historical developments briefly summarized at the end of Chapter 2 must wait for fuller development until Chapters 6–10. Even though the footnotes in Chapter 2 express Professor Orme's intention to explain the historical half of his subject in subsequent chapters, the notes do not ameliorate the reader's justified annoyance at finding early school history discussed midway through the book.

Since Professor Orme's point of view is essentially that of the medieval historian, his study has limited significance for students of the Renaissance. Chapters 9 and 10 describe the end of a distinctly medieval era of English education, not the birth of a new educational philosophy:

> . . . what particularly characterized the medieval era in education has now disappeared. The old grammarians and poets are no longer read in the classrooms. The schools of the cathedrals, colleges and chantries have all undergone reforms, while those of the religious orders have utterly ceased to exist. Education has become a matter of concern to the civil power, and the conditions under which the schoolmasters do their work are becoming very different. It is a suitable moment for the *medieval* historian to conclude his work.
>
> (p. 289)

Obviously, Tudor clerics and laymen inherited valuable curricular and administrative principles from the medieval educational system, but Professor Orme's primary purpose is to characterize the medieval parent, not its Renaissance offspring.

Appended to the study is "A List of Medieval English Schools, 1066–1530," which comprises "secular schools, both public and private, including the schools of collegiate churches and private households, which are known to have existed or to have been projected between the Conquest and the beginning of the Reformation in 1530" (p. 293). Arranged alphabetically by location (253 places are cited), the entries provide such information as is known about the school's range of study, its foundation or endowment, the period of time during which its operation can be traced, and appropriate references to it in primary and secondary sources. Although Professor Orme acknowledges that the list is both preliminary and incomplete, it provides telling and conveniently arranged support for the considerable influence of secular schools on English education. Together with a useful twenty-six-page bibliography, the list enables medievalists to study further the growth, continuity, and influence of medieval English schools. Indeed, those whose research and interest compel them to investigate any area of medieval English education will have to take into account Professor Orme's thoroughly documented and extensive survey of the subject.

Shakespeare and the Lawyers by O. Hood Phillips. Methuen & Co., 1972. Pp. x + 214. $10.00.

Reviewer: Raymond V. Utterback.

   Legal aspects of Shakespeare's life and works as well as lawyers' reactions to Shakespeare comprise the material surveyed in this volume. A distinguished legal scholar at Birmingham University, Phillips incorporates valuable references and an extensive bibliography, but aside from the description of legal minds' preoccupations in editing and interpreting Shakespeare, his book is primarily a compilation rather than a contemporary addressing of the legal issues. Shakespeare's life is treated first, consideration being given to such matters as the legal implications of his marriage by special license, his purchases of property (although the 1613 Indentures with Henry Walker for purchase and mortgage of a house at Blackfriars, with which legal documents two of the authentic Shakespeare signatures are associated, are not mentioned), and Shakespeare's will. Subsequent chapters are devoted to legal matters in the plays and to describing lawyers' contributions to Shakespeare scholarship; the latter section moves from the first lawyer-critic, Rymer, through the great legally-trained editors of the eighteenth century, Rowe, Theobald, Capell, Steevens, and Malone, to such recent commentators as P. S. Clarkson, C. T. Warren, and particularly George W. Keeton. The work concludes with a chapter entitled "Did Shakespeare have a Legal Training?" which indicates that the weight of legal opinion lies in the negative.
   No strict principle of selecting material seems to have been imposed. Although usually concerned only with comments by lawyers, the book occasionally recounts arguments by persons who are primarily Shakespeare scholars (Wilson, Knights, Draper) while omitting other scholarly discussions of major significance for understanding legal matters in the plays. Ernest Schanzer is cited on the marriage contracts in *Measure for Measure* but not W. W. Lawrence or Davis P. Harding; Lilian Winstanley's *Hamlet and the Scottish Succession* is not found even in the bibliography. Chapter divisions are somewhat arbitrary and overlapping, resulting in duplication and scattering of material. One would expect explanation of the various meanings of the term "divorce" (in *3 Henry VI*, *Richard II*, and *Henry VIII*) in Chapter 3, "Legal Terms, Allusions and Plots," but it occurs in Chapter 9, "Criticism of Shakespeare's Law." The Oliver Wendell Holmes-Sir Frederick Pollock correspondence is described twice, each time quoting the

same passage from Pollock (pp. 138–39, 168). Often simply the reporter of
what a legal expert has claimed, Phillips makes no evaluation of Holmes's
naïve criticism that Shakespeare disregarded dramatic fitness and violated
probability by inserting eloquent passages, such as Macbeth's "Tomorrow
and tomorrow" speech, whenever he was struck by the mood to write
something profound. While Phillips presents a lucid explanation of *Hales v.
Petit* (1563), in which a suicide is judged a criminal, and relates it carefully
to the matter of Ophelia's doubtful death, the material appears four times
in four different chapters. On the other hand, the affairs of Sir William
Allen (Lord Mayor of London in 1571) and his daughters, or of Sir Brian
Annesley (declared lunatic in 1603 by his elder daughters and defended by
his youngest daughter, Cordell) are not mentioned at all, though their situations had legal connections and may have influenced the writing of *King
Lear*. One wishes Phillips had given more emphasis to Shakespeare's use of
Ser Giovanni Fiorentino for the pound-of-flesh story in *The Merchant of
Venice*, whose trial scene perpetually attracts interest. The lawyers who
dismiss as invalid Portia's arguments about shedding blood or about an
exact pound of flesh seldom note that they are not Shakespeare's invention. Phillips cites an analogous judgment recorded in Leti's *Life of Pope Six-
tus the Fifth* (1521–90). When a Roman merchant seeks a pound of a Jew's
flesh, the Pope uses the stricture of an exact pound, subsequently finds
both parties guilty of criminal behavior tantamount to murder and suicide,
and finally commutes each death penalty to a fine for support of a hospital.
Phillips repeats without comment the translator's view (in 1754) that
Shakespeare borrowed his story from Leti, as if it were probable Shakespeare had reconstructed Ser Giovanni's story by considerably rearranging
Leti's.

   The book contains disturbing inconsistencies. While flatly declaring that
aside from Lord Chief Justice Gascoigne (*2 Henry IV*) "there are no com-
plimentary references to lawyers . . . in any of the plays" (p. 62), Phillips
later reports James D. Teller's approval of Shakespeare's tributes to the
most worthy expounders of the law and John Light's conclusion that
Shakespeare speaks well of lawyers and their duties to their clients. Phillips' own statement is not consistent with Shakespeare's text—Bellario's letter, which is read aloud on stage, praises the young legal expert
(Balthasar/Portia), as do Shylock and Gratiano at later moments, and for
contrary reasons; praise is liberally applied to the "brother justice[s],"
Angelo and Escalus (*Measure for Measure*, III.ii.265), though of course only
one deserves it. Again, early in the book Phillips supports the claim that
two thirds of the plays have strong legal foundations, though he actually

names only about one third, but later he cites Benjamin F. Washer's argument that none of the plays is founded on a legal plot or story and merely labels this view unusual.

The book would have profited from a clearer conception of its audience. While part of the work discusses Shakespeare's use of the law from the lawyers' professional point(s) of view, other portions rehearse quite general comments by prominent lawyers or illustrate the fascination of lawyers with Shakespeare, and others introduce rather basic information about Shakespeare's use of such sources as Holinshed's *Chronicles*. The reader is left to sort out a good deal for himself. But though Phillips is not entirely systematic or comprehensive, he distinguishes, as some lawyers have not, between the dramatic worlds of different plays, set in various countries and diverse historical times with differing degrees of realism. He does not assume all legal questions in the plays must be referred to one legal standard, the complex legal system of late Tudor England, though he allows the lawyers to explain many examples of how the customs and language of Elizabethan law are reflected in the plays and to argue many a case or technical point with each other. Indeed, Phillips recognizes that Shakespeare fulfills his own profession of dramatist by using the law dramatically, if not always the way a lawyer would.

Shakespeares Stil: Germanisches und Romanisches Vokabular by Jürgen Schäfer. Athenäum Verlag, 1973. Pp. 240.

Reviewer: H. M. Klein.

Glancing at the title of Dr. Schäfer's work, one might at first recoil and think: "not again," dimly remembering earlier unsatisfactory or even annoying etymological dissections of Shakespeare's vocabulary. Reading the book, one is relieved to see that the author actively—and without any obnoxious bias—retrieves this approach. Combining an impressive command of computation techniques, general linguistic theory, stylistics, and knowledge of the period with a felicitous practical sense of style and dramatic craftsmanship, he manages to make a highly instructive, indeed often fascinating, contribution both to the basic problems involved in merging statistics and to literary criticism, to our appreciation of Shakespeare's use of words, and more specifically to the interpretation of innumerable scenes, even some entire plays. In several respects the seven chapters and three appendices that form the book seem an early and powerful exploitation of the new possibilities opened to the study of Shakespeare's language by Marvin Spevack's computer-based *Complete and Systematic Concordance*, though the impetus behind Schäfer's work presumably antedates the *Concordance* and certainly antedates and exceeds Spevack's own presentation of these possibilities (cf. *Shakespearean Research and Opportunities*, 5–6 [1970–71], 46–51).

Considering the caliber of the book (it was originally written as a Münster *Habilitationsschrift*) one is, in the main, agreeably surprised to find that Schäfer refrains from overloading his text with references. He travels relatively lightly, restricting his material and rigorously excluding earlier contributions to aspects on which more recent work is available. Thus, of course, he refers to *The English Dictionary from Cawdrey to Johnson* by D. T. Starnes and G. E. Noyes, but not to Murray's 1900 Romanes Lecture on *The Evolution of English Lexicography*. Similarly, he uses R. C. Alston's *Bibliography* but not G. A. Kennedy's—perhaps a less obvious decision, as the two do not yet completely overlap. One is struck, especially in the four later chapters which are wholly devoted to Shakespeare's plays, by how well he gets on without studies that would appear to suggest themselves, such as Empson's *Structure of Complex Words*, H. M. Hulme's *Explorations in Shakespeare's Language*, P. A. Jorgensen's *Redeeming Shakespeare's Words*, or G. D. Willcock's "Shakespeare and Elizabethan English" (*Shakespeare Survey*, 7 [1954], 12–24) and with only very loose contact with C. Ehrl, B. I. Evans and F. P. Wilson. That this could be feasible plainly illustrates that Schäfer's approach is important in its own right. In fact, Schäfer's exclusiveness—which is, one must hasten to add, more than balanced by the enormous amount of literature he does consider—sometimes tends to justify his view even where contributions are concerned which (as opposed to those mentioned above) have a direct bearing on his immediate subject. A case in point is D. S. Bland, who lays such emphatic stress on Shakespeare's use of the "ordinary" word (c.f. *Shakespeare Survey*, 4 [1951], 49–55). When one looks more closely at Bland's random collection of examples of these ordinary, simple words—mostly, as he points out, "active" verbs of pictorial quality in their context, such as *blab, duck,* and *fret*—one sees that they all are of Germanic origin, an observation Bland does not make, perhaps does not think worth making, but which appears indicative of a phenomenon warranting systematic investigation.

In the first three chapters Schäfer maps out his fundamental positions.

Chapter I, "The Etymological Consciousness of Shakespeare's Contemporaries" (pp. 1–25), illustrates the development, in the Renaissance, from the classical interest in etymology as an "absolute" investigation of the meaning of words to the modern "evolutionary" search for their derivation. He rightly stresses that the transition does take place in the period—something not always recognized—although it is by no means completed. When Schäfer relates the old, "static" concepts of language generally to the Ptolomaean cosmology, however, he overestimates, like Tillyard, the unity of the Elizabethan world picture. Especially interesting is Schäfer's discussion of copious Dutch material on the origins and status of diverse languages (pp. 5ff) and of the Dutch influence on English thought. This is obviously particularly useful to his approach but might have been complemented by the inclusion of more French and, ultimately, Italian theorists (cf. P. Villey, *Les Sources italiennes de la "Deffence et Illustration"* [Paris: H. Champion, 1908]). Nevertheless, the demonstration of the powerful etymological interest among the Elizabethans convincingly corrects the impression given by Starnes and others. And one tends to agree with Schäfer's thesis that the discussion in England focuses more and more on the differentiation of Romance and Germanic derivation (p. 24), even though these very terms have an uncomfortably anachronistic ring about them.

Chapter II, "The Problems of Statistical Analysis: Quantitative Distribution of the Germanic and Romance Vocabularies" (pp. 26–42), is excellent. Briefly mentioning that single and multiple count do not render parallel results, single count always yielding a higher Romance percentage, he decides on the multiple count for his purposes, as it allows a direct comparison of passages of varying length (p. 29; there are, ultimately, obvious limits to this also, but they are beside the point here, as Schäfer is not interested in averages of huge portions of text). Schäfer's discussion of previous multiple counts of Shakespeare's Romance and Germanic words and assertions of percentages, mainly going back to G. P. Marsh, R. G. Kent, and L. Hannauer (90, 79, 86% Germanic vocabulary) is brief and necessarily cruel: they all averaged up on far too small a basis, underestimating Shakespeare's enormous range of distribution. However, Schäfer makes an even more important point: such averages, even when arrived at transparently, correctly, and supported by masses of the text—indeed the entire text—are misleading and practically useless from the literary point of view because they blur not only the difference between verse and prose (the Romance element tends to be higher in verse) but the all-important factors of speaker, context, and specific dramatic situation. Appendix I (p. 183), consisting of a short list of percentage figures in selected passages ranging from 3 to 40% Romance words (which Schäfer gives throughout in his statistics as the lower and thus easier figures) in verse, from 2 to 30% in prose, confirms this sound view probably more by accident than by design: the extremely low figures turn out, on inspection, to be taken from samples rather brutally torn away from longer speeches. However, the reader, duly cautioned, is glad to accept Schäfer's firm assignment to quantitative analysis (of a rough indicatory value only) to be complemented by qualitative considerations.

In Chapter III, "Level of Style and Choice of Words: The Stylistic Differentiation of Germanic and Romance Words" (pp. 43–72), the discussion of attitudes towards the expansion of the English vocabulary could have profited, to name only longer contributions, from such early, possibly unsophisticated, studies as W. Prein, *Puristische Strömungen im 16. Jahrhundert* (Eickel i. W., 1909) and J. L. Moore, *Tudor-Stuart Views on the Growth, Status and Destiny of the English Language* (Halle: M. Niemeyer, 1910), certainly from V. L. Rubel, *Poetic Diction in the English Renaissance* (New York: MLA, 1941), and even a little from B. Groom's continuation of Rubel. From the primary material Schäfer gives a good selection of differing views. When touching on the currency of words, his concentration on English dictionaries to the virtual exclusion of bilingual ones (from Elyot to Cotgrave) and translators' glossaries entails the loss of valuable information. Thus, for example, Schäfer comments on the passage about *accommodated* in *2 Henry IV*, III.ii.72–88; it is intriguing to note that, in 1572 at any rate, according to Richard Huloet and John Higgins' *Dictionarie, accommodated* was no "usual word." With regard to one principal point in this chapter Schäfer, although he is of course not alone, differs from a formidable array of opinions: he categorically states that there was as yet no standard language (materially disagreeing with scholars like H. C. Wyld, R. F. Jones or Willcock, who see this standard as clearly emerging, and radically disagreeing with A. H. King, who in his study of *Poetaster* takes it for granted) and that the frequent references and appeals to such a norm are indications not of its existence but of its being felt as an acute desideratum. The other main contentions are neither very controversial nor very surprising for the most part. Already in Chapter II (p. 39) Schäfer had pointed out that even Sir John Cheke's vocabulary is by no means as purely Saxon as one might expect, and in his discussion of this and other examples he consolidates by precise information more or less J. L. Moore's statement that "There were no Purists, only Latinists of varying degrees of Purism" (p. 46; cf. also, more recently, J. Sledd, "A Footnote on the Inkhorn Controversy," *Tulane*

Studies in English, 28 [1949], 49–56). We are furthermore confirmed in the knowledge that actual usage—indeed fashion—decided, often rapidly, on a wide if sometimes ephemeral acceptance or disuse of a certain word (p. 58), that unfortunately Elizabethan rhetorics do not give examples of words in connection with the *genera dicendi* (p. 53), that an etymological differentiation did not influence stylistic assessment (p. 50), and that words were generally neutral in value, depending for their status and effect on the function assigned to them in specific contexts. Groom had already remarked on this and furnished excellent examples in *golden* and *silver* (*The Diction of Poetry from Spenser to Bridges*, pp. 31f); Schäfer, here restricting himself to the Romance element, gives equally convincing ones: *retrograde, intrinsicate, egregious*.

Most important, however, for the later course of the book are some plain statements of fact which might, to the unbelieving, amount to admissions: neither the Germanic nor, more markedly, the Romance element represents a homogenous stylistic entity (p. 43); some (one should really say many) Romance words were as common as Germanic ones (p. 44); monosyllables were, whether valued or despised on principle, generally regarded as Saxon (p. 48); and it is usually polysyllables that are liable to be labelled "hard words." It is very well for Schäfer to assert that the fact of a Romance word being monosyllabic and/or having already been introduced in the Middle English period does not allow us automatically to assume that it was fully accepted and usual around 1600 (p. 45). It is equally well for him to adduce powerful instances of dramatic juxtapositions like *Macbeth*, II.ii.60–63, ending with "The multitudinous seas incarnadine / Making the green one red" (which admittedly is far more relevant than Bland's juxtaposition of "The multitudinous seas incarnadine" with Lear's "Pray you, undo this button," p. 53). The suspicion remains that for the literary interpretation one might possibly do just as well to go by the perhaps amateurish criteria of simpleness, "ordinariness" versus complexity, unusualness, "hardness." This is strongly suggested, e.g., by the passage with which F. P. Wilson closes his 1941 British Academy Shakespeare Lecture on "Shakespeare and the Diction of Common Life" (rpt. in A. Ridler, ed. *Shakespeare Criticism, 1935–1960* [Oxford: Oxford Univ. Press, 1963], pp. 90–116). Lear's speech "Pray, do not mock me" (IV.vii.59–70) which Wilson rightly presents as a paradigm of inspired and moving simplicity is, with 96 words (excluding Cordelia as a proper name) conveniently close to 100, Schäfer's minimum unit. Analysis shows that there are no words of more than three syllables, 2 words of three, 11 words of two and 83 words of one syllable, and the multiple etymological count gives the not extremely low figure of 13, 6% words of Romance origin—all of them already introduced into Middle English.

In Chapter IV, "Types of Germanic-Romance Distribution: The Function of Decorum and Dramatic Situation" (pp. 73–96) Schäfer proceeds to put his approach into practice. Acknowledging the necessary qualifications, he reaffirms his belief in the significance of etymological distribution and proposes that there may exist, in between the extremes (shown in Appendix I, see above) levels which mark a definite style. The subsequent detailed analyses of many passages show that the diction of low characters (pp. 74–78, e.g., the two Carriers in *1 Henry IV*) usually, that of children (pp. 78–80) progressively, tends to have low Romance percentages, as is the case with comic dialogue and comic figures (pp. 80–84, Beatrice and Benedick, Falstaff). The Romance portion rises in courtly-formal language (pp. 84–87, examples from *Hamlet* and *Lear*), particularly in opening speeches and set speeches generally (pp. 87–90), whereas the language of real love is predominantly Germanic in origin (pp. 90–93). The impression voiced over Chapter III gradually recedes, Schäfer proves his point, especially as his analyses always consider the qualitative weight of the words and closely investigate the specific structure of the speech in question (e.g. Launce in *Two Gentlemen*, II.iii.1–35, pp. 74f; Son to Macduff, p. 80). The juxtaposition, for example, of Romeo's language relating to Rosaline and to Juliet (pp. 91f), or Cordelia's reply as opposed to Goneril's and Regan's, and a more extensive discussion of Portia's language (pp. 94f) carry further conviction. Following these interpretations, even the skeptic will have to agree that the distribution of Romance and Germanic words in Shakespeare is neither chaotic nor irrelevant (p. 95). Moreover, Schäfer successfully demonstrates that the various types of distribution are not primarily dependent on subject (p. 89) or on person (p. 92)—rendering a statistical average of distribution by character as useless as that by play—but are clearly governed by decorum and, progressively more, by the dramatic situation, emotional implications and atmosphere prevailing at any given moment (pp. 95f).

After this chapter, which both in position and impact forms the center of the book, there follow two others illustrating the role of the two vocabularies from the point of view Schäfer calls "dramatic-dynamic." Chapter V, "The Uneducated Speaker: Actual Speech, Literary Tradition, and Dramatic Genre" (pp. 97–115) sides with those scholars who sharply distinguish between actual speech and its creation on the stage (p. 97; cf. pp. 76f), thus complementing others like Wyld (*A History of Colloquial English*, 3rd ed. [Oxford: B. Blackwell, 1936], pp. 99f) and Hulme (*Modern Language*

Review, 41 [1946], 108–12; *Review of English Studies*, ns 6 [1955], 128–40) who, conversely, mistrust the stage language even of "low" realistic comedy as an unqualified guide to everyday language. Consequently Schäfer assigns considerable weight to the idea that the satirical representation of the general inclination toward impressive, but imperfectly understood, ponderous polysyllables became a specifically literary topos from the second half of the sixteenth century onwards (pp. 103f—to the point of surmising a literary influence on instances in nonliterary documents which appear to mirror reality). Keeping tightly to his approach he feels obliged to exclude bowdlerizations of Latin words and macaronic speech (as equally to be met in other languages, p. 98), errors like "Arthur's bosom" (as manifestations of ignorance not directly linguistic, p. 99) and grammatical mistakes (as not morphologic–semantic in nature, p. 99). Thus he is left with four groups: the mistaking of two morphologically similar Romance words (e.g. *preposterous* for *prosperous*), the deformation of Romance words (e.g. *pulsidge* for *pulse*—the borderline to bowdlerizing must surely be often difficult to establish), substitution of Germanic for Romance words on the basis of sound (e.g. *honey-suckle* for *homicidal*), and finally the mistaking of two Germanic antonyms (e.g. *blunt* for *sharp*—which he assumes to be a secondary effect of errors concerning Romance words, p. 99). He concentrates on the first group which is the most numerous and important. As Schäfer's ultimate aim is always interpretation rather than pure linguistic analysis, one regrets these limitations but is left with enough significant material to make an interesting contribution to the field of comic effects. He is not disturbed by the fact that contemporary rhetoricians fail to cope properly with these mistakes—taking the view, here as elsewhere (cf. pp. 99f, n. 9, 104f, 137) that there are various gaps between classical models and terminology and the actualities of Elizabethan speech. He also rejects malapropism as an irrelevant term on sociological grounds (p. 106), as he finds the comic errors largely limited to persons of low rank. Schäfer assembles a very useful list of the intended and the chosen words in Shakespeare (pp. 100f, n. 10) which shows that about 80% of the intended words were introduced before 1500 and presumably, in many cases certainly, well known in Shakespeare's day. This is good to know but can hardly surprise in view of the dramatic use to which these words are put, as well as in view of the audience situation. The study of various examples leads Schäfer to perceive a development of Shakespeare's exploitation of these linguistic effects: they are increasingly used in the characterization of very few persons and are progressively integrated into the context. A remarkable interpretation of *Much Ado* (pp. 113–15) shows both tendencies at their peak, supporting the main action and themes of the play.

Of the entire book, Chapter VI, "Germanic-Romance Synonyms in Shakespeare: The Given Language Structure and Poetic Realization" (pp. 116–51), is the portion most confined to straight linguistic survey and most directly based on Spevack's *Concordance*. Schäfer stresses the Germanic-Romance differentiation in this manifestation of the Elizabethan desire for and pride in *copia verborum*, which leads him to lay heavier emphasis, later on, on the two-member synonyms, albeit they are not recognized under the contemporary rhetorical term *synonymia*. Correctly from the dramatic point of view he restricts himself to the study of synonyms discernibly correlated in the text, though not necessarily syndetically linked (p. 124). He acknowledges our still uncertain information in this field but nevertheless tentatively suggests, under substitution, author-specific variations from general usage in that he shows some unusual combinations to be frequent (e.g., *love/amity*, p. 119) and some usual ones missing (e.g., *ghostly/spiritual* which do not overlap at all, pp. 119f, and, especially interesting, *dale/vale*, which, as opposed to Spenser's indiscriminate use, have opposed associations in Shakespeare, pp. 120–23). In his discussion of the much more frequent variation synonyms (pp. 126ff) the most interesting observations concern the pun (pp. 127f), the occasional underscoring of social distinctions (e.g. Antony: *descend*, crowd: *come down*, p. 128), and the development from often great rigidity to an enormous degree of flexibility in the employment of variation synonyms, something which is paralleled in the use of collocation (p. 143). With regard to collocation in general (pp. 135ff) Schäfer admits that the Elizabethans preferred structures of four and even more of three members (p. 136) and do not seem to have been guided by the Germanic-Romance differentiation (p. 138). However, he discerns this differentiation especially in what he terms "contrastive collocation" under which he includes, departing from the narrow definition of synonym, expressions like Iago's "duteous and knee-knocking knave" (*Othello*, I.i.45—contrast of concrete image and abstract concepts, p. 145). This expansion—a defensible and fruitful move—then enables him to penetrate beyond categorizing and analyzing the linguistic phenomena to literary appreciation in that he sees several such contrastive collocations linked to the imagery of certain situations (e.g., Claudius' "hatch and disclose," *Hamlet*, III.i.174), others to imagery of leitmotiv character (e.g. "Th' expectancy and rose," III.i.160). Nevertheless, the whole chapter strikes as rather bitty, but no doubt a number of Schäfer's lines of enquiry will prove stimulating. Chapter VI is complemented by a systematic table of Shakespeare's synonyms in Appendix II (pp. 184–203).

Chapter VII is again more general and cohesive, concluding the book with a study of "The Great Tragedies Period: A Stylistic Experiment" (pp.

152–80) which may prove to attract perhaps the most intensive, if not un-controversial, attention. Here Schäfer concentrates on qualitative aspects, such as the effects of accumulated polysyllables and particularly the concentration of polysyllabic neologisms as lending (independently of an over-all numerical count) a decisively Romance character to certain plays. Pursuing the widely recognized concept of this period in Shakespeare's work as one of intense stylistic experiment and achievement and following up in particular ideas put forward by Chambers and V. Salmon (*Shakespeare Survey*, 23 [1970], 13–26), Schäfer confirms this concept—which had hitherto been based on a variety of criteria—afresh from his findings. He is conscious, also in this respect, of the *OED*'s and our general limitation of knowledge but sees enough evidence for linguistic unity of the plays from *Hamlet* to *Coriolanus*, characterized by an extraordinarily high proportion, especially in the Romance element, of hapaxlegomena and first instances of words (in connection with which he adds Appendix III, pp. 204–20, containing an unusually extensive and practical list of what seem, at the present time, Shakespeare's coinings). And he demonstrates that this feature is not one of genre but really of the period (roughly from 1600 to 1608, pp. 154–59). Only *Timon* will not fit into the pattern of a sudden apex in *Hamlet*, followed by a high level and a gradual decrease, so Schäfer cautiously proposes placing it after *Coriolanus* (p. 159). The information gathered from these two criteria tallies with an exceptionally high Romance portion in many prominent passages (p. 160), both in verse and prose (p. 170). A series of apt and sensitive interpretations of texts corroborates the thesis, frequently revealing astonishing contrasts and tensions between the Germanic and Romance elements. Of these, the discussion of Iago and Othello (who is proved to be anything else but "rude" in his speech, pp. 165–69) is highly illuminating to read in conjunction with Empson (pp. 218–47) and Jorgensen (pp. 3–21)—the three are hunting such different game. It is true, Schäfer cannot operate with the etymological argument alone; he uses other terms like "simple" and "unobtrusive" (p. 160), "sonorous" (p. 163), "far-fetched," "choice" and "precious" (p. 164), the concreteness or abstractness of imagery (p. 173), etc. However, he nowhere claims that the etymological differentiation alone suffices to describe Shakespeare's style, least of all in the great tragedies (cf. p. 180). However, such doubts as may have remained after Chapter IV will now have disappeared.

Finishing Schäfer's book, one cannot but accept it as very important and valuable, in many ways as a model, study. One accepts it not simply in the sense that almost any approach to Shakespeare will, if intelligently and intensively pursued, reveal arresting facets of his art but in the sense that the

varying use of Germanic and Romance vocabulary represents one of the
fundamental data of his style, the combined quantitative and qualitative or
dramatic analysis of which can yield significant insights. We could clearly
do with a great number of similar studies, although it remains to be seen
whether the results with other authors will prove equally rewarding from
the literary point of view.

Shakespeare's Patterns of Self-Knowledge by Rolf Soellner. Ohio
State University Press, 1972. Pp. xxi + 454. $15.00.

Reviewer: Roland Mushat Frye.

Since Socrates identified the importance of self-knowledge for human
life, the theme has continued to hold an honored place in occidental
thought and culture. During and after the Renaissance, Socrates' admonition to "know thyself" (often in the Latinized form *nosce teipsum*) figured
importantly in philosophical, theological, devotional, and ethical writings
as a seminal and/or organizing conception. Problems of self-knowledge
were at least equally evident in creative literature, and the dramas of
Shakespeare repeatedly deal with the subject, whether as leitmotif or as
minor theme. Professor Soellner has addressed himself to the important relations between Renaissance developments of this concern and Shakespeare's poetic employments of it. Recognizing the expansive nature of the
subject, he analyzes only twelve of the thirty-six canonical plays, four each
from the early, middle, and late periods of the dramatist's creative life.
Even when so restricted, the effort is ambitious, and in a number of ways
the result is creditable.

The first chapters of the book briefly chart the intellectual backgrounds,
after which the author turns to his primary interest in the analysis of his
three sets of four plays each (*Err. LLL, R2, H5; JC, Ham., Tro., MM; Oth.,
Lr., Mac., and Tmp.*). Each chapter is built around a scaffolding of pertinent
citations from Shakespeare's cultural milieu, but most of the effort is devoted to character analyses for each play. In this regard there is a tendency
on Professor Soellner's part to slip into Bradleyan preoccupations and to
move away from a tight focus upon self-knowledge as such, but even so
his critiques are generally marked by responsible judgment and a balanced

view which rejects oversimplification. I cannot but regret, however, that he did not restrict himself with greater rigor and so have space for treating the *nosce teipsum* theme in the remainder of Shakespeare's canon.

I also wish that Soellner's analyses were more attuned to the Elizabethan theater and to the all-pervasive implications of the fact that Shakespeare's works were plays, designed for stage performances; too often he reads them in ways more appropriate to narrative poems or novels. The only reference to Granville-Barker concerns the stoicism of Brutus, where Soellner has something of value to say, but he could have profited from the dramatic critic's persistent consciousness of the theatrical milieu for which the characters were created. A sense of the dramatic possibilities and limits within which Shakespeare developed self-searching characters never figures here: there is no consideration, for example, of the audience conditions which Bentley and Harbage have treated so helpfully, or of theatrical conditions at the Globe which Beckerman studied—nor indeed are there even references to these scholars. There is also a regrettable lack of attention to differences between genres and consequent differences in the operations of self-knowledge. Professor Soellner may be correct when he concludes that "for Shakespeare there was no separate comic, tragic, or historical man, nor were there different kinds of self-knowledge" (p. xvii), but even if so there are still important differences between the arena for *nosce teipsum* provided by comedies in which "Jack shall have his Jill; / Naught shall go ill; / The man shall have his mare again, and all shall be well" (*MND* III.ii.461–63) and tragedies in which Gertrude declares of the dead Ophelia that "I hop'd thou shouldst have been my Hamlet's wife," (*Ham*. V.i.244), or a distraught Othello cries out "My wife, my wife! what wife? I have no wife. / O, insupportable!" (*Oth*. V.ii.97f). The basic conditions of soul-testing are so radically different between comedy and tragedy (not to mention the other genres) that there is an impelling need to consider how the processes, if not the ends, of self-knowledge differ from one form to another.

Professor Soellner's treatment of Hamlet takes no notice of Eleanor Prosser's theologizing *Hamlet and Revenge* (Stanford: Stanford Univ. Press, 1967)—a very curious omission, since if Prosser is correct, then Soellner's analysis is scarcely acceptable. I find Prosser pervasively wrong-headed, but Soellner's subject should have required him to consider her arguments. If the Ghost is indeed the devil bent on damnation, as she maintains and as Robert West and Dover Wilson admit as a strong possibility, then Hamlet has a very different problem from that which Soellner recognizes.

Soellner denies Macbeth any genuine goodness even early in the play, and instead affirms his "real moral worthlessness" from beginning to end

(p. 337). That premise ineluctably reduces the tragic impact of the play. Furthermore, it leads Soellner to find Macbeth's late reluctance to shed Macduff's blood "puzzling" (p. 353). His assurance that Macbeth "blames the witches, not himself" (p. 353) fails to take any account of the King's passionate asseveration "Damned [be] all those that trust them" (*Mac.* IV.i.139). As for conscience, Soellner divests Macbeth of it entirely, largely because the word does not appear in the play, and finds fear operating in its stead. Here the interpretation is demonstrably wrong. In the light of Christian doctrines almost universally held in Shakespeare's time, all the talk about fear up to Act IV would have appeared to Jacobeans to be a clear sign of the operation of a bad conscience. When the preoccupation with "saucy doubts and fears" subsides after the willful visit to the Weird Sisters at Acheron, Macbeth has entered a radically new stage of development, which may be characterized by Hooker's reference to "that pit wherein they are sunk that have put far from them the evil day, that have made a league with death and have said, 'Tush, we shall feel no harm' "—the pit "wherein souls destitute of all hope are plunged" (Sermon IV in *Works*, ed. Keble, II, 377). Had Soellner acquired a more serviceable acquaintance with theology, he would not have fallen into this major misinterpretation of the play. He might also have recognized the radical difference between Edgar's pagan "ripeness is all" and Hamlet's Christian "readiness is all" (pp. 193, 303) and numerous other issues of various import, all directly relevant to our understanding of the characters and their understanding of themselves.

On the positive side, Soellner's work makes numerous contributions, of which a few may be cited here. His defense of Banquo against Bradley's aspersions is quite successful. So too is his more elaborate and critically impressive argument for Henry V, not only as an ideal but also as a more complex character than he is usually taken to be in our age of leaden antiheroism. His treatment of Lear is admirably perceptive and balanced, while his analysis of Edgar is full of valuable insights. The understanding of Miranda is fine, and the revelation of Prospero as a complicated and unpriggish character is especially impressive. How well Soellner can use historical evidence for interpreting Shakespeare's characters may be seen in his application of Perrott's writings to Lear and of Bacon's to Prospero (pp. 307, 373).

In sum, though the book is not so successful as I had hoped, it is nonetheless a serious and responsible contribution. The subject of self-knowledge in Shakespeare is an important one, which will certainly continue to inspire interest and attract critical attention. Future explorers of this field will find much to correct in Soellner but also much to admire.

Modesty and Cunning: Shakespeare's Use of Literary Tradition by
Karl F. Thompson. The University of Michigan Press, 1971.
Pp. 176. $6.95.

Reviewer: W. F. Bolton.

   The method is familiar: description of a pervasive intellectual or literary
convention from former times; demonstration that the audience of those
times felt at home with the convention, no matter how arcane it seems to
us; application of the convention to our understanding of this or that
literary classic. The convention, and the classic, can vary—oral formulism,
patristic exegesis, numerology, courtly love; *Beowulf,* Chaucer, Spenser,
Shakespeare. In form and content, however, this kind of literary history
has become a literary convention in its own right.
   Karl F. Thompson's book follows this method. His first chapter gives an
"Introduction," defines his terms, sets out his assumptions, sketches his
scenario. The second describes "The Chief Conventions of Shakespeare's
Plays" as "The Gifts of Time." The third turns to "A Ready Audience,
Well Taught"—the Globe clientele who, primed with the contents of
Chapter 2, came to see what Shakespeare did with them. The latter half of
the book traces chronologically in three further chapters the use of literary
convention in Shakespeare's plays: "The Upstart Crow," "The Globe
Plays," "The Last Plays: A Quality of Strangeness." Footnote
documentation occupies five pages at the back of the book, and there is an
index.
   The convention of convention criticism has its canons too: they are
mostly those of verification. Was there such a convention, in life or in literature, at the time and place we are considering (for this is historical
criticism, and the details of time and place are crucial)? Did the known or
assumed audience have command of this convention? Does the convention
make a meaningful appearance in the work we have before us? And if the
answer to any of these is "no" or "not proved," is the failure in the case or
in its advocate?
   In contrast to that of some earlier students of Shakespearean conventionality, Thompson's purpose is "to focus more directly on Shakespeare's
method of incorporating conventional material and traditional patterns into
his plays" (p. 5). That would be a large order, but he goes on to limit it:
"Four such aspects of the tradition promise to afford sufficient sound
examples to show how Shakespeare used these familiar conventions and to

what effect" (p. 6); the four are courtly romance, revenge tragedy, didactic purpose, and the doctrine of natural correspondences.

The assumption underlying such treatment Thompson sums up early in his book:

> . . . there are some aspects of Shakespeare's drama for which the most industrious and ingenious researchers have found no one source. And if Shakespeare creates on his own, without model, source, or analogue, a play (*Love's Labour's Lost*, for example) similar in its use of conventions to a play taken from a well-known source (as *As You Like It* from Lodge's *Rosalynde*), what else can we suppose than that Shakespeare was so used to employing the conventions and so skillful in extracting from them the maximum dramatic value that in filling out any plot he called upon his mastery of the entire tradition and waited not the instruction of particular sources.
>
> *(p. 12)*

In this case, obviously, the tradition is that of courtly romance. On the following page Thompson refers to it as "the courtly tradition," but the index reference to that page lists it under "courtly love," and that is clearly what all three terms mean for Thompson. In his characterization of the courtly love tradition Thompson depends especially on C. S. Lewis' *Allegory of Love* for his secondary source and, later, on Chrétien de Troyes as his primary source: "in all literature, popular as well as aristocratic, the conventions held full sway relatively unchanged since their formulations by medieval romancers like Chrétien de Troyes" (p. 50). Unfortunately, he makes no use of F. X. Newman's symposium *The Meaning of Courtly Love* (Albany: State Univ. of New York Press, 1968), where the real character of the tradition receives up-to-date and authoritative study. The oversight is important because, of the four traditions he lists, it is to courtly romance that Thompson devotes by far the largest part of his study.

For Thompson, convention is "any detailed familiar character type, turn of phrase, tag line, stock situation, expression, or metaphor," while tradition is "a body of such conventions that, taken together, make up a coherent, recognizable theme, or type of drama or story, or poetic statement of doctrine, such as the revenge play or courtly romance" (p. 4). But later (pp. 149–50) he writes "Of these conventions the one he principally settles on is the religion of love," "In its religion-of-love theme," "Hear her . . . play with the religion-of-love metaphor," "For the metaphors of the religion of love," suggesting that a tradition may also be

a convention, a theme, metaphor, or metaphors. Since for Thompson
courtly love, courtly romance, and the courtly tradition (and code of love,
religion of love, *fin amour*) are all one item, while convention and tradition
are all one category—one that includes so much—the taxonomic aspects of
his method are not very clear.

Thompson's assessment of Shakespeare's audience raises similar doubts.
The unqualified assurance of his opening generalizations, "They also had a
lively memory of themes and conventions, stock characters and situations,
and accustomed metaphors in the many plays they had seen" (p. 26) or
(about Reynolds' *Triumph of Gods Revenge*) "No playgoer at the London
theaters was indifferent to this problem, and none would deem morally
sound any play about revenge that did not in some way reinforce the same
beliefs that Reynolds urged" (p. 36) wanes a bit when it comes to specifics:
"we do have *considerable* indication that the Globe audience was *pretty
much* a cultural unity. First, we have a record of what kind of education a
large part of this audience was *likely* to have had. Second, we can *infer* its
preferences *fairly* accurately" (p. 29; italics mine) or "The literary
conventions of the books read in considerable number by the Globe audience (or at least offered by the London book trade in considerable numbers
to that audience) . . ." (p. 46). The more general notion of "a ready audience, well taught" does not, in any case, seem to have been shared by
Jonson, whose audience struck him as notably ill-taught and unready for
coping with the traditions underlying his plays, especially his tragedies.
(Thompson's comment about the absence of the doctrine of natural correspondences in *Sejanus* [p. 122] is one I directly contradicted in my edition of
that play as long ago as 1966.)

I have used over half of this review on Thompson's three methodological
chapters, for it is in them that he presents the rationale on which his
interpretations are based; but he devotes 120 of the book's 167 pages of
exposition to the final three chapters, a sort of vade mecum to The
Complete Plays of William Shakespeare (Chapter 5 alone extends to fifty-
two pages, virtually a third of the book). He accords five pages to *Romeo
and Juliet*. Out of their larger context, the following quotations may be
vulnerable to unfairly severe judgment, but I think they speak for
themselves:

> Actually, the cause of the disaster should be Romeo's disobedience to
> the code of love—a point never made quite clear in the play. . . . For
> to put revenge and honor above love is to betray the code of love,
> and thus cause the ensuing disaster. This is what, I believe,

Shakespeare set out to tell. . . . The brilliancies as well as the inadequacies of *Romeo and Juliet* spring in large part from Shakespeare's filling in the pattern and expanding the plot and characterizations of the source story with aspects of courtly conventions and revenge-play conventions.

(pp. 74–76)

Thompson has this to say about *Measure for Measure*:

The duke is one of the most enigmatic of Shakespeare's characters—not because his thoughts are profound or his psychology inordinately complex. Such impressions arise, as we have already seen in Shakespeare's apprentice plays, when two or more stereotypes are joined in one.

(p. 115)

And this about *Coriolanus*:

This special quality results largely from the absence of either conflict of conventions or synthesis of conventions. Conventions of romance do not appear, even for occasional motivations; nor do the natural correspondences appear in the expected form of portents foreshadowing disasters to the state. The play seems, consequently, barren and unenriched, and Coriolanus himself brittle, the least poetically minded, hence the least amiable of Shakespeare's heroes.

(p. 146)

Thompson's discussion includes quotations of nine lines from *Romeo and Juliet*, four from *Measure for Measure*, and none from *Coriolanus*. Space will not permit, of course; but it is remarkable nonetheless that his method can proceed to its conclusions, and such conclusions, with so little quotation from the texts it seeks to explicate.

There are typographical errors on pp. 81, 126, 149, 154, 167, and, if by "adjure" Thompson intends "abjure," 84. Some of his assertions are also in error: "Heroes of romance may not question the justness of their ladies' commands; Lancelot never allowed himself to think that the whims of the capricious Guenevere were sometimes excessive" (p. 69), with substantiation again from Chrétien de Troyes. Yet in Malory, a far more proximate and hence relevant source, Lancelot thinks as much and says as much. Or,

The explanation that Lady Anne, like actual women of medieval times [sic], is merely a pawn of feudal interests for whom women were convenient means of acquiring rights of inheritance and holding of fiefs or preventing disseisin will not suffice. True, for actual women of the fifteenth century the protection of men was their only way of surviving. . . .

(p. 91)

No, not true. The social role of fifteenth-century women was determined by civil status among other things, and his summary is historically false of propertied *un*married women. But Anne is a widow, and her suitor Richard made her so; hence the irony of his "courtly" devotion to her; hence the inadequacy of Thompson's judgment that "Shakespeare never intimates any other motive for Lady Anne than that provided by the courtly tradition" (p. 91).

It is too bad that Thompson repeatedly takes to task modern Shakespearean producers and critics whose interpretations differ from his. For in the end it is the interpretations that matter, their worth depending on their soundness, their soundness on their verifiability. The method as Thompson employs it is unequal to the task of dealing with the literary traditions that Shakespeare used. It is not securely grounded in the traditions themselves or in modern scholarship about them; it makes insufficient distinctions in the times, places, genres, audiences, and plays it surveys; and it shows too little incredulity of its own reductionist conclusions.

The Quarto Copy for the First Folio of Shakespeare by J. K. Walton. Dublin University Press, 1971. Pp. 306. $12.50.

Reviewer: J. S. Dean.

In this book Professor Walton sets out to "discover the nature of the copy used for the printing of the First Folio in all those instances where a good quarto existed before the Folio was printed" (dustjacket), thus following in the choppy wakes of W. W. Greg and Alice Walker. He has expended considerable energy in trying to solve some basic Shakespearean textual cruces by means of "new methods of investigation, which are based on the evaluation of substantive readings" (Preface). Walton engages the bibliographers in battle over method, particularly Fredson Bowers over whether accidentals or substantive variants provide the better evidence for determining how a text was transmitted. Their controversy over method is a long-standing one. Some years ago W. W. Greg, in reviewing Walton's *The Copy for the Folio Text of 'Richard III,'*[1] supported Walton's thesis that Q3 and not Q6 underlies F *Richard III.*[2] Bowers first accepted that thesis,[3] then later rejected it because of what seemed to him an arbitrary handling of evidence that at times proved nonexistent or insufficient.[4] Greg began his review by saying: "Mr. Walton is right: we have been weaving fantastic theories to account for imaginary evidence" (p. 125). The question to be raised with *The Quarto Copy for the First Folio of Shakespeare* is whether Walton has not perhaps followed the course of some of his predecessors in employing a suspect method that relies upon questionable evidence. There is much that is valuable in this second book, but in such a speculative field it is wishful thinking for Walton to claim with such certainty the results he does for his method.

From the first, Professor Walton takes on the bibliographers, who, he feels, have abandoned the evidence of substantive for accidental errors in arguing the genetic relationship of one text to another: "Their lack of interest in the critical evaluation of readings as a method of establishing genetic relationship means that they failed to see the role of contamination, which, necessarily involves an evaluation of readings" (p. 61). According to Walton, following the classicist George Thomson (p. 51), it is essential to collect and classify substantive variants if we are to solve the three long-standing problems of Shakespearean textual transmission: (1) determining which quarto served as printer's copy for the the Folio when we know that some quarto did, (2) determining whether for certain F texts corrected quartos or manuscripts served as printer's copy, and (3) determining how efficiently quartos were collated with manuscripts before the quartos were used as copy for F. These three issues prompt the arguments of the remaining three chapters of the book.

In Part One Walton defines his problem and sets forth his reasons for relying on substantive variants, rather than accidentals, to solve certain textual questions. Textual bibliographers have generally relied upon coincidence of variant readings to show genetic relationships. For most cases, this practice is valid, but when the compositor has collated his text with another with authority, but of a different textual tradition, it becomes difficult to tell which reading is closest to what the author wrote. First it is

necessary to establish general textual authority before resolving the particular case. As W. W. Greg noted in "The Rationale of Copy-Text" (*Studies in
Bibliography,* 3 [1950–51], 19–36), an individual text may vary in its authority
between its substantive and accidental readings. His classic theory of divided authority effectively ended the tyranny of the copy-text that had resulted when editors overextended McKerrow's principle. Within this field
of activity Walton attempts to establish the genetic relationships of Shakespeare's Folio texts where a good quarto preceded F. Both Bowers and Walton claim that the evidence often used to determine these relationships has
been too limited, but where Bowers favors the further examination of accidentals, Walton would employ substantives.

Substantive readings in Walton's view are "readings regarded not as
inked shapes but as possessing meaning" (p. 27). To Walton they are
superior to the physical evidence of book production in establishing the
genetic relationships of texts, for we

> . . . cannot study the history of a text as we would, say, the history of
> a fossil. A literary document, considered as a material object, is not
> transmitted: its readings are transmitted. In other words, the physical
> aspect of the relationship of texts is not of the essence of their rela-
> tionship when we are thinking in terms of the descent of one from
> another. . . . The existence of any physical "fact" concerning the pro-
> cesses followed in the printing-house before the actual moment of
> impression of the inked types has to be *inferred*: such facts no longer
> themselves exist. . . . On the other hand, the readings in a text, con-
> sidered as entities possessing meaning, are surviving "facts," whose
> existence does not have to be inferred; and they thus provide the
> primary evidence of the history of the text.
>
> (*pp. 28–29*)

Walton places his faith in the significance of substantive variants since
these, he feels,

> . . . are the only evidence we have in any one text which takes us
> back to and indicates these intervening agents of transmission, be-
> cause if an agent of transmission transmits an original reading he
> leaves no mark. Hence errors are essential evidence concerning the
> history of any text, and it is in general only through errors that we
> can determine the relation of one text to another.
>
> (*p. 29*)

In this argument, then, he runs counter to the idea of Professor Bowers and others that the compositor's unconscious variations are the more reliable evidence for studying the relationships between texts.

Walton prepares his case for using substantive readings by placing Shakespearean textual criticism in historical perspective. He sketches the progress of major editions from the days of subjective editors like Rowe and Pope (Edmond Malone's great corrupter of Shakespeare's text) to current ways of bibliographical editors who, in his view, err in ignoring meaning: they "are not primarily interested in the evaluation of readings and, indeed, they usually try to avoid if possible having to rely on it" (p. 61). Walton chides the nineteenth-century editors of the Old Cambridge Shakespeare, Clark and Wright, for once having determined the precedence of the "Pied Bull" to the "N. Butter" quarto of King Lear, to call the question (in their words) "one rather of bibliographical curiosity than of critical importance" (quoted, p. 10). A very Daniel himself, Walton finds that P. A. Daniel's study of Richard II and Richard III in 1885 contains "grave errors in procedure and logic" (p. 10) and "is still in essentials followed by some present-day scholars" (p. 68). Daniel's error, says Walton, is to treat the quartos printed before the Folio not as "monogenous," where after the first quarto each succeeding quarto is printed from the one preceding it, but as "polygenous," where none of the quartos is a descendant of any other (p. 69). The quartos must be treated in toto when dealing with cruces. Walton takes Greg's early definition of Bibliography—"the study of books as material objects," a study "which has nothing whatever to do with the subject or literary content of the book" (quoted, p. 11)—as being the current bibliographers' gospel, despite Greg's later broader interpretation of the bibliographer's role in exercising editorial judgment. As for the arguments of A. W. Pollard and R. B. McKerrow, they are not bibliographical: "rather are they economic, legal, psychological, and textual" (p. 16). Walton makes these distinctions among the kinds of evidence to show that bibliographical analyses such as those by Bowers can be of only limited help in establishing texts.

Still preparing his case historically, Walton goes on to dispose of six aspects of textual studies in the present century: good and bad quartos, Elizabethan and Jacobean theatrical manuscripts, and conditions of printing and publishing (in three pages) and, suggesting greater importance, bibliography, accidentals, and substantive readings (in thirty-two). Walton has harsh words for the bibliographer's use of accidentals, and no doubt he has Bowers' criticism of his earlier book in mind when he says: "Bowers would here seem to wish to exalt bibliography into a dogma which is above discussion and substitute for reason bibliographical pontification" (p. 23). Walton may well be right in asserting that it is not the class of evidence (whether the "physical" evidence of bibliography or conceptual evidence from substantive readings) that determines the validity of the conclusion but the method of evaluation applied to it. But then some areas are less open to question than others. The quarrel lies in the nature of the final perimeter governing editorial judgment. Bowers, in his *Textual & Literary Criticism* (not with "and" for the ampersand, as Walton has it, p. 289) (Cambridge: Cambridge Univ. Press, 1959), would use bibliography to delineate the limits of choice an editor may have:

> Let us not mistake the bibliographical contribution to textual criticism. Under no circumstances is it designed to substitute other means for eclecticism. Instead . . . textual bibliography takes as its end the logical scientific control of the eclectic method and the supplementing of the methods of literary criticism applied to choice of readings. The control takes the form of requiring the purely critical judgement to operate within fixed bounds of physical fact and logical probability. This union of the critical judgement with the bibliographical method is the hope of the future. Bibliography alone will carry one a long way towards good editing, but it is no magic carpet to the Promised Land.
>
> *(p. 115)*

Is it possible that Professor Walton's suspicions about bibliographers arise from a misunderstanding of how the wiser ones conceive of their function? Does he see the science of bibliography not just in pursuit of but devouring art? The bibliographer G. Thomas Tanselle concedes that "writers on textual criticism, after outlining various procedures for minimizing the role of subjective judgment in the analysis of variant readings, have been forced to admit that certain issues cannot be decided without the exercise of judgment."[5] What we have, for example, in Walton's examination of the efficiency of the collations made between quarto and manuscript, is a study in which the "possible" is too often taken for the "demonstrable" or the "probable," to borrow Bowers' terms.[6]

As for accidentals, Walton (unlike Bowers) finds them subject to the same changes as substantives as they pass through the mind of the compositor. According to Walton, "Bowers consistently fails to give due weight to the fact that evidence arises only when a transmitter introduces variation, which is itself a less mechanical process than the correct reproduction of copy, and that the person who least mechanically reproduces a text is not necessarily the person who will most mechanically vary from it" (p.

35). Accidentals are difficult to use as evidence, says Walton, since they must be differentiated from the compositor's usual practice. And though after much painstaking work it is sometimes possible to identify the compositor and his regular habits, substantive variants for Walton still provide the best evidence, since they are directly concerned with the transmission of meaning. His method derives from the genealogical method that Karl Lachmann and others used mainly with classical manuscripts, a progress or progressive elimination of error dependent upon the absence of contamination. One critical stage in this process (and Walton's) is to find the variants and then decide if they are visual or linguistic. Walton would have it that since genetic relationships in Shakespeare's collateral substantive texts are subject to contamination (the complication of manuscript consultation), the best way to solve the three main problems noted earlier is to analyze substantives.

Rather than rehearse the particular criticisms others have had of Professor Walton's theories,[7] I should like to comment on what seems to be his tendency in this book to resort to hunches based on divination of the Elizabethan printer's psyche, or to take a few facts and then with elaborate statistical formulas determine degrees of probability—two ways to argue from insufficient evidence. Walton's major proof for his method is his analysis of the printing of F *Richard III*, the matter of Walton's earlier book, where he had set out to disprove Daniel's thesis. Since its publication in 1955, though, there has been no general acceptance of its hypothesis that Q3 and not Q6 served as printer's copy; indeed, it has sparked off much inconclusive controversy between Walton and Bowers. T. H. Howard-Hill has said of the Walton-Bowers "skirmishes" that "when two able bibliographers can neither agree on the facts of the case nor persuade the other to see the light . . . to persist in unedifying debate is an abuse of 'bibliographical method.' "[8] Despite the continuing disagreement, Walton in this latest book repeatedly refers to Q3 *Richard III* as F printer's copy as if it were undisputed fact. Surely he begs the question.

Furthermore, although Walton criticizes Daniel's method of handling variants in the texts of *Richard III* to show coincidence between certain quartos antecedent to F, Walton's own statistical analyses depend upon a sometimes personal distinction between "indifferent" variants (where two readings have a similar meaning) and definite errors. Walton takes the case for Q3 as closed and chooses to regard Greg's acceptance of his argument as sufficient approval. Bowers' main criticisms, though, remain unanswered, despite Appendix B (pp. 287–88). Why cannot F *Richard III*'s "Newes" (Through Line Number 3342 [IV.iv.536]), where Q3 has "tydings" and Q6 "newes," simply be a common definite error, especially since Bowers has shown that the previous "newes" two lines above in F was set by another compositor and thus could not have influenced the later "Newes"? To consider, as Walton does, "tydings / newes" to be indifferent because the two words mean approximately the same thing is certainly a debatable distinction. Is it not also possible, as Robert K. Turner suggests (see n. 7), that the Q3–F coincidence of "I bury" (Q4–6 read "Ile burie") in the passage, "But in your daughters wombe I bury them" (TLN 3214 [IV.iv.423]) could be interpreted as an indifferent change if we think of "I bury" as expressing a future action? Are there really any definite errors peculiar to Q3 and F? Even if we could clearly distinguish one sort of variant from another, would there be enough indifferent variants between the quarto and Folio versions of *1 Henry IV, Romeo and Juliet, The Merchant of Venice*, and *Richard II*, four plays "which have only a small number of 'indifferent' variants" (p. 85), to provide a statistically significant sampling for Walton's proportional analysis? Even the plays with a relatively large number of indifferent variants between the quarto and Folio versions—*Othello, Hamlet, King Lear*, and *Richard III*—contain what most statisticians would consider too few items for obtaining valid results. For instance, Walton bases his conclusions about *Richard III* in part upon his finding 18 indifferent variants introduced in Q4, 11 in Q5, 58 in Q6, 121 in Q7, and 57 in Q8 (pp. 104–13). But Walton feels "it is all the more permissible" not to take variants that probably resulted from compositorial oversight, since what are important are the "proportions of the different kinds of error rather than the actual total number of errors" (p. 194; see also pp. 134f). How much weight can be placed on this type and degree of information? Walton, whose method is essentially rhetorical, does not so much prove his case after disproving all others, but rather seeks to discredit opposing views, leaving his own to stand—a battery of disjunctive propositions.

Opinion rather than fact also colors the problem of determining whether for certain F texts corrected quartos or manuscripts served as printer's copy. Walton establishes three classes of error: Class I, "made up of instances where there is evidence specifically indicating the printing of the F text from a corrected quarto"; Class II, graphic errors, "errors which arose through a misreading of handwriting or through the kind of failure of penmanship to which an author or transcriber is prone"; and Class III, "errors which are not included in either of the two previous classes" (pp. 194–95). The real difficulty comes in interpreting Class II graphic errors. They could, as Turner has said, result from reading heavily annotated quarto as well as manuscript copy. And could not typographical errors sometimes be interpreted as graphical errors?

In determining the substantive errors common to Q and F texts found in the plays with good quartos that differ from the F version, Walton has a

problem. He accepts secondhand the list of errors compiled by others—
Alice Walker's for *King Lear, 2 Henry IV, Othello*, and, with J. Dover Wilson,
Hamlet, and Peter Alexander's for *Troilus and Cressida*—but must make up
his own list of Q3–F readings for *Richard III*, since other editors have taken
Q6 to be the copy text for F. Whether those variant readings are truly sub-
stantive in all cases is open to question.

The results of the analysis of the common errors in these six plays can
depend upon some fine distinctions between what is graphic and what
nongraphic. Then too, the case may rest upon only a few examples, as in
Richard III, with twenty-two common, but only four (questionable) graphic
errors, the others being Class I or III. With just these data, can we accept
Walton's proportions of graphic to nongraphic errors to indicate the nature
of the printer's copy? Can we be certain, as Walton claims to be, that the
Folio versions of *Othello, Hamlet*, and *2 Henry IV* were printed from manuscript copy and *Richard II* and *Richard III* entirely from their respective third
quartos? Such, in any case, is the premise of the last part of his book.

In Part Four Walton considers the collator's efficiency in checking manuscript against quarto copy to be used in setting F. Put simply, it varied
within plays and from play to play. Here, Walton's suppositions are
psychological. For instance, at the end of *Richard III*, with the turmoil of
the stage action representing the Battle of Bosworth Field, Walton suggests
that "the collator may have persuaded himself that the dialogue is there of
less importance than it is earlier in the play" (p. 268). Walton calculates the
percentages of errors corrected in F *Richard II* (59, 54, 39, 33, and 55% for
each act) and predictably finds that "the efficiency of the collation declined
during the first four Acts but increased in Act V to something near its initial level" (p. 245). Why? A matter of the horse nearing home: "It is in fact
easy to assume that the collator's energies progressively waned but that,
when he had got over half way and saw the end of his task in sight, his
efficiency began to increase and finally reached a point not far below its
initial level" (p. 254; see also the assumptions on pp. 226–27). Why increase? Why not decrease in efficiency? Later, however, Walton admits that
"of course his mind may not have functioned in the way I have suggested"
(p. 268). The collator's erratic work "becomes all the more likely if we take
it that he felt free to decide which parts of the play were least deserving of
his attention. Since there can in fact have been no effective supervision of
the work of collation (assuming that the lack of correction was not due to a
damaged manuscript), a collator may well have felt free to exercise his
judgment in this matter" (pp. 268–69). How do we know there could be
"no effective supervision" and on what basis can we take it that collators
doubled as critics? Walton speculates about the printer's habits in a way
that led Greg to criticize the earlier book: "a psychological explanation of

his erratic behaviour, which leaves me cold and sceptical."[9]

Mr. Walton has obviously brought all of his guns to bear on some major Shakespearean textual problems that scholars would like to see overcome. His wide reading from the techniques of classical and medieval textual editors to the proportional formulas of mathematicians, his ability to pick holes in the arguments of others, and his statement of the bibliographical problems in the plays under question are the chief virtues that appear in this book, once Walton's facts and logic are sifted from the persuasive aspects of his argumentative rhetoric. He could convince as well without engaging in the polemics of categorical judgments against the work of others to whom he owes no little debt: Daniel's "initial mistakes" (p. 60) and "fundamental blunders" (p. 71), Miss Walker's "fundamental error" (p. 215), Greg's "rather cumbersome assumption" (p. 242, n. 1), Bowers' "errors in logic and also linguistically unsound assumptions" (p. 23), his "surely desperate attempt" (p. 34), his "attempted demonstration" (p. 41), his "still hopeless" position (p. 42). Such pontification is not necessary and will not win converts.

A book that makes its bid upon the minutiae of what compositors and proofreaders did or did not do would also be helped if it were itself more accurate in page references and titles of books. For example, besides the case of the expanded ampersand noted earlier, Walton in his list of references cites Philip Williams' review of Alice Walker's *Textual Problems* (p. 295) as on pages 482–83, instead of 481–84—small change, of course, but such is the stuff that bibliography grows on. A book that argues the merits of substantive versus indifferent variants needs to be carefully proofread if it means to be accepted.

Studies in textual bibliography must, I suppose, have stipulative definitions, graphs, "if . . . then" clauses, lists of fragmented words and phrases, abbreviations, numbers, and abstract diction. But in the name of Shakespeare, could there not be more grace in the delivery? At one extreme Walton halts and repeats:

> In drawing up the following lists of "indifferent" variants introduced into these quartos, it was important to achieve consistency in what is to be included as an "indifferent" variant. In general I have taken an "indifferent" variant to be a variant reading which gives a meaning similar to that of the reading with which it is variant. I have considered as a variation in reading any change in grammatical form. A variation in grammatical form sometimes gives rise to a difference in meaning, small though this difference may be.
>
> (*p. 83*)

At the other extreme, he can run on in labyrinthine fashion to tell us about *Othello*'s famous misplaced line, "And hell gnaw his bones": "The explanation given above of the misplacement of 'And hell gnaw his bones' and the substitution of a comma for the full stop which should come after 'bones' is confirmed by the fact that the assumption which it makes concerning the length of a page of the manuscript is consistent with what information we are given on this point by *More* D" (p. 222). Apparently Compositor B glanced at the top of the wrong leaf of manuscript copy (averaging about fifty lines) and set the passage fifty lines early—an explanation to Walton's credit.

Notes:

1. Monograph Series, No. 1 (Auckland, New Zealand: Auckland University College, 1955).
2. *Library*, 5th ser., 11 (1956), 125–29.
3. *Shakespeare Quarterly*, 10 (1959), 91–96.
4. "The Copy for the Folio *Richard III*," *Shakespeare Quarterly*, 10 (1959), 541–44.
5. "Textual Study and Literary Judgment," *Publications of the Bibliographical Society of America*, 65 (1971), 109.
6. *Bibliography and Textual Criticism* (London: Oxford Univ. Press, 1964).
7. See besides the reviews by Greg and Bowers of Walton's earlier book on *Richard III*, some reviews of this later one: by Richard Proudfoot, *Shakespeare Survey*, 25 (1972), 193–98; Albert Smith, *Library*, 5th ser., 27 (1972), 354–59; Robert K. Turner, Jr., *Modern Philology*, 71 (1973), 191–96; Hermann Heuer, *Shakespeare-Jahrbuch* (Heidelberg, 1973), 204–05; and Martin Lehnert, *Shakespeare-Jahrbuch* (Weimar), 109 (1973), 199–201.
8. In reviewing Fredson Bowers' *Bibliography and Textual Criticism* and *On Editing Shakespeare, Shakespeare Studies*, 4 (1968), 380–83.
9. Greg, *Library*, 5th ser., 11 (1956), 128.

White Magic and English Renaissance Drama by David Woodman. Fairleigh Dickinson University Press, 1973. Pp. 148. $8.00.

Reviewer: D'Orsay W. Pearson.

This study, originally accepted as a Columbia University dissertation in 1968, contributes no new insights into the complex topic of "white magic" during the Renaissance; if anything, it obscures rather than enlightens. It proceeds on the basis of dogmatic and undocumented assertion, facile oversimplification, generalization on the basis of limited evidence, and an occasional, but nevertheless serious, misrepresentation of fact or of materials cited. It is highly derivative and cannot substitute for some of the excellent studies from which it is obviously drawn—for example, Frances B. Yates's *Giordano Bruno and the Hermetic Tradition* (Chicago: Univ. of Chicago Press, 1964); D. P. Walker's *Spiritual and Demonic Magic from Ficino to Campanella* (London: Routledge & Kegan Paul, 1958), or E. M. Butler's *The Myth of the Magus* (Cambridge: Cambridge Univ. Press, 1948) or *Ritual Magic* (Cambridge: Cambridge Univ. Press, 1949).

Dr. Woodman's most obvious technique, that of the dogmatic, undocumented assertion, appears first in the Introduction, where he declares, without any reference to either primary or secondary sources, that the scope of white magic includes alchemy, natural astrology, the raising of Neoplatonic demons, and healing with herbs (pp. 12–13). Why cite alchemy as an adjunct of white magic?[1] In citing herbal healing as one of the pursuits of the white magician, is he amalgamating the roles of the learned theurgist and the village "cunning woman" of the Renaissance? Is he assuming that actions carried out in conjunction with purification rituals and with beneficent ends in mind can all be called "white magic"? And does his "white magician" involve himself in all four pursuits, or will only one qualify him for discussion? As the reader proceeds further into the study, it becomes apparent that Dr. Woodman, through eclectic borrowing and synthesis, has created his own version of white magic, a version which is at once highly inclusive and oversimplified. For example, in his introduction he observes that the white magician could practice three kinds of magic: divine, celestial, and natural. These, though he does not say so, are the three kinds of magic explored in Cornelius von Agrippa's *De Occulta Philosophia*. But the "natural magic" he defines is definitely not the natural magic of Agrippa's first book, for the reader is told that "natural magic" is "primarily alchemy, which explored the sympathetic virtues and properties that could be discovered in tangible things, especially metals" (p. 14). The claim that "natural magic" is primarily alchemy will not correspond with that art described by Marsiglio Ficino or Pico della Mirandola any more than it will fit the definition Sir Walter Ralegh gives in his *History of the World*.[2] By incorporating alchemy into natural magic, Woodman has definitely expanded its traditional limits and at the same time has limited an understanding of it by ignoring the talismanic and incantatory elements which its practice frequently involved.

By setting up his own criteria for what constitutes white magic, Dr. Woodman does derive an advantage; he can include in his study such chapters as "Healers in Shakespeare," "The Jacobean Court Masque: The King as White Magician," and "Jonson: Alchemy Satirized." Having set up his own guidelines, he is free to discuss any characters or incidents which fit into his definition, wherever they appear in drama.

He finds himself forced to qualify almost from the beginning. At the end of his initial chapter on "White Magic and the Church," which appears to owe a good deal to Miss Yates and Mr. Walker, Woodman concludes: "In England, a few of the cognoscenti had heard of the Florentine Neo-platonists through translations and word of mouth. Free of the Inquisition, white magic could survive there in a somewhat more tolerant atmosphere, though this hardly put the subject in the public domain. More familiar were those legendary prototype figures whose lives embraced wonder working and white magic" (pp. 33–34).[3] He then plunges into a chapter dealing with "The Legendary Magician" (which is, incidentally, very heavily dependent upon Miss Butler's *The Myth of the Magus*), concentrating on three characteristics of that tradition especially: the possession of a magic ring, the burning of the magician's books, and the magicians' contest. Of the ring, he claims it could "bring fertility and health, act as a preventive, or fend off death" (p. 29).[4] The discussion of the magicians' contest gives him the opportunity to review such combats in *Friar Bacon and Friar Bungay*, *John a Kent and John a Cumber*, *1 Henry IV* (where Glendower's activities do not involve a contest) and *The Birth of Merlin*. Generalizing on the basis of *John a Kent and John a Cumber* alone, he claims, "the white magician reaffirms the natural order of true love in society and denounces the contrived unnatural plans of the parents" (p. 47).[5] This generalization he will later pick up at the end of his chapter on "Healers in Shakespeare" and amplify in relation to *The Tempest*.

"Healers in Shakespeare" continues to illustrate Dr. Woodman's technique of formulating generalizations on the basis of little or no evidence. The author admits that the "art of healing in Shakespeare is in most cases bound up with the remedies of folk medicine that were documented in herbals" (p. 51) and then says, "Shakespeare utilizes this overlapping [of the physician's, herbalist's, and healer's arts with white magic and wonder working] to create several characters who function as both healers and wonder workers; their role is not that of the white magician . . . but their actions suggest an awareness of white magic" (p. 54). He then proceeds to discuss Friar Lawrence in *Romeo and Juliet* (where the reader is told that since the potion given to Juliet was intended for a benevolent outcome, "it might be seen as a use of white magic by some of the audience", p. 56), Cornelius in *Cymbeline*, Cerimon in *Pericles*, Helena in *All's Well* ("Possibly Helena's deceased father, Gerard de Narbonne, had been a white magician and his 'prescriptions' were still effective in her hands," p. 60), and Paulina in *The Winter's Tale*. Of the scene of pseudo-necromancy in Act V of this play, the reader is told, "By emphasizing the lawfulness of magic, Shakespeare asks the audience to accept the whole ceremony as if it were created solely for a benevolent reunion" (p. 61). Dr. Woodman sees Paulina's role as similar to that of the white magician's role of "infusing powers and life into statues he has created" (p. 61), and his failure to recognize the necromatic overtones results, in this reviewer's opinion, in a very cursory and erroneous interpretation of a scene which depends for its audience impact upon those very overtones.

At the end of his analysis of Shakespeare's healers, Dr. Woodman admits that Shakespeare does not provide any details about white magic in association with his healers, but then goes on to assert, "Healing through the art of white magic, moreover, brings natural order to the physical body, just as it can bring health and good government to the disordered body politic" (pp. 62–63). That white magic has been used in the plays under discussion has been hinted at but never proved, and the materials discussed in the chapter will not substantiate such a claim. Yet the claim is made and serves as the basis for discussing Prospero as the healer par excellence.

"Prospero as the White Magician" depends heavily upon Frank Kermode's introduction to the Arden edition of *The Tempest* (Cambridge: Harvard Univ. Press, 1958) for defining Prospero's role as white magician and upon Rose A. Zimbardo's "Form and Disorder in *The Tempest*," (*Shakespeare Quarterly*, 14 [1963], 49–56) for interpretation of the play. Professor Zimbardo's claim that "Prospero's art then can order what is amenable to order, but it can only affect temporarily that which is fundamentally chaotic" (p. 53), becomes, under Dr. Woodman's pen, an assertion that the art becomes "in Prospero's hands a crucial instrument for curing the disordered minds of rebels and usurpers as well as the body politic" (p. 86), a claim which leads into "The Jacobean Court Masque: The King as White Magician." In this chapter, Dr. Woodman again flouts the very criteria he sets up; if he accepts, as he indicates, the symbolic and allegorical nature of the masque, then the "symbolic crisis" he envisions cannot be taken literally. And only on the literal, realistic level can he justify calling the resolution of the masque's movement an act of white magic. Included in this chapter are discussions of masques which use the machinery of theurgy (Jonson's *The Fortu-*

nate Isles and their Union) and black magic (Jonson's *The Masque of Queenes*) but which do not in any sense use the king as white magician. In discussing *The Masque of Queenes*, Dr. Woodman isolates the ninth hag, who had been gathering henbane, adder's tongues, nightshade, moonwort and leopard's bane and claims, "To make it clear that these particular herbs belong more to the enchantress than to the white magician, Jonson provides scrupulous footnotes about them, stating that Paracelsus, Della Porta and Agrippa believed these particular poisonous agents to be used in sorcery and not in white magic" (p. 94). Such a contrast is not a part of Jonson's gloss or his intent. As he stated in his dedication to Prince Henry, the purpose of the gloss was "to retriue the particular *authorities* (according to yor gracious command and a desire borne out of iudgement) to those things, wch I writt ovt of fullnesse, and memory of my former readings. . . ."[6] And to cite, in the gloss, that the herbs mentioned "are common *veneficall* ingredients, remembered by Paracelsus, Porta, Agrippa, & others" (p. 293) is not necessarily to draw a contrast between the elements of black and white magic.[7]

Other examples of careless handling of source materials exist. In discussing Ariel's role in *The Tempest*, Woodman tells his reader, "Not so rebellious as Lucifer, and not used by Shakespeare as a fallen angel, Ariel does belong partially to that disobedient band God expelled from heaven" (p. 80). The footnote reference at the end of this confusing sentence is to C. S. Lewis's *The Discarded Image* (Cambridge: Cambridge Univ. Press, 1964), pp. 134–38. A check on these pages reveals that Lewis is exploring four conflicting theories about the *longavei* or long-lived ones—whether they are elemental spirits, demoted angels, spirits of the dead, or fallen angels or devils. Lewis' only reference to Ariel in the passage identifies him as a "tetrarch of air" (pp. 134–35). Again, when the reader is told, "Apart from Christ, Calvinism denied intermediary beings between man and God" (p. 25), what is one to do with Calvin's own *Institutes of the Christian Religion*, I.xiv.6: "But the point on which the scriptures specially insist is that which tends most to our comfort, and to the confirmation of our faith, namely, that angels are the ministers and dispensers of the divine bounty towards us"?[8] Or, when one reads that Prospero's art "allows him to perform miraculous operations over nature" (p. 73), what about the distinction between "miracle" and "marvel" which was, and still is, applicable to a judgment of Prospero's actions?[9]

Enough has been said about *White Magic and English Renaissance Drama* to indicate that however topical the subject, the study itself presents serious problems in conception, scholarship, and technique. It repeats some valid

insights reached earlier by other scholars or expands through assertion
insights reached by them; it tends toward oversimplification in areas where
qualification is essential; it is dogmatic rather than analytical. One wishes it
were otherwise.

Notes:

1. Of the various individuals one might consider Renaissance magi in the
    sixteenth and seventeenth centuries, only two, John Dee and Paracelsus,
    showed any deep interest in alchemy; in complaining to Queen Elizabeth I
    about the losses suffered when his home in Mortlake was ransacked in 1583,
    Dee cited the loss of a lump of thrice-refined material, obviously the result of
    some alchemical experiment. Dr. Woodman may be including alchemy in the
    field of white magic as a result of Mis Yates's statement that "the Hermetic
    science *par excellence* is alchemy" and that "In the Renaissance, a new style
    'Alchymia' becomes associated with the new magia and cabala" (p. 150).
2. For a summary of the "natural magic" systems of Ficino, Pico, and Agrippa,
    see Yates, pp. 62–83, 87–97, 130–34. Or see Book I of Agrippa's *Three Books of
    Occult Philosophy or Magic*, trans. J. F. (1651), ed. W. F. Whitehead (Chicago,
    1898). Ralegh defined "natural magic" as nothing other "than the absolute
    perfection of natural philosophy"; see *The History of the World*, 2nd ed.
    (London, 1677), p. 160. Or see Wayne Shumaker, *The Occult Sciences in the
    Renaissance: A Study in Intellectual Patterns* (Berkeley: Univ. of California Press,
    1972), pp. 108–109, for a discussion of the two main meanings of "natural
    magic" in the Renaissance. Shumaker treats alchemy as an occult art separate
    from white magic, while Richard Cavendish, *The Black Arts* (New York:
    Capricorn, 1968), pp. 143–80, groups it among poetic pursuits.
3. Woodman's claim that white magic could survive in a more tolerant atmosphere
    in England should be set against Herbert Berry's more solidly documented
    claim, in "Dr. Fludd's Engravings and Their Beholders" (*Shakespeare Studies*, 3
    [1967], in which Berry examines Flood's complaints that his works received
    more attention abroad than they did from his own countrymen. Berry
    concluded, "Fludd's fascination with the occult was neither new nor unique in
    England, but it was not very saleable there, and it bordered on being illegal
    and heretical, as an English parson, William Foster, rudely pointed out" (p.
    113).
4. Dr. Woodman returns to the ring motif later (p. 66) when he discusses its use
    in *The Wisdome of Dr. Dodypoll*; here, he notes that Lucilla's father "possesses a
    ring that contains magical virtues, and, in what approximates an act of white
    magic, overcomes the Enchanter and puts him to flight." By citing only positive
    appearances of the ring, Dr. Woodman implies it is a definite apurtenance of
    the white magician. However, this is not strictly true. In an anonymous play,
    which Bullen entitled *The Distracted Emperor*, a magic ring worn under the
    tongue of Theodora is responsible for Charlemagne's doting upon her even in
    death. Discovered there by Turpin, it causes Charlemagne to become enamored
    of him when he appears with it on his person. At the conclusion of the play,
    Charlemagne refers to it as "a rynge, a wytchcraft rynge," and Ganelon, the
    purveyor of it, declares," . . . the sorcerer / That made it I did murder

conynglye, / And at her [Theodora's] deathe had I recompast it / I had been kynge of *Fraunce*"; see A. H. Bullen, ed. *A Collection of Old English Plays* (1882–85; rpt. New York: B. Blom, 1964), II, 260. Throughout the play, the ring is associated with usurpation, adultery, falsehood, love madness, murder, and injustice.

5. John Lyly's *Mother Bombie* employs a "cunning woman" or "white witch" as a major figure to bring about a positive dramatic resolution; Mother Bombie, like John a Kent, does not become in the end a scapegoat figure. However, even a generalization based on these two plays would be dangerous. See *The Complete Works of John Lyly*, ed. R. Warwick Bond (Oxford: Clarendon Press, 1902), III.

6. *Ben Jonson*, ed. C. H. Herford and Percy and Evelyn Simpson, VII (Oxford: Clarendon Press, 1941), 283. Since James I did not himself participate in the masques, Dr. Woodman is pushed to find masques to fit his thesis, and he ignores what is perhaps his most likely masque for argument, *The Vision of Delight*, Christmas, 1617 (VII, 463–71) in which the accolade to James was, "Behold a king / Whose presence maketh this perpetuall *Spring*, / The glories of which Spring grow in that Bower, / And are the marks and beauties of his power" (p. 469).

7. Jonson appears to use the term *veneficall* to include all witchcraft; the term also appears in his explanation of the antimasque, where he refers to the hags appearing with "spindells, timbrells, rattles, or other *veneficall* instruments" (VII, 283). Unlike many of his contemporaries, he does not then distinguish between *veneficium*, or poisoning, *sortilegium*, or foretelling the future, often by casting lots, and a variety of other forms of witchcraft.

8. Trans. Henry Beveridge (Grand Rapids, Mich.: Eerdmans, 1966), I, 145.

9. See St. Thomas Aquinas, *Summa Theologicae*, Ia, Q. cv ff., or Paul Kocher, *Science and Religion in Elizabethan England* (San Marino: Huntington Library, 1953), pp. 104–11. N. S. Bushnell's argument in "Natural Supernaturalism in *The Tempest*" (*PMLA*, 47 [September, 1932], pp. 684–98) would also throw doubt upon Woodman's claim.

The Rosicrucian Enlightenment by Frances A. Yates. London and Boston: Routledge & Kegan Paul, 1972. Pp. xv + 269. 30 plates. $15.00.

Reviewer: Wayne Shumaker.

The reader of this interesting but disturbing book will discover only seven references to Shakespeare, none of them very substantial. He will nonetheless find much which may change rather basically his understanding of the dramatist's age and the thought-currents which were abroad in it. In recent decades scholars like P. O. Kristeller, Eugenio Garin, D. P. Walker, and Miss Yates, together with specialists in such subjects as alchemy, astrology, Neoplatonism, the Cabala, and witchcraft, have given us an entirely new picture of the Renaissance which is basically in conflict with the traditional one. The Renaissance now appears to have been far more backward-looking than had been thought, far less the earliest stage of modernity. It was, in fact, the heyday of all the occult sciences, which it rediscovered in antiquity and attempted—though with what effect on the general attitudes of both educated men and the public is still in dispute—to harmonize with Christianity and substitute for the current Aristotelian philosophy and Catholic or Protestant theology. Miss Yates's enormous merit is that she knows, perhaps, as much as, or more than, any other living person about an immense body of relevant documents written predominantly in Latin, although sometimes also in the vernaculars, and has propagandized their importance effectively. For this we owe her deep gratitude. A serious drawback, which I will attempt to illustrate in due course, is that she now sees occultism wherever she looks and has herself apparently come to believe that the occult systems are in some sense "true" and ought, if not to replace modern science, at least to be incorporated into it. The tendency is not unusual among students of the occult and is glaringly present, for example, in the voluminous writings of A. E. Waite. A second weakness is that she is too often persuaded by masses of converging possibilities. Nevertheless I think it important, in a review which will be largely critical, to say in advance that Miss Yates's service to Renaissance scholarship is great and will probably be lasting.

The arresting thesis of the first two chapters is that in accepting the crown of Bohemia in 1619 the Elector Frederick V of the Palatinate, or his advisors, had in mind the substitution for the repressive Hapsburg Catholicism of a "Rosicrucian" Protestantism drenched in Hermetic symbolism and sympathetic to alchemy, numerological mysticism, and Cabalism. This "liberal" Protestantism was expected to have strong English support because the Elector, in 1613, had married Elizabeth, the daughter of James I, and he had also been invested with the Order of the Garter. The support, however, was not forthcoming because James, with characteristic caution, was attempting to hedge his bets by marrying Prince Charles to a Spanish princess. When the Empire reacted strongly and, at the battle of the White Mountain near Prague, decisively defeated Frederick on November 8, 1620, the "Winter King and Queen" of Bohemia fled to The Hague, where they were to spend the rest of their years in exile. The result of the Imperial victory was the disastrous Thirty Years' War (though its rumblings had in fact preceded Frederick's acceptance of the Bohemian throne) and a massive rearrangement of power structures which altered the subsequent history of Europe. The hoped-for "Renaissance, or premature Enlightenment, or misunderstood Rosicrucian Dawn" (p. 28) was therefore not, after all, to come. It is a chief purpose of Miss Yates's book to explore, "within the sphere of influence of the movements around Frederick of the Palatinate and his bid for the Bohemian crown," "the stimulus which had set in motion the movement leading to the so-called 'Rosicrucian manifestos' with their strange announcements of the dawn of a new age of knowledge and insight" (pp. 29, 28–29).

The search carries us far and into many odd corners—so many, indeed, and in such rich detail, that only a very general summary is possible. The third chapter attempts to connect John Dee, who had spent much of his time between 1583 and 1589 in Bohemia, with the manifestos published in 1614 and 1615 but first heard of in 1610: "the Rosicrucian movement in Germany was the delayed result of Dee's mission in Bohemia over twenty years earlier, influences from which became associated with the Elector Palatine" (p. 40). The fourth chapter is on the manifestos themselves, the *Fama Fraternitatis* and the *Confessio Fraternitatis*, and the fifth is on a related document, the *Chymische Hochzeit Christiani Rosencreutz* (1616, but purportedly written in 1459). Chapter VI is about Johann Theodore De Bry, publisher of the esoteric works of Robert Fludd and Michael Maier; his location at Oppenheim, in the Palatine, is regarded as significant. Chapters VII and VIII trace a Rosicrucian "Furore" (sic) in Germany and "Scare" in France. Subsequent chapters attempt to draw into the circle of Rosicrucian thought and influence Francis Bacon; Italian liberals like Paolo Sarpi, Traiano Boccalini, Giordano Bruno, and Tommaso Campanella; certain Utopian plans for a *Societas Christiana*; Johann Comenius; the Royal Society; Elias Ashmole; Isaac Newton; and Freemasonry. Finally, an appendix contains translations of the two Rosicrucian manifestos together with valuable bibliographical information about them.

The information—as opposed to some of the inferences—contained in the book is reliable; the writing is lucid, if sometimes repetitive; the insights, because of Miss Yates's knowledge and sympathy, are often profound; the enthusiasm is contagious. Also, the library resources available to her—chiefly, I think, at the Warburg Institute and the British Museum—are exceptional, and her linguistic equipment is adequate for all the relevant documents except, pardonably, whatever may be written in Czech. (Hopefully, some day a competent Czech scholar will ransack library and private holdings in Prague and elsewhere for traces of Dee's visit in the 1580s.) I propose, however, to ask the essential scholarly question, "Are the conclusions as well as the information true?" The answer, regrettably, must be that in the opinion of the present reviewer many of them are not. I intend to explain why, not only in order to permit readers to arrive at their own judgments but also to suggest to the author—whom I respect—what aspects of her method raise basic questions for persons who share her interests but not her strong occultist sympathies.

The sympathies occasionally become very clear. For example, on pp. 226–27 she says that "The combination of a Hussite-Protestant type of religious liberalism with very strong infusion of Hermetic–Cabalist tradition should have produced interesting and original results. And when there came in with John Dee's movement an infusion of such traditions as they had developed in Elizabethan England, the results, in original scientific and religious attitudes, might have been phenomenal." The implication is plainly that Hermetic-Cabalist thought could profitably have replaced the emerging empiricism popularly accredited to a Baconian influence. Again, after commenting neutrally about Gabriel Naudé's attacks on occultists (pp. 106–109) she writes, "Two years later, in 1625, Naudé showed more courage by publishing his famous work, 'Apology for Great Men Suspected of Magic' " (p. 109). It is courageous to support magic and presumably cowardly to oppose it. Once more, Fludd's parallels between the macrocosm and the microcosm are asserted to be "made even closer than they were in the time of Pico and Ficino through the influence of Paracelsus who had made these correspondences more precise through his medico-astral theories" (p. 79). If Miss Yates does not believe that the macrocosm-microcosm parallels were "real" and that Paracelsus' whole grotesque system, including his alchemical theories and the three "principles" of salt, sulphur, and mercury, was preferable to modern chemistry, and if she does not also believe that the modern physician should "fortunen the ascendent / Of his ymages for his pacient," as Chaucer's Doctor of Physic did, the phrasing is, to say the least, untactful.

I shall not belabor the point, although it might be supported by other citations and by analysis of a pervasive tonality, for I have come to believe that the danger of a revived occultism is less acute than I thought it at the time I wrote the preface to my *Occult Sciences in the Renaissance* (Berkeley: Univ. of California Press, 1972). Neither am I altogether certain that Miss Yates does not simply allow herself occasionally to be swayed too much by her empathy with the writers she is discussing. In itself, empathy is an excellent thing, for its obverse is a tendency to misunderstand by imposing one's own ideas upon whatever one is reading, a practice which, in writers who deal with temporally remote thought, is disabling. Nevertheless I urge that it is possible to empathize at a distance, as Miss Yates's colleague at the Warburg, D. P. Walker, has consistently done, and that the resulting coolness favors accuracy without impeding insight.

More important is the author's tendency to draw inferences which favor a preestablished hypothesis. No doubt the hypothesis has itself resulted from a preliminary sorting of evidence, but, once formed, it can distort perception.

A typical example appears on p. 80, where she says that Michael Maier, the alchemical theorist, visited England about 1612 and was "almost certainly in contact with Robert Fludd, though exactly when or under what circumstances is not known." The only evidence given is that Maier's *Arcana arcanissima* (1614) was dedicated to the English physician Sir William Paddy, who knew Fludd. This is like saying that I must be "in contact with" all the Renaissance scholars who are acquainted with any of my friends. The guess about Maier may (or may not) be correct, but "almost certainly" is an overstatement. Another example appears on p. 77, where we are told first that Fludd "must have been invited" to publish his works through the De Bry firm in Oppenheim and then that this "may mean that his defense of the R. C. Brothers against Libavius had been recognized as proof of his support of Palatinate policies." But we do not know that the initiative was not Fludd's; if it was, his support of the Palatinate policies is pure guesswork. In fact, according to Fludd himself he published abroad for the perfectly credible reason that "the De Bry firm gave him far better illustrations than would have been possible in England" (pp. 78–79). Once more, an argument for Bacon's connection with Rosicrucianism is found in the dedication of his *Advancement of Learning* (1605) to "James I, the same monarch as he to whom the Rosicrucian movement in Germany so vainly pinned its hopes" (p. 118). Moreover, the dedication calls for "a fraternity or brotherhood in learning," and the Rosicrucians were a *fraternitas* (ibid.). The first observation counts for nothing unless Miss Yates is right in supposing that the Rosicrucians were behind Frederick's Bohemian venture— precisely what the association is intended to help prove. The second requires us to accept literally the Rosicrucian claim to skill in all languages, for the *Advancement* was written in English. Straightened out, the sequence of events would run as follows. In 1605, or shortly thereafter, the men who were subsequently to invent the Rosicrucian *ludibrium* were struck not only by Bacon's suggestion of a learned academy but also by the dedication of the *Advancement* to James. Nine years later, after James's daughter had married Frederick, they remembered both Bacon's program and his dedication and published a mystical manifesto (written before the marriage) which they expected to gain the sympathy of a rabidly antimystical king. It is not enough for Miss Yates that Bacon's description of Solomon's house in the *New Atlantis* (1627) may conceivably owe something to the Rosicrucian commitment to group research. Typically, she wishes to multiply the connections by running them both backwards and forwards to enrich them.

The pages are strewn with such dubious connections. It is, in fact, one mark of Miss Yates's recent writings that she deals continuously with them. Although it would be ungracious to dwell tiresomely on the point, I am anxious to make clear the kind of scholarly procedures to which I am objecting. The second Rosicrucian manifesto, the *Confessio Fraternitatis*, is connected with Dee through the fact that it was published in the same volume with another document, the *Consolatio Brevis*, which draws upon Dee's *Monas Hieroglyphica* (p. 61). The two may have been bound together for no better reason than that each was too short for separate publication and both were expected to appeal to the same audience. A Latin prayer with which the *Consolatio* ends is "reminiscent of Dee's prayers" (47) regardless of the fact that prayers notably characterize only one of Dee's writings, the *True Relation*, which was not published until 1659. George Herbert's poem "The Elixir" suggests the German Rosicrucian movement because, apparently, it uses the word "tincture" and the phrase "This is the famous stone / That turneth all to gold" (p. 225). But Herbert's tincture repudiates alchemy, for it is the attitude expressed in the phrase "for thy sake," the willingness to see God in all things, including the sweeping of a room, and to act always for Him and in Him. Similarly, it is extremely doubtful, despite Donne's figurative use of many occult notions, that his metaphysical poetry is "in many ways the counterpart of Maier's emblematics, expressing in a different medium a philosophical and religious outlook which may be closely parallel" (p. 231). Donne's occultist allusions are mostly "witty." The vast body of his sermons would yield small evidence of his acceptance of a "spiritual alchemy" like Maier's.

The same tendency to stretch facts and then to build on the extrapolations is visible even in details which bear little weight in Miss Yates's demonstration of her thesis. If she has learned of several occasions on which messengers passed between Heidelberg and London after Elizabeth's marriage, is it a fair extension to speak of "The constant going and coming of messengers" (p. 79)? Is the emphasis exactly right in the observation that Maier's publications "begin in 1614, the year after the wedding of Frederick and Elizabeth; they end in 1620 (though there is one later one), the year of the brief reign of Frederick and Elizabeth in Bohemia" (p. 87): The *Cantilenae Intellectuales*, with a dedication dated in 1622, is acknowledged only grudgingly in the parenthesis; its existence destroys the generalization, which is made notwithstanding. Even such a glancing phrase as "the Palatinate, so close to Venice . . ." (p. 132) betrays an impulse to force the evidence. The citation appears in the chapter on "Italian Liberals and Rosicrucian Manifestos" and is intended to increase our disposition to widen the circle of Palatinate influence.

A passion to draw disparate events and personages together, to pull everything into a single complex pattern, is apparent everywhere. Two characteristic phrases are "was in touch [*or* in close touch] with" and "was in contact with." Such contacts and touchings constitute a sizeable part of Miss Yates's demonstrations, but the evidence given for them is only occasionally firm. Again, the pages are thickly sprinkled with phrases like "may have been," "must surely," "may be looking back to," "Can it be true that?" "This . . . need not necessarily imply," "it could merely mean," "would have observed that," "would have realized that," "seems to have been," "is pretty certainly," "might be," and so on. (The examples are from pp. 198–201). Miss Yates herself perhaps does not realize how often what at one point is frankly speculative on a later page has become indisputably true. On pp. 2–3 it is "suggested" (by somebody else) that the masque at the end of *The Tempest* was added for a special performance, "perhaps" on the night of Frederick's and Elizabeth's betrothal. By p. 19, where an ambassador's report from Heidelberg is quoted as praising the couple, the two have become "the Shakespearean pair." On p. 111 all the careful subjunctives and conditionals which have preceded are forgotten in the recapitulatory sentence beginning, "We have seen that the Rosicrucian movement, or its manifestos, was connected with the movement for the installation of Frederick, Elector Palatine, in Bohemia. . . ." It appears, alas, to be characteristic of much highly speculative scholarship that innumerable guesses add up to certainty. Occasionally the interpretation of an illustration is persuasive until one takes the trouble to check details. Thus Plate 30, which reproduces an engraving from Thomas Sprat's *History of the Royal Society*, is said (p. 192) to show an angel blowing a trumpet and Francis Bacon under an angel's wing. The trumpet, however, is held across the angel's shoulder riflewise, with the mouthpiece down, and to my perception the wing is "behind" Bacon, not over him. In scholarship of this kind the temptation to make subtle distortions is sometimes irresistible. It is only fair to add, however, that the interpretations of lions, roses, garters, and much else in the plates are not only consistently interesting but usually credible. Iconology is highly developed at the Warburg, and Miss Yates is skilled at it.

Before proceeding to a general summary I pause briefly on a single detail which I believe to be clearly mistaken: almost the only factual error I have detected. Trithemius's *Steganographia* (1606, but circulated in MS much earlier) is said to "associate" the Rosicrucian Brothers with angel-magic (pp. 107–108). The elaborate apparatus of angelic messengers, however, is a *ludibrium* like that of the manifestos, the angels' names being keys to the ciphers which it is the purpose of the book to explain in a veiled and confusing way. A partial, but helpful, explanation of how this works is given by W. Schneegans in *Abt Johannes Trithemius und Kloster Spanheim* (Kreuznach: Schmithals, 1882, p. 192f.). Trithemius himself professed in a letter (see ibid., pp. 189–91) to be able to communicate a message to a man confined under guard three miles beneath the earth's surface "auf natürlichem Wege, ohne abergläubische Mittel und ohne Hülfe von Geistern"; and it is clear from the *Clavis* or *Schlüssel* sometimes printed with Trithemius's *Polygraphia* (1518, 1550, 1564, 1571, 1600) that the angelic apparatus, although invented partly for the purpose of sheer mystification, is a part of the cipher. We learn also from Gustavus Selenus's *Cryptomenytices et Cryptographiae Libri IX* (Lunaeburgi, 1624), which is an *enodatio* of Trithemius, that the angelic names Samaël, Anaël, and Veguaniël stand, respectively, for codes in which b, c, and d represent a, and so on to the end of the alphabets. The error is forgivable, however, since contemporary readers also misinterpreted the work and the Inquisition condemned it immediately upon publication.

I come now to one of the book's major theses, that "the Rosicrucian movement in Germany was the delayed result of Dee's mission in Bohemia over twenty years earlier" (p. 40). Although no blanket denial is possible, the chances are that the theory is mistaken.

The reason, briefly, is that Dee's own record of his continental residence is one of steady frustration. To be sure, his son Arthur later reported having played at quoits in Bohemia with pieces of gold produced by alchemical transformation, and on his return trip Dee presented the Landgrave of Hesse with twelve horses—a rich gift which sorts oddly with frequent reports of poverty and the selling of equipment and clothing for food. The general impression given by the *True and Faithful Relation* (London, 1659; ed. Meric Casaubon), which contains the chief part of Dee's notes on the Polish and Bohemian adventure (a few scattered entries in the *Private Diary* are relevant), is that the trip was disastrous. The Emperor Rudolf II, of whose occultist sympathies Miss Yates speaks frequently, not only professed inability to understand the copy of Dee's *Monas Hieroglyphia* which was presented to him but was so unfriendly that on February 28, 1585, the Archangel Michael promised to fulfill a request—whether Dee's or Edward Kelly's is unclear—that the Emperor be destroyed (*True Relation*, p. 380). Elsewhere than in Prague, Dee's luck was no better. He was shunted about from court to court, from nobleman to nobleman, was banished from the Emperor's dominions, and found real patronage, after the collapse of Laski's support, only from Count Rožmberk, who was clearly eccentric. The "mission" to which Miss Yates refers so honorifically might better be judged as aimed less at the spreading of an esoteric, "liberal" gospel than as a determined effort to gain wealth and the European fame to which Dee thought he was entitled.

It remains, of course, possible that Dee made a few unknown converts who subsequently had a direct or indirect influence on the Rosicrucian furor, but I think it highly improbable. Luigi Firpo, in "John Dee, Scienziato, Negromante e Avventuriero" (*Rinascimento*, III, 1952, 25–84) discusses the Bohemian (and Polish) venture so thoroughly, in such an appropriate tone, and with such minuteness that it is hard to imagine anyone's being able to do a better job on the basis of published resources. His summary of Dee's character and achievements can be put into useful contrast with the favorable—not to say worshipful—judgment implied everywhere by Miss Yates and asserted explicitly by Peter French in *John Dee: The World of an Elizabethan Magus* (London: Routledge & Kegan Paul, 1972). Dee, says Firpo,

> did not have any awareness of the infinite humility and patience to which the experimental researchers were later to submit in order to pursue small, partial, and provisional truths at the cost of painful toil: what he sought restlessly was a quick, short, infallible way to rise to a total knowledge which would bestow upon man an illimitable knowledge over nature. This sin of impatient pride reduced natural philosophy to occultism and led him to a presumed arcane science upon which there seemed to open enticing spiracles (*spiragli*)—rare and distant Alexandrine, Hebrew, or Arabic texts, once unknown to the systematizers of the traditional doctrines and now taken up again with avid curiosity and jealous secrecy. . . . There lived in him a certainty of the special favor of God, which from his earliest years had aroused in his heart both an infinite love of truth and an insatiable desire for knowledge, so that he did not despair of receiving a superhuman faculty by the gift of infusion and consented to develop the most hid-

den secrets of nature and to join them to the treasures of celestial
wisdom.

(*p. 29*)

The "short, infallible way" was to obtain messages directly from angels by
means of his skrying-glass, though he himself saw and heard nothing and
depended on the intermediation of the unscrupulous Kelly. Miss Yates's
book does not so much as hint that Dee's chief preoccupation throughout
the whole of his continental residence in 1583–89 was not alchemy, not
mathematics, not research into natural science, but precisely these conversations, which he interrupted with alchemical experiments only in the hope
of obtaining money—hopefully by success, but more confidently through
noble or royal patronage. It would be strange indeed if such activities,
which led neither Dee nor anybody else anywhere, resulted, after the lapse
of twenty-odd years, in a Rosicrucian movement purported to have led to
political upheavals of broad scope and devastating consequences.

In the same way Miss Yates's other major thesis may be doubted, that
the "politico-religious aspect of the message contained in the Rosicrucian
manifestos" was "an apocalyptic message of universal reformation leading
to a millennium and associated with movements around the Elector
Palatine which were eventually to lead to the Bohemian enterprise." The
Bohemians, we are told, "who 'married the Palatine' to the world, expected world reformation to be the result" (pp. 57–58). That the Hapsburg
emperors hoped to force a return to Catholic orthodoxy is, so far as I
know, indisputable; that the Elector and his advisors meant to achieve an
earthly Utopia on the basis of "spiritual alchemy," Hermetic philosophy,
the parallels between microcosm and macrocosm, numerological mysticism,
and—one may add—angelic conversations is hardly credible. How is the
world to be united by means of an occultism whose essence is secrecy and
limitation to a small band of initiates? The Rosicrucians, if they ever existed, remained invisible, and the fraternity was described as envisaging
not a government but a kind of Academy which might aspire to a gradual
perfection of knowledge. At best, the rule of ignorant subjects by an enlightened monarch determined to produce a Hermetic Utopia might have
led to a benevolent tyranny; at worst, it would have issued in a series of
administrative measures roughly comparable to the substitution of a National Board of Faith Healers for a system of socialized medicine. If Frederick had such a program in mind, his defeat at White Mountain may
have spared the world a ludicrous chapter of history.

There is not space to consider in detail the professed influence of Dee and the Rosicrucians on Bacon, the Italian liberals, the Christian Utopias, Comenius, the Royal Society, Newton, and Freemasonry. The justest summary comment might be that Miss Yates is always lively and imaginative and sometimes persuasive.

There is a class of readers who prefer excitement to historical reliability. To them, *The Rosicrucian Enlightenment* may be recommended without qualification. For others, the book will appear to be flawed by the author's advocacy of the ideas she discusses and by her tendency to let the accumulation of honest guesses result too often in conviction. The advocacy causes her to find heroes and saving truths where some may perceive only deluded men and happily abandoned misconceptions. The tendency to forget the tentative quality of her inferences leads to overly confident assertion of the centrality of occultism in serious Renaissance thought, where it had, to be sure, an astonishing vogue without, I think, ever ceasing to be marginal. But there are also strong positive values in this book, as in all the others by the same author: enormous learning, linguistic competencies which open to her resources to which more limited scholars are forbidden entry, insights born of the marriage of wide reading with a subtle and sympathetic mind, a praiseworthy industry, and a prose style which is consistently clear and vigorous. I repeat that Renaissance scholarship owes her much and that its debt is likely to be permanent. No serious student of the period should fail to read the book. He should approach it, in the present reviewer's opinion, with skepticism, but he will carry away from his reading knowledge that will alter his understanding of much he had thought he knew.

The Heart's Forest: A Study of Shakespeare's Pastoral Plays by David Young. Yale University Press, 1972. Pp. xi + 209. $7.95.

Reviewer: Robert P. Merrix.

Recent Shakespearean studies dealing with dramatic structure and genre keep revealing the immense contribution made by William Empson in *Some Versions of Pastoral*. His analysis first of all of the double plot in *Henry IV* led to an understanding of the parodic function of the low comic structure in Elizabethan drama and was the basis for numerous structural studies.[1]

Now, with the publication of David Young's *The Heart's Forest*, Empson's influence is evident in reshaping scholarly attitudes about genre, especially the pastoral.[2] As Professor Young notes, the tendency to identify pastoral with sheep, sheephooks and other traditional machinery was "abruptly reversed" by Empson whose approach—a study of pastoral "in terms of emotional focus"—led to "a new understanding of the subject matter of pastoral, and, to . . . its typical structure" (pp. 8–9). Recognizing the specific dramatic implications inherent in Empson's general study of pastoral "versions," Professor Young rejects the traditional study of pastoral drama exemplified by W. W. Greg's *Pastoral Poetry and Pastoral Drama* (London: A. H. Bullen, 1906) which is concerned primarily with the "trappings of pastoral" and accepts Empson's discovery of pastoral's "vitality and essential vision" and its function of "putting the complex into the simple." Thus he chooses to "settle between the stools of Empson and Greg" and to treat the pastoral as an "extraordinarily fluid and adaptable" literary genre (pp. 10–11).

Such an approach is applied to four of Shakespeare's plays, *As You Like It, King Lear, The Winter's Tale* and *The Tempest*, which Professor Young insists are "versions of pastoral in a sense more literal than that used by Empson" (p. 36). Each play exhibits the standard plot pattern of pastoral—"the exile of some of its central characters into a natural setting; their sojourn in that setting; and their eventual return" (p. 27). Moreover the plays exhibit the various themes earlier associated with such a structure, such as "man's relation to the natural world; his search for harmony with his environment; his tendency to idealize, alternately, the life of the city and that of the country; his dreams of escape, retirement, and a self-contained life hospitable both to the sensual gratification and to spiritual fulfillment; and the origin of good and evil in terms of opposition between the civilized and the primitive" (p. x). Finally, the plays reveal "certain external features, mainly stylistic" (p. 27) such as various antitheses—of Nurture and Nature, of Nature and Art, of Nature and Fortune—and paradox, which, like antithesis, is "inherent in the initial contradictions of the genre" (p. 36). Following his analysis of the plays and his "Epilogue" in which he reaffirms Shakespeare's "imaginative fertility, his restless experimentation, and his ability to transform and transcend convention" (p. 193), he appends an interesting chapter on "Producing the Pastorals."

In Chapter One, prior to his treatment of the individual plays, Professor Young briefly discusses the background of both dramatic and nondramatic pastoral modes. In addition he outlines the "meanings and extensions of the pastoral" as they might have aided the artist. And finally, though somewhat dubiously, he explains his reasons for choosing the four plays under study while excluding others which have been termed "pastoral." In tracing the rise of pastoral drama Professor Young rejects the general assumption that the structural patterns informing the eclogue and court entertainments led to the development of Renaissance pastoral drama. The eclogue "hardly provided useful dramatic models" while the dramatist who used the pastoral in court entertainment "ran the risk of falling victim to a specialized genre . . . reflecting court needs and values alone" (p. 13). Although Peele and Lyly (especially in *Gallathea*) reveal some aspects of pastoral drama in their plays, Peele's plays are primarily court entertainment and Lyly's plays are only a partial step in the development of the genre. The solution to the dramatic problem was to combine narrative romance and the pastoral, "an amalgam which could be traced back to *Daphnis and Chloe*" and which may be inherent in such works as Montemayor's *Diana*, Spenser's *The Faerie Queene* and the novels of Sidney, Greene and Lodge (pp. 13–16). It was this type of pastoral—filled with "a tremendous variety of incident that included love, fighting, disguising, clowning, singing and dancing, shipwrecks, wild animals, shepherds, savages and kings"—which became successful, while the type exemplified by Fletcher's *The Faithful Shepherdess*, based on pure Italian models, failed. The episodic, the melodramatic and the spectacular features of medieval and Renaissance romance effectively merged with pastoral to provide new directions. It was Sidney's *Arcadia*, Professor Young asserts, which established the English example of this genre with the pattern of the pastoral sojourn of characters into a rural or wilderness setting until their restoration and return. Early plays exemplifying this combination of romance and pastoral are *The Maid's Metamorphosis, The Thracian Wonder* and *Mucedorus*. Elizabethan pastoral drama then, when Shakespeare turned to it, "was not a courtly and elegant genre based on Italian models, but a rough-hewn and ramshackle affair" (p. 26).

In his section on the "meanings and extensions" of pastoral Professor Young stresses "pastoral's function as an alternative, born of dissatisfaction" with the "complex, hectic, urban present" (p. 27). The pastoral setting which provides the alternative is subjective and expressionistic and the alternative function creates a dialectic—"a kind of discourse between reality and the imagination" (p. 32). The subsequent stylistic features include social, psychological and aesthetic antitheses.

Professor Young's rationale for exclusion of other "pastoral" plays by Shakespeare is, like the pastoral, somewhat subjective and equivocal. *Timon* is excluded because it does little with its natural setting once the hero arrives; *Cymbeline* is only briefly touched on in the chapter on *The Winter's Tale* "since two late romances are treated fully"; *A Midsummer Night's Dream* is excluded because it was treated "in considerable detail elsewhere" by Professor Young, it does not fit the pastoral pattern because "one night does not . . . amount to a sojourn," and it was not "Shakespeare's first direct engagement with the pastoral tradition" as was *As You Like It* (pp. 36–37). Obviously each critic has a right to circumscribe the material in his study; but one must question such reasoning which excludes *Midsummer Night's Dream* on temporal grounds when the very essence of pastoral, as Professor Young insists, is "subjective and general." In dramatic time and intensity a night may serve as well as sixteen years.

In his chapter on *As You Like It*, Professor Young accepts Shakespeare's adaptation of Lodge's romance as a serious rather than satiric attempt to perfect and embellish the source ("The Tale of Gamelyn"). Shakespeare wrote the play "out of a sympathetic interest in pastoral." Thus, *As You Like It* is a "survey of the wonderful diversity and folly of human life and an affirmation of its ability, despite all shortcomings, to retain its resilience and renew itself" (p. 39).

Shakespeare's contributions to Lodge's source are, of course, most significant. His changes include making the two dukes brothers, matching them with Orlando and Oliver, thus strengthening "the parallel between the violations of natural bonds and the relationships which lead to the pastoral sojourn"; assigning the "bad" brothers "arbitrary evil and equally arbitrary conversion to good" in order to emphasize the larger forces (e.g., Fortune) controlling the play (p. 42), and, while retaining conventional elements, emphasizing rather than concealing their artificial aspects: Arden is deliberately established as a mythic setting "stylized and sparsely pictured, whose literary and artificial character is kept always before us" (p. 43). Shakespeare's additions are orchestrated with his changes: by adding Corin, Audrey, and William we have more realistic characters who either bring the pastoral closer to "real" country life or who expose its artificiality; Touchstone and Jaques introduce both the satiric and equivocal tendencies of pastoral; Duke Senior introduces a romantic element and native strain; and Rosalind and Orlando provide courtly love games and wit combats (pp. 40–41). It is this mingling of opposites which establishes the dialectic within the play.

The artifice of *As You Like It* is linked closely to the subjectivity and relativity of the sojourn. A "subjective" setting like Arden, thus, reveals the relativity of human experience: the forest becomes a kind of mirror which reflects the image of the self and its true preoccupations (e.g., Adam and

Orlando find Arden hostile because they are lost; Corin, who is secure, sees peace and contentment). But the characters are also mirrors, especially Touchstone who, as a "parodist supreme," participates in and simultaneously parodies everyone else's "subjectivity" (p. 52). Like its subjective nature, Arden's relative nature rejects "blanket judgments and rigid categories" so that while opposites such as Nature and Nurture and Nature and Fortune are expressed, "we are not allowed to use them for easy classification or to feel that they are immutable" (p. 55). Thus while Rosalind has described herself as "one out of suits with fortune" she has earlier with Celia contributed to the "witty disintegration of the Nature-Fortune dichotomy" (p. 55). "There is," concludes Professor Young, "scarcely an element in *As You Like It* unaffected by a sense of relativity. Sex, rank, fortune, the ages of man, the forest itself, are all seen as variables rather than constants" (p. 58).

In addition to the equivocal treatment of themes and characters in *As You Like It*, the play exhibits other stylistic traits, especially paradox and the rhetorical techniques of meiosis and encomium. Quoting Touchstone's conversation with Corin on the shepherd life (III.ii.13–22) and Phebe's comments following her encounter with "Ganymede" (III.iv.110–14), Professor Young asserts that such paradoxes are "part of the play's vision of human experience and a corrective to the tendency of pastoral to deal in rigid categories and simple judgments" (p. 62). Reduction is evidenced by Celia's transforming the goddess Fortune to a "spinning peasant"; expansion is exhibited "when Celia argues that banishment is really liberty, when the Duke discourses on the sweet uses of adversity, and when Jaques decides that 'motley's the only wear' " (pp. 62–63).

The final aspect of *As You Like It* in relation to pastoral is the generalizing tendency, "its habit of drawing back to survey the ways of the world and the human condition" (p. 64). Because of its special structure, setting up hypothetical alternatives, there is an "oscillation between the general and the particular." It is Rosalind who excels at this generalizing activity, effectively steering a course "between the excessive subjectivity" of Jaques and the excessive objectivity of Touchstone. And it is Rosalind who embodies, through such a balance, the ideals of love and the values of pastoral. "The great subject, when the real has been taken into account, will be the ideal, and its microcosm will be Rosalind" (pp. 66–68).

As You Like It, concludes Professor Young, is unique and our discoveries in the play "about the complicated relations of Nature and Art, our growing sense of the relativity of experience, our abandonment of doctrines and categories in favor of a recognition of the equivocal and paradoxical elements of life and love, all lead to remarkable widening of judgment, a new tolerance" (p. 71).

In his chapter on *King Lear*, Professor Young, recognizing the apparent incompatibility of tragedy and pastoral, uses several motifs and examples in order to subsume the play under the pastoral rubric. He quotes Polonius' famous generic hyperbole—"tragical-comical-historical-pastoral" and the pastoral elegiac tradition—exemplified by the death's head icon and motto, *"Et in Arcadia ego."*[3] *King Lear* is also related to pastoral structurally. While Professor Young admits that few surface details are related to the "conventional trappings of pastoral," and that the "use of pastoral is submerged, eccentric" and unconventional (pp. 74–75), the play, nevertheless, reveals the pastoral form—exclusion of characters, their sojourn and eventual return. Moreover it exhibits other features of pastoral romance—disguises, bizarre emotions, errors, allegiances "which disrupt the normal social bonds," and antitheses. The three-part pastoral pattern is exemplified in both plots (the *Leir* source for the main plot suggests a pastoral setting by referring to a "thicket" and "a good sheep's russet seagown") but the subplot, strongly linked to the *Arcadia*, is primary since the Gloucester plot, unlike the King Lear plot, follows the "normal curve of the pastoral, with the ceremonious defeat of the bad brother by the good brother and the good brother's restoration to society" (pp. 76–78). That Shakespeare intended a pastoral mode is evident in his unconcern with careful cause and effect relationships and the "tragical-pastoral tension in the play." Finally Professor Young "measures" *King Lear*'s relation to pastoral by comparing it with *As You Like It*. In addition to sharing "plot features" and themes (love and justice), the two plays are paired by "their concern with the nature of Nature" and by similarities of detail (e.g., the Fool, the banished ruler, the mirror setting). It is setting, however, which gives Professor Young difficulties in his comparison: in *King Lear* "the pleasant and fanciful settings of Arden are gone, and into their place rushes a natural world that is inscrutable, unpleasant, and intensely realized"; the comedy, "emphasizing the artifice of pastoral, was the natural predecessor of *Lear*; the road to the heath had been pointed out by Touchstone" (pp. 81–84). But Professor Young's analytical journey down the road reveals some intentional fallacy detours: "We are tempted to hypothesize. What if Duke Senior were not in a position to speak quite so calmly", and "what if Adam and Orlando did not stumble on friendly outlaws and their convenient banquet?" (p. 81). Surely that is precisely the point: if such actions had not happened *As You Like It* would have been a "pastoral tragedy."

Professor Young returns to the road in his analysis of the pastoral pattern in *King Lear* and the complex treatment of Nature. *King Lear*'s world is indeed "Poor Tom's world" and Nature is, if nothing else, "certainly indifferent and, to those who are unaccommodated, harsh and fearsome" (p. 83). Edgar's speeches—revealing his relation to Nature as Oswald's reveal the servant's relation to society—graphically show us "the world of the play, and its pastoral triad of man, society, and nature"; while "from Lear's unfettered imagination" we obtain a "vision of man as creator and victim of corrupt social institutions" (p. 86).

The pastoral pattern in *King Lear* is employed primarily to negate it, to deny its "characters and audience the consolations supposed to accompany poverty, isolation and humiliation," and to suggest "that renunciation is no insurance against suffering" (p. 93). Such negation is achieved by sudden peripeties directed against the pastoral norm. Following Lear's extrusion, rather than "the decorous withdrawals of pastoral romance, we are given a scene of astonishing emotional power" of three hundred lines, followed by the terrifying heath scene—only to be followed by a reversal in which "the play seems likely to turn toward pastoral again" in Lear's "recognition" that he must accept his lot (p. 89). But before Lear can achieve the calm of Duke Senior he is swept violently away from the norm by the entrance of Edgar. Like Lear, Edgar's character oscillates from one "echoing a traditional defense of pastoral" (i.e., being brought low in being out of Fortune's way) to one of shock upon seeing his blind father. But the worst peripety in the play is Cordelia's death, which also "is preceded by an affirmation of pastoral value"—Lear's renunciation of the world—that "is bound to give us hope." But rather than taking Lear and his daughter out of Fortune's way, Lear's speech is simply a prelude to "Kent's horrified question" ("Is this the promis'd end?"): at once a reference to the Last Judgment and "a final reminder of shattered expectations" (pp. 91–92). For Professor Young, this last scene is not an assertion of "Christian consolation"; just the opposite, it enables the play to keep us "uncertain," to destroy "guarantees," and to expose "assumption."

It is in his short but perceptive analysis of Nature in *King Lear* that Professor Young most clearly reveals the concept of "pastoral tragedy." He points out that Nature is largely *not* what the characters think it to be, that is, "a material and metaphysical backing for their own needs and desires"; both good and evil characters are deluded by Nature, and "direct appeals to Nature, in whatever form, do not work for anyone" (pp. 93–94). That the play ends "with a failure to identify man and nature, with a vision of human isolation, surely gives a full and final meaning to the notion of pas-

toral tragedy." Quoting from Edwin Muir's *Autobiography*, Professor Young
suggests that the meaning is grounded in "the conflict between the sacred
tradition of human nature, which is old, and nature, which is always new,
for it has no background" (p. 97).

How then can we see *King Lear* in any but pessimistic terms, especially
since the final scene "shows only a few men, struggling to communicate
among themselves"? Professor Young suggests three "oblique and tentative" answers. First is the recognition of our common conditions, the recognition that all share "the fact of birth and the burden of death" (p. 99).
Also there is man's kinship with other men which leads to "bonds and
ties" between them and a "regard for the value of human relationship."
Finally, there is the human imagination which "separates him from the
beasts" and sustains "his sacred tradition." Man's imagination protects him
from the truth (Lear's "happy" death, believing that Cordelia lives) and
helps him to accept suffering (pp. 100–101). That imagination, operating in
aesthetic terms, makes possible a dramatic experience "and a set of insights" which "we can balance against the darkness when we face the
'promised end.' " Though Lear as man is "the natural Fool of fortune," he
expresses "the bond of human life to the natural rhythms" (pp. 94–95); the
play itself "offers the miracle of recurrent experience . . . stripped of its destructive character," and like Keats' nightingale, is "timeless and timely"
(p. 103).

In his chapter on *The Winter's Tale* ("The Argument of Time") Professor
Young first discusses the late Romances in general, with some emphasis on
Cymbeline. He notes that the plays have been granted their "right to
uniqueness" but that "they do not differ as radically from Shakespeare's
works as had often been supposed." What distinguishes them from other
plays "is the prominence given to the patterns and conventions of narrative romance"—primitivism, composed of folktales, episodic structure and
other archaic features (p. 105). Such preoccupation with the primitive results in "the emphatic and open use of artifice" deliberately employed by
Shakespeare. These late plays are thus "experiments in the fabulatory" and
"celebrations of the human imagination" (p. 108). Our critical confusion
about the plays results from our inability to understand the playwright's
conscious use of "engagement and detachment"—the former pulling us
psychologically into the plays and the latter (like Brecht's theory of epic
theater) increasing our distance from the play, enabling us to evaluate and
appreciate the aesthetic experimentation. These experiments may be seen
in *Pericles*, which, while not really a pastoral (it has no "sojourn"), is a
"crucial piece of groundwork" (p. 110). Such a pattern, especially in *Cym-*

beline, where a "spirit of detachment seems to prevail," sends us "skidding between sorrow and amusement" and proves that Shakespeare's art culminated in the late plays (p. 111). Most importantly, pastoral is restored in the late plays "in such a way that we are left unmistakably aware of its fictitious and ideal character" (p. 115).

The "outlines of pastoral romance" with the variegated structure of contrasts, and improbable yet harmonious conclusions, "playfully subverted" in *As You Like It* and "grimly" used in *King Lear* for unpleasant facts, are employed for their own sake in *The Winter's Tale*, where they are heightened and refined by Shakespeare (p. 120). The playwright's additions (e.g., the bear and the sheep-shearing feast) in Greene's source, *Pandosto*, are deliberately designed, as is the "bifurcated" structure which is "emphatically exposed" by the use of an archaic chorus (p. 116).

Such a structure—the "juxtaposition of the tragic and comic sections"—in *The Winter's Tale* is a natural outgrowth of the comic and tragic genres in *As You Like It* and *King Lear* and both stresses the generic opposition, emphasizing the arbitrary aspects of genre, and also polarizes the play's elements—"good and evil, life and death, loss and restoration, creation and destruction," and so on. The effect is dual: "a widening of the meaning of pastoral by bringing its antinomies into line with . . . clearly defined opposites, and a stress on the arbitrary and artificial character of all such distinctions in light of the play's exaggerated outlines" (pp. 117–18).

Professor Young's analysis of the major themes—the interrelation of art and nature and time—is geared to the engagement-detachment theory. The first part of the play, involving the apparently unmotivated jealousy of Leontes, seems typical of the "pastoral romance tradition of violent and inexplicable passion." But the "remarkable tension" emerging from this "conventional pattern and the psychological verisimilitude" moves us "from the detachment of recognizing the implausible circumstances surrounding this passion to the engagement of sharing its intensity" (pp. 121–22). Such ambivalence also affects Leontes: Is his jealousy real or unreal? Does he, like Othello and Macbeth, "desperately try to remake" his world to fit his "horrible imaginings" or does he "unconsciously and insistently" remind us of his "plunge into illusion"? (pp. 123–24).

In the second part of the play, introduced by the appearance of Time, "we are thrust more and more toward the emblematic" and "will not be asked again to engage ourselves in the same way to the dramatic action" (p. 125). This second part "seems capable of containing everything from the Jacobean underworld practices of Autolycus" to the "great seasonal myths of Flora and Persephone" and because Shakespeare has been "steadily closing the distance between art and nature," the two themes are "becoming indistinguishable and reality and imagination seem to be intertwining and merging within a framework of artifice" (pp. 126–29). Nature itself is an "artist-creator" and its masterpiece is Perdita, a "living likeness" of Hermione and a "dead likeness" of the statue. These "likenesses" in the final scene are used to draw Nature and Art together (p. 130).

Time in *The Winter's Tale* is also related to the play's structure. The two halves of the play present two kinds of time thematically suited to the differing genres: the first ("tragic") part "linear, impetuous, irrevocable" and the second (pastoral comedy) "cyclic, leisurely, restorative" and harmonious (p. 134). Professor Young notes how frenzied is the activity in the first three acts (e.g., Polixenes' hasty trip, Hermione's speedy trial and "execution"); how both Leontes and Hermione are "outside time," suspended until they are merged with the comic cyclic phase of part two; and how the leisurely fourth act, especially the sheep-shearing scene, "marks time" by a seasonal event and is thus "an affirmation of man's relation to natural rhythms and seasonal cycles" (pp. 135–37). The final act "completes the traditional pastoral romance pattern of extrusion and return by reassembling all the characters" and once again increases the dramatic pace. Thematically then we see the restorative value of Time "through an extremely artificial and arbitrary mode" (p. 139). Finally it is Time's speech which best expresses Shakespeare's concept of Nature and Art: "the staleness of a tale . . . is something that can overtake the freshest things"; Time himself tells us that we must decide "whether listening to him and a story which is his 'argument' is a profitable way to spend *time*." It is, thus, "Time's overview" which refers us once more to the uniqueness that arises from the very structure of *The Winter's Tale*: "its striking rehandling, through juxtaposed genres, of the pattern of extrusion and restoration" (pp. 143–45).

Professor Young's chapter on *The Tempest* ("Rough Magic") is both his longest and most difficult to appraise. In order to fit the play into his finished pattern he must reassess basic attitudes about the play's setting and origin, and, most importantly, its theme of magic. Admitting that a desert island "may differ from the more traditional pastoral landscapes," he insists that it nevertheless embodies features which permit the "same ambivalence between a desire to escape to a simpler form of existence and a fear of being cut off from society, civilization, indeed all human company" (p. 146). Moreover, even though Shakespeare may have drawn upon the Bermuda pamphlets for some details, he places the island in the Mediterranean, so that the "old" civilization and traditions of such a setting may be "simultaneously invoked" with the "True Declaration" and the

Bermuda pamphlets, both of which represent the "new" civilization.

It is with Professor Young's analysis of the play's analogue or "influence" that one begins to sense some critical straining. He accepts and further emphasizes K. M. Lea's discussion of the play's relationship to the "shipwreck pastorals" of the *Commedia dell 'Arte*. While conceding, as Lea also does, that one cannot find an *Ur-Tempest* among even one existing scenario, he nevertheless asserts that the plays evince enough "standard features" (e.g., castaways on an enchanted isle inhabited by a magician) that we may accept them as an important source. Why they have not been widely accepted by scholars, he insists, is because of the "traditional preference of Shakespearean source hunters for nondramatic as opposed to dramatic sources, and for textual as opposed to nontextual influences" (p. 150). Such a "back door" approach to *The Tempest* by way of the *commedia* is important because it permits Shakespeare to transform "crude and unlikely materials," and reveal rather than conceal "the artifice on which his theater is inevitably based"; we are moreover allowed "to differentiate sharply between this play and the other late romances in the matter of structure" (p. 153). Even though professor Young admits that such claims can be made for *The Tempest* "without the recognition of the *commedia* influence," he insists that Shakespeare was "deliberately resorting" to the structure and manner of the source. In fact such a structure—the highly flexible setting; the fortuitous assembling of characters; and a magician whose "omnipotence excused wild improbabilities"—may explain the "unusually tight" structure of *The Tempest*. Like the *commedia, The Tempest* in "adhering to the unities becomes a kind of game" (p. 154).

Such a fictive structure exemplifies a kind of "playful double-consciousness"—e.g., the opening storm which is "realistic" but in fact an illusion; Prospero's expository speech to Miranda (I.ii) which deliberately calls attention to the artifice in the play; and the fact that Prospero's "magicianship" is only a role of which we are well aware (p. 155). As we shall see, says Professor Young, "Shakespeare's handling of the magician and his magic," the "dreamlike and unstable world" and the "treatment of the great pastoral themes of art and nature" are related to the "deliberately unrealistic materials from which the play is shaped" (p. 159). But while one may agree, generally, with Professor Young's own treatment of the last two assumptions of his thesis, one must seriously question the first: Shakespeare's use of magic and the magician.

Professor Young's analysis of Prospero is based on the concept of "white" magic in which Prospero "does not traffic with devils or endanger his soul" and is "a kind of cross between Friar Bacon"—a magician alternating between castigating those who cross him, and helping those who come to him for aid—and "John a Kent on the one hand, and Doctor Faustus on the other" (p. 161). While Professor Young admits that Prospero's role "disturbs" the magician "enough that he is inclined to give it up" (as Bacon renounces his magic) and that the magic tends "to weaken, to cramp, confine, and imprison" (p. 167), he nevertheless suggests that the "rough magic" is essentially benign (it determines the structure of the play, isolating groups of characters for study), and that Prospero is a "kind of metaking whose power, based on knowledge, extends to nature and is, paradoxically, more real because it is grounded in illusion" (p. 162). In short, the magic "is plainly analogous to the world of the theater in which it all takes place" (p. 166). Thus, as Professor Young admits, it is "surprising" when Prospero "appears in the Epilogue, claiming the same symptoms as his victims," especially since he "seems the only person in the play who is invulnerable to the effects of the magic he eventually renounces" (p. 169).

How Professor Young escapes this "paradox" is itself paradoxical: "we are not listening to Prospero, really" in the speech, "but rather the actor who played him"; and the paradoxical speech both puts us in Prospero's vacated role—the benevolent tyrant—and also didactically suggests "the existence of a curious process whereby confinement, rightly borne, can lead to freedom" (p. 169).

Unfortunately we cannot employ a structural analysis to explain and justify the function of Prospero. While one may, with Professor Young, reject previous attempts to "impose allegorical meanings on the play," thereby exonerating the magician or "explaining" his role, we cannot exonerate him by casually linking him to "white" magic or by translating the theurgic themes of the play into an aesthetic process. As several scholars have shown recently,[4] the use of magic by Renaissance man regardless of what qualifying adjectives we impose on it was demonic. Donald Seltzer, for example, notes that "any power which could call up spirits—be they neoplatonic 'daemons' or necromantic 'demons'—would not claim the assistance of God, and must, therefore receive the aid of the devil."[5] The very fact that Prospero, unlike Faustus, ultimately understands that "the illusion of mastery" is "bondage to greater powers" is not employed simply as a recognition of paradoxes (e.g., confinement and freedom, mastery and servitude) which are "mutually complementary aspects of the same thing" (p. 170). His recognition, whether it be put in the "actor's" mouth or Prospero's, surely suggests, as did Bacon's, that trafficking with spirits is contrary to the laws of God and may be physically or spiritually destructive.

"Good ends," as the essentially anti-Machiavellian audience knew, did not justify evil means.

In his sections of the "dreamlike and unstable world" of *The Tempest* and the treatment of "the great pastoral themes of Art and Nature," Professor Young returns to more substantial critical ground, except when discussing Prospero's magic as the artistic side in the Art-Nature duality. Briefly stated, the subjective world of *The Tempest* is reflected in the dissolution of the normal physical and mental barriers, leading to "problems of identity and belief"; these problems in turn are "linked with problems of reality" (p. 177). The uncertainty of reality leads to the possibility that nothing is real (p. 178). The dissolution of the physical and mental barriers leads to reversal or "transfers" "whereby mental experience takes on physical characteristics and vice versa" (p. 172). The culminating effect of these "transfers" is to establish a structure "whereby realities are not merely juxtaposed, but tend to give way to one another," thereby creating "a reality so shifting and impermanent that only a man . . . like Prospero can have any mastery of it" (p. 178). Finally the illusory and unstable condition of the play is embodied and explained in Prospero's famous speech (IV.i.146–63) which is the "central vision of the play" and "the justification for the play's style, tone, and structure" (p. 180).

Professor Young's final section on *The Tempest*, in which he analyzes its pastoral content in terms of dualities of Nature-Art and Nature-Nurture, exhibits his theory of the play's "fictive conjunction of opposites," as well as his brief, perhaps unaware, sojourn to allegorical interpretation. For example, "Ariel and his cohorts are neither demons nor angels, but spirits of wind, water, earth and fire"; or they are "billows, winds and thunder" (pp. 181–82); or finally they are aspects of Nature: "Ariel—delicate, quicksilver, sympathetic," and "Caliban—heavy, clumsy, grotesque and deformed" (p. 186).

As for the Art-Nature duality, he suggests that "the union of Art and nature" exists throughout the play "until the end, when the partnership is dissolved, as if to suggest that such ideal conjunction is temporary at best" (p. 181). Such a harmony of Art and Nature is dependent on Prospero's magic which itself is an "art." Moreover Prospero's magic "is not contrary to nature but very much a part of it"—a "harmony between a human will and natural processes and forces" (p. 181).

Just as the Art-Nature duality is complex, so too is the Nature-Nurture "question." While evil seems certainly to reside on the lower savage scale with Caliban, "we are confronted with Antonio and Sebastian" also; "what in Caliban is physical, natural, and open deformity recurs as spiritual, acquired, and hidden deformity" in the Italian aristocrats (p. 187). The same is true of innocence. Ariel and Miranda, "presumably a manifestation of the best qualities of the natural world," are counterpoised by Ferdinand and Gonzalo, the more refined and civilized characters.

How are we to assess Professor Young's contribution to Shakespearean scholarship in general and to the pastoral in particular? In a sense both parts of this question are answered in Professor Young's Epilogue and in the Appendix. In general, he denies that he has "revolutionized our understanding of Shakespeare or invented an entirely new way of approaching his plays" but he suggests, among other things, that his approach gives us an insight into Shakespeare's sensitive awareness of his own literary heritage. Specifically, Professor Young suggests that his approach to the plays reveals a Shakespeare who "was able to transcend genre and convention, turning them to his most original uses, making them uniquely his" (p. 193).

To these insights we can essentially agree. While genre to be valid as a critical tool must be circumscribed, that delimitation may be as broad as the playwright's imagination permits. No play of Shakespeare's is an either-or product but a mingling of elements and conventions as diverse as the playwright's own milieu. As Professor Young states, "the dialogue between works of art and critical categories is, and ought to be, an endless one" (p. 7). And while we may disagree with Professor Young's individual interpretations of some plays, especially *The Tempest*, he has demonstrated the basic pastoral pattern of exclusion, sojourn and return in each play. Finally he has provided us an explanation for the artifice in the plays and the curious stylistic techniques—paradox and antithesis. Because of the work of Professor Maynard Mack and Professor Young's own analysis, one begins to understand the ambivalence in *King Lear*. That insight, in itself, is contribution enough.

Notes:

1. See Richard Levin, *The Multiple Plot in English Renaissance Drama* (Chicago: University of Chicago Press, 1971), pp. 3–4 and his bibliography, pp. 252–53. Among those influenced directly or indirectly by Empson are Muriel Bradbrook in her *Themes and Conventions of Elizabethan Tragedy* (Cambridge: Cambridge Univ. Press, 1935); Norman Rabkin, "The Double Plot: Notes on the History of a Convention," *Renaissance Drama*, 7 (1964), 55–69; Robert Ornstein, "The Comic Synthesis in *Doctor Faustus*," *ELH*, 22 (1955), 165–72; Glynne Wickham, *Shakespeare's Dramatic Heritage* (New York: Barnes and Noble, 1969); Jonas Barish, "The Double Plot in *Volpone*," *Modern Philology*, 51 (1953), 83–92.

2. In addition to Young's book see Thomas McFarland, *Shakespeare's Pastoral Comedy* (Chapel Hill: Univ. of North Carolina Press, 1972), p. 24 and passim.

3. See Erwin Panofsky, "*Et in Arcadia Ego*: Poussin and the Elegiac Tradition," in *Meaning of the Visual Arts* (Garden City, N.Y.: Doubleday, 1955), pp. 295–320.

4. See e.g., Frank Towne, " 'White Magic' in *Friar Bacon and Friar Bungay*?" *Modern Language Notes*, 66 (1952), 9–13; Donald Seltzer in his edition of *Friar Bacon and Friar Bungay* (Lincoln: Univ. of Nebraska Press, 1963), pp. xiv–xv; and especially D'Orsay W. Pearson, " 'Unless I Be Reliev'd by Prayer': *The Tempest* in Perspective," *Shakespeare Studies*, 7 (1974), 253–82. Professor Pearson argues that the Epilogue is an integral and thematic part of the play and is "both conclusion to and summation of *The Tempest*" (p. 278).

5. Seltzer, pp. xiv–xv.

Books Received

(Inclusion of a book in this list does not preclude its being reviewed in this or a subsequent volume.)

Adamczowski, Jan. *Nicolaus Copernicus and His Epoch*. Philadelphia: Copernicus Society, 1974. Pp. 161.

Adams, Robert M. *The Roman Stamp: Frame and Facade in Some Forms of Neo-Classicism Stamp*. Berkeley: Univ. of California Press, 1974. Pp. 254.

Alexander, Sidney. *Lions and Foxes: Men and Ideas of the Italian Renaissance*. New York: MacMillan, 1974. Pp. xi + 357.

Barkan, Leonard. *Nature's Work of Art: The Human Body as Image of the World*. New Haven: Yale Univ. Press, 1975. Pp. x + 291.

Barroll, J. Leeds, Alexander Leggatt, Richard Hosley and Alvin Kernan. *The Revels History of Drama in English, Vol. III, 1576–1613*. London: Methuen, 1975. Pp. xxxiii + 526.

Beaumont, Francis and John Fletcher. *Philaster*, ed. Dora Jean Ashe. Lincoln: Univ. of Nebraska Press, 1974. Pp. xxxii + 152.

Bergeron, David M. *Shakespeare: A Study and Research Guide*. Lawrence, Mass.: St. Martin's, 1975. Pp. vii + 145.

Bluestone, Max. *From Story to Stage: The Dramatic Adaptation of Prose Fiction in the Period of Shakespeare and His Contemporaries*. The Hague: Mouton, 1974. Pp. 341.

Breakworth, E. R. C. *Shakespeare and the Bawdy Court of Stratford*. London: Phillimoreo, 1972. Pp. viii + 184.

Brock, D. Heyward and James M. Welsh. *Ben Jonson: A Quadricentennial Bibliography, 1947–1972*. Metuchen, N.J.: Scarecrow, 1974. Pp. x + 166.

Brooke, Nicholas, ed. *Shakespeare, "Richard II": A Selection of Critical Essays*. London: Macmillan, 1973. Pp. 256.

Bryant, J. A., Jr. *The Compassionate Satirist: Ben Jonson and His Imperfect World*. Athens: Univ. of Georgia Press, 1972. Pp. ix + 195.

Bullough, Geoffrey. *Narrative and Dramatic Sources of Shakespeare*. Vol. VIII: *Romances*. New York: Columbia Univ. Press, 1975. Pp. xiv + 423.

Clark, Sandra, and T. H. Long, eds. *The New Century Shakespeare Handbook*. Englewood Cliffs, N.J.: Prentice-Hall, 1974. Pp. x + 291.

Clifford, Gay. *The Transformations of Allegory*. London: Routledge, 1974. Pp. viii + 132.

Colie, Rosalie L. *The Resources of Kind: Genre Theory in the Renaissance*, ed. Barbara K. Lewalski. Berkeley: Univ. of California Press, 1974. Pp. ix + 137.

———. *Shakespeare's Living Art*. Princeton: Princeton Univ. Press, 1974. Pp. ix + 370.

——— and F. T. Flahiff, eds. *Some Facets of "King Lear": Essays in Prismatic Criticism*. Toronto: Univ. of Toronto Press, 1974. Pp. xi + 236.

Colman, E. A. M. *The Dramatic Use of Bawdy in Shakespeare*. New York: Longman, 1974. Pp. xi + 230.

Danson, Lawrence. *Tragic Alphabet: Shakespeare's Drama of Language*. New Haven: Yale Univ. Press, 1974. Pp. xii + 200.

Davis, Arthur G. *The Royalty of Lear*. New York: St. John's Univ. Press, 1974. Pp. xiii + 168.

Dekker, Thomas. *The Shoemaker's Holiday*, ed. D. J. Palmer. London: Bern, 1975. Pp. xxv + 101.

Dent, Alan. *World of Shakespeare: Sports and Pastimes*. New York: Taplinger, 1974. Pp. 111.

Dias, Walter. *Shakespeare: His Tragic World: Psychological Investigations*. New Delhi: S. Chand, 1973. Pp. xxiii + 532.

Doebler, John. *Shakespeare's Speaking Pictures: Studies in Iconic Imagery*. Albuquerque: Univ. of New Mexico Press, 1974. Pp. xix + 236.

Dudley, Edward, and Maximilian E. Novak, eds. *The Wild Man Within: An Image in Western Thought from the Renaissance to Romanticism*. Pittsburgh: Univ. of Pittsburgh Press, 1973. Pp. xi + 333.

Egan, Robert. *Drama Within Drama: Shakespeare's Sense of His Art in "King Lear," "The Winter's Tale," and "The Tempest."* New York: Columbia Univ. Press, 1975. Pp. ix + 128.

Ellis, Herbert A. *Shakespeare's Lusty Punning in "Loves Labour's Lost."* The Hague: Mouton, 1973. Pp. 239.

Garber, Marjorie B. *Dream in Shakespeare: From Metaphor to Metamorphosis*. New Haven: Yale Univ. Press, 1974. Pp. x + 226.

Goldberg, S. L. *An Essay on "King Lear."* Cambridge: Cambridge Univ. Press, 1974. Pp. 192.

Granville-Barker, Harley. *More Prefaces to Shakespeare*, ed. Edward M. Moore. Princeton: Princeton Univ. Press, 1974. Pp. 167.

Green, Martin. *The Labyrinth of Shakespeare's Sonnets: An Examination of Sexual Elements in Shakespeare Language*. London: Charles Skilton, 1974. Pp. ix + 193.

Hawkes, Terence. *Shakespeare's Talking Animals: Language and Drama in Society*. Totowa, N.J.: Rowman and Littlefield, 1973. Pp. viii + 193.

Heninger, S. K., Jr. *Touches of Sweet Harmony: Pythagorean Cosmology and Renaissance Poetics*. San Marino, Calif.: Huntington Library, 1974. Pp. xvii + 446.

————. *English Prose, Prose Fiction, and Criticism to 1660: A Guide to Information Sources*. Detroit: Gale Research Co., 1974. Pp. ix + 255.

Hibbard, G. R., ed. *The Elizabethan Theatre IV*. Hamden, Conn.: Shoestring, 1974. Pp. xv + 175.

Jonson, Ben. *The Alchemist*, ed. Alvin B. Kernan. New Haven: Yale Univ. Press, 1974. Pp. ix + 246.

Kermode, Frank. *Shakespeare, Spenser, Donne*. New York: Viking, 1971. Pp. vii + 308.

Kinney, Arthur F. *Elizabethan Backgrounds: Historical Documents of the Age of Elizabeth I*. Hamden, Conn.: Shoestring, 1975. Pp. xi + 412.

———. *Titled Elizabethans: A Directory of Elizabethan State and Church Officers and Knights, With Peers of England, Scotland and Ireland, 1558–1603*. Hamden, Conn.: Shoestring, 1973. Pp. ix + 89.

Kinsman, Robert S., ed. *The Darker Vision of the Renaissance: Beyond the Fields of Reason*. Berkeley: Univ. of California Press, 1974. Pp. 352.

Kozlenko, William, ed. *The Disputed Plays of William Shakespeare*. New York: Hawthorne, 1974. Pp. xi + 371.

Leggatt, Alexander. *Shakespeare's Comedy of Love*. London: Methuen, 1974. Pp. xiv + 272.

May, Robin. *Who Was Shakespeare?* Newton Abbot: David and Charles, 1974. Pp. 143.

McAlindon, T. *Shakespeare and Decorum*. New York: Barnes and Noble, 1973. Pp. viii + 227.

McManaway, James G., ed. *Shakespeare and England*. Review of National Literatures, ed. Anne Paolucci. Jamaica, N.Y.: St. John's Univ., 1972. Pp. 196.

McMullan, Frank A. *Directing Shakespeare in the Contemporary Theatre*. New York: Richards Rosen, 1974. Pp. 175.

Middleton, Thomas. *Three Plays*, ed. Kenneth Muir. Totowa, N.J.: Rowman and Littlefield, 1975. Pp. xix + 217.

——— and William Rowley. *A Fair Quarrel*, ed. R. V. Holdsworth. London: Ernest Benn, 1974. Pp. xiv + 130.

Nelson, William. *Fact or Fiction: The Dilemma of the Renaissance Storyteller*. Cambridge: Harvard Univ. Press, 1973. Pp. 121.

Nichols, J. G. *The Poetry of Sir Philip Sidney: An Interpretation in the Context of His Life and Times*. New York: Barnes and Noble, 1974. Pp. x + 171.

Ornstein, Robert. *A Kingdom for a Stage: The Achievement of Shakespeare's History Plays*. Cambridge: Harvard Univ. Press, 1972. Pp. xii + 231.

Oyama, Toshikazv, ed. *Shakespeare Translation: Annual Publication on Shakespeare Translation*. Tokyo: Yushodo Shoten, 1974. Pp. xiii + 97.

Peterson, Douglas L. *Time, Tide and Tempest: A Study of Shakespeare's Romances*. San Marino, Calif.: The Huntington Library, 1974. Pp. xv + 259.

Phillips John. *The Reformation of Images: Destruction of Art in England, 1535–1660*. Berkeley: Univ of. of California Press. 1973. Pp. xiii + 228.

Pinciss, Gerald M. *Christopher Marlowe*. New York: Ungar, 1975. Pp. iii + 138.

Quinn, David Beers. *England and the Discovery of America, 1481–1620*. New York: Knopf, 1974. Pp. xxiv + 497.

Randall, Dale B. J. *Jonson's Gypsies Unmasked: Background and Theme of "The Gypsies Metamorphos'd."* Durham, N.C.: Duke Univ. Press, 1975. Pp. xiii + 200.

Salingar, Leo. *Shakespeare and the Traditions of Comedy*. Cambridge: Cambridge Univ. Press, 1974. Pp. x + 356.

Schoenbaum, Samuel. *William Shakespeare: A Documentary Life*. New York: Oxford Univ. Press, 1975. Pp. xviii + 273.

Shakespeare, William. *The Tragedy of Othello the Moor of Venice*, ed. Lawrence J. Ross. New York: Bobbs-Merrill, 1974. Pp. xxxix + 304.

Simmons, J. L. *Shakespeare's Pagan World: The Roman Tragedies*. Charlottesville: Univ. Press of Virginia, 1973. Pp. xi + 202.

Smith, James. *Shakespearian and Other Essays*. Cambridge: Cambridge Univ. Press, 1974. Pp. vii + 351.

Speaight, Robert. *Shakespeare on the Stage: An Illustrated History of Shakespearian Performance*. Boston: Little, 1973. Pp. 304.

Swinden, Patrick. *An Introduction to Shakespeare's Comedies*. London: Macmillan, 1974. Pp. x + 188.

Tobias, Richard C., and Paul G. Zolbrod, eds. *Shakespeare's Late Plays, Essays in Honor of Charles Crow*. Athens: Ohio Univ. Press, 1975. Pp. xiv + 235.

Todd, D. K. C. *I Am Not Prince Hamlet: Shakespeare Criticism and Schools of English*. New York: Barnes and Noble, 1975. Pp. iii + 199.

Turner, Robert Y. *Shakespeare's Apprenticeship*. Chicago: Univ. of Chicago Press, 1974. Pp. vii + 293.

Ure, Peter. *Elizabethan and Jacobean Drama*, ed. J. C. Maxwell. New York: Barnes and Noble, 1974. Pp. viii + 258.

Varma, R. S., ed. *Papers on Shakespeare*. New Delhi: S. Chand, 1973. Pp. viii + 89.

Vickers, Brian, ed. *Shakespeare: The Critical Heritage, Vol. I, 1623–1692*. London: Routledge, 1974. Pp. xi + 448.

––––––. *Shakespeare: The Critical Heritage, Vol. II, 1693–1733*. London: Routledge, 1974. Pp. xi + 549.

J. A. Ward, ed. *Renaissance Studies in Honor of Carroll Camden. Rice University Studies*, Vol. 60, No. 2. Pp. ix + 169.

Watkins, Ronald, and Jeremy Lemmon. *In Shakespeare's Playhouse: The Poet's Method*. Newton Abbot: David and Charles, 1974. Pp. 207.

––––––. *In Shakespeare's Playhouse: "Hamlet."* Newton Abbott: David and Charles, 1974. Pp. 150.

––––––. *In Shakespeare's Playhouse: "Macbeth."* Newton Abbot: David and Charles, 1974. Pp. 164.

––––––. *In Shakespeare's Playhouse: "A Midsummer Night's Dream."* Newton Abbott: David and Charles, 1974. Pp. 150.

Wine, M. L., ed. *The Tragedy of Arden of Faversham*. London: Methuen, 1973. Pp. xcvi + 180.

Wilson, Katherine M. *Shakespeare's Sugared Sonnets*. New York: Barnes and Noble, 1974. Pp. 382.

Zeeveld, W. Gordon. *The Temper of Shakespeare's Thought*. New Haven: Yale Univ. Press, 1974. Pp. xv + 266.